WRITER'S CHOICE

GRAMMAR AND COMPOSITION

Turner Wins Crown for Second Time

The district finals for track and field were held last Saturday at Armstrong Memorial Field. Representatives from the high schools in the tri-county area competed in a total of twenty events, and hotly contested

The most publicized event was the women's mile run. Defending champion Katy Turner of Midview High was undefeated in regular-season competition. All eyes were on her as she went up against Mai Komoro, a student transfer at River View High who missed the early part of the season.

Before she transferred, Komoro was the San Diego city league champion in the mile last year. She finished this season undefeated in all meets in which she competed. Turner slipped as she started but quickly regained her balance. She soon overcame Komoro's early lead, but Komoro hung in, putting the pressure on Turner in the last quarter mile. Turner was able to kick out the last few yards to win the title for the second year in a row. Komoro came in second, and Anna Perez took the third position.

Turner, a senior, is scheduled to attend the University of North Carolina on a track scholarship. Komoro, still a junior, will have another chance at the title next year.

from Fairview High

Student Advisory Board

Rachel Hansen

Claire Monty

Maritza Pagán

Maurice Phifer

David Ojeda

Michael Kim

Charles Dayton

Yahna Awazu

Chris Fickes

WRITER'S CHOICE

GRAMMAR AND COMPOSITION

Vincent van Gogh, *The Starry Night*, 1889

Consulting Author for Composition
William Strong

Grammar Specialist
Mark Lester

Visual-Verbal Learning Specialists
Ligature, Inc.

New York, New York   Columbus, Ohio   Woodland Hills, California   Peoria, Illinois

Send all inquiries to:
Glencoe/McGraw-Hill
936 Eastwind Drive
Westerville, Ohio
43081

ISBN 0-02-635882-4
(Student Edition)
ISBN 0-02-635883-2
(Teacher's Wraparound Edition)

6 7 8 9 10 11 12   071   01 00 99 98 97

Consulting Author for Composition

William Strong is Professor of Secondary Education at Utah State University, Director of the Utah Writing Project, and a member of the National Writing Project Advisory Board. A nationally known authority in the teaching of composition, he is the author of many volumes, including, most recently, *Writing Incisively: Do-It-Yourself Prose Surgery* (McGraw-Hill, 1991).

As Consulting Author, Dr. Strong helped to develop the structure and content of Part 1: Composition. He reviewed and edited all Composition units. Dr. Strong also conceived and wrote Unit 8: Style Through Sentence Combining. He collaborated on Sentence Combining Blackline Masters, which accompanies *Writer's Choice*.

Grammar Specialist

Mark Lester is Professor of English at Eastern Washington University. He formerly served as Chair of the Department of English as a Second Language, University of Hawaii. He is the author of Grammar in the Classroom (Macmillan, 1990) and of numerous professional books and articles.

As Grammar Specialist, Dr. Lester reviewed student's edition material from Part 2: Grammar, Usage, and Mechanics. He collaborated on Grammar Reteaching Blackline Masters, which accompanies *Writer's Choice*.

Associate Consultant in Writing

Bonnie S. Sunstein is Associate Professor of English and Director of the Master of Arts in Teaching Program at Rivier College in Nashua, New Hampshire. Dr. Sunstein has taught extensively in New England in colleges and secondary schools, as well as in the New Hampshire Reading and Writing Program. She has published in the area of writing and teaching and is the coeditor of Portfolio Portraits (Heinemann, 1992) and the author of a forthcoming book about teachers and writing (Boynton/Cook).

As Associate Consultant in Writing, Dr. Sunstein established the theoretical framework for integrating writing portfolios into *Writer's Choice*.

Contributing Writers

Larry Beason is Assistant Professor of English at Eastern Washington University. Dr. Beason is the writer of Grammar Reteaching Blackline Masters, which accompanies *Writer's Choice*.

Willis L. Pitkin Jr. is Professor of English at Utah State University. Dr. Pitkin is the writer of Sentence Combining Blackline Masters, which accompanies *Writer's Choice*.

Visual-Verbal Learning Specialists

Ligature, Inc., is an educational research and development company with offices in Chicago and Boston. Ligature is committed to developing educational materials that bring visual-verbal learning to the tradition of the written word.

As visual-verbal and curriculum specialists, Ligature collaborated on conceiving and implementing the pedagogy of *Writer's Choice*.

Acknowledgments

Grateful acknowledgment is given authors, publishers, photographers, museums, and agents for permission to reprint the following copyrighted material. Every effort has been made to determine copyright owners. In the case of any omissions, the Publisher will be pleased to make suitable acknowledgments in future editions.
Continued on page 838

Composition Advisers

The advisers reviewed Composition lesson prototypes. Their contributions were instrumental in the development of the Writing Process in Action lessons.

Michael Angelotti
Head of Division of Teacher
 Education
College of Education
University of Oklahoma

Charles R. Duke
Dean of the College of Education
 and Human Services
Clarion University

Carol Booth Olson
Director
University of California, Irvine,
 Writing Project

Judith Summerfield
Associate Professor of English
Queens College, City University of
 New York

Denny Wolfe
Professor and Associate Dean
Darden College of Education
Old Dominion University
formerly Director, Tidewater Writing
 Project

Educational Reviewers

The reviewers read and commented upon manuscripts during the writing process. They also critiqued early drafts of graphic organizers and page layouts.

Lenore Croudy
Flint Community School
Flint, Michigan

John A. Grant
St. Louis Public Schools
St. Louis, Missouri

Vicki Haker
Mead Junior High School
Mead, Washington

Frederick G. Johnson
Georgia Department of Education
Atlanta, Georgia

Sterling C. Jones Jr.
Detroit Public Schools
Detroit, Michigan

Barry Kincaid
Raytown School District
Kansas City, Missouri

Evelyn G. Lewis
Newark Public Schools
Newark, New Jersey

M. DeAnn Morris
Crescenta Valley High School
La Crescenta, California

Anita Moss
University of North Carolina
Charlotte, North Carolina

Ann S. O'Toole
Chesterfield County Schools
Richmond, Virginia

Suzanne Owens
Glendale High School
Glendale, California

Sally P. Pfeifer
Lewis and Clark High School
Spokane, Washington

Marie Rogers
Independence High School
Charlotte, North Carolina

Barbara Schubert
Santa Clara County Office of
 Education
San Jose, California

Ronnie Spilton
Chattahoochee High School
Alpharetta, Georgia

Robert Stolte
Huntington Beach High School
Huntington Beach, California

Student Advisory Board

The Student Advisory Board was formed in an effort to ensure student involvement in the development of *Writer's Choice*. The editors wish to thank members of the board for their enthusiasm and dedication to the project.

The editors also wish to thank the many student writers whose models appear in this book.

Thanks are also due to Miami University of Ohio for help in the selection of models from student portfolios and to *Merlyn's Pen* for cooperation in providing student models.

Contents

Part 1 Composition

UNIT 1 Personal Writing

> **Grammar Link**
>
> When you write, avoid shifting verb tenses for no reason.
>
> In the literature model on page 10, note that N. Scott Momaday starts his recollection in the present tense and then sticks to that tense.
>
> Revise each sentence below to make the verb tenses consistent.
>
> 1. We went to the movies yesterday, and we see a double feature.
> 2. Sam's birthday party will be next week; it was a bowling party.
> That ~~~ol bus ~~ long Main Stree~

UNIT 2 The Writing Process

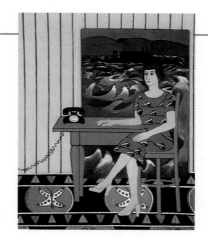

Grammar Link

Use vivid verbs in your narratives.

Effective sports stories contain verbs that let
the reader "see" what is happening. Rewrite
the sentences below, replacing all bold-faced
words with more vivid action verbs.

1. The Phoenix Suns **went** out onto the
   basketball court as the overflow home-
   town crowd **clapped**.
2. Charles Barkley **got** the tip and immediately **ran** to the basket.
3. The crowd **applauded** as Barkley **moved**
   around the opposing center to score.

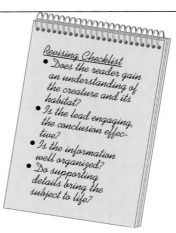

Revising Checklist
• Does the reader gain an understanding of the creature and its habitat?
• Is the lead engaging, the conclusion effective?
• Is the information well organized?
• Do supporting details bring the subject to life?

UNIT 5

Expository Writing

Grammar Link

Double negatives, such as *can't. . .no,* cancel each other out. Avoid them.

In the final paragraph of the model on page 284, the writer correctly uses only one negative word to express a negative idea.

Rewrite the sentences below, eliminating the double negatives.

¹There isn't no reason why the school can't sponsor a computer club. ²We don't have none now, but we could easily organize one. ³People who don't have no computer games could share them. ⁴People who don't know nothing about using a computer could get help. ⁵Since we don't

UNIT 7
Research Paper Writing

Four Types of Research Paper

Summary	The writer explores a topic by summing up the opinions of other writers and researchers.
Evaluative	The writer states an opinion and backs it up with evidence found in primary and/or secondary resources.
Original	The writer does original research on a topic and reports on his or her findings.
Combination	The writer combines approaches in one paper, such as summarizing opinions, then conducting original research.

Sentence Combining

Skills and Applications

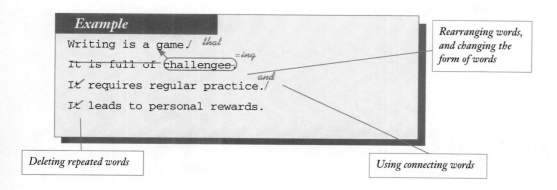

Example

Writing is a game./ *that*

It is full of ⌢challenges.⌡ *=ing*

It̸ requires regular practice./ *and*

It̸ leads to personal rewards.

Rearranging words, and changing the form of words

Deleting repeated words

Using connecting words

UNIT 9 Troubleshooter

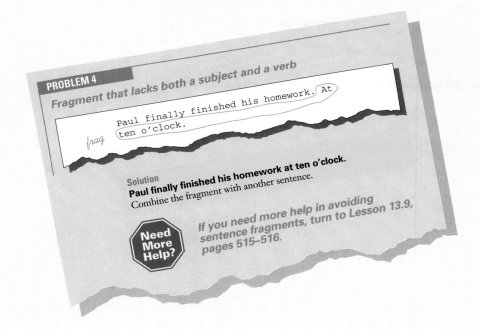

PROBLEM 4

Fragment that lacks both a subject and a verb

frag   Paul finally finished his homework. At ten o'clock.

Solution
Paul finally finished his homework at ten o'clock.
Combine the fragment with another sentence.

Need More Help? If you need more help in avoiding sentence fragments, turn to Lesson 13.9, pages 515–516.

Part 2 Grammar, Usage, and Mechanics

UNIT 10

Parts of Speech 400

UNIT 11

Parts of the Sentence 456

Part 3 Resources and Skills

Literature Models

Composition Models

Each literature selection is an extended example of the mode of writing taught in the unit.

Skill Models

Excerpts from outstanding works of fiction and nonfiction exemplify specific writing skills.

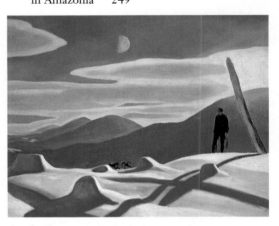

Language Models

Each Grammar Review uses excerpts to link grammar, usage, or mechanics to literature.

Fine Art

Fine art—paintings, drawings, photos, and sculpture—is used to teach as well as to stimulate writing ideas.

Case Studies:
Writers at Work

Each case study focuses on a real writer working on a
real-life writing project. Come on backstage!

Lisa Twyman Bessone
Sportswriter
Sportswriting, *Bessone
Profiles a Winner*
Page 166

Sandra Cisneros
**Poet and Fiction
Writer**
Letter Writing,
*A Letter from
Sandra Cisneros*
Page 4

Lorenzo Chavez
Feature Writer
Feature Writing,
*Chavez and the Quest
for Human-Interest
Stories*
Page 54

Gary Ross
Screenwriter
Fantasy Writing, *Ross
Scripts* Big
Page 124

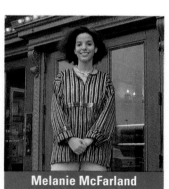

Melanie McFarland
Movie Reviewer
Movie Review, *At the Movies*
Page 276

Suzanne Winckler
Science Writer
Nature Writing, *Winckler
Tracks Cactus*
Page 214

Part 1

Composition

Hallways
- Wax bright on linoleum
- Rows of lockers, classroom doors for pun[c]tuation
- The click-clack sound of heels and rubber squeal of tennis shoes
- White, old-fashioned porcelain drinking fountains
- Voices calling to friends long out of earshot
- School smells: cafeteria, gym, chlorine, erasers, papers, books
- Frosted glass windows

Part 1 Composition

Personal Writing in the Real World

A Letter from Sandra Cisneros

F O C U S: Writing letters can help you communicate with someone, teach you something about yourself, and stimulate new writing ideas.

Author Sandra Cisneros

On a windy spring day, Sandra Cisneros stole some time from her busy schedule to write a letter to her friend, Pulitzer prize-winner and poet laureate of Illinois, Gwendolyn Brooks. Cisneros had just published a new book of fiction called *Woman Hollering Creek.* She says, "This was right before my book tour began. For some reason, I always tour with Brooks's book *Maud Martha.* That morning I'd read one of the stories. I thought, 'I should tell Ms. Brooks how much I like her book.'"

Cisneros had not written to Brooks for a long time, but she says, "I wanted her to know how happy her book made me at this moment and how important it's been to me. I'm sure I'll get a response from her further down the line."

Cisneros learned how to write a proper letter in the fifth grade, but she has struggled all her life to forget that lesson. The writer recalls, "In school they gave us all the parts of a model letter to a friend—and they taught us to write it as if it were an essay. It was a lesson in how to sound like someone we're not."

Now Cisneros only writes letters in which she is free to be herself. The author says her letters are "not the kind of conversations you have when

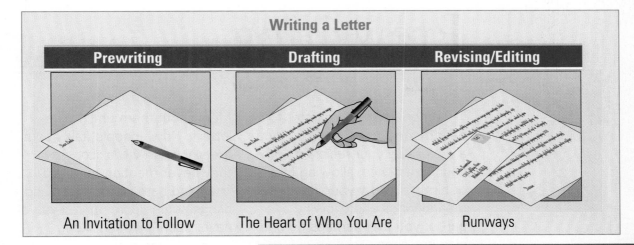

Writing a Letter

Prewriting	Drafting	Revising/Editing
An Invitation to Follow	The Heart of Who You Are	Runways

you're dressed in your suit, but the kind you have sitting at your kitchen table wearing your pajamas, talking to someone who's very dear to you."

Cisneros often writes her letters on "pretty paper, that delicious creamy kind with texture. Not intimidating paper, but paper you can do anything on. I'm very fussy about my pens and my papers."

For her letter to Gwendolyn Brooks, Cisneros sat at her typewriter for a couple of hours. She says, "When it's someone as special as Gwendolyn Brooks, you can't just dash off a postcard."

"I could call people, but I just love to write letters. When I write a letter I'm forced to shine my shoes and capture my experiences in the most accurate way possible for someone who's not present. It takes me a long time to write a letter. I want to write something very beautiful to give as a gift, the way an artist would give a sketch."

—Sandra Cisneros

Gwendolyn Brooks's novel Maud Martha *was published in 1953.*

Prewriting

AN INVITATION TO FOLLOW

When you write a letter to a dear friend, says Cisneros, "You are blessing your recipient with your confidence, allowing [her or him] to follow your inner meanderings and showing a part of you that perhaps no one else has seen."

Cisneros had recently moved to New Mexico when she began her letter to Gwendolyn Brooks. "When I get to a new place, I like to sift through the events that are affecting me. I don't know how I feel about them until I write letters. Now, [people] talk about the sky in New Mexico, but they never mention the wind. The wind here just rolls out and bangs porch doors open. I've never seen anything like it."

So Cisneros opened her letter to Gwendolyn Brooks by talking about the wind in New Mexico. As Cisneros says, "People don't realize that you can start a letter from whatever comes into your head."

Cisneros begins her letter by describing the wind over the mesa.

Drafting

THE HEART OF WHO YOU ARE

Drafting letters can reveal hidden or private aspects of yourself. Cisneros calls letter writing her "way of meditating, of listening inside my heart to how I'm being affected by the outside world. The heart of who you are comes out when you truly write."

This writer considers her letters to be a much more accurate reflection of her life than any other kind of record, including her journal, which she uses primarily as a place to write "shorthand" notes to herself.

Cisneros says, "In my letters, I can plunge right into that deeper level where my poems come from. Unless you talk for a very long time to someone you know very well, you can't reach that level. I often surprise myself by what I pull up. Then I make copies of my letters and they become longer journal entries."

A copy of Cisneros's letter to Gwendolyn Brooks will probably end up in Cisneros's journal under the title, "The Windy Day—Letter to Gwendolyn Brooks."

In the letter's second paragraph, Cisneros reminds Brooks of a book Brooks had given her.

March 5th, 1991

Dear Ms. Brooks,

It is what Winnie the Pooh would call a blustery day here. Or what Miss Emily would designate a wind like a bugle. From over and over the mesas, snapping dust and terrifying trees.

I am in my pajamas though it's past mid-day but I like my leisure to dream a little longer when I am asleep, and continue dreaming on paper when I am awake. I am rereading your wonderful MAUD MARTHA again, a copy you gave me, and which I am very grateful to have. I remember when I first discovered that book, in the American library in Sarajevo, across from the famous river where the archduke was shot that started a world war. And it was there too that I read T.S. Eliot's collected poems. If you go to Sarajevo, and look at the chapter on PRACTICAL CATS you'll see a cherry stain on one of the pages—because I was reading the book on the opposite bank of the river, under a row of cherry trees in front of my American friend Ana's apartment house, and at the moment I was reading about one of Eliot's cats—the Rum Tum Tigger?—a wind shook a cherry loose that landed with a startled plop on the page. And my heart gave a little jump too because the book wasn't mine. A wine-colored stain against the thick creamy pages.

Revising/Editing

RUNWAYS

Cisneros often revises and edits her letters on a typewriter.

In the second page of the letter, Cisneros tells Brooks about what is happening in her life.

Although Cisneros often writes her drafts by hand, she says, "Then I need to get to a typewriter, I need to see it typed to do the editing."

Even after she mails a letter, Cisneros keeps marking the copy she makes for herself. She says she often uses a letter as a "runway" to the creative writing process.

She says, "Sometimes I'll go through copies of my letters and I'll underline with a marker some nugget I'm going to save to reuse. When I'm stuck with a story, I might go through all my old letters and just read. I'll ask, 'Where can I put this?' Sometimes I start by writing a letter and then realize I've got a story. Other times, as I'm writing a story, I'll have a character rant or rave or whine or howl or laugh or swoon, and I'll realize that was really a letter to someone, but it's not going to get sent and it doesn't matter."

She continues, "I might use part of this letter to Gwendolyn Brooks in an essay that would include the anecdote of the cherry stain. What this letter particularly sparked for me was how I would like [to teach] the book *Maud Martha* in a course."

I mean to teach it one day along with other books that use a series of short inter-related stories. Perhaps with Ermilo Abreu Gomez's CANEK and Nellie Campobello's CARTUCHO albeit the translation of both is crooked. The form fascinates. And I'd done as much with MANGO STREET, though I hadn't met your MAUD yet. Perhaps I was "recollecting the things to come."

Ms. Brooks, please know I haven't quite disappeared altogether from the land. I've been migrant professor these past years, guest writer-in-residence at UC Berkeley, UC Irvine, the Univ. of Michigan at Ann Arbor and now here for one semester. All for the sake of protecting my writer-self. Some years dipped low and some reeled to high heaven. But now the days are good to me. I have a new book due out from Random (see enclosed reviews) and I have sold my little house on Mango to the big house of Vintage. Both books slated for this April. And it seems my life is in a whirl like the wind outside my window today. Everything shook and snapped and wind-washed and fresh, and, yes, that is how it should be.

I only wanted to say this to you today. That your book gives me such pleasure. That I admire it terribly. I think of you often, Ms. Brooks, and your spirit is with me always.

un abrazo fuerte, fuerte,

Sandra Cisneros

Responding to the Case Study

1. Discussion

Discuss these questions about Sandra Cisneros's writing.

- What are some differences between the letters Cisneros learned to write in school and those she writes now?
- In what way does Cisneros feel that writing a personal letter helps her to learn about herself?
- How does Cisneros use her letters as a source of ideas for her other writing?
- In her letter to Gwendolyn Brooks, what details does Cisneros include that help you understand her feelings?

2. Personal Writing

Write a one-page letter to your best friend. Choose a setting that is comfortable for you—perhaps one similar to that shown in the photo. Write to your friend about anything you wish. In your letter, express yourself as honestly as you can. Compare the experience of writing a letter to that of talking with your friend on the telephone. Which do you prefer? Why? How do you express yourself differently?

Grammar Link

Use subordinate clauses to create variety in sentence structure.

A *subordinate clause* has a subject and a predicate, but it cannot stand alone as a sentence. It must be attached to a main clause to make sense.

*I am in my pajamas **though it's past mid-day**....*

Use each subordinate clause below in a sentence. Start by thinking whom or what the clause might describe.

1. who moved away last year
2. after I had finished supper
3. although I have a desk in my room
4. before I was halfway through
5. when I get a chance

See Lesson 13.2, page 502.

Personal Writing
Writing to Discover

Self-discovery can happen in many ways. Former Beatle John Lennon expressed his identity in this self-portrait. N. Scott Momaday, in the model below, writes to discover something about himself.

John Lennon, *Self Portrait*

Literature Model

What uncertainties does Momaday give voice to here? In your opinion, who is this writing for?

Oh I feel so dumb . . . I don't know how to be a Kiowa Indian my grandmother lives in a house . . . only it doesn't have lights . . . and you have to carry wood in from the wood pile . . . but that isn't what makes it Indian its my grandma the way she is the way she looks her hair in braids the clothes somehow yes the way she talks she doesn't speak English so well . . . wait I know why it's an Indian house because . . . there is Indian stuff all around blankets and shawls bows and arrows everyone there . . . talks Kiowa and the old people wear Indian clothes . . . and there is laughing Indians laugh a lot and they sing oh yes they love to sing . . . there are drums too and it goes on through the night *that's* Indian . . .

Recalling specific details of sights and sounds helps Momaday deal with his uncertainties.

N. Scott Momaday, *The Names*

Learn by Writing

Asking personal questions is one way to get started writing about yourself. In the model, Momaday began with questions about his Kiowa heritage and then found answers as he recalled experiences, feelings, and observations. You can review elements of your own life to learn more about who you are, as the diagram below illustrates.

Personal Questions Chart (with Sample Answers)

Q. What are some of the central things that make me *me*?
A. African American, teenager, oldest kid in my family, member of soccer team

Q. How do I feel as a typical day goes on?
A. I usually feel pretty good; too much homework gets me down, though. I feel warm and secure at home but free and more myself with my friends.

Q. What kinds of lessons have I learned recently?
A. I've learned about friendship, about dating, and about being a good loser in soccer.

Q. What do I enjoy most lately?
A. Hanging out with friends, playing soccer, vegging out to dumb TV shows, and, believe it or not, my world history class

Observations
Our dog, Sparky, is getting pretty old. He sleeps most of the time and doesn't play catch anymore.

Memories
Oatmeal always reminds me of breakfasts with my grandmother.

Some sources for personal writing

Experiences
The first time Alissa and I went downtown alone, we got lost.

Reactions
I get so angry when Mom expects me to babysit my little sister, Mandy.

Feelings
I feel completely in control when I strike out a batter.

Journal Writing

John Lennon's self-portrait on page 10 emphasizes three features: his hair, his nose, and his eyeglasses. In your journal, draw a simple sketch of yourself. Emphasize three simple attributes, either physical characteristics or personality traits. Then write to answer this question: What does your self-portrait reveal about who you are?

Write About Yourself

Whatever your sources, often the easiest way to begin personal writing is simply to begin—let your thoughts run free and write whatever comes to mind. Don't worry about spelling or grammar. Set a definite time limit—say, ten minutes—and keep writing until the time is up. If you get stuck, write anything, even "I'm stuck!" Just keep going. Before you know it, a word will spark a memory or another idea, and you'll be on your way. In the process, you may clarify your thoughts and even discover something about yourself. The chart below shows how this might happen.

A Stroll Through Personal Writing

1 Simply begin. How do I begin?

2 Keep writing. Begin began begun . . .

3 A word will spark an idea. What have I begun lately?

4 The idea grows. Started babysitting next door

5 Idea leads to a memory. My favorite babysitter when I was five

6A Memory leads in direction A. Helped me make funny snowmen

6B Memory leads in direction B. Wonder what he's doing now

7 Finally, writing takes a focus. I liked sculpting snow, making funny faces. It's like the cartoons I draw for the school paper . . . that's part of who I am, "the cartoonist"!

Your experiences, feelings, memories, observations, and reactions are your best sources for personal writing. See what student Vallery McCann learned about herself.

How would you assess the honesty of Vallery's writing? Does it sound authentic?

This journal entry helps Vallery think about plans for her future. What plans might you write about?

Student Model

Well, today is a milestone in my life. Yeehah. Three years ago today I was ending an old life and beginning a new one, & I didn't even know it. The freedom I have today is incredible. I am not ashamed of me. I have gotten to know myself. I was thinking on my way to school today maybe the difference between a romantic relationship & a friendship is that in a friendship the only commitment is unconditional love. I'm getting ready to graduate. Life looms ahead. I'm finding myself believing in education. I want to teach and give that opportunity of freedom to others. So today is my third anniversary drug free! I will not back down! I am free!

Vallery McCann, Hamilton Heights High School, Arcadia, Indiana

1.1 Writing Activities

Freewrite About Yourself

Choose one of the following opening phrases, or use one of your own, to write about freely for five minutes. Remember, keep writing. If you get stuck, repeat a word over and over until something else comes to you.

- If only I could . . .
- The one word that best describes me is . . .
- I would never give up my . . .
- No one knows that I . . .
- The one thing I would like to change about myself is . . .

When you are finished, review what you have written. Underline any parts that help you learn about yourself. Did you discover anything new? Then circle phrases or ideas that you might want to use in a composition and save them for future reference.

PURPOSE	To express your viewpoint on a topic that interests you
AUDIENCE	Adult and teen-age newspaper readers
LENGTH	3–4 paragraphs

Cross-Curricular: Social Studies

Spend several minutes writing about your town, city, or community, and how it has contributed to making you who you are. Include some of the following points:

- How does the size of your community affect you? Do you live in a crowded city, always surrounded by other people, or in an isolated, rural environment?
- Do your friends and neighbors share a similar cultural background, or is it a very mixed neighborhood? What have you learned from this?
- How have the schools and other institutions in your neighborhood affected you?
- How do the characteristics of your community contribute to making you the kind of person you are?

Summarize your answers to these and any other questions you think of in a paragraph or two.

Grammar Link

When you write, avoid shifting verb tenses for no reason.

In the literature model on page 10, note that N. Scott Momaday starts his recollection in the present tense and then sticks to that tense.

Revise each sentence below to make the verb tenses consistent.

1. We went to the movies yesterday, and we see a double feature.
2. Sam's birthday party will be next week; it was a bowling party.
3. That school bus goes along Main Street and turned right on Linden.
4. When I got to school, I meet my friend before science class.
5. Pat likes this book because she enjoyed the author's style.

See Lesson 15.6, page 556.

Personal Writing
Keeping a Journal

A writer's journal can be a place to examine feelings, record daily events, or even try out new ideas. During World War II, thirteen-year-old Anne Frank and her family were forced to hide in a cramped attic to avoid capture by the Nazis. Frank's journal became her refuge during those terrible times.

Literature Model

Notice that Frank dates the journal entry.

Friday, 24 December 1943

When someone comes in from outside, with the wind in their clothes and the cold on their faces, then I could bury my head in the blankets to stop myself thinking: "When will we be granted the privilege of smelling fresh air?" And because I must not bury my head in the blankets, but the reverse—I must keep my head high and be brave, the thoughts will come not once, but oh, countless times. Believe me, if you have been shut up for a year and a half, it can get too much for you some days . . . . Cycling, dancing, whistling, looking out into the world, feeling young, to know that I'm free—that's what I long for; still, I mustn't show it. . . . I sometimes ask myself, "Would anyone, either Jew or non-Jew understand this about me, that I am simply a young girl badly in need of some rollicking fun?" I don't know, and I couldn't talk about it to anyone.

Frank is first inspired to write by thoughts of sensory details—"cold on their faces," "smelling fresh air."

Frank uses this brief journal entry to ask important questions, give herself advice, and vent her feelings. In your opinion, what is the value of such expression?

Anne Frank, *The Diary of a Young Girl*

Why Keep a Journal?

Keeping a journal is like thinking out loud—on paper. In your journal you might record daily events, but you also are free to follow an idea wherever it leads. By writing about your experiences, reactions, and observations, you can make discoveries about yourself and the world.

It just dawned on me! In only five days my sister will be nineteen years old! The last year of teen-agism. What happened to the little girl who would play Barbies with me, to my best friend who had been by my side for the last sixteen years? I miss her so much! Growing up can really hurt. It really is painful how everyone must part and make their separate way.

Kimberly Daniel, Jefferson Davis High School, Montgomery, Alabama

Freewriting can go wherever the writer's mind goes. Notice how Kimberly even makes up a word—"teen-agism."

Kimberly expresses an important lesson about growing up and moving on. Perhaps she'll develop this idea more fully later.

You can choose from a number of different kinds of journals, each with a different purpose. A diary, for example, is a personal record of daily events that the writer doesn't usually plan to share. A student may also keep a learning log to record thoughts and impressions of school courses and what's going on in those courses.

Your journal can also serve as a writer's journal—that is, a source for ideas to inspire your writing. These might be brief notes on writing ideas, a collection of words or phrases, even news clippings, jokes, or photographs. Here's a story idea that came from one student's journal.

I was thinking about something rather funny the other day. I wondered what it would be like to have grown old overnight and pass up all the hardships of life (develop this as the opening of my story). I would already be retired and I wouldn't have to worry about finishing school or getting a job . . . I would be able to go places and do things without having to worry about getting somewhere on time (give examples and go into more detail) . . . (All of this could be developed into a story about a boy who has grown old and finds out . . . that he has missed the best parts of life.)

Matthew Porter, Jefferson Davis High School, Montgomery, Alabama

Do you find Matthew's idea for writing interesting?

Notice how Matthew uses his writing to come up with a concrete idea for a story. This can work for you, too.

Journal Writing

Compare the two student models on this page. What do they reveal about their writers? What kinds of materials are included in each? Record your reactions in your own journal.

How Do You Keep a Journal?

Journal writing has no set rules. You just need to find a system that works for you. Here are some tips that might help you get started on your own journal.

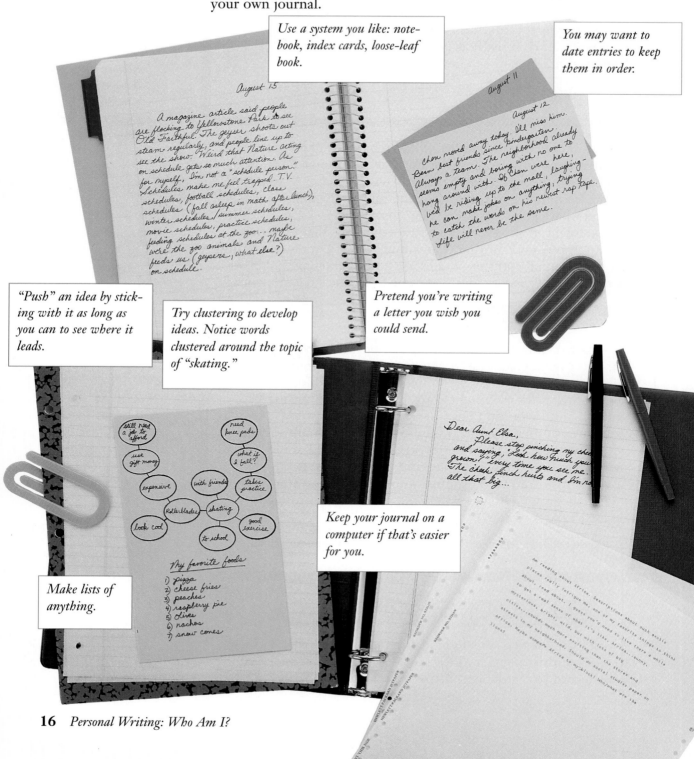

Use a system you like: notebook, index cards, loose-leaf book.

You may want to date entries to keep them in order.

"Push" an idea by sticking with it as long as you can to see where it leads.

Try clustering to develop ideas. Notice words clustered around the topic of "skating."

Pretend you're writing a letter you wish you could send.

Keep your journal on a computer if that's easier for you.

Make lists of anything.

Write a Journal Entry

Look at the painting on this page. Create a journal entry based on this painting. Write, for example, about what you see in the painting. Does it evoke any memories? Any feelings or ideas for writing?

- Think aloud on paper.
- Let one idea lead you to another.
- Date your entry.

PURPOSE To free-associate from a picture
AUDIENCE Yourself
LENGTH 1–3 paragraphs

Berthe Morisot, *The Cherry Tree*, c. 1891

Cooperative Learning

In a small group, brainstorm about travel experiences that have helped you discover something about yourself. Talk about places you have seen, people you have met, or experiences you have had away from home. Let others take notes as each person talks. Use the notes to write a journal entry about how these experiences have changed you or taught you something about yourself.

Grammar Link

In personal writing, be sure you use the correct pronoun, *I* or *me*, in a compound subject or object.

Use *I* or *me* to complete each sentence below.

1. Dan and _____ are working on a history project.
2. His grandfather has sent some old family documents for him and _____ to use.
3. My sister drove Dan and _____ to the main library on Saturday.
4. He and _____ each used the computer and microfiche to locate information.
5. Our adviser told Dan and _____ that we can exhibit our project in the media center.

See Lesson 17.1, page 595.

Personal Writing
Writing a Personal Essay

A personal essay offers opinions about something the writer has experienced or takes a personal interest in. In the model below, Robert Fulghum tells why he thinks certain household experiences are crucial to growing up.

Law?
Medicine?
Getting Married?
Paying Bills!
Buying a Car?
Killing Bugs Myself!

Literature Model

After the dishes are washed and the sink rinsed out, there remains in the strainer at the bottom of the sink what I will call, momentarily, some "stuff." A rational, intelligent, objective person would say that this is simply a mixture of food particles too big to go down the drain. . . . But any teenager who has been dragooned into washing dishes knows this explanation is a lie. That stuff in the bottom of the strainer is toxic waste—deadly poison—a danger to health. In other words, about as icky as icky gets.

One of the . . . reasons I had . . . respect for my mother when I was thirteen was because she would reach into the sink with her bare hands—BARE HANDS—and pick up that lethal gunk and drop it into the garbage. . . .

Never mind what any parent or objective adult might tell me, I knew that the stuff in the sink drainer was lethal. . . .

But now. Now, I am a grown-up. And have been for some time. And I imagine making a speech to a high school graduating class. . . . I would give them this list of things that grown-ups do: clean the sink strainer . . . clean up the floor when the baby throws strained spinach, clean ovens and grease traps and roasting pans. . . . I'd tell the graduates that when they can do these things, they will be adults. Some of the students might not want to go on at this point. But they may as well face the truth . . . Being an adult *is* dirty work.

But someone has to do it.

Robert Fulghum, *It Was On Fire When I Lay Down On It*

What effect do words like "toxic" and "icky" have on you? What other words contribute to Fulghum's vivid, humorous picture?

Why do you suppose Fulghum saved the main point for the end of his piece?

What Is a Personal Essay?

A personal essay expresses your viewpoint about a subject you have experienced—a subject other than yourself. The personal essay is not directly about you. You may write your personal essay in a traditional essay format—introduction, body paragraphs, and conclusion—or you may write it in a freer way, following your own train of thought. As you write your essay, you can follow Fulghum's example and use humorous anecdotes and exaggeration to express your views.

What Can I Write About?

If you have an assigned topic, explore the aspects that especially intrigue you. Otherwise, write about whatever interests you.

Select a Topic   Your journal, newspapers, and magazines are sources of essay ideas. Here are two other ways to find a topic.

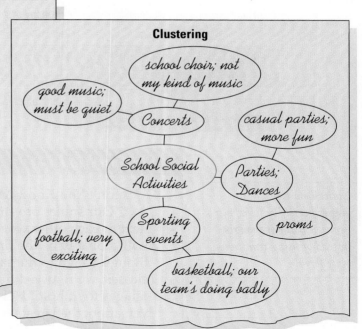

Freewriting
Write freely to find a topic. Write on whatever we want...write on write on write on...right on! Old slang phrase. Not totally awesome or even groovy--more tubular? Slang words mean different things. "Bad" means good (drove Dad crazy with that one!) Where did all those words come from? (requires research) What does slang do for me? Why slang? with friends? with adults? It'S LANG uage isn't it? TOPIC!

Clustering

good music; must be quiet

school choir; not my kind of music

Concerts

casual parties; more fun

School Social Activities

Parties; Dances

proms

football; very exciting

Sporting events

basketball; our team's doing badly

Journal Writing

In your journal, try creating a cluster diagram to help you think of an essay topic. Begin with a base word about something that interests you, and see where you end up. If you need help getting started, look around the room, and write the name of an object.

Compose a Thesis Statement   A thesis statement conveys your main point. It may also explain how you intend to support your main point. To develop a thesis statement, ask yourself questions about your topic. Focus on a specific aspect of the subject, and condense it to a basic statement. Consider Fulghum's thesis statement: "Being an adult *is* dirty work."

How Can I Make My Essay Come to Life?

By letting your enthusiasm for your topic influence your choice of words and details, you can make your essay lively. Support your thesis statement with vivid details and examples. Use these tips and model.

How Can I Make My Essay Interesting?	
Tip	**Example**
Answer offbeat questions about the subject.	What might views on this subject have been a hundred years ago? A hundred years ago, people might have thought that . . .
Include personal anecdotes.	I won my first carnival goldfish when . . .
Pretend to be a reporter covering a news story.	We are at the local video arcade to . . .
Compare your topic to something familiar and fun.	Doing algebra problems is a little like working out crossword puzzles.

Student Model

Notice how Keshia expresses herself by following her own train of thought instead of using traditional essay form.

Like Fulghum, Keshia presents her main point at the end of the essay.

Don't You Know Me?
Our smiles are simple smiles. As we both sit down next to each other we realize that smile that was shared will probably be the first and last between us. Even though we go to the same school and have the same classes, we're two different people with two different images to uphold. Hers is the jet set world of witty conversation, the latest styles, and dates. The purse, the walk, and the friends she keeps tell her lifestyle and identity. The buzzing in the halls, the shared glances between them let you know you are the outsider looking in.

As we step off the bus we put on our "masks" for the stage we'll be on. One's mask is a little bit brighter, the other one's dull, but each a character just the same.

Keshia White, Hyde Park Career Academy, Chicago, Illinois

1.3 Writing Activities

Write a Personal Essay

Use one of the following topics or one of your own choosing to write a personal essay that could be published in your school or home-town newspaper: How becoming a teenager changed my life style; what one U.S. teenager thinks about the future of the country; what I wish someone had told me when I was five.

- Include a thesis statement.
- Use vivid details and examples.

PURPOSE Self-discovery
AUDIENCE Yourself
LENGTH 3–4 paragraphs

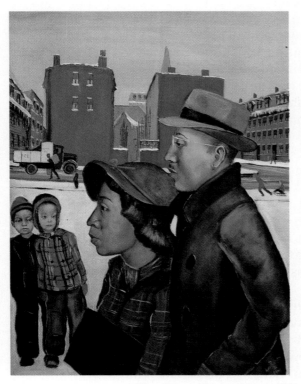

Allan Crite,—*Harriet and Leon*, 1941

Grammar Link

Use strong, specific verbs to make your personal writing clear and effective.

For example, Robert Fulghum speaks in his essay of a teenager who is ***dragooned into washing dishes.***

In each sentence, replace the general verb with one that is more precise.

1. The student volunteers worked all day at the new community center.
2. Some cleaned floors and windows.
3. Others moved lumber and cinder blocks from the yard into the meeting room.
4. Most of the students like the results of the day's efforts.
5. Only a few spoke about the difficulty of the work.

See Lesson 10.3, pages 414–422.

Cooperative Learning

In a small group, study the painting on this page. Discuss similarities and differences between your neighborhood and that shown in the painting. Consider how the artist might have painted your street if he had used you or your neighbors as subjects, and write an essay about this topic. Use the group discussion to help you write your individual essays. Then regroup, and consider how you might present the essays to the whole class.

Personal Writing
Writing Autobiography

Autobiographies are first-person accounts of important moments in an individual's life. In the model below, Lynn Griffey describes a personal experience.

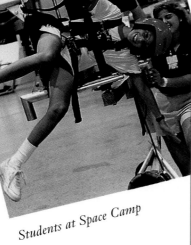

Students at Space Camp

Student Model

*E*ver since I was a child, I've been fascinated with space. So in the fall of my junior year my parents sent me to the United States Space Camp. I was so excited; I thought this was going to be the beginning of great things to come. This was my dream come true. I always had dreams of me in space, and I always knew I could do it.

Immediately after I got there, I looked around. I saw how every one of those kids had the same dreams and feelings I had. It was incredible.

After sitting through lecture after lecture, and going through experiment after experiment, I realized that I wasn't sure of my feelings anymore. I knew I was having a great time learning and exploring, but I also knew that I didn't have the same look in my eye that one boy did. He was having more than just a "good time"; he lived to be doing this.

I began feeling guilty because I started thinking of all the money my parents had spent for me to go there. Then I realized they want me to be happy. That's why they spent all the money, to see if this was what I wanted to do for the rest of my life.

I think I learned a lot about myself that week. I discovered that at sixteen it's not necessary to know precisely what the future holds. Maybe I'll still want to be in space some day. However, right now I just want to be sixteen and explore all the exciting careers I have to choose from.

Lynn Griffey, Hamilton Heights High School, Arcadia, Indiana

Notice how Lynn introduces the subject, setting, and main idea early on. Where do you first sense what might happen? Which words help to create this sense?

Lynn concludes by relating how her experience changed her perception of herself as well as her goals and expectations.

What Is an Autobiography?

An autobiography is a person's written account of his or her own life—experiences, thoughts, feelings. An autobiographical sketch, like Lynn's, is personal writing about a significant event or period in the writer's life. It should give readers a sense of who the author is, how the author came to be that way, and what the author has experienced.

How Do You Find Autobiographical Material?

Your autobiographical material comes from your life—anything you have done, felt, thought, dreamed, experienced, or learned. We all have mental files of our experiences. Each of us uses a variety of different filing systems. We file events by emotional content—happy, sad, exhilarating. We file them according to the time in our lives they occurred—before school age, during elementary school. We even file them according to the areas in our lives to which they relate—school, family, friends.

To search through your mental files, start by making a list of general categories, or file labels, you might find in each of the filing systems listed below. Then brainstorm, freewrite, or use other prewriting techniques to retrieve some of the specific experiences you have stored in these files. Refer to Lesson 2.2, pages 64–68, for other prewriting techniques.

Your Autobiographical Files		
Filing System	**Sample File Labels**	**Sample Experience**
By emotional content	Happy, sad, afraid, angry	Getting a new bicycle
By time they occurred	Early childhood, junior high	Beginning junior high school
By area in life they relate to	Family, friends	Taking car trips with my family

Journal Writing

In your journal, create a "life map." From left to right, draw or write important events from your life in chronological order. Shape your map any way—straight line, peaks and valleys, loops.

How Do You Present Your Material?

There are many ways to present autobiographical material. You can begin with "I remember" and then recount a particular event. You can structure your story as an interview or you can use one of the methods shown in the chart. You may need to explain the significance of an event, as Kareem Abdul-Jabbar does in the model.

Two Ways to Present Your Material			
Flashback	**Present** Shopping with Gloria —we both loved the same clothes.	**Past** Even as 4-year-olds, she and I wanted the same toys.	**Present** I hope that we don't start to like the same boys now.
Successive Journal Entries	**Feb. 8** Nelsons asked me to go skiing with them —sort of scared.	**Feb. 9** Best day ever! I skied quite well- for my first time out.	**Feb. 10** Couldn't get out of bed. It hurt to walk.

Literature Model

Abdul-Jabbar sets the scene and presents the main idea immediately.

What kind of words does Abdul-Jabbar use to create a vivid picture of the event?

In the final sentences of this autobiographical sketch, Abdul-Jabbar sums up the significance of this event.

I t was that summer [after seventh grade] that I grew so many inches and started at least to *look* like a basketball player. I started to be able to do things like palm a basketball and touch the rim, and it was soon obvious that the long frame could be put to use in places other than the baseball diamond. Around this same time, one event changed my view of basketball and how to play it dramatically. I went to see a high school all-star game at the Brownsville Boys Club in Brooklyn. Guys like Connie Hawkins, Roger Brown, Billy Burwell, and other All-City players were on the court doing their thing, and I was awestruck. I had never seen people dunk and soar and change direction in midstride the way these guys did. . . . The warm-up was awe-inspiring, and I feel that evening in Brooklyn changed my concept forever of what is possible on the court. Baseball would remain close to my heart, but here was a game that was best played by individuals with *my* physical attributes. The possibilities seemed endless.

Kareem Abdul-Jabbar with Mignon McCarthy, *Kareem*

1.4 Writing Activities

Write an Autobiographical Sketch

Think of an event or period in your life that you feel had an impact on the kind of person you are now. You might remember making or losing a friend, visiting a new place, or learning a new skill or sport. Once you have chosen a topic, decide on the most effective technique to tell your story.

- Provide all the information your readers will need to understand your sketch.

- Be sure the story conveys a sense of who you are.

- Make clear why the episode you are describing had such an effect on you.

- Tell what happened; don't just comment on it.

PURPOSE To tell about an important event in your life
AUDIENCE Classmates and teacher
LENGTH 5–6 paragraphs

COMPUTER OPTION

You may wish to share your autobiographical sketch with family members or friends. If so, your computer's page makeup capability can help you to design a professional-looking document. You might design the page with the title of the essay or poem as the headline, in boldface type.

Grammar Link

In general, avoid sentence fragments in your writing.

A **sentence fragment** is an error that occurs when an incomplete sentence is punctuated as a complete sentence. Often the fragment can be joined to the sentence that comes before or after it. Read this example:

Ever since I was a child. (fragment) I've been fascinated with space.

Ever since I was a child, I've been fascinated with space. (complete sentence)

In the paragraph below, change each sentence fragment to form a complete sentence.

I want to make my career in music. [1]Because I love playing trumpet. I play in the band and orchestra. [2]And the jazz band, too. Next, I want to learn to play the French horn. [3]Maybe during summer vacation. [4]If my job leaves me enough time to practice. My parents say I should plan a different career. [5]Something dependable, like accounting or teaching. We'll see.

See Lesson 13.9, pages 515–516.

Personal Writing
Writing a Poem

Whether rhymed or unrhymed, poems often convey personal feelings through the use of strong, precise language.

Langston Hughes wanted to express his feelings about his people, African Americans. Notice how powerfully he does so—and with so few words—in this brief poem.

> ### Literature Model
>
> *My People*
>
> The night is beautiful,
> So the faces of my people.
>
> The stars are beautiful,
> So the eyes of my people.
>
> Beautiful, also, is the sun.
> Beautiful, also, are the souls of my people.
>
> Langston Hughes

This free-verse poem does not have regular rhyme or rhythm patterns, but the repetition gives it a rhythmic feeling.

Poetry as Self-Expression

Effective poets like Hughes put together words to create sounds and images that express much more than what the words alone actually say. Such sounds and images help poets actively engage their readers' memories, emotions, and imaginations.

Traditional and Free Verse

In free verse such as Hughes's poem, there are no set patterns of rhyme or rhythm. More traditional poems, however, do follow set rhyme and rhythm patterns. Compare the following humorous poem with Hughes's poem. Notice the regular rhyming and rhythmic patterns in "Song of the Open Road" and the freer form and style of "My People." One thing both poems do have in common is a strong central image.

Song of the Open Road

I think that I shall never see
A billboard lovely as a tree.
Indeed, unless the billboards fall
I'll never see a tree at all.

Ogden Nash

The Special Language of Poetry

The language of poetry is one of vivid sounds and images. Just think of how Langston Hughes's images of night, stars, and sun linger and overlap with the images of his people's faces, eyes, and souls. Poets create such memorable pictures with a variety of techniques such as those explained in this chart.

Some Poetic Devices		
Device	**Definition**	**Example**
Sensory detail	A detail that appeals to one of the senses: sight, touch, taste, smell, or hearing	Slivers of frosty grass crunched underfoot.
Simile	A comparison between two unlike things, using the words *like* or *as*	Sleep, like a soft, dark blanket, comforted him.
Metaphor	A comparison between two unlike things, without using the words *like* or *as*	Her dress was a pink cloud of crepe.
Personification	The giving of human qualities to objects, animals, or things	Flowers saluted the morning sun.
Sound effect	A pattern of sound (e.g., rhyme, rhythm, repetition) used to help create an image	The raspy snarl of a motorcycle awakened him.

Journal Writing

Find a single word in one of the poems in this lesson or in the list of examples above, and use it as the center for brainstorming. Generate associations, in the form of words or phrases, with this word as fast as you can. Then use some of your associations to create a brief poem.

Forms of Poetry

Like most traditional haiku, this one has five syllables in lines 1 and 3 and seven in line 2.

Literature Model

There was a young person from Perth
Who was born on the day of his birth.
He was married, they say,
On his wife's wedding day
And died when he quitted this earth.

Anonymous

Literature Model

Butterfly, these words
from my brush are not flowers,
only their shadows.

Soseki

Like most limericks, this one begins "There was a . . ." and ends with a funny or unusual rhyming line.

In the poems above, notice the limerick's rhyming pattern and the haiku's syllable pattern. Following is a free verse poem.

Student Model

Intimate Calm

There—
With the soft rays of the lamp
Resting on the pallid walls
And the earthen carpet—
With the falling leaves and the dark, dewy dusk
Enveloping me
Like my grandmother's familiar afghan—
With the comforting sounds of the television
Capturing my attention with its witty charm—
With the beautiful willowing wisps
Of my brother's laughter in the kitchen
With my body
Propped against my favorite pillow
Sunken into the billowing cushions
Curled like the kitten
Asleep in my lap
Underneath that familiar yarn
Which conceals the memories of my mother's mother—
I lay
With a peaceful mind—
Eating refried beans

Heather Robertson, Jefferson Davis High School, Montgomery, Alabama

Why do you suppose Heather chose to repeat the word "with" at the beginning of several lines?

The repetition of the k and hard c sound provides a rhythm to these two lines.

Write Your Own Poem

Try freewriting to come up with an idea for a poem. Begin by focusing on a subject about which you have strong feelings. Underline any words or phrases that are especially descriptive of your topic or your feelings about it. Use some or all of the underlined items in your poem.

- Use at least two of the poetic devices in the chart on page 27.
- Give your poem a pattern of some kind.

PURPOSE To write an original poem
AUDIENCE Students and teachers
LENGTH 5–15 lines

Rufino Tamayo, *Hombre Ante el Infinito (Man Contemplates Infinity)*, 1950

Grammar Link

Use precise adjectives to bring your sentences to life.

Notice how Heather Robertson, in her poem "Intimate Calm," uses precise *adjectives* to create vivid images:

pallid** walls;* ***billowing *cushions*

Revise the lines below by adding vivid adjectives to modify nouns.

1. two people standing on a hillside overlooking a lake
2. a baby sleeping in its stroller
3. the chair in the dentist's office, surrounded by tools and equipment
4. wind in the trees outside the cabin
5. a potted plant on the table near the window

See Lesson 10.4, pages 423–428.

Cooperative Learning

In a small group brainstorm ideas for a poem about the painting on this page. Use some of the poetic techniques discussed in this lesson (similes, metaphors, personification). List all the suggested ideas and phrases. To get started, imagine yourself the central figure in the painting. What do you see? What are you thinking about? Write your own poem, adapting and arranging the ideas as you wish. Use free verse or follow a pattern of rhyme and rhythm. Meet again as a group to share and discuss your poems.

Writing About Literature
Keeping a Reader-
Response Journal

A reader-response journal is a place where you can record your reactions to what you are reading.

When Mitchell Kittlaus, a student from Illinois, finished reading Katherine Mansfield's story "The Doll's House," he was prompted to write in his reader-response log. Read the "letter-to-the-character" letter Mitchell wrote. See what it was that impressed him about the character Kezia.

Student Model

Dear Kezia,

What word choices in Mitchell's letter suggest the degree of his involvement in the story?

I admire you greatly for the courage you displayed. . . . You took a big risk by inviting the Kelvey girls into your courtyard to see the doll house. Do not be intimidated by your aunt's punishment. Although you should obey your elders, it was right of you to question their negative opinion of the Kelveys. If you do not understand their attitude, take the initiative to talk with your parents and relatives, so that together you can discuss their views. You may not agree with what they believe, but it is important that you fully comprehend their feelings.

Mitchell expresses his personal feelings about the story's main incident.

I also respect you for the kindness that you showed to Lil and Else Kelvey. It is always easier to hurt someone's feelings by acting in an inconsiderate way, especially when such thoughtless behavior is encouraged by one's peers. . . .

I encourage you to continue to keep an open mind in your relations with others. People should only be judged by the content of their character. Hopefully, you can set a positive example for others to follow.

Mitchell Kittlaus, Evanston Township High School, Evanston, Illinois

---

Respond Personally

A reader-response journal can be a special section in a larger personal journal or a journal in itself. In a reader-response journal, you can write about what interests, puzzles, angers, or even bores you about your reading. The journal can help you keep track of what's going on in the work you are reading. More importantly it can help you relate your reading to your own life. For example, you might write about similarities you find between a character's view of life and your own.

Respond Creatively

Think of new ways to respond to your reading. You might write a letter of encouragement (or complaint) to the main character. You could rewrite a scene from a play to make it take place in your home town. Some of these ideas may inspire you to write your own creative pieces.

Responding to What You Read	
Idea	**Sample**
1. Write a news flash.	Flash! Three local children disappeared last night from their backyard. Relatives say the three had been talking about time travel just prior to their disappearance. (response to *A Wrinkle in Time* by Madeleine L'Engle)
2. Imagine yourself as a main character.	Here I am shipwrecked on a deserted island with just a bunch of other boys my own age. I'd better make a plan for survival. (response to *Lord of the Flies* by William Golding; the photo on the right is from a movie based on that novel)
3. Write about the character visiting your home.	As Mrs. Luella Bates Washington Jones came through the door, she filled our living room with her powerful presence. (response to "Thank You, M'am" by Langston Hughes)

In your reader-response journal, you could suggest what might have happened if two characters had never met or if one event hadn't taken place. What if the setting were changed? Be creative in finding ways to write about your reading.

Journal Writing

Choose a book or story you have read recently. In your journal, respond to the story in any way you wish.

Respond to Learn About Yourself

An important part of any story, novel, play, essay, or poem is what you, the reader, bring to it. When you reflect on it in light of your personal experiences and impressions, literature can actually change you.

Keeping a reader-response journal gives you a chance to think more about a work of literature—to consider the relevance of the story or poem to your own life. What do you think about . . . ? How would you change it to make it more real? What if . . . ? Would you have done what the characters did?

By considering these kinds of questions, you come to a new, deeper understanding of the story. Michelle Kalski learns about herself by responding to Shel Silverstein's poem "Reflection" in two different ways.

REFLECTION

Each time I see the Upside-Down Man
Standing in the water,
I look at him and start to laugh,
Although I shouldn't oughtter.
For maybe in another world
Another time
Another town,
Maybe HE is right side up
And I am upside down.

Shel Silverstein

Student Models

Just a reflection of myself.
Or so it seems.
What stares back is a person
Full of peace and at ease.
A backward image of me.

Dear Mr. Silverstein,

Finally, someone has managed to step into the world of a reflection. As a curious youngster, I was always fascinated with reflections and looked for ways to prove that the person in the pool of water or the mirror was somehow different than me. I thought it was wonderful of you to reveal the idea of a reflection being in the world right side up.

Michelle Kalski, Evanston Township High School, Evanston, Illinois

Notice how Michelle relates Silverstein's poem to her own life by telling of a childhood fascination of hers.

1.6 Writing Activities

Write a Reader-Response Journal Entry

Read the poems below. Then choose one of them or one of your own choosing. Respond to the poem you select in a creative way as you would in a reader-response journal.

Old Mary

My last defense
Is the present tense.

It little hurts me now to know
I shall not go

Cathedral-hunting in Spain
Nor cherrying in Michigan or Maine.

Gwendolyn Brooks

My People

The night is beautiful,
So the faces of my people.

The stars are beautiful,
So the eyes of my people.

Beautiful, also, is the sun.
Beautiful, also, are the souls of my people.

Langston Hughes

Keep these questions in mind as you respond to the poem:

- How does the poem relate to your life?
- What feelings does it suggest?
- How do you agree or disagree with it?

PURPOSE To explore your reactions to a poem
AUDIENCE Yourself
LENGTH 1–3 paragraphs

COMPUTER OPTION

If you are entering your reader-response entries into a computer file, you will need some way to identify your entries for retrieval. A good plan is to date each entry. Or you might add a code word, such as *poems* or the author's name. Then you can use the Search function to retrieve a particular entry.

Grammar Link

When using pronouns, do not shift person or number without a good reason.

Notice how, in his letter on page 30, Mitchell consistently uses the pronoun *you* when addressing Kezia.

Supply appropriate pronouns in the following sentences.

1. I especially like reading science fiction, where _____ appreciate the combination of fact and fantasy.
2. When one reads a play, _____ must visualize the action of the characters.
3. We enjoyed his poetry because _____ can clearly understand his feelings.
4. If you don't like the major characters in a book, it is hard for _____ to take much interest in what happens to _____.
5. They love Agatha Christie's stories because _____ never get tired of her characters.

See Lesson 17.5, pages 602–606.

Writing About Literature
Writing About Biography

When you are reading a biography, one way to respond is to relate events in the subject's life to your own life. Shella Calamba does this in the model below.

Amelia Earhart, 1933

Student Model

I never thought Amelia Earhart and I could have so much in common. Although, as a little girl, I was outfitted in frilly doll dresses and constantly reminded to be "lady-like," I, like Amelia, preferred to do things that were branded as "tomboy" activities, such as climbing trees, which was hard, but feasible, while wearing a pink dress. Amelia's roller coaster project reminded me of my own skateboard dashes down a hill in sledding fashion. As Amelia did, I, too, often employ the phrase "because I want to," to justify actions that may seem inane or highly psychotic to others.

Not only did Amelia's childhood remind me of mine, she also made me think of a friend from grammar school who dreams of becoming a pilot. She will undoubtedly be forced to deal with sexism in pursuing her goal, but I think reading Amelia's biography would prevent her from being discouraged in achieving her ambitions. Even by today's standards, what Amelia accomplished was remarkable and unprecedented by any man or woman. However, Amelia is not someone to be admired exclusively by pilots. Her courage, determination, and persistence set an inspiring example for anyone with a dream.

Shella Calamba, Lincoln Park High School, Chicago, Illinois

> *What words signal the many comparisons between Shella and Amelia in the first paragraph?*

> *Shella shows the relevance of the biography to others in today's world, moving from personal meanings to more general ones.*

Respond Personally to a Biography

When you respond personally to a biography, you are responding to the subject of the biography and to his or her world. You can try to get to know the subject by focusing your reader-response journal entries on the subject's attitudes, values, and behavior. What does the subject care about? What motivates her or him in life? Relate your discoveries to your own life. Do you care about the same kinds of things as the subject? What qualities does the subject have that you admire? What do the subject's accomplishments teach you about your own life?

The chart below shows some ways you can respond personally to a biography. Try any of the following suggestions or come up with other ways of thinking about a biography's subject.

Some Formats for Responding to Biography	
Format	**Example**
Write a skit showing how the person might act in a new and unusual situation.	Ben Franklin at an electrical plant
Write an encouraging letter helping the subject with a problem.	To Mohandas Gandhi encouraging his efforts to win independence for India
Write an editorial endorsing the person for public office.	Michael Jordan for mayor of your town
Bring a historical figure into the modern-day world.	Queen Isabella visiting NASA and learning about space exploration
Write a diary entry from a crucial day in the person's life.	Amelia Earhart's diary from the day her plane was lost over the Pacific Ocean
Rewrite an incident from the subject's life, changing one part slightly.	Abraham Lincoln not going to the theater where he was assassinated
Enact an on-the-spot news story with your subject.	A news interview with Clara Barton immediately after a Civil War battle

Journal Writing

In your journal respond to a biography you have read or seen. Use one of the ideas from the chart on this page.

"Interview" Your Subject

One way to get to know the subject of a biography is through an imaginary interview. To develop such an interview, work with a classmate and role-play. One of you should take the role of the interviewer and the other should portray the subject of the biography. Ask questions that get at the whys and hows of the person's life. Tailor your questions to your particular subject. Base the subject's responses on what you know from your reading.

Feel free to be creative and have fun with the interview. For example, you might choose the form of a late-night talk show discussion, such as Jay Leno interviewing Leonardo da Vinci. You might pretend that a historical character is visiting the present-day world, as Elizabeth Chen did an imaginary interview with Dr. Martin Luther King Jr. for a made-up newspaper, the *Chronicle*.

Sample Interview Questions

- What was the accomplishment you were most proud of?
- What was your greatest challenge?
- What surprises you most about today's world?
- If you could tell the people of today one thing, what would it be?

Student Model

Chronicle: Dr. King, what you did for the civil rights movement in the 1950s and 1960s obviously had an enormous impact then, but do you think it affects society today?

MLK: What the people did then, promoting the cause of civil rights through peaceful means, has led the way toward a day of equal rights for all people.

Chronicle: Do you think there is equality now?

MLK: Under the law, yes, but in the hearts and minds of some Americans, no. I cannot say there is equality when I hear of racial violence every day. There will not be equality until everyone is treated the same in practice as well as under the law.

Chronicle: But how can we change that?

MLK: Through education. Through the help of all people— black, white, red, and yellow—to show that the only difference between us is skin color. By showing that all people can achieve the same success if given an equal opportunity.

Elizabeth Chen,
Downers Grove North High School, Downers Grove, Illinois

1.7 Writing Activities

Write a Response to a Biography

Choose a major event or decision in the life of a person whose biography you have read. Write a response to share with your classmates. You can use one of the formats suggested in the chart on page 35; you can write an imaginary interview; or you can write a more personal response.

- Show that you understand your subject.
- Make your response interesting to your audience.

PURPOSE To explore a section of a biography
AUDIENCE Your classmates
LENGTH 2–4 paragraphs

Cooperative Learning

In a small group select a famous scientist, artist, or author whose work is familiar to everyone in the group. Divide up the task of researching the person's life, one member of the group taking the person's childhood, another the person's early career, and so on. Write a paragraph on the area you researched, and share your paragraph with the others in the group. Combine the paragraphs into group essays, with individual writers adding their own beginning and concluding paragraphs.

Grammar Link

When the subject of a sentence is a compound joined by *and* that refers to two or more different things, the verb that agrees with it must be plural.

Notice subject and verb in this sentence:

*Her courage, determination, **and** persistence **set** an inspiring example. . . .*

Add the correct verb form.

1. Washington and Adams _____ the first two presidents of the United States.
2. John Adams and his son, John Quincy Adams, _____ both presidents.
3. Both the House of Representatives and the Senate _____ in the Capitol.
4. The Declaration of Independence, the Constitution, and the Emancipation Proclamation _____ kept in the U.S. Archives.
5. The secretary of state and the attorney general _____ members of the president's cabinet.
6. Ulysses Grant and Dwight Eisenhower _____ generals.
7. John Quincy Adams and Andrew Jackson _____ born in 1767.
8. Kennedy, F. D. Roosevelt, and Wilson _____ students at Harvard.
9. Dwight Eisenhower and Lyndon Johnson _____ born in Texas.
10. Gerald Ford and Richard Nixon _____ born in 1913.

See Lesson 16.5, pages 578–579.

UNIT 1

WRITING PROCESS IN ACTION

PERSONAL WRITING

In preceding lessons you've learned about using personal writing for a variety of purposes. Now it's time to make use of what you learned. In this lesson you're invited to write an autobiographical sketch about an incident or a personal interaction that made a positive difference in your life—an event or a relationship that provided a good "lesson in living."

• Assignment •

Context	*Everyday People* magazine plans a special issue featuring autobiographical sketches by students. You are invited to write an uplifting story about a person or an incident that made a real difference in your life. Focus on your personal feelings and on why the event or person was so important to you.
Purpose	To write a vivid personal account that will allow readers to understand the impact of this event
Audience	"Everyday" people—students, parents, teachers, other townspeople
Length	1 to 2 pages

The following pages can help you plan and write your autobiographical sketch. Read through them and then refer to them as you need to, but don't feel limited by them. You are in charge of your own writing process.

Prewriting

Begin by choosing an incident to write about. It might be from any period in your life. It might have taken place over several weeks or months, or it may have happened quickly. It may have been dramatic or quiet, serious or humorous. If you can't think of an incident, use some of the suggestions on the notepad to help you get started. Once you have an idea in mind, try to recall what happened as fully as possible. You might begin by writing your answers to *who*, *what*, *when*, *where*, and *why* questions.

Part of your goal is to explain the significance of the event. One way to do this:

Prewriting Options
- Read over your journal entries.
- Make a list of important people in your life.
- Look through scrapbooks and photographs at home.
- Search your mental files for possible topics.
- Freewrite to discover your thoughts.

- List things that describe yourself, your attitudes, and your circumstances *before* the event or interaction took place.
- Then note the ways in which things were different afterward. Write a statement that summarizes what the experience meant to you, how it changed you, or what you learned from it.

Notice how these lines from Kareem Abdul-Jabbar's autobiography vividly describes the life-changing effect of his seeing a particular basketball game when he was young.

Literature Model

I was awestruck. I had never seen people dunk and soar and change direction in midstride the way these guys did. . . . The warmup was awe-inspiring, and I feel that evening in Brooklyn changed my concept forever of what is possible on the court. Baseball would remain close to my heart, but here was a game that was best played by individuals with *my* physical attributes. The possibilities seemed endless.

Kareem Abdul-Jabbar with Mignon McCarthy, *Kareem*

Drafting

Drafting Tip

For more information about enlivening your personal writing, see Lesson 1.3, page 20.

Start with your summary statement about the significance of the event. This will help you focus your thoughts as you write. It will also prepare your readers for what follows. Then add sentences and paragraphs to tell your story. Write freely, referring to your prewriting notes, but try to organize your thoughts in some logical way. If your experience involves a clear sequence of events, you might present the details in straight chronological order—the order in which they occurred.

As you write, look for ways to make your sketch come to life. What anecdotes, descriptions, comparisons, or other details can make your story vivid? Consider using dialogue to help bring your characters to life. To be sure the dialogue sounds natural, read your draft aloud.

Revising

Revising Tip

For help with adding significant details and finding a suitable structure for your sketch, see Lesson 1.4, pages 22–25.

To begin revising, look back at the assignment; then read your draft to see if you have met the goals. Next, have a **writing conference**. Read your draft to a partner or small group. Use your audience's reactions to help you evaluate your work so far. The following questions can help you and your listeners:

- Does my writing qualify as an autobiographical sketch?
- Is my sketch easy to follow?
- Is my sketch vivid and accurate?
- Is my tone natural? Does it sound like me talking?
- Does my writing show how this incident or interaction changed my life for the better?
- Is my writing appropriate for my audience?

Editing

Once you are happy with the basic content and set-up of your autobiographical sketch, **proofread** it carefully for errors in grammar, usage, mechanics, and spelling. Use the questions at the right as a guide.

In addition to proofreading, use the self-evaluation list below to make sure your autobiographical sketch does everything you want it to do. When you're satisfied, make a clean copy of your sketch, and proofread it one more time.

Self-Evaluation
Make sure your autobiographical sketch—

- Focuses on an incident or interaction that improved your life
- Conveys the significance of this incident or interaction
- Answers the *who, what, where, when, why,* and *how* questions
- Reflects your spoken rhythms and phrases
- Follows correct grammar, usage, and mechanics

Editing Checklist
- Have I avoided sentence fragments?
- Are all my verb forms and tenses correct?
- Have I used *I* and *me* correctly in compounds?
- Are my pronoun references clear?
- Have I checked spellings of any words I'm unsure of?

Presenting

Proofreading

For proofreading symbols, see page 100.

You can use the autobiographical sketches you and your classmates have written to produce an issue of *Everyday People*. Create a cover and a table of contents. Add illustrations if you wish. Make it available for others to read. If you feel your sketch is too personal to share publicly, keep it with your journal so that you can refer to it later.

Journal Writing

Reflect on your writing process experience. Answer these questions in your journal: What do you like best about your personal writing? What was the hardest part of writing it? What did you learn in your writing conference? What new things have you learned as a writer?

Personal Writing
Literature Model

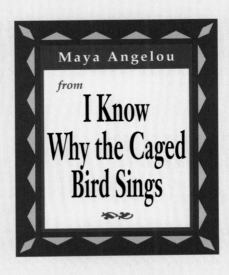

Maya Angelou

from
I Know Why the Caged Bird Sings

Maya Angelou, best known for her autobiographies I Know Why the Caged Bird
Sings *and* Gather Together in My Name, *has also been a poet laureate, playwright, movie
and television writer, journalist, dancer, actress, director, composer, and civil rights worker.
As you read this autobiographical sketch, see if the turning point she descibes reminds you of
any significant event in your own life. Then try the activities in Linking Writing and Literature
on page 51.*

For nearly a year, I sopped around the house, the Store, the
school and the church, like an old biscuit, dirty and inedible.
Then I met, or rather got to know, the lady who threw me my
first life line.
Mrs. Bertha Flowers was the aristocrat of Black Stamps. She had
the grace of control to appear warm in the coldest weather, and on
the Arkansas summer days it seemed she had a private breeze which
swirled around, cooling her. She was thin without the taut look of

wiry people, and her printed voile[1] dresses and flowered hats were as right for her as denim overalls for a farmer. She was our side's answer to the richest white woman in town.

Her skin was a rich black that would have peeled like a plum if snagged, but then no one would have thought of getting close enough to Mrs. Flowers to ruffle her dress, let alone snag her skin. She didn't encourage familiarity. She wore gloves too.

I don't think I ever saw Mrs. Flowers laugh, but she smiled often. A slow widening of her thin black lips to show even, small white teeth, then the slow effortless closing. When she chose to smile on me, I always wanted to thank her. The action was so graceful and inclusively benign.[2]

She was one of the few gentlewomen I have ever known, and has remained throughout my life the measure of what a human being can be.

Momma had a strange relationship with her. Most often when she passed on the road in front of the Store, she spoke to Momma in that soft yet carrying voice, "Good day, Mrs. Henderson." Momma responded with "How you, Sister Flowers?"

Mrs. Flowers didn't belong to our church, nor was she Momma's

1 voile (voil) a thin, sheer fabric; often made of cotton

2 benign (bi nīn') good-natured

Harriet Powers, *Pictorial Quilt*, c. 1895–1898

familiar. Why on earth did she insist on calling her Sister Flowers? Shame made me want to hide my face. Mrs. Flowers deserved better than to be called Sister. Then, Momma left out the verb. Why not ask, "How *are* you, *Mrs.* Flowers?" With the unbalanced passion of the young, I hated her for showing her ignorance to Mrs. Flowers. It didn't occur to me for many years that they were as alike as sisters, separated only by formal education.

Although I was upset, neither of the women was in the least shaken by what I thought an unceremonious[3] greeting. Mrs. Flowers would continue her easy gait up the hill to her little bungalow,[4] and Momma kept on shelling peas or doing whatever had brought her to the front porch.

Occasionally, though, Mrs. Flowers would drift off the road and down to the Store and Momma would say to me, "Sister, you go on and play." As I left I would hear the beginning of an intimate conversation. Momma persistently using the wrong verb, or none at all.

"Brother and Sister Wilcox is sho'ly the meanest—" "Is," Momma? "Is"? Oh, please, not "is," Momma, for two or more. But they talked, and from the side of the building where I waited for the ground to open up and swallow me, I heard the soft-voiced Mrs. Flowers and the textured voice of my grandmother merging and melting. They were interrupted from time to time by giggles that must have come from Mrs. Flowers (Momma never giggled in her life). Then she was gone.

She appealed to me because she was like people I had never met personally. Like women in English novels who walked the moors (whatever they were) with their loyal dogs racing at a respectful distance. Like the women who sat in front of roaring fireplaces, drinking tea incessantly from silver trays full of scones and crumpets. Women who walked over the "heath"[5] and read morocco-bound[6] books and had two last names divided by a hyphen. It would be safe to say that she made me proud to be Negro, just by being herself.

She acted just as refined as whitefolks in the movies and books and she was more beautiful, for none of them could have come near that warm color without looking gray by comparison.

It was fortunate that I never saw her in the company of powhitefolks. For since they tend to think of their whiteness as an evenizer, I'm certain that I would have had to hear her spoken to commonly as

---

3 unceremonious (un' ser ə mo′ nē əs) impolite

4 bungalow (buŋ′ gə lō′) a small house, usually one story high plus an attic

5 heath (hēth) an expanse of wasteland, especially in Britain, covered with heather and shrubs

6 morocco-bound (mə rä′ kō) having a leather cover

Beverly Buchanan, *Bogart, Georgia*, 1989

Bertha, and my image of her would have been shattered like the unmendable Humpty-Dumpty.

One summer afternoon, sweet-milk fresh in my memory, she stopped at the Store to buy provisions. Another Negro woman of her health and age would have been expected to carry the paper sacks home in one hand, but Momma said, "Sister Flowers, I'll send Bailey up to your house with these things."

She smiled that slow dragging smile, "Thank you, Mrs. Henderson. I'd prefer Marguerite, though." My name was beautiful when she said it. "I've been meaning to talk to her, anyway." They gave each other age-group looks.

Momma said, "Well, that's all right then. Sister, go and change your dress. You going to Sister Flowers's."

The chifforobe[7] was a maze. What on earth did one put on to go to Mrs. Flowers' house? I knew I shouldn't put on a Sunday dress. It might be sacrilegious.[8] Certainly not a house dress, since I was already wearing a fresh one. I chose a school dress, naturally. It was formal without suggesting that going to Mrs. Flowers' house was equivalent to attending church.

I trusted myself back into the Store.

"Now, don't you look nice." I had chosen the right thing, for once.

"Mrs. Henderson, you make most of the children's clothes, don't you?"

"Yes, ma'am. Sure do. Store-bought clothes ain't hardly worth the thread it take to stitch them."

"I'll say you do a lovely job, though, so neat. That dress looks professional."

Momma was enjoying the seldom-received compliments. Since everyone we knew (except Mrs. Flowers, of course) could sew competently, praise was rarely handed out for the commonly practiced craft.

"I try, with the help of the Lord, Sister Flowers, to finish the inside just like I does the outside. Come here, Sister."

I had buttoned up the collar and tied the belt, apronlike, in back. Momma told me to turn around. With one hand she pulled the strings and the belt fell free at both sides of my waist. Then her large hands were at my neck, opening the button loops. I was terrified. What was happening?

"Take it off, Sister." She had her hands on the hem of the dress.

"I don't need to see the inside, Mrs. Henderson, I can tell . . ." But the dress was over my head and my arms were stuck in the sleeves. Momma said, "That'll do. See here, Sister Flowers, I French-seams around the armholes." Through the cloth film, I saw the shadow approach. "That makes it last longer. Children these days would bust out of sheet-metal clothes. They so rough."

"That is a very good job, Mrs. Henderson. You should be proud. You can put your dress back on, Marguerite."

"No ma'am. Pride is a sin. And 'cording to the Good Book, it goeth before a fall."

"That's right. So the Bible says. It's a good thing to keep in mind."

I wouldn't look at either of them. Momma hadn't thought that taking off my dress in front of Mrs. Flowers would kill me stone dead. If I had refused, she would have thought I was trying to be "womanish" and might have remembered St. Louis. Mrs. Flowers

---

7 chifforobe (shif′ ə rōb′) a combination of wardrobe and chest of drawers

8 sacrilegious (sak′ r ə lij′ ə s) involving the violation of something holy

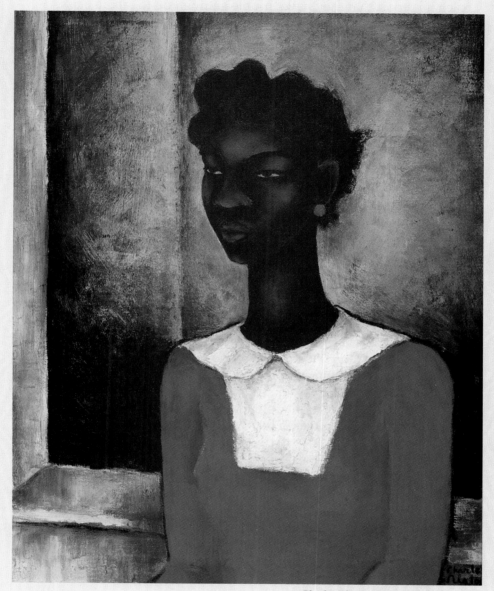

Charles Alston, *Girl in a Red Dress*, 1934

had known that I would be embarrassed and that was even worse.
I picked up the groceries and went out to wait in the hot sunshine.
It would be fitting if I got a sunstroke and died before they came
outside. Just dropped dead on the slanting porch.

There was a little path beside the rocky road, and Mrs. Flowers
walked in front swinging her arms and picking her way over the stones.

She said, without turning her head, to me, "I hear you're doing
very good school work, Marguerite, but that it's all written. The

teachers report that they have trouble getting you to talk in class." We passed the triangular farm on our left and the path widened to allow us to walk together. I hung back in the separate unasked and unanswerable questions.

"Come and walk along with me, Marguerite." I couldn't have refused even if I wanted to. She pronounced my name so nicely. Or more correctly, she spoke each word with such clarity that I was certain a foreigner who didn't understand English could have understood her.

"Now no one is going to make you talk—possibly no one can. But bear in mind, language is man's way of communicating with his fellow man and it is language alone which separates him from the lower animals." That was a totally new idea to me, and I would need time to think about it.

"Your grandmother says you read a lot. Every chance you get. That's good, but not good enough. Words mean more than what is set down on paper. It takes the human voice to infuse them with the shades of deeper meaning."

I memorized the part about the human voice infusing words. It seemed so valid and poetic.

She said she was going to give me some books and that I not only must read them, I must read them aloud. She suggested that I try to make a sentence sound in as many different ways as possible.

"I'll accept no excuse if you return a book to me that has been badly handled." My imagination boggled at the punishment I would deserve if in fact I did abuse a book of Mrs. Flowers's. Death would be too kind and brief.

The odors in the house surprised me. Somehow I had never connected Mrs. Flowers with food or eating or any other common experience of common people. There must have been an outhouse, too, but my mind never recorded it.

The sweet scent of vanilla had met us as she opened the door.

"I made tea cookies this morning. You see, I had planned to invite you for cookies and lemonade so we could have this little chat. The lemonade is in the icebox."

It followed that Mrs. Flowers would have ice on an ordinary day, when most families in our town bought ice late on Saturdays only a few times during the summer to be used in the wooden ice-cream freezers.

She took the bags from me and disappeared through the kitchen door. I looked around the room that I had never in my wildest fantasies imagined I would see. Browned photographs leered or threatened from the walls and the white, freshly done curtains pushed against themselves and against the wind. I wanted to gobble up the room entire and take it to Bailey, who would help me analyze and enjoy it.

"Have a seat, Marguerite. Over there by the table." She carried a platter covered with a tea towel. Although she warned that she hadn't tried her hand at baking sweets for some time, I was certain that like everything else about her the cookies would be perfect.

They were flat round wafers, slightly browned on the edges and butter-yellow in the center. With the cold lemonade they were sufficient for childhood's lifelong diet. Remembering my manners, I took nice little lady-like bites off the edges. She said she had made them expressly for me and that she had a few in the kitchen that I could take home to my brother. So I jammed one whole cake in my mouth and the rough crumbs scratched the inside of my jaws, and if I hadn't had to swallow, it would have been a dream come true.

As I ate she began the first of what we later called "my lessons in living." She said that I must always be intolerant of ignorance but understanding of illiteracy. That some people, unable to go to school, were more educated and even more intelligent than college professors. She encouraged me to listen carefully to what country people called mother wit. That in those homely sayings was couched the collective wisdom of generations.

When I finished the cookies she brushed off the table and brought a thick, small book from the bookcase. I had read *A Tale of Two Cities* and found it up to my standards as a romantic novel. She opened the first page and I heard poetry for the first time in my life.

"It was the best of times and the worst of times . . ." Her voice slid in and curved down through and over the words. She was nearly singing. I wanted to look at the pages. Were they the same that I had read? Or were there notes, music, lined on the pages, as in a hymn book? Her sounds began cascading gently. I knew from listening to a thousand preachers that she was nearing the end of her reading, and I hadn't really heard, heard to understand, a single word.

"How do you like that?"

It occurred to me that she expected a response. The sweet vanilla flavor was still on my tongue and her reading was a wonder in my ears. I had to speak.

I said, "Yes, ma'am." It was the least I could do, but it was the most also.

"There's one more thing. Take this book of poems and memorize one for me. Next time you pay me a visit, I want you to recite."

I have tried often to search behind the sophistication of years for the enchantment I so easily found in those gifts. The essence[9] escapes but its aura[10] remains. To be allowed, no, invited, into the private

---

9 essence (es′ ′əns) the basic nature or most important quality

10 aura (ôr′ ə) the atmosphere or feeling that seems to surround a certain person or thing

Wilmer Angier Jennings, *Landscape*, 1945

lives of strangers, and to share their joys and fears, was a chance to exchange the Southern bitter wormwood[11] for a cup of mead[12] with Beowulf or a hot cup of tea and milk with Oliver Twist. When I said aloud, "It is a far, far better thing that I do, than I have ever done . . ." tears of love filled my eyes at my selflessness.

On that first day, I ran down the hill and into the road (few cars ever came along it) and had the good sense to stop running before I reached the Store.

I was liked, and what a difference it made. I was respected not as Mrs. Henderson's grandchild or Bailey's sister but for just being Marguerite Johnson.

Childhood's logic never asks to be proved (all conclusions are absolute). I didn't question why Mrs. Flowers had singled me out for attention, nor did it occur to me that Momma might have asked her to give me a little talking to. All I cared about was that she had made tea cookies for *me* and read to *me* from her favorite book. It was enough to prove that she liked me.

11 **wormwood** (wᵾrm′ wood′) a bitter oil

12 **mead** (mēd) a drink made of honey and water

Linking Writing and Literature

Readers Respond to the Model

What makes Maya Angelou's autobiographical account appealing?

Explore Maya Angelou's personal writing by answering these questions. Then read what other students liked about Angelou's autobiographical story.

1. Do you share Marguerite's admiration for Mrs. Flowers? Explain.
2. How does Maya Angelou's use of imagery make her writing intensely personal? Name some specific images that you found memorable.

3. Do you find a connection with your own life in this description of a special childhood relationship?
4. How might reading this selection affect your personal writing? Does it give you any specific ideas? Explain.

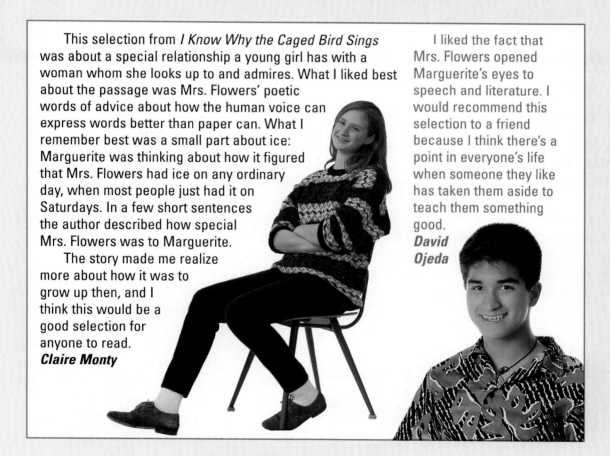

This selection from *I Know Why the Caged Bird Sings* was about a special relationship a young girl has with a woman whom she looks up to and admires. What I liked best about the passage was Mrs. Flowers' poetic words of advice about how the human voice can express words better than paper can. What I remember best was a small part about ice: Marguerite was thinking about how it figured that Mrs. Flowers had ice on any ordinary day, when most people just had it on Saturdays. In a few short sentences the author described how special Mrs. Flowers was to Marguerite.

The story made me realize more about how it was to grow up then, and I think this would be a good selection for anyone to read.
Claire Monty

I liked the fact that Mrs. Flowers opened Marguerite's eyes to speech and literature. I would recommend this selection to a friend because I think there's a point in everyone's life when someone they like has taken them aside to teach them something good.
David Ojeda

Unit 1 Review

Reflecting on the Unit

Summarize what you have learned in this unit by answering the following questions.

- In what ways can personal writing help you make discoveries about yourself?

- What can you keep in a personal journal and how can it serve as a valuable source of writing ideas?

- What strategies can you use to explore ideas for personal essays?

- What are some of the different methods you can use to present autobiographical materials?

- What are some devices poets use to create memorable word pictures?

- What is the purpose of a reader-response journal and how can it help you learn?

Adding to Your Portfolio

Follow this procedure to choose selections for your portfolio:

Look over the personal writing you have done during this unit. Select two pieces of writing to put into your portfolio. Each piece should demonstrate that you have worked with one or more of the concepts listed above. In other words, look for pieces of writing that show some or all of the following:

- a valuable self-discovery, or something special that makes you *you*
- an idea source for a future personal essay
- ideas generated by freewriting, clustering, or creating an idea map
- your own personal thoughts and feelings in poetic form

Reflect on your choice.
Attach a note to the piece you chose, explaining briefly why you chose it and what you learned from writing it.

Set goals.
How can you improve your writing? What skill will you focus on the next time you write?

Writing Across the Curriculum

Make a civics connection.
Think about an experience you had with someone quite different from yourself—in age, culture, or economic status. Make brief notes about how the person was different from you and what you learned from the encounter. Then, using those notes, write a paragraph demonstrating how encountering this new person affected your life or beliefs.

The Writing Process in the Real World

Chavez and the Quest for Human-Interest Stories

F O C U S: Writing a can't-put-it-down feature story takes careful research, creative writing, and hard-nosed editing.

E veryone knows what a news story is. The papers brim with fast-paced accounts of the day's international tensions, business ups and downs, personal triumphs and tragedies. But what's a feature story?

One quick way to answer that question is to scan a fifteen-foot magazine rack in a big grocery store. Almost every magazine carries feature stories—information pieces that are "softer, more personable, less direct . . . and that lean more toward entertainment," according to Lorenzo Chavez, a freelance writer and writing teacher. Chavez writes on subjects as diverse as Latin America, the arts, education, and business for newspapers and for *Vista,* a magazine for Hispanic readers inserted in about 20 Sunday newspapers nationwide.

Feature writer Lorenzo Chavez

> "*The feature story tries for a more humane point of view, to draw in the reader, to get the reader to see that people are not statistics. . . . A feature story can make us more sensitive to what's really happening.*"
>
> – Lorenzo Chavez

rootsearch

From Abadía to Zúñiga, Hispanic surnames tell the story of a people in a restless migration over the centuries from the Old to the New World. Every month VISTA traces the history of Hispanic family names to help its readers in their quest for beginnings.

ALARGON

This surname comes from th lage of Alarcón in Cuenca, S When the town was recaptured f the Moors by Fernán Martínez Ceballos in 1176, King Alfonso allowed Martínez to change his s name to that of the city as a rewar After that he was known as Fernă Martínez de Alarcón, and his de scendants spread throughout the Spanish-speaking world.

The Alarcons from Cuba trace back directly to the village in central Spain. Don Lope de Alarcón, mayor of the town, had a daughter named Teresa who married Gonzalo de Ocaña in 1492. When he died, the children were given the right to use their mother's maiden name as their primary surname. One de scendant, Antonio de Alarcón Ocaña, took the name to Havana, where he died in 1664, leaving many

As Chavez will tell you, feature stories can cover anything: sports stars, science breakthroughs, tips on buying cars— even tracing your family history, or genealogy, a subject Chavez covered for *Vista*.

Chavez will also tell you that ideas for feature stories are everywhere; in fact, there are "just too many," laughed Chavez. And, of course, you have to be alert and open to ideas. The idea for Chavez's story on family histories, "The Quest for Hispanic Roots," came from *Vista* readers. Over the years, hundreds of *Vista* readers had written in to "Rootsearch,"

a popular genealogy column devoted to tracing family histories. In this case, with so many readers writing in to the column, the *Vista* staff decided to run an article that could help people do family research on their own. But before Chavez could help others with their research, he had to go through his own research. Chavez began his writing process by narrowing his focus and doing some research.

Writing the Feature Story

Prewriting	Drafting	Revising/Editing
Collecting the Facts	Telling the Story	Getting Ready for Publication

Prewriting

COLLECTING THE FACTS

Before Chavez could start researching the article on genealogy, he had to narrow his original idea to a few key points—no more than he could cover in the allotted space of 1,500 words, or about six pages in *Vista* magazine. Ultimately, he chose to write about the biggest and most active genealogical societies and libraries in Texas and California, states from which the majority of reader letters had come.

With story idea in hand, Chavez had to gather the facts, and he began by listing a few questions to direct his research: Why do people search for their pasts? What libraries or associations can help?

It took Chavez about a week to get the answers. Some information came from newspaper clippings, but most of it came from 30 or 40 phone calls he made to libraries and researchers.

Drafting

TELLING THE STORY

After his interviews, Chavez had 20 pages of notes, several taped conversations, a few newspaper clips, and a head full of ideas. Before sitting down at the computer, Chavez reminded himself of one key thing: He had to picture the people he was writing for, a "middle-aged to older generation, people of Mexican descent, mostly retirees, who have spare time and an interest in history and politics." To engage his readers, Chavez had to put himself in their shoes and anticipate questions they might ask.

Now Chavez was ready to write. To grab the reader, he used an anecdote about Mickey Garcia, a Texas genealogist who researches family histories. He portrayed Garcia as a treasure hunter. "She's searching for a valuable thing, not gold, but a family history," Chavez said. "I used that [approach] because I didn't want to frighten the reader by saying this was a long, time-consuming, arduous task."

From there Chavez stitched the story together in a clever way. Using quotes, descriptions, and explanations, he told readers what sparked people's interest in genealogy, introduced top researchers, described huge family reunions, and explained how to find family records.

To close the story, Chavez quoted researcher George Ryskamp, who said: "To be a good genealogist, you have to be a good detective. You never know what you're going to find."

Human interest is a key element in a good feature story. In his feature story Chavez included a photo of the Vela family reunion, which boasted nearly 1,500 participants.

Revising/Editing

GETTING READY FOR PUBLICATION

After writing for three days, Chavez had a rough draft. "It was messy, but I knew I had everything I wanted there," he said. Now he was ready to revise.

At this stage, Chavez worked on a printout of his story. On hard copy he could see problems more clearly. "Problems pop up more. You can see poor structure [when there are] too many prepositions. If the lead is too long, you can see

How do you know if your copy is dull or lively? If your story excites you, it will probably excite the reader.

it—the paragraph is all gray. No one is going to get through that first paragraph," he explained.

Before printing out a copy of his story, Chavez checked the length on the computer so he knew if he needed to cut sentences or paragraphs. Then he checked his facts, spelling, and grammar. "If you have poor spelling and grammar or the facts are wrong, the reader will ask, 'Why should I read this guy? He doesn't know what he's talking about.'"

After that, Chavez worked to improve his style. He rewrote dull sentences to make them bold and active. He varied sentence lengths to create rhythm, so the story sounded interesting, not monotonous. Finally, he checked to be sure the story had some mystery. "You can't put all the information at the top or the reader doesn't have anything to look forward to," Lorenzo said. "You have to have some suspense, something pushing the reader forward."

Finally, Chavez turned his copy over to staff editors, who reviewed his work before publication. His editors, he said, catch mistakes and other problems because they have a fresh point of view.

Responding to the Case Study

1. Discussion

In a small group, discuss these questions about Lorenzo Chavez's writing.

- In what ways is a feature story different from a news story?
- Why did Chavez choose genealogy as the topic of his story?
- What sources of facts did Chavez use for his story? What are some other possible sources he might have used?
- Before he started to draft his story, what did Chavez need to know about his audience?
- Why did Chavez revise and edit on a printout rather than on the computer?

2. Expository Writing

Write a paragraph analyzing a feature story.

Clip a feature story on a topic of your choice from a newspaper or magazine. Review the story and rate its success. Begin by brainstorming three or four criteria to use in making your evaluation. Next to each item, note a specific example from the story. Then write a paragraph analyzing the strategies used to grab and hold your interest.

Grammar Link

Vary sentence lengths.

Lorenzo Chavez writes that he varied sentence lengths to create rhythm, so the story sounded interesting, not monotonous. You can vary sentence lengths by using a variety of sentence patterns: simple, compound, complex, and compound-complex.

Revise each item below by combining each pair of simple sentences in two different ways. Add or change words or phrases as needed.

1. Feature story ideas are everywhere. Ideas often come from news articles.
2. Chavez writes for *Vista* magazine. *Vista* is targeted to Hispanic readers.
3. Chavez interviewed genealogists. He collected taped conversations.
4. Chavez improved his draft. He changed words and sentences.
5. Genealogists share their research findings. There are many genealogical societies.

See Lessons 13.3 and 13.4, pages 503–506.

The Writing Process
Overview of the Writing Process

Michelangelo, detail of the Sistine Chapel ceiling, 1508–1512

Writing is a way for you to explore your thoughts and mental images. It is also a way to discover more about yourself and the people and experiences that helped make you who you are.

Discover the Stages in the Process

After Michelangelo had begun painting the Sistine Chapel in Rome in the 1500s, he thought of new ideas and decided to resketch and repaint based on those new ideas.

A writer works in much the same way, exploring ideas in a rough draft, refining the draft, or even discarding it and searching for a new idea. Although no two writers approach the writing process in exactly the same way, most writers go through five basic stages: prewriting, drafting, revising, editing, and presenting.

Prewriting During prewriting, you decide what you want to write about by exploring ideas, feelings, and memories. You also begin to think about your audience and your purpose. Your audience is those who will read your work. Your purpose is what you hope to accomplish through your writing.

Drafting Writing a draft, or turning your ideas into paragraphs, is a stage in the writing process and a tool in itself. As you compose your draft, you find links between ideas which give new meanings to your words and phrases.

Revising The purposes of revising are to make sure that your writing is clear and well organized, that it accomplishes your objectives, and that it reaches your audience. To achieve these goals, you may need to cut or add to your writing. Mark these changes right on your draft, and then incorporate them. Compare the writer's revised draft with her earlier draft to see what changes she incorporated during revising.

Editing The purposes of editing are to make sure that you've chosen the best possible words to communicate your ideas and that your sentences are grammatically correct. Finally, you proofread your writing and correct mistakes in capitalization, punctuation, and spelling. Note the editorial changes this writer has marked on her revised copy.

Presenting This is the stage at which you share your work with others. You might read what you've written aloud in class, submit it to the school newspaper, or give it to a friend to read. There are many avenues for presenting your work.

Prewriting

I remember when my dad finally took me fishing that summer. I was so afraid I would do something wrong. But even though it didn't turn out the way I hoped, it was great to... boat, to... sides,... back,... and... any...

Drafting

It was the summer I turned twelve. My father loved fishing and for months I had begged him to take me with him fishing. I wanted to be a part of his world. Mostly I wanted his praise. We took a boat out on a...

Revising and Editing

It was the summer I turned twelve. For months I had begged my father to take me with him fishing. He loved fishing, and I hoped that by joining him I would win his afection. Finally he agreed, and we took a boat out on a lake near our house. I baited the hook *myself* and held it up for my father's approval. The worm wiggled on the barbed tip, and I shut my eyes as I lowered ~~the hook~~ *it* into the water. As we sat there in silence, waiting, the sunlight beat down on my back, and I felt happy and sleepy. Then I felt a tug on my line - - I had caught a fish.

Journal Writing

In your journal explain the stages you went through on a recent writing assignment. How do they compare with the stages described above?

Follow the Process

At any point in the writing process, you may return to any of the preceding stages. For example, if you're having trouble drafting a paragraph, you may go back to the prewriting stage and outline it first. If you get stuck as you revise, you may redraft some of your writing. You may even need to gather more information or reevaluate your purpose.

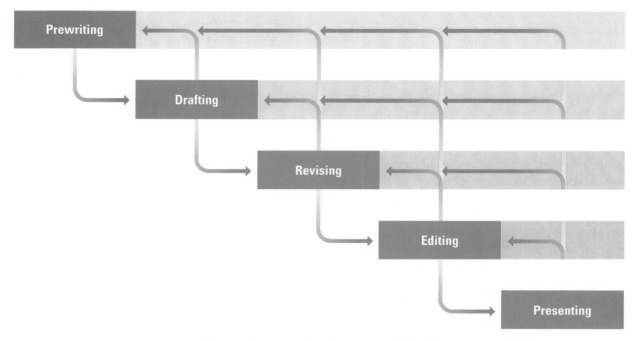

Remember, too, that because writing is a process of discovery, you may be surprised by what you find when you write. Like Alice Walker, you may discover something new about yourself, your world, and the forces that have shaped your life.

What did Walker discover about her mother through her writing?

Literature Model

*S*o many of the stories that I write . . . are my mother's stories. Only recently did I fully realize this: that through years of listening to my mother's stories of her life, I have absorbed not only the stories themselves, but something of the manner in which she spoke, something of the urgency that involves the knowledge that her stories—like her life—must be recorded.

Alice Walker, *In Search of Our Mothers' Gardens*

After years of listening to her mother's stories, Walker decides she wants to write about them.

2.1 Writing Activities

Write a Comparison

Writer Lawrence Osgood noted that "writing is like exploring. . . . As an explorer makes maps of the country he has explored, so a writer's works are maps of the country he has explored." Use Osgood's analogy to suggest how writing is like another process, such as producing a school play, making a dress, or constructing a birdhouse.

Consider each stage of the two processes. Write a paragraph or two explaining what the two have in common. If there are ways in which the two processes are not alike, be sure to point that out as well.

- List the five basic stages of the writing process.
- Explain in your own words the activities that should take place during each step in the writing process.
- Give at least three reasons a writer might have for repeating one or more steps in the writing process.

PURPOSE To compare two processes
AUDIENCE Your classmates
LENGTH 1–2 paragraphs

COMPUTER OPTION

A visual diagram can often help you compare two things or two processes. You can use your computer to put the information into a comparative chart or, using a series of boxes, into a cluster diagram. Consult the Help function on your machine to find out how to create such visual aids on your machine.

Grammar Link

Add commas to avoid run-on sentences.

In the Revising and Editing model on page 61, the writer uses a comma to avoid a run-on sentence.

The worm wriggled on the barbed tip, and I shut my eyes . . .

Revise the sentences below, correcting the run-on sentences by adding commas where needed.

1. It was the summer I turned thirteen and I longed to be independent.
2. My parents said the highway was too dangerous so they wouldn't let me ride my bike to the mall.
3. One day temptation grew too strong and the lure of my bike became irresistible.
4. Gasoline fumes made me feel queasy and the noise gave me a headache.
5. I got really tired and I thought I would never get there!
6. I finally arrived but I was totally exhausted.
7. The mall looked cool so I parked my bike and ran inside.
8. I threw myself onto a bench and the icy mall air cooled my damp body.
9. An ice cream cone tasted good and I was on my way again.
10. I strolled outside to the bike rack but my bike was gone!

See Lesson 13.10, pages 517–519.

The Writing Process
Prewriting: Getting Started

Ideas for writing are everywhere. In prewriting you can use a variety of techniques to find and focus on a writing topic.

Prewriting is the stage during which you generate ideas. During prewriting you unleash your imagination to allow promising writing topics to emerge. Among the techniques that writers find useful for generating writing ideas are freewriting and collecting.

Begin with Ideas

Freewriting   To freewrite, choose a topic and a time limit and then just start writing your ideas as they come to you. Don't worry about grammar, spelling, punctuation, or logic. If you run out of ideas, repeat the same word over and over until a new idea occurs to you. When the time is up, review what you've written. The ideas that most interest you are likely to be the ones that will be most worth writing about.

Take a look at the freewriting generated by one writer. Note how many ideas she came up with in just a few minutes.

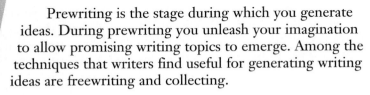

Model

Is the writer more interested in the quick flow of ideas or in following grammar or punctuation rules? How do you know?

I love spending time with my uncle Edward. He always has stories to tell—like how he used to roller-skate to work when he first got out of college. And stories about my father—his little brother—that make me laugh but that seem like they're about somebody else because I can't imagine my dad as a kid but I can imagine Uncle Edward as a kid, even though he's a lot older than my dad. Probably because he's so easy to talk to—he's more like my friend than my uncle. I told him that I wanted to ➡

be a writer someday, but he didn't laugh—he said I should start now. I wonder if I could write a story about Uncle Edward on skates.

The writer has discovered an idea for a possible writing project: her uncle's early experiences.

Collecting   Books, magazines, newspapers, movies, and even conversations with other people are valuable sources of ideas and information. A good source of raw material is your journal. Based on a journal entry, Moses Thomas Greene II wrote the following reaction to a TV show.

Student Model

As a young person in America, I think of death as something that will occur when I am in my eighties or older. However, an episode of *A Different World* made me realize that I can't take this longevity for granted anymore.

In this episode, a group of college students in a public speaking class were given a unique assignment: they were asked to deliver their own eulogy. Although most of the students gave humorous speeches, one student took the assignment more seriously because she had Acquired Immune Deficiency Syndrome, or AIDS. Up until then, the student had kept her condition a secret, but she decided to tell her classmates the truth when she delivered her eulogy. As a result, the rest of the students began avoiding the young woman and didn't want to hear about how she was dealing with her condition.

What I liked best about the episode was that it handled the issue realistically. The students' reactions reflected the attitude of many "real" people toward the disease—ignore it and it will go away. However, the episode made me see that AIDS is a problem that needs to be dealt with and that can't be ignored.

Moses Thomas Greene II
Brentwood High School, Brentwood, New York

How does Moses "hook" you in the first paragraph of his essay?

Writing about this difficult subject helped Moses sort out his feelings about it.

Journal Writing

Pick one idea you find interesting from your own collection of raw material and freewrite about it for five minutes. What new ideas did your freewriting generate? Note these in your journal.

Explore Your Ideas

Explore your ideas to clarify your thinking and find a focus for your writing. Two useful techniques for exploring ideas are making lists and asking questions.

Making Lists   Start with a key word or idea, and list other ideas as they occur to you. Don't worry about the order; just let your ideas flow freely from one to the next. This kind of free-association activity is also often referred to as brainstorming.

One writer used the technique of list making to generate the ideas shown below. What other ideas come to mind as you read through each list?

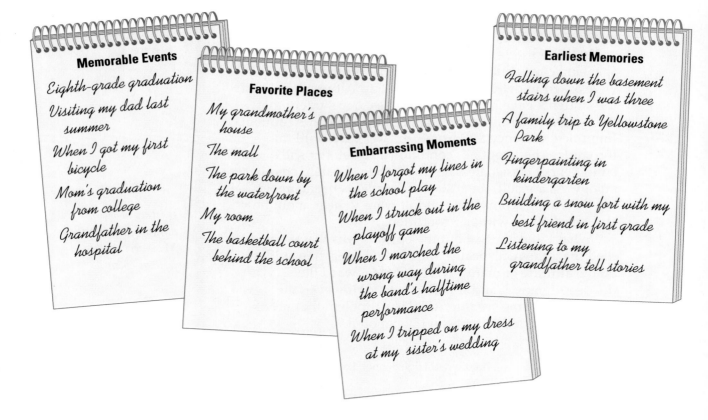

Memorable Events

Eighth-grade graduation

Visiting my dad last summer

When I got my first bicycle

Mom's graduation from college

Grandfather in the hospital

Favorite Places

My grandmother's house

The mall

The park down by the waterfront

My room

The basketball court behind the school

Embarrassing Moments

When I forgot my lines in the school play

When I struck out in the playoff game

When I marched the wrong way during the band's halftime performance

When I tripped on my dress at my sister's wedding

Earliest Memories

Falling down the basement stairs when I was three

A family trip to Yellowstone Park

Fingerpainting in kindergarten

Building a snow fort with my best friend in first grade

Listening to my grandfather tell stories

Once you've finished your lists, look them over and underline the ideas that seem most interesting to you. Draw lines between related ideas. Did any unexpected ideas appear? Did you recall events you had not thought about for a long time? Did you learn something new about yourself? These ideas may be worthwhile writing topics.

Asking Questions To explore a topic by asking and answering questions about it, begin with six basic questions: *who? what? where? when? why?* and *how?* In the chart below, the writer explored an idea generated through list making by asking and answering questions based on these six questions.

Questions to Explore Ideas

Who

Q. Who or what do I want to write about?
A. My 73-year-old grandfather, who grew up in Vietnam and came to the United States after the Vietnam War.

What

Q. What happened to my subject?
A. During the war he was separated from his family. He finally escaped from Vietnam. He spent a long time in a refugee camp, until family members in the United States could arrange for him to come here.

Where

Q. Where did this happen?
A. In a small village in Vietnam and later in a refugee camp just across the border of Thailand.

When

Q. When did this happen?
A. He escaped in 1973 and lived in a makeshift tent in Thailand until 1978.

Why

Q. Why did this happen?
A. He escaped from Vietnam because of the war. Many people left Vietnam because they were afraid of the new Communist leaders. They fled to nearby Thailand because it wasn't under Communist rule.

How

Q. How did this happen?
A. He was able to escape from Vietnam and start a new life in the United States partly because of his determination to see his family again and partly because of luck.

Journal Writing

Choose a family member you might like to write about. In your journal pose *who, what, where, when, why,* and *how* questions to explore your subject. Think of possible answers and record them in your journal.

Narrow Your Topic

Once you've chosen a general topic to write about, you need to narrow its scope. You can use a network tree to help you narrow your writing topic. Start by listing your general topic at the top of the tree. Then use the same free-association technique that you used in list making to generate ideas to fill out the tree. Notice in the network tree below how many ideas the writer identified by using the questions on page 67 to explore an idea generated during list making.

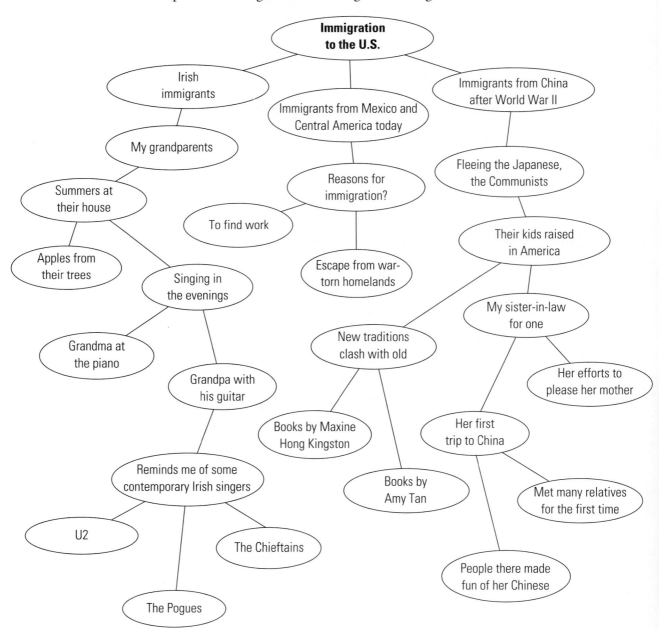

Generate Story Ideas

In this unit you will be writing a human-interest feature story. Use the prewriting methods discussed in this lesson to choose three possible topics for your story.

- Freewrite or collect ideas from other sources.
- List ideas and see how they relate to each other.
- Ask questions to explore and clarify ideas.
- Create a network tree to narrow a topic.

PURPOSE To explore story ideas
AUDIENCE Yourself
LENGTH 1–2 pages

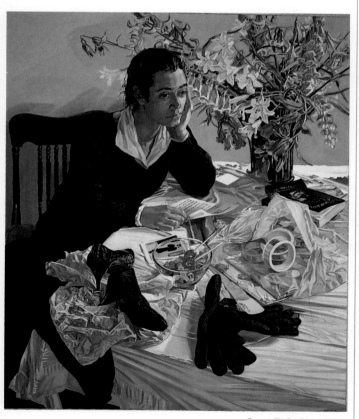

Janet Fish, *Kara,* 1983

Cooperative Learning

In a small group, study and discuss the young woman pictured in the art on this page. What do the details in the painting reveal about the life of this young woman? Then brainstorm possible topics for human-interest stories suggested by the painting. Choose a group member to record the topics so that they can be shared with the entire class.

Grammar Link

Make collective nouns and verbs agree.

A *collective noun* takes a plural verb when it refers to individual members of a group and a singular verb when it refers to the group as a whole. In the second paragraph of the student model on page 65, Moses uses a plural verb, *were given,* with the collective noun, *group.*

Find the subject in each sentence and write it on your paper. Then write the verb in parentheses that agrees with the subject.

1. A group in English class (is/are) interested in brainstorming ideas related to writing a family history.
2. The committee (is/are) quick to agree among themselves on several topics.
3. The class (agree/agrees) to pursue two or three of the suggested ideas.
4. The majority (enjoy/enjoys) writing stories about their families.
5. A panel (is chosen/are chosen) to evaluate the essays.

See Lesson 16.4, page 576.

The Writing Process
Prewriting: Identifying Purpose and Audience

You can focus your ideas by defining the reason for your writing (your purpose) and determining the people for whom you are writing (your audience).

The earlier you determine the audience and purpose for your writing, the more focused your final product will be. Here is how one writer narrowed her topic to establish a purpose. How will her choice of audience focus her topic still further?

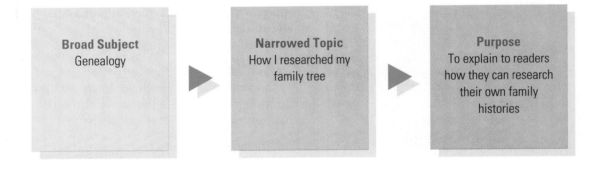

Broad Subject	Narrowed Topic	Purpose
Genealogy	How I researched my family tree	To explain to readers how they can research their own family histories

Determine a Purpose

Consider the primary purpose for your writing: to inform or explain, to persuade, to amuse or entertain, to narrate, or to describe. Sometimes, however, you may write to accomplish more than one purpose. For instance, if you write a letter to the editor of your school newspaper praising a campaign to raise money for a shelter for the homeless, your primary purpose might be to inform your fellow students about the campaign and the shelter. Your secondary purpose might be to persuade students to help with the campaign. To determine the primary purpose of your writing, answer the questions on the next page.

In the following paragraphs, writer Yoshiko Uchida explains her purpose in writing about the lives of Japanese Americans during World War II. At that time, the United States was at war with Japan. Many Japanese American families were forced to leave their homes and live in camps run by the U.S. government. Uchida often speaks to schoolchildren about her own experiences in one of the camps.

Literature Model

I always ask the children why they think I wrote *Journey to Topaz* and *Journey Home,* in which I tell of the wartime experiences of the Japanese Americans. "To tell about the camps?" they ask. "To tell how you felt? To tell what happened to the Japanese people?"

"Yes," I answer, but I continue the discussion until finally one of them will say, "You wrote those books so it won't ever happen again."

And that is why I wrote [*Desert Exile*]. I wrote it for the young Japanese Americans who seek a sense of continuity with their past. But I wrote it as well for all Americans, with the hope that through knowledge of the past, they will never allow another group of people in America to be sent into a desert exile ever again.

Yoshiko Uchida, *Desert Exile*

What is Uchida's primary purpose? Do you think Uchida believes that "the pen is mightier than the sword"?

Uchida considers the needs of her two audiences: Japanese Americans and all other Americans.

Journal Writing

Choose a topic that appeals to you. How might you approach that topic if your purpose were to inform? To persuade? To entertain? To narrate? To describe? In your journal, jot down ideas about different ways to approach the same topic.

Address Your Audience

To best communicate with your audience, put yourself in their place. Think about what your readers need or want to know about the subject. Consider also the language that would best communicate your ideas to them.

Find the Right Level   Identify the various aspects of the subject that will most interest your readers. For example, an audience of tennis enthusiasts may enjoy reading about the specific shots a player used to win a game. However, an audience that is less familiar with the sport may be more interested in reading about the player's personality.

Then consider how much your audience already knows about the topic you've chosen. This will help you avoid explaining something most of your readers already know or writing about something they don't understand.

Find the Right Language   Choose words that are appropriate to your audience and purpose. For a research paper or a letter to the principal, you would use formal English, paying attention to rules of standard grammar and usage. For a letter to a friend, conversational English would be more appropriate.

To make sure that your writing will reach its intended audience you can ask yourself several questions. The questions below helped one writer determine how to address his audience. The writer chose to write on the following topic: "How My Sister Ann Drives Me Crazy." His basic purpose was to entertain.

Questions to Help You Address Your Audience	
1. Whom am I writing for?	My English class, other ninth-graders
2. How much do they know about Ann?	Not much. I'll have to present a vivid description and character sketch of my sister.
3. What writing style should I use?	I'll use a humorous, informal, conversational style to help keep them interested in what I'm saying.
4. What vocabulary is appropriate?	Words they understand, especially some contractions and slang to get across the way my sister talks.

Identify Purpose and Audience

For each of the possible topics you listed in Lesson 2.2, ask yourself the questions on page 71 to define your purpose for writing. Likewise, use the questions on page 72 to help you identify your audience and determine how to address that audience. Then select a final topic for your human-interest story.

- Determine if your purpose is to inform, persuade, entertain, or describe.
- Consider the language and aspects of a topic suitable for your audience.

PURPOSE To choose a final topic
AUDIENCE Yourself
LENGTH 1–2 pages

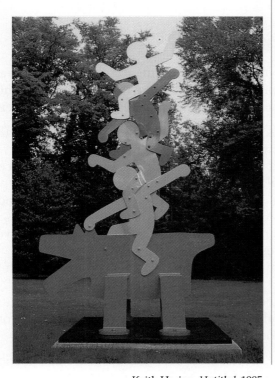

Keith Haring, *Untitled*, 1985

Cooperative Learning

Work in small groups to prepare short presentations describing the sculpture pictured on this page. Each group member should choose a different purpose and audience for the presentation. For example, one student might describe the piece of art to a kindergarten class with the purpose of warning against unsafe behavior. Another student might describe the piece to a group of artists with the purpose of explaining how the sculpture was created. The group discussion that follows should focus on how vocabulary, sentence structure, content, and other elements vary with differences in purpose and audience.

Grammar Link

Revise sentences to suit an audience.

Revise each complex sentence into two simple sentences to make it more suitable for a young audience.

1. When our big family reunion took place last August, we all looked forward to a good time.
2. Because we had planned so many special events, there was scarcely time to visit with everybody.
3. Despite the fact that some of the younger cousins ate too much, no one became ill.
4. We tried to include a picture of everyone in the big photo album that we made to record the event.
5. Because our next reunion will probably be in Florida, most of us hope to get a chance to go to Disney World.

See Lesson 13.3, pages 503–504.

The Writing Process
Prewriting: Gathering Information

Whatever your writing project is, you will need some type of information. Using the library and interviewing people can usually provide you with the information you need.

Use the Library

If your writing project requires information that you do not already have, your school or public library is the best place to find the information you need. Use these tips to make your research more efficient.

- Search for books by title, subject, or author, using either the card catalog or the on-line computer system.
- Use the subject headings for each listing as cross-references to related material.
- Browse among other books in the section in which you locate a useful book.
- Jot down the author, title, and call number of each book you think you will use.
- Record books that *don't* provide help (so you won't search for them again).
- Examine each book's bibliography for related titles.
- Try to be an independent researcher, but ask a librarian for help if you cannot locate much information on your topic.

See pages 760–771 in Resources and Skills for more information on using library resources.

Conduct Interviews

Some of your best sources for information may be people. Use interviews to find out about a person's ideas, feelings, and experiences.

Informational Interviews   In an informational interview, you ask a person to speak about a subject he or she knows well. The interview may be informal—that is, a casual conversation—or formal—that is, one for which you need to make an appointment.

Whether your interview will be formal or informal, prepare for it carefully. Learn as much as you can about your subject and about the person you are going to interview. Think about what your readers will want to know. Then write down at least four or five major questions that will help you get at this material. Use *who, what, where, when, why,* and *how* questions so that you get answers that provide information, not just a yes or no response.

During the interview, listen carefully so that you can ask intelligent follow-up questions. Often the most interesting information emerges in response to a question you had not planned to ask. Take notes or tape-record the interview.

As soon as possible after the interview, write up a full account of it, based on your notes or your tapes. Write down everything you remember. If necessary, contact the person you interviewed to clarify any confusing ideas or questionable facts.

Before the Interview
- Make the appointment.
- Research your topic and find out about your source.
- Write out four or five basic questions.

During the Interview
- Ask informational questions (*who, what, where, when, why,* and *how*).
- Listen carefully.
- Ask follow-up questions.
- Take accurate notes (or tape-record).

After the Interview
- Write a more detailed account of the interview.
- Contact source for any needed clarification or to double-check facts.

Journal Writing

You are researching services for senior citizens in your community for a class assignment. In your journal write down four or five informational questions you might ask a senior citizens' program director during an interview.

Oral Histories   To obtain information about an event in recent history, you might interview someone who lived through the event. For example, if you want information about your family history, interview a relative who can tell you about the lives of other family members. Such "spoken memories" are called oral history.

Family stories can tell you a great deal about both the story-teller and life in the past. The following is an excerpt from the oral history *Hannah's Daughters.* Hannah Lambertson Nesbitt, who lived from 1876 to 1974, describes life on her grand-father's farm.

Literature Model

*I*n my grandaddy's time it was different than it is now. It was all hand labor, and men could support their families. . . . We had poorhouses, yes. A lot of men lived on a poor farm. I used to know a portion of a song about a son who persuaded his parents to deed him their farm. Well, they yielded to him and he turned them out. They had to go "over the hills to the poorhouse." That's what the song was called. There's many children did that to their folks.

But I'm talking about what *my* folks done. They looked after those that needed help. If a man took sick or died, they looked after his family. Grandaddy sent Grandma to different places; she had several families she used to keep. She'd clothe them and everything else. She'd just go to visit and see what they had to have. . . . And if they needed a barrel of flour, they got it. . . . The farmers just did it. They helped those that needed it. Not like it is today.

Dorothy Gallagher, *Hannah's Daughters*

Observation

One tool that newswriters use is observation—witnessing an event and recording it. Trials, ball games, and congressional debates are example of events that are described for millions by people observing the events. Careful observation requires the use of the observer's five senses to gather information. The observer takes notes, writing down the important points so that nothing is forgotten or overlooked. The notes then are the basis for the written report of the event—perhaps in a newspaper or magazine article.

2.4 Writing Activities

Gather Information About Your Topic

Think carefully about your topic. What kind of information do you need? What is the most effective method of gathering that information? Make these decisions and then, using the method you have chosen, start making notes that contain information that you might include in your paper. You may want to record your notes on note cards, notebook paper, or your computer (see the Computer Option that follows). Be sure to write down anything that might be useful.

- Locate the best sources of information.
- Make arrangements to interview sources.
- Prepare a list of questions you will ask in an interview.
- Include enough information in your notes.

PURPOSE To gather information
AUDIENCE Yourself
LENGTH Varies

COMPUTER OPTION

Your computer can be an excellent tool to save valuable information for research projects. You can use it when compiling a family history or any research project for which you will gather information over a long period of time. Establish a classification system, and use it to list the information you've obtained, the source, and the date. As you gather additional data, create subheads to classify, store, change, and retrieve information as needed.

Grammar Link

Use quotation marks to indicate speech.

When taking notes during an interview, be sure to use quotation marks to enclose the exact words of the speaker.

Rewrite each of the sentences below, adding quotation marks wherever they are necessary.

1. When I first began teaching, said my former teacher Mrs. Moody, things were very different.
2. Can you tell me about some of those differences? I asked.
3. Well, she said, for one thing, many classes were bigger.
4. We really didn't do much group work, she added.
5. I also remember, she continued, that there was time for physical education as well as art and music.
6. We used to rely on filmstrips and movies, she reminisced.
7. Now, Mrs. Moody went on, teachers use computers, VCRs, and television.
8. What about homework, Mrs. Moody? I asked. Is it more or less important today than it was years ago?
9. Homework is just as important today as it was years ago, Mrs. Moody replied.
10. In fact, she concluded, I would call homework one of the cornerstones of the educational system.

See Lesson 21.7, pages 714–718.

The Writing Process
Drafting: Turning Notes into Paragraphs

When you draft, you use your prewriting notes to create a piece of writing.

Family ties, sometimes I feel like I've got so many responsibilities to my family I don't have a life of my own. Babysitting my brothers. If I have to do that again next weekend I'll just scream. And when they do something wrong, I get the blame. Can't Mom see I need to have some time to myself? Wasn't she ever my age? Life must have been so different when she was growing up.

Prewriting Notes

Swimming

First experience—nearly drowned when I fell into a pond when I was four years old

Learning to swim was a nightmare for me

If we were meant to swim, we'd have gills and fins

The time my uncle taught me how to tread water— he was so patient, didn't laugh at me

Overcame fears

Wonder what a wave-action pool is like . . .

Prewriting Notes

Your first draft will not be perfect. It's your first try at presenting your ideas in an order that makes sense and shaping them into paragraphs.

Put Your Ideas in Order

One way to put your ideas in order is to sort them into categories. If an idea doesn't seem to fit anywhere, leave it out. If a new idea occurs to you while you are sorting, include the idea if it fits. Look at the way one writer organized her ideas on the topic "I always like my Aunt Alicia best."

Organizing Ideas

- My Aunt Alicia
- Her mysterious apartment in the city
- Apartment filled with books and the little clay animals she found in Mexico
- I got lost once on my way there
- Her embroidered jeans jacket
- Her flashy jewelry
- Long dark hair, held up with a comb
- Treated me like a person, not just her niece
- Listening to her old rock-and-roll records

Introductory Material
- My Aunt Alicia
- Her flashy jewelry
- Her embroidered jeans jacket
- Long dark hair, held up with a comb

Body
- Her mysterious apartment in the city
- Listening to her old rock-and-roll records
- Apartment filled with books and the little clay animals she found in Mexico

Concluding Material
- Treated me like a person, not just her niece
- One place in the world I felt at home

Write Paragraphs

Each paragraph in your draft should be organized around one main idea—or controlling idea. Often the main idea is stated in a topic sentence. The supporting details develop the main idea by proving, clarifying, or expanding upon it. Like building blocks, the supporing ideas provide the foundation on which the main idea rests.

There is no magic formula for writing a paragraph. One approach is to write supporting sentences first to help determine a main idea and then write a topic sentence to express that idea. An alternative approach is to write the topic sentence first. Keep in mind that you can revise any part of your paragraph at any point in the writing process.

Journal Writing

Look through your journal for possible main ideas for paragraphs. Pick one idea, and list supporting details that you might use to develop that idea in a paragraph.

A topic sentence may be a statement or a question. Whatever its form, a good topic sentence expresses the main idea clearly and makes the reader want to keep reading. Your choice of topic sentence also helps determine how you will develop the paragraph.

Try out several possible topic sentences before choosing the one that best expresses your main idea. Each of the following topic sentences is based on the painting shown here. Note how each would take a paragraph in a different direction.

Eastman Johnson, *The Hatch Family*, 1871

- Just a century ago, several generations of a family often lived together under one roof.
- Although a frail man, my grandfather still ruled the family.
- The dark wood paneling glowed in the firelight.

Notice how the writer in the model below relates every detail to the idea stated in the topic sentence.

Literature Model

Why do you suppose O'Connor puts a topic sentence up front and reinforces it at the paragraph's conclusion?

N o one was particularly glad that Mary Fortune looked like her grandfather except the old man himself. He thought it added greatly to her attractiveness. He thought she was the smartest and the prettiest child he had ever seen and he let the rest of them know that if—IF that was—he left anything to anybody, it would be Mary Fortune he left it to. She was now nine, short and broad like himself, with his very light blue eyes, his wide prominent forehead, his steady penetrating scowl and his rich florid complexion; but she was like him on the inside too. She had, to a singular degree, his intelligence, his strong will, and his push and drive. Though there was seventy years' difference in their ages, the spiritual distance between them was slight. She was the only member of the family he had any respect for.

Details reveal physical resemblance and point out similarities in personality traits.

Flannery O'Connor, *A View of the Woods*

2.5 Writing Activities

Write a First Draft

Use your prewriting notes to get your ideas down on paper. Do not worry about spelling, grammar, or correct usage at this point.

- Arrange your ideas in an order that makes sense.
- Organize your draft into paragraphs.
- Make sure that each paragraph is organized around one main idea.

PURPOSE To write a first draft
AUDIENCE Yourself
LENGTH 1–2 pages

Cooperative Learning

In a small group, discuss the collage shown on this page. First describe it and then interpret its meaning. Each group member then (1) writes his or her own topic sentence focusing on some aspect of the picture, (2) lists details to support the topic sentence, and (3) drafts a paragraph, using the topic sentence and details.

Romare Bearden,
Blue Interior, Morning, 1968

Grammar Link

Use apostrophes with possessive indefinite pronouns.

Indefinite pronouns, such as *everyone* and *no one,* use apostrophes to form the possessive. *Personal pronouns,* such as *his* and *hers,* do not.

Rewrite the following sentences, underlining each personal and indefinite pronoun. Add apostrophes where they are needed.

1. Someones idea was to make a list of everybodys names and special skills for a school directory.
2. You and your classmates think about each others unique talents and strengths.
3. Under the letter *a,* you identify your classmates whose talents include athletics and art.
4. While you compile your list, others are working on theirs.
5. Your friend Carol says that no ones list is exactly like hers.

See Lesson 17.1, page 595, and Lesson 21.9, page 721.

The Writing Process
Drafting: Writing Unified Paragraphs

While every paragraph in your draft should be about one main idea, not every paragraph needs a topic sentence. What is the main idea of each paragraph in the model below?

The narrator, Esperanza, uses details from her great-grandmother's life to support the selection's main idea.

Do you like the way Cisneros has delayed stating the main idea until the last sentence? Why or why not?

Literature Model

My great-grandmother. I would've liked to have known her, a wild horse of a woman, so wild she wouldn't marry until my great-grandfather threw a sack over her head and carried her off. Just like that, as if she were a fancy chandelier. That's the way he did it.

And the story goes she never forgave him. She looked out the window all her life, the way so many women sit their sadness on an elbow. I wonder if she made the best with what she got or was she sorry because she couldn't be all the things she wanted to be. Esperanza. I have inherited her name, but I don't want to inherit her place by the window.

Sandra Cisneros, *The House on Mango Street*

Keep to the Main Idea

You can express a paragraph's main idea in a direct statement—that is, in a topic sentence. Or you can imply the main idea by suggesting it indirectly through your choice of supporting details.

Stated in a Topic Sentence There are several advantages to stating your main idea in a topic sentence. First, providing a clear statement of what the paragraph is about helps give your writing direction. Second, the sentence tells the reader what to focus on.

A topic sentence may appear anywhere in the paragraph. When a topic sentence appears at the beginning of a paragraph, it lets the reader know what's to come. When the topic sentence appears at the end, it summarizes the preceding supporting details and ensures that the reader has understood the main idea.

Implied In some paragraphs, particularly descriptive or narrative paragraphs, the main idea is implied, or stated indirectly. In these types of writing, the supporting details are so strongly linked by a main idea that this main idea shines through without having to be stated directly. Instead of saying "I was happy to be home," a narrative writer might use details to *show* he or she was happy.

Include Supporting Details

In a unified paragraph, each sentence provides one or more details that support the main idea. The supporting details can be sensory details, examples or incidents, facts, statistics, and reasons. Your purpose in writing will help you determine which kinds of supporting details to use.

Sensory Details Vivid sensory words describe how things look, sound, smell, feel, or taste. They draw your readers in and help them experience the scene or subject. To develop sensory details, try to visualize the scene you are describing and think about each of the senses in turn. For example, how would you use sensory details to describe the scene in this painting? First think about what you would see, hear, smell, feel, and taste if you could step inside it. Then decide what words you would use to make the scene come alive for your readers.

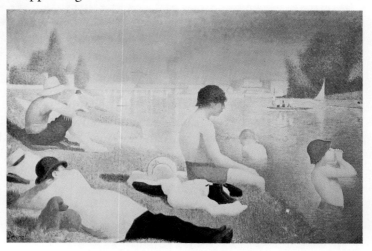

Georges Pierre Seurat, *The Bathers at Asnières*, 1883–1884

Journal Writing

Pick a place that's important to you or your family. Close your eyes and try to "see" it. Now listen for the sounds you hear there. Work your way through each of the other three senses. In your journal, jot down the sensory details that come to mind.

Examples or Incidents Sometimes the best way to develop a main idea is through describing examples or incidents. For example, to develop the main idea that "starting high school was one of the hardest things I've ever done," you might tell about something that happened when you started high school. Then, to explore a specific incident, ask yourself *who, what, where, when, why,* and *how* questions.

Facts and Statistics Another way to support a main idea is to use facts and statistics. A fact is a statement that has been proved by observation, experience, or study—for example, "Washington, D.C., is the capital of the United States." Statistics are facts that involve numbers—for example, "The average American sees 300 ads a day."

Suppose you wanted to write a paragraph with the following topic sentence: "There's not enough free time in the average high school student's life." Here's how one student used a time line to organize facts and statistics that could help support this topic sentence.

Facts and Statistics Organized on a Time Line								
Algebra: 25 word problems due tomorrow.		Track practice: 1 hour.		Eat dinner: 30 minutes. Then spend 30 minutes cleaning up, taking out the garbage.			Begin practicing lines for drama club play.	
1 P.M.	**2 P.M.**	**3 P.M.**	**4 P.M.**	**5 P.M.**	**6 P.M.**	**7 P.M.**	**8 P.M.**	**9 P.M.**
	English: essay assigned. Get 85% on quiz.		Go home. Take care of brother until Mom gets home in 1.5 hours.			Start homework.		

Reasons If your topic sentence expresses an opinion or gives an explanation, you can back it up with reasons. For example, if the topic sentence of your paragraph is "Husbands and wives should undertake an equal share of the housework and child care," you might use a graphic organizer like the one below to help you develop and outline reasons that document your topic sentence.

The notion that taking care of the home and children is "women's work" is sexist.

An equal relationship between parents presents a good model for their children.

Why should husbands and wives undertake an equal share of the housework and child care?

Spending more time together benefits both fathers and their children.

It is unfair to expect women employed outside the home to shoulder all of the domestic responsibilities as well.

2.6 Writing Activities

Check Your Paragraphs

Look over your draft to make sure that your paragraphs are unified. Ask yourself these questions:

- Does every paragraph have an implied or a stated topic sentence?
- Have I used sensory details?
- Have I used examples or incidents to help make my point?
- Would facts and statistics help support my main idea?
- If I am writing to express an opinion, is the opinion backed up with reasons?

PURPOSE To check paragraphs for unity
AUDIENCE Yourself
LENGTH 1–2 pages

Cross-Curricular: Science

Perform this simple experiment:

1. Equally fill two glasses nearly to the top with water.
2. Guess how many paper clips you will have to drop into each glass before the water overflows if you drop the paper clips one at a time into one glass and ten at a time into the other.
3. Explain whether you think there will be a difference and why.
4. Now drop one paper clip at a time into one of the glasses and ten paper clips at a time into the other glass. Take notes as you observe what happens.
5. Was your guess correct?

Draft a paragraph, using your guess or theory as your topic sentence. Use your observations to support or refute your topic sentence. Include any reasons you can provide for your results.

Grammar Link

Make sure subjects agree with verbs.

As you learned in this lesson, facts and statistics are good ways to support a main idea.

Rewrite the following paragraph. Choose the form of the verb in parentheses that agrees with each statistical subject.

[1]When 100 percent of the world's population (is/are) considered, more than 56 percent of the people (live/lives) in rural areas. [2]In the United States, however, the opposite is true; nearly 80 percent (live/lives) in metropolitan areas. [3]More than 971,000 people now (live/lives) in Las Vegas, Nevada, making it the fastest-growing area in the country. [4]In actual numbers, more than 500,000 people (was added/were added) to the population of Los Angeles from 1990 to 1992; 231,000 (was/were) the increase in Houston. [5]Only 20 of the 268 metropolitan areas in the United States (has/have) lost population since 1990.

See Lesson 16.4, page 576.

The Writing Process
Drafting: Ordering the Details

The way you organize details will depend on your purpose—whether you are narrating, explaining, persuading, or describing.

The computer screen below lists various methods of organizing supporting details and the most common purposes for which these methods are used. However, do not feel that you have to limit the organization of your writing to just what is shown here.

Chronological Order

Chronological order—giving events in the order that they happened—is often used to organize narrative writing. Notice how writer Jim Barnes uses chronological order to narrate the details of a frightening incident.

A deep, low moan—ghostly but unmistakably human— rolled up from the bowels of the black earth. There was for a moment, my brother recalls, a stillness like doom upon all of them. Then everybody was running, running. . . . A great shadow passed beside my brother. It was a horse. The moan persisted, even over the sound of thumping boots and racing hoofs. Now my brother passed the horse, and burst through the barbed wire fence at the edge of the field with one wild bound. He flung himself down the lane and plunged through the doorway of our house and hugged himself close to the dying coals in the fireplace. An hour passed before he began to cry.

Jim Barnes, "On Native Ground"

How many major events are signaled by transitions like "then," "now," and "an hour passed"?

Because the writer describes the action almost minute by minute, the reader feels drawn into the events.

Spatial Order

Spatial order—the order in which objects appear in a physical place—is often used to organize descriptive writing. To use spatial order, describe items as they appear from left to right, from top to bottom, from back to front, or in any other logical combination. Use words like *above*, *below*, *behind*, and *next to* to help readers "see" the scene you are describing.

For example, to describe the scene shown here, you might begin by identifying the chessboard in the middle of the room. From that starting point, you might go on to describe the two men on either side of the chessboard. Then you might move behind the men to the fireplace against the wall. Finally, you could describe the women.

Henri Matisse, *The Painter's Family*, 1911

Use spatial order to describe your favorite room. Identify a starting point in the room and use words like *next to* and *above* to indicate clearly the placement of each object in the room.

Order of Importance

Order of importance is an appropriate method to use when your supporting details are facts, statistics, incidents, or examples. For example, if you want to make an immediate impact on your reader, start with your most important detail. If you want to leave your reader thinking about your strongest point, build up to the most important detail.

Cause-and-Effect Order

When you want to show that one event took place because of another, you can use cause-and-effect order. In a cause-and-effect paragraph, the topic sentence may state the cause and the supporting details identify the effects. Conversely, the topic sentence may state the effect and the supporting details present the causes. This method works well when you write about science, history, or even about yourself. In the paragraph below, Ginger Lumpkin uses cause-and-effect order.

Student Model

The topic sentence prepares the reader for a cause-and-effect ordering of the supporting details.

A teacher who once doubted me ironically became a source of inspiration. In the seventh grade, I wrote a poem entitled "Lost on a Desert." After my teacher read my poem, she asked me who I had copied it from—she didn't believe that I had written it. Her remarks hurt me, but the experience made me feel determined to prove my creative writing abilities. As a result, I began to write a variety of poems, short stories, and plays, all of which my teacher praised. In the end, I not only showed my teacher that I could write well, but through my writing, I also gained a better understanding of myself.

How do these details support the topic sentence?

Ginger Lumpkin, Hyde Park Career Academy, Chicago, Illinois

The graphic below shows the cause-and-effect relationships presented in the paragraph. Note that most of the effects in turn act as causes.

I wrote a poem for my seventh-grade teacher.

My teacher read the poem but didn't believe I had written it.

Hurt but determined to prove my abilities, I continued to write.

The teacher liked my new work; I gained new self-knowledge.

2.7 Writing Activities

Check Organization

Read over your draft to make sure that the details in your paragraph are ordered. Remember that not all your paragraphs will be organized in the same way. As you look at each paragraph, ask yourself these questions.

- What type of order have I used?
- Is this the most effective way to organize the supporting details?
- Should I change the order?

PURPOSE To check order of details
AUDIENCE Yourself
LENGTH 1–2 pages

Cross-Curricular: Art

Use the glazed ceramic bowl on this page as a source of details for a paragraph. Decide on a topic sentence, and then write your paragraph. For example, you might want to speculate on the relationship between the king and his attendants on the left and the petitioners on the right. Use chronological order, spatial order, order of importance, or cause-and-effect order to organize your supporting details.

Iranian glazed ceramic bowl, c. 1200

The Writing Process
Drafting: Writing Coherent Paragraphs

In a coherent paragraph, all the sentences are clearly and logically connected to one another. Transitional words, repeated words, synonyms, and pronouns are the "glue" or "mortar" you can use to link together sentences and build a better paragraph.

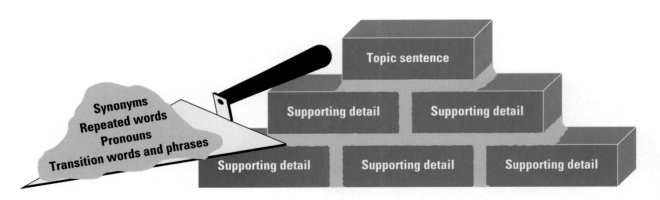

Build a Coherent Paragraph

Use the following checklist to help make sure your paragraphs are coherent.

Checklist for Writing Coherently
1. Are all the sentences linked clearly and logically to one another?
2. Can I repeat any words to help show the connections between ideas?
3. Have I used synonyms that my readers will be able to understand?
4. Does each pronoun refer back to some antecedent?
5. Are there any transitions I can use to link the sentences?

Use Transition Words and Phrases

Use transitions—words or phrases that show relationships between ideas—to help you write coherent paragraphs. Transitions create logical links between sentences in a paragraph and help the reader follow your train of thought. The chart below shows some common transitions.

Transitions			
Kinds	**Examples**		
Time	after first	before meanwhile	finally then	next when
Place	above below	beside here	next to near	there opposite
Importance	first primary	second mainly	more important	most important
Cause and effect	as a result so	consequently therefore	for that reason	because
Comparison and contrast	although similarly	in contrast however	on the other hand like	in the same way unlike
Example	for example together with	for instance along with	namely likewise	that is

You can also use transitions to link paragraphs in a longer piece of writing. Transitions such as *first, second,* and *most important* can help readers understand the relative importance of each paragraph. Other transitions can help the reader understand relationships between paragraphs. Transitions such as *finally* and *therefore* often create a successful link to the concluding paragraph.

Journal Writing

Look through your journal, and select a paragraph. Then use the list of questions on page 90 to make sure the paragraph is coherent. Insert transitions listed in the chart above to create links between your sentences.

Use Repetition and Synonyms

Another way to link sentences is to repeat the same word from sentence to sentence. But be careful: too much repetition will bore your readers. One way to avoid too much repetition is to read your work aloud. If you hear the same word too often, it's probably time to use synonyms—words that have similar meanings. Keep your audience in mind, however. Unfamiliar synonyms may make your ideas more difficult to follow.

In the paragraph below, N. Scott Momaday repeats words and phrases and uses synonyms to link his sentences.

Repetition of words such as "they" and "there" helps link sentences.

What effect does the use of synonyms have?

Effective repetition of "they" results in parallel structure.

> ### Literature Model
>
> My grandmother lived in a house near the place where Rainy Mountain Creek runs into the Washita River. Once there was a lot of sound in the house, a lot of coming and going, feasting and talk. The summers there were full of excitement and reunion. The Kiowas are a summer people; they abide the cold and keep to themselves, but when the season turns and the land becomes warm and vital they cannot hold still; an old love of going returns upon them. The old people have a fine sense of pageantry and a wonderful notion of decorum. The aged visitors who came to my grandmother's house when I was a child were men of immense character, full of wisdom and disdain. They dealt in a kind of infallible quiet and gave but one face away; it was enough. They were made of lean and leather, and they bore themselves upright. They wore great black hats and bright ample shirts that shook in the wind. They rubbed fat upon their hair and wound their braids with strips of colored cloth. Some of them painted their faces and carried the scars of old and cherished enmities. They were an old council of war lords, come to remind and be reminded of who they were.
>
> N. Scott Momaday, *House Made of Dawn*

Use Pronouns

To avoid the boring repetition of specific nouns, substitute pronouns for a word, a group of words, or an idea that appears in a preceding sentence. Note the use of pronouns in the literature model above. As an experiment, mentally substitute nouns for the pronouns. How does the selection read?

Check Your Paragraphs for Coherence

Look over your draft to make sure that your paragraphs are coherent.

- Circle your transition words and phrases. Where can you use more?
- Draw a box around the repeated words and synonyms you have used to link your sentences and paragraphs.
- Underline the pronouns you have used to avoid unnecessary repetition.

Make any changes to your paragraphs that will make them more coherent.

PURPOSE To make paragraphs coherent
AUDIENCE Yourself
LENGTH 1–2 pages

Aaron Douglas, *Building More Stately Mansions*, 1944

Grammar Link

Use conjunctive adverbs to show relationships.

These words in the chart on page 91 are *conjunctive adverbs: so, consequently, therefore, similarly, however,* and *likewise.* They are used between clauses to show the relationship between them. They are preceded by semicolons and followed by commas.

Use a conjunctive adverb to join each pair of sentences below into one.

1. When she grew older, Amy Tan decided to become a writer. Her parents did not encourage her in this pursuit.
2. As time passed, she sold several stories she had written. She decided to become a full-time writer.
3. Today Amy Tan is the author of two best-selling novels. She is researching a third book.
4. She often writes of the conflict between her Chinese culture and her American one. Another theme in her work is mother-daughter conflict.

See Lesson 10.7, page 441.

Cross-Curricular: Art

The painting on this page is the work of Aaron Douglas, one of the foremost artists of the Harlem Renaissance. What might this painting be saying about the creation of huge historically significant structures? What might the title mean? Write a paragraph that expresses the message you think Douglas wanted to convey in this painting. Use repetition to keep your paragraph strong and coherent.

2.8 Drafting: Writing Coherent Paragraphs **93**

The Writing Process
Revising: Improving Paragraphs

Revising is the stage of the writing process in which you step back and take a new look at your work. You evaluate it, get the reaction of others, and then rewrite your draft to solve any problems.

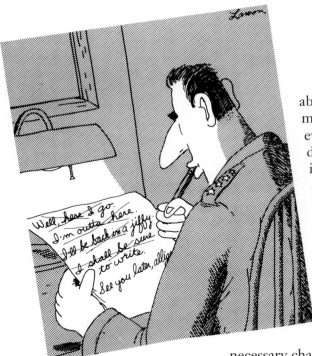

As you revise, you may learn something new about your piece of writing. You may clarify its meaning, find a way to say it more effectively, or even discover entirely new ideas. Sometimes you don't get the words quite right the first time. For instance, it may have taken General MacArthur several tries before he came up with his memorable farewell line: "I shall return."

Revise in Stages

One useful strategy for revising is to break the process down into three parts. First, put yourself in the place of your readers and go through the draft quickly, checking to make sure that your meaning is clear. Make any necessary changes.

Next, read your draft aloud to a partner or small group. Often, ideas that seem clear to you will need to be rephrased for an audience. Take notes on the questions your peer reviewers ask and on their suggestions.

Finally, go back to your draft and read it carefully one final time. Look at the notes from your writing conference. Now is the time to decide what changes you want to make.

Check for Meaning

After you finish your first draft, set it aside for a while. Then, when you pick it up to revise it, you'll see it with fresh eyes.

Read it through once quickly and jot down notes or ideas in the margins. Don't worry about word choices, grammar, spelling, or punctuation. Use the following checklist to help you focus on the big picture—the meaning.

Meaning Checklist
1. Have I presented the main idea clearly? What is the main idea? (Hint: If you cannot easily answer the question after reading your writing, chances are you have not presented the main idea clearly enough.)
2. Have I achieved my purpose through my writing?
3. Who is my audience? Have I written this piece with their needs in mind?
4. Do I need to give my readers more information?

If you have trouble answering any of these questions, you may need to return to the prewriting or drafting stages to rework your ideas. Don't be discouraged. Going back and forth between the stages is part of the writing process. Even writers like Joan Didion rework their ideas: "My writing is a process of rewriting, of going back and changing and filling in. In the rewriting process you discover what's going on."

Prewriting

Drafting

Revising

Journal Writing

Review an entry in your journal that you have not looked at recently. Following the entry, write any suggestions you now have for clarifying the main idea of the entry.

Have a Writing Conference

Read your draft to a peer reviewer or reviewers. Ask them to read the checklist below and keep it in mind as they listen.

Unity Checklist
1. Does every detail I have selected support the main idea?
2. Have I organized the supporting details in the most logical way?
3. Have I included any sentences that are unnecessary because they simply restate the main point without adding any new information or meaning?
4. Have I made the relationships between my ideas clear?

After you have read your draft aloud, ask your listeners these questions.

- What was the strongest part of my writing?
- What, if anything, was not clear?

Then go over the questions in the checklist with them. They may ask you to read your draft again as they listen carefully.

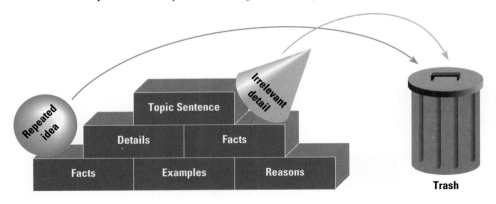

Do a Final Reading and Revise

Use the checklist for your final reading. Make your revisions, using your notes from the writing conference and from your own checking of your draft.

Coherence Checklist
1. Have I written sentences that flow logically and clearly?
2. Would repeated words, pronouns, synonyms, or transitions improve the flow of my writing?
3. Have I made appropriate word choices?
4. Have I used specific nouns and active verbs?
5. Have I deleted all unnecessary words?

2.9 Writing Activities

Revise Your Draft

Follow these steps for your revision.

- Read your draft over once for meaning.
- Have a writing conference, and take notes.
- Do a final reading and make changes.

Use circles and arrows, taped-on additions, cross-outs—whatever works for you—to show your revisions.

PURPOSE To revise your draft
AUDIENCE Yourself, peer reviewers
LENGTH 1–2 pages

Cross-Curricular: Social Studies

For a class project, you have been asked to revise the following paragraph about families in western Sumatra in Indonesia. Use the checklists presented in this lesson to help you.

> The society is matrilineal. All inherited property and family names are handed down from mother to daughter. Most of the people are rice farmers. The grandmother is the most powerful member of the family. Children are given the name of their mother's family. All the descendants of one grandmother live together in one big house. Up to thirty family members live in one house. A woman marries and the husband moves in with his wife's family.

Grammar Link

Use active and passive voice.

When revising your writing, make sure that most verbs are in the *active voice*. Use the *passive voice* when you do not know or do not want to call attention to the performer of an action.

Rewrite each sentence below that you think should be in the active voice. If you think a sentence is belongs in the passive voice, write *passive*.

1. Great tennis talent is being developed by a young Californian named Venus Ebonistarr Williams, trained by her father to become a tennis star.
2. At the age of ten, Venus was ranked by some tennis experts as number one in southern California in the girls' twelve-and-under division.
3. This ranking was attained only after a great deal of hard work.
4. As part of her routine, she is coached by her father at the tennis courts every day.
5. Great discipline is required to practice tennis skills on a daily basis.
6. Net shots, as well as forehand and backhand drills, are some of the skills practiced by this rising star.
7. Tennis is played by Venus's entire family.
8. In the family's life, an important role is played by tennis.
9. A journal has been kept by Venus's father of the important events in her life.
10. A winning future is predicted by coaches and pros for this young player.

See Lesson 15.7, page 558.

The Writing Process
Editing: Checking Words and Sentences

Editing is the stage in which you make sure that you've used words correctly. You also check your writing for errors in grammar, word usage, punctuation, capitalization, and spelling. The goal of editing, like the other stages in the writing process, is to communicate your ideas clearly to your readers.

COMPLAINTS ABOUT NBA REFEREES GROWING UGLY

It is bad manners to break your bread and roll in your soup.

Plunging 1,000 feet into the gorge, we saw Yosemite Falls.

GRANDMOTHER OF EIGHT MAKES HOLE IN ONE

TUNA BITING OFF WASHINGTON COAST

No bear feet allowed.

Edit Your Draft for Sense

To edit for sense, make sure that your words and sentences say what you want them to say. For example, you check that you have not used unclear or misplaced modifiers like the examples on this page. Use the checklist on page 99 to help identify and correct errors in your writing.

Editing Checklist

Question	Example
1. Are all words used correctly?	She could ~~of~~ *have* waited.
2. Do subjects and verbs agree?	Each of my brothers drive*s* a truck.
3. Are verb tenses correct?	If you wanted it, you should ~~say~~ *have said* so.
4. Are pronoun references clear and correct?	~~Ann~~ *she* called her mother every day, when *Ann* ~~she~~ *W* was away at camp.
5. Have I corrected all run-ons and fragments?	She turned on the radio*, but* she heard only static, *W*hich was annoying.

Self-Editing To edit your own writing, you need to approach your work objectively and critically. Reading your work aloud is crucial. Note the changes Rachelle Netkow chose to make.

Student Model

My family is *a*typical ~~of a~~ family *of* *in* the 1990s. Both of ^ my parents work, which means many of the household responsibiliti*e*s are left to my brother and *me* ~~I~~. We do them, of course ^ even though we don't like ~~it~~ *the extra work*. Since ^ *everyone in* my family is busy with *various* ^ activities, it is unusual for all of us to be home at the same time. ~~But~~ *O*ccasionally though, we try to do special things *together*. ^ My family is very close even if we don't see each other *very* ~~all that~~ often.

Rachelle Netkow, Centennial High School, Pueblo, Colorado

Change makes pronoun reference grammatically correct.

Why did Rachelle add "everyone in" here?

Journal Writing

How can you make sure that your changes in one sentence do not alter the meaning of the following sentence? Write down a few general tips that will help you edit any writing project.

Peer Editing To edit another's writing, focus on the ideas and organization of a piece of writing rather than on its grammar and mechanics. Be honest, but respect the writer's feelings. Identify strengths as well as weaknesses. Offer suggestions for improvement, not just criticisms. Note the peer editor's comments on the paragraph below.

Avoid repetition of pronouns.

Good transition!

Expand — tell us what she talked about.

Rearrange sentences.

Last fall, my family drove my older sister Shana to college. It was her freshman year, and even though she didn't say so, I could tell ~~she~~ *Shana* was scared and sad to leave home. For one thing, she talked more during the drive than she has for the past three years. She didn't even yell at me when I helped carry her stereo equipment to her room. Normally, ~~She~~ *Shana* has a fit if I so much as touch one of her records. It really was a day full of surprises. When it was time to go, she even hugged me.

Proofread and Mark Your Draft

Proofreading is reading closely to find errors in spelling, punctuation, and capitalization. For marking corrections, use a set of basic proofreading symbols. The chart below shows a few.

Proofreading Marks		
Mark	**Meaning**	**Example**
∧	Insert	My granmother is eighty-six years old.
ℒ	Delete	She grew up on a dairry farm.
#∧	Insert space	She milked cows every morning.
⌒	Close up space	She fed the chickens in the barn yard.
≡	Capitalize	times have changed.
/	Make lowercase	Machines now do the Milking.
⌒ sp	Check spelling	Chickens are fed autommatically.
⁀	Switch order	Modern farms are like more factories.
¶	New paragraph	Last year I returned to the farm.

Edit Your Human-Interest Story

After you have prewritten, drafted, and revised your story, you must edit it. Check to make sure your story makes sense (see the checklist on page 99). Then proofread your draft for spelling, grammar, and usage errors. Use editing symbols as you proofread (see the chart on page 100).

- Edit your sentences so they make sense.
- Be objective when editing your own work.
- Proofread closely to find errors.

PURPOSE To "polish" your paper
AUDIENCE Yourself
LENGTH 1–2 pages

COMPUTER OPTION

A useful proofreading tool is the spell-checker in your word-processing program. It will probably identify your name as a spelling error until you enter your first and last names into the computer's spelling dictionary. If your spell-checker does not give you the option of adding a word to its dictionary, consult your manual to find how to do so. Once the computer recognizes your name, you can concentrate on correcting real spelling and typographical mistakes.

Remember that the spell-checker feature on your personal computer cannot be relied on as the only method of proofreading your work. For example, the computer will not tell you when you typed *form* but meant *from*.

Grammar Link

Correct dangling and misplaced modifiers.

Some of the headlines at the beginning of this lesson contain dangling or misplaced modifiers. Dangling modifiers modify no word at all; misplaced modifiers modify the wrong word.

Rewrite the following sentences, correcting the misplaced or dangling modifiers in each.

1. The large mural attracts the visitor's eye on the wall.
2. Working out too long, the volleyball practice session made me feel stiff and sore.
3. We bought souvenirs at the main lodge that only cost $5.50.
4. Tacos and enchiladas were served at the buffet covered with salsa.
5. The air was released from the balloon with a hissing sound.
6. Antiques are sold by the shop owner with chipped paint and broken legs.
7. Milking cows and feeding chickens, farm life gave Jamaica a sense of fulfillment.
8. The art fair attracted several hundred thousand visitors, which only lasted three days.
9. The birthday cake was presented to Thad with pink icing and chocolate sprinkles.
10. Driving through the rain, the trip took me longer than usual.

See Lesson 18.7, pages 632–637.

The Writing Process
Presenting: Sharing Writing

The last stage in the writing process is sharing or presenting your work. A school newspaper, such as that shown below, is just one of the many places, or forums, in which you can present your writing.

---

 10 ╱╱╱ **SPORTS** ╱╱╱ The Peninsula Outlook November 20, 1990

Forever a Seahawk: Erstwhile PHS football great shines with Seattle Seahawks

by Cain Claxton

Twelve years have passed since Paul Skansi played split end for Peninsula High School.

Since Skansi played football in high school, he has gone on to play the sport for the University of Washington Huskies, the Pittsburgh Steelers, and the Seattle Seahawks. Along the way he impressed many people: his coaches, his friends and relatives, and even people who have never met him.

"In the sixth grade you could see that he was a blue chipper," Key Peninsula Middle School teacher John Leverett said. Leverett, who taught Skansi in the sixth grade at Goodman Middle School, threw passes to him before any professional quarterbacks did.

"That was one of the funnest years I've had growing up," Skansi said, adding that Leverett "was a teacher that I'll never forget. We did a lot of math, a lot of social studies, and played a lot of football."

Skansi's small size worried his parents, Nick and Patti Skansi. They were concerned that he might get injured playing against larger players. They didn't let Skansi play his freshman and sophomore years, and were reluctant to let him play his junior year.

"He was engaged in all the other athletic events

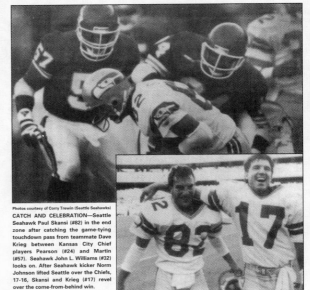

Photos courtesy of Corry Trewin (Seattle Seahawks)
CATCH AND CELEBRATION—Seattle Seahawk Paul Skansi (#82) in the end zone after catching the game-tying touchdown pass from teammate Dave Krieg between Kansas City Chief players Pearson (#24) and Martin (#57). Seahawk John L. Williams (#32) looks on. After Seahawk kicker Norm Johnson lifted Seattle over the Chiefs, 17-16, Skansi and Krieg (#17) revel over the come-from-behind win.

that were offered," Skansi's father said. "I just thought that was enough."

When Skansi finally got a chance to play his junior year, 1977, former Head Football Coach Larry Lunke, now coaching Anacortes High School, already had Mike Bos, a star receiver in his senior year. Lunke needed Skansi to play in other areas and placed him at

Skansi's Collegiate Records

Paul Skansi
... ... Bowl Pla... 1978

Present Your Writing

Because presentation often depends on your particular audience, you should begin thinking during the prewriting stage about where and how you'd like your writing to appear. You have many options for presenting your work to others: at school, in your community, and in the wider world.

School Forums   The diagram below shows some of the presenting options that may be available at your school. Consider the nature of your writing project to help you determine its forum. For example, a short story or poem might be ideal for a class anthology. A movie review might appear in a school newspaper.

Community Forums   If you'd like to reach a wider audience, find out what's being published in your community. Community newspapers may print feature stories about local people and events. Community groups, too, may publish newsletters that accept student work.

Contests   Magazines, such as *Redbook, Seventeen,* and *Merlyn's Pen,* and organizations, such as the National Council of Teachers of English, often sponsor writing contests. The winners may receive prizes and have their work published.

Journal Writing

In your journal, create a diagram like the one shown on this page. Put a check mark next to each of the school forums in which you currently present your work. Circle those to which you would like to submit your work. Find out more about each new forum you have circled.

Open-Market Forums   If you're interested in writing for periodicals, you might target magazines aimed at teenagers, such as *Seventeen*, *Sassy*, or *'Teen*. You also might choose special-interest magazines, such as *Bicycling* or *American Photo*.

Start with something you've already written and try to find a market for it, or do the reverse: find a magazine first and then write a piece for that publication. *Writer's Market* and the *Market Guide for Young Writers* list publications that accept material from young writers. The latter reference describes the type of material each publication accepts, explains how to prepare a manuscript for submission, and often tells about writing contests.

> *The first paragraph lists the name of the publication, the publisher's name and address, and a description of the publication and its audience.*

> *The second paragraph describes the type of material published.*

> *The third paragraph explains how to submit material. Note that "SASE" stands for "self-addressed, stamped envelope."*

---

* PURPLE COW, Signa Publications, 3423 Piedmont Road N.E., Ivy Place Suite 320, Atlanta, GA 30305. Monthly tabloid (ten issues) covering any subject of interest to 13 to 18 year olds.

Publishes: General articles of interest to teens; book, movie, and record reviews; humor; interview/profile; sports (general and anecdotal—no "How to Play Soccer"); personal experience: coping with problems . . . ; and seasonal interest material.

Submission Info: All manuscripts must be typed and accompanied by SASE. Articles should be 500–3,000 words. Pays \$5–\$40. Maximum length for fillers is 150 words. Pays \$5–\$10 for fillers and photos.   Send complete manuscript or query with published clips of published work.

Give Oral Presentations

The most common forum for oral presentation is the classroom, where you may give an oral report or your teacher may read your writing aloud. Other opportunities in your school may include:

- a drama club (for presenting your original play)
- a competitive tournament (for presenting a speech)
- a school radio station

Present Your Human-Interest Story

You have followed all the steps in the first four stages of the writing process: prewriting, drafting, revising, and editing. You are through with the actual writing of your piece. Now you must decide how to present your story.

Maybe you wish to present your paper in another way. You might submit it to a newspaper or magazine or decide to present it orally to a group. If you have made any of these decisions, then the paper must be prepared in a way that best fits the requirements of the presentation. Refer to the lesson for help in preparing your presentation.

- Decide the best way to share your writing, considering all the options, written and oral.
- Prepare a final version suited to your audience, such as school, community, open-market, forums, or contests.
- Check that your draft meets the requirements of the presentation.

PURPOSE   To make a final version of a human-interest story for presentation
AUDIENCE   Varies with the type of presentation
LENGTH   1–2 pages

COMPUTER OPTION

When appropriate, use your computer program function to italicize, underline, or boldface words, phrases, and sentences. For example, to distinguish stage directions from dialogue in a script, you can write the instructions for action in italic type. To emphasize words or phrases in a speech or a letter, use the underlining or bold-faced type.

Grammar Link

Italicize or underline titles.

Note that the titles of publications to which you might submit materials are italicized in this lesson. Titles of books, newspapers, magazines, lengthy poems, plays, and films should always be italicized. If you are typing or handwriting a paper, indicate italics by underlining.

Rewrite the sentences below, underlining the parts that should be italicized.

1. I have submitted my story to Reader's Digest.
2. Who is the book editor of the Boston Globe?
3. I have just finished reading Palace Walk by Naguib Mahfouz.
4. Her poems have been published in The Norton Anthology of American Literature.
5. That was a very interesting Time magazine article.
6. The drama club is performing Death of a Salesman.
7. Did you see the movie version of The Color Purple?
8. In English class we are reading Hamlet.
9. We spent last week analyzing Walt Whitman's famous poem, Song of Myself.
10. Have you ever used the Readers' Guide to Periodical Literature?

See Lesson 21.8, pages 719–720.

Writing About Literature
Explaining Theme

To analyze a piece of literature, you must first identify a theme, or underlying meaning, in the work. In the model below, Tad Burton identifies a theme in Louise Erdrich's poem "Indian Boarding School"—the meaning of freedom—and uses that theme to analyze the piece.

Student Model

Tad states Edrich's theme idea in his topic sentence: freedom does not depend upon physical restrictions for it is a state of mind.

Tad uses specific details as well as lines from the poem to support his main idea.

How does Tad broaden his theme? How does he link this theme to his original one?

*I*n Louise Erdrich's poem "Indian Boarding School," the poet suggests that freedom is a state of mind. Although the Native American girls who live in the boarding school are subjected to physical abuse and are forced to deny their heritage, their will is not crushed. The girls imagine what a real home would be like and visit it in their dreams. In addition, even though they really have no chance to escape from their captors, some of the boarding school's inmates feel free when they hide out for a brief time in the enclosed boxcar of a train.

The idea that freedom is in one's mind is also extended to encompass a broader scope. In the last line of the poem, speaking about "the old injuries of the past," Erdrich compares the girls' situation with the experience of the Native American people at the hands of the early settlers. Like the girls in the school, the Native Americans underwent much suffering. They were taken away from their homes and placed on reservations. Nonetheless, the poet believes that the Native American people ultimately remained free because no one could manipulate their thoughts.

Tad Burton, Rangeview High School, Aurora, Colorado

Identify a Theme

A theme is a generalization about life or human nature that the writer communicates through the piece of literature. For example, one theme in Shakespeare's play *Macbeth* is that evil eventually destroys the evildoer.

To discover themes in a piece of literature, you need to see what messages the writer is trying to communicate. One way to discover a theme is to use prewriting techniques, such as freewriting. For example, begin with the line "What [title of work] tells me" and freewrite for five minutes. Another way to close in on a theme is to brainstorm. For example, in a small group, take turns completing the following: "I think one of the author's messages is . . ." Discuss each group member's answer.

Freewriting

What Romeo and Juliet tells me is that love can spring up in the most unlikely circumstances, that love can triumph over hate, that love and hate are closely related, that strong emotions can lead to violent ends.

Brainstorming

Maria: I think one of Shakespeare's messages is that hatred can destroy lives.

Jamal: I think one of Shakespeare's messages is that even though hatred can destroy lives, love can triumph over hatred.

Journal Writing

What other strategies—besides the freewriting and brainstorming techniques described above—might you use for discovering the themes in a piece of literature? Write your ideas in your journal.

Support the Theme with Evidence

Once you have identified a theme, look to the piece of literature for details that reflect or support that theme. You need to provide evidence to convince your readers that the message you have discovered is indeed one that the author was trying to convey.

The basic elements of any piece of narrative literature are character, setting, and plot. Use prewriting techniques to examine each of these elements as you seek details to support the theme you have found. Your evidence may include quotations, descriptions, summaries of key events, and explanations of passages in the text.

A scene from the movie *Romeo and Juliet*

Characters To support your analysis of a theme, study the characters' physical descriptions, thoughts, actions, words, and relationships with other characters. For example, to show that one of Shakespeare's themes in *Romeo and Juliet* is that love can triumph over hate, you might describe Romeo's impulsive behavior at the masked ball.

Setting The setting—time of day, place, mood, and other details—can also help develop a theme. Try to determine what message the author is conveying through the choice of setting. For example, Romeo and Juliet first meet at a masked ball. Perhaps, in choosing this setting, Shakespeare is saying something about the senselessness of a feud based only on appearances and one's last name.

Plot The plot—the sequence of events in the story being told—can also reveal the theme. Generally, the plot begins with a central conflict and develops it to its climax and resolution. Romeo and Juliet's meeting at the ball triggers the central conflict—that is, the conflict between their love and the hatred between their families.

Write About the Theme

Once you have identified a theme and have gathered the details to support it, you're ready to draft your paragraph. Like any other paragraph you write, your analysis should be unified and coherent. Generally, you will want to state the theme in your topic sentence and then present the supporting details in a logical order—perhaps in order of importance. As you revise your work, be sure to use transitions to help the reader understand relationships between ideas.

Write a Literature Analysis

Choose a piece of literature with which you are familiar. Freewrite for five minutes to try to discover a theme that you can then write about. Use quotations, descriptions, and summaries of events in the story to support your analysis. Use the five stages of the writing process to write a paragraph based on the theme.

- Look for a generalization about life or human nature.
- Support the theme with details of character, setting, and plot.
- Check that your paragraph is unified and coherent.

PURPOSE To analyze literature
AUDIENCE Your teacher
LENGTH 1 paragraph

Grammar Link

Capitalize proper nouns.

Rewrite the following paragraph, correcting errors in capitalization.

[1]In william shakespeare's play *macbeth*, the writer suggests that the lust for power corrupts people. [2]Witches tell macbeth that he will eventually become king of scotland. [3]Convinced that the witches have told the truth, he and his wife, lady macbeth, murder king duncan. [4]Macbeth then becomes involved in other murders, including those of the wife and son of macduff. [5]By the time macbeth is killed by the scots, the desire for power has corrupted him completely.

See Lesson 20.2, pages 675–681.

Cross-Curricular: Art

Identify those features of the painting that attract your interest or attention, or that evoke memories or mental images. Freewrite for five minutes or use a cluster map to define the painting's theme. To find details that support the theme, look for elements of character, setting, and plot. Use the theme and details to write one or two paragraphs analyzing the painting.

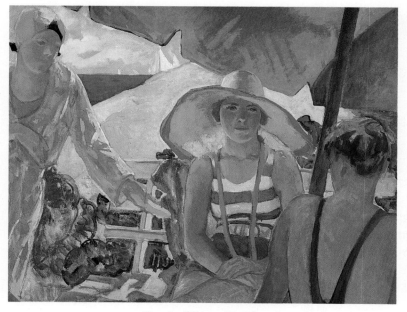

Beatrice Whitney Van Ness, *Summer's Sunlight*, c. 1936

UNIT 2

WRITING PROCESS IN ACTION

THE WRITING PROCESS

In the preceding lessons you've learned about the stages of the writing process. Now it's time to make use of what you learned. In this lesson, you are invited to retell a story a family member has told you—whether the story has been in your family for generations or is a new addition to your family's collection of favorites.

• Assignment •	
Context	Your cousin has decided to create a written collection of memorable family stories so that future generations will be able to know about their ancestors and their past. You have been asked to contribute your favorite family tale to the collection.
Purpose	To write a story that captures something of your family members and their experiences.
Audience	Family members, friends, and future generations
Length	1–2 pages

The following pages can help you plan and write your family story. Read through them and then refer to them as you need to. But don't be tied down by them. You're in charge of your own writing process.

Prewriting

Where will you get your story idea? Talk with your family, look through old pictures, and think about your own memories. Once you've identified a story, use freewriting, list making, or questioning to brainstorm for details.

To bring your story into sharper focus, think about your purpose and audience, and keep them in mind as you gather details to provide a full and accurate account. In the literature example below, notice how the author uses story details to reinforce the theme of the writing.

Prewriting Options
- Check your journal. What have you already written about family members or personal experiences?
- Talk with your family. What family stories have they especially enjoyed?
- Look at family albums. What clues do faces and places provide?

Literature Model

*T*he aged visitors who came to my grandmother's house when I was a child were men of immense character, full of wisdom and disdain. . . . They were made of lean and leather, and they bore themselves upright. They wore great black hats and bright ample shirts that shook in the wind. They rubbed fat upon their hair and wound their braids with strips of colored cloth. . . . They were an old council of war lords, come to remind and be reminded of who they were.

N. Scott Momaday, *House Made of Dawn*

Now that you have a story in mind, think about your purpose. You want to tell a memorable story, but is there anything else you want to accomplish? Do you want to make your readers laugh? Persuade them to be proud of their roots? If you do have a secondary purpose, identify it so that you can keep it in mind as you draft.

Next, consider your audience. Friends and future generations might lack your and your family's current familiarity with your subject. So you might add to your prewriting notes any information these readers would need to understand your story.

Finally, gather any remaining details you may need to tell your story effectively. You want to provide a full and accurate account of your chosen tale.

Drafting Tip

For help writing coherent paragraphs, see Lesson 2.8, pages 90–92.

Drafting

A good way to start drafting is to just jump in. Let the story tell itself, flowing naturally from beginning to end. As you draft, refer to your prewriting notes for details that will make your story stick in the reader's mind.

If you have trouble starting your story, think about the main idea you're trying to communicate and write it as a topic sentence. Then try to develop your idea by describing incidents that support it. Ask yourself *who, what, where, when, why,* and *how* questions to help you think of details about the event.

If you're telling the story in chronological order, consider ordering the details in the same way. Sometimes, however, using cause-and-effect order works well, too. Do not be too concerned with spelling and grammar at this point. Your goal at this stage is to get the story and supporting details down on paper.

Once you've finished your draft, put it away for a while. You will return to it later with a fresh perspective.

Revising

Revising Tip

To check the paragraphs in your story for unity and coherence, use the checklists in Lesson 2.9, pages 94–96.

To begin revising, read over your draft to make sure that what you have written fits your purpose and your audience. Then have a **writing conference.** Read your draft to a partner or small group. You might also ask a family member who is familiar with the story to read your draft to help you identify whether any important details are missing or whether you have told anything incorrectly. Then revise the story to strengthen it. You can use the questions on this pad to help you.

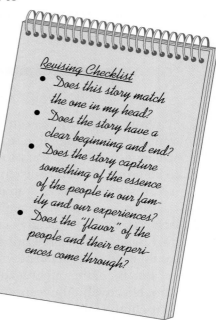

Revising Checklist
- *Does this story match the one in my head?*
- *Does the story have a clear beginning and end?*
- *Does the story capture something of the essence of the people in our family and our experiences?*
- *Does the "flavor" of the people and their experiences come through?*

Editing

After you're satisfied with the basic content and flow of your story, **proofread** it carefully to correct errors in grammar, usage, mechanics, and spelling. Use the Editing Questions as a guide. You'll also need to consider these special questions:

- If you used any foreign words or names, did you spell and capitalize them correctly?
- If you used any family expressions, dialect, or slang, did you include enough explanation so that readers will be able to understand them?

Editing Questions

- Have I used commas to avoid run-ons with "and"?
- Have I used quotation marks to enclose all direct quotes in the dialogue?
- Have I punctuated possessive pronouns correctly?
- Have I capitalized names, groups, and places correctly?
- Have I used my spell-checker or checked the spelling of any unfamiliar words?

Self-Evaluation

Make sure your family story—

- focuses on a tale about a family member or experience
- hooks interest early on by establishing relevance to the reader
- uses vivid sensory details and realistic dialogue
- provides any needed explanations
- follows correct grammar, usage, mechanics, and spelling

Proofreading

For proofreading symbols, see page 100.

Presenting

You can use your story to start your own family collection. Send your story along with a request to members of your family, asking them to send you *their* favorite family tales in return. You can also tell your story at your next family gathering.

Journal Writing

In your journal write down the names of three or four characters from your story. Under each name, list as many words and phrases as you can that describe that character.

Descriptive Writing
Literature Model

Amy Tan

from

The Kitchen
God's Wife

Amy Tan, who was born of Chinese parents in the United States, uses incidents from her own family history as the raw material of her writing process. In this excerpt, Tan depicts the differences between the narrator, Pearl, and Pearl's mother, while at the same time emphasizing the ties that bind them together. Pay special attention to how the author uses detail in the dialogue to bring the characters to life. When you finish the excerpt, try the activities in Linking Writing and Literature on page 121.

My mother is standing outside the house when we return. "I tried to chase you, but you were too fast," she says as soon as I get out of the car. "And then I knew you would remember and come back." Tessa and Cleo are already racing up the stairs.

"Remember what?"

"Grand Auntie's farewell gift. Remember? Two, three days ago I told you not to forget. Yesterday I said, Don't forget. You forgot?"

"No, no," I say. "Where is it?"

"In back, in the laundry room," she says. "Very heavy, though. Better ask your husband to carry it." I can just imagine what it must be: the old vinyl ottoman Grand Auntie used to rest her feet on, or perhaps the set of chip-proof Melmac dishes. As we wait for Phil to come back with the girls, my mother hands me a cup of tea, waving off my protests. "Already made. If you can't drink it, I only have to throw it away."

I take a few quick sips. "This is really good." And I mean it. I have never tasted tea like this. It is smooth, pungent, and instantly addicting.

Tomie Arai, *Laundryman's Daughter*, 1988

"This is from Grand Auntie," my mother explains. "A few years ago she bought it for herself. One hundred dollars a pound."

"You're kidding." I take another sip. It tastes even better.

"She told me, 'If I buy myself the cheap tea, then I am saying my whole life has not been worth something better.' So she decided to buy herself the best tea, so she could drink it and feel like a rich person inside."

I laugh.

My mother looks encouraged by my laughter. "But then she thought, If I buy just a little, then I am saying my lifetime is almost over. So she bought enough tea for another lifetime. Three pounds! Can you imagine?"

"That's three hundred dollars!" I exclaim. Grand Auntie was the most frugal[1] person I knew. "Remember how she used to keep all the boxes of See's candies we gave her for Christmas, telling us they were too good to eat? And then one year, she gave a box back to us for Thanksgiving or something. Only it was so old—"

My mother was nodding, already laughing.

"—all the candies were white with mold!"

"Bugs, too!" my mother adds.

"So she left you the tea in her will?" I say.

"Already gave it to me a few months ago. She was thinking she was going to die soon. She didn't say, but she started to give things away, good things, not just junk. And one time we were visiting, drinking tea. I said, 'Ah, good tea!' same as always. This time, Grand Auntie went to her kitchen, brought back the tea. She told me, '*Syau ning*, you take this tea now.' That's what she called me, *syau ning*, 'little person,' from the old days when we first knew each other.

"I said, 'No, no! I wasn't saying this to hint.' And she said, '*Syau ning*, you take this now so I can see how happy you are to receive it while I am still alive. Some things can't wait until I'm dead.' How could I refuse? Of course, every time I came to visit, I brought back her tea."

Phil returns with Cleo, Tessa is right behind. And now I am actually sorry we have to leave.

"We better hit the road," says Phil. I put the teacup down.

"Don't forget," my mother says to Phil. "Grand Auntie's present in the laundry room."

"A present?" Cleo says. "Do I have a present too?"

Phil throws me a look of surprise.

"Remember?" I lie. "I told you—what Grand Auntie left us in her will."

---

1 frugal (froo' gəl) thrifty

He shrugs, and we all follow my mother to the back.

"Of course it's just old things," says my mother. She turns on the light, and then I see it, sitting on the clothes dryer. It is the altar for Grand Auntie's good-luck god, the Chinese crèche.[2]

"Wow!" Tessa exclaims. "A Chinese dollhouse."

"I can't see! I can't see!" Cleo says, and Phil lifts the altar off the dryer and carries it into the kitchen.

The altar is about the size of a small upturned drawer, painted in red lacquer. In a way, it resembles a miniature stage for a Chinese play. There are two ornate[3] columns in front, as well as two ceremonial electric candles made out of gold and red plastic and topped by red Christmas tree bulbs for flames. Running down the sides are wooden panels decorated with gold Chinese characters.

"What does that say?" I ask my mother.

She traces her finger down one, then the other. *"Jye shiang ru yi.* This first word is 'luck,' this other is another kind of luck, and these two mean 'all that you wish.' All kinds of luck, all that you wish."

"And who is this on the inside, this man in the picture frame?" The picture is almost cartoonlike. The man is rather large and is seated in regal splendor, holding a quill[4] in one hand, a tablet in the other. He has two long whiskers, shaped like smooth, tapered black whips.

"Oh, this we call Kitchen God. To my way of thinking, he was not too important. Not like Buddha, not like Kwan Yin, goddess of mercy—not that high level, not even the same level as the Money God. Maybe he was like a store manager, important, but still many, many bosses above him."

Phil chuckles at my mother's Americanized explanation of the hierarchy of Chinese deities.[5] I wonder if that's how she really thinks of them, or if she's used this metaphor[6] for our benefit.

"What's a kitchen god?" says Tessa. "Can I have one?"

"He is only a story," answers my mother.

"A story!" exclaims Cleo. "I want one."

My mother's face brightens. She pats Cleo's head. "You want another story from Ha-bu? Last night, you did not get enough stories?"

---

2 **crèche** (kresh) a display representing the birth of Jesus
3 **ornate** (ôr nāt') heavily decorated and ornamented
4 **quill** (kwil) a pen made from the stem of a feather
5 **the hierarchy of Chinese deities** (hī' ə rär' kē) (dē' ə tēz) the order of importance of all the Chinese gods
6 **metaphor** (met' ə fôr) a comparison of two unlike things used to clarify the more unfamiliar one

"When we get home," Phil says to Cleo. "Ha-bu is too tired to tell you a story now."

But my mother acts as if she has not heard Phil's excuses. "It is a very simple story," she says to Cleo in a soothing voice, "how he became Kitchen God. It is this way."

And as my mother begins, I am struck by a familiar feeling, as if I am Cleo, again three years old, still eager to believe everything my mother has to say.

"In China long time ago," I hear my mother say, "there was a rich farmer named Zhang, such a lucky man. Fish jumped in his river, pigs grazed his land, ducks flew around his yard as thick as clouds. And that was because he was blessed with a hardworking wife named Guo. She caught his fish and herded his pigs. She fattened his ducks, doubled all his riches, year after year. Zhang had everything he could ask for—from the water, the earth, and the heavens above.

"But Zhang was not satisfied. He wanted to play with a pretty, carefree woman named Lady Li. One day he brought this pretty woman home to his house, made his good wife cook for her. When Lady Li later chased his wife out of the house, Zhang did not run out and call to her, 'Come back, my good wife, come back.'

"Now he and Lady Li were free to swim in each other's arms. They threw money away like dirty water. They slaughtered ducks just to eat a plate of their tongues. And in two years' time, all of Zhang's land was empty, and so was his heart. His money was gone, and so was pretty Lady Li, run off with another man.

"Zhang became a beggar, so poor he wore more patches than whole cloth on his pants. He crawled from the gate of one household to another, crying, 'Give me your moldy grain!'

"One day, he fell over and faced the sky, ready to die. He fainted, dreaming of eating the winter clouds blowing above him. When he opened his eyes again, he found the clouds had turned to smoke. At first he was afraid he had fallen down into a place far below the earth. But when he sat up, he saw he was in a kitchen, near a warm fireplace. The girl tending the fire explained that the lady of the house had taken pity on him—she always did this, with all kinds of people, poor or old, sick or in trouble.

"'What a good lady!' cried Zhang. 'Where is she, so I can thank her?' The girl pointed to the window, and the man saw a woman walking up the path. Ai-ya! That lady was none other than his good wife Guo!

"Zhang began leaping about the kitchen looking for some place to hide, then jumped into the kitchen fireplace just as his wife walked into the room.

"Good Wife Guo poured out many tears to try to put the fire out. No use! Zhang was burning with shame and, of course, because of the hot roaring fire below. She watched her husband's ashes fly up to heaven in three puffs of smoke. Wah!

"In heaven, the Jade Emperor heard the whole story from his new arrival. 'For having the courage to admit you were wrong,' the Emperor declared, 'I make you Kitchen God, watching over everyone's behavior. Every year, you let me know who deserves good luck, who deserves bad.'

"From then on, people in China knew Kitchen God was watching them. From his corner in every house and every shop, he saw all kinds of good and bad habits spill out: generosity or greediness, a harmonious nature or a complaining one. And once a year, seven days before the new year, Kitchen God flew back up the fireplace to report whose fate deserved to be changed, better for worse, or worse for better."

"The end!" shouts Cleo, completely satisfied.

"Sounds like Santa Claus," says Phil cheerfully.

"Hnh!" my mother huffs in a tone that implies Phil is stupid beyond words. "He is not Santa Claus. More like a spy—FBI agent, CIA, Mafia, worse than IRS, that kind of person! And he does not give *you* gifts, you must give *him* things. All year long you have to show him respect—give him tea and oranges. When Chinese New Year's time comes, you must give him even better things—maybe whiskey to drink, cigarettes to smoke, candy to eat, that kind of thing. You are hoping all the time his tongue will be sweet, his head a little drunk, so when he has his meeting with the big boss, maybe he reports good things about you. This family has been good, you hope he says. Please give them good luck next year."

"Well, that's a pretty inexpensive way to get some luck," I say. "Cheaper than the lottery."

"No!" my mother exclaims, and startles us all. "You never know. Sometimes he is in a bad mood. Sometimes he says, I don't like this family, give them bad luck. Then you're in trouble, nothing you can do about it. Why should I want that kind of person to judge me, a man who cheated his wife? His wife was the good one, not him."

"Then why did Grand Auntie keep him?" I ask.

My mother frowns, considering this. "It is this way, I think. Once you get started, you are afraid to stop. Grand Auntie worshipped him since she was a little girl. Her family started it many generations before, in China."

"Great!" says Phil. "So now she passes along this curse to us. Thanks, Grand Auntie, but no thanks." He looks at his watch and I can tell he's impatient to go.

Ch'ing dynasty, porcelain teapot and beaker, c. 1700

"It was Grand Auntie's gift to you," my mother says to me in a mournful voice. "How could she know this was not so good? She only wanted to leave you something good, her best things."

"Maybe the girls can use the altar as a dollhouse," I suggest. Tessa nods, Cleo follows suit. My mother stares at the altar, not saying anything.

"I'm thinking about it this way," she finally announces, her mouth set in an expression of thoughtfulness. "You take this altar. I can find you another kind of lucky god to put inside, not this one." She removes the picture of the Kitchen God. "This one, I take it. Grand Auntie will understand. This kind of luck, you don't want. Then you don't have to worry."

"Deal!" Phil says right away. "Let's pack 'er up."

But now I'm worried. "Are you sure?" I ask my mother. She's already stuffing the plastic candlesticks into a used paper bag. I'm not exactly superstitious. I've always been the kind who hates getting chain letters—Mary used to send them to me all the time. And while I never sent the duplicate letters out as instructed, I never threw the originals away either.

Phil is carrying the altar. Tessa has the bag of candlesticks. My mother has taken Cleo upstairs to find a plastic neon bracelet she left in the bathroom. And now my mother comes back with Cleo and hands me a heavy grocery sack, the usual care package, what feels like oranges and Chinese candy, that sort of thing.

"Grand Auntie's tea, I gave you some," my mother says. "Don't need to use too much. Just keep adding water. The flavor always comes back."

Linking Writing and Literature

Readers Respond to the Model

How does Amy Tan use details to develop her theme?

Explore Amy Tan's use of detail to develop her theme and bring her characters to life. Then read what other students liked in Tan's story.

1. What terms might you use to describe Pearl's mother? Which details in the story led you to select those terms?
2. How do the details in the dialogue point out the differences between the mother's and daughter's generations?
3. The theme of this story deals with relationships between generations and between cultures. Freewrite or list some details Amy Tan has used to develop this theme.
4. The story of the Kitchen God's Wife is a detail within the larger story. How has Tan related this tale to her overarching theme?

The scene that I remember most clearly was when Zhang went before the Jade Emperor, who decided that Zhang should be Kitchen God to look over people's households and to see whether they were decent people. The writer kept my attention because of the interesting story of the Kitchen God and the wonderful detail in the story.

I enjoyed the portrayal of the Chinese American family, where the husband was Caucasian and his wife and her family were Chinese and very loyal to their culture. The story showed how cultures relate and clash at the same time.

Rachel Hansen

I enjoyed the story because it informed me of another religion and culture. I thought the facts and details surrounding the story of the Kitchen God's origin, however, seemed very far-fetched. I would have made Phil's doubts of the grandmother's story more critical so that there would have been a logical response to a story that seems illogical.

Michael Kim

Unit 2 Review

Reflecting on the Unit

Summarize what you learned in this unit by answering the following questions:

- What are the five stages of the writing process?

- What are the important elements of each stage of the process?

- What strategies and techniques can help you at each stage of the writing process?

- What are some ways to analyze theme in a piece of literature?

Adding to Your Portfolio

Choose a selection for your portfolio.
Look over the writing you did for this unit. Select a completed piece for your portfolio. The writing you choose should show some or all of the following:

- ideas generated by using such techniques as freewriting or listing
- words and ideas chosen with a particular audience in mind
- a clear topic sentence that controls appropriate supporting details
- careful revising and editing
- development through all five stages of the writing process, including presenting

Reflect on your choice.
Attach a note to the piece you chose, explaining briefly why you chose it and what you learned from writing it.

Set goals.
How can you improve your writing? What skill will you focus on the next time you write?

Writing Across the Curriculum

Make a social studies connection.
Choose a family member who lived either in another country or who lived in the United States during the early 1900s. Write a paragraph comparing one or two important aspects of this person's daily life with your daily life today.

Descriptive Writing in the Real World

Ross Writes Script for *Big*

F O C U S: Screenwriters depend upon descriptive writing to let the director know exactly how they envision the finished movie.

W riting a screenplay about a boy who got his wish to be big seemed like a natural transition to Gary Ross. The screenwriter explains, "I grew up in Los Angeles, and my father is a screenwriter. I'd written novels and a couple of other scripts that people hired me to do. I realized I wanted to do something I cared about."

Ross worked on the *Big* script with his friend Anne Spielberg. Describing their process, he says, "First, we outlined the whole movie. We

*Screenwriter
Gary Ross*

planned out every scene in detail, and we each wrote our own scenes. Then we'd discuss and rewrite each other's scenes until the script was unified into one voice."

As they worked their way through the writing process, they needed to make each scene vibrant and alive on the page. They could achieve this goal to some extent through dialogue, but detail and description are key to providing actors and directors with a script that conveys a real sense of mood.

Ross says, "Every image you describe must be chosen to bolster a particular point." Ross puts it another way: "The screenwriter has to take the reader to the movie before it's made." In this Case Study, Gary Ross talks in detail about three scenes with vivid descriptions that gave the director a clear idea of the story he and Spielberg had imagined.

*"Every child says, 'I wish I were a grown-up.' The screenplay for **Big** came out of wondering what would happen if that wish were ultimately fulfilled."*

— Gary Ross

Descriptive passages in a movie script generate specific images that help to establish mood.

Scripting a Movie

Prewriting	Drafting	Revising/Editing
Outlining the Whole Movie	Detailing a Scene	Choosing the Right Words

Prewriting

OUTLINING THE WHOLE MOVIE

Even in the early stage of outlining the movie, Ross and Spielberg were aware of the mood they wanted the finished film to evoke. This awareness helped them select appropriate details and develop them into descriptive paragraphs in the script.

Ross recalls the scene near the beginning of the movie, when the main character, Josh, goes to an amusement park on the shore with his family. Earlier, the twelve-year-old has been thwarted by not being grown-up enough to have a date with the girl he likes or even being big enough to go on the roller coaster.

As Josh walks alone near the beach, he hears a huge wave. Ross says, "That wave is meant to be a little ominous. It isolates Josh from the carnival, and it also serves as a portent of what's coming."

The boy walks past "the most modern games" to get to the machine that will eventually change him into an adult. This antique fortune-telling machine, "Zoltar Speaks," contrasts sharply with the newness of the video games.

Ross and Spielberg's vivid description of Zoltar provided a blueprint for the invention of the Zoltar machine featured in the finished movie. Ross says, "We wrote this description to give a dangerous, timeless, and lonely feeling. Of course, that's very much what the journey from childhood to adulthood is about. It's mysterious to embark on that, and these are the qualities we wanted to evoke."

Drafting

DETAILING A SCENE

Another of Ross's favorite scenes shares the seaside carnival setting of the Zoltar scene. Now Josh has been transformed to an adult.

As Josh and his girlfriend stand on the boardwalk, they hear music coming from an old dance pavilion. "The pavilion is shown for only a couple of seconds in the film," Ross says, "but I'm proud of our description. I was inspired by something I'd read in an F. Scott Fitzgerald book, about life on the French Riviera. We wanted to evoke the same romance and magic but also the decline and the sadness that's coming."

Ross and Spielberg had a particular, real-life amusement park

in mind for this scene. Ross says, "After writing this description, we lobbied for this particular location. We asked them to shoot it there, and they did."

Ross and Spielberg's description of the old dance pavilion in the script creates a mood of faded grandeur.

JOSH AND SUSAN

They look at it awkwardly for
each other. It seems like each
something, but neither one does
second, when Susan cocks her he

                                   SUSAN
        You hear that?

                              JOSH
    What?

                              SUSAN
        Music.

EXT. BOARDWALK

The sounds of Big Band Music drift out of the old dance
Pavilion. Built near the turn of the century, it is part
Mosque, part Opera Hall, part Seaside Pleasure Palace. All
the obelisks have flagpoles for the banners that have long
since gone away. The sound of Moonlight Serenade echoes up
the boardwalk as the ocean pounds in the distance.

EXT. ARCADE

Josh and Susan walk out of the arcade onto the nearly
deserted boardwalk. Towering above them is the dark metal
hulk of a roller coaster, closed for the winter. Further
on is the latticework of an empty Ferris wheel.

                              SUSAN

Revising/Editing

CHOOSING THE RIGHT WORDS

When editing the script to unify it into one voice, Ross and Spielberg were aware that the words would need to be precise to evoke a particular mood in a scene. For example, near the end of the film, Josh revisits a scene from his childhood; the mood needed to be nostalgic. Ross says, "We knew if we wrote this scene poetically, the director would end up putting the poetry into the film.

EXT. BASEBALL FIELD

It's late afternoon as the sun turns the field a light gold. Two boys stand alone on the grass, shagging flies in the fading light. There is silence, then the crack of a bat, then the distant pop of a ball hitting leather. Josh watches silently from the side of the field leaning back in his business suit. There is no conversation as the ritual continues between them — just the swing of the bat and the long lazy arc of a fly ball as it goes from one boy to another. Josh loosens the knot of his tie as he stares at the boys in front of him. A light breeze ruffles his hair.

This paragraph from the script describes a scene Josh revisits from his childhood.

Usually you have to write lean for the screen, but this time we really pulled out all the stops and went for it. We even used a poetic device, alliteration, to describe the 'long lazy arc' of the fly ball."

This scene takes place in what Ross calls "that mystical, magical, temporal instant between day and night. The sun turns the field gold for only a few minutes a day, so there's a fragile, fleeting quality of something that's there for only an instant and then is lost."

Ross continues, "The fact that the two boys stand alone gives the scene a beautiful, isolated quality. There's nothing in the world except them." For a while the scene is shot from Josh's point of view. Ross says, "Josh is privy to this scene, but he's lost the beauty of it because of his wish to be big. Showing Josh in a business suit emphasizes that he's constrained by being an adult. And when he loosens his tie, he shows that being big is constricting him. That's what I mean by writing description that bolsters a point. When the light breeze ruffles his hair, it harkens back to the magical wind that blew when he first wished to be big. This time the wind shows he's drawn back to the world of childhood."

Responding to the Case Study

1. Discussion

Discuss these questions about Gary Ross's writing.

- Besides dialogue, what other elements does Ross say are essential to making each scene of a screenplay vibrant?
- Why does Ross think it is important to have a mood in mind before writing a scene?
- Describe how Ross chose the details for the scene in which Josh discovers the Zoltar machine.
- Which details in the baseball scene convey nostalgia?

2. Descriptive Writing

Write a paragraph describing a scene or mood. The details a screenwriter chooses help the director "see" how a film will look. Imagine a scene that conveys a specific mood, or use the picture below for inspiration. Write a paragraph describing either the painting or an imaginary scene in detail so clear that your writing could be used by a director in a movie. Try to have every image in your scene fit with the mood you are trying to create.

Grammar Link

Use participles to create active descriptions.

A *participle* is a verb form used as an adjective:

fading light.

In this description of the baseball field, Gary Ross uses participles to convey a sense of movement as well as describe what the boys are doing:

*"Two boys stand alone on the grass, **shagging** flies in the **fading** light."*

Write a sentence using each participial phrase below. Start by thinking of a noun or pronoun for each phrase to modify.

1. wandering through an unfamiliar neighborhood
2. blowing wildly through the bare-limbed trees
3. nervously clutching
4. scratching against the darkened window
5. whispering fearfully behind the broken gate

See Lesson 12.3, page 485.

Joan Miró, *Carnival of Harlequin*, 1924–25

Descriptive Writing
Writing a Descriptive Paragraph

In the model below author J. R. R. Tolkien uses his descriptive skills to transport you to an eerie scene. Notice how Tolkien creates a mood in his topic sentence and then uses well-ordered details to paint a vivid picture that reinforces the mood.

Literature Model

Tolkien's first sentence conveys the overall impression of the scene.

What is Tolkien's writing strategy, as indicated by words like "before his feet," "on the further side," and "far beyond it"?

H ard and cruel and bitter was the land that met his gaze. Before his feet the highest ridge of Ephel Dúath fell steeply in great cliffs down into a dark trough, on the further side of which there rose another ridge, much lower, its edge notched and jagged with crags like fangs that stood out black against the red light behind them: it was the grim Morgai, the inner ring of the fences of the land. Far beyond it, but almost straight ahead, across a wide lake of darkness dotted with tiny fires, there was a great burning glow, and from it rose in huge columns a swirling smoke, dusky red at the roots, black above where it merged into the billowing canopy that roofed in all the accursed land. ➡

Sam was looking at Orodruin, the Mountain of Fire. Ever and anon the furnaces far below its ashen cone would grow hot and with a great surging and throbbing pour forth rivers of molten rock from chasms in its sides. Some would flow blazing toward Barad-dûr down great channels; some would wind their way into the stone plain, until they cooled and lay like twisted dragon-shapes vomited from the tormented earth. In such an hour of labor Sam beheld Mount Doom, and the light of it, cut off by the high screen of the Ephel Dúath from those who climbed up the path from the West, now glared against the stark rock faces, so that they seemed to be drenched with blood.

J. R. R. Tolkien, *The Return of the King*

Grammar

Revising Tip

When your revise your writing, you can add vivid adjectives to help create a mood and draw a picture. Refer to Lesson 10.4, page 423.

Create an Overall Impression

There are many ways to begin putting together a description. One way is to think of the overall impression, or mood, you want to communicate. Then, in your topic sentence, use words and phrases that will help convey this mood to your reader.

Mood   Your descriptive paragraph will have greater impact if it evokes a particular mood rather than just describes details that aren't unified. Perhaps you want to express horror or inspire fear, as Tolkien does. Maybe you intend to communicate a happy, light-hearted feeling or a sad, nostalgic one. Whatever impression you choose, carefully write your paragraph to present that impression clearly.

Concentrate on conveying a single, effective picture to the reader. In the Tolkien model, for example, the author creates a picture of a forbidding, polluted, "accursed land." He appeals to the reader's senses with images of dull fires, smoke, jagged rocks like fangs, and a "lake of darkness." The overall impression in the reader's mind is of a grim, tormented, and frightening landscape.

Journal Writing

Think of a powerful scene in a book or movie—one that was incredibly beautiful or scary or hilarious. In your journal jot down the overall impression, or mood, the scene conveyed. Make a list of the details in the scene that supported the overall impression.

Topic Sentence   In a descriptive paragraph, the topic sentence should "overview" the scene and summarize the content of the paragraph. In doing so, it can also help establish the paragraph's mood. The rest of the paragraph should contain details that support the topic sentence. You might want to envision the parts of your paragraph like this.

Vocabulary

Revising Tip

In the revising stage of your work, check to make sure the details you have used actually support your topic sentence.

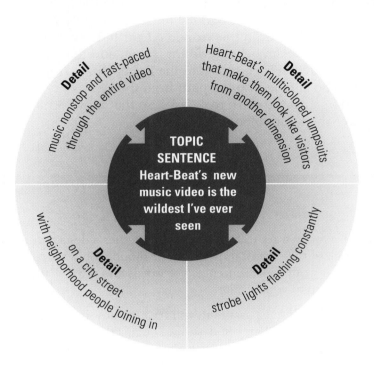

Detail music nonstop and fast-paced through the entire video

Detail Heart-Beat's multicolored jumpsuits that make them look like visitors from another dimension

TOPIC SENTENCE Heart-Beat's new music video is the wildest I've ever seen

Detail on a city street with neighborhood people joining in

Detail strobe lights flashing constantly

Notice that the topic sentence of the literature model on page 130 is at the very beginning of the paragraph. A topic sentence at or near the beginning of the paragraph lets the reader know what's coming. On the other hand, a topic sentence at or near the end of a paragraph, as in the model below, can summarize what you have just described.

Model

In what order are details mentioned in this description? Does the writer rely only on visual details?

Ambassador Aleesa Aguilar entered the control room of the Galavian spacecraft, guided wordlessly by two of the craft's security officers. As the first earthling to meet the Galavians and to see a Galavian craft, she instinctively did a quick scan of her surroundings. A whirring sound directed her eyes to the far left of the brightly lit, cavernous white room. There she saw the "pilots," actually two androids—robots—who monitored the ship's course. Her ➡

experienced eyes next followed a series of about fifteen "space windows," computer screens that simulated the view off into space in fifteen directions. At five of these "windows" sat groups of Galavians, as expressionless as the androids, rapidly making calculations and plotting courses. Then a sharp voice to her right blared "All rise," as the craft's commander entered. In these few seconds, the savvy Ambassador Aguilar learned much about these hard-working, severe, highly regimented aliens.

The topic sentence at the end summarizes the importance of this brief description.

Orient the Reader

In writing a descriptive paragraph, your goal is to transport the reader to the scene. Yet you must also help to orient the reader by providing a sense of direction and of where things are. Describing items in spatial order is one way to help orient the reader.

Spatial Order   There are many kinds of spatial orders. For example, the Tolkien model on pages 130–131 uses near-to-far spatial order. The author begins by describing what lies nearest the character and proceeds to describe things farther and farther away. In fact, he follows the order your own eyes might move in if you were looking at the scene. Other ways your eyes might move include left to right (or right to left), as in the model on pages 132–133, and top to bottom (or bottom to top).

Prewriting Tip

Before you begin drafting, decide how you want to arrange the details in your description.

Left to right

Near to far

Top to bottom

Journal Writing

What are some other ways to look at and describe a scene? In your journal suggest two alternatives to spatial order. Then write a brief description of your room, the street you live on, or your school, using spatial order or one of your alternative suggestions.

Transitions   Transitions are words that connect one sentence or idea to the next and help show the relationship between the two—words like *before, then, next, under, in front of, to the right of,* and *inside.* In descriptive writing, transitions can help the reader keep track of where things are. What transitions might you use in describing the scene pictured below?

© Nancy Thill

The excerpt below, by Mary Stewart, is from a story about Merlin, teacher and friend of the legendary King Arthur. Notice how the author ties together her description with spatial-order transitions.

Stewart uses the following spatial-order transitions: "behind," "against," "over," "around," "in front," "a few paces away," "between," "above," "beyond," "to the peak," "at," "where we had seen."

Literature Model

At first, after the blaze of the guard-room, I could see nothing. I shut the door behind me and leaned back against the damp wall, while the night air poured over me like a river. Then things took shape around me. In front and a few paces away was a battlemented wall, waist high, the outer wall of the castle. Between this wall and where I stood was a level platform, and above me a wall rising again to a battlement, and beyond this the soaring cliff and the walls climbing it, and the shape of the fortress rising above me step by step to the peak of the promontory. At the very head of the rise, where we had seen the lighted window, the tower now showed black and lightless against the sky.

Mary Stewart, *The Crystal Cave*

Write a Descriptive Paragraph

Imagine your school gymnasium or some other sports arena at night, after a game is over and the crowd has left. Write a one-paragraph description that gives the reader a clear visual picture of the place.

- Decide on the mood you will create.
- Write a strong topic sentence.
- Use spatial order.
- Select precise transition words.

PURPOSE To describe a place and evoke a mood
AUDIENCE Other students
LENGTH 1 paragraph

Cross-Curricular: Art

Look closely at James Doolin's *Last Painter on Earth*. How do the title and the shadow create mood? How do the colors and form of the landscape contribute to the painting's mood? Identify specific details in the painting, and write a paragraph that vividly describes the scene. Create a mood so that a different artist reading your paragraph could create a painting with a mood similar to this one.

Grammar Link

Use prepositional phrases to show spatial relationships.

A *prepositional phrase* is made up of a preposition such as *under, over,* and *above* plus an object.

Revise the following sentences by adding at least one prepositional phrase to each sentence to clarify a spatial relationship.

1. The vase fell.
2. A flock of Canada geese flew.
3. There was a bright flash of lightning.
4. The artist painted.
5. The sun set and the moon rose.

See Lesson 12.1, page 481.

James Doolin, *Last Painter on Earth*, 1983

Descriptive Writing
Using Descriptive Language

In the model below, Madeleine L'Engle seems to choose just the right words to convey a feeling or a vision. Notice how she uses precise nouns and vivid modifiers to capture your attention and help you picture the experience she is describing.

What is the combined effect of such phrases as "delicious fragrance," "when the sun's touch is gentle," and "golden with light"?

With the words "tender," "new," and "tiny," L'Engle suggests that the world of Uriel is innocent, unsullied, and young.

Literature Model

She looked around rather wildly. They were standing in a sunlit field, and the air about them was moving with the delicious fragrance that comes only on the rarest of spring days when the sun's touch is gentle and the apple blossoms are beginning to unfold. She pushed her glasses up on her nose to reassure herself that what she was seeing was real.

They had left the silver glint of a biting autumn evening; and now around them everything was golden with light. The grasses of the field were a tender new green, and scattered about were tiny, multicolored flowers. Meg turned slowly to face a mountain reaching so high into the sky that its peak was lost in a crown of puffy white clouds. From the trees at the base of the mountain came a sudden singing of birds. There was an air of such ineffable peace and joy all around her that her heart's wild thumping slowed.

Madeleine L'Engle, *A Wrinkle in Time*

Choose Words for Their Connotations

Connotations are the feelings and the values readers usually associate with any given words—associations that go beyond the simple dictionary definition of the word. In her first paragraph, L'Engle writes of a "delicious fragrance." Why didn't she use the word *odor*, since *odor* and *fragrance* have the same basic meaning—smell? The answer is simple: most readers associate *odor* with an unpleasant smell and *fragrance* with an appealing one.

In choosing words for your descriptive writing, remember that many words come loaded with such connotations. Just as L'Engle chose "delicious fragrance," you should choose the best words you can find to re-create your vision.

Use Precise Nouns

Precise, vivid nouns are an important tool for re-creating your vision and making your writing more lively. By choosing nouns that are specific (*cloak*, for example) instead of general (*clothes*), you convey a clearer, more complete picture to your reader. The chart below shows some examples of nouns going from general to specific.

Nouns		
General	Specific	More Specific
monster	vampire	Count Dracula
animal	amphibian	bullfrog
rain	storm	hurricane

Grammar
Drafting Tip

When drafting a description, you can refer to the material about concrete nouns in Lesson 10.1, page 401.

Journal Writing

How specific can you get? In your journal write the words *plant*, *machine*, *person*, *music*, *art*, *sport*, and *game* down the left side of one page. Next to each word, write as many nouns as you can think of that are increasingly specific examples of the general word.

Select Vivid Adjectives and Adverbs

Revising Tip

When revising your writing, you can use a thesaurus to help you find more colorful and appropriate modifiers. A thesaurus lists words with their synonyms and antonyms.

Vivid modifiers—that is, adjectives and adverbs—can bring your descriptions to life. Make sure each word's connotation fits the impression you want to create. For example, a *shining* sword gives a different impression from a *blazing* one.

Don't settle for dull, overused modifiers, like *good* or *bad*. Select more colorful and original modifiers, such as *honorable* and *wicked*. Sometimes you may even want to use exaggeration to make your description more colorful. You might say, for example, "My date last night was horrendous—everything went wrong." For help finding more colorful and appropriate words, you can check the listings in a thesaurus.

Making Your Modifiers More Lively		
funny	amusing	hilarious
heavy	weighty	ponderous
well	adequately	expertly

Here's how one student used precise nouns and lively modifiers in her writing. Notice how the carefully chosen words re-create an eerie scene from her imagination.

Student Model

Notice the dramatic effect created by "nightmarish," "looming shadow," and the narrator "flattened . . . against the far wall."

*I*t was after me again. I kept on running, my heart beating wildly. But it kept on coming, more determined than ever to catch me. I ran into a small hut near the end of the village, hoping I could find protection there; but the hut was empty and that horrible, nightmarish creature grew closer with every step. When I saw its looming shadow in the doorway, I flattened myself against the far wall. It came toward me, my screams for help growing louder with every step it took. Finally, it was but mere inches from my face. I closed my eyes and prayed for a quick demise. It reached slowly with its massive claws toward me and said, "You're it!"

What is the effect of the words "massive claws"? What impact does this effect have on the ending?

Nikki Phipps, Hamilton Heights High School, Arcadia, Indiana

3.2 Writing Activities

Write a Vivid Paragraph

Imagine you will write a story in which you wake up one day in an imaginary world. Write a paragraph describing the place. Perhaps you are inside a television and have the freedom to jump from channel to channel. You could be in your own house but only one inch tall. Create a believable fantasy world for your readers.

- Use precise nouns.
- Select vivid modifiers.
- Be aware of connotation.

PURPOSE To write a vivid description of a fantasy world
AUDIENCE Readers of a journal
LENGTH 1 paragraph

Cooperative Learning

In a small group, brainstorm about the painting at the right. Identify specific details, such as the heart in the man's palm. Work together to come up with vivid and specific nouns and modifiers to describe these details. Then write individual paragraph descriptions of the scene. As a group, decide how best to present the paragraphs to the class.

Grammar Link

Use specific language to write effective descriptions.

Revise this descriptive paragraph, using precise nouns and adding vivid modifiers.

¹They entered the woods at night. ²Trees stood all around and blocked out the sky. ³The air smelled. ⁴As they walked farther, they could hear noises behind and beside them. ⁵The ground under their feet felt soft. ⁶Lights flickered ahead of them, then died. ⁷Something flew into one girl's face. ⁸Then they heard another sound and tried to run out of the woods.

See Lesson 10.1, page 401, Lesson 10.4, page 423, and Lesson 10.5, page 429.

Marc Chagall, *Paris Through the Window*, 1913

Descriptive Writing
Describing an Imaginary Place

In the excerpt below Ray Bradbury orders details to create a mood and allow the reader to picture an imaginary place.

Literature Model

They had a house of crystal pillars on the planet Mars by the edge of an empty sea, and every morning you could see Mrs. K eating the golden fruits that grew from the crystal walls, or cleaning the house with handfuls of magnetic dust which, taking all the dirt with it, blew away on the hot wind. Afternoons, when the fossil sea was warm and motionless, and the wine trees stood stiff in the yard, and the little distant Martian bone town was all enclosed, and no one drifted out of their doors, you could see Mr. K himself in his room, reading from a metal book with raised hieroglyphs over which he brushed his hand, as one might play a harp. And from the book, as his fingers stroked, a voice sang, a soft ancient voice, which told tales of when the sea was red steam on the shore and ancient men had carried clouds of metal insects and electrical spiders into battle.

Mr. and Mrs. K had lived by the dead sea for twenty years, and their ancestors had lived in the same house, which turned and followed the sun, flower-like, for ten centuries.

Mr. and Mrs. K were not old. They had the fair, brownish skin of the true Martian, the yellow coin eyes, the soft musical voices. Once they had liked painting pictures with chemical fire, swimming in the canals in the seasons when the wine trees filled them with green liquors, and talking into the dawn together by the blue phosphorus portraits in the speaking room.

Ray Bradbury, *The Martian Chronicles*

"Fossil sea," "motionless," "stiff," "bone town"—what is the overall feeling created by this description?

How does the order in which various activities are described contribute to the overall effect of the description?

Create Your Own Imaginary Place

You might already have an idea for an imaginary place. If not, try brainstorming, freewriting, or clustering to come up with an idea. A few words that might help you focus on imaginary places include *beneath*, *beyond*, *inside*, *before*, and *after*. Let your mind wander or simply let yourself wonder, "What would it be like there?" Look at something familiar, like your school, from a different point of view—such as through the eyes of a bug. Maybe one of the following topics will start you on the way to your own imaginary place:

fantasy lands	future societies	glacial caves
under the sea	behind the wall	a laboratory
an ancient castle	inside a chrysanthemum	alien planets

Grammar

Prewriting Tip

To explore the details of your imaginary place, think about vivid adjectives and adverbs that help evoke clear images. See Lessons 10.4 and 10.5, pages 423–434.

Explore Your Imaginary Place

Mentally exploring your imaginary place will help you see it in greater detail, and these details will enable you to describe the place to your reader. One good way to explore a place in detail is by asking and answering questions about it. What are its inhabitants like, if there are any? What can I see, hear, smell, feel, and taste here? What, if anything, does this place resemble? Don't be afraid to ask creative questions, such as the ones below.

Creative Questions and Answers
Q: What colors do I see here?
A: Neon-green atmosphere, acid-yellow swampland, and orange vines
Q: What do the inhabitants do for fun?
A: March stiffly in long lines around the main swamp
Q: What presents the greatest danger here?
A: Deadly purple vapors from the swamp
Q: What do the inhabitants eat?
A: Yellow vapors that spray from the swamp vines

Journal Writing

In your journal, list questions you could use to explore any imaginary place. Try to come up with questions about specific, even unusual, details of the place. Keep the list. You can use it when you begin planning and creating your own imaginary world or place.

Determine the Mood of Your Place

The description you write of your imaginary place will be more effective if it conveys a strong mood. A chart like the one below can help you come up with sensory details that will help you create a mood. Some of the most effective details are those that appeal to a reader's senses. What details can you add to the ones below?

Vocabulary
Revising Tip

As you revise, eliminate details that detract from the mood of your description. Do the sounds of your words help create the feeling you want? To review how to create mood, see Lesson 3.1, page 131.

Using Details to Create a Mood	
Feeling	**Sample Details**
Loneliness	utter silence, dusty furniture, ticking clock, dead air, musty odors
Mystery, horror	secret passages, distant moaning, creaking floors
Excitement	fast pace, lively music, bright colors, laughter
Warmth, safety	glowing lights, crackling fire, steaming tea kettle, soft cushions

Organize the Details of Your Place

After you've decided on what details you want to use to create a mood, the next step is to choose the method of organization that will best convey your description to the reader. What is the most important feature of the scene—a castle, a tree, clouds of purple mist? How does that feature relate to other details? You can organize objects and also other descriptive elements, as Ray Bradbury does when he describes actions in a "winding-down" form in the literature model on page 140.

As you draft your description, follow the spatial order that works best for your scene. If, for example, a tree or tall building dominates the picture, top-to-bottom spatial order might work best. What kind of organization would you choose to describe the place pictured to the left?

3.3 Writing Activities

Describe a Scene

Write a paragraph describing a backyard barbecue, from the point of view of a fly. In your description, include details that appeal to each of the five senses—sight, hearing, touch, taste, and smell. Taken together, the details should convey a single, specific mood or idea.

- Decide on the mood you wish to evoke.
- Select sensory details to convey the information.
- Use appropriate spatial order.

PURPOSE To write a description of a place from an unusual perspective
AUDIENCE Your classmates
LENGTH 1–2 paragraphs

Cross-Curricular: Music

Music can evoke a scene or setting in one's imagination. Listen to a piece of classical or other instrumental music with your eyes closed. Then write a paragraph describing the setting the music evokes for you. Use specific sensory details in your description. You may wish to exchange papers with a classmate for peer review.

Grammar Link

Use appositives to clarify.

An *appositive* is a noun or pronoun that follows another noun or pronoun to identify or give additional information:

*a house of crystal pillars on the planet **Mars.***

Expand each of the following sentences. Add an appositive or an appositive phrase—an appositive plus a modifier or modifiers—to follow each italicized term. Remember to add commas where necessary—when the appositive is not essential to the meaning.

1. An excerpt from Ray Bradbury's *book* can be found on page 140.
2. Although the description is imagined, the reader can almost see the *place*.
3. The description of the place includes a description of some of its *inhabitants*.
4. The way the *author* arranges details that appeal to the senses helps evoke a mood.
5. One *character* liked to read.
6. His *wife* cleaned house with magnetic dust.
7. The inhabitants had lived by the dead sea a *long time*.
8. They used to have a *shared interest*.
9. The *book* is science fiction.
10. *Ray Bradbury* has a rich imagination.

See Lesson 12.2, page 483.

Descriptive Writing
Describing an Imaginary Person

To describe a fictional character, first imagine the character. Then think up details of appearance, movement, or personality that will help bring that character to life.

Nam June Paik, *Family of Robot: Grandfather*, 1986

Imagine a Character

To create an imaginary character, begin by deciding on the type of character you want to create. Your own imaginary character can be based on just about anything—from your wildest fantasy to someone you observe on the bus. Then ask yourself some creative questions to help develop details about your character. Questions like the following might help.

Questions for Developing Character Details
1. What are my character's most prominent features?
2. How does my character move and communicate?
3. What trait or traits set my character apart from others?
4. Does my character's appearance fit his, her, or its personality?

In the model below an aged woman from the imaginary town of Gont is trying to help a child. The observer, Tenar, has doubts about this woman.

Literature Model

Tenar was not at all sure what she wanted Aunty Moss to be, finding her unpredictable, unreliable, incomprehensible, passionate, ignorant, sly, and dirty. But Moss got on with the burned child. Perhaps it was Moss who was working this change, this slight easing, in Therru. With her, Therru behaved as with everyone— blank, unanswering, docile, in the way an inanimate thing, a stone, is docile. But the old woman had kept at her, offering her little sweets and treasures, bribing, coaxing, wheedling. "Come with Aunty Moss now, dearie! Come along and Aunty Moss'll show you the prettiest sight you ever saw. . . ."

Moss's nose leaned out over her toothless jaws and thin lips; there was a wart on her cheek the size of a cherry pit; her hair was a gray-black tangle of charm-knots and wisps; and she had a smell as strong and broad and deep and complicated as the smell of a fox's den. "Come into the forest with me, dearie!" said the old witches in the tales told to the children of Gont. "Come with me and I'll show you such a pretty sight!" And then the witch shut the child in her oven and baked it brown and ate it, or dropped it into her well, where it hopped and croaked dismally forever, or put it to sleep for a hundred years inside a great stone, till the King's son should come, the Mage Prince, to shatter the stone with a word, wake the maiden with a kiss, and slay the wicked witch. . . .

"Come with me, dearie!" And she took the child into the fields and showed her a lark's nest in the green hay, or into the marshes to gather white hallows, wild mint, and blueberries.

Ursula K. LeGuin, *Tehanu: The Last Book of Earthsea*

LeGuin contrasts unpleasant aspects of Moss's appearance with her good side, both here and later in the selection.

What is the picture of Aunty Moss created by such details as "toothless jaws," "thin lips," and "gray-black tangle"?

By contrasting Moss's behavior with that typically attributed to witches, LeGuin helps us to see her more as an individual than as a stereotype.

Journal Writing

In your journal describe a fantasy or science-fiction character with whom you are familiar. Explain how the character's personality does or does not fit his or her appearance.

Make a Character Come to Life

Grammar
Editing Tip

When editing a character sketch, make sure you have used pronouns correctly. See Lessons 17.5 and 17.6, pages 602–609.

If you were to describe your best friend, you would probably mention your friend's looks and personality. You might also note some of your friend's unique quirks, strengths, or habits. Such details would help other people to envision your friend as a real live person.

When describing an imaginary character, you want to include these same kinds of details to make your character come to life. Note that the details that are most unusual or most inconsistent with the rest of the description will do the most to make your character real. Such details will help give your character a three-dimensional quality that a character with no inconsistencies might lack. In addition, inconsistencies will tend to arouse your reader's interest and curiosity. Aunty Moss, in the model on page 145, is interesting because she seems to look like a witch, but she does not behave as we might expect a witch to behave.

Here's a character description from the imagination of student Todd Crusey. How does he bring life to his character? Think about what inconsistencies you might add to make the character more interesting, yet still believable.

How would you describe the overall impression created by sensory details such as sweat rolling down his forehead "like an avalanche" and "the carved stones he called hands"?

Crusey holds our interest by waiting until the very end to reveal who the character really is.

Student Model

Sweat rolled like an avalanche down his broad, sloping forehead. It collected on the ledge of his square jutting brow and was then absorbed by the dense brown forest of his eyebrows. Slowly the perspiration dripped down into the large sockets that housed his squinting onyx eyes. From his hollow temples ran a flood of exhaustion that made his whole face glisten in the dark amber light of the prison wall. His nose was a wide, flat wedge, beaten down by the fists of over a hundred men. From his broad shoulders to the carved stones he called hands, he was a warrior. He had done battle in countless brawls and riots and had the scars to show for it. His only reward was his heartbeat; he had survived. This mean and relentless beast of a man always prevailed and was feared by all sane men. That's why they brought him here. Within these prison walls he reigned. He was truly a giant; he made the rules and he had the power to enforce them. That's why they called him warden.

Todd Crusey, Jefferson Davis High School, Montgomery, Alabama

3.4 Writing Activities

Write About an Imaginary Person

Observe someone while you are riding on a bus or looking out your window or from another location of your choice. Take notes on the person's appearance, and use your notes to create a description of an imaginary person you could later write a short story about.

- List unique physical traits.
- Create possible personality quirks.
- Describe inconsistencies between appearance and personality.

PURPOSE To create an imaginary person based on a real one
AUDIENCE Your teacher and classmates
LENGTH 1–2 paragraphs

Grammar Link

Use correct forms of verbs.

Write the correct form of the verb in parentheses to complete each sentence.

1. When you edit your character sketch, make sure that you have (do) all you can to bring the character to life.
2. The details Ursula K. LeGuin used in writing about Aunty Moss (bring) the character to life.
3. I have (feel) that I've known many of the characters I've read about.
4. I also have (write) about characters I have created myself.
5. Some of these imaginary characters (begin) to seem like friends as I wrote about them.

See Lesson 15.2, page 544.

Cooperative Learning

Brainstorm in a group to come up with details that describe the character in this painting. What does the environment add to your perceptions of the character? After each person writes a one-paragraph description, combine the paragraphs into a group description.

Remedios Varo, *Useless Science or the Alchemist*, 1958

Describing an Imaginary Person **147**

Writing About Literature
Analyzing Character Descriptions

When you write to analyze a character in literature, pay attention to what you can learn from the character's physical appearance, thoughts, words, and actions.

One student writer chose a dragon to describe. The dragon is a character from "The Rule of Names" by science-fiction writer Ursula LeGuin. As you read the model below, notice the aspects of the dragon Arthur Housinger focuses on.

Student Model

O ne common desire links one living being to another, to be happy. Some find happiness with friends and money. In this respect, the dragon in "The Rule of Names," Yevaud, was no different from a man. He was a slightly egocentric being who just wanted some friends and some treasure.

Yevaud showed his egocentricity several times. As Blackbeard told Birt, Yevaud attacked the island of Pendor and killed many men just so he could have a treasure all for himself. After one hundred years, he ran away from the island with the treasure. He locked it in his inner chamber at Sattins Island.

Yevaud knew that this would not be enough to ensure happiness, but he had a few more tricks up his sleeve. First, he changed his appearance. Yevaud knew the unfortunate truth that people often judge a book by its cover; therefore, he changed his cover to a "little fat man of fifty who waddled along with his toes turned in." By changing ➡

Housinger notes the importance of this character's change in appearance.

his appearance, Yevaud, also known as Mr. Underhill, not only made a few friends, but he covered his tracks as the thief of the treasure. Blackbeard accurately called him a "wise, cunning monster, full of strength and subtlety."

Yevaud's tricks lacked perfection, though, just as many of his elixirs did. Since Yevaud was constantly showing a false front, a barrier came between him and the villagers. His smiles were even false and made the village girls feel nervous. Yet since he was such a bumbling wizard, the townspeople simply treated Mr. Underhill as a fellow villager. This too was a falsehood, as was shown when Yevaud used his great powers to fight Blackbeard.

Yevaud tried to be something he wasn't, a friendly, inept wizard called Mr. Underhill. Once this barrier of deceit disappeared, Yevaud's true self, along with his true name, could spread its wings. Although Blackbeard's description of Yevaud was accurate, it was not complete. Yevaud was also a friendly being who found a home where he felt comfortable, one who wanted friends and treasure.

Arthur Housinger, Rich East High School, Park Forest, Illinois

Here Housinger shows the villagers' reactions to Yevaud/Underhill.

Housinger next analyzes Yevaud/Underhill's actions and how these actions affected other characters.

Consider a Character's Appearance

A character's physical appearance can suggest a great deal about the nature and background of the person. In "The Rule of Names," for example, the details of the main character's appearance are especially significant, since they hint at his true nature and background.

The order and way in which these physical details are presented may also be important. An author may put the most important facts about a character first or describe them in the greatest detail so as to impress them upon you. In *Robin Hood: Prince of Thieves,* for example, novelist Simon Green first describes Robin Hood's friend Azeem as follows: "Tall and heavily muscled, he had dark skin covered with intricate tattoos. Even his shaved head was ornamented with them." Thus, Green emphasizes Azeem's strength and his exotic quality, suggesting that these are important features. As the story unfolds, readers learn that these are, in fact, among the most important things to know and remember about Azeem.

Presenting Tip

When you present your description orally, you can create or emphasize a mood with vocal techniques such as lowering your voice or drawing out a phrase or word.

Journal Writing

In your journal jot phrases to describe someone you know. Circle the most significant details.

Note Thoughts, Words, and Actions

Because a character's thoughts, words, and actions might not always be consistent with his or her appearance, you should consider all information you have about the character. For example, although Azeem looks like a powerful and exotic person, his thoughts, words, and actions reveal him also to be a loyal, honorable, and loving friend.

Thoughts		Words		Actions		Conclusion
"Not for the first time, Azeem realized he was a long way from home, and those he had loved."	**+**	"It is because I love them so dearly that I cannot dishonor them by breaking my vow."	**+**	"Azeem examined Fanny's swollen belly… and then looked at her compassionately." He then delivered Fanny's baby.	**=**	These thoughts, words, and actions indicate that Azeem is a loving, loyal, and compassionate man.

When you analyze a character's thoughts, words, and actions, you may want to ask yourself how you feel about what the character says and does. You might also ask such questions as these: How would I feel around this person? What qualities does this character have that I admire or dislike? Asking and answering such questions will help you get to "know" the character personally and will help make your writing about the character fresh and stimulating.

Think About Reactions of Other Characters

An author can also reveal much about a character by showing how other people react to that character. Be aware of these reactions as you analyze a character, but be sure to consider the nature of each person who is doing the reacting, too. For example, the character's enemies would naturally dislike him or her, while the character's friends would be biased in his or her favor. The reactions of neither would be completely accurate. The chart below shows two reactions to Azeem. Which do you think shows the truer picture?

Reaction A
Robin Hood tells his men his opinion of Azeem: "I trust him."

Reactions to Azeem

Reaction B
Friar Tuck and the others distrust Azeem and call him a savage because his ways are so different from their own.

3.5 Writing Activities

Write a Character Analysis

Select a character from one of the books or stories mentioned in this unit or from another work you know and like. Imagine that the character was a dinner guest in your home last night. Write in your journal about your family's reactions to the character as well as any discussions or activities that may have happened during the evening.

- Describe the character's appearance.
- Analyze his or her words and actions.
- Describe reactions of family members

PURPOSE To analyze what you can learn about a character from literature who has been put in another setting

AUDIENCE Yourself

LENGTH 3–4 paragraphs

COMPUTER OPTION

You can help organize the details for your character analysis with the help of your word processor. Type in each significant detail you discover about the person. Hit the return key after each note you type. Then you can later rearrange your details without having to retype the pieces of information into your file. You can use each detail wherever you want as you develop your writing structure.

Grammar Link

Make pronoun references clear.

When you write to analyze a character, use clear, consistent, and unambiguous pronoun references. In the model on pages 148–149, Arthur Housinger tries to provide the antecedent for each use of "he" and "his."

Rewrite the sentences below to correct each unclear pronoun reference.

1. Arthur writes about Yevaud and Blackbeard, and he says that he called him a "wise, cunning monster."
2. Yevaud and Mr. Underhill are really the same character, since he turns himself into him.
3. When writers describe characters, they should make them come alive.
4. Azeem, who was a friend of Robin Hood, had an exotic appearance, and he told his men his opinion of him.
5. It is important to write clearly when you analyze a character one has read about.

See Lesson 17.6, page 607.

UNIT 3

WRITING PROCESS IN ACTION

DESCRIPTIVE WRITING

In preceding lessons you've learned about describing imaginary places and characters and about the kinds of words and details that can make descriptions effective. You've also had a chance to write your own descriptive paragraphs. Now it's time to make use of what you learned. In this lesson you're invited to create a place in your imagination and then describe it. This place may be one that could actually exist in this world or it may be an entirely fantastical place—one that's out of this world.

• Assignment •

Context	*You are a staff writer for <u>Vicarious Voyager</u>, a magazine of descriptive writing that lets "even dedicated couch potatoes expand their horizons." You have been asked to write an article describing an imagined place. Focus on describing personal impressions and sensations.*
Purpose	*To write a description of a place you've imagined that is so vivid that it helps readers feel transported there*
Audience	*Teenagers who want the experience of visiting new places*
Length	*1 to 2 pages*

The following pages can help you plan and write your description. Read through them and then refer to them as you need to—but don't be tied down by them. You're in charge of your own writing process.

Prewriting

What kind of place will you be describing—an exotic country, an alien wilderness, a landscape that might exist on the head of a pin? Use a place that you think up yourself, or review the literature models in this unit for possible ideas. Then start exploring your place by mentally wandering through it. The questions on the notepad may help you get started.

As you wander, write down your impressions, using as many sensory details as you can. Think too about the mood you want to create and what details you could accentuate to convey this mood. For example, to communicate a sense of nostalgia in describing the ruins of an imaginary castle, T. H. White uses details that describe not only the ruins, but also the living things that still inhabit them.

Prewriting Questions

- What type of place is it?
- Who or what lives here, if anything?
- What do the inhabitants do?
- Do natural laws as we know them hold here?
- What is the overall mood of the place?

Literature Model

*T*he castle of the Forest Sauvage is still standing, and you can see its lovely ruined walls with ivy on them, standing broached to the sun and wind. Some lizards live there now, and the starving sparrows keep warm on summer nights in the ivy, and a barn owl drives it methodically, hovering outside the frightened congregations and beating the ivy with its wings, to make them fly out. Most of the curtain wall is down, though you can trace the foundations of the twelve round towers which guarded it. . . .

T. H. White, *The Once and Future King*

Drafting

To begin drafting, think of a likely place of entry to your place. One approach is to choose a spot from which you could easily orient your readers to the surroundings. For example, you could be crouched behind a door, or you might be up on a hill, with an overview of a whole scene below.

Now visualize your place from your chosen point of entry and, using your prewriting notes, begin drafting. Don't stop writing just to find the absolutely "right word." For now, just keep your ideas flowing.

As you may have done in prewriting, you can let your "journey" be guided by your reaction to various sensations, or you can use one of these methods of organization:

Drafting Tip

For more information about using spatial order, see Lesson 3.1, page 133.

- **Spatial order.** To organize details spatially, describe all of the elements in a place by their location as you perceive them—top to bottom, left to right, or front to back.
- **Order of importance.** Start by describing key details and then move on to less important ones. This method works well if your readers need to grasp certain basic elements of your world first.

Once you have everything down on paper, even if you're not totally happy with how you said it, put your draft aside. A few hours' or even a day's time away from it can help you see its strengths and weaknesses more clearly.

Revising

To begin revising, read over your draft to make sure that what you've written fits your purpose and audience. Then have a **writing conference**. Read your draft to a partner or small group. Use your audience's reactions to help you evaluate your work.

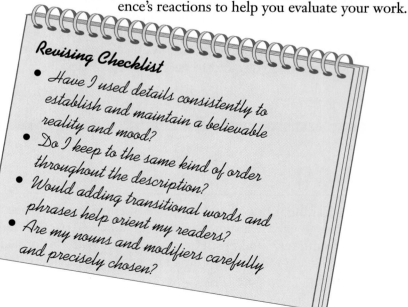

Revising Checklist
- Have I used details consistently to establish and maintain a believable reality and mood?
- Do I keep to the same kind of order throughout the description?
- Would adding transitional words and phrases help orient my readers?
- Are my nouns and modifiers carefully and precisely chosen?

Revising Tip

For help with transitions and word choice, see Lesson 3.1, page 134, and Lesson 3.2, pages 136–138.

Editing

Once you are happy with the basic content and set-up of your description, **proofread** it carefully for errors in grammar, usage, mechanics, and spelling. Use the questions at the right as a guide.

In addition to proofreading, use the self-evaluation list below to make sure your description does all the things you want it to do. When you're satisfied, make a clean copy of your description and proofread it one more time.

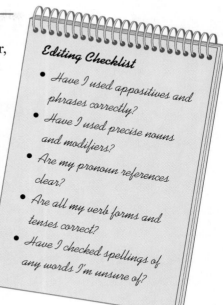

Editing Checklist

- Have I used appositives and phrases correctly?
- Have I used precise nouns and modifiers?
- Are my pronoun references clear?
- Are all my verb forms and tenses correct?
- Have I checked spellings of any words I'm unsure of?

Self-Evaluation
Make sure your description—

- focuses on an imagined place
- orients readers by presenting details in logical order
- uses vivid sensory details and appropriate figurative language
- uses first person point of view consistently
- follows correct grammar, usage, mechanics, and spelling

Proofreading

For proofreading symbols, see page 100.

Presenting

You can use the descriptions you and your classmates have written to create your own magazine of travel writing. Form an editorial board to select the best descriptions based on the criteria in the text; then create a cover, a table of contents, and an introduction for your collection, and make it available for others to read.

Journal Writing

Reflect on your writing process experience. Answer these questions in your journal: What do you like best about your description? What was the hardest part of writing it? What did you learn in your writing conference? What new things have you learned as a writer?

Descriptive Writing
Literature Model

MARY STEWART

◆◆◆◆ FROM ◆◆◆◆

THE **CRYSTAL**
CAVE

In The Crystal Cave, *Mary Stewart vividly describes the world of King Arthur's sixth-century England through the eyes of the magician Merlin. She calls these imaginative stories "somewhere between legend and truth and fairy tale and known history." As you read, pay special attention to Stewart's effective use of descriptive language. Then try the activities in Linking Writing and Literature on page 163.*

This was bigger than had appeared from outside. Only a couple of paces inside the archway—and my paces were very short— the cave opened out into a seemingly vast chamber whose top was lost in shadow. It was dark, but—though at first I neither noticed this nor looked for its cause—with some source of extra light that gave a vague illumination, showing the floor smooth and clear of obstacles. I made my way slowly forward, straining my eyes, with deep inside me the beginning of that surge of excitement that caves have always started in me. Some men experience this with water; some, I know, on high places; some create fire for the same pleasure: with me it has always been the depths of the forest, or the depths of the earth. Now, I know why; but then, I only knew that I was a boy who had found somewhere new, something he could perhaps make his own in a world where he owned nothing.

Next moment I stopped short, brought up by a shock which spilled the excitement through my bowels like water. Something had moved in the murk, just to my right.

I froze still, straining my eyes to see. There was no movement. I held my breath, listening. There was no sound. I flared my nostrils, testing the air cautiously round me. There was no smell, animal or human; the cave smelt, I thought, of smoke and damp rock and the earth itself, and of a queer musty scent I couldn't identify. I knew, without putting it into words, that had there been any other creature near me the air would have felt different, less empty. There was no one there.

I tried a word, softly, in Welsh. "Greetings." The whisper came straight back at me in an echo so quick that I knew I was very near the wall of the cave, then it lost itself, hissing, in the roof.

There was movement there—at first, I thought, only an intensifying of the echoed whisper, then the rustling grew and grew like the rustling of a woman's dress, or a curtain stirring in the draft. Something went past my cheek, with a shrill, bloodless cry just on the edge of sound. Another followed, and after them flake after flake of shrill shadow, pouring down from the roof like leaves down a stream of wind, or fish down a fall. It was the bats, disturbed from their lodging in the top of the cave, streaming out now into the daylight valley. They would be pouring out of the low archway like a plume of smoke.

I stood quite still, wondering if it was these that had made the curious musty smell. I thought I could smell them as they passed, but it wasn't the same. I had no fear that they would touch me; in darkness or light, whatever their speed, bats will touch nothing. They are so much creatures of the air, I believe, that as the air parts in front of an obstacle the bat is swept aside with it, like a petal carried downstream. They poured past, a shrill tide of them between me and the wall. Childlike, to see what the stream would do—how it would divert itself—I took a step nearer to the wall. Nothing touched me. The stream divided and poured on, the shrill air brushing both my cheeks. It was as if I did not exist. But at the same moment when I moved, the creature that I had seen moved, too. Then my outstretched hand met, not rock, but metal, and I knew what the creature was. It was my own reflection.

Hanging against the wall was a sheet of metal, burnished[1] to a dull sheen. This, then, was the source of the diffused[2] light within the cave; the mirror's silky surface caught, obliquely,[3] the light from the cave's mouth, and sent it on into the darkness. I could see myself moving in it like a ghost, as I recoiled[4] and let fall the hand which had leapt to the knife at my hip.

Behind me the flow of bats had ceased, and the cave was still. Reassured, I stayed where I was, studying myself with interest in the mirror. My mother had had one once, an antique from Egypt, but then, deeming such things to be vanity, she had locked it away. Of course I had often seen my face reflected in water, but never my body mirrored, till now. I saw a dark boy, wary, all eyes with curiosity, nerves, and excitement. In that light my eyes looked quite black; my hair was black, too, thick and clean, but worse cut and groomed than my pony's; my tunic and sandals were a disgrace. I grinned, and the mirror flashed a sudden smile that changed the picture completely and at once, from a sullen young animal poised to run or fight, to something quick and gentle and approachable; something, I knew even then, that few people had ever seen.

Then it vanished, and the wary animal was back, as I leaned forward to run a hand over the metal. It was cold and smooth and freshly burnished. Whoever had hung it—and he must be the same person who used the cup of horn[5] outside—had either been here very recently, or he still lived here, and might come back at any moment to find me.

1 burnished (bʉr′ nish′d) polished
2 diffused (di fyooz′ ′d) spread out in every direction
3 obliquely (ə blēk′ lē) indirectly
4 recoiled (ri koil′ ′d) fell back
5 cup of horn a cup made from an animal's horn

I was not particularly frightened. I had pricked to caution when I saw the cup, but one learns very young to take care of oneself, and the times I had been brought up in were peaceful enough, at any rate in our valley; but there are always wild men and rough men and the lawless and vagabonds to be reckoned with, and any boy who likes his own company, as I did, must be prepared to defend his skin. I was wiry, and strong for my age, and I had my dagger. That I was barely seven years old never entered my head; I was Merlin, and, bastard or not, the King's grandson. I went on exploring.

The next thing I found, a pace along the wall, was a box, and on top of it shapes which my hands identified immediately as flint and iron and tinderbox,[6] and a big, roughly made candle of what smelled like sheep's tallow.[7] Beside these objects lay a shape which—incredulously and inch by inch—I identified as the skull of a horned sheep. There were nails driven into the top of the box here and there, apparently holding down fragments of leather. But when I felt these, carefully, I found in the withered leather frameworks of delicate bone; they were dead bats, stretched and nailed on the wood.

This was a treasure cave indeed. No find of gold or weapons could have excited me more. Full of curiosity, I reached for the tinderbox.

Then I heard him coming back.

My first thought was that he must have seen my pony, then I realized he was coming from further up the hill. I could hear the rattling and scaling of small stones as he came down the scree[8] above the cave. One of them splashed into the spring outside, and then it was too late. I heard him jump down on the flat grass beside the water.

It was time for the ring-dove again; the falcon was forgotten.[9] I ran deeper into the cave. As he swept aside the boughs[10] that darkened the entrance, the light grew momentarily, enough to show me my way. At the back of the cave was a slope and jut of rock, and, at twice my height, a widish ledge. A quick flash of sunlight from the mirror caught a wedge of shadow in the rock above the ledge, big enough to hide me. Soundless in my scuffed sandals, I swarmed on to the ledge, and crammed my body into that wedge of shadow, to find it was in fact a gap in the rock, giving apparently on to another, smaller cave. I slithered in through the gap like an otter into the river-bank.

---

6 **tinderbox** (tin' dər bäks') a metal box holding the materials to make a fire

7 **tallow** (tal' o) animal fat used to make candles

8 **scree** (skrē) a slope covered with rock fragments

9 **It was time for the ring-dove again; the falcon was forgotten.**
Unlike the ferocious falcon, the ring-dove was a bird that kept quiet and knew when to run away. While Young Merlin was often called "falcon," one character had told him that he was still a ring-dove.

10 **boughs** (bouz) tree branches

It seemed that he had heard nothing. The light was cut off again as the boughs sprang back into place behind him, and he came into the cave. It was a man's tread, measured and slow.

If I had thought about it at all, I suppose I would have assumed that the cave would be uninhabited at least until sunset, that whoever owned the place would be away hunting, or about his other business, and would return only at nightfall. There was no point in wasting candles when the sun was blazing outside. Perhaps he was here now only to bring home his kill, and he would go again and leave me the chance to get out. I hoped he would not see my pony tethered[11] in the hawthorn brake.[12]

Then I heard him moving, with the sure tread of someone who knows his way blindfold, towards the candle and the tinderbox.

Even now I had no room for apprehension,[13] no room, indeed, for any but the one thought or sensation—the extreme discomfort of the cave into which I had crawled. It was apparently small, not much bigger than the large round vats they use for dyeing, and much the same shape. Floor, wall and ceiling hugged me round in a continuous curve. It was like being inside a large globe; moreover, a globe studded with nails, or with its inner surface stuck all over with small pieces of jagged stone. There seemed no inch of surface not bristling like a bed of strewn flints, and it was only my light weight, I think, that saved me from being cut, as I quested about blindly to find some clear space to lie on. I found a place smoother than the rest and curled there, as small as I could, watching the faintly defined opening, and inching my dagger silently from its sheath into my hand.

I heard the quick hiss and chime of flint and iron, and then the flare of light, intense in the darkness, as the tinder caught hold. Then the steady, waxing[14] glow as he lit the candle.

Or rather, it should have been the slow-growing beam of a candle flame that I saw, but instead there was a flash, a sparkle, a conflagration[15] as if a whole pitch-soaked beacon was roaring up in flames. Light poured and flashed, crimson, golden, white, red, intolerable into my cave. I winced back from it, frightened now, heedless of pain and cut flesh as I shrank against the sharp walls. The whole globe where I lay seemed to be full of flame.

11 **tethered** (teth' er'd) tied with a rope or chain
12 **brake** (brāk) a thicket
13 **apprehension** (ap' rə hen' shən) dread
14 **waxing** (waks' ing) slowly growing larger
15 **conflagration** (kän' flə grä' shən) an enormous fire

It was indeed a globe, a round chamber floored, roofed, lined with crystals. They were fine as glass, and smooth as glass, but clearer than any glass I had ever seen, brilliant as diamonds. This, in fact, to my childish mind, was what they first seemed to be. I was in a globe lined with diamonds, a million burning diamonds, each face of each gem wincing with the light, shooting it to and fro, diamond to diamond and back again, with rainbows and rivers and bursting stars and a shape like a crimson dragon clawing up the wall, while below it a girl's face swam faintly with closed eyes, and the light drove right into my body as if it would break me open.

I shut my eyes. When I opened them again I saw that the golden light had shrunk and was concentrated on one part of the wall no bigger than my head, and from this, empty of visions, rayed the broken, brilliant beams.

There was silence from the cave below. He had not stirred. I had not even heard the rustle of his clothes.

Then the light moved. The flashing disc began to slide, slowly, across the crystal wall. I was shaking. I huddled closer to the sharp stones, trying to escape it. There was nowhere to go. It advanced slowly round the curve. It touched my shoulder, my head, and I ducked, cringing. The shadow of my movement rushed across the globe, like a wind-eddy[16] over a pool.

The light stopped, retreated, fixed glittering in its place. Then it went out. But the glow of the candle, strangely, remained; an ordinary steady yellow glow beyond the gap in the wall of my refuge.

"Come out." The man's voice, not loud, not raised with shouted orders like my grandfather's, was clear and brief with all the mystery of command. It never occurred to me to disobey. I crept forward over the sharp crystals, and through the gap. Then I slowly pulled myself upright on the ledge, my back against the wall of the outer cave, the dagger ready in my right hand, and looked down.

He stood between me and the candle, a hugely tall figure (or so it seemed to me) in a long robe of some brown homespun stuff. The candle made a nimbus[17] of his hair, which seemed to be grey, and he was bearded. I could not see his expression, and his right hand was hidden in the folds of his robe.

---

16 wind-eddy (wind′ ed′ ē) a current of wind
17 nimbus (nim′ bəs) a bright cloud or aura surrounding a person or object

I waited, poised warily.

He spoke again, in the same tone. "Put up your dagger and come down."

"When I see your right hand," I said.

He showed it, palm up. It was empty. He said gravely: "I am unarmed."

"Then stand out of my way," I said, and jumped. The cave was wide, and he was standing to one side of it. My leap carried me three or four paces down the cave, and I was past him and near the entrance before he could have moved more than a step. But in fact he never moved at all. As I reached the mouth of the cave and swept aside the hanging branches I heard him laughing.

The sound brought me up short. I turned.

From here, in the light which now filled the cave, I saw him clearly. He was old, with grey hair thinning on top and hanging lank over his ears, and a straight growth of grey beard, roughly trimmed. His hands were calloused and grained with dirt, but had been fine, with long fingers. Now the old man's veins crawled and knotted on them, distended[18] like worms. But it was his face which held me; it was thin, cavernous almost as a skull, with a high domed forehead and bushy grey brows which came down jutting over eyes where I could see no trace of age at all. These were closely set, large, and of a curiously clear and swimming grey. His nose was a thin beak; his mouth, lipless now, stretched wide with his laughter over astonishingly good teeth.

"Come back. There's no need to be afraid."

"I'm not afraid." I dropped the boughs back into place, and not without bravado[19] walked towards him. I stopped a few paces away. "Why should I be afraid of you? Do you know who I am?"

He regarded me for a moment, seeming to muse. "Let me see you. Dark hair, dark eyes, the body of a dancer and the manners of a young wolf . . . or should I say a young falcon?"

My dagger sank to my side. "Then you do know me?"

"Shall I say I knew you would come some day, and today I knew there was someone here. What do you think brought me back so early?"

18 **distended** (dis tend' 'd) swollen
19 **bravado** (bre vä' dō) pretended confidence or courage

Linking Writing and Literature

Readers Respond to the Model

What makes Mary Stewart's descriptions effective?

Explore Mary Stewart's descriptions by answering these questions.
Then read what other students liked about Stewart's descriptions.

1. Mary Stewart's description of a child's experience is told from an adult's memories of that experience. How does that perspective affect the telling of the story?

2. How did you react when you read the line "Then I heard him coming back"? What descriptive words caused you to have this reaction?

3. Choose a descriptive paragraph from the selection that you particularly like. What specific words or images make this description work?

I always enjoy exploration type scenes, so the scene during which the boy explores the cave was the one I liked most. The dominant mood was one of curiosity and suspicion. The writer created that mood by making all things very odd or at least out of the ordinary. The meeting of the old man and the boy seemed for a second to be the end for one of them.

The old man is the sort of character I usually enjoy. He laughs at the over-inventive and imaginative people. He is quite likely a cynic. The scene in which the boy, Merlin, met the old man was by far the most memorable.

Charles Dayton

The owner of the cave had an easy-going, relaxed feeling about him. He laughed when he saw the kid running out instead of being angry for his being there. Stewart made the old man seem real by giving such a detailed description of his face and of what he did each moment. I also liked the description Stewart gave of the moment when the man lit the candle and the "diamonds" were sparkling brightly.

Yahna Awazu

Unit 3 Review

Reflecting on the Unit

Summarize what you learned in this unit by answering the following questions.

- What are the important elements of a well-written descriptive paragraph?

- In what ways does word choice affect the quality of descriptive writing?

- What are the important aspects of describing an imaginary place? Of creating a convincing character?

- What are some things to keep in mind when you analyze a fictional character?

Adding to Your Portfolio

Follow this procedure to choose selections for your portfolio.

Look over the descriptive writing you have done during this unit. Select a completed piece of writing to put into your portfolio. The writing you choose should show some or all of the following:

- descriptive details that contain a strong overall impression
- precise, vivid language that has the appropriate connotations
- a well-defined mood
- attributes that convey a character's uniqueness

Reflect on your choice.

Attach a note to the piece you chose, explaining briefly why you chose it and what you learned from it.

Set goals.

How can you improve your writing? What skill will you focus on the next time you write?

Writing Across the Curriculum

Make a geography connection.

Decide on a real country where you'd like to situate the imaginary place you just wrote about. Choose your country because of such things as its climate and terrain, its political system, or any other factors you think are relevant. Then write a paragraph explaining some of the attributes of the country that made you think your place belongs in it.

Narrative Writing in the Real World

Bessone Profiles a Winner

F O C U S: Most sports narratives focus on character and conflict—conflict between players or between teams, or an individual's struggle to overcome personal limitations.

L isa Twyman Bessone grew up in a family that took its sports seriously. Her father, Jack Twyman, played basketball for the Cincinnati Royals, and the whole family traveled to many of his games. At Dartmouth, Bessone became the captain of the rowing crew. The "incredibly unbiased" sports stories she wrote about her team helped her land a job on a suburban paper in Cincinnati. A few years later, in 1981, Bessone joined the staff of *Sports Illustrated.*

"You start as a fact checker," Bessone recalls. "You're trying to get the story exactly right before it's published." Later, when she started actually writing stories for *Sports Illustrated*, Bessone sharpened her interest in "what's going on behind the field. You try to get to know what motivates the athlete, what makes these people so driven and so disciplined."

*Sportswriter
Lisa Bessone*

Prewriting	Writing the Sports Story Drafting/Revising	Editing/Presenting
Finding and Researching the Narrative	Getting the Story Down Right	Sharing with the World

Prewriting

FINDING AND RESEARCHING THE NARRATIVE

Lisa Bessone knew she'd found a great story when she watched a triathlon in 1989. She recalls, "A couple of my friends were running. Along comes this guy running with a prosthesis [artificial leg] and doing incredibly well. We all remarked on how amazing it was. A small feature appeared in the paper the next day about this football player, Jim MacLaren, who had lost his leg in a motorcycle accident and was now running triathlons in excellent times." So Bessone's idea for the nonfiction narrative came from her observation of MacLaren running in the triathlon and from reading the newspaper feature story about him later.

> *"Sports are about games, but they can be a metaphor for so much more. When I write sports stories, I try to look beyond to something that's not readily apparent. I really want to tell a story, not just who won. And when I empathize with the person I'm writing about, I can make my readers feel something, too."*
>
> —Lisa Twyman Bessone

Once she got the idea for the narrative, Bessone sent a query letter to her editor at *Sports Illustrated* requesting approval to pursue the story. Bessone's editor gave her an enthusiastic go-ahead. Now she was ready to research her narrative.

Armed with a tape recorder, Bessone flew to New England to interview Jim MacLaren. Before an interview Bessone always writes down questions she calls "touchstones to remind myself of the direction I want to go. Usually one question will spark a half-hour discussion."

At first, MacLaren didn't want to talk about the injury that destroyed his leg and nearly took his life. Bessone was willing to wait. "As a sportswriter, you learn the art of hanging out.

The more people know you, the more they trust you. After a while Jim told me about the accident. . . . It was obviously traumatic that he'd lost his leg, but most of the other aspects of his story were really upbeat."

In addition to interviewing MacLaren, his mother, and several of his friends, Bessone sought statistics from the Triathlon Federation: "You need that kind of stuff to give your story a factual basis. Instead of just saying MacLaren is a really good runner, for example, I could say he finished the race only twenty-four minutes behind the winner. And the triathlon is a grueling race with two legs, let alone one." Even as she was collecting information, Bessone considered how best to arrange those crucial elements of character and conflict into a compelling narrative.

An interviewer's tools often include a tape recorder and a notebook of key questions.

The Ironman Triathlon is a race consisting of a 2.4-mile swim, a 112-mile bike ride, and a 26-mile run.

Drafting/Revising

GETTING THE STORY DOWN RIGHT

Lisa Bessone listened to her tapes, noting the things she wanted to include in her narrative. The sportswriter usually has some idea of the organization she's going to use. "That's like a road map you're following the whole time," Bessone says. "Once you have the organization down, the whole piece works." Bessone's "road map" for this narrative was MacLaren's progression from his accident and rehabilitation to competing in races.

After Bessone had completed her first draft, however, MacLaren ran the 1989 Ironman Triathlon, and Bessone decided to revise her story. At this triathlon, held annually in Hawaii, MacLaren bested the previous amputee record by almost two hours. Bessone also wanted to include an anecdote MacLaren later told her about an incident that occurred during the marathon leg of the triathlon; Bessone decided to use this anecdote in her lead paragraph.

This lead paragraph sets a scene that arouses curiosity, creates drama, and then reels the reader in with its last sentence. Bessone comments, "At first you don't know why you're reading; then you find out. It's like holding a card back. Then in

In the marathon leg of the 1989 Ironman Triathlon in Hawaii, Jim MacLaren, a 27-year-old professional triathlete and a former linebacker for Yale, fell in step with 41-year-old Ken Mitchell, who played the same position for the Atlanta Falcons from 1972 to '75. Given the demands of the race (a 2.4-mile swim, a marathon run, and a 112-mile bike ride), conversation had to be minimal, but the two talked a bit about Mitchell's 11 knee operations, the result of his football career. After about a mile MacLaren decided to pull ahead. "I'm saying a little prayer for you, Jimmy," Mitchell called out as he dropped farther and farther behind. MacLaren, you see, was running with a prosthesis on his leg.

the next paragraph, I explain why MacLaren merits this story." Bessone also used her conclusion to drive home the message of her narrative, that there are no limits on any of us.

Editing/Presenting

SHARING WITH THE WORLD

A newspaper sportswriter's story usually appears almost exactly as it is written. But it's the rare magazine story that gets published without being changed.

Bessone explains, "The editors cut this piece a lot. The main section they cut was about why it's so phenomenal that MacLaren does what he does. A biophysicist I talked to said that the fact MacLaren runs so fast defies medicine. In the original story I also had him coming back, finishing the Ironman with tears in his eyes. I was sad to see these things go. But there are space constraints on any magazine piece."

The magazine editors and designers wrote the heading and subheading for the story and sent a photographer to take pictures of MacLaren. One of the two photographs they used shows MacLaren with his wife. "She, too, played a larger role in my original story," Bessone says. "But the editors decided to let the visual carry that part of the story."

In response to her article about MacLaren, Bessone says she got many telephone calls, including one from someone who wanted to do a movie about Jim MacLaren. "He's a heroic figure," says Bessone. "It was a happy story."

Responding to the Case Study

1. Discussion

Discuss these questions about Lisa Bessone's writing.

- Why does Lisa Bessone feel that knowing "what's going on behind the field" and "what motivates the athlete" is essential for writing good nonfiction sports narratives?
- How did Bessone conduct research for her narrative about Jim MacLaren?
- What did Bessone use as her "road map" for the narrative?

2. Narrative Writing

Write the lead paragraph for a sports narrative.

Think about a sports event that you witnessed at school, in a local park, or on television. Make notes about what happened and what you saw. Decide how you would organize your material to write a narrative about the event. Then write a lead paragraph that arouses curiosity or creates drama.

Grammar Link

Capitalize proper nouns.

In her writing, Lisa Bessone uses many proper nouns naming athletes, places, and teams. Correct the following sentences, capitalizing proper nouns as necessary.

1. The ironman triathlon, the grandfather of all triathlons, is held annually in hawaii.
2. The contestants run more than 26 miles after bicycling on hot lava flats and swimming miles in the pacific.
3. Famous marathons are held each year in new york city and boston, massachusetts.
4. The marine corps marathon in washington, d.c., passes the lincoln memorial and the capitol.
5. Ewing of the new york knicks helped the United States win the Olympic basketball gold in 1992.

See Lesson 20.2, pages 675–681.

Case Study **171**

Narrative Writing
Writing Simple Narratives

A narrative is a story that relates a sequence of events. The story may be true—nonfiction—or imagined—fiction. A successful narrative involves realistic characters and situations brought to life with specific details. In the following narrative, Jamaica Kincaid tells the true story of how her mother came to live on the island of Antigua.

Literature Model

Notice that the story has a beginning—the departure from Dominica; a middle—the journey; and an end—the safe arrival in Antigua.

W hen my mother, at sixteen, after quarreling with her father, left his house on Dominica and came to Antigua, she packed all her things in an enormous wooden trunk that she had bought in Roseau for almost six shillings. She painted the trunk yellow and green outside, and she lined the inside with wallpaper that had a cream background with pink roses printed all over it. Two days after she left her father's house, she boarded a boat and sailed for Antigua. It was a small boat, and the trip would have taken a day and a half ordinarily, but a hurricane blew up and the boat was lost at sea for almost five days. By the time it got to Antigua, the boat was practically in splinters, and though two or three of the passengers were lost overboard, along with some of the cargo, my mother and her trunk were safe.

What vivid images help you "see" Kincaid's story?

Jamaica Kincaid, *The Circling Hand*

Understand the Basics of Narrative

All narratives contain characters, setting, and plot. Characters are the individuals in a story. In the narrative above, the characters include Kincaid's mother and grandfather. Setting establishes a story's time and place, such as the boat bound for Antigua. Finally, the events that occur in a story make up its plot.

Narratives may contain a conflict, a struggle that triggers the action. The conflict in Kincaid's story relates to the mother and the hurricane.

Generate Ideas for Writing

The best narratives contain believable characters and situations. Therefore, it's a good rule of thumb to base the narratives you write on what you know, drawing on the ordinary and not-so-ordinary experiences that shape your life. A family trip, for example, probably contains all the basic elements of a narrative. Here are some ways to get started.

Talking Talking about what you've done and where you've been can help you discover what you want to say in writing. In addition, reaction to your stories can help you gauge their audience appeal. Listening to other people's stories might also trigger writing ideas.

Freewriting You can also freewrite as a way to generate a topic for a story. Then, when you come up with an idea that interests you, use freewriting again to explore it. Write down whatever comes into your mind about your topic for about five minutes. In the following model of freewriting, a writer decided to explore an everyday experience: a routine trip to the dentist.

Model

*T*error. What else do you feel when you go to the dentist? Sitting in that waiting room, trying to read a magazine. Muffled groans and screams—and some not so muffled—foretell the horrors awaiting me. If only I'd flossed regularly, not just two or three days before this torture session. That doesn't fool anybody. Certainly not my dentist. I think he enjoys poking around in my mouth, making me squirm. He puts on his gloves, snapping the elastic loudly to watch me jump. Then, grinning sadistically like the crazed dentist in *Little Shop of Horrors*, he says the most frightening words in the English language: "Open wide."

This freewriting contains some narrative elements. Can you identify them?

Grammar
Revising Tip
Use personal pronouns correctly when you write a personal narrative. See Lesson 17.1, page 595.

Journal Writing

Look through your journal to find story ideas. Underline any incidents that seem significant or interesting to you. Freewrite about each incident for five minutes to generate more story ideas.

Build on Your Ideas

Prewriting Tip

Jot down ideas for possible narratives in your journal. Anything can serve as inspiration: talking to people, reading, even watching television.

You can build on your ideas by answering questions about your story's basic elements and by constructing a framework of your story's events. Remember, however, that you may not even discover your story until you begin writing it. As writer Flannery O'Connor once said, "I write because I don't know what I think until I read what I say."

Answering Questions If you want to flesh out the basic elements in your narrative before you begin drafting, try answering the following questions. If you would prefer to just begin drafting, you may want to refer to these questions as you write your draft.

Questions to Flesh Out the Basic Narrative Elements

1. Who are my characters? About whom do I want to write?
2. What conflict(s) will my characters be involved in?
3. When does my story take place?
4. Where does my story take place?
5. Why do my characters get involved in their conflict(s)?
6. How does the setting affect my characters? How do they overcome their conflict(s)?
7. Do my characters change in any way during the course of the story? If so, in what ways and why?

Constructing a Framework Most narratives are organized in chronological order, the order in which the events happened. Try plotting the events in your narrative in chronological order along a time line. Keep asking yourself the question, *What happened next?* This will help you keep track of the events and write them down in order.

1:30 P.M. First Event	**4:45 P.M.** Second Event	**9:00 P.M.** Third Event	**7:00 A.M.** Fourth Event	**8:00 A.M.** Final Event
Paul and Carlos set off to ride their mountain bikes through the woods near their home.	They become confused by the many trails and take a wrong turn. As night falls, they are hopelessly lost.	They try to keep warm and build a shelter with branches. They spend a miserable night in the woods.	The next day, they continue to try to find their way back home. They came upon old railroad tracks.	By following the tracks, they reach town and safety.

4.1 Writing Activities

Write a Personal Narrative

You've decided to enter a writing contest sponsored by a national teen magazine. The contest rules state that you must write a one-page narrative about an experience that did not turn out as you expected. Use the prewriting techniques described in this lesson to help you explore your topic and build on your narrative's basic elements. Refer to your prewriting samples as you draft your narrative, but don't feel limited by the ideas you came up with at that stage in the writing process.

- Include believable characters, setting, and plot.
- Test out your ideas by talking them through or freewriting.
- Ask yourself questions to fill out the details of your narrative.
- Construct a time line or another organizational framework for your narrative.

PURPOSE To write a personal narrative for a contest
AUDIENCE Editors of a teen magazine
LENGTH 2–4 paragraphs

COMPUTER OPTION

If your word processor has an outlining feature, you can use it to outline your personal narrative. As you create your outline, this feature simultaneously creates a skeleton draft of your writing. In addition, as you come up with new ideas and enter the changes on your outline, the draft also changes. After you have completed your outline, "flesh out" your skeleton draft. Then use the cut-and-paste feature on your computer to help you revise and edit the draft.

Grammar Link

Use strong adverbs to make writing more precise.

Note how the writer on page 173 notes that the dentist "puts on his gloves, snapping the elastic loudly to make me jump."

Revise the following sentences by adding at least one strong adverb to each.

1. Murmurs seep from under the dentist's door.
2. I imagine that the dentist has told someone to "open wide."
3. My own teeth begin to vibrate as the buzz of the drill reaches my ears.
4. I can feel the pull and push of some sharp instrument in my mouth.
5. I remember that I'm waiting for my brother to have his braces checked.

See Lesson 10.5, page 429.

Narrative Writing
Developing Conflict in Narrative

In a narrative, as in a movie, it is often the conflict, or struggle, that keeps the audience interested. There are several types of conflict. Choose the one that works best with your characters and situations.

Use Events to Develop Conflict

The conflict, or struggle, in a story is what sets events in motion and makes the audience want to find out what happens. In the movie *Jaws*, for example, the uncertain outcome in the struggle between men and shark creates a gripping story.

Conflict plays the same role in a narrative that a main idea plays in other types of writing. Just as all supporting details help develop a main idea, all events in a narrative help develop its conflict.

As a character grapples with the conflict, the plot builds to a climax, the high point of the story. The resolution, in which the aftermath of the climax is revealed, brings the narrative to an end. The graph on the opposite page shows how the development and eventual resolution of a conflict form the basis for the plot.

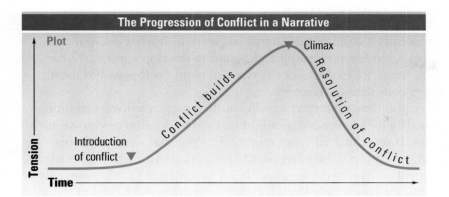

The Progression of Conflict in a Narrative

Learn the Types of Conflict

Drafting Tip

As you draft the conflict in your narrative, remember that a conflict with a less predictable climax and resolution is more likely to involve your readers.

Conflicts can be internal or external. External conflicts involve one or more characters and an outside force. Internal conflicts occur within a character. The chart below lists four types of conflicts, three external and one internal.

Four Types of Conflict	
Conflict	**Examples**
Person Against Person The narrative pits one character against another.	One character exposes a flaw in another. One character attempts to harm another. One character opposes the beliefs of another.
Person Against Nature A character struggles against a dangerous animal, place, or condition.	A character is attacked by a rampaging elephant. A character tries to scale a dangerous peak. A character is threatened by a hurricane.
Person Against Society Society or tradition stands in the way of a character's desires.	Society prevents a character from doing something. An ethnic or religious group imposes its beliefs on a character who no longer wants to follow them.
Person Against Self The conflict is within the character's mind.	A character struggles with a lack of ambition. A character seeks to achieve an unrealistic goal. A character tries to overcome a fear of flying.

Journal Writing

Think about a narrative you've read in which a character (or characters) faced a particular conflict. How was the conflict resolved? Write your answer in your journal.

Develop Conflict

To identify a conflict for a narrative, start with what you want to write about and use prewriting techniques to develop conflict. For example, freewrite to discover the types of conflicts that would most challenge your main characters.

Once you have identified a main conflict, use prewriting techniques to generate a list of events that might be used to develop or resolve such a conflict. If you think an event might affect the characters or forces involved, try listing some of its possible effects. As you write, keep pushing yourself to answer the question *What happens next?* until your story is complete. See how writer Russell Baker presents two conflicts in the following selection.

Literature Model

Baker sets up two types of conflict: Baker versus his own fear of deep water and Baker versus the Navy instructor.

Baker uses dialogue to develop the conflict between himself and the Navy instructor.

What is the climax of each conflict? How are the conflicts resolved?

On the first day in the pool an instructor with a voice like a bullhorn ordered fifty of us to climb a high board and jump in feet first. . . . A line was formed to mount the ladder and jump. I drifted to the end of the line, then stepped out when the splashing started and introduced myself to the instructor.

"I'm a nonswimmer," I said. "You want me to go to the shallow end of the pool?" At City College I'd spent four years in the shallow end of the pool.

"This pool doesn't have a shallow end," the instructor said.

"Well, what am I going to do?"

"Get up on that platform and jump," he said.

The pool depth was marked as fifteen feet at that point.

"I'm not kidding. I can't swim a stroke."

"Up! Up!" he shouted.

"But I'll drown."

"This pool's got the best lifesaving equipment in the Navy," he said. "Don't worry about it."

"Come on."

"I'm giving you an order, mister. Up!" . . .

I stepped to the edge, closed my eyes, and walked into space. The impact of the water was like being smacked on the bottom by a two-by-four, then I was sinking, then—my God! —I was rising irresistibly to the surface. My head broke water. The water was actually supporting me, just as everybody had always said it would.

Russell Baker, *Growing Up*

4.2 Writing Activities

Write a Narrative

You've decided to contribute a one-page narrative to a booklet entitled *Common Conflicts Encountered by Teens*. The booklet is prepared by and designed for students at your school.

Consider the following as possible topics for your narrative:

a student is afraid to speak out when her friend is jeered at by fellow classmates; a student wants to try out for a part in the school play but isn't sure if he's good enough; a student feels pressured by her friends to remain at a party after her curfew.

- Include events that develop the conflict for your readers.
- Build your plot to a climax.
- Create a resolution to the conflict.

PURPOSE To write a narrative
AUDIENCE Students at your school
LENGTH 3–4 paragraphs

César A. Martinez, *Mestizo*, 1987

Cross-Curricular: Art

The drawing below is a self-portrait by César A. Martinez. Entitled *Mestizo*, it shows the artist flanked by a jaguar, native to the Americas, and a Spanish bull, which represents Europe. The drawing reflects Martinez's struggle to come to terms with his own cultural identity, rooted in both North America and Spain. Generate events that might be used to develop and eventually resolve the conflict. Then write a brief narrative based on the drawing.

Grammar Link

Avoid sentence fragments.

Each item below contains a *sentence fragment*, or incomplete sentence. Rewrite the item to eliminate the fragment. Change words as necessary.

1. The conflict in a narrative engages a reader's interest. Because a reader wants to find out how the conflict will be resolved.
2. The plot is set in motion by the conflict. Which can be an internal conflict or an external one.
3. The plot building to a climax, the high point of the story. After the climax, the resolution ends the narrative.
4. A conflict within the character's mind. Internal conflict pits the character against himself or herself.
5. Much of the conflict in young adult literature is internal. Adolescents experiencing the pains of growing up.

See Lesson 9.1, page 376, and Lesson 13.9, page 515–516.

Narrative Writing
Writing Dialogue

Dialogue, or conversation between characters, brings the characters in a story to life. Like the cartoon below, a story would be hard to follow without the dialogue.

"Mom, can I drive on the way back?"
"Of course not, Calvin."

"Can I just steer then? I promise I won't crash."
"No, Calvin."

"Can I work the gas and brakes while you steer?"
"No, Calvin."

"You never let me do anything."

Discover the Uses of Dialogue

You can use dialogue to help advance a narrative's plot. For example, if the plot involves an argument between two characters, you can let the characters speak for themselves rather than summarizing their dispute.

You can also use dialogue to reveal your characters' personality traits or to show relationships between characters. For instance, instead of telling the reader, "Robert was shy," use Robert's actions and words to reveal his shyness: "Robert shuffled uneasily, looked at his feet, and mumbled, 'Nice to meet you.' "

Additionally, you can use dialogue to make the reader feel closer to the action, to help the reader "see" the story as it unfolds rather than to hear about it from a narrator. Dialogue can also help establish character and conflict, and it can make a conflict more powerful and real to the reader.

Think About Real People to Develop Dialogue

When you're writing dialogue for a story about something that really happened, try to remember as closely as possible what each person said. If your story is fictional, you'll need to invent dialogue. To do so, you might try to imagine that you are one of the characters and freewrite about the conflict from that character's point of view. Keep in mind the character's age, background, and personality and how those qualities may be reflected in speech.

Sometimes my mother makes me want to scream. Why won't she let me get an after-school job? All my friends are working and making their own money. Why does Mom still treat me like a kid?

If the conflict involves two characters, you might try freewriting a letter from each character to the other. Each letter should reflect the letter writer's point of view and feelings about the conflict.

Dear Angela,

    I know you're angry with me because I won't let you work after school. But I'm afraid a job would interfere with your studies. You know you won't get into a good college if your grades are poor. Besides, I'd worry when you'd be coming home after dark.

Dear Mom,

    I promise you a job won't hurt my grades. I'll be home every day by 7:00, which gives me tons of time to do my homework. And Carla's already said she can give me a lift home after work. Best of all, I'll be able to buy that winter jacket I saw at the mall with my own money.

Dialogue should sound like real speech. In real speech, people often interrupt each other, ignore each other's comments, speak in fragments, and break the rules of grammar. To test whether your dialogue sounds natural, read it aloud.

Journal Writing

In your journal write down three pieces of dialogue that you have overheard and that struck you as interesting. Why do you think you remembered these particular conversations? What made them interesting? Write your ideas in your journal.

Develop Your Story with Dialogue

Dialogue can bring your writing to life. In Matthew Cheney's short story "The Nauga Hunters," Hank invites his younger brother Chucky to hunt for a nauga, an imaginary beast. Note how Cheney uses dialogue to develop his characters and advance the story.

Student Model

*C*hucky stood next to his brother without saying anything. Then he asked quietly, "Is it about Mom and Dad?"

"Jus' beat it!"

"What's gonna happen? Is Dad gonna leave?"

"You wanna know? You really wanna know, you little jerk? Las' night I heard Mom and Dad talkin'."

"Fightin'?"

"Nope, jus' talkin'. Dad said he's gonna leave and go ta New York and take me, and Mom can have you. So I brought you out here jus' ta be nice 'cause I may never really be able ta do anythin' like this again. Okay? Satisfied?"

"You sure yer tellin' the truth?"

Hank stood up and jumped on his brother; they fell to the damp ground. His eyes were sparkling and his lips were unfirm. "Would I lie about that, you little . . ." His voice faded as he pulled his arm up to punch Chucky. Chucky was crying now. Hank stood up. "Forget it," he said. "Supper'll be almost ready." Chucky was still on the ground. "You comin'?"

Chucky pulled himself up and brushed off his rear end. His face was streaked with tears. "Yup," he said softly.

Matthew Cheney, New Hampton School, New Hampton, New Hampshire.
First appeared in *Merlyn's Pen: The National Magazine of Student Writing*

Dialogue effectively reveals the story's central conflict and its climax: the boys' parents are getting a divorce.

How does Cheney use dialogue to convey Hank's anger and confusion?

Try to make your dialogue as realistic as possible. As you write it, keep the following guidelines in mind.

Prewriting Tip

To develop your ability to write realistic dialogue, watch a favorite television show. Note how the dialogue reflects the ages, backgrounds, and personalities of the characters.

Dialogue Guidelines

- Use language that reflects the age, background, and personality of each character.
- Make sure your dialogue has a purpose—to advance the action, to reveal a character's personality or relationships between characters, or to show the conflict.
- Begin a direct quotation with a capital letter, and enclose it in quotation marks.
- Begin a new paragraph each time the speaker changes.

4.3 Writing Activities

Write a Dialogue

You've been chosen to write the dialogue for a skit for your school's theater group. Use the information below to develop the dialogue.

Chen and Kirby are best friends, but their personalities are very different. Chen is an optimist, always able to see the bright side. Kirby is a pessimist, always assuming the worst. Both are on the track team. For the first time in years, the team has a chance to win the state title. As they warm up before the championship race, Kirby admits to Chen that he wants to withdraw. He's afraid he'll cause the team to lose. Chen inspires Kirby with his own enthusiasm. By the time the starting signal sounds, both friends are ready to give their personal best.

As you develop your dialogue, read it aloud to find out how it sounds. Try to imagine yourself in each character's place.

- Let the characters speak for themselves.
- Use dialogue for a purpose.
- Write dialogue that sounds like real speech.
- Use language appropriate to the character.

PURPOSE To write dialogue for a skit to be performed by your school's theater group
AUDIENCE Your school's student body
LENGTH 1 page

Cooperative Learning

In a small group, choose a scene from American history to dramatize. First discuss the personalities and backgrounds of the characters. Then meet with your group to write dialogue that develops the action and accurately reflects each character's personality and background. After all the dialogue has been written, present your group scene to the rest of the class.

Grammar Link

Know when and how to use quotation marks.

Dialogue, the exact words of a speaker, is written with quotation marks.

Rewrite the sentences below, using quotation marks to enclose every direct quotation. Make other changes in capitalization and punctuation as necessary.

1. My little sister stamped her right foot and exclaimed I'm so mad.
2. Nibbling at the cuticle of her right thumb, my older sister whispered why is Alicia so mad?
3. Don't ask me I answered, lowering my voice.
4. People who have something to say my angry sister hissed should have the courage to say it so that other people can hear.
5. This is a new idea I murmured in return.

See Lesson 21.9, pages 714–718.

Narrative Writing
Using Anecdotes

An anecdote is a short narrative used to illustrate a point or reveal character. In the model below the writer uses an anecdote to demonstrate poet Langston Hughes's scorn for the so-called Jim Crow laws.

Most anecdotes instruct or entertain, and they often contain dialogue. Although anecdotes can stand on their own, they are frequently used as supporting details in longer pieces of writing.

This anecdote contains a plot—Hughes is trying to get served dinner; characters—Hughes, the steward, the naval officer; and a setting—a train's dining car.

How is dialogue used to reveal Hughes's attitude toward the Jim Crow laws?

Literature Model

B y this time he unquestionably had become bolder in confronting Jim Crow. Always now he entered the dining car at the first call, instead of shrinking back and waiting for the last as blacks were supposed to do.

Picking a center table, he usually tried to brazen it out before incredulous but discreetly supportive black waiters and often indignant, but often yielding, white stewards. "Are you a Puerto Rican?" a steward demanded in Alabama. "No, hungry!" The man handed over a menu. "Are you Cuban?" a curious white Navy officer then asked. "No, American," Langston coolly replied. "Are you Cuban?"

Arnold Rampersad, *The Life of Langston Hughes, Volume II: 1941–1967*

Generate Anecdotes

You can generate anecdotes by drawing on real-life experiences or by using prewriting techniques to invent them. Keep in mind that you will use the anecdote to illustrate a point in a longer piece of writing.

Anecdotes Based on Fact Some anecdotes are based on incidents that actually happened. To generate true-life anecdotes, think about significant or entertaining incidents from your own life. You might want to look through your journal for ideas. Then think about the point each anecdote could make in a longer piece of writing.

Factual Anecdotes	
Anecdote	**Point**
The time I stood up for myself even though my friends disagreed	To show that you should voice your opinions, even if they are unpopular
The time my brother first went away to college	To show that life is a process of change
The time I struck out and my team lost the game	To show that true friends stand by you even when you fail

Invented Anecdotes When you're writing a fictional narrative, you can invent anecdotes. First decide on the point you want to make. Then freewrite to come up with an anecdote that could illustrate that point.

Invented Anecdotes	
Point	**Anecdote**
To show a character's selfishness	A character thinks only of himself or herself at the expense of others
To show that two characters have different values	An argument between two characters
To show that you have to confront a fear to overcome it	A character confronts his or her fear of heights by climbing a mountain

Vocabulary

Drafting Tip

When you draft your anecdote, be sure to present the events of the story in chronological order. Helpful transition words include *after*, *before*, *as soon as*, *first*, *next*, *now*, *soon*, and *then*. See Lesson 2.8, page 91.

Presenting Tip

One effective method to present an anecdote is to read it aloud.

Journal Writing

Look through your journal for incidents that could be written up as possible anecdotes. Then list the incidents, and identify the point each could make in a longer piece of writing.

Decide Where and How to Use Anecdotes

Prewriting Tip

If you are writing about yourself, you might ask family members to discuss their early memories of you. Their stories could supply you with useful anecdotes.

Once you have an anecdote, you need to consider whether or not to use it to make a specific point in a longer piece of writing. To help you decide, ask yourself the following questions.

Questions to Determine the Usefulness of an Anecdote
1. Does this anecdote make the point I want to make?
2. Does the anecdote advance the narrative?
3. Is the anecdote brief, yet meaningful?
4. Does the anecdote instruct or entertain?

In Jennifer Tuck's short story "My Grandmother's House," the narrator dreads returning to her grandmother's house after her grandmother dies. As a little girl, she had been afraid of the house because it was so large and dark. As this anecdote reveals, however, on one particular occasion her grandmother helped her overcome her fears.

Student Model

What does the anecdote reveal about the narrator's grandmother?

I had been sitting on the porch for nearly an hour when my grandmother came out, quietly letting the screen door creak on its old rusty hinges and then sigh as it came to rest against the crooked door frame Grandpa was always saying he would fix.

"Why don't you come inside?" she said. "We are going to eat dinner soon and I would hate to think of sitting at the table without you."

"I'm afraid." I barely whispered this shameful feeling, and stared straight down at my untied shoes.

Notice that the anecdote could stand on its own as a brief narrative, complete with plot, setting, and characters.

"That's OK. I was afraid when we first moved here, too. You just have to remember that this house is a lot like your house, only there's love from many families here instead of just our own. Did you ever stop to wonder who could have lived here before? There must be so many memories within these walls!"

We talked on and on and gradually my fear began to fade. When my mother called us inside, I didn't hesitate for an instant before following my grandmother inside.

Jennifer Tuck, Central High School, Manchester, New Hampshire
First appeared in *Merlyn's Pen: The National Magazine of Student Writing*

Write an Anecdote

Your English class is collecting an anecdote from each class member for a get-to-know-your-classmates project. The collection will be distributed to all of the students in the class. Write a one-page anecdote that reveals something about your personality. You may choose to write about a time when you made a fool of yourself in front of someone you wanted to impress or a time when your sense of humor helped relieve an unpleasant situation. You might choose to reveal another aspect of your personality.

- Make sure that your anecdote supports your point.
- Include significant details.

PURPOSE To write an anecdote that reveals something about yourself.
AUDIENCE The members of your class
LENGTH 3–4 paragraphs

Joan Brown, *After the Alcatraz Swim #3*, 1976

Grammar Link

Use comparative and superlative forms of adjectives and adverbs correctly.

Comparative adjectives and adverbs compare two things—for example, Langston Hughes's becoming "bolder" in confronting Jim Crow. *Superlative forms* of adjectives and adverbs compare more than two things.

Complete each sentence below with the correct form of the word in parentheses.

1. After some time, Langston Hughes entered the dining car _____ than he first had. (courageously)
2. Who were _____ (amazed): the white stewards or the black waiters?
3. Perhaps _____ of all were the fellow passengers Hughes encountered in the dining cars. (surprised)
4. Some passengers moved to the _____ corner of the dining car when they saw the poet approach. (far)
5. They showed _____ what they thought than did those passengers who just ignored Hughes. (clearly)

See Lessons 18.1–18.3, pages 621–626.

Cross Curricular: Art

Look at the painting on this page. What ideas for anecdotes does it suggest? Freewrite or list to generate ideas for anecdotes and for the points they could illustrate. Finally, draft your anecdote, using dialogue.

Narrative Writing
Writing a Sports Narrative

A good sports narrative, such as the model below, contains all the elements of any good narrative: character, setting, and conflict that builds to a climax and resolution.

Student Model

The conflict in a sports narrative is often person against person, as each athlete struggles to win the sports event.

What is the climax in this sports narrative? How is it resolved?

T he pop of the gun sets the swimmers' legs in motion and arms flawlessly scooping pockets of water. Their heads bob rhythmically, each straining to reach the end of the pool. At the end of each lane, fellow swimmers stand and cheer their teammates, with a single exception. One blond-haired swimmer receives cries from teammates who lean close to the water, straining to show the swimmer their enthusiasm and their lips. The swimmer is deaf, and the encouraging motions of her friends urge her to go faster.

The race is close. The blond head edges out in front, neck and neck, with another swimmer beside her. However, with a last, powerful stroke, the blond swimmer breaks the tie and hits the timer seconds before her competitor. As she rests against the wall of the pool, accepting the congratulations of her teammates, an ear-to-ear grin appears across her face.

Charissa Adelman, Quartz Hill High School, Quartz Hill, California

Begin with Intensifying Action

You'll want to begin your sports narrative at the point in the event when conflict starts to build. Usually this is the moment when the action intensifies. For example, to tell the story of a team's dramatic, come-from-behind victory, you might begin at the point in the game in which the team seized control and began its push for victory.

Include Supporting Details

Like other narratives, most sports narratives develop a conflict to its climax and resolution. You may want to chart the action that develops the conflict. This technique can help you identify the important events —the supporting details—that you'll want to include.

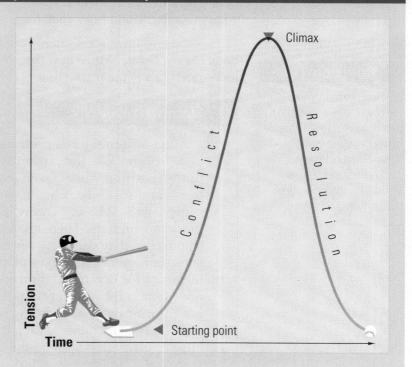

Development of Conflict in a Sports Narrative

Starting Point:
A baseball game is tied at the bottom of the ninth inning, with two outs. A runner on third represents the winning run.

Conflict:
The pitcher stares at third base. The base runner, determined to break the record for stolen bases, boldly stares back.

Climax:
As the pitcher fires the ball, the base stealer makes a dash for home and plows into the catcher.

Resolution:
When the dust clears, the umpire waves his arms and yells, "Safe!" The crowd roars with delight.

Journal Writing

Watch a sports event at school or on television. Use it as the basis for preparing a sports narrative. Choose a starting point, graph the development of the conflict to its climax and resolution, and then write a brief summary of each point in the plot.

Build a Memorable Story

Prewriting Tip

When prewriting about a sports event, try list making to generate details. Use the significant details to develop your narrative.

After you've chosen a sports event, determined your starting point, and charted the action, you're ready to draft your sports narrative. Begin by considering your lead. A **lead** is a strong opening sentence that grabs the reader's attention and gets the story moving. Examine your story's starting point. Is there anything dramatic, amusing, or surprising about it? If so, you might use that for your lead. Remember, however, that a narration of the event will only make up part of your article. (For tips on how to write a sports feature, see the Unit 4 Case Study on pages 166–171.)

State the Facts Clearly Be sure that you have presented the sequence of events and all the facts clearly. Double-check quotations for accuracy, and make sure each source is identified.

Use Vivid Language Wherever possible, show the action rather than telling about it. Vivid action verbs and sensory details can bring your story to life and hold your readers' interest.

Read the following selection from baseball writer Roger Angell's book *Season Ticket*. Notice how Angell makes even a seemingly actionless stretch of a game interesting.

Vocabulary
Revising Tip

When revising your writing, use a thesaurus to help you find more precise, vivid verbs. A thesaurus lists words with their synonyms and, if applicable, their antonyms.

Literature Model

A base runner leads cautiously away from first, then trots back as the pitcher steps off the rubber. The third-base ump walks seven steps out toward left field, turns, and strolls back again. Another foul ball, bounced softly past first base. "Throw it *straight*," somebody in the press box mutters. There are spatters of applause in the stands, but they die away for lack of hope. . . . I can see some fans getting up, in twos and threes, and heading up the aisles for home and dinner. The park is half empty by now. Out in the sloping right-field sector of the seats, there is a thin, a-cappella rendering of "Happy Birthday," for somebody—her name is Ella, it turns out—and other fans around the park join in on the last "happy birthday to you-ooo!" and Ella gets a little round of applause, too. But that ends as well (a coach is out talking to the pitcher now), and even the everyday noises of the baseball park— the hum of voices, the undercurrent of talk and cheers and laughter and vender cries—drop and fade, and Fenway Park is almost silent, just for a minute.

Roger Angell, *Season Ticket*

What verbs does Angell use to help the reader "see" the action in the ballpark?

4.5 Writing Activities

Write a Sports Narrative

The editor of your school newspaper has asked you to write a sports narrative based on an important basketball game. Use the following information to write the narrative.

> West High and East High, long-standing rivals, face each other in the state basketball finals. The game is close until the fourth quarter, when East High pulls ahead with a 78–70 lead. Finally, West High comes from behind to win the game 82–80, with a basket in the final seconds of the fourth quarter.

- Begin your narrative where conflict starts to build.
- Bring your conflict to a climax and provide a resolution.
- State the facts clearly in vivid language.

Elaine de Kooning, *Campy at the Plate*, 1953

PURPOSE To narrate an exciting sports event for a school newspaper
AUDIENCE Student and teacher sports fans
LENGTH 3–6 paragraphs

Cooperative Learning

Use the image on this page to develop a sports narrative. Work in small groups to brainstorm ideas for a story. Chart the action. Then have one group member begin the story, someone else write the next section, and so on till everyone has written a section and the story is brought to a conclusion.

Grammar Link

Use vivid verbs in your narratives.

Effective sports stories contain verbs that let the reader "see" what is happening. Rewrite the sentences below, replacing all bold-faced words with more vivid action verbs.

1. The Phoenix Suns **went** out onto the basketball court as the overflow home-town crowd **clapped**.
2. Charles Barkley **got** the tip and immediately **ran** to the basket.
3. The crowd **applauded** as Barkley **moved** around the opposing center to score.
4. When Dan Majerle **made** 6 of 13 three-point shots, the arena **shook**.
5. After Danny Manning **took** the ball from an opposing player and scored to win the game for Phoenix, the Phoenix coach, Paul Westphal, **got up** from the bench.

See Lesson 10.3, page 414.

Writing About Literature
Writing About Suspense

Grant Wood, *Death on the Ridge Road*, 1935

Two of the most common ways to build suspense in a narrative are to use foreshadowing and to withhold information from the reader. In this painting the artist effectively creates suspense, or anxiety about what will happen next.

Ways to Create Suspense

- **Foreshadowing** Foreshadowing gives clues about what is going to happen later in the story. Writers often use this technique to prepare the reader for an ominous turn of events. The clues may include details of setting, characters, or plot. In the example on the opposite page, note how writer Mario Vargas Llosa uses a character's fearful imaginings to foreshadow events to come.

- **Withholding Information** In withholding information from the reader, a writer creates a puzzle with a few pieces missing, a mystery to be solved. Curious to find out what will happen, the reader reads on. Mystery writers often withhold some key piece of information until the final scene when the mystery is solved.

*A*fter swimming for a few minutes Miguel felt the cold that had momentarily vanished coming over him again, and he speeded up his strokes because it was in his legs, especially in his calves, that the water had a greater effect, first making them insensitive, then stiffening them. He was swimming with his face in the water, and each time his right arm rose out of it, he turned his head to expel air and breathe in another supply, at which he submerged his face and chin once more, just barely, so as not to hinder his own progress but, on the contrary, to split the water like a prow and make his forward movement easier. With each stroke he glanced at Rubén swimming smoothly, effortlessly on the surface, not splashing now, with the delicacy and ease of a seagull gliding. Miguel tried to forget Rubén and the sea and the breakers, which must still be far off, for the water was clear and calm, and they were swimming only through newly risen surf. He wanted to remember nothing but Flora's face and the down on her arms that sparkled on sunny days like a little forest of golden threads. But he could not prevent another image from succeeding to that of the girl—the image of a mountain of raging water . . . in a real ocean stirred by inner cataclysms in which were thrown up unusual waves that could have swamped an entire ship and upset it with astonishing rapidity, hurling passengers, lifeboats, masts, sails, sailors, porthole covers, and flags into the air.

Mario Vargas Llosa, "Sunday"

The writer builds suspense by describing Miguel's progress, stroke by stroke. As a result, the reader feels the character's weariness and fear.

What image does the author use to foreshadow the possible dangers ahead for Miguel?

Journal Writing

Sometimes a writer withholds information from the character(s) in a story but reveals it to the readers. What effect does this have on the reader? How does it create suspense? Write your ideas about this technique in your journal.

Write About a Suspenseful Story

Drafting Tip

Sensory details can add immediacy to your suspense writing and draw the reader into your story. See Lesson 2.6 on page 83 to help you develop these details.

Grammar
Editing Tip

When you edit your writing, check to see that you have formed all possessive nouns, such as *General Zaroff's* island, correctly. You may want to refer to Lesson 9.10, page 394, and Lesson 21.11, pages 721–723, for help.

When you analyze a suspenseful story, focus on the ways in which the writer creates suspense. Provide examples from the text to support your ideas. As you read, ask yourself the following questions.

Questions to Determine How a Writer Creates Suspense
1. What details in the descriptions of the characters help build suspense?
2. Which events in the plot help build suspense?
3. What aspects of the setting build suspense?
4. What are the characters' reactions as suspense builds?
5. What atmosphere or mood does the writer create? How does the mood change?
6. In what ways does the writer foreshadow events to come?
7. What information does the writer withhold from the characters?

By exploring your answers to these questions through freewriting or brainstorming, you can develop a focus for an analysis of a suspense story. In the model below, Elizabeth Chen analyzes some of the techniques writer Richard Connell uses to build suspense in his short story "The Most Dangerous Game."

Student Model

Chen uses specific examples from the story to develop the focus of her essay.

Richard Connell uses foreshadowing to heighten suspense in "The Most Dangerous Game." When Rainsford falls off his yacht and swims to General Zaroff's island, he is relieved to reach its "dense jungle." However, the narrator states, "What perils that tangle of trees and underbrush might hold for him did not concern Rainsford just then." This statement suggests that the character will soon be in danger. By foreshadowing this future event, the author creates a sense of anticipation in the reader and compels him to read on.

Connell also draws the reader into the story by withholding information. When Zaroff asserts that he hunts "the biggest" game on his island, he does not at first reveal what that game might be. As a result, Rainsford and the reader are forced to guess. The diabolical answer, which directs the course of the rest of the story, becomes clear to both at about the same time.

At the end of her essay, how does Chen herself withhold information in order to pique the reader's interest in the story?

Elizabeth Chen
Downers Grove North High School, Downers Grove, Illinois

4.6 Writing Activities

Write to Analyze Setting

Read the following selection from Edgar Allan Poe's short story "The Pit and the Pendulum." Then use the questions from page 194 to help you write an analysis.

> So far I had not opened my eyes. I felt that I lay upon my back, unbound. I reached out my hand, and it fell heavily upon something damp and hard. There I suffered it to remain for many minutes, while I strove to imagine where and *what* I could be. I longed, yet dared not, to employ my vision, I dreaded the first glance at objects around me. It was not that I feared to look upon things horrible, but that I grew aghast lest there should be *nothing* to see.

Edgar Allan Poe, "The Pit and the Pendulum"

Patricia Gonzalez, *Fountain View*, 1985

PURPOSE To identify the details in a story's setting that help create suspense
AUDIENCE Your classmates
LENGTH 1–2 paragraphs

Grammar Link

Use possessive nouns correctly.

Words like *Flora's* and *General Zaroff's* are *possessive nouns*.

Possessive nouns can be singular or plural. Revise the following sentences about the student model on page 194 by creating possessives using the words in boldface.

1. **The story of Richard Connell** uses foreshadowing to heighten suspense.
2. **The conflict of Rainsford and General Zaroff** is a serious one.
3. Only one man can win **the contest of the two men.**
4. The suspense of the situation grabs **the interest of the readers.**
5. **The analysis of Elizabeth Chen** does not reveal the outcome of the contest.

See Lesson 9.10, page 394, and Lesson 21.11, pages 721–723.

Cross-Curricular: Art

The scene in the painting is the setting for a suspense story. Introduce the story by describing the scene in a way that creates mystery and suspense. Then make notes as to what might happen in the rest of the story.

Writing About Literature
Analyzing Point of View in a Narrative

Just as a performer on the stage and a person in the audience would describe a rock concert differently, so would different narrators tell a story differently. The author's choice of narrator determines how a particular story is told and how, in turn, a reader understands the story.

Identify the Point of View

The writer of a narrative selects a point of view, or a perspective, from which to tell the story. The author has three basic points of view from which to choose.

In a story told from a first-person point of view, the narrator is a character in the story. This type of narrator uses first-person pronouns, such as *I* and *we*, in telling the story. A first-person narrator knows only what he or she is thinking and describes only the events he or she witnesses.

In a story told from a third-person limited point of view, the narrator stands outside the story. This type of narrator uses third-person pronouns such as *he*, *she*, *it*, and *they*. The third-person limited narrator describes the actions and words of all the characters but the thoughts and feelings of only one character.

In a story told from a third-person omniscient point of view, the narrator stands outside the action but knows all and sees all. A third-person omniscient narrator can relate everything that happens in the story, including the thoughts and feelings of all the characters.

Examine the Effect of Point of View

After identifying the point of view of a narrative, notice what effect the choice of point of view has on the presentation of the story. Then use examples from the text to support your opinion.

Grammar

Editing Tip

When writing about point of view, be sure to refer to the narrator rather than the author of the narrative. As you edit your writing, check that all pronoun references are clear. See Lessons 9.5–9.6, pages 386–388.

- **First-Person Narrator** Stories told by a first-person narrator tend to draw the reader into the action because the reader identifies with the "I" who is telling the story. As you evaluate the effect of point of view of a narrative, remember that the first-person narrator may be a biased or unreliable witness. In the following selection from Eugenia Collier's short story "Marigolds," the first-person narrator recalls how she felt after hearing her father cry for the first time.

Literature Model

*T*he world had lost its boundary lines. My mother, who was small and soft, was now the strength of the family; my father, who was the rock on which the family had been built, was sobbing like the tiniest child. Everything was suddenly out of tune, like a broken accordion. Where did I fit into this crazy picture? I do not now remember my thoughts, only a feeling of great bewilderment and fear.

Eugenia Collier, "Marigolds"

Notice that the first-person narrator only reports her own pain and confusion. She does not consider how her father must be feeling.

Do you identify with the child telling the story? Why?

- **Third-Person Limited Narrator** A third-person limited narrator stands outside the story but relates events as if he or she were looking over the shoulder of one of the characters. Because the narrator is so close to this one character, the reader tends to identify with and sympathize with the character. Be aware, however, that this narrator may withhold information or tell more than the character would tell.

Journal Writing

Choose a piece of narrative writing told by a third-person limited narrator. Now imagine the same piece told by a first-person narrator. What effect might the change in point of view have on the story? Write down your ideas in your journal.

In the following example, Mathew Isaac analyzes the effect of a third-person limited narrator in O. Henry's "The Gift of the Magi."

Student Model

Isaac maintains that O. Henry uses a third-person limited narrator to make the story's ironic ending more effective.

I n O. Henry's "The Gift of the Magi," a third-person limited narrator primarily relates the actions, thoughts, and feelings of the character Della. The narrator withholds information from the reader about her husband, Jim, and thereby sets up the story's final, ironic twist.

The story's narrator is also used to comment ironically on the characters themselves. For example, when Della cries because she doesn't have enough money to buy Jim a present, the narrator remarks that "life is made up of sobs, sniffles, and smiles, with sniffles predominating." . . .

What specific examples and quotations from the story does Isaac use to support his opinion?

Although we are encouraged to laugh at Della and Jim, at the story's end, the reader is the object of the narrator's irony. There it is implied that the reader who only laughs at the pair, without recognizing their deep love, is the real fool.

Mathew Isaac, Rich East High School, Park Forest, Illinois

- **Third-Person Omniscient Narrator** The third-person omniscient narrator stands outside the action of the story but relates the thoughts, feelings, words, and actions of all the characters. Although this narrator seems objective, keep in mind that he or she still tells only as much or as little as the author wants to reveal.

In the selection below, Ethan and his daughter Becky ride a ski lift. As you read, consider what the narrator does and doesn't tell about the story's events and characters.

Literature Model

The narrator doesn't reveal what happens to the out-of-control skier. What effect does this have on the reader?

A dark figure with spreading legs veered out of control beneath them, fell forward, and vanished. Ethan cried out, astonished, scandalized; he imagined the man had buried himself alive. Becky was barely amused, and looked away before the dark spots struggling in the drift were lost from sight. As if she might know, Ethan asked, "Who was that?"

What words and phrases suggest that the narrator may not be telling the reader everything about the characters' thoughts?

"Some kid." Kids, her tone suggested, were in plentiful supply; one could be spared.

John Updike, "Man and Daughter in the Cold"

4.7 Writing Activities

Write to Analyze Point of View in a Story

Write a letter to a friend in which you discuss a short story you have read recently. Give the story's title and author, and tell your friend about the story by analyzing its point of view. What effect does the story's viewpoint have on the conflict? What effect does its point of view have on the resolution? How would the story be different if it had been written from another point of view? Close your letter by telling whether or not you recommend the story to your friend.

- Clearly identify the point of view of the narrator: first person, third-person limited, or third-person omniscient.
- Use examples from the text to discuss the effect of the point of view.

PURPOSE To analyze the effect of point of view on a short story
AUDIENCE Your friend
LENGTH 1–2 paragraphs

COMPUTER OPTION

When you're ready to edit your analysis, use the spelling checker on your computer to help you proofread your work. Remember that the checker can't catch correctly spelled words that are used incorrectly. If you write *their* when you mean to say *there*, for example, the checker won't recognize the error. Therefore, it's a good idea to proofread your work yourself line by line to find the less obvious mistakes.

Grammar Link

Avoid incorrect pronoun shift.

When you write, avoid shifting pronouns from one person to another.

Incorrect: If *one* works hard, *you* can succeed.

Revise the sentences below to eliminate the incorrect shifts in person.

1. One's point of view is reflected in your understanding of an event.
2. You choose your narrator to present one's point of view.
3. One may choose one of three basic points of view to tell their story.
4. When one has a first-person narrator, you use pronouns such as *I* and *we*.
5. As you evaluate the effect of first-person point of view, try to determine how much we can trust the first-person narrator.
6. They enjoy first-person narration because you feel close to the action.
7. If one writes from a third-person limited point of view, you can describe the thoughts and feelings of only one character.
8. I use a third-person omniscient narrator so you can relate everything that happens in a story.
9. An author entertains me best by capturing your interest.
10. One's interest will most likely be captured if their curiosity is aroused.

See Lesson 9.6, page 388, and Lesson 17.5, page 602.

UNIT 4

WRITING PROCESS IN ACTION

NARRATIVE WRITING

In preceding lessons you've learned the basics of narrative—characters, setting, plot, and conflict. You've also had the chance to analyze anecdotes and elements of suspense and to create dialogue. Now it's time to put into practice what you've learned. You're invited to write a narrative that is based on a central conflict and its resolution.

• Assignment •

Context	You have been asked to contribute to an anthology of student writing called Resolutions, a book of stories about various kinds of conflicts. Your story, which can be happy or serious, may be based on a real incident or may be wholly imaginary. It may be told in the first or the third person.
Purpose	To write a true or fictionalized narrative about a conflict.
Audience	High school students and teachers throughout the nation
Length	1–2 pages.

You will find the next few pages helpful for planning and writing your narrative. Begin by reading through the pages, but don't feel you have to remember everything on them. You can refer to the pages when you need to. Use the suggestions, but don't feel limited by them. Remember, you're in charge of your own writing process.

Prewriting

What to write about—something imaginary or something that has actually happened to you or someone you know? Something amusing, suspenseful, or unusual? Your first task is choosing a problem or incident in which a character faces a conflict that needs to be resolved.

The ideas on the notepad may help you think of a conflict you can use.

Prewriting Options

- List events that you remember.
- Skim your journal for ideas.
- Brainstorm imaginary conflict situations.
- Freewrite about an issue or topic you feel strongly about.
- Narrow your choices to conflicts your characters can resolve.

Once you have selected an incident, map out the sequence of events involved in it. Next, arrange these details on a time line, even though you don't have to tell your story in strictly chronological order. Finally, decide what point of view you will use: first-person, third-person limited, or omniscient narrator.

Drafting

To begin drafting, envision the scene in which the conflict of your story reaches its crisis point. If you've chosen to write from a particular character's point of view, get inside that character's head. Then begin writing about that crisis moment. Use vivid action verbs and strong sensory details to describe what is going on. Notice the language Julia Alvaraz uses to convey how a crisis erupts:

Prewriting Tip

If you want to review information about third-person narration, see Lesson 4.7, pages 196–198.

Drafting Tip

For more information about developing conflict in a narrative, see Lesson 4.2, pages 176–178.

Literature Model

*T*he expression on his face shocked both mother and daughter. Carlos's toothless mouth had collapsed into a dark zero. His eyes bored into Yoyo, then shifted to Laura. In barely audible Spanish, as if secret microphones or informers were all about, he whispered to his wife, "You will permit her to read *that*?"

Julia Alvarez, *How the García Girls Lost Their Accents*

Next, work backward from your central paragraph. Try to fill in the information about characters, setting, and events the reader needs to know to understand what leads up to this scene.

- Who appears in the scene?
- Why are these characters there?
- How did these characters get there?
- Where does this scene take place?
- Why does it take place in this particular setting?

Then work forward from your central scene. Write about the events that resolve the complication. If you get stuck, focus on answering "What happens next?" Once you have drafted the pieces of your story, refer to your time line to arrange them. Finally look for good places to add dialogue or anecdotes.

Drafting Tip

To help you identify where to add dialogue and anecdotes, see Lessons 4.3 and 4.4, pages 180–186.

Revising

Revising Tip

To review ideas that can help you create suspense, see Lesson 4.6, pages 192–194.

To begin revising, read over your draft to make sure that what you've written fits your purpose and audience. Then have a **writing conference**. Read your draft to a partner or small group. Use your audience's reactions to help you evaluate your work.

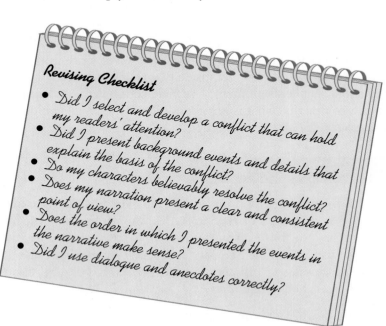

Revising Checklist
- Did I select and develop a conflict that can hold my readers' attention?
- Did I present background events and details that explain the basis of the conflict?
- Do my characters believably resolve the conflict?
- Does my narration present a clear and consistent point of view?
- Does the order in which I presented the events in the narrative make sense?
- Did I use dialogue and anecdotes correctly?

Editing

When you are satisfied with your narrative, **proofread** it carefully for errors in grammar, usage, mechanics, and spelling. Use the questions at the right as a guide.

In addition to proofreading, use the self-evaluation list below to make sure your narrative does all the things you want it to do. When you feel that it does, make a clean copy of your story and proofread it one more time.

Self-Evaluation

Make sure your conflict narrative—

- focuses on an interesting conflict
- hooks interest by establishing setting, characters, and conflict early
- uses dialogue, anecdotes, and figurative language effectively
- uses point of view consistently
- follows correct grammar, usage, mechanics, and spelling

Editing Checklist

- Have I capitalized all proper names?
- Have I avoided sentence fragments?
- Have I correctly punctuated direct quotations?
- Have I avoided pronoun shifts?
- Have I checked spellings of any words I'm unsure of?

For proofreading symbols, see page 100.

Presenting

Although for this assignment you have written a narrative for a fictitious anthology, there's no reason you can't submit it to a real anthology. You might have your story published in your school literary magazine. If you want to submit it for publication for a wider audience, ask your teacher or librarian to suggest suitable journals.

Journal Writing

Reflect on your writing process experience. Answer these questions in your journal: What do you like best about your narrative? What was the hardest part about writing it? What did you learn in your writing conference? What new things have you learned as a writer?

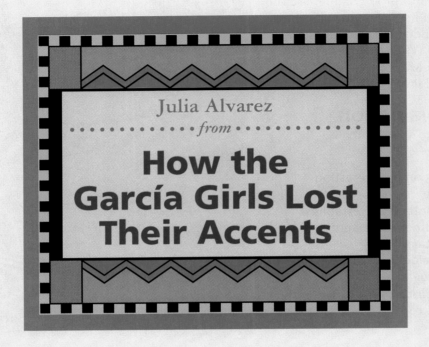

Julia Alvarez
· · · · · · · · · · *from* · · · · · · · · · · · ·

How the García Girls Lost Their Accents

Born in the Dominican Republic, Julia Alvarez came to the United States with her family when she was 10. In this selection from "Daughter of Invention," one of the short stories in Alvarez's first book of fiction, How the García Girls Lost Their Accents, *the author presents a simply structured narrative about her family. As you read, focus on characters and conflict. Then respond in the activities in Linking Writing and Literature on page 211.*

T he weekend before the assembly Monday morning Yoyo went into a panic. Her mother would just have to call in tomorrow and say Yoyo was in the hospital, in a coma.
Laura tried to calm her down. "Just remember how Mister Lincoln couldn't think of anything to say at the Gettysburg, but then,

bang! *Four score and once upon a time ago,"* she began reciting. "Something is going to come if you just relax. You'll see, like the Americans say, *Necessity is the daughter of invention.* I'll help you."

That weekend, her mother turned all her energy towards helping Yoyo write her speech. "Please, Mami, just leave me alone, please," Yoyo pleaded with her. But Yoyo would get rid of the goose only to have to contend with the gander. Her father kept poking his head in the door just to see if Yoyo had "fulfilled your obligations," a phrase he had used when the girls were younger and he'd check to see whether they had gone to the bathroom before a car trip. Several times that weekend around the supper table, he recited his own high school valedictorian speech. He gave Yoyo pointers on delivery, notes on the great orators and their tricks. (Humbleness and praise and falling silent with great emotion were his favorites.)

Laura sat across the table, the only one who seemed to be listening to him. Yoyo and her sisters were forgetting a lot of their Spanish, and their father's formal, florid diction was hard to understand. But Laura smiled softly to herself, and turned the lazy Susan at the center of the table around and around as if it were the prime mover, the first gear of her attention.

That Sunday evening, Yoyo was reading some poetry to get herself inspired: Whitman's poems in an old book with an engraved cover her father had picked up in a thrift shop next to his office. *I celebrate myself and sing myself. . . . He most honors my style who learns under it to destroy the teacher.* The poet's words shocked and thrilled her. She had gotten used to the nuns, a literature of appropriate sentiments, poems with a message, expurgated[1] texts. But here was a flesh and blood man, belching and laughing and sweating in poems. *Who touches this book touches a man.*

That night, at last, she started to write, recklessly, three, five pages, looking up once only to see her father passing by the hall on tiptoe. When Yoyo was done, she read over her words, and her eyes filled. She finally sounded like herself in English!

As soon as she had finished that first draft, she called her mother to her room. Laura listened attentively while Yoyo read the speech out loud, and in the end, her eyes were glistening too. Her face was soft and warm and proud. "*Ay,* Yoyo, you are going to be the one to bring our name to the headlights in this country! That is a beautiful, beautiful speech. I want for your father to hear it before he goes to sleep. Then I will type it for you, all right?"

Down the hall they went, mother and daughter, faces flushed with accomplishment. Into the master bedroom where Carlos was propped up on his pillows, still awake, reading the Dominican papers, already days old. Now that the dictatorship had been top-

---

1 expurgated (eks' pər gāt' 'd) with objectionable passages removed pled, he had become interested in his country's fate again. The interim government was going to hold the first free elections in thirty years. History was in the making, freedom and hope were in the air again! There was still some question in his mind whether or not he might move his family back. But Laura had gotten used to the life here. She did not want to go back to the old country where, de la Torre or not, she was only a wife and a mother (and a failed one at that, since she had never provided the required son). Better an independent nobody than a high-class houseslave. She did not come straight out and disagree with her husband's plans. Instead, she fussed with him about reading the papers in bed, soiling their sheets with those poorly printed, foreign tabloids. "*The Times* is not that bad!" she'd claim if her husband tried to humor her by saying they shared the same dirty habit.

The minute Carlos saw his wife and daughter filing in, he put his paper down, and his face brightened as if at long last his wife had delivered the son, and that was the news she was bringing him. His teeth were already grinning from the glass of water next to his bedside lamp, so he lisped when he said, "Eh-speech, eh-speech!"

"It is so beautiful, Cuco," Laura coached him, turning the sound on his TV off. She sat down at the foot of the bed. Yoyo stood before both of them, blocking their view of the soldiers in helicopters landing amid silenced gun reports and explosions. A few weeks ago it had been the shores of the Dominican Republic. Now it was the jungles of Southeast Asia they were saving. Her mother gave her the nod to begin reading.

Yoyo didn't need much encouragement. She put her nose to the fire, as her mother would have said, and read from start to finish without looking up. When she concluded, she was a little embarrassed at the pride she took in her own words. She pretended to quibble with a phrase or two, then looked questioningly to her mother. Laura's face was radiant. Yoyo turned to share her pride with her father.

The expression on his face shocked both mother and daughter. Carlos's toothless mouth had collapsed into a dark zero. His eyes bored into Yoyo, then shifted to Laura. In barely audible Spanish, as if secret microphones or informers were all about, he whispered to his wife, "You will permit her to read *that*?"

Laura's eyebrows shot up, her mouth fell open. In the old country, any whisper of a challenge to authority could bring the secret police in their black V.W.'s. But this was America. People could say what they thought. "What is wrong with her speech?" Laura questioned him.

"What ees wrrrong with her eh-speech?" Carlos wagged his head at her. His anger was always more frightening in his broken English. As if he had mutilated the language in his fury—and now there was nothing to stand between them and his raw, dumb anger. "What is wrong? I will tell you what is wrong. It show no gratitude. It is boastful. *I celebrate myself? The best student learns to destroy the teacher?*" He mocked Yoyo's plagiarized words. "That is insubordinate.[2] It is improper. It is disrespecting of her teachers—" In his anger he had forgotten his fear of lurking spies: each wrong he voiced was a decibel[3] higher than the last outrage. Finally, he shouted at Yoyo, "As your father, I forbid you to make that eh-speech!"

Diego Rivera, *Tina Modotti*, 1927

Laura leapt to her feet, a sign that *she* was about to deliver her own speech. She was a small woman, and she spoke all her pronouncements standing up, either for more projection or as a carry-over from her girlhood in convent schools where one asked for, and literally, took the floor in order to speak. She stood by Yoyo's side, shoulder to shoulder. They looked down at Carlos. "That is no tone of voice—" she began.

But now, Carlos was truly furious. It was bad enough that his daughter was rebelling, but here was his own wife joining forces with her. Soon he would be surrounded by a houseful of independent American women. He too leapt from the bed, throwing off his covers. The Spanish newspapers flew across the room. He snatched the speech out of Yoyo's hands, held it before the girl's wide eyes, a vengeful, mad look in his own, and then once, twice, three, four, countless times, he tore the speech into shreds.

"Are you crazy?" Laura lunged at him. "Have you gone mad? That is her speech for tomorrow you have torn up!"

"Have *you* gone mad?" He shook her away. "You were going to let her read that . . . that insult to her teachers?"

---

2 insubordinate (in' sə bôr′ d'n it) disobedient
3 decibel (des′ ə bel′) a numerical measure of the loudness of sound

"Insult to her teachers!" Laura's face had crumpled up like a piece of paper. On it was written a love note to her husband, an unhappy, haunted man. "This is America, Papi, America! You are not in a savage country anymore!"

Meanwhile, Yoyo was on her knees, weeping wildly, collecting all the little pieces of her speech, hoping that she could put it back together before the assembly tomorrow morning. But not even a sibyl[4] could have made sense of those tiny scraps of paper. All hope was lost. "He broke it, he broke it," Yoyo moaned as she picked up a handful of pieces.

Probably, if she had thought a moment about it, she would not have done what she did next. She would have realized her father had lost brothers and friends to the dictator Trujillo. For the rest of his life, he would be haunted by blood in the streets and late night disappearances. Even after all these years, he cringed if a black Volkswagen passed him on the street. He feared anyone in uniform: the meter maid giving out parking tickets, a museum guard approaching to tell him not to get too close to his favorite Goya.

On her knees, Yoyo thought of the worst thing she could say to her father. She gathered a handful of scraps, stood up, and hurled them in his face. In a low, ugly whisper, she pronounced Trujillo's hated nickname: "Chapita! You're just another Chapita!"

It took Yoyo's father only a moment to register the loathsome nickname before he came after her. Down the halls they raced, but Yoyo was quicker than he and made it into her room just in time to lock the door as her father threw his weight against it. He called down curses on her head, ordered her on his authority as her father to open that door! He throttled that doorknob, but all to no avail. Her mother's love of gadgets saved Yoyo's hide that night. Laura had hired a locksmith to install good locks on all the bedroom doors after the house had been broken into once while they were away. Now if burglars broke in again, and the family were at home, there would be a second round of locks for the thieves to contend with.

"Lolo," she said, trying to calm him down. "Don't you ruin my new locks."

Finally he did calm down, his anger spent. Yoyo heard their footsteps retreating down the hall. Their door clicked shut. Then, muffled voices, her mother's rising in anger, in persuasion, her father's deeper murmurs of explanation and self-defense. The house fell silent a moment, before Yoyo heard, far off, the gun blasts and explosions, the serious, self-important voices of newscasters reporting their TV war.

A little while later, there was a quiet knock at Yoyo's door, followed by a tentative attempt at the doorknob. "Cuquita?"

4 sibyl (sib' 'l) a fortune teller

her mother whispered. "Open up, Cuquita."

"Go away," Yoyo wailed, but they both knew she was glad her mother was there, and needed only a moment's protest to save face.

Together they concocted a speech: two brief pages of stale compliments and the polite commonplaces on teachers, a speech wrought by necessity and without much invention by mother and daughter late into the night on one of the pads of paper Laura had once used for her own inventions. After it was drafted, Laura typed it up while Yoyo stood by, correcting her mother's misnomers[5] and mis-sayings.

5 misnomers (mis nō′ mərz) errors in naming persons or places

Adrián Luis González, Painted pottery typewriter, c. 1980

Yoyo came home the next day with the success story of the assembly. The nuns had been flattered, the audience had stood up and given "our devoted teachers a standing ovation," what Laura had suggested they do at the end of the speech.

She clapped her hands together as Yoyo recreated the moment. "I stole that from your father's speech, remember? Remember how he put that in at the end?" She quoted him in Spanish, then translated for Yoyo into English.

That night, Yoyo watched him from the upstairs hall window, where she'd retreated the minute she heard his car pull up in front of the house. Slowly, her father came up the driveway, a grim expression on his face as he grappled with a large, heavy cardboard box. At the front door, he set the package down carefully and patted all his pockets for his house keys. (If only he'd had Laura's ticking key chain!) Yoyo heard the snapping open of locks downstairs. She listened as he struggled to maneuver the box through the narrow doorway. He called her name several times, but she did not answer him.

"My daughter, your father, he love you very much," he explained from the bottom of the stairs. "He just want to protect you." Finally, her mother came up and pleaded with Yoyo to go down and reconcile[6] with him. "Your father did not mean to harm. You must pardon him. Always it is better to let bygones be forgotten, no?"

Downstairs, Yoyo found her father setting up a brand new electric typewriter on the kitchen table. It was even better than her mother's. He had outdone himself with all the extra features: a plastic carrying case with Yoyo's initials decaled below the handle, a brace to lift the paper upright while she typed, an erase cartridge, an automatic margin tab, a plastic hood like a toaster cover to keep the dust away. Not even her mother could have invented such a machine!

But Laura's inventing days were over just as Yoyo's were starting up with her school-wide success. Rather than the rolling suitcase everyone else in the family remembers, Yoyo thinks of the speech her mother wrote as her last invention. It was as if, after that, her mother had passed on to Yoyo her pencil and pad and said, "Okay, Cuquita, here's the buck. You give it a shot."

---

6 reconcile (rek′ ən sĭl′) to make up; to settle a disagreement

Linking Writing and Literature

Readers Respond to the Model

How does Julia Alvarez use characters and conflict to make her narrative effective?

Explore Julia Alvarez's story by answering these questions. Then read what other students liked about Alvarez's narrative.

1. What is the basic conflict in Alvarez's narrative? What background information does the author provide to set up this conflict and make it appear more realistic?

2. Choose a character that you particularly liked in the story. Explain how Alvarez's description of this character contributes to the narrative.

3. Alvarez wrote this story in the third person. Analyze how this point of view affects the story. How would the story have changed if the author had told it in the first person?

My favorite character was Laura. I really enjoyed her enthusiasm for her daughter's speech and how she stood up to her husband, a forbidden act in the Dominican Republic. The author set up the conflict by telling how the family's life had been in the Dominican Republic and then contrasting that culture with the American culture.

I would have written the story in first person. Maybe the author wrote it in third person because it was based on a personal experience and brought back too many memories, so she had to distance herself by writing in third person.
Rachel Hansen

My favorite character was Laura, the mother, because she was kind-hearted and open-minded. She reminded me of my mother. The writer made Yoyo's mother seem real by making her passionate. The scene I remembered most clearly was when the father ripped up Yoyo's speech. His reaction seemed so unjust and unfair.
Maritza Pagán

Unit 4 Review

Reflecting on the Unit

Summarize what you learned in this unit by answering the following questions.

- What are the basic elements of narrative writing?

- What is the role of conflict in a plot?

- What purposes do dialogue and anecdotes serve in a narrative?

- What are the three narrative points of view and the characteristics of each?

- What are some important elements and techniques in writing a sports narrative? In writing about suspense?

Adding to Your Portfolio

Choose a selection for your portfolio.
Look over the narrative writing you have done during this unit. Select a completed piece of writing to put into your portfolio. The piece that you choose should show some or all of the following:

- believable situations and characters
- clear, realistic dialogue
- a clear sequence of events

Reflect on your choice.
Attach a note to the piece you chose, explaining briefly why you chose it and what you learned from writing it.

Set goals
How can you improve your writing? What skill will you focus on the next time you write?

Writing Across the Curriculum

Make a Literature connection.
Think about Julia Alvarez's story from *How the García Girls Lost Their Accents.* What other short stories have you recently read and enjoyed that involved conflict? Choose one of these stories and write a paragraph or two about it, narrating the basic conflict and explaining how the conflict was resolved.

You may wish to share your completed piece with a small group or with the whole class. Consider setting up a book and story display so that students can read each other's recommended stories.

Expository Writing in the Real World

Winckler Tracks CACTUS

F O C U S: The expository writer informs and explains and must keep in mind what the audience needs to know.

The day of the big cactus hunt started early, at 4:30 A.M. actually, when a group of Cassin's kingbirds set up a racket outside Suzanne Winckler's tent. "I lay there thinking how they sounded like a pack of overindulged miniature poodles . . . ," she later wrote.

Annoying as they were, the kingbirds provided the perfect indecorous start to a slightly wacky day in nature study: the first and perhaps the only big day in cactus.

Big day? Winckler, a freelance writer and passionate bird watcher, got the idea from the big day tradition in the bird world. In bird watching a "big day" means choosing teams, heading into the field, and trying to spot as many feathered species as possible in 24 hours. "I wanted to take that idea, poke a little fun at it, and apply it to another organism, in this case cactus," she explained. For Winckler, this particular big day would result in a piece of writing published in a national magazine.

"I selected cacti as my subject because I love them, although I didn't know a great deal about them," Winckler said. "I also love the landscape they're in and the fact that they're sort of the antithesis of birds: they don't fly, and except for their gorgeous flowers, they're retiring. I was also attracted by the strong conservation angle, the greedy way

Suzanne Winckler,
Freelance writer

Writing the Cactus Story

Prewriting	Drafting	Revising/Editing
Stalking the Facts	Crafting the Story	Sorting the Prickly Details

> *"I started out by watching birds, and then I followed birds into nature and found a larger, more complicated world there—a world that is being compromised by our behavior. I wanted to write about that."*
>
> —Suzanne Winckler

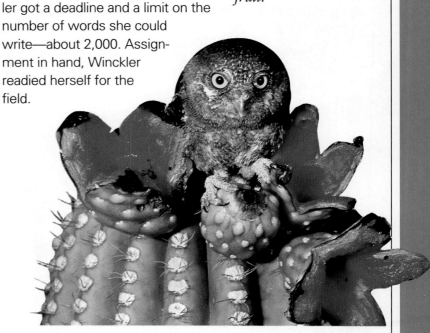

An elf owlet sits on a saguaro cactus that blooms with red, edible fruit.

people will go in and steal these cacti. I wanted to make a point about that."

Winckler's first step was to approach Dr. Allan Zimmerman to see if he'd participate in her wry adventure. "Allan is one of the premier taxonomists in the world of cactus," Winckler explained, "but he's also an avid birder, so he immediately understood what the joke was."

Then Winckler called an editor she knew at *Audubon,* an environmental magazine, and talked the idea through, a common practice for her. With the go-ahead, Winck-

ler got a deadline and a limit on the number of words she could write—about 2,000. Assignment in hand, Winckler readied herself for the field.

Prewriting

STALKING THE FACTS

The setting for Winckler's big day was, Big Bend, a vast desert area in southwest Texas. In this region of varied soils and terrains, the team could find the biggest number of species in the world with the least amount of driving. Winckler staged her big day over a long weekend and invited Zimmerman and three other biologists.

On the day of the hunt, the team started out before daylight and worked intensely until after dark. They searched dry arroyos, grassy pastures, and searing desert flats, using the characteristic field posture of the cactologist—running around in circles with heads bowed in close exploration. In the end, they got better acquainted with 43 species, from chollas and prickly pears to living rocks and barrel cacti.

For Winckler, the day was a juggling act—stalking rare cacti with the team, then stepping back to record the experience as a writer for a magazine. Winckler jotted information in a hard-bound record book. She also sketched all the cacti and asked Zimmerman to tell her their scientific names.

When Winckler got back home, she interviewed several more cactus experts by phone. "I talked to some people who not only grow rare cacti but are also involved in the legal aspects of protecting rare species. I used that information as background—as a larger landscape to set this piece in."

Next Winckler organized her notes and transcribed tapes from a friend who had carried a recorder on the hunt. Because the article would be short and personal, Winckler didn't develop an outline as she does for longer stories. Instead she mentally mapped out a rough structure for the piece.

Southwest Texas

NEW MEXICO

Pecos R.

TEXAS

• Odessa

• Fort Stockton

Marathon

• Sanderson

Rio Grande

• Del Rio

Big Bend National Park

Eagle Pass

MEXICO

These pages of Winckler's journal reveal some of her detailed notes.

top snatch"

(Asclepia) -
(Esclepia) -   Funnastrum.

turning
Esclepia   dusky pink

pale pink

Two-leaf senna - yellow flower
Cassia rhoemini

- leaf angel wing like

P.P. seedlings starts out cylindrical

(926.4 - pottseii)

Drafting

CRAFTING THE STORY

With her rough plan clearly in mind, Winckler "sat down, took a deep breath, and started writing." It would take her about five mornings at the computer to craft the story.

Winckler led off her story with the noisy kingbirds. "I wanted to emphasize that what I was picking up on in the landscape was birds—not cacti—and the sense that it was an incredible experience in the tent. I think that not many people are aware of how alive the world is at unexpected hours of the day," she said. "I also didn't want anyone to think I was an expert on cacti, because I wasn't."

From there, Winckler worked to entertain readers, teach them about Big Bend and rare cacti, and leave them caring about the place and its garden of obscure, strange plants. How did she do it?

By comparing unfamiliar cacti to everyday things, Winckler helped readers experience the spiny plants firsthand. Chollas, readers learned, "grow out on the desert like enormous candelabras," while *Echinocereus viridiflorus davisii* look like "a tiny hairball." A blooming *Coryphantha vivipara* smelled like "floor polish" to Winckler, old tuna-fish cans to someone else.

With all her descriptions, Winckler resisted the urge to go overboard. "In describing an organism, a landscape, or an organism in a landscape, you must not get carried away in a purple sense," she said. "I mean you shouldn't be too flowery, too cute, too gorgeous for what the situation really is."

As a nature writer, Winckler also stressed the importance of going beyond beautiful description. "It's very easy to love nature and get sentimental about it," she said. "You can use description to get readers involved in an expository article. But you can't just ride on that. You have to introduce the science of nature so people will understand how things function in the larger planetary sense."

There are about sixty species of cactus in west Texas out of a family total of two or three thousand. Some of them, like the chollas, which grow out on the desert like enormous candelabras, are quite common and widespread, while other species exhibit a fierce partiality to small and scattered plots of certain soils. Needless to say these finicky ones are, first, rare and, second, highly prized by cactus fanciers, a situation that has helped put them on that old proverbial brink. One finds these rare cacti by knowing something about the Mix-

Even though Winckler conveys much technical information about cacti in her article, she makes the subject lively and enjoyable through her first-person point of view and informal style.

To convey scientific information, Winckler developed simple, clear examples. For instance, she pointed out how every cactus is adapted to a special location and soil: "We drove hither and yon that day from a hummock of limestone to a hill of gypsum, each of which harbored its own brand of cactus."

Winckler closed her story with an update on laws protecting cacti. Though far from perfect, Winckler explained, the laws have had some effect. "I am told that cacti are no longer leaving the Trans Pecos by the tons as they used to," she wrote. That was good news for Winckler—and readers, newly concerned about *E. v. davisii* and all the others.

Revising/Editing

SORTING THE PRICKLY DETAILS

Once Winckler finished her first draft, she began to revise—adding some details, deleting other information. She also finished working on her sentence structure. "I spend a lot of time writing a sentence and then turning it on its head, putting something in the middle. I play at it a lot."

That kind of effort resulted in strong, clear sentences, like the one Winckler used to begin a paragraph on pink, neon-colored cactus flowers. "One complaint I have about birds is that too few of them are pink," she wrote.

Once Winckler's editor read the story, she had relatively few changes to suggest because the story had little complex detail and touched on no major legal issues. Most of Winckler's larger pieces do take more editing and fact checking, however, something she appreciates. "I wish I were edited more heavily," Winckler observed. "The world needs more editors. I'm aware of how much other people can help your writing."

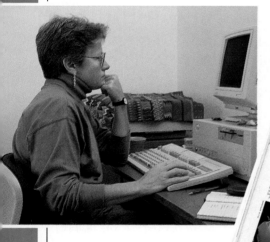

Winckler loves working at her computer, where she plays with the language, revising and editing each sentence until it's just what she wants.

Responding to the Case Study

1. Discussion

Discuss these questions about Suzanne Winckler's writing.

- How did Winckler gather information for her expository article about nature?
- What were Winckler's purposes in writing the article?
- What were two strategies Winckler used to make scientific information clear to her readers?

2. Expository Writing

Write a short research report.

In a group of three or four, choose a natural area that is threatened in some way. Explore the natural systems at work there and how they are threatened. List research questions in three or four categories, such as how the ecosystem works, what threatens it, and why it should be saved. Have each group member research one set of questions and write a 500- to 1000-word report. Pool your information and present a report to the class.

Grammar Link

Make subject and verb agree in an inverted sentence.

In inverted sentences, the subject follows the verb:

*There **are** about sixty **species** of cactus in west Texas. . . .*

An inverted sentence may also begin with a prepositional phrase:

*On a saguaro cactus **sits** an **elf owlet**.*

Find the simple subject in each sentence below. Then write the verb that agrees with the subject.

1. Outside Winckler's tent (scream, screams) the annoying kingbirds.
2. Here (come, comes) Zimmerman.
3. In southwestern Texas (grow, grows) many kinds of cacti.
4. There (was, were) cactuses Zimmerman had never heard of before.
5. There (is, are) similarities between bird watching and cactus watching.

See Lesson 16.3, pages 574–575.

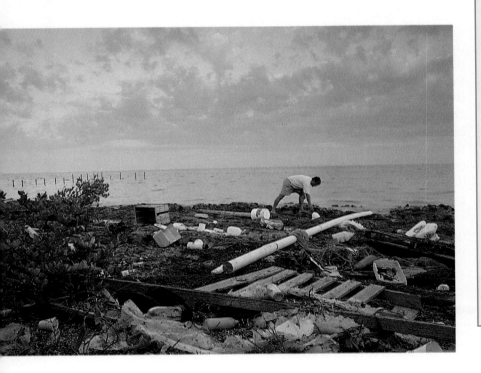

Expository Writing
Explaining and Informing

Expository writing is writing that explains and informs. In the model below, a science writer explains what really happens when a person gets out of bed.

Literature Model

Bodanis introduces the cause of the surprising chain of tiny, imperceptible events that follows the simple act of getting out of bed.

Whack thump bam! The man's foot extends out of bed and lands on the floor. The floorboards jam down and their vibrations travel sideways like pond waves to the wall. The whole house compresses in the new loading—bricks where the floor fits into the wall shrinking smaller by 1/100,000 inch from the weight.

The writer uses examples to make his point memorable.

Any impact that doesn't get lost in the walls stays quivering in the floor. The chest of drawers starts lifting up and down, as does the bed, the chair, the table with its plant on top, the stack of magazines and Sunday papers in the corner, and even the old coffee cup left down on the floor. All lift up and bounce down, rebound up and crash down again as the floor reverberates to get rid of its buzzing energy. In a particularly energetic leap out of bed this bouncing of furniture can be seen (lampshades especially are prone to being knocked over in such moments), but even with a softer landing the furniture shaking takes place.

Then the second foot touches down, the waker stands up, and he steps to the double-glazed window to see what is happening outside.

David Bodanis, *The Secret House*

The Nature of Expository Writing

Bodanis's explanation of the strange and jarring events caused by stepping out of bed is an example of expository writing. The student model below shows another type of expository writing. It describes the step-by-step process of a flower sprouting, growing, and blooming. Although there are different kinds of expository writing, all writers of exposition share one goal: to present a clear, concise explanation that readers will find interesting and informative.

Vocabulary
Revising Tip

As you revise, make your explanations livelier and more informative by replacing general verbs with more precise action verbs. Bodanis, for example, uses *bounce, reverberates,* and *rebound* in his explanation. See Lesson 10.3, pages 414–422.

Student Model

The flower, one of nature's many miracles, is created through a series of complex steps. With an embryo, a supply of stored food, and a protective covering, the seed begins the process. Most seeds remain dormant at first, usually because conditions are not favorable for growth. Seeds have been known to stay dormant from one week to fifty years and still germinate properly. Germination occurs when there is an abundant supply of water, an adequate amount of oxygen, and the proper temperatures. Crucial to the plant's life, water begins the next step in the process. The seed absorbs large amounts of water, causing the protective coating to soften. The internal tissues then swell and break through the coating. This new life, this plant, immediately begins to burn food, and it produces the energy necessary for growth. The vulnerable plant now becomes susceptible to sunlight. Too much or too little can harm it. However, the sun helps make the food for the plant to burn and receive energy. This process continues even after the first leaves develop. The plant grows stronger and more mature each day. Finally, the full-grown plant is ready to receive its crowning glory—the flower.

Billy McKnight, Jefferson Davis High School, Montgomery, Alabama

McKnight introduces this paragraph with a clear statement of what he will explain.

McKnight ties his process explanation together with transitions that show chronological order. What are some transitions that he uses?

Journal Writing

Look through some books and magazines for three expository paragraphs on different topics—for example, the development of a frog or the construction of a house. In your journal briefly explain why each is an expository paragraph.

Drafting Tip

For help with drafting a topic sentence, see the chart on this page and Lesson 2.5, page 80.

The Varieties of Expository Writing

The essay is one of the most common forms of expository writing. Usually, it consists of an introduction, body, and conclusion. The **introduction** includes a thesis statement—a one-sentence summary of your purpose for writing. The **body** consists of one or more paragraphs of details that support the thesis. The **conclusion** summarizes or gives the implications of what you've said in your essay.

You probably use other forms of expository writing quite often without even realizing it. You are using expository writing if you write out instructions for a neighbor on taking care of your cat while you are on vacation or if you jot down directions for a friend.

The chart below presents the various kinds of expository writing, the basic purpose of each kind, and an example of each. While each variety has a distinct purpose, you can use two or more varieties in combination to explain and inform.

Kinds of Expository Writing		
Kind	**Basic Purpose**	**Example**
Definition	To define a term or give the basic tenets of a theory	A supernova is a star that explodes, becoming extremely bright before fading and leaving a huge cloud of dust and gas.
Process	To give the steps in a process or explain a sequence of events	To locate their prey, bats use a process called echolocation, in which they send out high-pitched sound waves. These waves bounce off insects and echo back to the bat.
Cause and Effect	To explain how or why one or more events or actions cause other things to happen	The rubbing and grinding of the Earth's crustal plates against one another causes earthquakes.
Classification	To break down a broad topic into narrower categories	There are two main types of whales: toothed whales and baleen whales.
Comparison-Contrast	To discuss similarities in and differences between two related phenomena or events	Venus's flytraps and pitcher plants are both meat-eating plants. Venus's flytraps trap insects in their leaves. Pitcher plants capture insects that drown in their jug-shaped leaves.

Write an Expository Paragraph

Pick a simple process or event to explain or define. Be sure that you are familiar enough with the parts of it to explain it clearly. Write a paragraph or two about it.

- Give a clear, concise explanation.
- Use a clear opening and conclusion.
- In the body, use details to support your thesis.

> **PURPOSE** To explain the details of a process or event
> **AUDIENCE** Your teacher and classmates
> **LENGTH** 1–2 paragraphs

Cross-Curricular: Art

The fresco on this page is *The Making of a Fresco Showing the Building of a City* by Diego Rivera. Examine each section of the fresco carefully. Then write a short paper explaining the processes that the fresco illustrates. Organize the parts of your explanation in some reasonable order.

Grammar Link

Use precise verbs.

In both models the writers use precise action verbs to make their explanations vivid as well as informative. Use precise verbs to revise the sentences below.

1. The Aries spacecraft is off the Cape Canaveral launch pad.
2. Crowds look at the craft atop its pillar of flame.
3. In the third booster stage, the capsule goes from Earth's orbit.
4. Through their porthole, the astronauts see the red planet Mars.
5. Endless plains and jagged chasms are on Mars.

See Lesson 10.3, pages 414–422.

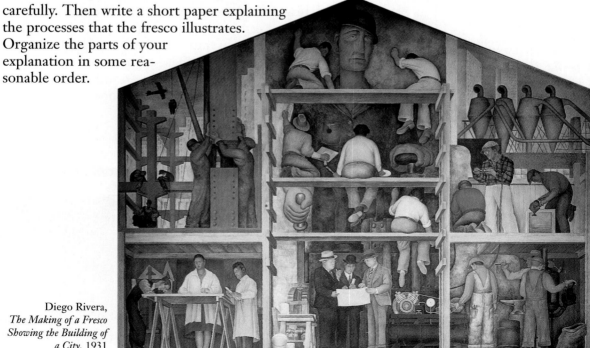

Diego Rivera,
The Making of a Fresco Showing the Building of a City, 1931

Expository Writing
Going into Detail

Supporting details are essential elements in expository writing. Note how a science writer uses statistics and specific examples to explain the relationship between scents and human behavior.

Literature Model

> We have already developed a system to control the environment by fragrance," says Junichi Yagi, vice president of S. Technology Center-America, a subsidiary of Shimizu, Japan's largest architectural, engineering, and construction firm. . . . Experiments in Japan with thirteen keypunch operators, monitored eight hours a day for thirty days, showed that the average number of errors per hour dropped by 21 percent when office air was scented with lavender (it reduces stress) and by 33 percent when laced with jasmine (it induces relaxation); a stimulating lemon scent reduced errors by 54 percent. . . .
>
> Shimizu researchers also find that orange, peppermint, eucalyptus, chamomile, and Japanese cypress are soothing, while scarlet sage and rosemary are stimulating. (I would add Play-Doh and Rockin' Roger's Bar-B-Q Sauce to the stimulating list.)
>
> Judith Stone, *Light Elements*

Here Judith Stone provides statistics to illustrate her point.

Stone adds two scents to the list. Which smells might you add?

Kinds of Supporting Details

Supporting details give expository writing its strength. Note the types of supporting details listed in the chart.

Prewriting Tip

To help come up with supporting details, you can brainstorm with other students. To learn more about brainstorming, see Lesson 2.2, page 66.

Supporting Details for Expository Writing	
Kinds	**Example of Use in Exposition**
Facts	Alligators live largely in fresh water, while crocodiles live mostly in salt water or in at least slightly salty water.
Statistics	The world's largest tree is a giant sequoia called the General Sherman tree. It measures 101.5 feet at the base, is 272.4 feet tall, and weighs about 12,334,000 pounds.
Examples/ Incidents	The chimpanzee is an example of an animal that makes and uses tools. Chimpanzees cut pieces of grass to specific lengths for fishing termites out of termite mounds.
Sensory details	The aurora borealis appears as a glimmering curtain of light flashing in the night sky.
Reasons	One reason some people think penguins are mammals rather than birds is that their feathers are short and fluffy and, from a distance, resemble hair.

Journal Writing

Read a magazine or newspaper article. Next, without reviewing the article, list in your journal the supporting details you recall. What makes these details memorable? Write your ideas.

How to Select Supporting Details

Common sense will help you select supporting details. For example, if you are explaining a process, you will want to present all the steps. The following factors are the most important for selecting types of supporting details for a particular exposition:

- the type of exposition you are writing
- your purpose for writing, especially your secondary purpose (see examples of secondary purpose in the chart on page 226)
- the level of knowledge or expertise of your audience

The chart shows how to analyze key factors in selecting appropriate supporting details for two kinds of exposition.

Using Supporting Details		
Factor	Situation #1	Situation #2
Main purpose and type of your exposition	To explain the cause and effects of a natural phenomenon	To compare two theories about a natural phenomenon
Your secondary purpose	To interest your audience in the topic	To show your knowledge of the theories
Level of knowledge of your audience	Audience unfamiliar with the topic	Most of targeted audience (scientists) familiar with the topic
Kinds of supporting details you might rely on most heavily	Incidents and interesting sensory details	Facts and statistics that provide convincing support

How to Organize Supporting Details

How you organize your supporting details depends in part on the type of exposition you are writing. For example, if you are writing about a cause and its effects, you might present the least important effect first and the most important effect last.

Model

In what order does the writer list supporting details?

The writer concludes with a prime example of one urban gardener.

Urban gardens—plots overflowing with juicy red tomatoes, shiny green cukes, crisp beans, and myriad flowers—have been popping up in greater numbers all over our neighborhood since spring. You've probably seen them in backyards, empty lots, even on rooftops. Rising vegetable prices, up 35 percent from last year, are surely one reason behind the spread of these garden plots. Even more important reasons include the desire for healthful, pesticide-free vegetables and for the better taste of the home-grown vegetables. Delia Jackson exemplifies this trend. She even took a course called City Gardens at the local community center. Soon after the class ended, she began a roof garden atop the high-rise where she lives. "My friends joked about it at first," she says, "but now the same ones are coming over for my vine-ripened tomatoes."

Write a Background Information Article

Rearrange and use the following details to write an explanation of the term *hurricane*. Plan your writing as a background information piece for your community newspaper. In addition to explaining what a hurricane is, you want to impress the audience with a hurricane's great destructive power.

1. In 1992 hurricane Andrew hit southwestern Florida, causing $20 billion in damage and killing at least 38 people.
2. The winds of a hurricane can exceed 75 miles per hour.
3. Hurricanes develop over warm tropical ocean waters.
4. The winds and rain produce massive waves, called a storm surge, which bring floods.
5. A hurricane is a powerful, swirling storm.
6. The most destructive part of the hurricane is the area of wall clouds that surround the eye, where winds may reach 150 miles per hour.
7. A hurricane may cover an area of 200 to 300 miles in diameter.
8. At the center of a hurricane is the eye, an area of calm about 20 miles in diameter.

- Choose memorable statistics and sensory details to get the attention of your audience.
- Define new terms for a general audience.
- Order your details for their best effect.

PURPOSE To explain what a hurricane is and to describe its destructive power
AUDIENCE Newspaper readers
LENGTH 2–3 paragraphs

Grammar Link

Use commas correctly in a series.

In the literature model, note how Judith Stone uses commas to separate items in a series.

Rewrite the following sentences, adding commas to separate three or more words or phrases.

1. Peppermint orange jasmine and chamomile are scents commonly used in teas.
2. Popular dessert coffees include those flavored with hazelnut Dutch chocolate or Swiss mocha.
3. She ground the coffee beans scooped them into the filter added four cups of water and turned on the coffeemaker.
4. Coffee is a tree or shrub native to tropical Africa Asia and Central and South America.
5. Coffee trees grow about fifteen feet tall have long leaves and produce white or cream flowers.

See Lesson 21.5, page 700.

Cooperative Learning

You need to explain a natural process, such as soil erosion, for a Science Room reference notebook. Work with a small group. Together, make a list of the supporting details that you will use to explain the process, and then write a draft of your explanation. Your audience will be students who need help to understand a process, so write your exposition as clearly as possible and define difficult terms.

Expository Writing
Explaining How To . . .

A "how to" paper, a common form of expository writing, is used to teach a skill or just to share knowledge. Usually the writer presents the instructions as a series of steps. What process is Patrick McManus explaining in the model below?

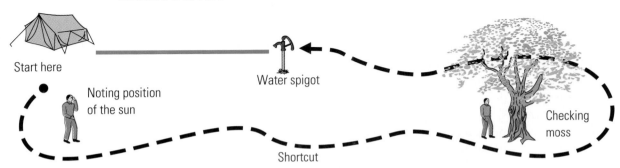

Start here

Noting position of the sun

Water spigot

Shortcut

Checking moss

Literature Model

In his introductory sentence, McManus identifies the process he will be explaining.

N ow how should you go about getting lost? . . . If you are camped in a public campground, simply say that you are going to take a shortcut to the communal spigot [water faucet] to fill the water bucket. . . . Shortcuts rank number one among ways to get lost quickly and thoroughly. . . . Before starting your shortcut, take careful note of the position of the sun. This will give the impression that you know what you're doing. . . . [Also,] always study on which side of the trees the moss is growing. Guides and other experienced woodsmen are fond of giving this advice, because looking at moss helps even them to get lost.

McManus gives tips to help a camper get lost. Have you gotten lost anywhere besides the woods? What tips would you give to get lost where you did?

Patrick McManus, *Rubber Legs and White Tail-Hairs*

How do you steer a canoe? How do bees make honey? Any process can be explained clearly, step by step.

Think About Your Purpose

Sometimes you explain a process in order to teach a skill, such as how to feed a pet snake.

Sometimes you may explain a process just to share knowledge, for example, how fireflies make their flashing lights.

Suppose you wanted to explain how to bathe a dog. During prewriting, list all the steps in a chart similar to this one.

Grammar
Editing Tip

Some transitions useful in process writing are *after, always, as soon as, before, first, following, in order to, now, soon, so that, then, until.* To learn when to punctuate these transitions, see Lesson 21.5, page 697.

Planning a "How to" Paper

1. Choose topic: how to bathe a dog.

2. Define audience: first-time dog owners.

3. Gather information: read manuals, interview, observe.

4. List steps of the process in chronological order.

a. Set up safe bathing area—rubber mat in the tub, nonskid rug on floor.

b. Gather shampoo, sponge, bucket or shower head, towels, comb or brush, and other equipment you need.

c. If you don't have a hand-held shower head, fill tub half-full with lukewarm water.

d. Plug dog's ears with cotton to prevent water from entering. (Remember to take cotton out after bath.)

e. Wet dog all over with lukewarm water.

f. Shampoo dog, using your fingers to scrub.

g. Rinse dog with water, using bucket or shower head.

h. Wash dog's face with sponge dipped in clear water.

i. Let dog shake off excess water.

j. Rub dog dry with towels, or use hair dryer.

k. Comb dog when coat is dry.

5. Note any special instructions.

6. Tell result of process: clean, happy dog.

Journal Writing

In your journal list five possible topics for a process explanation. Then write a brief statement explaining whether the purpose of each would be to teach a skill or simply to share knowledge.

Write About a Process

You can use the chart you made during the prewriting stage to help you write the first draft of your explanation. First, make sure the steps in the process are clear. You may need to combine steps for simplicity, as illustrated in the diagram below. Next, show the relationships between these steps with appropriate transitional words and phrases. The diagram indicates some transitions you might use to create a smooth chronological flow.

In your **introduction** state the process you are explaining and the relevance of the process. This will help capture your reader's interest. Also, you can often use humor to engage your readers. In your **conclusion** emphasize the importance of the process you have explained, identifying its benefits to your audience. This will help you to leave your reader with a strong impression.

5.3 Writing Activities

Write a Brief Report

Think of something you know how to make or do that you could demonstrate to the class. Write a short paper about the process. Be prepared to give the demonstration in class.

- List all the materials you'll need.
- List all the steps in order.
- Use transitional words and phrases.
- Include an introduction and conclusion.

PURPOSE To explain a process that involves a demonstration
AUDIENCE Your teacher and classmates
LENGTH 1–2 paragraphs

Cross-Curricular: Science

Think of a process you have learned about in your science class. Write an explanation of the process for students in a fifth-grade science class. Assume that the students have little or no background knowledge about the subject. Make sure to define all the unfamiliar terms you use. Use short, simple sentences that fifth-graders will be able to understand. Use transitions so that the readers can understand where they are in the process. If you wish, include a diagram or other illustration to help explain the process. Then present your paper to a fifth-grade science class.

Cross-Curricular: Health

Think of a process you have learned about in your health class. Write an explanation of the process as you would for an essay test given by your health teacher. Use transitions to show your teacher that you understand the steps in the process and the order in which they occur.

Grammar Link

Do not shift verb tenses unnecessarily.

Rewrite the following steps, using consistent verb tenses throughout the instructions.

How to Start Up the Computer
1. Found the ON and OFF power switch. This switch was somewhere on the monitor—at the bottom front, on one side, or in the back.
2. Move the power switch to the ON position.
3. After a few seconds the monitor screen will brighten.
4. Adjust the brightness control, usually located at the side or the bottom of the monitor, if it was not set at a level you preferred.
5. From the main menu or desktop, select the software program in which you wished to work.
6. If you are inserting a diskette, make sure that you inserted the diskette with the metal end first and the side with the arrow facing up.
7. If you experienced problems starting up, ask yourself the following questions:
8. Was the computer plugged into an electrical outlet?
9. Is the ON/OFF power switch turned to the ON position?
10. Had the brightness control been properly adjusted?

See Lesson 15.6, page 556.

Expository Writing
Explaining Cause and Effect

Cause-and-effect writing helps a reader understand the relationships between events or facts. In the model below, two science writers explain the surprising effects of gravity.

Literature Model

Sagan and Druyan describe a general effect and explain its cause in the first sentence.

Sagan and Druyan use this simple comparison to help make their point.

Do you think Sagan and Druyan's hypothetical example of Mount Everest is effective? Explain why or why not.

T he Earth and the other planets tend to be almost perfect spheres because, as Newton showed, gravity is a central force—it pulls everything equally toward the center of the world, itself held together by the force of gravity. The mountains sticking up above the spherical surface of the Earth represent less of a deviation from a perfect sphere than does the layer of paint or enamel on the surface of a typical globe that represents the Earth. If you were able to pile a sizable mountain on top of Mount Everest, it would not just sit there, poking in solitary magnificence into the stratosphere. The additional weight you had added would crush the base of Everest, and the new composite mountain would collapse until it was no larger than Everest is today. The Earth's gravity severely limits how much deviation from a perfect sphere our planet is permitted.

Carl Sagan and Ann Druyan, *Comet*

The explanation in the model focuses mainly on effects. As the chart on the next page shows, cause-and-effect writing may also focus on the causes.

Earthquake: Cause and Effects

Cause

Massive plates that make up the earth's surface move, putting great pressure on the rocks at the plates' edges. Sometimes the pressure becomes too great for the rocks to bear.

Effects

Rocks along the edges break and shift when pressure becomes too great, creating an earthquake.

▼

The earthquake releases energy in the form of waves, or vibrations.

▼

The waves shake the earth's surface, buildings, and bridges, sometimes causing great damage.

Link Cause and Effect

Cause-and-effect writing explains how one event causes another. Note how each effect listed on the diagram above serves as the cause for the next effect. While some cause-and-effect writing is based on a complex series of causes and effects, some deals with only one cause and only one effect, giving a clear, detailed explanation of the relationship.

Beware of false cause-and-effect relationships. If one event follows another, the second wasn't necessarily caused by the first. Consider the sentence "The moon eclipsed the sun; then clouds covered the sky." This sentence does not show cause and effect, only sequential events. The eclipse did not cause the clouds to cover the sky.

An important way to make a true cause-and-effect relationship clear is with a thesis statement—a clear statement of your main idea—presented in a topic sentence. A thesis statement for an essay on earthquakes might be the following: "Great pressure along the edges of the earth's moving plates causes rocks to break and shift, creating an earthquake that can bring its destructive shock waves to the earth's surface."

Grammar

Drafting Tip

When writing a cause-and-effect explanation of a recurring event or a natural phenomenon such as an earthquake, use the present tense. For information on other times present tense should be used, see Lesson 15.3, pages 548–550.

Journal Writing

If you can use the word *because* to show the relationship between events or facts, the relation is causal, not just sequential. In your journal write possible causal relationships, such as effects caused by watching television or causes for earning good grades, and try the "*because* test" on them.

Organize Causes and Effects

Once you have a thesis statement, you can begin organizing your draft. You can follow either a cause-to-effect pattern or an effect-to-cause pattern. For example, you might organize a piece about the greenhouse effect by listing and explaining the many causes and concluding with the possible effects. A piece on the tides might first describe tides and the changes they bring to coastlines and then discuss their cause.

Whichever form of organization you use, you will need to connect your events, facts, and ideas with effective **transitions.** The chart below shows two types of transitions you may need to use.

Some Transitions for Cause-and-Effect Writing		
Cause and Effect	as a result because consequently	due to if, then since	so therefore thus
Degrees of Certainty	certainly likely maybe	necessarily possibly probably	undoubtedly unquestionably of course

Your cause-and-effect piece will also need an **introduction** and a **conclusion.** In your introduction you should catch the reader's attention and give your purpose. Your thesis statement can serve as the introduction. Then you can conclude by summarizing the cause-and-effect relationship or extending the information you have presented. Note the introduction, transitions, and conclusion in the selection below by Eric Koszyk.

Koszyk begins with a topic sentence that clearly states the causal relationship he plans to explain.

What are some words in addition to "believe" that Koszyk uses to stress the uncertainty of the theory?

In his conclusion Koszyk restates his cause-and-effect relationship but again stresses its uncertainty.

Student Model

*A*n ice age usually occurs every couple of million years or so, but some scientists now believe that the current warming of the earth is likely to speed up this process. They believe that the warming of the planet will melt the polar ice caps. This, then, will change the level of water in the planet's oceans, which, therefore, will change the salt composition of the oceans. This altered salt composition would bring about a change in the jet stream winds that circle the earth. And this change in the jet stream would bring about the cooling trend that could well speed up the coming of the next ice age. Some scientists disagree, but a large number of other scientists and environmentalists believe in this theory.

Eric Koszyk, Quartz Hill High School, Quartz Hill, California

5.4 Writing Activities

Write a Cause-and-Effect Paragraph

Plan and write a cause-and-effect paragraph on the relationship between hours of study and good grades, or on another cause-and-effect topic of your choice.

- Decide whether to focus on causes or effects.
- Write a clear thesis statement.
- Use appropriate transitions.
- Include an introduction and a conclusion.

PURPOSE To explain a cause-and-effect relationship

AUDIENCE Your teacher and classmates

LENGTH 1 paragraph

Cross-Curricular: Art

Study the painting below. Write a brief cause-and-effect paragraph explaining what has occurred in this scene, presenting at least two causes and two effects.

Grammar Link

Make subjects and verbs agree.

Subjects must agree with verbs no matter how many words come between them.

Rewrite the sentences below to make subjects and verbs agree.

1. According to environmentalists, current temperature changes of the earth signals the coming of the next ice age.
2. Thousands of years ago, many parts of the earth's surface was covered by ice sheets.
3. The movement of glaciers cause erosion.
4. Rocks buried in the ice scrapes and digs at the land.
5. Scientists at the local university is preparing reports on climate changes.

See 16.1, pages 571–572.

Henry O. Tanner, *After the Storm*, c. 1880

Expository Writing
Classifying a Subject

When you classify, you group items into categories based on common attributes, or qualities. Notice how loon calls are classified in the passage below.

Literature Model

What does Hubbell tell the reader in her first sentence?

Hubbell describes the hoot, the wail, the tremolo, and the yodel as the four basic types of loon calls.

What do you learn from Hubbell's conclusion?

I n recent years, loon calls have been studied by researchers and it is now generally accepted that there are at least four basic calls in the loon's vocabulary, with gradations and combinations and shading to refine the meanings. Within a family, loons call to one another with a soft hoot. The wail, the cry with which the nightly chorus commences, is used when one loon is trying to establish contact with other loons. The tremolo calls that are supposed to sound like a madman's laughter are alarm calls. . . . The yodel is the song of the male loon, a complex series of rising notes followed by an undulation [pulsating tone]; it is gorgeous to human ears but a loon uses it to define and defend his territory. Very recently, researchers have discovered that male loons' yodels are distinctive, each from the other, and can be used as aural tags to study and follow individuals.

Sue Hubbell, "For the Love of Loons," *Smithsonian* magazine

Why Do You Classify?

Classification is an effective way to organize ideas. In the diagram on page 237, one writer has classified clouds according to their general shapes. She has done so to help organize her ideas about clouds. With that type of classification, she will be able to provide a clear overview of the topic, make information accessible, and better inform or instruct her audience.

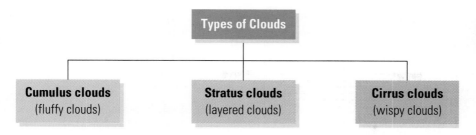

Types of Clouds

| Cumulus clouds (fluffy clouds) | Stratus clouds (layered clouds) | Cirrus clouds (wispy clouds) |

How Do You Plan a Classification?

Your most important task in planning a classification is to create meaningful categories appropriate for your purpose and audience. The chart below shows how different purposes and audiences may affect the way items are classified. Look at the common feature that ties together each category of trees in the chart.

Three Ways of Classifying Trees		
Audience	**Classification**	**Common Feature**
Scientists	• Cone-bearing trees • Seed-bearing trees • Spore-bearing trees	Methods of Reproduction
Landscape Architects	• Shade trees • Trees for windbreaks • Ornamental trees	Usefulness
Wild-food Collectors	• Trees that bear edible nuts • Trees that bear edible fruits • Trees that have edible sap	Source of food

Journal Writing

Think of a subject for which you will plan a classification, such as types of writing in your journal or types of music. In your journal create a diagram like the one at the top of this page in which you classify your subject. Make sure your categories are mutually exclusive and based on a common feature.

How Do You Write a Classification?

As you draft your classification, follow the organization shown in the chart on page 238. Study the organization of the student model that follows.

Introduction
Include a thesis statement or topic sentence and a list of categories.

Body Paragraph(s)
Identify and explain each category, one by one, and include examples.

Conclusion
Summarize your classification and its significance.

Student Model

On what feature does Arnold base the categories she introduces in her first sentence?

Wildflowers, admired for their beauty and magnificence, include flowers from woodlands, mountains, prairies, deserts, and swamps.

Woodland flowers rely on humus, the product of decaying leaves and wood, for food. Unable to grow in bright sunlight, they favor early spring for growth. Typical woodland flowers include rhododendron and violets. Mountain flowers flourish on any high mountaintop, but grow only after the ice and snow melt. Examples are alpine roses and saxifrages. Prairie flowers are voluptuous and plentiful; their bright colors represent the stereotypical wildflower.

Arnold's body paragraph includes images such as "beardtongues clothe the prairie."

Masses of globemallows, sunflowers, and beardtongues clothe the prairie. The beauty of desert flowers is only temporary, as they quickly grow and flower after infrequent rains, then wither in the blinding sun. They have thorny branches, no leaves or very few, and thick, fleshy, water-holding stems. Desert plants include octillos and cacti. Finally, swamp flowers, such as lizard's-tails and willows, love wet meadows and ponds. Others, including pitcher plants and spider lilies, thrive in marshes.

From reading her conclusion, how would you explain Arnold's own attraction to this topic?

Their simple dignity and elegance make wildflowers an unequaled natural phenomenon and a worthy topic of study.

Alli Arnold, Henry Clay High School, Lexington, Kentucky

5.5 Writing Activities

Write a Classification

Choose a group of items to classify. Select any group that interests you. You may wish to use one of the following topics: rocks and minerals; friends; movies; popular music groups; precipitation. Write a paragraph classifying the items.

- Classify the items in a way that fits your purpose and your audience.
- Include an introduction and a conclusion.

PURPOSE To classify items
AUDIENCE Your classmates; an audience of your choice
LENGTH 1 paragraph

Pablita Velarde, *Old Father Story Teller*, 1960

Grammar Link

Use specific concrete nouns.

Alli Arnold uses precise concrete nouns in her classification of wildflowers on page 238. Instead of writing that wildflowers grow in "many places," she names these places—"woodlands, mountains, prairies, deserts, and swamps."

In the sentences below, replace the underlined words with specific concrete nouns.

1. As I hiked, I heard some strange <u>sounds</u>.
2. <u>Beautiful</u> <u>flowers</u> grew wild along the trail.
3. During the storm, <u>a few pieces of camping gear</u> were damaged.
4. <u>Many things</u> in my backpack were ruined.
5. Next year, I plan to visit <u>tourist attractions</u> in Washington, D.C.

See Lesson 10.1, page 401.

Cooperative Learning

In a small group discuss the painting on this page. Have each group member then choose a different way to classify the items in the painting. Together, make a chart showing your classifications.

Expository Writing
Comparing and Contrasting

Comparing involves discussing similarities between two or more related things. Contrasting involves discussing differences between such items. In the model below, a nature writer uses comparison and contrast to present information about two extinct birds.

Literature Model

In the first sentence the writer introduces the main idea—that two related birds suffered a similar fate on Mauritius.

The Dodo was not the only pigeon to suffer extinction on Mauritius. There was also the striking crested Pigeon Hollandaise, which is commonly called the Mauritius Blue Pigeon (*Alectroenas nitidisima*). Like the Common Dodo, it was endemic [native only] to Mauritius. This exotic Blue Pigeon did not suffer from the Dodo's inability to fly, nor did it nest on the ground. It was a graceful forest bird that fed on fruit, berries and seeds. It lived in large flocks and nested communally in trees. Again, unlike the Dodo, this bird was delicious to eat. "Shooting parties" were often organized by the resident Europeans for sport and food.

How were the birds alike? How were they different?

David Day, *The Doomsday Book of Animals*

How might you compare and contrast two creatures with which you are familiar? How are a dog and a cat alike and different? What features do a goldfish and a shark have in common? How are they different?

Dodo Bird

- Flightless
- Nested on the ground
- Not good to eat
- Gawky
- Lived and nested alone

Similarities

- Members of the pigeon family
- Native only to Mauritius
- Killed off by Europeans

Mauritius Blue Pigeon

- Flying bird
- Nested in trees
- Good to eat
- Graceful
- Lived and nested in large groups

Think About Similarities and Differences

One technique you can use to explore similarities and differences between two subjects is a Venn diagram. The Venn diagram above shows the similarities and differences between the two extinct birds described in the model on page 240. To set up a Venn diagram, follow these steps:

1. Draw two intersecting circles.

2. Title the circles with the subjects to be compared.

3. List unique features of each subject.

4. List the similarities of the two subjects in the space where the circles intersect.

Vocabulary

Drafting Tip

Transitions like the following help you organize a comparison-contrast: *but, however, in the same way, like, unlike, similarly.*

Journal Writing

What are some other tools you could use to explore similarities and differences between two subjects, such as you and your best friend? In your journal try creating a chart or other tool to help you compare two subjects of your choosing.

Organize a Comparison-Contrast

Grammar

Editing Tip

When you edit your comparison-contrast, make sure that your comparisons are complete. See Lesson 18.4, page 628.

Once you have explored similarities and differences between two subjects, you can organize your comparison-contrast. The chart below shows two methods of organization: (1) by subject and (2) by feature. Notice how the writer organized the essay in the model that follows.

Comparison-Contrast: Elephants and Hippos		
By Subject	**Subject 1: Elephants** Feature A: Anatomy Feature B: Size Feature C: Habitat Feature D: Endangered	**Subject 2: Hippos** Feature A: Anatomy Feature B: Size Feature C: Habitat Feature D: Endangered
By Feature	**Feature A: Anatomy** Subject 1: Elephants Subject 2: Hippos **Feature B: Size** Subject 1: Elephants Subject 2: Hippos	**Feature C: Habitat** Subject 1: Elephants Subject 2: Hippos **Feature D: Endangered** Subject 1: Elephants Subject 2: Hippos

Model

Does the writer's use of organization by subject successfully create a vivid comparison between elephants and hippos? Explain.

T wo of the world's most wondrous and enormous animals, the elephant and the hippopotamus, may one day disappear. Just think of the majestic elephant, the largest land-dwelling animal. A typical African bull, or male, measures eleven feet tall at the shoulders and weighs about four tons. African cows, or females, and Asiatic elephants are only slightly smaller. And, as you picture an elephant, you probably think of its thick gray skin, long trunk, fan-shaped ears, and great ivory tusks. The valuable ivory of the tusks presents the greatest danger for elephants, as ivory-seeking hunters kill thousands each year.

Note the writer's use of visual details in this comparison-contrast.

Not quite as massive as the elephant, the hippo is the third largest land animal, just behind the rhino. A typical hippo weighs about 2,500 to 3,000 pounds and is about five feet tall at the shoulders. Besides its huge body, among the hippo's most recognizable features are its bulging eyes, allowing it to submerge most of its head yet still keep its eyes above water. Farmers and hunters kill many hippos each year to protect farmlands and to sell the animals' meat, hide, and tusklike ivory canine teeth.

5.6 Writing Activities

Write a Comparison-Contrast Paper

Choose a pair of places or items to compare, such as big cities and small towns, board games and video games, or another pair of your choice. Write a brief paper comparing and contrasting the items.

- Choose items that are related.
- Use a Venn diagram to clarify their similarities and differences.
- Organize your paper by comparing subjects or by comparing features.

PURPOSE To compare and contrast two items
AUDIENCE Your teacher and classmates
LENGTH 2 paragraphs

Katsushika Hokusai, *The Great Wave off Kanagawa*, c. 1830

Grammar Link

Make compound subjects and verbs agree.

When compound subjects are joined by *either . . . or* or *neither . . . nor*, the verb always agrees with the subject nearer the verb.

Rewrite each sentence below so that the compound subjects and verbs agree.

1. Neither the dodo bird nor the blue pigeon were safe from European hunters.
2. Either Mauritius or other islands in the Indian Ocean was home to the dodo.
3. Either farmers or hunters has killed the hippos for their hides and teeth.
4. Either the African bull or the Asiatic elephant weigh about four tons.
5. Neither Kenya nor other African nations protects these animals adequately.

See Lesson 16.5, page 578.

Cross-Curricular: Geography

Study the painting on this page, and look again at the painting *After the Storm* on page 235. Each depicts a different mood of the sea. Write a two to three-paragraph comparison-contrast of the two paintings in the form of a report for geography class.

Expository Writing
Writing with Graphics

Sometimes words alone can't convey enough information about a topic. Notice how the map and text work together in this magazine feature, a piece of exposition.

Literature Model

I n March 1989 the world watched in horror as the *Exxon Valdez* disgorged 10.8 million gallons of North Slope crude [oil] into the pristine waters of Prince William Sound. It was the largest spill ever off the United States. But whatever lessons may have been learned about preventing spills were not effectively applied in 1990. Hardly a week passed without news of yet another disturbing spill. The first ten months of the year saw an estimated 28 million gallons of oil discharged around the world, which makes 1990 a typical year. . . . On our oil-soaked map you'll see the spills that reached at least 10,000 gallons, whether from tanker accidents caused by human error . . . or storage tanks struck by lightning.

"Another Crude Year," *Discover*, January 1991

Why do you think the writer uses the term "oil-soaked map"?

Here the writer explains to the reader what the map shows.

Know Your Basic Options

Graphics come in four main forms: maps, diagrams, tables, and graphs. Each type can help illustrate your expository writing.

Maps A map is a graphic most commonly showing all or part of the earth's surface. Maps often show what might take many paragraphs to describe. Whenever you use a map, be sure to include its legend, which explains the map's symbols.

Diagrams Diagrams use pictures to clarify the relationship among parts of a whole or to show how something works. The diagram at the right shows how the water cycle works. Such a diagram can help your reader visualize a process.

Tables By examining the information in the rows and columns of a table, you can see how a subject changes under different conditions, such as time or location. The table on page 246, for example, compares temperature range and precipitation among four of the world's biological zones, or biomes (regions divided according to climate and soil conditions).

Graphs Often the best way to convey numerical information will be a graph. Graphs can reveal patterns of information, showing relationships among different facts or statistics. They can thus be a useful tool in comparison-contrast writing: a bar graph, for example may compare the wealth of three nations. Graphs can also show how something develops over time. The line graph at the right shows how the number of sunspots changes over 36 years.

Journal Writing

Try using a graphic to explain something about yourself, for example, your study habits, eating habits, or how your tastes have changed.

Use Graphics for Greatest Impact

Whenever you use graphics in your writing, place them and refer to them so that they make the greatest impact on the reader.

Revising Tip

As you read your first draft, check all references to graphics to be sure that they are helpful to the reader—that is, that they really add to the explanation.

Positioning Graphics   Where you place a graphic depends on the function of the graphic and your purpose for using it. For example, to capture the reader's attention and establish a basic framework, you could put a graphic at the beginning of your piece. Imagine you're writing an explanation of cells. You might use a diagram of a basic cell, with all its parts labeled, as part of the opening paragraph.

In the middle of the essay, you might include graphics that convey a great amount of information in a concise way, reinforce information, or serve as a handy reference for the reader. In the example of an essay on cells, a table showing the variation in sizes of different types of cells might appear in the middle.

At the end of your explanation, you will probably want to summarize your main points. For example, in the conclusion of an essay on cells, you could include a table comparing and contrasting plant and animal cells. Wherever and however you use graphics, you need to let the reader know why they are there and when to look at them.

Referring to Graphics   In referring to a graphic, you might simply tell the reader to look at it when the graphic helps illustrate a point you are making. For example, with a table of cell sizes, you might write, "Different kinds of cells vary in size, as shown in the table." You can also instruct the reader to use the information from a graphic in a specific way. If you were using the table below in a piece of exposition about biomes, you might tell the reader to use the table to compare the different levels of precipitation in *each biome*.

Whatever your purpose, title graphics clearly when you present more than one. In that way you will be sure that the reader is not confused and can refer to the appropriate graphic easily.

Four Biomes: Temperature and Precipitation		
Biome	**Avg. Yearly Temperature**	**Avg. Yearly Precipitation**
Deciduous forest	6°C to 28°C	75 to 125 cm
Grassland	0°C to 25°C	25 to 75 cm
Desert	24°C to 34°C	less than 25 cm
Tropical rain forest	25°C to 27°C	200 to 400 cm

5.7 Writing Activities

Write a Paragraph with a Graphic

Look through your school textbooks, or think of something you have learned about recently. How could the information be shown in a graphic? Create a graphic to show the information.

- Make a map, diagram, table, or graph.
- Write a paragraph about the subject, and in your paragraph refer to your graphic.

PURPOSE To use a graphic to show a concept
AUDIENCE Your classmates
LENGTH 1 page

COMPUTER OPTION

Some graphics can be created using your computer's word-processing program. You might also be able to use illustration software to create graphics. Experiment with different arrangements and styles to see which presents your information most clearly.

Grammar Link

Avoid using run-on sentences.

Run-on sentences occur when two or more complete sentences are written without proper punctuation between them.

Rewrite the run-on sentences below to make them grammatically correct.

1. Graphics come in four basic forms each type can enhance a piece of exposition.
2. Information in a table is organized in a concise, systematic way, it is presented in rows and columns.
3. Be sure to label all parts of your graphic clearly labels help the reader recognize and understand data.
4. Diagrams clarify relationships among parts of a whole and graphs reveal patterns of information.
5. There are many kinds of graphs, line, bar, and pictographs are among them.
6. A map needs a legend and it may need a scale, too.
7. Check all references to graphs in your writing they really add to the exposition.
8. The data in the table was easy to understand, the diagram was confusing.
9. He positioned the map in the middle of the essay and he used a table in his conclusion.
10. The water cycle is shown in the diagram you can find it on page 245.

See Lesson 13.10, pages 517–519.

Expository Writing
Writing a Feature Article

A feature story in a newspaper or magazine presents in-depth information on a topic related to a current issue or event. The feature story often includes photographs, such as the ones below, that focus on the setting and the subject of the story.

Usually longer than a news article, the feature story may try to capture a mood or a moment, or it may highlight a person, experience, or other topic of general human interest. Since feature writers use description, narration, and exposition, their stories tend to be both entertaining and informative. The literature models in this lesson are excerpts from a feature story, "Searching for Medicinal Wealth in Amazonia," published in *Smithsonian* magazine. Note how the writer, Donald Dale Jackson, opens his story with a detailed description of the rain forest and a scientist.

*A*n hour and a half had passed since we had seen any human scratches on the great green kingdom below us, the rain forest of southern Suriname at the northern fringes of Amazonia. Since then our Cessna six-seater had droned over an unforgiving landscape of jungle dotted with cloud-shadow puddles and tree-choked arroyos [stream beds] streaked by brown rivers. Even at 4,000 feet I could feel the oppressive heat, and we were beginning to descend. The lumpy carpet of rain forest gradually metamorphosed into a canopy of high trees that hid the ground.

Mark Plotkin leaned forward and squinted. Three plumes of smoke stained the horizon ahead. A few seconds later a clearing suddenly materialized, dun-colored and impossibly puny amid the green sea. Now I saw a village of about 80 thatched huts clustered beside a chocolate river. . . . Plotkin grinned. "Welcome to Kwamalasamutu," he said. "The first time I came here I thought I'd found paradise. I still think it's as close as we're apt to get."

Plotkin—New Orleans born, Harvard trained and Washington based—was coming home, in a sense, to this tiny settlement in Amazonia. . . . Plotkin has assigned himself the task of collecting and documenting the plants the Tiriós [Amazonian Indians] use before the mixed blessings of creeping civilization supplant the tribal medicine men and their wisdom. . . .

As a field ethnobotanist . . . Plotkin is the most visible exponent of a discipline that has only recently come into its own. Where ethnobotany was once mainly concerned with plant identification, it is viewed today as a potential lifesaver. The chemical components of plants that medicine men use in healing rites could conceivably be building blocks for new drugs or even cures for such scourges as cancer and AIDS.

Donald Dale Jackson, "Searching for Medicinal Wealth in Amazonia," *Smithsonian* magazine

What do you learn from the opening sentence of Jackson's feature article?

The writer's direct quotes and sensory details give the reader an intimate view of people and places.

How would you define "ethnobotany" and explain its importance, based on Jackson's fourth paragraph?

Journal Writing

Look through a newspaper for an interesting feature story. In your journal note what types of writing are used.

Plan a Feature Article

Feature writers face two basic challenges. First, they must identify current topics that will interest their readers. Then they must gather the information and uncover the details to bring that topic to life and give readers important background to the news.

Find a Topic   Feature articles can be on just about anything. Many, but not all, feature articles focus on current news stories, casting them in new light with important background or interesting approaches. Feature writers may also provide information not related to the news. For example, they might tell of intriguing people or share personal experiences.

Coming up with a good topic for your own feature article requires insight into your audience. You need to know their general age, their interests, what they might hope to learn, and what it might take to capture their imaginations.

The best way to find an interesting topic is to think about things in the news or in your own life that are of special interest to you. What are you curious about? If an idea seems intriguing to you, it may also fascinate your audience. The following tips may help you think of fresh feature ideas.

Prewriting Tip

When you interview, double-check the correct spelling of the person's name and his or her exact title or position. If you plan to use a statement from the interview or from printed material as a direct quotation, be sure you have permission. For more tips on interviewing, see Lesson 2.4, pages 75–76.

Some Ways to Get Ideas for Your Feature Story

- Take a different route to school. What new things do you see?

- Go someplace you don't usually go. Listen to conversations. Watch what people do. What questions do these people spark?

- Sit in a familiar spot, and note anything that seems out of the ordinary about the people or the place. What did you see that you didn't expect to see?

- Put yourself in the place of someone in the news, a character in a book, a person you see on the street. What ideas do you get from looking at the world through their eyes?

- Leaf through a type of book or magazine you don't generally read. What new topics spark your interest?

Gather Information   Once you have settled on an idea for a feature story, you need to gather information. Reading will give you background. Visiting places related to your topic may help you write descriptions with greater detail and authority and even re-create a mood. The list on the next page will provide the most valuable information for your feature story. It presents some questions a writer might ask when interviewing a scientist such as Mark Plotkin about the rain forest.

Some Questions for a Rain Forest Scientist

- How did you first become interested in rain forests?

- How would you summarize the importance of your work in the rain forest?

- In what parts of the world do you think the rain forest is most likely to survive? Why?

- What is the most surprising thing you have seen on all your trips to the rain forest?

Draft a Feature Article

After you have gathered information for your feature, you can begin writing a draft of your article. Construct an outline to organize your ideas. Then use the following advice to create a lively article.

Begin with a Lead That Pulls   Journalists use the term *lead* to describe the opening of a story. An effective lead sets the story in motion and draws the reader into the writing. The chart below lists some ways to create a successful lead.

A Lead for Your Feature Story

- a surprising detail

- an anecdote that gets at the story's essence

- a revealing image that indicates the direction of the story

- a vivid description of the place

- a summary of the central conflict

- a portrait of one of the main people

- a lively quote

- an event that kicks off the story

Revising Tip

When you revise, have a friend look for places where your story lacks supporting details (see Lesson 5.2, pages 224–227) or doesn't flow smoothly.

Editing Tip

Make sure your quotes are accurate and you have been fair to everyone. You might phone the people involved in the story to read them the final version.

Presenting Tip

When your feature story is complete, present it in a form and a place that will reach the appropriate audience. Choose illustrations for the feature that will add useful information to the story as well as catch the attention of the intended audience.

Journal Writing

Look through newspapers and magazines for feature stories. Clip some leads that catch your attention. Tape these clippings into your journal.

Grammar
Editing Tip

When editing your article, make sure that your quotations are punctuated correctly. For tips on when and how to use quotation marks, see Lesson 21.9, pages 714–718.

Jackson uses sensory details to make this scene come to life.

What do you learn about the people in this article from the quotations Jackson presents?

Add Lively Details   The details you include in your feature will make or break your story. Pick details that make your main points vivid and memorable. Include anecdotes that create empathy for your subject. Include quotes that let the reader hear your subject speaking in his or her own voice. Craft explanations that give your audience a clear understanding of the history, significance, or inner workings of a topic. Notice the details Jackson includes in this excerpt from his article.

Literature Model

The Indians mobbed him [Plotkin] as he climbed out of the plane. Boys tugged at his arms and grabbed his luggage. Speaking Sranan tongo, the trading language of Suriname, Plotkin had a smile or joke for each of them. "We thought you forgot us," one boy said—he hadn't been there for two years. "We were crying." Here in this exotic outpost light-years removed from his own culture, in a remote corner of a country that few Americans can identify or pronounce, the kid from New Orleans was among friends. "It feels terrific," he said.

Use an Effective Ending   The ending of your feature should be as fresh and vigorous as the lead. It should tie the feature together and, if possible, leave the reader with a new thought to ponder.

Some of the best ways to begin a feature are also good ways to end it. Quotes, humorous anecdotes, close-up portraits, lively details, and vivid scenes work as well at the end of a story as at the beginning. Why do you suppose Jackson concludes his article with an image of the rain forest as seen from the airborne Cessna?

Jackson uses strong sensory details to help bring his ending to life.

Note Jackson's use of adjectives to tell his story, especially the string of adjectives in the concluding sentence.

Literature Model

The Cessna finally appeared in the northeast sky and touched down five minutes later. Thirty tense minutes ensued before the pilot could get the engine started for the return trip. The plane's cabin felt like a broiler. . . .

A few minutes later we were airborne. The dust-brown clearing that was Kwamalasamutu became smaller and smaller until it was a tiny brown speck lost in the great green, and then it was gone and there was only the green, the endless, timeless, pitiless, life-giving, suffocating green of the rain forest.

5.8 Writing Activities

Write a Feature Story

Choose a topic that interests you and write a feature story for publication in your school paper or a community newspaper. The chart on page 250 can help you select a topic. Use illustrations with your feature if you wish.

- Create a strong lead.
- Use lively details.
- Include a quotation.
- Use an effective ending.

PURPOSE To create a feature story
AUDIENCE Students or adults
LENGTH 5–8 paragraphs

Cooperative Learning

In a small group, discuss your individual impressions of the 53-foot-high sculpture shown below. Generate 10 quotations about the work. Then have each member write a feature story that uses a quotation about how viewers react to the sculpture, which stands in the Federal Center Plaza in Chicago.

Alexander Calder, *Flamingo*, 1974

Grammar Link

Use commas to set off nonessential appositives and adjective clauses.

Feature writers often use appositives and adjective clauses to add informative details. Appositives and adjective clauses that are not essential to the meaning of the sentence should be set off by commas.

Rewrite the sentences below, adding commas where they are needed.

1. The Amazon Basin a region two-thirds the size of the United States is home to thousands of plant species.
2. Field ethnobotanist Mark Plotkin lives and works among the Tiriós.
3. Plotkin who is Harvard trained and Washington based is also a speaker about conservation.
4. Ethnobotany is a complex field that I do not understand.
5. Ethnobotany which was once mainly concerned with plant identification is today viewed as a potential lifesaver.

See Lesson 21.6, pages 703–704.

Expository Writing
Answering an Essay Question

When you take an essay test, plan your time carefully, and write answers that demonstrate your knowledge. In the model below, columnist Cecil Adams's response to "Why Do Cats Purr?" gives you an idea of what it takes to answer an essay question successfully.

Literature Model

Adams begins his answer by explaining one thing he knows for sure about cats' purring: when they do it.

What does Adams mean when he says purring "seems to be a kind of homing device"? Does this hypothesis make sense to you?

Adams concludes with a theory that highlights all that we don't know about cats' purring.

Cats don't purr just when they're feeling chipper—they also purr when they're frightened or badly hurt. Purring doesn't have any specific emotional connotation; rather it seems to be a kind of homing device. Cats learn the signal in the first few days of kittenhood, when they can't see, hear, or smell very well. The mother cat purrs to call the kittens to nurse—unable to hear the sound, the kitten can feel the vibrations.

There are two schools of thought on exactly *how* a cat purrs. One theory traces the vibrations to a set of "false vocal chords," a bundle of membranes that lies above the genuine vocal chords and seems to have no other clear function. The other opinion locates the purr in the vibrations of the hyoid apparatus, a series of small bones connecting the skull and the larynx that nominally serves to support the tongue. Since it's very difficult to induce a cat to purr while you are examining his hyoid apparatus, the truth may never be known.

Cecil Adams, *The Straight Dope*

Look for Key Words in the Question

Answers to essay questions follow a basic format—the format of the essay. The **introduction** contains a **thesis statement,** a one-sentence summary of the thrust of your answer. The **body of** the answer supports the thesis statement with facts, examples, details, and reasons. The **conclusion** summarizes or gives the implications of your answer. The essay question itself often gives strong clues as to how the answer should be structured. The chart below can help you decipher the clues.

Grammar
Drafting Tip

Restate the essay question as the beginning of your thesis statement. "What were the causes of the Civil War?" becomes "The Civil War was caused by . . ." For information on using active and passive voices of verbs, see Lesson 15.7, page 559.

What Essay Questions Tell You	
Clue Verb	**Action to Take**
Describe	Paint word pictures by providing precise details of an event, a process, or a person.
Explain	Tell why or how by using facts, examples, or reasons, and emphasize cause-and-effect relationships or step-by-step processes.
Compare	Show how two or more subjects are alike.
Contrast	Highlight the differences between two or more subjects.
Classify	Group and label the important features of a subject, and discuss the different categories into which you have grouped them.
Analyze	Break something down into the parts that compose it, show the relationship between the parts and the whole, and tell the function or significance of each of the parts.

Journal Writing

For each clue verb in the chart above, identify one or more prewriting tools, such as a Venn diagram, that could help you answer that particular kind of essay question efficiently. List each tool in your journal next to the corresponding clue verb.

Focus Your Answer

By taking time to identify and organize your information, you can avoid the common mistake of writing down everything you know about a subject in a haphazard, disjointed fashion.

Organize Your Information The following diagram details the process you might use to answer a "take home" essay question.

Answering an Essay Question

Question

Describe hail, and explain how and when hailstones form.

Underline clue verbs and other key words.

Describe hail, and explain how and when hailstones form.

List notes.

- Hail: form of precipitation made up of lumps of ice
- Begins as tiny ice crystal in thundercloud
- Strong winds in cloud toss crystal up and down; water condenses around crystal and freezes, forming layers of ice on the crystal, thus creating a hailstone and making it grow larger and heavier.
- Hailstone becomes too heavy to remain aloft, falls to ground.
- Size of stone depends on strength of wind, length of time in cloud.
- Most hailstones smaller than one inch in diameter, but some larger than a baseball
- Large hailstones smash windows, dent cars, destroy crops.
- Hailstorms usually occur in summer, when thunderstorms are more frequent, violent.

Develop thesis statement.

Hail is a form of precipitation made up of lumps of ice that form within thunderclouds.

Outline answer and develop conclusion.

Organize your answer into main points and supporting details. The conclusion might summarize the answer.

Hail: What is it and how and when does it form?

What? —————————————————————— *When?*

- *A form of precipitation made up of lumps of ice*

How?

- *Begins as crystal in thundercloud*
- *Strong winds toss it up and down*
- *Water condenses around crystal, freezing into layer of ice*
- *Layers of ice build up around crystal, creating a hailstone, which continues to get larger and heavier*
- *Hailstone becomes too heavy to stay aloft, falls to ground*

- *Usually forms in summer, when thunderstorms are more frequent and violent*

Write Your Answer   If you follow a process like the one just laid out, writing an answer to an essay question will become a much easier task. Your plan for your answer will help you focus your ideas, write quickly, and avoid including unnecessary information. Follow the steps below when writing your answer to an essay question.

Writing Your Essay Answer

1. Express your thesis in the opening sentence to show that you understand the question. Writing your thesis at the beginning will also help you focus your answer.

2. Use your notes, thesis statement, and organizational plan to develop your major points and supporting details. You can draw additional supporting details from your notes.

3. Include transitions between each major point.

4. Do not stray from your plan unless you realize some point is incorrect or unworkable. Do not add information that does not support your thesis.

5. Provide an ending that reflects the basic answer you have written.

Journal Writing

In your journal copy two essay questions from your science textbook, or make up two sample questions. For each question do some research to list enough notes to form an answer, and then write a thesis statement to help focus your answer.

Revise and Edit Your Answer   Leave time to read over your answer once you have finished. Make sure that your thesis statement is clear and that you have covered all important points. Correct any content errors first. Add details by inserting sentences where necessary. You can clarify a relationship between ideas by adding or changing a transitional word.

Now look at Jason Larmore's essay answer to the question "Into what three general classes do astronomers group stars? What are the characteristics of each class of stars?"

How does Larmore's first paragraph demonstrate that he understands the question?

What supporting details does Larmore use to point out the characteristics of the stars in each of the three groups?

In his conclusion Larmore stresses the relationship among the different classes of stars.

Student Model

*A*stronomers group stars into three general classes: the main-sequence, the giant and supergiant, and the white dwarf. Each class has its own characteristics; size, brightness, and color all help determine a star's group. Of these three factors, size is the most important because size differences between classes are dramatically obvious.

Main-sequence stars are the most common. The yellowish main-sequences form an average between the white dwarves and the "red" giants, but because of the giant's immensity, everything seems microscopic in comparison.

The enormousness of the giant-class stars can be shown by comparing them to our own solar system. A single supergiant, placed where our sun is, would engulf all of the inner planets and some of the outer planets. Because the giant stars are so massive, they sometimes are unable to burn gases at a normal temperature. A decrease in this temperature causes them to have a reddish color, common to many giants. There are, however, exceptions to the "red" giant pattern. Deneb is a giant that shines with a blue light. This indicates an extremely high temperature. These exceptions comprise the brightest stars in the night sky.

The final class of stars is the white dwarf. These stars are the result of giant stars that collapsed because they couldn't maintain their mass. The white dwarves are very dense and shine white. These stars are much smaller than our sun, yet they outweigh it exponentially. The fact that white dwarves come from giant stars shows that even though stars are divided into classes, they are in some ways related.

Jason Larmore, Henry Clay High School, Lexington, Kentucky

5.9 Writing Activities

Write an Essay Answer

Find an end-of-chapter question in your history or science book that could be answered in a short essay. Review the chapter; then write your essay.

- Decide exactly what the question is asking.
- Recast the question as a thesis statement.
- Make notes and organize them.
- Write your answer.
- Revise and edit your answer.

PURPOSE To write an essay answering a history or science question
AUDIENCE Your teacher
LENGTH 1–2 paragraphs

Cooperative Learning

Work together in a small group, and brainstorm your own list of "imponderables," questions about the natural world like those Cecil Adams might answer in his column. (See the model on page 254.) What parts of the natural world puzzle or mystify you? Here's your chance to have someone else find the answers for you. Exchange lists with another group. Select one question from their list for your group to research and answer. Each group member should research and write an answer individually, but then put everyone's information together into one group answer. Give the final version of your answer to the other group. They may wish to grade your paper based on how well they think you have answered their question.

Grammar Link

Make pronouns and their antecedents agree.

In this passage from the student model, note how the indefinite pronoun and the antecedent agree: "Astronomers group stars into three general classes . . . *each* . . . has *its* own characteristics."

Use each indefinite pronoun below and an antecedent in a sentence.

Sample several
Answer *Several* of the astronomers explained *their* theories.

1. everything
2. everyone
3. both
4. few
5. each
6. no one
7. many
8. one
9. either
10. neither

See Lesson 16.7, page 581, and Lesson 17.5, pages 602–606.

Writing About Literature
Comparing and Contrasting Two Myths

A myth is an ancient story that offers an explanation about some aspect of the natural world. Notice the similarities in the Sioux and Zulu creation myths.

According to a myth of the Sioux, Native Americans of the Plains, the first man sprang from the soil of the Great Plains. As he emerged, he saw only the sun. After freeing himself from the clinging soil, he began to take halting steps. The sun shone on his body, toughening his skin and making him strong. The Sioux descended from this man.

A myth of the Zulu people of Africa describes how the sky god created the first people. After his marriage to the earth goddess, the sky god walked through a swamp. He broke off reeds of different colors and fashioned a man and a woman from each different colored reed. A different tribe descended from each pair of reed people.

Student Mathew Isaac read these ancient stories and pondered their similarities and differences. Here's what he came up with.

Student Model

Isaac finds a central point of comparison between the two myths—the fertile soil.

What central difference does Isaac find between the two myths?

The Sioux and Zulu myths attempt to explain the creation of mankind. The setting and the characters in the myths reveal a great deal about these groups. Both deeply revered their soil, for their pastoral life-styles revolved around it. This reverence may be inferred from the fertile land, the setting for both myths. The Sioux man emerged from the soil, while the Zulu were created from reeds in a swamp. The Zulu people recognized a god as their creator. The Sioux did not, at least according to this myth, although their myth notes the importance of the sun for continued life.

The beliefs and values of the Sioux and Zulu, some of which were shared, are visible in their creation myths.

Mathew Isaac, Rich East High School, Park Forest, Illinois

Explain a Myth

Myths sometimes offer explanations for why things happen as they do. Science provides one kind of explanation, but myths offer alternative views. The ancient Romans explained the seeming movement of the sun across the sky as the work of a heavenly charioteer circling the earth daily. The ancient Japanese explained the creation of their islands with a myth about the spear of a god named Izanagi. In fact, there are probably as many distinctly different mythologies as there are different cultures.

Drafting Tip

In a comparison of two stories, use a feature-by-feature comparison. This form will help you weave together your points of comparison. See Lesson 5.6, page 242.

Find Similarities and Differences

The chart below shows the common elements of literature, which all myths share. You can cite these elements to compare myths from different cultures.

Common Elements of Literature	
Element	**Definition**
Setting	The place and time in which the action of the story occurs The location can be real or imaginary. In a myth, the time is usually the past.
Characters	The people, animals, or gods that participate in the action of the story
Conflict	The struggle that is central to the story It can be a struggle between characters or forces.
Plot	The story's sequence of events A plot revolves around a conflict and builds to a climax that is later resolved.
Theme	The message or main idea of the story The theme may or may not be stated directly.

Journal Writing

Think about a myth with which you are familiar. In your journal write a brief summary of the myth, and then, in a short list, identify each of the literary elements in that myth.

Use a Comparison Frame

How did the sun and the moon get into the sky? Here are two answers in the form of myths, one ancient Mexican and one ancient Nigerian.

According to the Mexican myth, the gods were arguing about who among them should light the earth by day and who by night. After four days of arguing, two gods volunteered. One was rich and strong, and the other was poor and feeble. The gods then built a huge bonfire, and the two volunteers stepped toward it. The rich god was afraid of the flames and drew back from the fire. The poor god jumped right into the fire and was catapulted high into the sky. He became the sun. The bonfire began to die. The rich god still wanted a share of the glory. He leaped into the embers, sailed into the sky, and became the moon.

According to the Nigerian myth, before there were people, the sun and the moon were married and lived on earth. The sun was good friends with the water and one day invited him to his village to meet his wife. The water flowed into the village, with the fish, the crabs, the whales, and all the other living things swimming in the seas. Soon the sun and the moon had to climb on top of the village huts because of all the water. But the water kept coming and began lapping the rooftops. The sun and the moon had to flee to safety. They each took a bounding leap into the sky, and there they remain.

The comparison frame below will help you compare and contrast the two myths.

Grammar
Drafting Tip

When explaining a myth or describing past events, be consistent in your choice of verb tense. For more information on consistent tenses, see Lesson 15.6, page 556.

Comparison of Two Myths		
Element	**Mexican Myth**	**Nigerian Myth**
Setting	A long time ago on earth	A long time ago on earth
Characters	The Mexican gods	The sun and moon, a married couple, and the water
Conflict	Which of the gods will get to be the sun and which the moon?	Water threatens to drown the sun and moon when he visits.
Plot	The gods argue. Two gods volunteer, one rich and strong, the other poor and feeble. . . .	The sun invites water to his village. Water flows into the village, rising up to the rooftops. . . .
Theme	Bravery, not wealth, brings great glory.	Some guests can't be accommodated in one's home.

Write a Comparison-Contrast Essay

Imagine that you are writing a paper entitled "Some Common Themes in World Mythology" for your literature class. Write a comparison-contrast of the two myths below.

Iroquois myth: Four animals, bound on leashes by a giant, are responsible for the winds. A strong, fierce bear brings on the north winds of winter. A gentle fawn brings on the south winds of summer. An angry panther brings on the west winds that accompany storms and whirlwinds. A moose brings on the east winds with their chilling mists. The giant unleashes these animals to match his moods. But he tries to keep to his duty and unleash each wind in its proper season and time.

Italian myth: The north wind is a woman who at one time wanted to marry the south wind. But the south wind was lazy and comfortable in his bachelorhood and told the north wind that he couldn't marry her without a dowry [the riches a woman brings to a marriage]. The north wind blew for three days and nights, covering the land with a blanket of silver snow. This she presented as her dowry. The south wind, not wanting to marry, blew for three days and nights. His hot breath melted all the snow. The north wind decided that she no longer wanted to marry the south wind, because he had frittered away her entire dowry in only three days.

- Compare and contrast the literary elements of the two myths.
- Weave your points of comparison together with a feature-by-feature treatment.

PURPOSE To compare two myths
AUDIENCE Your high school literature teacher
LENGTH 1–2 paragraphs

Grammar Link

Make clear comparisons.

The comparisons in a comparison-contrast essay must be clear and complete. Rewrite each sentence below to correct the incomplete or unclear comparison.

1. There are more myths about creation than about any subject.
2. The Zulu myth is more religious in tone than the Sioux.
3. Did the ancient Greeks worship more gods than anyone?
4. The cleverness of the gods was always greater than the people.
5. Myths explaining the natural world are more ingenious than scientists.

See Lesson 18.4, page 627.

COMPUTER OPTION

Use the copy feature of your word-processing program to preserve the first draft of your comparison-contrast essay as you work to improve it. When your first draft is complete, save it. Make a copy of it (either as a new file or as a new page in the existing file). Continue to work on improving your essay. Do the same with each successive draft. In this way, you'll always have a record of your earlier ideas and the changes you've made. Thus, you will be able to reinstate previous ideas and even earlier drafts if later changes don't work.

WRITING PROCESS IN ACTION

EXPOSITORY WRITING

In preceding lessons you learned about the different types of expository writing, the purpose of each, and ways to make expository writing informative and appealing. You have written cause-and-effect explanations, comparison-contrasts, and essays. Now it is time to apply what you have learned. In this lesson you are invited to write about an insect or animal that repels most people, presenting information in a way that will help your reader better understand and empathize with the creature.

• Assignment •

Context	A science teacher has a problem: this year most of his sixth-grade students seem to be afraid of or disgusted by the creatures about which he wants to teach them. He wants your class to write brief articles about the insects and animals. The articles should help his students appreciate these creatures.
Purpose	To write a brief article about a creature people often label "bad" to help children experience and appreciate this animal in its own right
Audience	Sixth-grade science students
Length	1–2 pages

The guidelines on the following pages can help you plan and write your article. Read through them, and then refer to them as you complete this assignment. Don't be tied down by the guidelines, however. Remember, you're in charge of your own writing process.

Prewriting

What would you like to write about—wolves, sharks, spiders, bats? Any of these creatures are fair game, but see what other ideas you can come up with. Brainstorm with classmates to generate a list of "vicious," "disgusting," or just misunderstood creatures. From this list select a subject that both interests you and is likely to repel or intrigue your audience.

Once you have identified your subject, freewrite or brainstorm to create an inventory of what you already know about this creature. The questions on the notepad will help you get started.

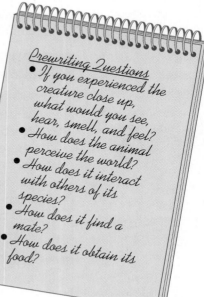

Prewriting Questions
- If you experienced the creature close up, what would you see, hear, smell, and feel?
- How does the animal perceive the world?
- How does it interact with others of its species?
- How does it find a mate?
- How does it obtain its food?

Next, do research to find the facts. Start by checking encyclopedias, magazines, and videotapes to determine the accuracy of each characteristic you listed in your initial inventory. Expand your inventory by interviewing authorities on this creature. These experts might include zookeepers, animal trainers and breeders, pet store owners, farmers, or rangers. Record your findings on note cards or in a journal.

Once you have gathered your data, look over your notes to determine how you can best organize your information. The notes themselves may suggest a particular kind of organization. However, if they don't, look for a main idea or focus, and consider weeding out all details not related to that focus. Select the most interesting details to use in your lead, or introduction, and then try to determine what would most logically flow from that.

Drafting

For this assignment, you need to grab and hold your readers' attention. You might want to start with a fact or myth that is likely to intrigue young readers.

As you write the body of your paper, be sure to support the points you want to make with specific details. Try also to bring your subject to life with facts, analogies, and other evidence. Read the passage on page 266 to see how natural history writer Barry Lopez brings to life the relationship between the wolf and his habitat.

When you've accomplished the purpose of your feature, conclude your article. If you chose to present one animal's life from birth to death, your conclusion might focus on the death. If you wrote your feature as a flashback, your conclusion would bring readers back to the present. Your conclusion should give your feature a sense of closure or completeness.

Drafting Tip

For suggestions about how to find an effective lead for your story, see Lesson 5.8, page 248.

Literature Model

*T*he wolf is tied by subtle threads to the woods he moves through. His fur carries seeds that will fall off, effectively dispersed, along the trail some miles from where they first caught in his fur. And miles distant is a raven perched on the ribs of a caribou the wolf helped kill ten days ago, pecking like a chicken at the decaying scraps of meat. A smart snowshoe hare that eluded the wolf and left him exhausted when he was a pup has been dead a year now, food for an owl. The den in which he was born one April evening was home to porcupines last winter.

Barry Holstun Lopez, *Of Wolves and Men*

Revising

Revising Tip

For examples of vivid supporting details, see Lesson 5.2, page 225, and Lesson 5.8, page 248.

To begin revising, read over your draft to make sure that what you've written fits your purpose and audience. Then have a **writing conference**. Read your draft to a partner or small group. Use your audience's reactions to help you evaluate your work.

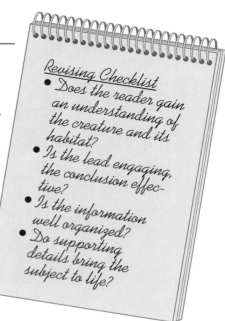

Revising Checklist
- Does the reader gain an understanding of the creature and its habitat?
- Is the lead engaging, the conclusion effective?
- Is the information well organized?
- Do supporting details bring the subject to life?

Editing

When you have revised your article for basic content and organization, **proofread** it carefully for errors in grammar, usage, mechanics, and spelling. Think again about your audience. You may find that you will need to simplify or shorten some of your sentences and make your tone more informal. Use the questions at the right as a guide.

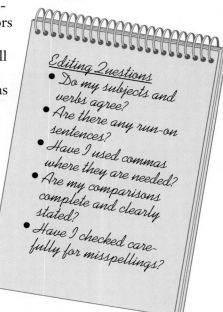

Editing Questions
- Do my subjects and verbs agree?
- Are there any run-on sentences?
- Have I used commas where they are needed?
- Are my comparisons complete and clearly stated?
- Have I checked carefully for misspellings?

Self-Evaluation

Make sure your article—

- focuses on a creature likely to repel young students
- uses vocabulary and a writing style appropriate for your audience
- develops in a logical, natural way
- supports points with specific details
- follows correct grammar, usage, mechanics, and spelling

Presenting

Think about how you can make your essay easy for sixth graders to read and understand. Would a map help you explain your animal's habitat? Would a graph help you present statistical information about your subject?

Proofreading

For proofreading symbols, see page 100.

Presenting Tip

For information about how to enhance your paper with graphics, see Lesson 5.7, pages 244–247.

Journal Writing

Reflect on your writing process experience. Answer these questions in your journal: What do you like best about your article? What was the hardest part of writing it? What did you learn from talking to others about it? What new things have you learned as a writer?

Expository Writing
Literature Model

Barry Holstun Lopez

from

Of Wolves and Men

Barry Lopez writes about natural history and the environment in short fiction, articles, essays, and books. Among his many books is Of Wolves and Men, *which grew out of a 1974 article he wrote for* Smithsonian *magazine. As you read, notice how Lopez's explanations help his reader "see" the wolf in its own right and its own world. Then try the activities in Linking Writing and Literature on page 273.*

I magine a wolf moving through the northern woods. The movement, over a trail he has traversed many times before, is distinctive, unlike that of a cougar or a bear, yet he appears, if you are watching, sometimes catlike or bearlike. It is purposeful, deliberate movement. Occasionally the rhythm is broken by the wolf's pause to inspect a scent mark, or a move off the trail to paw among stones where a year before he had cached[1] meat.

1 cached (kashd) stored up

The movement down the trail would seem relentless if it did not appear so effortless. The wolf's body, from neck to hips, appears to float over the long, almost spindly legs and the flicker of wrists, a bicycling drift through the trees, reminiscent of the movement of water or of shadows.

The wolf is three years old. A male. He is of the subspecies *occidentalis*, and the trees he is moving among are spruce and subalpine fir on the eastern slope of the Rockies in northern Canada. He is light gray; that is, there are more blond and white hairs mixed with gray in the saddle of fur that covers his shoulders and extends down his spine than there are black and brown. But there are silver and even red hairs mixed in, too.

Nancy Schutt, *Encroachment*, 1987

It is early September, an easy time of year, and he has not seen the other wolves in his pack for three or four days. He has heard no howls, but he knows the others are about, in ones and twos like himself. It is not a time of year for much howling. It is an easy time. The weather is pleasant. Moose are fat. Suddenly the wolf stops in midstride. A moment, then his feet slowly come alongside each other. He is staring into the grass. His ears are rammed forward, stiff. His back arches and he rears up and pounces like a cat. A deer mouse is pinned between his forepaws. Eaten. The wolf drifts on. He approaches a trail crossing, an undistinguished crossroads. His movement is now slower and he sniffs the air as though aware of a possibility for scents. He sniffs a scent post, a scrawny blueberry bush in use for years, and goes on.

The wolf weighs ninety-four pounds and stands thirty inches at the shoulder. His feet are enormous, leaving prints in the mud along a creek (where he pauses to hunt crayfish but not with much interest) more than five inches long by just over four wide. He has two fractured ribs, broken by a moose a year before. They are healed now, but a sharp eye would notice the irregularity. The skin on his right hip is scarred, from a fight with another wolf in a neighboring pack when he was a yearling. He has not had anything but a few mice and a piece of arctic char[2] in three days, but he is not hungry. He is traveling. The char was a day old, left on rocks along the river by bears.

The wolf is tied by subtle threads to the woods he moves through. His fur carries seeds that will fall off, effectively dispersed, along the trail some miles from where they first caught in his fur. And miles distant is a raven perched on the ribs of a caribou the wolf helped kill ten days ago, pecking like a chicken at the decaying scraps of meat. A smart snowshoe hare that eluded the wolf and left him exhausted when he was a pup has been dead a year now, food for an owl. The den in which he was born one April evening was home to porcupines last winter.

It is now late in the afternoon. The wolf has stopped traveling, has lain down to sleep on cool earth beneath a rock outcropping. Mosquitoes rest on his ears. His ears flicker. He begins to waken. He rolls on his back and lies motionless with his front legs pointed toward the sky but folded like wilted flowers, his back legs splayed,[3] and his nose and tail curved toward each other on one side of his body. After a few moments he flops on his side, rises, stretches, and moves a few feet to inspect—minutely, delicately—a crevice in the rock outcropping and finds or doesn't find what draws him there. And then he ascends the rock face, bounding and balancing momentarily

2 char (chär) a kind of trout

3 splayed (splād) spread out

Makah wolf mask, late nineteenth century

before bounding again, appearing slightly unsure of the process—but committed. A few minutes later he bolts suddenly into the woods, achieving full speed, almost forty miles per hour, for forty or fifty yards before he begins to skid, to lunge at a lodgepole pine cone. He trots away with it, his head erect, tail erect, his hips slightly to one side and out of line with his shoulders, as though hindquarters were impatient with forequarters, the cone inert in his mouth. He carries it for a hundred feet before dropping it by the trail. He sniffs it. He goes on.

The underfur next to his skin has begun to thicken with the coming of fall. In the months to follow it will become so dense between his shoulders it will be almost impossible to work a finger down to his skin. In seven months he will weigh less: eighty-nine pounds. He will have tried unsuccessfully to mate with another wolf in the pack. He will have helped kill four moose and thirteen caribou. He will have fallen through ice into a creek at twenty-two below zero but not frozen. He will have fought with other wolves.

He moves along now at the edge of a clearing. The wind coming down-valley surrounds him with a river of odors, as if he were a migrating salmon. He can smell ptarmigan[4] and deer droppings. He can smell willow and spruce and the fading sweetness of fireweed. Above, he sees a hawk circling, and farther south, lower on the horizon, a flock of sharp-tailed sparrows going east. He senses through his pads with each step the dryness of the moss beneath his feet, and the ridges of old tracks, some his own. He hears the sound his feet make. He hears the occasional movement of deer mice and voles.[5] Summer food.

Toward dusk he is standing by a creek, lapping the cool water, when a wolf howls—a long wail that quickly reaches pitch and then tapers, with several harmonics,[6] long moments to a tremolo.[7] He recognizes his sister. He waits a few moments, then, throwing his head back and closing his eyes, he howls. The howl is shorter and it changes pitch twice in the beginning, very quickly. There is no answer.

The female is a mile away and she trots off obliquely through the trees. The other wolf stands listening, laps water again, then he too departs, moving quickly, quietly through the trees, away from the trail he had been on. In a few minutes the two wolves meet. They approach each other briskly, almost formally, tails erect and moving somewhat as deer move. When they come together they make high squeaking noises and encircle each other, rubbing and pushing, poking their noses into each other's neck fur, backing away to stretch, chasing each other for a few steps, then standing quietly together, one putting a head over the other's back. And then they are gone, down a vague trail, the female first. After a few hundred yards they begin, simultaneously, to wag their tails.

In the days to follow, they will meet another wolf from the pack, a second female, younger by a year, and the three of them will kill a caribou. They will travel together ten or twenty miles a day, through the country where they live, eating and sleeping, birthing, playing with sticks, chasing ravens, growing old, barking at bears, scent-marking trails, killing moose, and staring at the way water in a creek breaks around their legs and flows on.

---

4 ptarmigan (tär′ mi gən) a kind of northern or alpine bird

5 voles (vōlz) field mice

6 harmonics (här män′ iks) overtones

7 tremolo (trem′ ə lō′) a pulsating tone

Linking Writing and Literature

Readers Respond to the Model

What techniques does Barry Lopez use to convey in-depth information in a lively and appealing way?

Explore Barry Lopez's exposition by answering these questions. Then read what other students like about Lopez's writing.

1. Barry Lopez uses third-person omniscient point of view. How does this point of view affect his writing?

2. What types of supporting details does Barry Lopez use to bring his subject to life?

3. How well do you feel you got to know the wolf from this exposition? Explain.

What I liked best about this selection from *Of Wolves and Men* was all the details the author used. Lopez's words made me realize exactly what the wolf was feeling. The mood was calm, but as a reader I still felt a sense of danger. The writer created that mood by carefully detailing the wolf's life—the danger that he had been through and that was yet to come.

I think Lopez's choice of third person was appropriate because it makes the reader an observer, watching the wolf and his movements rather than seeing the scene from the wolf's point of view. I would recommend this selection to a friend because it teaches you in an interesting way about the life of a wolf.

Claire Monty

The writer chose third-person point of view for an unbiased examination of the wolf's actions. The dominant mood of the selection was one of solemnity, which the writer created by always making the episode serene, not bringing out action.

Chris Fickes

Unit 5 Review

Reflecting on the Unit

Summarize what you learned in this unit by answering the following questions.

- What are the important characteristics of effective expository writing?

- What are the purposes of these types of expository writing: process explanation; cause-and-effect; classification; comparison-contrast? How does the writer organize each type?

- How do graphics serve expository writing?

- What are the important steps in preparing a feature article?

- What strategies are helpful for answering an essay question?

Adding to Your Portfolio

Choose a selection for your portfolio.

Look over the expository writing you have done in this unit. Select a favorite piece to put into your portfolio. The piece you choose should show some or all of the following:

- a clear expository purpose
- a well-formulated thesis statement
- supporting details appropriate for its purpose and audience
- in-depth information presented appealingly
- an interesting introduction and a conclusion that gives a sense of closure.

Reflect on your choice.

Attach a note to the piece you chose, explaining briefly why you chose it and what you learned from writing it.

Set goals.

How can you improve your writing? What skill will you focus on the next time you write?

Writing Across the Curriculum

Make a Social Studies connection.

Choose a recent event that has affected the environment in some way. The event can be a natural disaster, an accident such as an oil spill, or the passage of an environmental protection law. Then write a cause-and-effect paragraph explaining the event. Try to identify at least two causes of the event and two possible consequences. Include a suggestion for one or more graphics that will strengthen your writing. Don't forget to use vivid details.

Persuasive Writing in the Real World

At the Movies

F O C U S: Like all persuasive writers, movie reviewers rely on facts, examples, logic, and strong feelings to sway a reader's opinion.

The houselights dim, the crowd settles back, and after a few previews, *Dances with Wolves* begins. Minutes later, a wounded man's terror and the noise and confusion of combat have swept viewers onto a Civil War battlefield.

The high-voltage scenes grip everyone, including movie reviewers like Melanie McFarland, a high school senior at Morgan Park Academy in Chicago. But McFarland is working, too. She's looking for original scenes, believable characters, a high-quality experience. Her reviews, which appear in a monthly teen newspaper called *New Expressions,* help shape the opinions of Chicago-area high school students. The effect of these reviews can be as direct as determining readers' weekend movie-viewing plans.

Melanie McFarland

"When you see an advertisement for a movie, whether it's Out of Africa *or* The Garbage Pail Kids, *it's going to try to sell you on how good this movie is. And that's what a movie reviewer is for—to tell people, this is a really good movie, go see it, or this is terrible, stay away, don't waste your money."*

—Melanie McFarland

McFarland is a young reviewer, but her intense love of film puts her in the company of superb critics. Among them are reviewers who evaluate films for the consuming public—Roger Ebert of the *Chicago Sun-Times* and Roger Corliss at *Time.*

These and other top reviewers and critics share certain traits. They love films. They're film experts, having viewed and thought about thousands of performances. And they're skilled persuasive writers who bolster their points of view with vivid examples pulled from a broad knowledge of actors, directors, and moviemaking.

One thing critics don't always share, however, is their opinion of an actor or a film. "Every critic's verdict is going to be different because everyone has different tastes," McFarland observed.

What, then, does McFarland think of the films she's seen in the last few years? In her opinion, *Dances with Wolves* was the best film of 1990 because of its quality and its compassionate depiction of Native Americans. On the other hand, she finds most films aimed at teens disappointing, especially films that stereotype teens. "I'd like to see more films that deal with the real, everyday problems kids have to deal with growing up," she said.

Read about your peers' ideas and opinions in a monthly teen magazine.

Writing a Movie Review		
Prewriting	**Drafting**	**Editing**
Behind the Scenes	In the Theater	On Deadline

Prewriting

BEHIND THE SCENES/IN THE THEATER

Knowing films inside and out—that enables reviewers to spot clichés and innovations.

All of McFarland's behind-the-scenes preparation enables her to focus on the film when she sees it. Before McFarland ever sets foot in a movie theater, she does her homework. In part, that means gleaning information from the press kit that film companies send to reviewers and critics.

The press kit is a thick, glossy notebook-sized folder filled with background information, including biographies of the actors, writers, producer, and director. "I read the biographies of the actors so I can see what other work they've done," McFarland explained. "If I'm not familiar with [their work], I'll go out and rent some films."

Watching movies that constitute an actor's body of work is crucial for reviewers. By knowing an actor's skill and range, reviewers can spot new achievements or the lack of them in an actor's current work.

Reviewers begin their real work as they walk into the movie theater. "When you go to the movie, you should have some expectations [of the genre]," McFarland said. "For instance, if you're going to see a *Naked Gun* movie, you don't expect to see great acting because this is a campy film. You watch for how good the gags are."

During the film, reviewers look for original writing. "The lines should be imaginative," McFarland said. "They should make the actors glow." Reviewers also watch for strong directing and acting that's natural, not contrived. In a comedy McFarland notes how much of the audience is laughing—"the entire audience, not just the [person] in front of you." In a drama or action film, she considers the "grip factor"—how much the film grabs your emotions.

McFarland also makes a point of taking a friend to the movies "to get another opinion of the film," she said. After the film McFarland jots down notes about key scenes, dialogue, and acting, plus her insights and reactions. These prewriting notes will help McFarland to focus her ideas when she sits down to write. Reviewers strive to capture the high points—and low points—of their viewing experience for their readers.

Drafting/Editing

ON DEADLINE

Never gush. Quoted dialogue, colorful descriptions of characters and scenes—proof of your viewpoint gets readers to listen.

Before McFarland writes her review, she mulls over her reactions for a day. She jots down any important insights and reviews her background information and press kits.

When she's ready to write, McFarland imagines her audience—a few teenagers who want an intelligent opinion of the film she's seen. "I imagine what I would say to an audience right in front of me," McFarland said. "And then I write it down."

Like professional critics and reviewers, McFarland strives to grab readers with a strong lead. "I tend to set up scenarios in the opening paragraphs that lead into the actual critique."

Once McFarland finishes drafting the review on the computer and proofreading for spelling, grammar, and punctuation, she gives the review to one of her peer editors or supervising editors. In addition to proofreading, the peer editor checks the review for completeness, logic, and style. The supervising editor usually makes minor copyediting changes and, if there are major revisions needed, returns the manuscript to McFarland. After McFarland writes the final draft, the copy is imported from one computer system to another, and dummy electronic pages are created.

McFarland is always curious to see the layout and often returns to the office for one last check. A common error, she says, occurs when the copy is imported; text can "disappear" during the process, and she wants one last chance to proofread before press time.

Responding to the Case Study

1. Discussion

Discuss these questions about Melanie McFarland's movie reviewing.

- What does McFarland do before viewing a film she's going to review?
- What qualities of a movie does she look for as she watches and evaluates it?
- What strategies does she use in drafting her review?
- How might using a strong lead in a review help McFarland persuade her audience to accept her opinion?

2. Persuasive Writing

Write a summary of a movie review.

Read two or more movie reviews of the same film in newspapers or magazines, such as those shown below, or listen to television reviewers discuss the same movie. Write a summary paragraph of the review you thought was most persuasive and explain why.

Grammar Link

Use the correct word of a confusing pair.

Some confusing pairs of words are *homophones*—words like *their* and *there* that sound alike but have different meanings and spellings. Other words, such as *accept* and *except*, are easily confused simply because they sound similar.

Rewrite each sentence below, completing it with the correct word in parentheses. If you are in doubt, use your dictionary.

1. The theater reviewer was (formally, formerly) a movie critic.
2. Her opinion had no (affect, effect) on my decision.
3. Do you like horror movies better (then, than) comedies?
4. The scene was set in the lobby of the state (capital, capitol).
5. The group went to the movies (altogether, all together).

See Lesson 26.2, page 792.

P e r s u a s i v e   W r i t i n g
Writing Persuasively

Persuasive writing is writing that tries to influence a reader to accept an idea, adopt a point of view, or perform an action. Effective persuasive writing uses strong, relevant evidence to support its claims.

Use Persuasive Writing

Newspaper and magazine advertisements, as well as posters announcing events such as the concert pictured, are examples of persuasive writing. You might use persuasive writing to do any or all of the tasks in the following list:

- convince your principal to relax the school's dress code
- persuade others to see a movie or play
- advertise lawn-care services you can provide
- apply for a summer job

Construct a Logical Argument

An argument contains the body of evidence used to support a point of view. The purpose of the argument is to persuade readers to accept your point of view. When you present your evidence logically, you take your readers step by step through your argument.

The chief stages in the construction of a logical argument are detailed on the following pages.

Identify Your Purpose Before you begin constructing your argument, decide what you want your persuasive piece to accomplish. For instance, if you want to write a letter to your principal about the lack of sports opportunities for girls at your school, your purpose might be to ask the principal to help develop a girls' soccer team.

State Your Central Claim A claim is a statement that asserts something. In persuasive writing, your central claim usually makes clear your main purpose for writing, and this claim will often begin your argument. For example, the letter requesting increased sports opportunities for girls might begin, "Our school should organize a girls' soccer team." Identifying your claim at the beginning will help focus your argument.

Identify Supporting Evidence One way to start identifying evidence to support your claim is to ask yourself questions that begin, "What evidence do I have that . . . ?" Then look for answers to your questions.

For example, to support the claim that her school should organize a girls' soccer team, one writer asked herself, "What evidence do I have that . . ."

- enough girls are interested in joining a soccer team?
- the team would benefit the girls and the school?
- there is a need for additional sports activities for girls?
- the school can provide the necessary staff?

To answer these questions, the writer then conducted a survey of the girls at her school. As a result, she discovered overwhelming interest in a soccer team. She also talked to the coach of the girls' soccer team at a nearby high school and some of the gym teachers at her own school. As authorities on the subject, these people supplied the writer with expert testimony to support her claim. By using these kinds of sound evidence in her persuasive writing piece, the writer will improve her chances of persuading her audience.

> **Drafting Tip**
>
> As you draft, use transitions to show relationships between ideas and to lead your readers step by step through your evidence.

Journal Writing

Identify a situation in which you were persuaded to do something. In your journal note the evidence and tactics that were most effective in persuading you to take action. Then explain why these tactics may have been so effective.

Explain How the Evidence Supports Your Claim   If the link between your claim and the evidence you use to support it is obvious, you don't need to state it. If, however, the connection is not clear, you must explain how the evidence supports your claim and why the reader should accept your evidence.

Read the following model in which the writer presents her case for a girls' soccer team in a letter to her high school principal. Notice how the evidence supports her claim.

Model

The link between the survey results and the claim for a soccer team is obvious. The connection does not need to be stated.

Dear Mr. Lopez,

I strongly believe that our school should organize a girls' soccer team, and I am not alone in this belief. After conducting a survey among the junior and senior girls at our school, I found that fifty girls would be interested in trying out for a soccer team.

To discover how similar teams have worked out at other schools, I talked to Ms. Young, the girls' soccer coach at Fairfax High. When I asked her how the team has benefited the girls and the school, she said: "The girls on my team have become close friends. They help each other with everything—homework, personal problems." She added, "Their grades have improved—they've become all-around better students—and that's always good for a school."

What is the logical link between the girls at Fairfax High and the writer's claim?

A soccer team would be of equal benefit to the girls at our school. Just like the girls at Fairfax, many of the girls here have trouble making friends. A soccer team might help them adjust to school life.

Moreover, it would be simple to start a team. I've already talked to my gym teacher, Ms. Jordan. She's willing to take on the responsibility of coaching the team. The question of where to practice isn't a problem either, since the playing field isn't used after three o'clock on Tuesdays and Thursdays. All we need now is your support.

Reaffirm Your Claim   Conclude your argument by reaffirming your claim. You might suggest that, given the evidence you have presented, your claim is the logical conclusion. You might also explain how your claim could be put into action. In the model above, for example, the writer explains where and when the soccer team could meet and identifies a teacher who is willing to coach it.

6.1 Writing Activities

Write a Letter to the Editor

Write to the letters-to-the-editor section of your school newspaper about some aspect of school life that you would like to see changed. Be sure to construct a logical argument to support your claim.

- Identify your purpose.
- State your central claim clearly.
- Present evidence in a logical sequence.
- Explain how your evidence supports your claim.
- Conclude by reaffirming your claim.

PURPOSE To make a case for change in some aspect of school life

AUDIENCE Teachers and other students

LENGTH 1–2 paragraphs

Bronze plaque from Benin, date undetermined

Cooperative Learning

In a small group, discuss whether the plaque shown on this page should be shown in a school exhibit for students to view. Consider the subject and design of the work, as well as how students might react to it. Then divide the group into two teams. Have one team write a paragraph stating why the work should be exhibited in the school; the other should provide reasons not to exhibit it. Share your responses with the rest of the class to see who they think has presented the better argument.

Grammar Link

Double negatives, such as *can't. . .no*, cancel each other out. Avoid them.

In the final paragraph of the model on page 284, the writer correctly uses only one negative word to express a negative idea.

Rewrite the sentences below, eliminating the double negatives.

[1] There isn't no reason why the school can't sponsor a computer club. [2] We don't have none now, but we could easily organize one. [3] People who don't have no computer games could share them. [4] People who don't know nothing about using a computer could get help. [5] Since we don't need no more computers, we aren't going to need no new printers either.

See Lesson 18.6, page 630.

Persuasive Writing
Using Evidence Effectively

Just as an attorney must present sound evidence in a courtroom, you must use strong, reliable, and relevant evidence to prove your claim in a piece of writing.

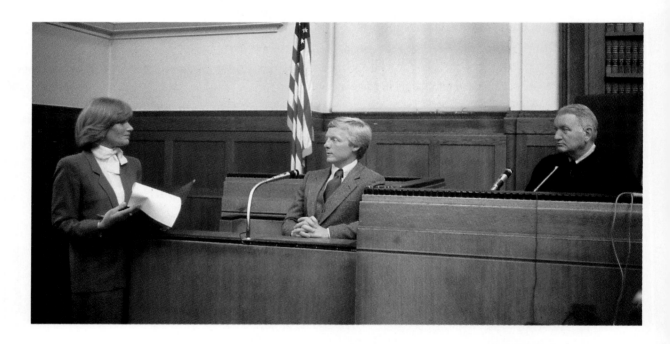

Identify the Evidence

The most common kinds of evidence used in persuasive writing include the following: facts, statistics, examples or incidents, opinions, and reasons. To collect these kinds of evidence, try freewriting, clustering, or making a list about your issue. You can also gather evidence by reading about your issue and by interviewing people. The more kinds of evidence you use to support your claim, the stronger your argument will be.

Evidence Used in Persuasive Writing		
Kind	**Definition**	**Example**
Fact	Something that is known to be true	Prehistoric dancers pictured on rock surfaces in Africa and southern Europe prove that dancing is one of the oldest forms of human expression.
Statistic	A fact that is expressed in numbers	When the musical *A Chorus Line* closed on Broadway in 1990, it had achieved a record of 6,137 performances.
Example or Incident	A particular case or event	In some societies, dancing plays a role in courtship. For example, in the United States, many high school students get to know one another at high school dances.
Opinion	A personal judgment based on what the person believes or feels to be true	A famous dancer once claimed, "The dance is a poem of which each movement is a word."
Reason	A logical argument	Many ballet dancers protest the use of toe shoes because the shoes cause permanent damage to the wearer's feet.

Assess the Accuracy of the Evidence

To assess the accuracy of your evidence, verify it in up-to-date sources. Check facts and statistics by consulting current encyclopedias, atlases, and other reference sources. Consult an expert on your subject to clarify something you don't understand or to obtain information that printed sources cannot provide. If you cannot verify a statement, or if the only source available to you is out of date, you may want to omit the statement from your argument. Your position will be greatly weakened if your readers spot inaccuracies in your argument.

Journal Writing

What do you think are the most reliable kinds of evidence you can use to support a claim? Why do you think this may be so? Write down your ideas in your journal.

Be sure that the people whose opinions you include are authorities on your subject. Resist using the opinions of well-known persons who have no connection to your subject. So-called testimonials do not have the validity of opinions supplied by authorities.

Grammar
Editing Tip

If you use statistics or number amounts in your evidence, be sure to check the subject-verb agreement. See Lesson 16.4, page 576.

Evaluate the Relevance of the Evidence

To assess the relevance of your evidence, examine each detail and ask yourself if it helps to develop the point you want to make. If not, you should probably discard the detail as irrelevant to your argument. For example, if you were writing to convince your audience that Spike Lee is a great movie director, you probably wouldn't include a statement naming his favorite restaurant. The statement has nothing to do with Lee's ability as a director and would only distract your readers from your central point.

Now read the following selection by editorial columnist Anthony Lewis. Notice that Lewis uses sound, relevant evidence to support his claim that the nicotine in cigarettes is as addictive as heroin or cocaine.

Lewis cites facts and statistics from a highly respected source, the U.S. Surgeon General, to support his claim.

In what way is each point Lewis uses in his argument relevant to his claim?

Literature Model

Dr. C. Everett Koop, the Surgeon General, was only spelling out in scientific terms what we all have observed about cigarette smoking. Users become dependent on the habit, and breaking it can be extremely difficult.

Of those who try to give up smoking, 80 percent have relapsed by the end of a year. Heroin users who try to give up their addiction have the same rate of failure.

"The pharmacologic and behavioral processes that determine tobacco addiction," the Koop report concluded, "are similar to those that determine addiction to drugs such as heroin and cocaine."

There is one profound difference between heroin and nicotine addiction. Tobacco kills 80 times as many people in this country. About 320,000 Americans die every year as a result of using tobacco products, while 4,000 die from the effects of heroin and related drugs.

Anthony Lewis, "Merchants of Death," *New York Times*

6.2 Writing Activities

Evaluate an Editorial

Find an editorial in a local or school paper and evaluate the evidence it uses to make its case. Write a brief review explaining why you think the editorial is or is not effective. Give clear reasons to support your opinion of the editorial's argument.

- Identify the evidence.
- Explain whether it is accurate.
- Decide whether it is relevant.

PURPOSE To evaluate the evidence in an editorial
AUDIENCE Your teacher and classmates
LENGTH 1–2 paragraphs

Cooperative Learning

In a small group discuss television shows that feature teenagers. Identify ways you think each show could be improved. Then have each group member choose one show and write a letter to its producers in which he or she proposes ideas for change. Finally, take turns presenting each letter to the rest of the group, who will act as the show's producers and assess the relevance of the evidence.

Grammar Link

Use verb forms correctly.

Past forms of verbs, such as *went*, should not be used with helping verbs; past participle forms like *done* should not be used alone.

Write the correct verb form to complete each sentence below.

1. The trial (began, begun) six weeks ago.
2. The judge had (gave, given) very clear instructions.
3. The lawyers had (chose, chosen) a jury in about three weeks.
4. They had (took, taken) their time because this trial was so important.
5. Both lawyers (did, done) their best to persuade the jury.
6. The defendant has (wrote, written) notes to her lawyer throughout the trial.
7. The newspapers said that the trial has (gone, went) on too long.
8. The courtroom (was, been) filled with spectators every day.
9. Has the foreman (spoke, spoken) for a unanimous jury?
10. The defense has (win, won) an acquittal.

See Lessons 15.1 and 15.2, pages 543–547.

Persuasive Writing
Checking Reasoning

Learning to recognize the logical flaws in an argument can help you eliminate these flaws from your own writing. There are several types of faulty logic that you should be able to recognize.

Eliminate Faulty Logic

Once you've chosen the evidence to support an argument, you need to make sure that the conclusions you draw from that evidence are logical or follow correct reasoning. Suppose, for example, that you try to persuade your parents to buy you an outfit because it's on sale and they could save by buying it now. Their logical response to this argument could be that they'd save even more money if they didn't buy it at all. If your conclusions are illogical, your readers may reject your entire argument—no matter how compelling your evidence and no matter how well written your argument. As you write, watch out for three of the most common errors in reasoning: red herrings, either/or thinking, and cause-and-effect errors.

Red Herrings   The term *red herring* derives from the practice of dragging a strong-smelling fish across a trail to confuse hunting dogs and throw them off the scent. In writing, a red herring is a topic or statement introduced to distract the reader's attention from the central issue or to hide a weak argument.

Read over your argument to check for red herrings. Make sure that each of your points is directly related to your claim. Anything that sends your reader in a different direction may be a red herring.

Either/Or Thinking   Either/or thinking results from oversimplifying your argument by assuming that the issue has only two sides. For example, a writer might make the following claim: "Schools should eliminate computer instruction and return to teaching students the basics—reading, writing, and arithmetic." This position, however, fails to take into account the possibility that computers may aid in teaching these basic subjects.

To make sure that you have not used either/or thinking in your writing, look for other reasonable positions between the two sides you have presented in the argument. If you find them, you are probably oversimplifying the issue.

Cause-and-Effect Errors   The fact that one event precedes another in time does not necessarily mean that the first event is the cause of the second. To make sure that you have identified true cause-and-effect relationships, plot your evidence on a cause-and-effect diagram. Check to be sure that each effect is the direct result of the cause you have listed.

In the cause-and-effect diagram shown below, one writer plots some evidence supporting the argument that the demand for ivory jewelry has endangered African elephants. Is each effect the direct result of its preceding cause? Review the "*because* test" described in the Journal Writing activity on page 233 for another way to check an argument for cause-and-effect errors.

Grammar

Presenting Tip

If you decide to present your argument orally, be sure it does not contain sentences with dangling modifiers, which will distract your audience. See Lesson 18.7, pages 625–629.

Consumers want ivory carvings and jewelry.

Hunters kill elephants to supply ivory.

Because old elephants with larger tusks have been killed, younger ones are hunted.

Younger elephants have smaller tusks, so more are killed to meet demand for ivory.

The killing of elephants accelerates, leading to possible extinction.

Journal Writing

Select an argument you have begun to write. In your journal plot its evidence on a cause-and-effect diagram like the one shown above. Then ask yourself if each effect you have listed is the direct result of the preceding cause. If it is not, correct your argument.

Analyze Your Opponent's Logic

Often you can strengthen your position in an argument by pointing out flaws in the opposing argument. To find the logical flaws in an argument, evaluate the information presented, point by point. Look for and identify any red herrings, oversimplifications, or faulty cause-and-effect relationships.

If, upon close examination, you find points in the opposing argument that are difficult to disprove, you may need to concede their worth or admit that those points are valid. Frequently, making reasonable concessions can make your argument more convincing. It gives readers the impression that they are reading a well-researched, unbiased argument.

In the following selection, Yona Zeldis McDonough points out some logical flaws in the argument against wearing fur coats. However, she also concedes some points to the opposition. Is her argument strengthened by the concessions she makes?

Literature Model

Notice that McDonough evaluates key points in the opposing view and points out their flaws.

As I walked along 57th Street in Manhattan, a woman hissed, "A lot of animals were tortured to make that coat!" I was surprised, not by her sentiment, which I understood and even respected, but by her need to express it, unsolicited, in public. In the following weeks, I discovered that my outspoken critic was not alone. . . . Like it or not, I realized I was going to have to defend my coat against detractors.

I understand the arguments against wearing fur and have decided to wear one anyway. Not only does fur solve, more efficiently than any other substance known to man, the need for warmth, it has also been with us for hundreds if not thousands of years.

What points does McDonough concede? How does she use them to expose weaknesses in her opponents' argument?

Since I eat meat, I find the distinction between wearing and eating arbitrary. Animals don't care whether their flesh is consumed or their skins are worn; the point is, they have died and we have killed them. This may sound cruel, but it is honest.

I would like to ask those women who keep shouting at me just how consistent they are: What about wearing leather and suede? Animals must be killed for those skins, too. Do all these women wear only sneakers and carry canvas bags?

Yona Zeldis McDonough, "Sisters Under the Skin," *The New York Times*

6.3 Writing Activities

Write a Persuasive Argument

Write a brief report accepting or rejecting each of these statements about relaxing a school's dress code. Evaluate each statement using sound logic.

1. The way students dress is one of the few things teenagers can control, and that independence shouldn't be restricted.
2. After the dress code at a nearby school was relaxed, the students' grade averages rose.
3. The dress code should be stricter because too many students concentrate on their looks rather than on their schoolwork.
4. Some students' dress expresses their ethnic and cultural diversity.
5. If students aren't given total freedom in determining their dress, they will strike.
6. In addition to determining the dress code, students should also have a voice in choosing the books they read in class.
7. Dress should be regulated only if a student's clothes create a disturbance or pose a danger.

- Identify the kind of error in each faulty statement.
- Explain how each faulty statement weakens the argument.

PURPOSE   To evaluate arguments regarding a
          school's dress code
AUDIENCE A panel composed of teachers and school
          administrators
LENGTH   1 page

■■■ **COMPUTER OPTION** ■■■

Some software programs can search a piece of writing for errors in grammar, usage, and mechanics. You might want to use such a program as you write your argument for the dress-code activity. Although the program can aid the revising process, you are still responsible for finding and correcting errors in reasoning.

Grammar Link

Use commas to set off parenthetical expressions and long introductory elements in sentences.

Find examples in Yona Zeldis McDonough's excerpt on page 292. Then rewrite the following sentences, adding commas where they are needed.

1. As you watch popular television programs you may ask yourself if they include too much violence.
2. During the course of the past few weeks a group has been monitoring programs to count the violent incidents.
3. The group's report shows that for the most part violence is depicted during prime time.
4. Although viewing violence may have no negative effects on older people constant exposure to violence may have a negative effect on young children.
5. Many parents as a matter of fact are convinced that they see evidence of violent behavior in their children.

See Lesson 21.5, pages 705–706.

Persuasive Writing
Using Language to Advantage

You can make your writing more precise by using limiting words, by replacing general words with specific ones, and by understanding the connotations of the words you use.

You can't always persuade an audience to accept your argument. Empty adjectives and wild promises such as those in the cartoon fool no one. However, using words that precisely express your meaning will give you a better chance of persuading your readers.

Use Limiting Words

Limiting words are words that allow you to account for exceptions when you state your point of view. Use limiting words to avoid over-generalizations, oversimplifications, or gross exaggerations of the facts. For example, if you said, "Today's rock singers depend on sophisticated sound equipment to make up for their lack of musical talent," many of your readers would recognize that your point of view is a gross over-statement. On the other hand, if you said, "Some of today's rock singers depend on sophisticated sound equipment to make up for a lack of musical talent," you'd probably stand a better chance of holding your audience's attention. *Some* is a limiting word. The following chart lists some common limiting words that you can use to avoid making overgeneralizations.

Limiting Words		
almost never	in most cases	occasionally
a minority of	less than half	often
as a rule	many	rarely
certain	more than half	seldom
few	most	several
frequently	mostly	some
half	nearly all	sometimes
hardly ever	nearly always	the majority of
in general	not all	usually

Use Specific Words

Make your persuasive writing more precise by replacing general words with specific ones whenever you can. For example, compare the following two sentences:

> "Certain types of television programs have really bad effects on young children."
> "Violent television shows cause violent behavior and nightmares in young children."

Because the second sentence provides more definite information and brings more vivid thoughts and images to mind, it is more likely to hold the reader's attention. You'll never convince your readers of anything if you can't hold their attention.

Vocabulary

Revising Tip

During revising, try using a thesaurus to help you find precise words that express your meaning exactly. See Lesson 24.2, page 776.

Journal Writing

What strategies might you use to help identify overgeneralizations? What strategies might you use to help you identify general words that could be replaced with more specific ones? Write your ideas in your journal.

Consider Connotations

Choose words that not only express your specific meaning but also have the right connotation. The connotation of a word is an idea or notion suggested by the word beyond its exact meaning. Suppose, for instance, that you describe the famous smile in Leonardo da Vinci's painting, the *Mona Lisa*, as "weird." The word *weird* implies that there is something unpleasant about the smile. If, on the other hand, you refer to Mona Lisa's smile as "mysterious," you suggest that it is interesting and attractive.

Emotionally loaded words—words with highly emotional connotations—cause strong negative or positive responses. Consider the words *bold* and *reckless*. Although they have similar meanings, these words prompt very different emotional responses. *Bold* excites positive feelings because it suggests a daring, confident spirit. *Reckless* stirs up negative feelings because it implies irresponsibility.

In the following model, the writer uses the connotations of words to praise the candidate he supports and to establish arguments against the opposition.

Leonardo da Vinci, *Mona Lisa*, 1503–1505

Model

Words such as "heroic" imply that Edwards nobly defends lost causes.

How would the tone of the piece be affected if you substituted the phrase "level charges" for "make petty allegations"?

What other words used in the model convey particular notions about Edwards and the candidate opposing him?

I heartily encourage you to vote for Don "Bud" Edwards, a man of action and notable accomplishments for mayor. As a former alderman, Bud battled tirelessly against the bureaucrats on the city council to guarantee inexpensive housing for the underprivileged. Furthermore, his heroic efforts on behalf of the elderly have been chronicled by prominent journalists across the country.

On the other side of the coin, we have Bud's opponent, Gus Badenough. Gus is notorious for his waffling stands on the issues and for his vicious opposition to Bud. In fact, he has attempted to obstruct Bud's valiant work for the homeless more than once. Now Gus has begun to make petty allegations, which our candidate will not lower himself to address.

Are we going to allow these smear tactics to succeed? I hope not. On election day, I believe that there will still be enough upstanding citizens to vote for a true gentleman and statesman, Bud Edwards.

6.4 Writing Activities

Write a Positive Description

Rewrite the paragraph describing Pablo Picasso's painting *Two Acrobats with a Dog* for your museum's newsletter. Try to inspire museum visitors to come see the painting.

> Picasso's painting of two young circus tumblers is depressing. The children's colorful costumes contrast pathetically with the miserable expressions on their faces. The older boy holds a tiny pack over his shoulder—probably containing both boys' meager rags of clothes. Perhaps the circus is traveling to yet another town, and the pair must move on, like homeless orphans seeking shelter. Even the dog looks wretched.

Pablo Picasso, *Two Acrobats with a Dog*, 1905

- Use limiting words to reword over-generalizations.
- Choose precise words.
- Choose words with positive connotations.

PURPOSE To make description of a painting more appealing and intriguing
AUDIENCE Potential art museum visitors
LENGTH 1 paragraph

Cross-Curricular: Music

Write a brief review of a record or song you have heard recently. Use connotative words to evoke either a positive or negative reaction in your readers and to persuade them to accept your opinion of the song.

Grammar Link

Use specific nouns and modifiers.

The sentences below describe a new cereal. Rewrite the sentences using specific nouns and vivid modifiers that will persuade readers to try this product. Consider the connotations of the words you substitute. Each sentence can be revised in more than one way.

1. You should buy this brand of breakfast cereal because it tastes good.
2. This cereal contains many things that are good for you.
3. The shapes of the flakes are interesting.
4. The flakes have a nice texture.
5. The cereal is more nutritious when served with different kinds of fruits.

See Lesson 10.1, page 401, and Lesson 10.4, page 423.

Persuasive Writing
Writing an Editorial

In an editorial, such as the one below, a writer expresses an opinion about a current news event or issue. An effective editorial is direct and absorbing and can move its readers to take a stand on or reevaluate an issue. Do you think the argument in the model is effective?

Literature Model

The writer uses comments such as "It's also overdue" to express an opinion on the use of steroids.

What pieces of evidence does the writer use to support his opinion?

Yesterday's announcement of a plan for U.S. and Soviet Olympic committees to test athletes for drugs is welcome news. It's also overdue. Sports organizations are fighting a losing battle against anabolic steroids, and the reason is that most don't have their hearts in the struggle. Only a handful of competitors, including Ben Johnson, the Canadian sprinter, were expelled from the Seoul Olympics for using the forbidden drugs. Yet, according to *The Times*'s recent series on drug use, probably half or more of the 9,000 athletes at Seoul had used steroids or similar drugs during training.

Steroid use has long been rampant, yet sports bodies from Olympic committees downward have been failing in their responsibility to deter it. Drug-using athletes set a dispiriting example to a society trying to fight drug abuse, especially to young people who are at grave risk of injury from the drugs. "The system is saying, do whatever it takes to win," says Bill Curry, football coach at Alabama.

. . . [D]iet and exercise are accepted ways of enhancing physical ability; drugs are not. Many athletes apparently take steroids not because they want to but from peer pressure or fear of losing to others who do. . . . Once the message is out that sports organizations are really serious about steroids, most athletes will probably abandon them with relief.

"Winking at Steroids in Sports," November 22, 1988, *The New York Times*

The New Television Season:
Another Winning Lineup

What's Right with Rap

Fair Fare for Films

**Whatever it is,
it isn't art**

*Why do dancers
always have to be
on their toes?*

Captive Audiences

Support your
local drama club

Choose an Issue

Choose one issue about which you feel strongly and state it in the form of a question. If you don't have an issue in mind, get a sense of controversial topics in your community by reading local newspapers, talking to people, and listening to local talk shows on radio or television. Then brainstorm to generate evidence that supports your viewpoint. In the following example, two writers with opposing viewpoints answered this question: "Are rock musicians who lip-sync at live concerts cheating their fans?"

Prewriting Tip

If you are having trouble coming up with evidence to support your argument, try to imagine a conversation on the subject with someone who holds an opposing view.

Yes, because . . .
Fans who pay high prices for concert tickets deserve to hear live music.
People go to live concerts to hear live music.
It's not as exciting for the fans; they might as well listen to a record.

No, because . . .
Today's concerts offer more than just singing.
It's exciting just to be there at a live performance.
The audience gets more for its money because shows are so extravagant.

Journal Writing

Generate a list of currently controversial issues that interest you, and choose one that could be the topic of an editorial you might write. Then brainstorm to generate evidence that you could use to support your viewpoint.

Appeal to Your Audience

Select evidence that will persuade your audience to take your stand. Keep in mind that a striking image can often speak more powerfully than a list of facts and statistics. For example, rather than saying "Thousands of people thronged the concert," you might say, "So many people attended the concert that the crowd that night formed the third largest city in the state."

You might also consider injecting some humor into your editorial. When you make your readers laugh, they may feel that they share common ground with you and therefore be more disposed to agree with what you're saying.

Draw a Conclusion

A good conclusion sums up the argument and spurs the reader to action. In the editorial below, Eugene Weresow makes his strongest point at the end.

Student Model

Weresow makes concessions to his opponents but counters their objections by discussing the intentions of the authors.

What is Weresow's strongest point?

*H*anging on my classroom wall is a long list of books that have been banned from certain schools. As I scanned the list, I recognized several that were among the best I've ever read, including *Catcher in the Rye, 1984,* and *Brave New World.* Although these books contain controversial language and situations, I believe it would be a mistake to ban them.

Admittedly, some of the characters in *Catcher in the Rye* use words that would be inappropriate in the classroom. But real people often swear and use slang expressions; the author is just trying to make his book realistic. Similarly, *1984* and *Brave New World* portray situations that some may consider unacceptable for political or social reasons. But the authors mean to convey a message with these works; the extreme situations they use make a more lasting impression upon the reader than would more acceptable situations.

I don't believe it is dangerous to expose students to the controversial material in these books. On the contrary, I believe the books should be valued for the ideas they express. Rather than protect impressionable students, those who ban these books do us a disservice: they deny us access to ideas.

Eugene Weresow, Edison High School, Edison, New Jersey

Write an Editorial for a TV Program

You have been asked to deliver an editorial on *Teen Say*, a television program for teenagers, on the issue "Should the academic year be extended through July?"

- Establish your position on the issue.
- Select evidence to persuade your audience.
- Summarize your argument with a strong conclusion.

PURPOSE   To persuade your audience to accept your views on extending the school year

AUDIENCE   Teenage TV viewers

LENGTH   2–3 paragraphs

COMPUTER OPTION

Suppose you want to send copies of your television editorial to several different teen magazines. Instead of typing multiple copies of your piece, use the Mail Merge feature of your word-processing program. Just type a list of the addresses to which you want to send the editorial. Then use Mail Merge to print as many copies as you want, each to a different address.

Grammar Link

Make verbs agree with indefinite pronoun subjects.

A verb must agree with an indefinite pronoun subject, such as *each* or *several*:

> **Several** *(plural)* **were** tested.
> **Each** *(singular)* **was** satisfactory.

Rewrite each sentence, choosing the correct form of the verb in parentheses.

1. I inquired about certain books and was told that some (was, were) not available in the school library.
2. All (is, are) literary classics and (has been, have been) in print for a long time.
3. No one in the library (has, have) time to help me use the computer catalog to locate other books by that author.
4. Most (is, are) in different editions and (has been, have been) reprinted several times.
5. Though there are two copies, neither (is, are) on the shelf.

See Lesson 16.7, page 581.

Writing About Literature
Writing a Movie Review

A movie review is one person's evaluation of a film. Although critics may differ in their opinions, most critics go through a similar procedure in developing their reviews.

Scene from *Dances with Wolves*

Provide Background Information

Most reviewers begin a movie review by expressing their opinion of the film. They then provide background information on the film by briefly summarizing the plot and identifying the characters, actors, director, and scriptwriter. To determine how much background information to include, ask yourself how much your audience already know about the film and what they need to know to understand your review of it.

Examine the Movie's Elements

Reviewers often evaluate certain elements of the film and measure the film's success by specific criteria. These criteria differ somewhat for different types of films. For example, a comedy can be judged according to how funny it is; an action film can be judged by how exciting it is. However, some criteria are useful for judging most movies. These are outlined in the chart below.

The Elements of a Movie	
Plot What happens in the film	Does it hold your interest? Does it seem plausible or contrived?
Theme What the film means	Is the movie's theme significant, worth pondering? Does the film develop the theme, or does it oversimplify a complex issue?
Characterization The way the characters are developed by the scriptwriter and the director	Do the characters seem real, believable? Are their motivations and actions true to their backgrounds and personalities?
Acting The way the actors portray their characters	Do the actors create believable characters? Do they evoke the intended responses in the audience—laughter, fear, sorrow?
Special Effects Techniques used to create illusions	Do the effects create the desired illusions? Do they enhance or overpower the story?
Sound Track The music that accompanies the visuals	Is the music appropriate to the scene in which it is used? What is the quality of the music? Is the sound track well recorded, clear?

Journal Writing

Choose a movie that you have seen recently. Use the questions in the chart above to examine the movie's elements and help you generate details that you could use in a movie review. Record the details in your journal.

Evaluate the Movie Critically

Although you can approach a movie review in many ways, using the questions below may help you develop your own perspective to evaluate a movie. Read the checklist, then study student Lina Chern's review.

Grammar

Editing Tip

When you edit your review, set off the movie title by underlining it. If you use a computer, input the title in italic type. Capitalize the movie title correctly. Refer to Lesson 20.2, page 677, to review capitalization rules.

A Critic's Checklist

1. Can I compare or contrast this film with another that explores the same theme?
2. Is this film adapted from a written work, such as a novel or a play? If so, can I compare it to the original work?
3. Can I compare my reactions with those of the audience?
4. Can I critique the film from a particular social or political perspective? Am I well informed enough to do so?

Student Model

I must admit that I was not expecting terrific results from *Terminator 2: Judgment Day*, the most eagerly awaited sequel of the summer. After all, its predecessor was one of the most thoughtful, understated action movies ever made, while *T2* was promising to be a typical overblown summer blockbuster. I was only half-correct—the story has lost some thought and subtlety and gained a great deal of special effects, but is still interesting and definitely entertaining.

What elements of T2 does Chern examine in her review?

Arnold Schwarzenegger (too marketable now to play the bad guy) stars as a reprogrammed Terminator cyborg that is ordered to go back in time to protect the still-adolescent John Connor (Edward Furlong); the boy is to become a key figure in the future war between humans and machines. After John and the Terminator rescue John's mother, Sarah (Linda Hamilton)—now a tough, hell-bent warrior—from a mental hospital, the three set out to prevent the coming nuclear holocaust, or Judgment Day. Meanwhile, they have to deal with another, more advanced Terminator that has been sent back to kill John.

What is Chern's opinion of the movie? Why do you think she compares T2 with the original Terminator to express her opinion?

In general, *Terminator 2* is engaging and creative, but in a more conventional way than the original. It is a clean, slick moneymaker, which should not deter anyone from seeing it.

Lina Chern, Maine East High School, Chicago, Illinois

6.6 Writing Activities

Write a Movie Review

Select a film known for its special effects and review it for the readers of your school newspaper. Base your review on an evaluation of the movie's use of special effects.

- Provide background information.
- Discuss whether special effects enhance or overpower the movie.
- Explain whether the effects create the desired illusions.
- Compare the special effects to those in another movie.
- Explain the audience's response to the movie.

PURPOSE To write a movie review
AUDIENCE Teenage readers of your school newspaper
LENGTH 1–2 paragraphs

Cross-Curricular: Literature

Choose one of the films listed below or another you have seen that is based on a work of literature. Then prepare a written review of the film in which you compare it with the original work of literature. If you like, submit the review for publication in your school's literary journal or newspaper.

- *Wuthering Heights*
- *A Raisin in the Sun*
- *The Grapes of Wrath*
- *Great Expectations*
- *The Color Purple*
- *The Age of Innocence*
- *Howards End*
- *Out of Africa*
- *Elmer Gantry*
- *A Passage to India*

Grammar Link

Use comparative and superlative forms of modifiers correctly.

more conventional, most eagerly awaited film, and *one of the most thoughtful*

Rewrite the following sentences. Use the correct degree of comparison of the modifiers in parentheses.

1. *The Nightmare Before Christmas* is one of the _____ films I have ever seen. (good)
2. It is _____ than other animated films. (thought provoking)
3. My little brother thought that the creatures in this movie sang _____. (beautifully)
4. The special effects in *Nightmare* are _____ than those in *E.T.* (imaginative)
5. The words of the songs are the _____ I have ever heard. (witty)
6. In the movie, Pumpkin Jack travels to the _____ town in all of Holiday World. (far)
7. He travels to Christmas, a town much _____ than his own. (nice)
8. In the film, Pumpkin Jack takes the _____ of all possible actions. (surprising)
9. Each gift Jack distributes is _____ than the next. (clever)
10. In the end, Jack learns that he is _____ of all when he is himself. (happy)

See Lesson 18.1, pages 621–622.

UNIT 6

WRITING PROCESS IN ACTION

PERSUASIVE WRITING

In this unit you've learned about writing to persuade and about the logical considerations that contribute to presenting a strong and well-supported argument. You've written reviews, articles, and editorials. Now it's time to apply what you've learned. In this lesson you will select a problem in your school or community and take a stand in favor of whatever corrective action you think is appropriate.

• Assignment •

Context	You are an editor of *Student Voices*, a monthly newsletter with a broad circulation in your school and community. You have been asked to write an editorial about a problem situation or an injustice you want to see changed. This is your opportunity to reach people who make policies and decisions that affect your life but who might not listen to you otherwise.
Purpose	To write an editorial that exposes a problem or injustice and encourages readers to take corrective action
Audience	Teenagers, teachers, school administrators, and community members
Length	2 paragraphs

The following pages can help you plan and write your editorial. Read through them and then refer to them as you need to. But remember, you're in charge of your own writing process.

Prewriting

What problems or injustices are on your mind? The suggestions on the notepad may help you explore your thoughts.

Choose one or two problems that you have identified. Using lists or questions, explore the problems you've identified (see Lesson 2.2). Write down everything you can think of related to each problem. Think about how each could be used to accomplish your purpose and influence your audience. Read what you have written about each problem. Then ask yourself the following questions, and use the answers to narrow your choices to one topic:

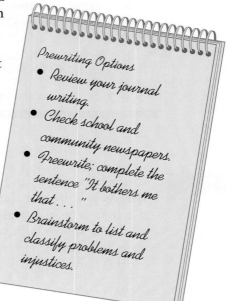

Prewriting Options
- Review your journal writing.
- Check school and community newspapers.
- Freewrite; complete the sentence "It bothers me that . . . "
- Brainstorm to list and classify problems and injustices.

- What problem do I care about the most?
- What claim do I feel the most confidence in making?
- About which topic are my readers most likely to share my concern?

Once you've narrowed your choice down to one topic, review your purposes—to persuade your readers that your claim is valid and to rouse them to take corrective action. Then take some time to think about your audience. Are your readers likely to agree or disagree with you? Do they already care about the issue, or must you persuade them to care? Persuading readers to act upon your argument may require meeting their needs and overcoming their attitudes.

Finally, begin to gather and evaluate statistics, opinions, examples, and other evidence that will help you back up your central claim.

Drafting

When you write persuasively, you want to present information in a way that will have a strong impact on your readers. To achieve this goal, use language that is forceful and direct. Choose specific words with strong connotations, as Clara Spotted Elk does in the following excerpt.

Drafting Tip

For help in summarizing your appeal, see Lesson 6.5, page 298.

Literature Model

W e are outraged that our religious views are not accepted by the scientific community and that the graves of our ancestors are desecrated. Many tribes are willing to accommodate some degree of study for a limited period of time—provided that it would help Indian people or mankind in general. But how many "specimens" are needed? We will not accept grave robbing and the continued hoarding of our ancestors' remains.

Clara Spotted Elk, "Skeletons in the Attic"

You might choose to state your claim forcefully at the start, then present the evidence and reinforce it with a strong conclusion. Alternatively, you can build up to your central claim, which you state last. As you present your evidence, address opposing arguments. Prove the arguments to be false or concede them in some way.

Once you've built your case, write a conclusion that will leave a strong impression. Summarize your main points, state or restate your central claim, and urge readers to take action.

Revising Tip

For suggestions on checking the logic of your arguments, see Lesson 6.3, pages 290–291.

Revising

To begin revising, read over your draft to make sure that what you've written fits your purpose and audience. Then have a writing conference. Read your draft to a partner or small group. Use your audience's reactions to help you evaluate your work.

Revising Checklist
- Have I presented my central claim clearly?
- Is my evidence accurate and relevant?
- Is my reasoning sound?
- Have I presented my case in a way that will appeal to my audience?

Editing

At this stage, look closely at your writing, paying special attention to your use of language. As you **proofread,** check for errors in grammar, spelling, usage, and mechanics. Use the questions on the notepad as a guide. Then use the self-evaluation list below to make sure that your editorial satisfies your purpose and communicates your message exactly as you want it to.

Editing Checklist
- *Have I chosen the correct word of a confusing pair?*
- *Have I used commas to separate introductory and parenthetical elements from the rest of a sentence?*
- *Have I used specific nouns and modifiers with appropriate connotations?*
- *Have I checked the spelling of any unfamiliar words?*

Self-Evaluation
Make sure your editorial—

- focuses on a school or community injustice
- contains a central claim and identifies a main purpose for writing
- supports the central claim with accurate and relevant evidence
- uses sound reasoning and addresses counter-arguments
- uses limiting words, specific words, and connotations to advantage
- uses correct grammar, usage, and mechanics

Proofreading

For proofreading symbols, see page 100.

Presenting

You can submit your editorial to the student newspaper, or you might consider using your article as the starting point for a campaign in support of your position. You can rework your editorial into a petition or a leaflet, or even present it as a speech.

Journal Writing

Reflect on your writing process experience. Answer these questions in your journal. What do you like best about your editorial? What was the hardest part of writing it? What did you learn in your writing conference? What new things have you learned as a writer?

Clara Spotted Elk

■ ■ ■

Skeletons in the Attic

Clara Spotted Elk has worked to help her fellow Native Americans regain the skeletal remains of their ancestors from museums, collectors, and federal agencies. In September of 1989, thanks in part to persuasive efforts such as hers, the Smithsonian Institution began returning some of these remains to their Native American descendants. As you read the following article, note how Spotted Elk expresses her point of view on this cultural issue. Then try the activities in Linking Writing and Literature on page 313.

Millions of American Indians lived in this country when Columbus first landed on our shores. After the western expansion, only about 250,000 Indians survived. What happened to the remains of those people who were decimated by the advance of the white man? Many are gathering dust in American museums.

In 1985, I and some Northern Cheyenne chiefs visited the attic of the Smithsonian's[1] Natural History Museum in Washington, D.C., to review the inventory of their Cheyenne collection. After a chance inquiry, a curator[2] pulled out a drawer in one of the scores of cabinets that line the attic. There were the jumbled bones of an Indian. "A Kiowa,"[3] he said.

Howling Wolf, Untitled drawing, 1876

Subsequently, we found that 18,500 Indian remains—some consisting of a handful of bones, but mostly full skeletons—are unceremoniously stored in the Smithsonian's nooks and crannies. Other museums, individuals, and federal agencies such as the National Park Service also collect the bones of Indian warriors, women, and children. Some are on display as roadside tourist attractions. It is estimated that another 600,000 Indian remains are secreted away in locations across the country.

The museum community and forensic[4] scientists vigorously defend these grisly[5] collections. With few exceptions, they refuse to return remains to the tribes that wish to rebury them, even when grave robbing has been documented. They want to maintain adequate numbers of "specimens" for analysis and say they are dedicated to "the permanent curation of Indian skeletal remains."

1 **Smithsonian** the Smithsonian Institution, a research organization administered by the United States government

2 **curator** (kyoo´rā tər) a person in charge of a museum

3 **Kiowa** (kī´ ə wä) a tribe of Plains Indians formerly of what is now Colorado, Oklahoma, Kansas, New Mexico, and Texas

4 **forensic** (fə ren(t)´ sik or fə ren´ zik) able to apply medical knowledge to legal matters

5 **grisly** (griz´ lē) horrible; ghastly

Indian people are tired of being "specimens." The Northern Cheyenne word for ourselves is "tsistsistas"—human beings. Like people the world over, one of our greatest responsibilities is the proper care of the dead.

We are outraged that our religious views are not accepted by the scientific community and that the graves of our ancestors are desecrated.[6] Many tribes are willing to accommodate some degree of study for a limited period of time—provided that it would help Indian people or mankind in general. But how many "specimens" are needed? We will not accept grave robbing and the continued hoarding of our ancestors' remains.

Would this be tolerated if it were discovered that it affected other ethnic groups? (Incidentally, the Smithsonian also collects skeletons of blacks.) What would happen if the Smithsonian had 18,500 Holocaust victims in the attic? There would be a tremendous outcry in this country. Why is there no outcry about the Indian collections?

Indians are not exotic creatures for study. We are human beings who practice living religions. Our religion should be placed not only on a par with science when it comes to determining the disposition of our ancestors, but on a par with every other religion practiced in this country.

To that end, Sen. Daniel K. Inouye (D.-HI)[7] will soon reintroduce the "Bones Bill" to aid Indians in retrieving the remains of their ancestors from museums. As in the past, the "Bones Bill" will most likely be staunchly resisted by the collectors of Indian skeletons—armed with slick lobbyists,[8] lots of money, and the mystique[9] of science.

Scientists have attempted to defuse this issue by characterizing their opponents as radical Indians, out of touch with their culture and with little appreciation of science. Armed only with a moral obligation to our ancestors, the Indians who support the bill have few resources and little money.

But, in my view, the issue should concern all Americans, for it raises very disturbing questions. American Indians want only to reclaim and rebury their dead. Is this too much to ask?

6 **desecrated** (de si krāt' d) treated something considered holy in an inappropriate manner

7 **(D.-HI)** Democrat, Hawaii

8 **lobbyists** (lä' bē ists) people who work to influence laws and government decisions in favor of one special-interest group

9 **mystique** (mi stēk') a set of mysterious feelings and attitudes surrounding a person, group, or activity

Linking Writing and Literature

Readers Respond to the Model

What evidence makes Spotted Elk's argument effective?

Explore Clara Spotted Elk's point of view by answering these questions. Then read how other students reacted to Spotted Elk's argument.

1. How does Spotted Elk's choice of words affect the tone of the article? What effect does the tone have on your reading of the article?

2. What is Spotted Elk's principle argument? What "evidence" does she provide to support her view?

3. How did you react to the description of those who Spotted Elk thinks will oppose the "Bones Bill"? What words or phrases triggered your reaction?

4. How does Spotted Elk use limiting words to prevent presenting an either/or situation? Give examples to support your answer.

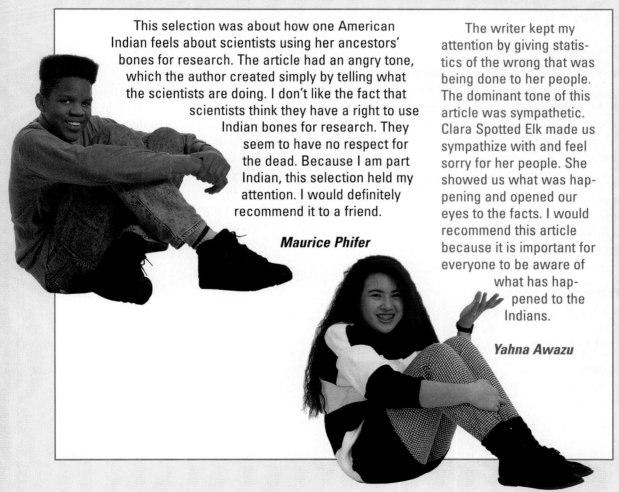

This selection was about how one American Indian feels about scientists using her ancestors' bones for research. The article had an angry tone, which the author created simply by telling what the scientists are doing. I don't like the fact that scientists think they have a right to use Indian bones for research. They seem to have no respect for the dead. Because I am part Indian, this selection held my attention. I would definitely recommend it to a friend.

Maurice Phifer

The writer kept my attention by giving statistics of the wrong that was being done to her people. The dominant tone of this article was sympathetic. Clara Spotted Elk made us sympathize with and feel sorry for her people. She showed us what was happening and opened our eyes to the facts. I would recommend this article because it is important for everyone to be aware of what has happened to the Indians.

Yahna Awazu

Unit 6 Review

Reflecting on the Unit

Summarize what you learned in this unit by answering the following questions.

- What are the most important elements of persuasive writing?

- What are some criteria for selecting, evaluating, and using evidence?

- How can choice of words make an argument more persuasive?

- What are some steps to take in constructing a logical argument?

- What are the purpose and the elements of an editorial?

- What criteria might you use to judge and review a movie?

Adding to Your Portfolio

Choose a selection for your portfolio.
Look over the persuasive writing you have done during this unit. Select a completed piece to put into your portfolio. The piece you choose should show some or all of the following:

- logical, accurate, relevant evidence to support a claim
- limiting words, specific words, and words with appropriate connotations
- strong evidence, a striking image, or humor to appeal to an audience

Reflect on your choice.
Attach a note to the piece you chose, explaining briefly why you chose it and what you learned from it.

Set goals.
How can you improve your writing? What skill will you focus on the next time you write?

Writing Across the Curriculum

Make a civics connection.
How do you feel about the large percentage of the population that does not vote in elections? Is voting a citizen's responsibility that should be encouraged? Is not voting a positive way to express dissatisfaction with the candidates? Develop an argument in which you define your position on this topic. Be sure to identify your purpose, state your claim, and support it with relevant and logical evidence.

Skills and Applications

Unit 7 Review

Research Paper Writing
Prewriting: Planning and Researching

George W. G. Ferris, the man who dreamed up the Ferris wheel, had a great challenge ahead of him: he had to turn his idea into a solid, working structure. After quite a bit of sketching and planning and a step-by-step approach, Ferris finally created this fantastic new contraption, the likes of which the world had never seen before.

In much the same way—with careful planning and a step-by-step approach—you can create a successful and engaging research paper.

What Is a Research Paper?

The research paper differs from many other kinds of writing because it includes factual information from a variety of sources. These sources may be primary (records of the people who took part in the event or period you are studying, such as journals, documents, or photos) or secondary (books and articles written about the event or period). Whatever the sources, you can write one of four basic kinds of research paper.

Four Types of Research Paper	
Summary	The writer explores a topic by summing up the opinions of other writers and researchers.
Evaluative	The writer states an opinion and backs it up with evidence found in primary and/or secondary resources.
Original	The writer does original research on a topic and reports on his or her findings.
Combination	The writer combines approaches in one paper, such as summarizing opinions, then conducting original research.

Choose a Good Topic

One of your first decisions is what to write about. Try to find a topic that interests you, one that you really want to learn about. If your teacher assigns a subject area, go to the library and skim some general articles covering that area in an encyclopedia. Look for any aspects of the subject that relate to your own interests and activities, or any personalities or events that sound intriguing and exciting. These can become topics to explore in the paper.

Also, keep in mind how much information will be manageable given the length of your research paper. If the topic is very broad, you'll have too much information, too many ideas to cover. If the library has a number of books on that particular topic, say, five to ten, or if the encyclopedia gives it more than two pages, the topic is probably too broad for a typical paper. On the other hand, some topics are so narrow that you won't be able to uncover enough material. If you write about such a topic, your paper will probably lack substance (unless you do original research). If you can only find one or two articles on the topic, for example, and if the encyclopedia doesn't cover it, you will almost certainly not have enough to write about.

Britta Waller, who wrote the model paper in Lesson 7.6, pages 342–347, was instructed to write about technology in history. She wanted to avoid run-of-the-mill topics but had to choose a subject on which there was enough information to write an adequate paper. After

Prewriting Tip

For information on library resources, see Unit 23, pages 760–771.

Too narrow: The gear mechanisms of a Ferris wheel

Appropriate: The history of the Ferris wheel

Too broad: Amusement parks and carnivals

some brainstorming and a trip to the library, she decided to write about the construction of the first Ferris wheel. It seemed an appropriate topic, since authors have devoted sections of books to it, and since she found articles on different aspects of the topic.

Find Information on Your Topic

Once you have a topic, you need to decide on your paper's central idea—the idea that will guide your thinking and your selection of research questions. Try to identify three to seven research questions, each question focusing on one aspect of the topic. Ask the *what*'s, *why*'s, and *how*'s about your topic (for example, "Why was this considered so important? What effect did it have on different groups in society? How did it come into being?"). As you begin to find answers, you'll come up with more sharply focused questions. Feel free to modify your central idea as you learn more about the topic.

The chart below lists and describes various sources of information that can help you answer your research questions in the area of science and technology.

Basic Sources of Science and Technology Information		
Type	**Description**	**Examples**
Periodicals	Newspapers, magazines, journals, and other sources that are published on a regular basis, either for general readers or for more specialized audiences	*Washington Post* *Scientific American* *National Geographic* *Science Digest* *Discover*
Government Agencies	Branches of federal, state, and local governments that publish reports, statistics, and other information on scientific topics	National Aeronautics and Space Administration U.S. Fish and Wildlife Service State and local departments of health
Nonprofit Organizations	Private groups that study certain scientific areas or topics and publish reports and statistics	World Wildlife Fund American Cancer Society American Dental Association Sierra Club
Computer Databases	General science information available through computer linkup for a fee	*Applied Science and Technology Index* *General Science Index* *Magazine Index*

Take Notes

Once you have found some sources, you can begin taking notes and collecting information. Taking notes efficiently and accurately is one of the most important steps in writing a good research paper. You will probably take many more notes than you will end up using, but don't worry—so do professional writers and researchers.

Develop a Working Bibliography   As you begin your research, assemble a record of the books, articles, and other sources you consult. This record is your working bibliography. When you find a useful source, record the publishing data on a three-by-five-inch index card, and number it. This way you can find and use the information more easily later. Complete bibliography cards will also help you write your final list of works cited.

Different kinds of sources need different data on their bibliography cards, as the samples below illustrate. Notice that at the top of each card, the writer identifies the bibliographic source with a number that will later serve as an easy way to identify the source.

Grammar

Editing Tip

When you edit your paper, you can check the accuracy of your spelling, punctuation, and capitalization of titles and authors by referring to your bibliography cards.

Kinds of Bibliography Cards

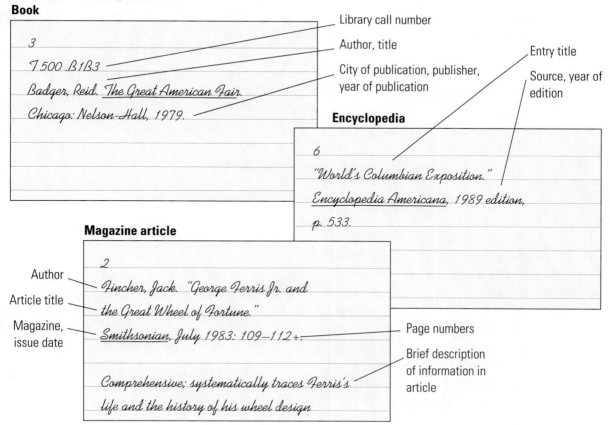

Book

3

T 500 .B1B3

Badger, Reid. *The Great American Fair.*

Chicago: Nelson-Hall, 1979.

Library call number
Author, title
City of publication, publisher, year of publication

Encyclopedia

6

"World's Columbian Exposition."

Encyclopedia Americana, 1989 edition,

p. 533.

Entry title
Source, year of edition

Magazine article

2

Fincher, Jack. "George Ferris Jr. and

the Great Wheel of Fortune."

Smithsonian, July 1983: 109–112+.

Comprehensive; systematically traces Ferris's

life and the history of his wheel design

Author
Article title
Magazine, issue date
Page numbers
Brief description of information in article

Prepare Note Cards Read your sources thoroughly for information, ideas, statements, and statistics that relate to your research topic. When you find something you can use, write it on a three-by-five card, with one piece of information per card, and record the number of that source's bibliography card. When making these note cards, you can either paraphrase, summarize, or quote the source directly.

International expositions are of recent origin. The first was the Great Exhibition held in London in 1851 which was the scene of Joseph Paxton's Crystal Palace—the first large-scale, prefabricated iron and glass building—which alone attested that fair's significance. From then until 1893 there were several European expositions, probably the most famous being that held in Paris in 1889, celebrated for its Eiffel Tower. The United States had hosted several trade fairs but only one full-scale international exposition, that held in Philadelphia in 1876, the celebration of the centennial of American independence. The World's Columbian Exposition would be the fifteenth world's fair and the second American one. But it was ~~of greater~~ scope than any of its predecessors. Early ~~simply~~ of one large exhibition hall, ~~or~~ of such a hall augmented with ~~t~~he main hall might be artfully de~~~~was made to lay out the surround~~~~~~lish the buildings with sculpture ~~~~Exhibition of 1867 originated both

To paraphrase, you rewrite the information in your own words.

Previous fairs

1. London, Great Exhibition, 1851

2. Philadelphia, 1876

3. Paris, 1889

Columbian Exposition was of a much larger scale.

6

Previous fairs

While it was built on the model of the other world's fairs, the 1893 Columbian Exposition was the grandest fair yet.

6

To summarize, you write down only the main ideas and key supporting material.

Previous fairs

"The World's Columbian Exposition would be the fifteenth world's fair and the second American one. But it was of vastly greater scope than any of its predecessors."

page xii

6

To use a passage exactly as written, write the direct quotation as it appears, and put it in quotation marks on your card.

Reading Sources Critically   As you read and research, think about sources critically. A source may be biased; that is, the writer may be prejudiced toward one particular viewpoint. Using a biased source without recognizing it as such can hurt your argument. To detect bias, ask yourself questions such as, "Does this writer have a hidden purpose?"

When you take specific notes, pay attention to each idea's context, or its relation to ideas before and after it. You may even want to note this context on your card. If you use information out of context, you may mislead the reader. For example, a political leader might have supported a shift to military rule—but only during wartime. If you don't mention that last fact, you present that leader's position out of context.

Avoid Plagiarism   Presenting someone else's ideas or statements as your own is plagiarism. You must avoid even accidental plagiarism. Writers sometimes begin to paraphrase but instead present an idea almost as it was originally written and then take credit for it. Read your sources critically, keep complete and well-documented notes, and credit other writers when you should. (See Lesson 7.4, "Citing Sources.") If you have doubts about whether you may be plagiarizing, try rewriting the passage again in your own words.

7.1 Writing Activities

Skills Practice

1. Write an explanation of why each topic below is too broad, too narrow, or about right for a five-page research paper:

- effects of the car on the United States
- 3-D movies—invention and refinement
- latest developments in contact lenses
- building the Great Pyramid at Giza

2. Suppose you wanted to write a report about the development of new, high-definition televisions. Which of the following sources do you think might have useful information on this topic? Choose the two best and the two worst sources, and explain each choice.

- *Newsweek* magazine
- *Encyclopaedia Britannica*, 1965
- *TV Guide*
- *Scientific American*
- *The Great Old Movies on TV*
- *Video Technology Review*, this year's annual edition

Your Research Paper

Select an appropriate topic for your own research paper—something you really want to know about. This will be the paper you will work on throughout the unit. Even though this unit uses examples from science and technology, the basic methods you learn will apply to the writing of any research paper. Begin by writing three to seven research questions. Then prepare bibliography cards, and begin taking notes for your paper.

Research Paper Writing
Prewriting: Outlining

WHAT PURE CHAOS! might be your thought, facing your mounds of research notes. But your notes are probably not any more impossible to sort out than is the pile of hardware shown here. All you need to bring order to the chaos is an organizing principle. For example, if you examine the hardware with the idea of function in mind, you might see that you could place all the items that hold things together in one pile, all the items that prevent leaks in another, and so on. Not only can an organizing principle help you bring order to your notes, it can help you develop an outline, which is a particularly useful tool for writing a research paper.

Create an Outline

A working outline—one that you continue to write and revise as you conduct your research—helps you think about your topic critically and makes your research efficient. The following tips will help you create such an outline.

Tips on Outlining

1. Look for similarities among notes: group note cards on similar topics together. Use each group as a main topic in your outline.

2. Within groups cluster similar note cards into subgroups that elaborate on the larger and more general main topic. Use these subgroups as the subtopics in your outline.

3. Arrange main topics to build on your central idea. And, under each main topic, arrange subtopics so they elaborate on the main topic in a logical way.

4. As you continue your research and learn more, revise and elaborate in your outline. Subdivide information in subtopics into outline entries as well.

5. Set aside note cards that don't fit under any heading.

6. Before you begin your first draft, prepare a final outline.

```
                    Title of Paper
    I. Main Topic
       A. Subtopic
          1. Division of a subtopic
             a. Subdivision of a subtopic
             b. Subdivision of a subtopic
          2. Division of a subtopic
             a. Subdivision of a subtopic
             b. Subdivision of a subtopic
       B. Subtopic
   II. Main Topic
```

Number main topics with roman numerals.

Notice the lettering, numbering, and indentation systems for subtopics and their divisions and subdivisions.

A subtopic doesn't have to have any subdivisions. But if you list any at all, you must list at least two.

How can you decide on the best way to arrange the ideas in your notes? Since ideas can be divided up many different ways, you have a number of options, depending on the nature of your information. In a history paper you might arrange ideas chronologically. In a science paper you might arrange ideas in causal order to show how one idea or event directly determines another, or in logical order to show how the presence of one item or idea makes another reasonably predictable. Britta Waller, writing on a topic that combines history and technology, creates an outline that proceeds from general to specific.

```
                 George W. G. Ferris
         The Man Who Re-invented the Wheel

    I. Background of 1893 Columbian Exposition
    A. Continued tradition of big fairs
       1. Previous world's fairs
          a. London and the Crystal Palace,
             1851
          b. Philadelphia, 1876
          c. Paris and the Eiffel Tower, 1889
       2. Chicago fair to be larger than
          earlier fairs
    B. Emphasized cultural achievements
       1. Planners D. H. Burnham and
          F. L. Olmsted
       2. Nation's top artists, inventors,
          industrialists
    C. Reflected values of the era
   II. Background of George W. G. Ferris
```

Waller provides a chronological account of the years leading up to the 1893 fair.

In what order does Waller present her topics? Is this a good way to arrange this paper?

Develop a Thesis Statement

Grammar

Drafting Tip

Thesis statements are often compound sentences. To review how to create compound sentences, see Lesson 13.3, pages 503–504.

So far, you have guided your research and outline according to your central idea, or the basic questions you've been exploring. You've probably rethought this idea as you have learned about the topic. Now, as you get ready to begin your first draft, it's time to turn that central idea into a thesis statement—that is, a concise idea that you try to prove, expand on, or illustrate in your writing. This statement gives your writing a focus from start to finish.

To create a thesis statement, look at your central idea critically. Is it as clear as it can be? Does it include all important aspects of your topic? Does it include historical background or new developments if these are relevant? Does it make the significance of your topic clear?

After asking these and other similar sorts of questions, write the idea again as a single sentence that describes your topic more precisely. This time include a mention of your approach to the topic. Are you comparing one topic with another, exploring a single topic in depth, trying to prove or disprove any common notions?

The chart below progresses from central idea to thesis statement. The chart on page 325 gives four basic kinds of thesis statements.

Example of a central idea:
The Ferris wheel was a unique engineering feat when it was constructed.

Examples of revising a central idea:
1. The Ferris wheel, a unique engineering feat in its day, came on the scene in time to help assert American superiority over Europe and became the most popular attraction at the Columbian Exposition.
2. The Ferris wheel, a unique engineering feat, was conceived at a time when America needed to show its superiority over Europe, but the wheel became the most popular attraction at the Columbian Exposition, overshadowing the many cultural exhibits.

Example of a thesis statement:
The unique engineering feat of the Ferris wheel was one of many assertions of American pride at the World's Columbian Exposition, but its huge popularity overshadowed the fair's cultural attractions.

Four Types of Thesis Statements		
Type	**Description**	**Example**
Original	Describes the background and results of original research to be presented in the paper	My survey of students and teachers at Lincoln High School has uncovered a desire for more and better computers and more instruction in computer science.
Evaluative	Identifies an issue and evaluates opinions on the issue that the writer will convey through the paper	Solar power provides our best option for future energy needs, taking into account both economic and environmental concerns.
Summary	Introduces the different perspectives on a topic for a paper that primarily summarizes the work of others	High-speed trains, traveling at speeds greater than 125 miles per hour, have revolutionized intercity travel in both France and Japan.
Combination	Combines any two or all three of the above approaches	Interviews with music-store salespeople and compact disc owners lead me to believe that the CD has replaced the record once and for all.

7.2 Writing Activities

Skills Practice

1. Organize the following pieces of information into three different categories. Then supply an outline heading for each, with sub-headings.

- Laser stands for *l*ight *a*mplification by *s*timulated *e*mission of *r*adiation.
- Lasers can be used in surgery.
- Compact discs are "read" by lasers.
- A laser creates a narrow beam of mono-chromatic and coherent light.
- Holograms rely on laser technology.
- Lasers help guide some "smart" bombs.
- Stores use lasers to ring up purchases.
- Laser light is the result of a chain reaction of atoms discharging photons.

- Manufacturing industries use lasers to inspect the quality of their products.

2. Rewrite the following into a concise, single-sentence thesis statement:

> The race to put an astronaut on the moon had numerous motivations. Many people thought it was a waste of money. Yet the space program has resulted in many inventions that improve our lives.

Your Research Paper

Prepare a working outline and a thesis statement for your own research paper.

Research Paper Writing
Drafting

Think of the simple light bulb—something we take for granted. Yet the light bulb was once just an idea in the mind of Thomas Edison. To make his idea a reality, Edison had to do research, make plans, examine the research of others, and then carefully refine his work.

A research paper requires much the same effort. Even as you turn your outline and notes into a draft, you still need to experiment, ask new questions, and refine your ideas.

Use Your Outline and Notes

Using the structure you have given your outline, you will be able to transform your piles of notes into a first draft. Look at your outline again to be sure you're satisfied with the way in which each idea leads to the next. Then begin drafting. The chart on the next page, "Some Tips on Drafting," may be helpful.

Sources

Anderson, Norman D., and Walter R. Brown. *Ferris Wheels*. New York: Pantheon, 1983.

Fincher, Jack. "George Ferris Jr. and the Great Wheel of Fortune." *Smithsonian,* July 1983.

Lee, William H. *Beautiful Scenes of the White City*. Chicago: Laird and Lee, 1894.

Notes

Admission 50 cents, the same as admission to fair. Still, 1.5 million rode it.
—Fincher, p. 14

Twenty-minute ride for 50 cents; two revolutions, six stops each time around; ran 8 A.M.–11 P.M.
—Anderson and Brown, p. 24

Lit by 3,000 electric bulbs at night, powered by generator in boiler house
—Anderson and Brown, p. 24

Drafting Tip

In your first draft, indicate the source of each borrowed idea by placing the author's name and the note card number in parentheses after that idea.

You don't have to include information from every note card in your draft. In fact, as the diagram shows, you are likely to develop the ideas from several note cards into one or two outline entries, and likewise into one or two ideas in your paper. As you put these ideas into your paper, identify the source of every borrowed idea, and try to use your own words wherever possible.

As you draft, use your outline as a "map" to help guide you in your writing. The outline should remind you of what comes before or after a particular idea. Furthermore, the outline should suggest the links, or transitions, you might use in your writing. After all, you have already begun linking ideas in your outline; now simply carry on that process, as the diagram below illustrates.

Outline

III. Specifics of Ferris Wheel
    A. Dimensions
    B. Built on principle of the bicycle wheel
    C. Riding
        1. Admission
        2. Hours
        3. Huge number of people riding
        4. Enthusiastic public response
IV. Early Criticism

Paragraph

A twenty-minute ride, or two revolutions with six stops each time around, cost 50 cents. The wheel ran from 8 A.M. to 11 P.M. At night, the wheel was lit by 3,000 electric light bulbs powered by a generator in the boiler house of the wheel (Anderson and Brown 24). One-and-one-half million people had ridden the wheel by Fair's end—a good number, considering that the 50-cent fee was equal to admission (Fincher 14).

Prepare the First Draft

Now that you're ready to write your first draft, read the chart below for solutions to some common drafting problems.

Vocabulary
Drafting Tip

For examples of transitions to link paragraphs, see Lesson 2.8, pages 90–92.

Solving Drafting Problems	
Problem	**Solution**
How can I overcome "writer's block" on my first draft?	Just begin writing and get the ideas down. Try writing for five minutes on whatever comes into your mind. Then, you'll be looser and ready to write your draft.
Do I have to write the first part of the paper first, the second part second, and so on?	Write any way that is easiest for you. If you write out of sequence, pay close attention to the transitions between sections as you revise.
What can I do with all these notes I have?	Set aside any note that duplicates another or is irrelevant to the main idea.
I have many notes on some aspects of my topic but few on others. What should I do?	Do more research, or look at your outline to see if you can write a good paper with the notes you now have. If so, revise your outline.
How can I avoid running out of time before I get very far into my writing?	Set aside at least three hours just for writing your paper. Eliminate distractions by going to a quiet place.
How can I best create transitions between my paragraphs?	Identify one major similarity or difference between the paragraphs. Try linking the paragraphs with a short phrase or sentence describing how they are similar or different.
What can I do to avoid being bogged down correcting spelling and grammar?	Ignore these problems until the next revision.

Write the Introduction and Conclusion

A good introduction should present your topic and approach. It should grab the attention of your readers and make them want to read on. Britta Waller begins her paper on the Ferris wheel with a quotation: "Ferris is a crackpot. He has wheels in his head."

Your conclusion should alert the reader that you are wrapping up. You might summarize your main points or mention any new questions your paper raises. Waller concludes by recounting the "true achievement" of Ferris's magnificent wheel.

7.3 Writing Activities

Skills Practice

Following the outline, use information in the notes that follow to write a few paragraphs about the elimination of yellow fever. Assume that your audience is a high school U.S. history class.

Outline
I. Eradication of yellow fever
  A. Walter Reed sent to Cuba
    1. Knows about Carlos Finlay's theories
    2. Sets up experiments
      a. Volunteer doctors and soldiers are intentionally infected and survive.
      b. Two others are infected accidentally and die.
      c. Experiments show disease is carried by mosquito.
  B. William Gorgas establishes mosquito control measures around Havana.

Notes
- 1881: Cuban physician Carlos Finlay suggested that a certain breed of mosquito carried the yellow fever disease.

- 1900: U.S. Army surgeon Walter Reed was sent to Cuba to investigate an epidemic of yellow fever among the U.S. troops there.

- Reed's fellow doctors and a number of soldiers volunteered for rather unconventional experiments:

  - Each was injected with yellow fever so Reed could study how the disease proceeds through the body.
  - All those intentionally injected contracted the disease but survived.
  - Two people who were infected accidentally came down with the disease and died.

- Reed's experiments proved that the disease was transmitted by the mosquito rather than by casual contact.

- 1905: William Gorgas developed and implemented measures to control mosquitoes, eliminating the disease as a major threat in Havana.

- Reed and Gorgas indirectly made the Panama Canal a reality by eliminating yellow fever in the Canal Zone.

Your Research Paper

Prepare a first draft of your own research paper.

Research Paper Writing
Citing Sources

While Ferris developed his wheel, others worked on some of the earliest automobiles. Yet unlike the Ferris wheel, the automobile has gone through amazing changes. The photo above and to the left shows Henry Ford's early Model T, while the one on the right shows a "car of the future."

Suppose you're writing a research paper about cars. For what kinds of information must you cite, or document, your sources? Most people know that Ford was one of the auto's early developers. You won't have to cite such common knowledge in your paper. But for information not so widely known, such as features planned for future cars, you need to document the source.

Document Information

In a research paper you need to be quite careful to indicate the sources of the information you present—including all ideas, statements, quotes, and statistics that you take from your sources and that are not common knowledge. One reason for documenting your sources is to enable the reader to check the source personally, in order to judge how believable or important a piece of information is. Another reason for proper documentation is to avoid plagiarism, as discussed in Lesson 7.1, page 321.

What to Document? What kinds of information need documentation? You should document your information whenever you use someone's exact words, or whenever you paraphrase a particular idea or series of ideas. You should also document any information that is not generally known or found in most books on the subject. Look at the chart below for tips on citing sources.

Documenting Your Information		
Information	**Citation?**	**Explanation**
"No single enterprise on the Midway or the grounds proper approached it either in patronage or in wonderment."	Yes	Direct quotations reflect an author's opinion. Readers may want to check the source for bias.
The fair signified economic ambition, the rise of the city, and rapid change.	Yes	This is a paraphrase of another author's opinion or research.
Ironically, there was a focus on cultural enlightenment and achievement.	No	This is a paraphrase of general information found in many sources.
The Ferris wheel cost $400,000 to build and turned a total profit of $733,086.	Yes	Specific cost and profitability of Ferris's wheel are not common knowledge.
The 1893 Columbian Exposition commemorated the four hundredth anniversary of Columbus's historic voyage.	No	This is common knowledge that would appear in most sources on the fair.
Ferris's name was forever matched with later machines.	No	Most people are aware that such rides are referred to as Ferris wheels.

Format Citations Properly

You can cite your sources in one of three basic formats: parenthetical documentation, footnotes, or endnotes. Your teacher may have a preference and assign one style for your paper, but each format serves the same purpose—to tell where you obtained your information.

Place each citation as close as possible to the idea, statement, or quotation in the text, to let your reader know what is being cited. You should generally place the citation where a pause would naturally occur, such as after a comma or at the end of a sentence.

When you wrote your first draft, you included author names and note card numbers for all the material you used from the cards. Now simply replace this information with complete citations in parentheses, or with consecutive numbers for footnotes or endnotes. For additional information needed in footnotes or endnotes, refer to your note cards and bibliography cards.

Parenthetical Documentation   One way to cite sources is to insert the author's name and a page reference in parentheses after the information from that author. Britta Waller uses this method. If the author is obvious from the text (for example, if the text reads "As Ferguson points out, . . ."), then you can merely insert the page number in parentheses. The chart below shows other forms of parenthetical documentation.

Examples of Parenthetical Documentation

1. **(Fincher 110)**
   Used when the source has a sole author, and only one work by that person is used in the paper. In our model paper this note refers to page 110 of the magazine article by Jack Fincher. If no single author is listed for a book or other source, use the name of the editor.

2. **(Anderson and Brown 18)**
   Used when the work cited has more than one author. If your source has three or more authors, just give the last name of the first author listed, followed by *et al.* ("and others"), such as (Lincoln et al. 151).

3. **(*Dream City, n. p.*)**
   When no author or editor is listed for the source, abbreviate the source's title for citation. This citation is for *The Dream City: A Portfolio of Photographic Views*. Since the book has no page numbers, *n.p.* is used in place of a page reference.

4. **(Badger, *American Fair* 14)**
   When the paper uses more than one work by the same author, abbreviate the book's title, and insert it after the author's name. If our model paper had used two books by Reid Badger, the citation for his book *The Great American Fair* might be made as shown above.

5. **(Lee 145; Anderson and Brown 26)**
   When you cite more than one source at the same place, include both sources, and separate them with a semicolon.

Footnotes   A footnote is a reference at the bottom of the text page that contains the information you are citing. You indicate the reference with a raised number, or superscript, and number notes consecutively throughout the paper. The footnote, unlike parenthetical documentation, contains the information from the bibliography card. Once you have cited a source, you can refer to it again in another footnote by using just the author's last name and the page reference.

Endnotes   Endnotes are similar to footnotes; however, endnotes appear on a separate page at the end of your paper instead of on the page with the documented material. Type your endnotes double-spaced, and present them under the heading "Notes."

Examples of Footnote and Endnote Entries

1. **Book with one author**
   David F. Burg, *Chicago's White City of 1893* (Lexington: UP of Kentucky, 1976) xii.

2. **Book with more than one author**
   Norman D. Anderson and Walter R. Brown, *Ferris Wheels* (New York: Pantheon, 1983) 16.

3. **Magazine article**
   Kate Holliday, "Big Wheels of the Fun Business," *Popular Mechanics,* Mar. 1969:229.

4. **Encyclopedia article**
   "World's Columbian Exposition," *Encyclopedia Americana,* 1989 ed.

5. **Article by an author in a book with an editor**
   Bernard S. Finn, "Electricity," *1876: A Centennial Exhibition,* ed. Robert C. Post (Washington D.C.: Smithsonian, 1976) 63.

6. **Book with an editor but no author**
   Frank H. Norton, ed., *Frank Leslie's Illustrated Historical Register of the Centennial Exposition* (New York: Frank Leslie's Publishing House, 1877) 29.

7. **Newspaper article**
   Ada Louise Huxtable, "You Can't Go Home to Those Fairs Again," *New York Times,* 28 Oct. 1973: Section II, p. 27, Col. 1.

8. **Unsigned article**
   "Higher Aspects of the Columbian Exposition," *Dial,* 1 Nov. 1892: 263–65.

9. **Pamphlet with no specified author**
   A Week at the Fair Illustrating Exhibits and Wonders of the World's Columbian Exposition (Chicago: Rand McNally, 1893) 163.

Editing Tip

Remember to underline or italicize titles of books, periodicals, and pamphlets. For more information see Lesson 21.10, pages 719–720.

Format Your List of Works Cited

Whether you cite your sources with parenthetical documentation, footnotes, or endnotes, your paper should include a complete list of the sources you used. This is your list of works cited, and, unlike your working bibliography, it contains only those sources that you use in your final version. While you may have consulted many additional sources for background and other general information, these sources shouldn't be included on this final list unless you use and cite ideas or data from the source in your paper.

From your bibliography cards, record the publishing information about the source. Alphabetize the source by the last name of the author or editor (use the first name listed, if there is more than one). If you use more than one work by the same author, you need not repeat the author's name for each entry; use a dash instead. If the source has no author or editor, alphabetize it by the title of the book or article. This chart shows the proper bibliographic style for various sources.

Compiling a List of Works Cited	
Source	**Entry**
Book with Single Author	Badger, Reid. *The Great American Fair.* Chicago: Nelson-Hall, 1979.
Book with Multiple Authors	Anderson, Norman D. and Walter R. Brown. *Ferris Wheels.* New York: Pantheon, 1983.
Magazine Article	Fincher, Jack. "George Ferris Jr. and the Great Wheel of Fortune." *Smithsonian* July 1983: 109–112+.
Encyclopedia Article	"World's Columbian Exposition." *Encyclopedia Americana*, 1989 ed.
Newspaper Article	"The Rays Take in the Columbian Exposition." *Chicago Tribune* 26 July 1984, sec. 5: 2.

Student Model

Works Cited

For works with more than one author, reverse the name of the first author only.

Anderson, Norman D., and Walter R. Brown. *Ferris Wheels.* New York: Pantheon, 1983.

Badger, Reid. *The Great American Fair.* Chicago: Nelson-Hall, 1979.

Indent text that runs more than one line.

Burg, David F. *Chicago's White City of 1893.* Lexington: UP of Kentucky, 1976. ➡

The Dream City: A Portfolio of Photographic Views. St. Louis: N. D. Thompson, 1893.

Holliday, Kate. "Big Wheels of the Fun Business." *Popular Mechanics* Mar. 1969: 144–146+.

Howells, William Dean. *Letters of an Altrurian Traveller* (1893–1894). Gainesville: Scholars' Facsimiles and Reprints, 1961.

"World's Columbian Exposition." Encyclopedia Americana. 1989 ed.

> *When alphabetizing a work by its title, ignore the words* a, an, *and* the.

> *Include the edition of the encyclopedia.*

7.4 Writing Activities

Skills Practice

1. For each of the following pieces of information, tell whether you think source documentation is necessary and explain why:

- Many more calls can be handled by cellular mobile phone service than were handled by earlier systems.
- The first licenses to build and operate mobile telephone systems were granted in 1982.
- Many advances in telephone technology have taken place since Alexander Graham Bell invented the receiver in 1876.
- One author laments, "Cellular phone technology eliminates one more place—inside your own car—where you can be free from interruptions."
- Most Americans today cannot conceive of life without the telephone.
- As a car equipped with a phone travels from cell to cell, the call is transferred via computer from one transmitter and receiver to another without interrupting the call.

2. Write proper entries for a list of works cited for the following sources:

- an article from the 1990 edition of the *World Book Encyclopedia* on jet propulsion engines
- an article entitled "The Concorde Tests the Skies," written by Janet Feldman, which appeared on page 30 of *Newsweek* on August 14, 1975
- an article by John Simons entitled "Breakthroughs in Jet Technology," which appeared on pages 70–84 of the book *Aviation and Space*, edited by M. W. Wister and published in New York by Little, Brown in 1982
- a book written by Richard Samson entitled *Jet Engine Basics*, published by MIT Press in Boston in 1975

Your Research Paper

Prepare a working bibliography of the sources you are using in your research paper.

Research Paper Writing
Revising

"Mr. Watson, come here. I want you!" said Alexander Graham Bell—the first sentence ever uttered over his new invention, the telephone. Yet despite this success, Bell continued to work on his invention and refine it so that it would communicate even better. Likewise, the first draft of your research paper will also "communicate" even better after you revise it.

Improve Your Paper

When you revise your first draft, you can improve your choice of words, your transitions, and—most importantly—the way you present your ideas. The following chart may help you do these things.

Grammar
Revising Tip

For suggestions on ways to vary your sentence structure, see the lessons in Unit 11, pages 457–471.

Solving Revision Problems	
Problem	**Solution**
How can I give my first draft a clearer focus?	Review your thesis statement; delete or rewrite anything in the paper that doesn't support it.
How can I make my argument easier to follow?	Add transitions, rearrange, and add ideas to make the paper more coherent. Delete irrelevant information.
How can I make my paragraphs flow smoothly from one to another?	Add or change transitions between paragraphs; rearrange paragraphs in a more logical order.
What if my introduction doesn't connect well with the rest of the paper?	Add transitions or rewrite introduction to conform with the purpose and main idea.
What can I do if my sentences sound repetitive?	Vary sentence structure. Use precise, lively language. Find synonyms for repeated words.

Take a look at some samples of the kind of revising you might need to do on your own research paper. First, look at the model below, which shows the revision to two paragraphs. Consider the reasons for each revision. Next, on page 338, follow the stages in the smaller-scale revision of one particular passage from another part of the same paper.

The Ferris wheel's was ~~very~~ popular. ~~This~~ was due to the ~~popularity of the Midway.~~ The Midway provided escape both from ~~the pressure and pains of~~ real life and from the culture ~~that was so~~ overwhelming ~~in~~ of the rest of the Fair. Couples ~~went~~ rushed to be married at the top of the wheel, but the closest they got was the superintendent's office on the ground below. ~~Rumors were started in the~~ newspapers started rumors of the wheel losing parts that then hurtled to the ground below. ~~Other rumors~~ or they told of the mechanism locking in place, trapping ~~with~~ the wheel's passengers ~~trapped~~ up in the air with no help. As ~~This~~ never happened, $such publicity made gigantic toy the ~~wheel~~ only more popular. (Howells 25). "No single enterprise on the Midway or the grounds proper approached it either in patronage or in wonderment" (Fincher 114).
The wheel did have its critics.
Howells accused the wheel of being a mere money-making contrivance--an

Change redundant sentence structures to make the paragraph more concise.

Does this change improve the paper? Why or why not?

Combine sentences that have the same subjects.

Why move this quotation?

Transition helps shift tone between paragraphs.

In an era hoping for a better world, grand engineering projects concentrated on building things other than weapons.

The 1890s and early 1900s were marked by a general wish for a better world. Engineering projects focused on new marvels of iron and steel, such as the Ferris wheel, instead of weapons.

The 1890s and early 1900s were marked by a universal wish for a better world, and most of all, "a world without war." Steel and iron were shaped into engineering marvels, such as the Ferris wheel, rather than weapons.

Revise a Science Paper

When you write a research paper on a scientific subject, you need to pay particularly close attention to certain questions. Presenting scientific data often requires even more precision than presenting other kinds of information, so you need to double-check any data you cite. Make certain that you use the most up-to-date information possible. If your topic is very current, look for more journal, magazine, and newspaper articles for late-breaking developments, and rely more heavily on these sources. Be sure you use specialized terms precisely. You may even want to use direct quotations from sources.

If you are using the research of others to draw your own conclusions on a topic, you have to be sure that the research is valid. Look closely at your sources to be sure that they are free from possible bias and that they have made logical, convincing arguments. Also, look at your own argument to be sure it is logical and complete. Science papers deal in facts, but facts can be arranged in confusing or illogical ways. Think about ways your information could be misinterpreted, and revise to make your meaning clearer.

Revising Tip

Many science papers are best organized in either visual or logical order. To review various methods of organization, see Lesson 7.2, page 323.

Checklist for Revising a Science Paper

1. Have I defined or explained technical terms adequately?
2. Have I used the latest information I can find on the subject?
3. Have all sources for quotations, theories, and technical information been credited?
4. Have I explained the scientific processes and reasoning so that an average reader can understand them?
5. Have I considered the validity of any opposing viewpoints? If those views contain important perspectives on my topic, have I mentioned them?
6. Have I considered any possible developments that may occur in the near future that may have an effect on my argument?

7.5 Writing Activities

Skills Practice

Revise the following passages for clarity, coherence, and readability.

Passage A

Compact discs are made of plastic coated with aluminum so that the signals can be read by a laser. Then they are coated in more plastic to protect the pits. Music is recorded on a compact disc in a series of minute pits of varying depths in an outward spiral. In the CD player a low-intensity laser is directed at the pits in their track. As the laser is alternately reflected or scattered off the pits, an optical sensor picks up these signals and converts the signals into sound impulses. The laser never touches the CD, so the CD doesn't wear down or scratch. Also, dust and fingerprints do not distort the laser beam. This results in almost no distortion in the playback. Not, surprisingly, CD recordings have become more popular than vinyl records.

Passage B

The first step for a spacecraft is to break away from Earth's gravity. This is a matter of speed, called the escape velocity.

The craft ascends into interplanetary space.

A craft going 25,000 miles per hour is released from Earth's gravitational pull. Then no force works to keep the spacecraft up. Gravity from Earth and the sun are still working to pull the craft down. As the craft gets farther from Earth, that planet's pull on it weakens. The gravity of the sun takes over. The craft is pulled into a solar orbit.

To reach the planets then, a spacecraft must leave Earth at a speed greater than escape velocity. Much velocity is used up in getting away from Earth. There must be enough velocity for the spacecraft to escape Earth's gravity, and enough left over to speed the spacecraft to another planet. The extra velocity makes the spacecraft orbit the sun at a different speed than Earth does.

Your Research Paper

Use what you have learned in this lesson to revise the paper you have been working on throughout this unit.

Research Paper Writing
Editing and Presenting: A Model Paper

George W. G. Ferris's marvelous wheel was at last a reality. After much planning and research, after construction and testing, Ferris put the finishing touches on his wheel and opened it to the public. And his efforts truly paid off, as the Ferris wheel became a symbol of nineteenth-century technological ingenuity and the world-renowned centerpiece of Chicago's 1893 Columbian Exposition.

In the same way, after much planning, research, and writing, you are about to put the finishing touches on your paper. With these final touches you should have a complete and clean research paper, one that is ready for presentation to your teacher and classmates.

Prepare the Final Copy

After revising your draft, type or print a new copy of it with your corrections included. Then you can give your paper one final proofreading, checking citations, grammar, spelling, punctuation, and word use. The checklist below can help you catch any remaining problems or errors.

Editing Tip

For additional editing tips, refer to Lesson 2.10, pages 98–101, and Unit 9, pages 375–398.

Prewriting Tip

During the prewriting stage, you may want to refer to the Final Copy Checklist on this page to remind yourself of the kinds of details you will want to gather and document carefully.

Final Copy Checklist

1. Have I organized my ideas clearly?
2. Have I explained or defined any words that may be unfamiliar to the reader?
3. Have I discussed my topic completely and fairly?
4. Have I corrected all grammar and spelling mistakes?
5. Have I documented my sources properly?
6. Have I considered the proper meaning(s) of the words I've used?
7. Have I spelled and capitalized everything correctly?
8. Have I prepared a neat and easy-to-read final copy?

Present the Complete Paper

Most research papers have a cover sheet, as shown here, containing the title of the paper as well as the writer's name and other identifying information. Your teacher may also ask you for other materials to check the extent of your research and the construction of your paper. You may be asked to include a clean copy of your final outline. If you type your outline, do not include the introduction or conclusion.

Your teacher may ask you to include a summary statement. This is basically a brief restatement of your thesis statement, no more than two sentences long and inserted before the main body of your text. Your teacher may also ask you to include an annotated list of works cited, which is simply your final list of works cited, with each source followed by your own remarks on the source's content and usefulness.

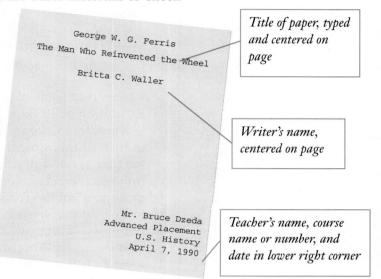

George W. G. Ferris
The Man Who Reinvented the Wheel

Britta C. Waller

Mr. Bruce Dzeda
Advanced Placement
U.S. History
April 7, 1990

Title of paper, typed and centered on page

Writer's name, centered on page

Teacher's name, course name or number, and date in lower right corner

7.6 Writing Activities

Skills Practice

1. Identify the grammatical mistakes in each of the following sentences, and correct them.

- Scientists should be sure that experiments do not merely reinforce his preconceived ideas.
- Henry Ford is aware of the European experiments in creating a "horseless carriage." He knew about them for many years when he began his work.
- People are often unaware of the scientific advance that take place in the era they live in.

2. Edit the following entries for a final list of works cited. You may need to refer to Lesson 7.4, pages 330–335, to review the proper forms of different types of entries.

- Encyclopaedia Britannica, 1991 ed., Cardiovascular System Diseases and Disorders.
- Cooke, Alistair. Alistair Cooke's America. Alfred A. Knopf, New York: 1973
- John Molinari, Hurricane Prediction: Catching the Waves, Science News, 21 October 1989, p. 262

3. Read the research paper by Britta Waller on pages 342–347. Then write a summary statement, about two sentences long, explaining the topic and purpose of her paper.

Your Research Paper

Use what you have learned in this lesson to complete and present the final version of your own term paper.

GEORGE W. G. FERRIS
THE MAN WHO REINVENTED THE WHEEL

Britta C. Waller

"Ferris is a crackpot. He has wheels in his head."
(Anderson and Brown 16)

Even officials of the famous World's Columbian Exhibition of 1893, such as the one quoted above, seemed to think that George Washington Gale Ferris's idea for an industrial monument to rival the Eiffel Tower was far-fetched, if not downright insane. Yet, when it was finally finished, Ferris's colossal wheel embodied the "can-do optimism" of the Exhibition (Fincher 109), America's industrial dominance, the American dream, and the flexibility of a capitalistic society. This paper will discuss turn-of-the-century America, how these times inspired the World's Columbian Exposition, and the birth, demise, and significance of the great Ferris wheel.

The 1890s and early 1900s were marked by a universal wish for a better world, and most of all, "a world without war" (Fincher 109). Steel and iron were shaped into engineering marvels, such as the Ferris wheel, rather than weapons. Chicago's World's Columbian Exposition of 1893 commemorated the 400th anniversary of Columbus's historic voyage and was the largest, most elaborate, and most magnificent World's Fair ever. The first international exposition was London's Great Exhibition of 1851, boasting Joseph Paxton's Crystal Palace—the first large scale iron and glass building and the ancestor of the modern skyscraper. The first American exposition was held in Philadelphia in 1876 to celebrate the country's centennial. However, it was the Paris Exhibition of 1889 that inspired the World's Columbian (Burg xii). Paris had produced the world-famous Eiffel Tower. America couldn't let Europe have all the limelight. In fact, this national rivalry was one of the prime moving forces behind the Fair. In addition, the Fair signified economic ambition, the rise of the city, and rapid progressive change (Badger 10). Ironically, there was a focus on cultural enlightenment and achievement. Buildings were in the "Greco-Roman-Oriental" style (Fincher 110). Under ➡

Why do you suppose Waller includes a quotation here?

Is the thesis statement effective? Why or why not?

Paper should be typed double-spaced, with one-inch margins on all sides.

Parenthetical documentation

the direction of Chicago architect Daniel H. Burnham and landscape architect Frederick Law Olmsted, the nation's best sculptors, architects, painters, writers, and musicians joined with industrialists and inventors to put their best work into the Exposition. Its achievement in the arts far surpassed its historical significance: "We have put aside individual taste and have united in an effort to carry out the several parts of a design which . . . was dominated by one idea," wrote Professor Halsey C. Ives, the Chief of the Department of Fine Arts (<u>Dream City</u>). The dual nature—industry and culture combined—of the Fair was a direct reflection of the era. Henry Steele Commager called the decade of the 1890s a watershed in American history:

> On the one side lies an America predominantly agricultural; concerned with domestic problems; conforming, intellectually, at least, to the political, economic, and moral principles inherited from the 17th and 18th centuries. . . . On the other side lies the modern America, predominantly urban and industrial; inextricably involved in world economy and politics . . . experiencing profound changes in population, social institutions, economy, and technology; and trying to accommodate its traditional institutions and habits of thought to conditions new and in part alien (Burg xiii).

Set off any quotations longer than three lines by indenting the entire passage.

The cultural idealism of the Fair was embodied in its alternate title—"The White City," so named because of a substance called "staff" which covered many of the buildings. Composed of plaster of Paris and jute fibers, staff closely resembled white marble ("World's Columbian Exposition" 533). Author William Dean Howells praised the Fair as "the perfect embodiment of human ingenuity and Christian brotherhood—the ideal of Grecian democracy in industrial America" (vii–viii). Howells saw the Fair as a glimpse of the future of America, and as a departure from the "Age of Accumulation"—a term he used to denounce the period before World War I (xii).

Including the author's name in the text lets Waller use only the page number in the parenthetical note.

However, Howells's altruistic ideals were pushed aside in favor of the Midway Plaisance, and its Queen—the Ferris wheel.

Early in 1892, Ferris sat quietly at Burnham's planning session for the fabulous exposition. A tunnel and trestle engineer and bridge builder from Pittsburgh, Ferris was 33 years old, tall, slim, and pale, with a bushy black ➡

moustache and a "resolute face" (Fincher 110). Born the eighth child of a Nevada farmer, Ferris attended military school in Oakland, California, at age 16 and attended college at Rensselaer Polytechnic Institute (RPI) in Troy, New York. Graduating in 1881, Ferris was said to have a great ability to meet a challenge. Burnham told those who assembled at the planning session: "Mere bigness is not what is wanted. . . . something novel, original, daring and unique must be designed and built if American engineers are to retain their prestige and standing" (Fincher 110). An evening soon after, Ferris sketched the design for his famous amusement ride on a scrap of paper at a Chicago restaurant. He determined all aspects of the wheel—size, number of passengers, price of admission—in his original sketch. He had "re-invented the wheel . . . big" (Fincher 110).

Ferris's wheel was 264 feet high and supported by two 140-foot pyramid-shaped steel towers (Burg 224). The wheel was 26 stories high, taller than any building on the grounds. It weighed, fully loaded, approximately 1,200 tons, or as much as three Boeing 747s (Fincher 111–112). Thirty-six passenger cars were suspended between two steel rims. Made of wood and iron, paneled with plate glass windows, and furnished with swivel chairs, the cars were approximately the size of train passenger cars (Burg 224). The wheel had a total capacity of 2,160 people (Lee).

The wheel was built on two 20-foot square, 35-foot deep concrete blocks. Plans were approved by the end of 1892. The thousands of parts needed for the steam-powered wheel were built by five different steel companies. In late March of 1893, five trains, each thirty cars long, brought all these parts to Chicago (Anderson and Brown 18). The most crucial was the huge axle—45 $\frac{1}{2}$ feet long, 33 inches in diameter, weighing 46 $\frac{1}{2}$ tons. Made by Bethlehem Iron Works of Bethlehem, Pennsylvania, the axle was the largest single piece of steel ever forged in the United States (Lee; Anderson and Brown 18).

Ferris built his ride based on the principle of the bicycle wheel. Heavy steel rods acted as the spokes and pulled toward the axle to keep the wheel's shape. By using tension, Ferris was able to build a lighter, stronger, and vastly larger structure than was ever before possible (Anderson and Brown 17).

A twenty-minute ride, or two revolutions with six stops each time around, cost 50 cents. The wheel ran from ➡

Logical organization shows how the combination of Ferris's personality and the standards set for the fair produced the Ferris wheel.

What do you suppose is the main purpose of this sentence?

Interesting analogy about the wheel's weight puts it in perspective for modern readers.

What kind of organization does Waller use here? Why might she have made this particular choice?

8 a.m. to 11 p.m. At night, the wheel was lit by 3,000 electric light bulbs powered by a generator in the boiler house of the wheel (Anderson and Brown 24). One-and-one-half-million people had ridden the wheel by Fair's end—a good number considering that the 50-cent fee was equal to admission to the entire Exposition (Fincher 114). One North Dakota farmboy wrote in a letter home: "Do whatever you have to do—even sell the kitchen stove—come to Chicago and ride the Ferris wheel!" (Anderson and Brown 26). A ride on the wheel, it was said, "may truly be called a round trip" (Lee).

Though an engineering milestone when completed, the wheel was not so well accepted in the early stages of its development. Burnham said it was not strong enough to withstand Lake Michigan winds, and even if it could, the public would be afraid to ride such a "rickety-looking contraption" (Fincher 112). Others doubted the wheel, too, but Ferris was finally allowed to build it if he could finance it. The Exposition had no better match for the Eiffel Tower. Ferris sold stock to wealthy Chicago businessmen (Fincher 112). The wheel cost $400,000 to build, and turned a total profit of $733,086 (Holliday 229).

What does this quotation contribute to the paragraph?

The Exposition was opened on May 1, 1893, by President Grover Cleveland, but the wheel was not completed. Work was done around the clock, but safety was still ensured. The wheel was powered by two 1,000-horsepower steam engines, one being held as a back-up (Anderson and Brown 21). It also had a huge air brake worked by two 10-foot steel bands which would tighten to stop the wheel in case it began to spin free (Fincher 111). With these features, the wheel was tested extensively. Wrote Ferris's partner and fellow RPI graduate William F. Gronau: "So perfect is the machinery that we did not feel the wheel move" (Fincher 114).

The Ferris wheel had its grand opening on Wednesday, June 21, 1893. Among the invited first riders were Mr. and Mrs. Ferris, the mayor of Chicago, and a 40-piece band, squeezed into one car (Anderson and Brown 23).

The Ferris wheel, and the Midway Plaisance where it was located, were both immediate successes. The Midway was a grand street of international displays and buildings meant to show the everyday life and oddities of all countries. The Midway was designed to "popularize" the Exposition, which it did very well, because many visitors ➡

Presenting Tip

Graphics, such as a labeled diagram of the Ferris wheel, will enhance a reader's understanding of a technical topic.

enjoyed its atmosphere much more than the cultural attractions (Badger 109). Ironically, Jackson Park, the location of the Midway, not the cultural Court of Honor, became the entrance to the University of Chicago, or the "Grey City," as it was known at the time (Badger 90). One anonymous limerick showed the true, educational value of the Fair to the University:

> Oh, there were more Profs than students,
> but then we didn't care;
> They spent their days in research work,
> their evenings at the Fair.
> and life upon the Campus
> was one continual swing,
> We watched the Ferris wheel go round
> and didn't do a thing.
> (Badger 157)

The Ferris wheel's popularity was due to the escape the Midway provided, both from real life and the overwhelming culture of the rest of the Fair. "No single enterprise on the Midway or the grounds proper approached it either in patronage or in wonderment" (Badger 108). Couples rushed to be married at the top of the wheel, but the closest they got was the superintendent's office on the ground below. Newspapers started rumors of the wheel losing parts that then supposedly hurtled to the ground below; or they told of the mechanism locking in place, trapping the wheel's passengers up in the air with no help. As this never happened, such publicity made the gigantic toy only more popular (Fincher 114).

Transitional sentence introduces the controversy surrounding the wheel.

The wheel did have its critics. Howells accused the wheel of being a mere money-making contrivance—an exploitation of the visitors (Howells 25). Others said Ferris had plagiarized the idea for the wheel, and that American, Asian, and European history was filled with similar, if less complex, models. This is true, but it was the design that made Ferris's creation unique (Anderson and Brown 37–38).

Transition shows the connection between the original wheel and those that followed.

Though not the first to build such rides, Ferris was forever associated with later machines. British engineer W. B. Basset sought to outdo Ferris's wheel in size and scope. American William Sullivan was also among those inspired by Ferris. Sullivan started the Eli Bridge Company in 1906 in Jacksonville, Illinois, largest current ➡

manufacturer of Ferris wheels. Sullivan, after riding the great wheel at the Exposition as many times as possible, capitalized on the commercial possibilities of the wheel. He made smaller, portable versions of about 45 feet in diameter which could be built in quantity (Anderson and Brown 41). George and Mary Tilyou wanted to buy Ferris's wheel and take it to their newly built Brooklyn amusement park—Coney Island, which was modeled after the Midway. The Tilyous couldn't afford the ride and instead built a 125-foot diameter "Wonder Wheel," which still stands. Though it wasn't the first or largest, as the signs claimed, Coney Island's Wonder Wheel established Ferris wheels and their many variations as a permanent fixture in modern American amusement parks (Fincher 117).

The criticism over the wheel's originality began the wheel's decline. Ferris's assets collapsed over lawsuits with the Exposition about the wheel's profits. During the winter of 1893–94, the wheel was left deserted. With a brief appearance at the North Clark Street Fair beginning in early 1895, the wheel regained some of its original standing, but it had simply lost its novelty. Neighbors in Clark Street campaigned to remove the wheel, ironically, complaining of its "undesirable industrialism" (Fincher 117). The wheel then appeared at the Louisiana Purchase Exposition of 1904 in Saint Louis and was still running perfectly. However, it remained unsuccessful. In 1906, following the Louisiana Exposition, the great wheel was brought tumbling down with 100 pounds of dynamite. The *Chicago Tribune* reported, "Within a few minutes, it was a tangled mass of steel and iron forty feet high" (Fincher 118). However, Ferris was not there to see its end. In November 1896, George W. G. Ferris had died unexpectedly in a Pittsburgh hospital at the age of 37. The cause was diagnosed as several different ailments, but mostly Ferris's death was due to depression over his potential bankruptcy and loss of hope (Fincher 118).

Story of wheel's demise is presented in chronological order.

The true achievement of the Ferris wheel lay not in how long it stood, but in its combination of pleasurable enjoyment and industrial achievement. It symbolized the ideals of the World's Columbian Exposition. Moreover, the Ferris wheel signified the industrial advancement of the times and provided an escape in the peaceful period before World War I.

What does Waller do in her conclusion?

Unit 7 Review

Reflecting on the Unit

Key concepts in writing a research paper include the following:

- Prewriting for a research paper involves finding a topic, getting information, developing a working bibliography, taking notes, preparing a working outline, and formulating a thesis statement.

- Drafting means using your outline and notes as you write an introduction, body, and conclusion.

- Proper documentation includes citations for specific ideas from sources as well as a list of works cited.

- Careful revision and proofreading prepare a research paper for its audience.

Adding to Your Portfolio

Choose a selection for your portfolio.
Look over the research paper you prepared during this unit, and put it into your portfolio. Your research paper should show the following:

- a topic that interests you and is neither too broad nor too narrow
- a strong thesis statement and a logical outline
- an introduction that presents a topic and approach
- a conclusion that wraps it all up
- proper citations for all sources
- careful revision and proofreading

Reflect on your choice.
Attach a note to your research paper, explaining what you learned from writing it.

Set goals.
- How can you improve your writing?
- What skill will you focus on the next time you write?

Writing Across the Curriculum

Make a social studies connection.
One type of research paper is a summary. Look through a newspaper or weekly news magazine. Choose a controversial issue that interests you. Look for different people's opinions on the topic. You can start with the editorial page. Then write a one-page report stating the issue, your position, and evidence supporting your position. Include a thesis statement and an effective conclusion, and be sure to cite your sources correctly.

Sentence Combining

Sentence Combining
Style Through Sentence Combining

Skillful writing is partly a matter of habit, just like skillful shooting on the basketball court. Both require practice. You can practice some aspects of sentence writing so that they become habit. The ability to write sentences smoothly frees your mind for other important tasks— like getting your ideas right.

Practice in Sentence Combining

This unit focuses on combining short sentences into longer, more complex ones. Remember that the goal is clear writing, not merely long sentences. Practice in sentence combining reveals your stylistic options, the choices you can make as you write. Long sentences are not always the best option.

Regular practice in sentence combining enables you to find clear ways to express your ideas. To write effectively, you must form good sentences consistently. Sentence combining can help you achieve that goal. By making you aware of writing choices, sentence combining also develops your writing style. As you try new types of sentence structures, your personal style will emerge naturally.

Develop Your Style

One way to develop a personal style, as you already know, is by writing regularly in a journal. Such writing helps unlock your ideas and find your own voice as a writer. Sentence combining is a second approach that has worked for millions of students.

Sentence combining presents you with clusters of short sentences and invites you to express their meanings in more interesting ways. Here's an example of a cluster:

Writing is a game.
It is full of challenges.
It requires regular practice.
It leads to personal rewards.

Scanning those four simple sentences, you can probably see different ways of combining them into a longer, more complex statement. Basically, there are four strategies for combining:

- deleting repeated words;
- using connecting words;
- rearranging words; and
- changing the form of words.

Look at one way of combining these sentences:

Example

Writing is a game. *that*
It is full of (challenges). *=ing*
I~~t~~ requires regular practice. *and*
I~~t~~ leads to personal rewards.

Rearranging words, and changing the form of words

Deleting repeated words

Using connecting words

Notice that this editing example produces sentence 1 below. Try reading it and the other variations aloud, listening to differences in style.

1. Writing is a challenging game that requires regular practice and leads to personal rewards.
2. Writing, a game full of challenges, leads to personal rewards through regular practice.
3. Requiring regular practice, the challenging game of writing leads to personal rewards.
4. The challenges of the writing game require regular practice, but lead to personal rewards.
5. Writing is a game that leads to personal rewards; overcoming its challenges, however, requires regular practice.

All of these sentences say basically the same thing, but they do so in different ways. In other words, each has a different emphasis. As a skilled writer, you choose the stylistic emphasis that best expresses your aims in the context of an emerging paragraph.

Sentence Combining Hints

Sentence combining is easy and fun. Here are some basic suggestions you might try as you explore style.

1. **Whisper sentences to yourself.** As you work with clusters of sentences, try combining them aloud. This process is faster than writing and helps you decide on a "best sentence" to write down.

2. **Work with a partner.** By trying out sentences on a partner—and hearing your partner's ideas—you often discover new, interesting ways to solve specific challenges. Don't be afraid to borrow ideas.

3. **Use context when choosing sentences.** Each paragraph has an emerging context—the sentences you have already combined. Reading this context aloud helps you decide on the best sentence option.

4. **Compare your sentences with those of other students.** Seeing how others have solved combining tasks broadens your awareness of sentence options. Keep asking: Which do I prefer?

5. **Look for stylistic patterns in your writing.** Calculate your average words per sentence; study your sentence openers; listen to rhythms in your style. Try new patterns to stretch yourself.

6. **Take risks.** Learning to make clear, effective sentences also means taking risks and making mistakes. So, strange as it may sound, it actually makes sense to accept mistakes—even *welcome* them—as you combine sentences. After all, mistakes provide feedback for your language learning. As you learn from them, you develop an expressive style, a voice of personal authority. You come to know yourself as a writer.

As you can see, sentence combining involves skills of talking to yourself, making judgments, and holding what you say in short-term memory so that you can transcribe it. These are oral skills as much as writing skills. Good writers trust an "inner voice."

A Workshop on Style

Looking ahead in this unit, you will find two kinds of sentence combining. The exercises in sections 8.1 through 8.4 present clusters of short sentences, with spaces between the clusters. The exercises in section 8.5, drawn from literature selections in this book, are set up in an unclustered format.

Sections 8.1 to 8.4 give you practice in writing descriptive, narrative, expository, and persuasive paragraphs. You can combine each cluster into a single sentence; but you can also leave a cluster partially combined—or combine clusters together. The idea, always, is to take risks and create the best sentences you can. Exercises on facing pages deal with the same topic or situation. Think of these exercises as "bookends" for the writing you will do. After you have combined sentences, your task is to connect the paragraphs into a longer essay or story. Doing so will help you transfer sentence-combining skills to your own writing.

Section 8.5 invites you to test your skills against those of a professional writer. As you do these unclustered exercises, you will need to figure out the ideas that logically belong together. After you have done the sentence combining, you can check your version against the author's original. By studying similarities and differences between the two passages, you will learn a great deal about your own style. Sometimes you will prefer the professional writer's sentences. Why, specifically, are they "better" than yours? But sometimes you will prefer your own style. Can you build on this writing skill, trying it out in your own stories and essays? Either way, you learn to write better.

Explore Your Own Style

The whole point of sentence combining practice is to improve your revising and editing skills—to help you see that sentences are flexible instruments of thought, not rigid structures cast in concrete. The simple fact that you feel confident in moving sentence parts around increases your control of the writing process. To acquire this sense of self-confidence in combining and revising sentences, you can try strategies like those shown below.

1. **Vary the length of your sentences.** Work for a rhythmic, interesting balance of long and short sentences, remembering that brevity often has dramatic force.

2. **Vary the structure of your sentences.** By using different kinds of sentence openers—and by sometimes tucking information in the middle of a sentence—you can create stylistic interest.

3. **Use parallelism for emphasis.** Experiment with repeated items in a series—words, phrases, and clauses—to understand how structural patterns work and how you can use them to your advantage.

4. **Use interruption for emphasis.** Colons, semicolons, dashes, commas, parentheses—all of these are useful tools in your stylistic tool kit; knowing how to use them well is important.

5. **Use unusual patterns for emphasis.** Reversing normal sentence patterns may never have occurred to you, but such a strategy can work—if you know how.

Description

Exercise A   First Date

Directions   Combine each cluster of numbered items into one or more sentences. Combine clusters, if you wish.

1.1 Tony sat on the edge of a sofa.
1.2 The sofa was plush.
1.3 The sofa was mauve.
1.4 He waited for his date to appear.

2.1 The room felt like a funeral parlor.
2.2 The room looked like a funeral parlor.
2.3 This seemed only fitting.
2.4 Her father was a mortician.

3.1 A gas log burned in the fireplace.
3.2 Its burning was cheerless.
3.3 It bathed the room with warmth.
3.4 The warmth was antiseptic.

4.1 Next to it stood a TV console.
4.2 Its screen reflected the firelight.
4.3 The firelight was flickering.

5.1 Gold draperies extended along one wall.
5.2 The draperies were heavy.
5.3 They were like a dark shroud.
5.4 A painting depicted fading sunlight.
5.5 The sunlight was over an ocean shore.

6.1 The quietness of the room seemed eerie.
6.2 Its suggestions of death seemed eerie.
6.3 Its suggestions of dying seemed eerie.

7.1 In front of him was a marble table.
7.2 It had networks of veins.
7.3 It had networks of capillaries.
7.4 The networks were polished.

8.1 He traced its lines with his eye.
8.2 He listened to a mantle clock.

Revising Tip

In cluster 4 try changing *reflected* to *reflecting* as you combine. A connector such as *with* may be useful in cluster 6.

Continue the Story   Whom does Tony meet—Mom, Dad, or the family pet? Writing further description will help you link "First Date" to "Ready to Party."

Ready to Party

Directions   Combine each cluster of numbered items into one or more sentences. Combine clusters, if you wish.

1.1 At school she was pretty.
1.2 Tonight she looked gorgeous.
1.3 Tonight she wore her hair pulled back.

2.1 She had olive skin.
2.2 She had facial features.
2.3 Her features were finely chiseled.

3.1 Her hair was combed past her ears.
3.2 Her hair was shoulder-length.
3.3 Her hair was black and lustrous.
3.4 Her eyes sparkled with laughter.
3.5 Her eyes were dark.

4.1 She wore earrings.
4.2 The earrings were gold loops.
4.3 She wore a denim jacket.
4.4 The jacket was over a red blouse.
4.5 She wore blue jeans.
4.6 The jeans were faded.

5.1 Even her boots looked ready for dancing.
5.2 The boots had pointed toes.
5.3 The dancing would be serious.

6.1 At school her image was low-key.
6.2 At school her image was conservative.
6.3 Tonight's outfit showed a personality.
6.4 The personality was outgoing.
6.5 The personality was fun-loving.

7.1 Tony felt awkward in his white shirt.
7.2 The white shirt was stiff.
7.3 He felt awkward in his sport coat.
7.4 He felt awkward in his slacks.
7.5 The slacks were carefully pressed.

Revising Tip

In clusters 1 and 6, try different connectors—*but, yet, however, while, although*—before settling on one; then check punctuation.

Continue the Story   Describe the scene that you see happening *after* this scene. Then share your text—"First Date" plus "Ready to Party"—with a writing partner.

Directions   Combine each cluster of numbered items into one or more sentences. Combine clusters, if you wish.

1.1 The day was only half over.
1.2 The student teacher was frustrated.
1.3 She was completely discouraged.

2.1 Morning classes had not cooperated.
2.2 This was despite her best efforts.
2.3 This was despite her planning.
2.4 Her planning was careful.

3.1 Now her mouth was tense.
3.2 It sagged with fatigue.

4.1 Her desk looked like a disaster.
4.2 It was cluttered with announcements.
4.3 It was cluttered with office notes.
4.4 It was cluttered with tardy slips.
4.5 It was cluttered with late papers.
4.6 The disaster was educational.

5.1 A buzzer echoed in the hallway.
5.2 It signaled a class change.
5.3 She still had not found a planner.
5.4 It contained her lecture notes.

6.1 She wore a badge of resignation.
6.2 The resignation was weary.
6.3 She watched the room fill with students.
6.4 They wanted lunchtime to continue.

7.1 The clock's second hand swept toward twelve.
7.2 She searched for a friendly face.
7.3 The face might help her through the period.

8.1 It was there near the back of the room.
8.2 This was much to her surprise.
8.3 This was much to her relief.

Continue the Story   Describe yourself as the person who saves the student teacher's day. Link this description to "Thunderstorm."

Exercise D   Thunderstorm

Directions   Combine each cluster of numbered items into one or more sentences. Combine clusters, if you wish.

1.1 The class moved to the windows.
1.2 The windows were half open.
1.3 The class waited for the show to begin.

2.1 Dust had turned the sky beige.
2.2 The dust was wind-blown.
2.3 The dust swirled up from the west.

3.1 Above the hills were shades of gray.
3.2 The gray was the color of gunmetal.
3.3 The gray darkened to purple.
3.4 The purple was ominous.

4.1 Lightning splintered the horizon.
4.2 The horizon was turbulent.
4.3 Its flash was followed by a boom.
4.4 The boom was heavy.
4.5 The boom rumbled.
4.6 The boom was like boxcars.
4.7 The boxcars were in the train yard.

5.1 Then the wind came up.
5.2 The atmosphere seemed luminous.
5.3 Its luminescence was strange.

6.1 Trees swayed like dancers.
6.2 Trees jerked like dancers.
6.3 The dancers were frantic.
6.4 Rain began to fall in drops.
6.5 The drops were fat.

7.1 They splattered the concrete.
7.2 They punched craters in the earth.
7.3 The craters were tiny.
7.4 The earth was thirsty.
7.5 They washed the air clean.

Continue the Story   Describe what happens next in this classroom scene. Share the text—"Student Teacher" plus "Thunderstorm"—with a writing partner.

Narration

Waking Up

Directions Combine each cluster of numbered items into one or more sentences. Combine clusters, if you wish.

1.1 The alarm rang at 6:30 A.M.
1.2 It brought Gary out of bed.
1.3 He had slept only a few hours.

2.1 He had thrashed about.
2.2 He had been unable to sleep.
2.3 He was worried about an interview.
2.4 The interview was for employment.

3.1 Now he blinked heavily.
3.2 He leaned against squares of tile.
3.3 The squares were smooth.
3.4 The tile was in the shower.
3.5 He tried to wake himself.

4.1 Warm spray stung his back.
4.2 It prickled his shoulders.
4.3 He only wanted to close his eyes.
4.4 He only wanted to go back to bed.

5.1 His brain had become sludge.
5.2 The sludge was thick.
5.3 The sludge was viscous.

6.1 He worked shampoo into his hair.
6.2 He turned under the shower head.
6.3 The shower head was hissing.
6.4 He hoped to revive himself.

7.1 He finally shut off the shower.
7.2 Cold drops spattered his back.
7.3 The drain sucked at his feet.

8.1 Then he pulled a towel from the rack.
8.2 He wrapped it around his waist.
8.3 He stumbled forward to meet the day.

Revising Tip

In cluster 1 use a *who* connector, making sure that sentence 1.3 follows *Gary.* Use a pair of commas for this relative clause.

Continue the Story What happens next? Narrate a transition from "Waking Up" to "Job Interview," perhaps using humor to build interest and tension.

Directions   Combine each cluster of numbered items into one or more sentences. Combine clusters, if you wish.

1.1 The waiting area was noisy.
1.2 The waiting area was cramped.
1.3 The waiting area was poorly lit.
1.4 It looked like a large broom closet.

2.1 Gary sat with two other applicants.
2.2 He tried to relax.
2.3 His insides felt tense.

3.1 He touched his fingers to his face.
3.2 He noticed they were ice cold.
3.3 This was a sure sign of nervousness.

4.1 His plan was to sell himself.
4.2 The selling would be straightforward.
4.3 It would be without arrogance.

5.1 He would emphasize his adaptability.
5.2 He would emphasize his friendliness.
5.3 He would emphasize his work habits.
5.4 His work habits were responsible.

6.1 The secretary called his number.
6.2 He wiped his palms dry.
6.3 He adjusted his new tie.
6.4 He arranged his face into a smile.
6.5 The smile was upbeat.

7.1 He strode into the interview room.
7.2 He told himself he had nothing to lose.

8.1 He shook hands with the interviewer.
8.2 He settled into an armchair.
8.3 He noticed his mismatched shoes.
8.4 One was light brown.
8.5 The other was black.

Revising Tip

In cluster 1 use *which* to create an adjective clause for sentence 1.4. For more on punctuating adjective clauses, see page 703.

Continue the Story   Narrate an interesting conclusion for this story. Then share your text—"Waking Up" plus "Job Interview"—with a writing partner.

Directions   Combine each cluster of numbered items into one or more sentences. Combine clusters, if you wish.

1.1 Sabrina lay on a blanket.
1.2 The blanket was in the backyard.
1.3 Her jacket was off.
1.4 Her sunglasses were on.

2.1 She had tried to study for an exam.
2.2 Last night's breakup was on her mind.
2.3 The breakup was sudden.

3.1 She had been sharing a pizza.
3.2 The pizza was after school.
3.3 She was with her boyfriend.
3.4 They had begun to argue.

4.1 Their voices grew louder.
4.2 Their voices grew more angry.
4.3 He had clenched a fist.
4.4 He had slammed it on the table.
4.5 This caused a stir in the restaurant.

5.1 He had leaned forward.
5.2 He had tried to hold her hand.
5.3 She had turned away.

6.1 Her rejection had been unexpected.
6.2 It had been a sharp blow.
6.3 The blow was to his pride.
6.4 His pride was masculine.

7.1 She had said he was immature.
7.2 He was unable to control his temper.

8.1 She had made her decision.
8.2 Her decision was to not see him again.
8.3 His apologies had been weak.
8.4 His apologies had been pathetic.

Continue the Story   Narrate what you imagine Sabrina to be thinking about. Is she having second thoughts? Use your narration as a link to "The Spider."

Directions   Combine each cluster of numbered items into one or more sentences. Combine clusters, if you wish.

1.1 Spears cushioned her notebook.
1.2 The spears were grassy.
1.3 A spider moved up a page.
1.4 The spider was long-legged.

2.1 The spider hesitated.
2.2 It then changed direction.
2.3 It was threatened by a pencil.

3.1 Its legs scurried for safety.
3.2 Its legs were delicate.
3.3 Sabrina grabbed one.
3.4 She picked up the spider.
3.5 The spider was thrashing.

4.1 She was amused by its dance.
4.2 The dance was frantic.
4.3 She made a two-fingered vise.
4.4 She moved in for the kill.

5.1 Death hung merciless.
5.2 Death hung poised.
5.3 It was above the spider's scream.
5.4 The scream was silent.

6.1 The afternoon was breathless.
6.2 The afternoon was warm.
6.3 She thought about her boyfriend.
6.4 She considered her own impulsiveness.

7.1 Sabrina felt the sun's warmth.
7.2 It was on her back.
7.3 It was on her arms.
7.4 Sabrina rolled over on her side.
7.5 She smiled to herself.
7.6 She let the spider go.

Revising Tip

In clusters 4 and 7 try participial phrases to open the sentences. For more on participles, see pages 485–486.

Continue the Story   Narrate a conclusion to this story. Then share your text—"Breakup" plus "The Spider"—with a writing partner.

Exposition

Exercise A   Dealing with Acne

Directions   Combine each cluster of numbered items into one or more sentences. Combine clusters, if you wish.

1.1 Acne is a common skin condition.
1.2 It is caused by oil glands.
1.3 Oil glands secrete too much sebum.
1.4 Sebum is a waxy lubricant.

2.1 Whiteheads result.
2.2 Excess sebum clogs the pores.
2.3 Excess sebum remains beneath the skin.

3.1 Plugs of sebum protrude above the skin.
3.2 Blackheads are the consequence.

4.1 Excess secretions cause red pimples.
4.2 Excess secretions invade other tissues.
4.3 Excess secretions inflame other tissues.

5.1 Simple steps can help you deal with acne.
5.2 They are mostly a matter of common sense.

6.1 Wash daily with soap and water.
6.2 Don't waste money on cleansers.
6.3 The cleansers are medicated.
6.4 Don't waste money on granular scrubs.

7.1 Use a drying lotion or cream.
7.2 This should contain benzoyl peroxide.

8.1 Wear your hair off your face.
8.2 This keeps it free of scalp oils.
8.3 Avoid hair dressings.
8.4 Hair dressings are greasy.

9.1 Don't pick at your face.
9.2 This increases inflammation.
9.3 This heightens your risk of pitting.
9.4 This heightens your risk of scarring.

Introduce the Article   Introduce the hygiene advice in "Dealing with Acne" by explaining why people need to understand this skin condition.

Exercise B   Protecting Your Skin

Directions   Combine each cluster of numbered items into one or more sentences. Combine clusters, if you wish.

1.1 Suntans may suggest good health.
1.2 They seriously damage your skin.
1.3 They destroy its elastic fibers.

2.1 Their consequence is premature aging.
2.2 No one wishes for the consequence.
2.3 This leaves skin dry and wrinkled.

3.1 Even less desirable are the health risks.
3.2 The risks include basal cell carcinoma.
3.3 The risks include malignant melanoma.

4.1 These skin cancers develop cumulatively.
4.2 These skin cancers develop irreversibly.
4.3 They are a result of sun exposure.

5.1 Early suntans can result in cancers.
5.2 Early sunburns can result in cancers.
5.3 The cancers are during adult years.

6.1 Many suntan salons promise safe tans.
6.2 They promise tans without burns.
6.3 They actually pose real health hazards.

7.1 Tanning booths use UVA radiation.
7.2 This penetrates the skin deeply.
7.3 This causes premature aging.
7.4 This increases susceptibility to cancers.

8.1 Protecting your skin requires something.
8.2 You reduce direct exposure to sunlight.
8.3 Use sunscreens rated at SPF 15 or higher.
8.4 Wear protective clothing in the sun.

9.1 Avoiding suntan salons is common sense.
9.2 It also saves you money.

Revising Tip

In clusters 2, 3, 4, 7, and 8, you can practice writing adjective clauses. For help on punctuating adjective clauses, see page 703.

Continue the Article   Create a transition paragraph after "Dealing with Acne" that links to "Protecting Your Skin." Share your text with a writing partner.

Taking Notes

Directions Combine each cluster of numbered items into one or more sentences. Combine clusters, if you wish.

1.1 There are many systems for notetaking.
1.2 Two have proved popular with students.
1.3 The students dislike traditional plans.

2.1 One system develops a spiderweb of words.
2.2 The system is sometimes called "webbing."
2.3 The system is sometimes called "mapping."
2.4 The words are from the reading.

3.1 Responses to reading trigger words.
3.2 The responses are personal.
3.3 Words are jotted down as "webs of meaning."

4.1 These webs may not make sense to someone else.
4.2 The webs speak clearly to us.
4.3 We are their authors.
4.4 We know what they are trying to say.

5.1 A second system also uses personal meaning.
5.2 The system is popular.
5.3 It is called the "dialogue journal."

6.1 The journal consists of two facing pages.
6.2 One page is for notes in outline form.
6.3 The other is for thoughts about the notes.

7.1 The notes record information objectively.
7.2 The facing page processes the information.
7.3 It provides emotional reactions.
7.4 It makes summaries.
7.5 It gives examples.
7.6 It asks questions.

8.1 A basic principle underlies both systems.
8.2 We bring unique experiences to reading.
8.3 We take away personal meanings.

Introduce the Article Develop a character sketch or dramatic incident that involves a student with poor study habits; use this sketch to introduce "Taking Notes."

Study Strategy

Directions Combine each cluster of numbered items into one or more sentences. Combine clusters, if you wish.

1.1 Many students have trouble studying.
1.2 They have not discovered principles.
1.3 The principles make it easy and fun.
1.4 They therefore get discouraged.

2.1 One approach is to get an overview.
2.2 The approach works for many students.
2.3 This is by flipping through a text.
2.4 This is by skimming major headings.
2.5 This is by reading the chapter summary.

3.1 This overview is like a road map.
3.2 This overview provides "the big picture."
3.3 This overview triggers personal knowledge.
3.4 This overview leads to questions.

4.1 A person turns headings into questions.
4.2 Questions arouse a sense of curiosity.
4.3 Questions provide a focus for reading.
4.4 Reading will follow in a few moments.

5.1 Questions engage one's thinking processes.
5.2 They are a tool for preparing the mind.
5.3 The tool is indispensable.
5.4 The preparation is to remember ideas.

6.1 Many students take notes as they read.
6.2 The students are highly successful.
6.3 They jot down answers to questions.
6.4 They challenge the author.

7.1 These students are active readers.
7.2 The readers recite key points to themselves.
7.3 The readers discuss ideas with others.
7.4 The readers review their notes.
7.5 They cannot help but learn the material.

Revising Tip

In cluster 5 try *because* as a sentence opener; then try an appositive, with dashes, after the word *questions*. Choose the sentence you prefer.

Continue the Article Write a conclusion for "Taking Notes" and "Study Strategy." Then share your text with a writing partner.

Persuasion

Directions Combine each cluster of numbered items into one or more sentences. Combine clusters, if you wish.

1.1 Most Americans worry about their weight.
1.2 Our culture says that "thin is in."
1.3 Advertisers sell us images of bodies.
1.4 The bodies are lean and handsome.

2.1 Forty percent of us are on diets.
2.2 This is at any given moment.
2.3 We are trying to shed excess pounds.

3.1 Losing weight is a major industry.
3.2 Promoters make a variety of claims.
3.3 The promoters seek quick profits.
3.4 The claims are given wide circulation.

4.1 One such myth centers on grapefruit.
4.2 It is supposed to contain enzymes.
4.3 The enzymes burn fats away.

5.1 No scientific evidence supports these claims.
5.2 Dozens of diets are based on this myth.

6.1 A second myth centers on diet pills.
6.2 The pills are touted as "sure cures."
6.3 The cures are for weight loss.

7.1 Pills sometimes have short-term effects.
7.2 No evidence supports long-term weight loss.

8.1 A third myth centers on electric stimulators.
8.2 These claim to provide "passive exercise."
8.3 These claim to trim fat in specific areas.

9.1 Scientific studies show something.
9.2 Such devices provide no change in body weight.
9.3 Such devices provide no change in body fat.
9.4 Such devices do not improve muscle tone.

Revising Tip

In cluster 1 try rearranging sentences to achieve emphasis; in cluster 9 delete *something* and use *that* as a connector.

Introduce the Article To introduce "Diet Myths," find an actual advertisement (from a Sunday supplement magazine, perhaps) and make it part of your paragraph.

More Diet Myths

Directions   Combine each cluster of numbered items into one or more sentences. Combine clusters, if you wish.

1.1 Some diet myths result from promoters.
1.2 Others seem to grow out of our folklore.
1.3 They are passed on by word of mouth.

2.1 There is a widely believed myth.
2.2 The stomach shrinks when you eat less.
2.3 This is simply untrue.
2.4 Your stomach cannot shrink.

3.1 Another myth is also quite common.
3.2 Potatoes are a fattening food.

4.1 A baked potato contains only 130 calories.
4.2 The potato is without butter.
4.3 The potato is without gravy.
4.4 The potato is without melted cheese.

5.1 Potatoes are a high-carbohydrate food.
5.2 The food has no fat or cholesterol.
5.3 The food has fewer calories than brown rice.

6.1 Yet another myth surrounds toast.
6.2 It is listed in many diets.
6.3 It may seem less fattening than untoasted bread.

7.1 Toasting bread removes only moisture.
7.2 It does not remove any calories.
7.3 This is contrary to popular belief.

8.1 A fourth myth concerns celery.
8.2 Some say it has "negative calories."
8.3 It takes so much work to chew celery.

9.1 Celery is a high-fiber vegetable.
9.2 It has only about six calories per stalk.
9.3 Chewing it does not use up extra calories.

Revising Tip

In either cluster 3 or 4, try dashes—as illustrated here—to achieve additional emphasis. In cluster 9 try *although* as an opener.

Continue the Article   Draw conclusions from "Diet Myths" and "More Diet Myths" that will persuade your reader. Then share your text with a writing partner.

Destroying History

Directions   Combine each cluster of numbered items into one or more sentences. Combine clusters, if you wish.

1.1 Homolovi is an ancestral home.
1.2 Homolovi means "Place of the Mounds."
1.3 The home is for many Hopi people.
1.4 The Hopi live in the desert Southwest.

2.1 This area has been plundered by looters.
2.2 The area covers 10,000 acres in Arizona.
2.3 The area is protected by federal and state laws.
2.4 The looters are in search of pottery.
2.5 The pottery is Native American.

3.1 The "pot hunters" use backhoes.
3.2 The "pot hunters" use other machinery.
3.3 The "pot hunters" leave a wake of destruction.

4.1 Hundreds of craters now scar the landscape.
4.2 Many buildings once stood there.
4.3 Two thousand people once lived there.
4.4 Two thousand people once worked there.
4.5 This was about 700 years ago.

5.1 The "pot hunters" rip the land.
5.2 The "pot hunters" gouge the land.
5.3 They destroy historical evidence.
5.4 The destruction is thoughtless.

6.1 Wealthy collectors support a black market.
6.2 The collectors are mainly from the United States.
6.3 The collectors are mainly from Japan.
6.4 The collectors are mainly from Germany.
6.5 The black market is flourishing.

7.1 Looters do the dirty work.
7.2 Private collectors are equally guilty.
7.3 They underwrite historical destruction.
7.4 They violate the heritage of Native Americans.

Revising Tip

In clusters 2 and 4 try *which* and *where as* connectors; in cluster 6 try a pair of dashes for stylistic emphasis.

Continue the Article   Should every culture have the right to record and document its own heritage? Make your case in a follow-up paragraph.

Directions   Combine each cluster of numbered items into one or more sentences. Combine clusters, if you wish.

1.1 Many Native Americans believe in spirits.
1.2 They deeply value ancient burial sites.
1.3 They deeply value ancestral dwellings.

2.1 They see the continuity in life.
2.2 They regard themselves as caretakers.
2.3 The caretakers have sacred duties.

3.1 Pots have significance to them.
3.2 Beads have significance to them.
3.3 Baskets have significance to them.
3.4 Projectile points have significance to them.
3.5 These objects help spirits find eternal peace.

4.1 Alaskan totem poles are cut up.
4.2 Alaskan totem poles are shipped overseas.
4.3 Native Americans shudder in disgust.

5.1 Someone tries to sell a Native American infant.
5.2 The Native American infant is mummified.
5.3 The price is $30,000.
5.4 Their jaws clench tight.

6.1 Anasazi pots bring nearly $100,000.
6.2 Anasazi baskets bring over $150,000.
6.3 They shake their heads sadly.

7.1 The black market angers Native Americans.
7.2 The market desecrates their past.
7.3 The market insults their values.
7.4 Their anger is understandable.

8.1 They look forward to a happier time.
8.2 Their heritage is accorded respect.
8.3 The black market collapses.
8.4 The market is now supported by looting.

Revising Tip

Try using *when* as an opener in clusters 4, 5, and 6. This effect is called *parallelism*.

Continue the Article   Imagine finding an arrowhead while hiking. Does it go into your pocket? Write about the personal reasons behind your decision.

Literature Exercises

Exercise A

Directions   Scan the sentences below. Some come directly from *The Crystal Cave* by Mary Stewart. The numbered sentences are adapted from Stewart's original. Combine the numbered sentences in your own way. Then compare your sentences with the originals on page 157.

Next moment I stopped short, brought up by a shock which spilled the excitement through my bowels like water. Something had moved in the murk, just to my right.

1. I froze still.
2. I strained my eyes to see.
3. There was no movement.
4. I held my breath.
5. I listened.
6. There was no sound.
7. I flared my nostrils.
8. I tested the air round me.
9. My testing was cautious.
10. There was no animal or human smell.
11. I thought something.
12. The cave smelt of smoke.
13. The cave smelt of damp rock.
14. The cave smelt of the earth itself.
15. The cave had a scent.
16. The scent was musty.
17. The scent was queer.
18. I could not identify it.

I knew, without putting it into words, that had there been any other creature near me the air would have felt different, less empty. There was no one there.

19. I tried a word in Welsh.
20. My try was soft.
21. The word was "Greetings."
22. The whisper came back at me in an echo.
23. The whisper came back so quickly.
24. I knew I was very near the wall of the cave.
25. Then it lost itself.
26. It was hissing in the roof.

Exercise B

Directions Scan the sentences below. Some come directly from *Of Wolves and Men* by Barry Lopez. The numbered sentences are adapted from Lopez's original. Decide which of the numbered sentences belong together, and combine them in your own way. Then compare your sentences with the originals on pages 270–271.

1. It is now late in the afternoon.
2. The wolf has stopped traveling.
3. He has lain down to sleep on cool earth.
4. The earth is beneath a rock outcropping.
5. Mosquitoes rest on his ears.
6. His ears flicker.
7. He begins to waken.
8. He rolls on his back.
9. He lies motionless.
10. His front legs are pointed toward the sky.
11. They are folded like wilted flowers.
12. His back legs are splayed.
13. His nose and tail are curved toward each other.
14. They are on one side of his body.

After a few moments he flops on his side, rises, stretches, and moves a few feet to inspect—minutely, delicately—a crevice in the rock outcropping and finds or doesn't find what draws him there. And then he ascends the rock face, bounding and balancing momentarily before bounding again, appearing slightly unsure of the process—but committed.

15. A few minutes pass.
16. He bolts suddenly into the woods.
17. He achieves full speed.
18. This is almost forty miles per hour.
19. This is for forty or fifty yards.
20. He begins to skid.
21. He begins to lunge at a lodgepole pine cone.
22. He trots away with it.
23. His head is erect.
24. His tail is erect.
25. His hips are slightly to one side.
26. They are out of line with his shoulders.
27. It's as if hindquarters were impatient with forequarters.
28. The cone is inert in his mouth.

Directions Scan the sentences below. Some come directly from *How the García Girls Lost Their Accents* by Julia Alvarez. The numbered sentences are adapted from Alvarez's original. Decide which of the numbered sentences belong together, and combine them in your own way. Then compare your sentences with the originals on pages 209–210.

"Go away," Yoyo wailed, but they both knew she was glad her mother was there, and needed only a moment's protest to save face.

1. Together they concocted a speech.
2. There were two brief pages of compliments.
3. The compliments were stale.
4. There were two brief pages of commonplaces.
5. The commonplaces were polite.
6. The commonplaces were on teachers.
7. It was a speech wrought by necessity.
8. It was a speech without much invention.
9. It was wrought by mother and daughter.
10. It was wrought late into the night.
11. It was wrought on one of the pads of paper.
12. Laura had once used the pads for her own inventions.
13. The speech was drafted.
14. Laura typed it up.
15. Yoyo stood by.
16. She corrected her mother's misnomers and mis-sayings.

Finally, her mother came up and pleaded with Yoyo to go down and reconcile with him [her father].

17. Yoyo found her father downstairs.
18. He was setting up a brand new typewriter.
19. The typewriter was on the kitchen table.
20. The typewriter was electric.
21. It was even better than her mother's.
22. He had outdone himself with all the extra features.
23. There was a plastic carrying case.
24. Yoyo's initials were decaled below the handle.
25. There was a brace to lift the paper upright while she typed.
26. There was an erase cartridge.
27. There was an automatic margin tab.
28. There was a plastic hood like a toaster cover.
29. The hood was to keep the dust away.

Directions   Scan the sentences below. Some come directly from *I Know Why the Caged Bird Sings* by Maya Angelou. The numbered sentences are adapted from Angelou's original. Decide which of the numbered sentences belong together, and combine them in your own way. Then compare your sentences with the originals on pages 48–49.

She took the bags from me and disappeared through the kitchen door. I looked around the room that I had never in my wildest fantasies imagined I would see.

1. Photographs leered from the walls.
2. Photographs threatened from the walls.
3. The photographs were browned.
4. The curtains pushed against themselves.
5. The curtains pushed against the wind.
6. The curtains were white.
7. The curtains were freshly done.
8. I wanted to gobble up the room entirely.
9. I wanted to take it to Bailey.
10. He would help me analyze it.
11. He would help me enjoy it.

"Have a seat, Marguerite. Over there by the table." She carried a platter covered with a tea towel. Although she warned that she hadn't tried her hand at baking sweets for some time, I was certain that like everything else about her the cookies would be perfect.

12. They were wafers.
13. The wafers were flat.
14. The wafers were round.
15. They were slightly browned on the edges.
16. They were butter-yellow in the center.
17. They came with the cold lemonade.
18. They were sufficient for childhood's lifelong diet.
19. I remembered my manners.
20. I took nice little bites.
21. The bites were lady-like.
22. The bites were off the edges.
23. She said something.
24. She had made them expressly for me.
25. She had a few in the kitchen.
26. I could take them home to my brother.

Directions   Scan the sentences below. Some come directly from "Skeletons in the Attic" by Clara Spotted Elk. The numbered sentences are adapted from Spotted Elk's original. Decide which of the numbered sentences belong together, and combine them in your own way. Then compare your sentences with the originals on page 311.

After a chance inquiry, a curator pulled out a drawer in one of the scores of cabinets that line the attic. There were the jumbled bones of an Indian. "A Kiowa," he said.

1. We subsequently found 18,500 Indian remains.
2. Some consisted of a handful of bones.
3. Most were full skeletons.
4. They were stored in the Smithsonian's nooks.
5. They were stored in the Smithsonian's crannies.
6. Their storage was unceremonious.
7. Other museums also collect the bones.
8. Other individuals also collect the bones.
9. Other federal agencies also collect the bones.
10. The agencies include the National Park Service.
11. The bones are of Indian warriors.
12. The bones are of Indian women.
13. The bones are of Indian children.
14. Some are on display as attractions.
15. The attractions are for tourists.
16. The attractions are by the roadside.

It is estimated that another 600,000 Indian remains are hidden away in locations across the country.

17. The museum community defends these collections.
18. Forensic scientists defend these collections.
19. Their defense is vigorous.
20. The collections are grisly.
21. There are few exceptions.
22. They refuse to return remains to the tribes.
23. The tribes wish to rebury them.
24. This is even when grave robbing has been documented.

They want to maintain adequate numbers of "specimens" for analysis and say they are dedicated to "the permanent curation of Indian skeletal remains."

Use Troubleshooter to help you correct common errors that you might make in your writing. You can indicate the errors on your paper using the handwritten codes in the left-hand column. Then the Table of Contents below will help you locate solutions to correct errors.

PROBLEM 1

Fragment that lacks a subject

frag   Sal put his best effort into his painting.
(Hoped it would win a prize.)

Solution

Sal put his best effort into his painting. He hoped it would win a prize.

Add a subject to the fragment to make it a complete sentence.

PROBLEM 2

Fragment that lacks a complete verb

frag   We heard a loud noise. (The fire alarm across the street.)

frag   The reviews are enthusiastic. (The critics encouraging us to put on future shows.)

Solution A

We heard a loud noise. The fire alarm across the street was wailing.

The reviews are enthusiastic. The critics are encouraging us to put on future shows.

Add a complete verb or a helping verb to make the sentence complete.

Solution B

We heard a loud noise—the fire alarm across the street.

The reviews are enthusiastic, with the critics encouraging us to put on future shows.

Combine the fragment with another sentence.

Fragment that is a subordinate clause

frag Maria was relieved. Because she found her notebook.

frag The restaurant is out of melon. Which I wanted for dessert.

Solution A

Maria was relieved because she found her notebook.

The restaurant is out of melon, which I wanted for dessert.
Combine the fragment with another sentence.

Solution B

Maria was relieved. She found her notebook.

The restaurant is out of melon. I wanted it for dessert.
Rewrite the fragment as a complete sentence, eliminating the subordinating conjunction or the relative pronoun and adding a subject or other words necessary to make a complete thought.

Fragment that lacks both a subject and a verb

frag Paul finally finished his homework. At ten o'clock.

Solution

Paul finally finished his homework at ten o'clock.
Combine the fragment with another sentence.

Need More Help?

If you need more help in avoiding sentence fragments, turn to Lesson 13.9, pages 515–516.

9.2 Run-on Sentence

PROBLEM 1

Comma splice—two main clauses separated only by a comma

run-on
> On vacation Luisa enjoys hiking in the mountains, Leon prefers swimming at the beach.

Solution A
On vacation Luisa enjoys hiking in the mountains. Leon prefers swimming at the beach.
Replace the comma with an end mark of punctuation, such as a period or a question mark, and begin the new sentence with a capital letter.

Solution B
On vacation Luisa enjoys hiking in the mountains; Leon prefers swimming at the beach.
Place a semicolon between the two main clauses.

Solution C
On vacation Luisa enjoys hiking in the mountains, but Leon prefers swimming at the beach.
Add a coordinating conjunction after the comma.

PROBLEM 2

Two main clauses with no punctuation between them

run-on
> Kim plays the guitar she writes music, too.

Solution A
Kim plays the guitar. She writes music, too.
Separate the main clauses with an end mark of punctuation, such as a period or a question mark, and begin the second sentence with a capital letter.

PROBLEM 3

Two main clauses with no comma before the coordinating
conjunction

run-on
```
Carla is planning to visit Yellowstone
National Park next summer and her sister
may join her.
```

run-on
```
The main course was boring but the dessert
was magnificent.
```

Solution
Carla is planning to visit Yellowstone National Park next
summer, and her sister may join her.

The main course was boring, but the dessert was magnificent.
Add a comma before the coordinating conjunction to separate the
two main clauses.

If you need more help in avoiding
run-on sentences, turn to Lesson 13.10,
pages 517–519.

9.3　Lack of Subject-Verb Agreement

PROBLEM 1

A subject that is separated from the verb by an intervening prepositional phrase

> *agr*　The sound of the nightingales (fill) the air.
>
> *agr*　The storms in winter (seems) severe.

Solution

The sound of the nightingales fills the air.

The storms in winter seem severe.
Ignore a prepositional phrase that comes between a subject and a verb. Make the verb agree with the subject, which is never the object of a preposition.

PROBLEM 2

A predicate nominative that differs in number from the subject

> *agr*　Bicycle races (was) his passion.

Solution

Bicycle races were his passion.
Ignore the predicate nominative, and make the verb agree with the subject of the sentence.

PROBLEM 3

A subject that follows the verb

> *agr*　Off the reef (lies) three sunken ships.
>
> *agr*　Here (comes) the first three volunteers.

Solution

Off the reef lie three sunken ships.

Here come the first three volunteers.
In an inverted sentence look for the subject *after* the verb. Then make sure the verb agrees with the subject.

PROBLEM 4

A collective noun as the subject

agr The chorus (sing) splendidly.

agr The jury (disagrees) among themselves.

Solution A
The chorus sings splendidly.
If the collective noun refers to a group as a whole, use a singular verb.

Solution B
The jury disagree among themselves.
If the collective noun refers to each member of a group individually, use a plural verb.

PROBLEM 5

A noun of amount as the subject

agr Ten months (are) the usual school year.

agr Ten dimes (makes) a dollar.

Solution
Ten months is the usual school year.

Ten dimes make a dollar.
Determine whether the noun of amount refers to one unit and is therefore singular or whether it refers to a number of individual units and is therefore plural.

A compound subject that is joined by and

aqr   Oxygen and hydrogen (is) essential to life.

aqr   Oil and vinegar (are) my favorite salad dressing.

Solution A
Oxygen and hydrogen are essential to life.
If the parts of the compound subject do not belong to one unit or if they refer to different people or things, use a plural verb.

Solution B
Oil and vinegar is my favorite salad dressing.
If the parts of the compound subject belong to one unit or if both parts refer to the same person or thing, use a singular verb.

PROBLEM 7

A compound subject that is joined by or *or* nor

aqr   Neither hardships nor danger (deter) him.

aqr   Either soup or sandwiches (makes) a good lunch.

Solution
Neither hardships nor danger deters him.

Either soup or sandwiches make a good lunch.
Make the verb agree with the subject that is closer to it.

PROBLEM 8

A compound subject that is preceded by many a, every, *or* each

aqr   Every nook and cranny (were) searched.

PROBLEM 9

A subject that is separated from the verb by an intervening expression

> *agr*   Carlos, as well as Dana, (love) baseball.

Certain expressions, such as *as well as*, *in addition to*, and *together with* do not change the number of the subject.

Solution

Carlos, as well as Dana, loves baseball.

Ignore an intervening expression between a subject and its verb. Make the verb agree with the subject.

PROBLEM 10

An indefinite pronoun as the subject

> *agr*   Each of the climbers (carry) a rope.

Some indefinite pronouns are singular, some are plural, and some can be either singular or plural, depending upon the noun to which they refer. (See page 413 for a list of indefinite pronouns.)

Solution

Each of the climbers carries a rope.

Determine whether the indefinite pronoun is singular or plural, and make the verb agree.

If you need more help with subject-verb agreement, turn to Lessons 16.1 through 16.7, pages 571–583.

9.4 Lack of Pronoun-Antecedent Agreement

PROBLEM 1

A singular antecedent that can be either male or female

> ant A good athlete must practice (his) routine daily.
>
> ant A parent and (his) child form a special bond.

Traditionally a masculine pronoun is used to refer to an antecedent that may be either male or female. This usage ignores or excludes females.

Solution A
A good athlete must practice his or her routine daily.

A parent and his or her child form a special bond.
Reword the sentence to use *he or she, him or her,* and so on.

Solution B
Good athletes must practice their routines daily.

Parents and their children form special bonds.
Reword the sentence so that both the antecedent and the pronoun are plural.

Solution C
Parents and children form a special bond.

Good athletes must practice routines daily.
Reword the sentence to eliminate the pronoun.

PROBLEM 2

A second-person pronoun that refers to a third-person antecedent

> ant Carlos and Jane love hiking because (you) benefit from vigorous exercise in peaceful, natural surroundings.

Be sure not to refer to an antecedent in the third person using the second-person pronoun *you*.

> **Solution A**
> **Carlos and Jane love hiking because they benefit from vigorous exercise in peaceful, natural surroundings.**
> Use the appropriate third-person pronoun.

> **Solution B**
> **Carlos and Jane love hiking because hikers benefit from vigorous exercise in peaceful, natural surroundings.**
> Use an appropriate noun instead of a pronoun.

PROBLEM 3

A singular indefinite pronoun as an antecedent

> *ant*   Each of the women had (their) own goal.
>
> *ant*   Neither of the men showed (their) surprise at the vote.

Each, *everyone*, *either*, *neither*, and *one* are singular and therefore require singular personal pronouns.

> **Solution**
> **Each of the women had her own goal.**
>
> **Neither of the men showed his surprise at the vote.**
> Don't be fooled by a prepositional phrase that contains a plural noun. Determine whether the indefinite pronoun antecedent is singular or plural, and make the noun agree.

If you need more help with pronoun-antecedent agreement, turn to Lesson 16.7, pages 581–583, and Lesson 17.5, pages 602–606.

9.5   Lack of Clear Pronoun Reference

PROBLEM 1

A pronoun reference that is weak or vague

ref   The traffic was snarled, (which) was caused by an accident.

ref   The room was stuffy and dimly lighted, and (that) made studying difficult.

ref   Some astronomers think that black holes are very numerous, but (it) is difficult to prove.

Be sure that *this*, *that*, *which*, and *it* have a clear antecedent.

Solution A
The traffic was snarled in a massive tie-up, which was caused by an accident.
Rewrite the sentence, adding a clear antecedent for the pronoun.

Solution B
The room was stuffy and dimly lighted, and those conditions made studying difficult.

Some astronomers think that black holes are very numerous, but their theory is difficult to prove.
Rewrite the sentence, substituting a noun for the pronoun.

PROBLEM 2

A pronoun that refers to more than one antecedent

ref   My sister always beats Susan at chess, but (she) still enjoys the game.

ref   When the dancers performed for the children, (they) were pleased.

My sister always beats Susan at chess, but Susan still enjoys the game.
Rewrite the sentence, substituting a noun for the pronoun.

The children were pleased when the dancers performed.
Rewrite the sentence, eliminating the pronoun.

PROBLEM 3

The indefinite use of you *or* they

ref   In Japan (you) go to school on Saturday mornings.

ref   In that school (they) have a fine music program.

Solution A
In Japan students go to school on Saturday mornings.
Rewrite the sentence, substituting a noun for the pronoun.

Solution B
That school has a fine music program.
Rewrite the sentence, eliminating the pronoun entirely.

If you need more help in making clear pronoun references, turn to Lesson 17.6, pages 607–609.

PROBLEM

An incorrect shift in person between two pronouns

pro They are going to the international fair, where (you) can sample foods from many nations.

pro I think life was easier when (you) had fewer possessions.

pro After one runs a marathon, (you) are exhausted and exhilarated.

Incorrect pronoun shifts occur when a writer or speaker uses a pronoun in one person and then illogically shifts to a pronoun in another person.

Solution A

They are going to the international fair, where they can sample foods from many nations.

I think life was easier when I had fewer possessions.

After one runs a marathon, one is exhausted yet exhilarated.
Replace the incorrect pronoun with a pronoun that agrees with its antecedent.

Solution B

They are going to the international fair, where people can sample foods from many nations.

I think life was easier when people had fewer possessions.
Replace the incorrect pronoun with an appropriate noun.

If you need more help in eliminating incorrect pronoun shifts, turn to Lesson 17.5, pages 602–606.

9.7   Shift in Verb Tense

PROBLEM 1

An unnecessary shift in tense

> *shift t*   Victor reads the newspaper and (noted) the sports scores.
>
> *shift t*   Nan arrived just as the play (begins).

When two or more events occur at the same time, be sure to use the same verb tense to describe each event.

Solution
Victor reads the newspaper and notes the sports scores.

Nan arrived just as the play began.
Use the same tense for both verbs.

PROBLEM 2

A lack of correct shift in tenses to show that one event precedes or follows another

> *shift t*   By the time the fire broke out, we (were) asleep for hours.

When events being described have occurred at different times, shift tenses to show that one event precedes or follows another.

Solution
By the time the fire broke out, we had been asleep for hours.
Shift from the past tense to the past perfect tense to indicate that one action began and ended before another past action began. Use the past perfect tense for the earlier of the two actions.

If you need more help with shifts in verb tenses, turn to Lesson 15.4, pages 551–553, and Lesson 15.6, pages 556–557.

9.8   Incorrect Verb Tense or Form

PROBLEM 1

An incorrect or missing verb ending

> *tense*   Yesterday I (walk) four miles in the morning.
>
> *tense*   Have you ever (watch) a soccer match?

Solution

Yesterday I walked four miles in the morning.

Have you ever watched a soccer match?
Add *-ed* to a regular verb to form the past tense and the past participle.

PROBLEM 2

An improperly formed irregular verb

> *tense*   Mike (teared) his pants on a nail.
>
> *tense*   Angela has (sweeped) every room.

Irregular verbs form their past and past participle in some way other than by adding *-ed*. Memorize these forms, or look them up.

Solution

Mike tore his pants on a nail.

Angela has swept every room.
Use the correct past or past participle form of an irregular verb.

PROBLEM 3

Confusion between the past form and the past participle

> *tense*   Mr. Yei has often (spoke) about life in China.

Mr. Yei has often spoken about life in China.
Use the past participle form of an irregular verb, not the past form,
when you use the auxiliary verb *have.*

PROBLEM 4

Improper use of the past participle

tense   We (rung) the doorbell several times.

tense   Jolene (swum) faster than anyone else
          on the team.

tense   We (begun) the trip without much advance
          planning.

The past participle of an irregular verb cannot stand alone as a verb.
It must be used with the auxiliary verb *have.*

Solution A
We have rung the doorbell several times.

Jolene has swum faster than anyone else on the team.

We have begun the trip without much advance planning.
Add the auxiliary verb *have* to the past participle to form a complete
verb.

Solution B
We rang the doorbell several times.

Jolene swam faster than anyone else on the team.

We began the trip without much advance planning.
Replace the past participle with the past form of the verb.

*If you need more help with correct
verb forms, turn to Lessons 15.1 and
15.2, pages 543–547.*

9.9   Misplaced or Dangling Modifier

PROBLEM 1

A misplaced modifier

mod   I got some fine pictures of the puppies (with my new camera.)

mod   (Dented and scratched,) Marta found her bicycle.

mod   We took a backpack on the train (stuffed with sandwiches and fruit.)

Modifiers that modify the wrong word or seem to modify more than one word in a sentence are called misplaced modifiers.

Solution

With my new camera I got some fine pictures of the puppies.

Marta found her bicycle dented and scratched.

We took a backpack stuffed with sandwiches and fruit on the train.

Move the misplaced phrase as close as possible to the word or words it modifies.

PROBLEM 2

The adverb only *misplaced*

mod   Carlos (only) eats spaghetti with clam sauce.

The meaning of your sentence may be unclear if *only* is misplaced.

Solution

Only Carlos eats spaghetti with clam sauce.

Carlos eats only spaghetti with clam sauce.

Carlos eats spaghetti only with clam sauce.

Place the adverb *only* immediately before the word or group of words it modifies. Note that each time *only* is moved in the sentence, the meaning of the sentence changes.

PROBLEM 3

A dangling modifier

mod (After working feverishly for days,) the
science project was completed.

mod (Watching television,) the screen suddenly
went blank.

mod (Hoping for a break from the heat,) a Canadian
cold front brought relief.

Dangling modifiers do not logically seem to modify any word in the sentence.

Solution

After working feverishly for days, Jan completed her science project.

Watching television, Yoshiko saw the screen suddenly go blank.

Hoping for a break from the heat, we were relieved when a Canadian cold front moved in.

Rewrite the sentence, adding a noun to which the dangling phrase clearly refers. Often you will have to add other words to complete the meaning of the sentence.

If you need more help with misplaced or dangling modifiers, turn to Lesson 18.7, pages 632–637.

9.10 Missing or Misplaced Possessive Apostrophe

PROBLEM 1

Singular nouns

poss   The (waitress) wallet held that (days) tips.

Solution

The waitress's wallet held that day's tips.

Use an apostrophe and an -*s* to form the possessive of a singular noun, even one that ends in -*s*.

PROBLEM 2

Plural nouns ending in -s

poss   The (soldiers) tents dotted the field.

Solution

The soldiers' tents dotted the field.

Use an apostrophe alone to form the possessive of a plural noun that ends in -*s*.

PROBLEM 3

Plural nouns not ending in -s

poss   The (childrens) bookstore is on Broadway.

Solution

The children's bookstore is on Broadway.

Use an apostrophe and an -*s* to form the possessive of a plural noun that does not end in -*s*.

PROBLEM 4

Pronouns

poss   I found ⟨somebodys⟩ watch.

poss   The best idea was ⟨her's⟩.

Solution A
I found somebody's watch.
Use an apostrophe and an -*s* to form the possessive of a singular indefinite pronoun.

Solution B
The best idea was hers.
Do not use an apostrophe with any of the possessive personal pronouns.

PROBLEM 5

Confusion between its *and* it's

poss   The boat has slipped ⟨it's⟩ mooring.

poss   ⟨Its⟩ a great day for a picnic.

The possessive of *it* is *its*. *It's* is the contraction of *it is*.

Solution
The boat has slipped its mooring.

It's a great day for a picnic.
Do not use an apostrophe to form the possessive of *it*. Use an apostrophe to form the contraction of *it is*.

If you need more help with apostrophes and possessives, turn to Lesson 17.1, pages 595–596, and Lesson 21.11, pages 721–723.

9.11 Missing Commas with Nonessential Element

Missing commas with nonessential participles, infinitives, and their phrases

com   Claude watched delighted as Cheryl accepted the award.

com   Marla finishing her work set out for a late afternoon jog.

com   To repeat the bus will leave promptly at five.

Solution

Claude watched, delighted, as Cheryl accepted the award.

Marla, finishing her work, set out for a late afternoon jog.

To repeat, the bus will leave promptly at five.

Determine whether the participle, infinitive, or phrase is truly not essential to the meaning of the sentence. If so, set off the phrase with commas.

Missing commas with nonessential adjective clauses

com   César who is also a licensed pilot is a certified scuba diver.

Solution

César, who is also a licensed pilot, is a certified scuba diver.

Determine whether the clause is truly not essential to the meaning of the sentence. If so, set off the clause with commas.

PROBLEM 3

Missing commas with nonessential appositives

com   Margaret Donelly⌒our letter carrier⌒is on vacation.

Solution
Margaret Donelly, our letter carrier, is on vacation.
Determine whether the appositive is truly not essential to the meaning of the sentence. If so, set off the appositive with commas.

PROBLEM 4

Missing commas with interjections and parenthetical expressions

com   Gosh⌒I enjoyed that game.

com   You know⌒of course⌒that the office is closed on Saturdays.

Solution
Gosh, I enjoyed that game.

You know, of course, that the office is closed on Saturdays.
Set off the interjection or parenthetical expression with commas.

If you need more help with commas and nonessential elements, turn to Lesson 21.6, pages 700–710.

9.12   Missing Comma in a Series

Missing comma in a series of words, phrases, or clauses

↓ com   The garden was a riot of zinnias⌒hollyhocks⌒
marigolds⌒and lilies.

↓ com   Reggie stopped⌒bent down⌒and picked up the
quarter he had dropped.

↓ com   Yuki ran down the street⌒around the corner⌒
and into the Murphys' garage.

            We watched the kites soaring into the sky⌒
↓ com   swooping back and forth⌒and gliding to earth.

↓ com   Angela plays the guitar⌒Bill sings⌒and José
accompanies them on the drums.

Solution

The garden was a riot of zinnias, hollyhocks, marigolds, and lilies.

Reggie stopped, bent down, and picked up the quarter he had dropped.

Yuki ran down the street, around the corner, and into the Murphys' garage.

We watched the kites soaring into the sky, swooping back and forth, and gliding to earth.

Angela plays the guitar, Bill sings, and José accompanies them on the drums.

When there are three or more items in a series, use a comma after each item that precedes the conjunction.

If you need more help with commas in a series, turn to Lesson 21.6, pages 700–710.

Part 2

Grammar, Usage, and Mechanics

Parts of Speech

10.1 Nouns

A **noun** is a word that names a person, a place, a thing, or an idea.

PERSON	teacher, uncle, niece, sister-in-law
PLACE	garage, city, park, school
THING	paw, giraffe, bicycle, ice cream, doorknob
IDEA	democracy, fame, love, disappointment

Exercise 1 **Identifying Nouns**

On your paper list the 25 nouns that appear in the following literary passage.

Literature: In a New Country

Hanging from a cord attached to the middle of the ceiling there was an electric bulb, low enough for an adult to reach and turn the black switch. I realized that this was our own electric light for us to turn on and off as we pleased. I pushed a chair under it and after some instruction from my mother proceeded to create lightning in the room by turning the switch as fast as I could.

Next I discovered the bedsprings. When I sat on the bed it sank deliciously. Jumping on it in my stocking feet, I held my balance dangerously as I made the bed creak and the mattress bounce. The head and foot of the bed were made of iron scrollwork in loops and rosettes painted white.

From *Barrio Boy* by Ernesto Galarza

Exercise 2 **Completing Sentences with Nouns**

On your paper write nouns to complete the following sentences. Be sure that your completed sentences make sense.

1. The _____ galloped by on her _____.
2. Ten of her _____ waved their blue _____.
3. The other _____ of her _____ cheered.
4. Her yellow _____ blew off her _____.
5. The _____ made her _____ fly wildly.
6. Three miniature _____ sat on the _____.
7. Their _____ were brushing their _____.
8. The _____ and her _____ approached the _____.
9. They walked their _____ and held their _____.
10. Everyone gathered around the tiny _____.

Singular and Plural Nouns

Nouns can be singular or plural, depending upon whether they name *one* person, place, thing, or idea or *more than one*.

To form the plural of most nouns, add -*s*. Other plural nouns are formed in different ways. For nouns ending in -*s*, -*ch*, -*sh*, -*x*, or -*zz*, add -*es* to form the plural. For nouns ending in -*y* preceded by a consonant, change the -*y* to -*i* and add -*es*. For most nouns ending in -*f* or -*fe*, change -*f* to -*v* and add -*es*. Other nouns have irregular plurals (e.g., *woman*, *women*). Some nouns do not change form from singular to plural (e.g., *sheep*, *sheep*).

SINGULAR	boy, body, watch, wife, ox
PLURAL	boys, bodies, watches, wives, oxen

Exercise 3 — Forming the Plurals of Nouns

Write the plural form of each noun below on your paper. Consult a dictionary if you need help.

1. victory
2. moose
3. lunch
4. box
5. mouse
6. video
7. man
8. half
9. goose
10. valley
11. business
12. batch
13. galaxy
14. radio
15. lens
16. chief
17. foot
18. deer
19. child
20. person

Exercise 4 — Completing Sentences with Singular and Plural Nouns

On your paper write singular or plural nouns to complete the following sentences. Be sure that your completed sentences make sense.

Heidelberg

1. The _____ of Heidelberg, Germany, is neither very large nor strategically important.
2. However, the _____ who live there boast of its beautiful _____.
3. Among the city's _____ are textiles, leather goods, and precision instruments.
4. A wide _____ flows through the _____.
5. Even the gabled _____ are an impressive _____.
6. The _____ is blessed with fertile _____ and a mild _____.
7. In the nineteenth century, the _____ of Heidelberg tripled.
8. Many modern _____ were constructed next to historic _____.
9. New _____ and _____ dotted the _____.
10. Nevertheless, the _____ remain committed to preserving their _____.

Possessive Nouns

The possessive form of a noun can show possession, ownership, or the general relationship between two nouns. Add an apostrophe and -*s* to form the possessive of a singular noun, even one that already ends in -*s*. Use an apostrophe alone to form the possessive of a plural noun that ends in -*s*.

SINGULAR POSSESSIVE	PLURAL POSSESSIVE
the **car's** hood	the **cars'** hoods
a **baby's** bottle	the **babies'** bottles
the **dish's** pattern	the **dishes'** patterns
a **valley's** towns	the **valleys'** towns
the **calf's** mother	the **calves'** mother
the **business's** payroll	the **businesses'** payrolls

Add an apostrophe and -*s* to form the possessive of a plural noun that does not end in -*s*.

the **women's** decision
the **children's** toys
the **sheep's** wool

Exercise 5	**Forming Possessive Nouns**

Rewrite each phrase below, using the possessive form of the italicized noun.

1. the *cat* food
2. the *wagons* wheels
3. the *mice* cage
4. the *parents* advice
5. the *child* toy
6. the *oxen* horns
7. the *book* cover
8. the *family* car
9. the *trolleys* whistles
10. the *boys* homework
11. the *cities* facilities
12. the *states* rights
13. the *mattress* springs
14. the *people* choice
15. the *wives* party
16. the *churches* steeples
17. the *deer* food
18. the *region* climate
19. the *fox* den
20. the *factories* smokestacks

Exercise 6	**Completing Sentences with Possessive Nouns**

On your paper write singular or plural possessive nouns to complete the following sentences. Be sure that your completed sentences make sense.

1. The _____ hearts began to pound as the chair lift brought them to the top of the _____ highest peak.
2. In the group behind them, their _____ face had a nervous look.
3. Only the young _____ voices sounded excited.
4. It had been the _____ idea to ski the _____ most challenging moguls.
5. Judy, the _____ most experienced skier, talked about the previous _____ trips.

Concrete and Abstract Nouns

A **concrete noun** names an object that occupies space or that can be recognized by any of the senses.

| petal | smoke | cough | orange | nook |

An **abstract noun** names an idea, a quality, or a characteristic.

| motion | humor | quantity | tact | rudeness |

Exercise 7   **Identifying Nouns as Concrete or Abstract**

On your paper identify each noun as *concrete* or *abstract*.

1. wisdom
2. sunshine
3. book
4. bravery
5. attitude
6. library
7. music
8. guitar
9. happiness
10. electricity

Exercise 8   **Using Abstract and Concrete Nouns**

For each concrete noun in items 1–10, write an abstract noun that names an idea associated with the concrete noun. For each abstract noun in items 11–20, write a concrete noun that has the quality of the abstract noun.

SAMPLE ANSWERS   rocket—power   taste—salt

1. bicycle
2. laughter
3. itch
4. home run
5. snow
6. summer
7. apple
8. in-line skates
9. applause
10. sundowns
11. haste
12. warmth
13. poverty
14. insight
15. sadness
16. joy
17. gratitude
18. distraction
19. eagerness
20. softness

Exercise 9   **Writing Sentences with Abstract Nouns**

On your paper write five sentences about what you think is important in life. In each sentence use at least one abstract noun to identify a goal, idea, or personal trait you admire. Underline each abstract noun.

Proper and Common Nouns

A **proper noun** is the name of a particular person, place, thing, or idea.

PROPER NOUNS	
PERSON	Sean Connery, Uncle Peter, Emily Dickinson
PLACE	Mexico, Lake George, Grand Canyon
THING	Statue of Liberty, *Great Expectations,* Thanksgiving
IDEA	Romanticism, Baroque Age, Judaism

A **common noun** is the general—not the particular—name of a person, place, thing, or idea

COMMON NOUNS	
PERSON	actor, uncle, poet
PLACE	country, lake, canyon
THING	statue, book, holiday
IDEA	movement, era, religion

Proper nouns are capitalized; common nouns are usually not capitalized.

Exercise 10   Matching Proper Nouns with Common Nouns

On your paper match each proper noun on the left with the corresponding common noun on the right.

1. Middle Ages	**a.** city
2. *Romeo and Juliet*	**b.** mountains
3. Cuba	**c.** building complex
4. *The Wizard of Oz*	**d.** team
5. Renoir	**e.** painter
6. Rocky Mountains	**f.** play
7. Chicago Cubs	**g.** river
8. San Francisco	**h.** island
9. Nile River	**i.** era
10. Houston Space Center	**j.** motion picture

Exercise 11   Naming Proper Nouns

On your paper add one more proper noun to each category below.

1. Wisconsin, North Dakota, New York, Georgia, _____
2. Atlantic, Antarctic, Indian, Arctic, _____
3. Michael, Pedro, Gregory, Joel, _____
4. *Chicago Tribune, New York Times, Milwaukee Journal, Trumptown Herald,* _____
5. France, Ghana, Malaysia, Argentina, _____

Collective Nouns

A **collective noun** names a group.

family	(the) senate
(the) public	(a) gaggle (of geese)
team	(an) audience
(the) press	(the) board (of directors)

A collective noun is sometimes considered singular and sometimes considered plural. You consider a collective noun singular when you talk about a group as a whole. You consider a collective noun plural when you talk about the individual members of a group.

SINGULAR   The audience shouts its approval.

PLURAL   The audience have arrived in small groups.

Exercise 12   **Identifying Collective Nouns**

On your paper list five collective nouns from each of the following paragraphs.

Porgy and Bess

[1]The Metropolitan Opera's 1985 production of George Gershwin's *Porgy and Bess* had a chorus of 70 voices. [2]The cast included such noted stars as Grace Bumbry and Simon Estes. [3]The orchestra was conducted by James Levine. [4]The audience had bought their tickets well in advance for all 16 performances. [5]The huge stage was filled with people representing the population of Catfish Row.

Animal Life in Africa

[1]In Africa a team of zoologists can observe many kinds of wild animals. [2]In a western forest might be seen a family of chimpanzees. [3]In the eastern grasslands, quiet watchers might spy a herd of roaming zebras. [4]In the northern desert, a flock of ostriches is not an uncommon sight. [5]The African continent has an extraordinary collection of animal life.

The Power of the Press

[1]The press plays an important and powerful role in contemporary life. [2]Television news programs, newspapers, and periodicals reach a large and eager audience. [3]As a result, journalists have a strong influence on society. [4]Sometimes a team of reporters can make or break a candidate's campaign for office. [5]To make an informed choice, the public must separate fact from opinion.

Identifying Nouns

On your paper identify each underlined noun as *common*, *proper*, or *collective*, depending upon how the noun is used in the sentence. Some nouns may belong in more than one category.

The Trail of Tears

In 1838, 16,000 Cherokee were forced from their [1]homes in the [2]Old South. Under armed guard, the [3]mass of Native Americans was pushed west across the [4]Mississippi River to Oklahoma's [5]Indian Territory. Other [6]cultures, including the Creek, Choctaw, and Chickasaw nations, were included in the removal [7]program. Many historians refer to this [8]journey west as the [9]Trail of Tears. They estimate that as many as a quarter of the [10]group may have died during the long and arduous migration.

Some [11]Native Americans rebelled against the removal program, while others fled to Canada or [12]Mexico. The Cherokee led the most organized [13]resistance. They had their own written language; their own [14]newspaper, the [15]*Cherokee Phoenix*; tax-supported schools; and a written [16]constitution. The Cherokee [17]nation also had the sympathy of some members of [18]Congress and of other government [19]officials. Although the Cherokee took legal action, they never were able to regain their [20]homelands.

Exercise 14 **Creating Sentences with Nouns**

On your paper write five sentences about a shop in your town or neighborhood. Use concrete nouns to convey a vivid picture of the place.

Exercise 15 **Completing Sentences with Nouns**

On your paper complete the paragraphs below by filling in each of the 20 blanks with the kind of noun specified in *italic* typeface. Be sure that your completed sentences make sense.

Thanksgiving Day

The festive 1*abstract* of the Thanksgiving 2*concrete* filled our 3*concrete*. 4*proper and concrete* told us the 5*common* of the 6*proper* who prepared the first Thanksgiving feast. All of the young 7*common* listened. The table, set with our best 8*concrete*, held steaming platters of 9*concrete* and 10*concrete*. For 11*common* each of us had a generous 12*common* of 13*concrete*.

After dinner we sat by the blazing 14*concrete*, and 15*proper and concrete* told us that it was President Lincoln who declared Thanksgiving an official holiday. Then we turned on the 16*concrete* and watched 17*proper and concrete*. Later that 18*common* we agreed that we had had so much good 19*abstract* we wished that 20*proper* came more than once a year.

10.2 Pronouns

A **pronoun** is a word that takes the place of a noun, a group of words acting as a noun, or another pronoun. The word or group of words to which a pronoun refers is called its **antecedent.**

> When James Baldwin was 14 years old, **he** became a preacher. [The pronoun *he* takes the place of its proper noun antecedent, *James Baldwin.*]
>
> When Georgia O'Keeffe and Alfred Stieglitz were married in 1924, **both** were famous artists. [The pronoun *both* takes the place of the nouns *Georgia O'Keeffe* and *Alfred Stieglitz.*]
>
> Although Georgia O'Keeffe **herself** was a painter, **her** husband was a photographer. [The pronouns *herself* and *her* take the place of the noun *Georgia O'Keeffe.*]

English pronouns fall into these categories: personal pronouns, reflexive and intensive pronouns, demonstrative pronouns, interrogative pronouns, relative pronouns, and indefinite pronouns.

Personal and Possessive Pronouns

A **personal pronoun** refers to a specific person or thing by indicating the person speaking (the first person), the person being addressed (the second person), or any other person or thing being discussed (the third person).

Personal pronouns also express number; they are either singular or plural.

Personal Pronouns		
	Singular	**Plural**
FIRST PERSON	I, me	we, us
SECOND PERSON	you	you
THIRD PERSON	he, him	they, them
	she, her	
	it	

FIRST PERSON	**I** kept the dog. [*I* refers to the person speaking.]
SECOND PERSON	The dog was afraid of **you.** [*You* refers to the person being addressed.]
THIRD PERSON	**It** ran away. [*It* refers to the dog mentioned in the previous sentence.]

Third-person pronouns also express **gender.** *He* and *him* are masculine; *she* and *her* are feminine; *it* is neuter (neither masculine nor feminine).

The personal pronouns include several forms that indicate possession or ownership.

A **possessive pronoun** takes the place of the possessive form of a noun.

Possessive Pronouns		
	Singular	**Plural**
FIRST PERSON	my, mine	our, ours
SECOND PERSON	your, yours	your, yours
THIRD PERSON	his	their, theirs
	her, hers	
	its	

Some possessive forms are used before nouns. Other possessive forms can be used by themselves. Notice that possessive pronouns do not contain an apostrophe.

USED BEFORE A NOUN   Take **your** bathing suit.

USED ALONE   That bathing suit is **yours.**

Exercise 16   **Using Personal and Possessive Pronouns**

Improve the following paragraph by replacing the underlined words or groups of words with personal or possessive pronouns. Write your answers on your paper.

Isamu Noguchi, Sculptor

Isamu Noguchi is famous for [1] Noguchi's striking abstract sculptures. [2] These sculptures can be seen in museums everywhere. Noguchi's father was a Japanese poet, and [3] Noguchi's mother was an American writer. As a young man in Paris, Noguchi studied with the sculptor Constantin Brancusi, who encouraged [4] Noguchi to work in abstract forms. In the 1930s Noguchi settled in New York. Soon [5] Noguchi's spare and elegant sculptures were being exhibited, and many people went to see [6] the sculptures. One admirer, Martha Graham, invited [7] Noguchi to create sets for [8] Martha Graham's dance company. [9] Noguchi also designed sculpture gardens, as well as furniture and lamps. Noguchi's later interest in architectural forms and design is reflected in the monumental *Red Cube* (1968). [10] *Red Cube* stands outside the Marine Midland Building in New York.

Exercise 17   Creating Sentences with Personal and Possessive Pronouns

On your paper write five sentences about someone or something that is special to you. Be sure to describe what you consider to be important or unique about the person or item. Use at least five personal or possessive pronouns. Then underline all the personal and possessive pronouns in your sentences.

Reflexive and Intensive Pronouns

Reflexive and intensive pronouns are formed by adding *-self* or *-selves* to certain personal and possessive pronouns.

Reflexive and Intensive Pronouns		
	Singular	Plural
FIRST PERSON	myself	ourselves
SECOND PERSON	yourself	yourselves
THIRD PERSON	himself, herself, itself	themselves

A **reflexive pronoun** refers, or reflects back, to a noun or pronoun earlier in the sentence, indicating that the same person or thing is involved.

A reflexive pronoun always adds information to a sentence.

You outdid **yourself** when you wrote that song.

Cathy always timed **herself** when jogging.

In dancing class we watch **ourselves** in the mirror.

The basketball players prepared **themselves** for the game.

An **intensive pronoun** adds emphasis to another noun or pronoun in the same sentence.

I **myself** ate the pizza.

The team **itself** chose the captain.

Maria **herself** opened the door.

George and Pedro planned the party **themselves.**

An intensive pronoun does not add information to a sentence. If the intensive pronoun is left out, the sentence still has the same meaning. An intensive pronoun usually comes immediately after its antecedent.

Demonstrative Pronouns

A **demonstrative pronoun** points out specific persons, places, things, or ideas.

Demonstrative Pronouns		
SINGULAR	this	that
PLURAL	these	those

This is your homeroom.

These are your classmates.

That will be your seat.

Carla's desk is cleaner than **those**. [*Those* refers to other desks.]

A demonstrative pronoun can come before or after its antecedent. Sometimes the antecedent is understood.

Exercise 18   Using Reflexive, Intensive, and Demonstrative Pronouns

Supply the appropriate reflexive, intensive, or demonstrative pronoun for each blank. Write your answers on your paper.

An Orchestra Performance

1. He reminded _____ to watch the conductor's baton.
2. The string, woodwind, brass, and percussion sections had prepared _____ during rehearsals.
3. Even the conductor _____ seemed nervous.
4. The air _____ seemed motionless in expectation.
5. We positioned _____ for the opening note.
6. Soon we found _____ listening anxiously for our cues.
7. _____ is a very moving piece of music.
8. We were so inspired by the occasion that our instruments seemed to play _____.
9. Afterward we all felt very proud of _____.
10. "Take _____," the concert manager said, handing several bouquets to the conductor.

Interrogative and Relative Pronouns

An **interrogative pronoun** is used to form questions.

who?   whom?   whose?   what?   which?

Who will lead the way?   **What** makes a good leader?
Whom would you choose?   **Which** of these paths is easiest?
Whose is the lightest pack?

The interrogative pronouns include the forms *whoever, whomever, whichever,* and *whatever.*

Whoever could have made such a mistake?

A **relative pronoun** is used to begin a special subject-verb word group called a subordinate clause (see Unit 13).

who   whoever   which   that
whom   whomever   whichever   what
whose   whosoever   whatever

The people **who** invented Monopoly were surprised by its success. [The relative pronoun *who* begins the subordinate clause *who invented Monopoly.*]

Dominoes is a game **that** many Texans play. [The relative pronoun *that* begins the subordinate clause *that many Texans play.*]

| **Exercise 19** | **Distinguishing Between Interrogative and Relative Pronouns** |

On your paper list the relative and interrogative pronouns that appear in the following sentences, and label each pronoun as *relative* or *interrogative*.

Harriet Tubman, a Courageous Woman

1. Harriet Tubman, who was born a slave in 1820, became a leader of the antislavery movement.
2. Who would have anticipated her development into one of the most powerful speakers in the United States?
3. Tubman, whose maiden name was Araminta Greene, married John Tubman.
4. She led hundreds of fugitive slaves along the Underground Railroad, a secret route that led from the South to Canada.
5. Which of her many talents did she use during the Civil War?
6. She did many jobs for the Union army, which fought to abolish slavery.
7. What did her fellow abolitionists call her?
8. Whatever she did, she lived up to her nickname, General Tubman.
9. Whom did she look after in the years following the Civil War?
10. She looked after orphans and old people, whom she loved dearly.

Indefinite Pronouns

An **indefinite pronoun** refers to persons, places, or things in a more general way than a noun does.

> **Everyone** needs food. [The indefinite pronoun *everyone* refers to people in general.]
>
> Did you get **enough** to eat? [The indefinite pronoun *enough* refers to a general, not a specific, amount.]
>
> After two hamburgers he did not want **another**. [The indefinite pronoun *another* has the antecedent *hamburger*.]

Some enjoyed the music.

Everyone went to the concert.

One had a crush on the lead singer.

Some Indefinite Pronouns				
all	each	many	nothing	somebody
another	either	most	one	someone
any	enough	much	other	something
anybody	everybody	neither	others	
anyone	everyone	nobody	plenty	
anything	everything	none	several	
both	few	no one	some	

Exercise 20   Creating Sentences with Indefinite Pronouns

On your paper write 10 sentences with indefinite pronouns. Use at least eight different indefinite pronouns; refer to the chart if you need help. Underline the indefinite pronouns in your sentences.

Exercise 21   Identifying Pronouns

(a) On your paper list in order the 25 pronouns that appear in the following paragraph. (b) Identify each pronoun as *personal, possessive, reflexive, intensive, demonstrative, interrogative, relative,* or *indefinite.*

A Great Magician

[1]Harry Houdini, a great magician who was born Erik Weisz, used a stage name borrowed from an earlier French magician called Houdin. [2]Whereas many of Houdin's illusions were optical ones, those that made Harry Houdini famous were daring escapes from complex traps—most of them designed by Houdini himself. [3]The most famous escape of all was the water-torture trick, in which Houdini, whose hands and feet were bound, was locked in a water-filled tank, only to emerge safe and free a moment later. [4]Audiences would ask themselves, What does Houdini do to free himself? [5]Wouldn't you wonder about this yourself? [6]Actually, Houdini created much of his magic by practicing yoga techniques, learning to survive on less oxygen than most of us need. [7]Whose name is synonymous with magic? [8]That is a question everyone can answer: it is Houdini's.

10.3   Verbs

A **verb** is a word that expresses action or a state of being and is necessary to make a statement.

The violinists **begin.**	Rehearsals **are** important.
A flutist **entered** late.	The conductor **seems** enthusiastic.

The primary characteristic of a verb is its ability to express time—present, past, and future. Verbs express time by means of *tense* forms.

PRESENT TENSE	They **walk** home together.
PAST TENSE	They **walked** home together.
FUTURE TENSE	They **will walk** home together.

Exercise 22   Identifying Verbs in Sentences

On your paper write the verbs that appear in each of the following sentences.

1. National parks in the American Southwest include Bryce Canyon, Zion, Mesa Verde, and Grand Canyon.
2. Over the centuries, water and wind erosion change the land dramatically.
3. Each park's natural features attract people of all ages.
4. An information center at the entrance to the park offers exhibits, maps, and publications.
5. Park rangers provide little-known facts about the history of the park.

Exercise 23   Completing Sentences with Verbs

On your paper write a verb to complete each of the following sentences.

The American Southwest

1. The Southwest _____ some of the most spectacular scenery in the country.
2. Deep canyons and tall mesas _____ the landscape.
3. Several Native American nations, including the Navajo and Hopi, _____ in the Southwest.
4. Many Native Americans still _____ the customs of their ancestors.
5. Some communities _____ in houses made of adobe (sun-dried earth and straw).
6. Even today many people in the Southwest _____ their own adobe homes.
7. Navajo women still _____ rugs on handmade looms.
8. The Hopi people still _____ ancient rain dances.
9. The Native Americans of the Southwest _____ proud of their heritage.
10. Despite modern intrusions, many of their traditions _____ unchanged.

Action Verbs

An **action verb** tells what someone or something does.

Some action verbs express physical action; others express mental action.

PHYSICAL ACTION   The catcher often **signals** to the pitcher.

MENTAL ACTION   A good catcher **understands** the batter's technique.

A **transitive verb** is an action verb that is followed by a word or words that answer the question *what?* or *whom?*

Cats **see** their prey in the dark. [The action verb *see* is followed by the noun *prey*, which answers the question *see what?*]

An **intransitive verb** is an action verb that is *not* followed by a word that answers the question *what?* or *whom?*

Cats **see** well in the dark. [The action verb is followed by words that tell *how* and *where*.]

Exercise 24	Identifying Action Verbs

On your paper write the action verbs that appear in the following sentences. Indicate whether each action verb is used as a *transitive* or an *intransitive verb*.

Sacajawea, an Intrepid Woman

1. After President Thomas Jefferson bought the Louisiana Territory from France, he arranged for its exploration.
2. In 1804 Meriwether Lewis and William Clark launched a search for an overland route to the Pacific Ocean.
3. Lewis and Clark hired a French Canadian fur trapper, Toussaint Charbonneau, as guide and interpreter.
4. Charbonneau's wife, Sacajawea, a Shoshone, also joined the expedition.
5. With her linguistic skills Sacajawea helped Lewis and Clark's communication with Native American tribes.
6. Four years earlier hostile Native Americans had abducted Sacajawea and later had sold her to Charbonneau.
7. In 1805 Lewis and Clark encountered a group of Shoshone, among them Sacajawea's brother, a chief.
8. He gave Lewis and Clark the horses they needed.
9. Sacajawea, her husband, and their infant son stayed with the expedition until Lewis and Clark had explored the Pacific Coast and returned to Wyoming.
10. Sacajawea and Charbonneau later returned to the Dakota Territory, where, some historians believe, Sacajawea died in 1812.

Completing Sentences with Action Verbs

On your paper write an action verb to complete each of the sentences below.

Stephen Crane

1. Stephen Crane _____ his first novel under the pen name Johnston Smith.
2. He _____ Syracuse University for a brief time, where he distinguished himself as a baseball player.
3. Crane's popular novel *The Red Badge of Courage* _____ the story of a young soldier during the Civil War.
4. The novel was widely acclaimed, and syndicated newspapers _____ Crane as a war correspondent.
5. The steamer on which Crane was traveling to Cuba, *The Commodore*, _____ off the coast of Florida.
6. He _____ his nearly fatal experience in *The Open Boat and Other Stories*.
7. Crane's natural writing style _____ an understanding of the realities of combat.
8. Crane _____ his varied life experiences in his writings.
9. Critics often _____ Crane's portrayal of war as realistic and powerful.
10. English writer Joseph Conrad _____ Crane when he moved to England in 1897.

Exercise 26   **Distinguishing Between Transitive and Intransitive Verbs**

On your paper complete the following sentences using the action verb in *italics*. In one sentence use it as a transitive verb. In the other sentence, use it as an intransitive verb. Add any other words that are necessary.

1. *hears*
    When hiking through the forest, Alicia _____. (transitive)
    When she pulls her hat over her head, she _____. (intransitive)
2. *studies*
    In the afternoon the class _____. (transitive)
    In order to do well in school, Paul _____. (intransitive)
3. *eats*
    For breakfast the baby _____. (transitive)
    When the baby is sick, she _____. (intransitive)
4. *practices*
    Before the concert Susan _____. (transitive)
    Because she wants to be in the band, she _____. (intransitive)
5. *play*
    In the afternoon the children _____ (transitive)
    Despite their age difference, the children _____. (intransitive)

Linking Verbs

A **linking verb** links, or joins, the subject of a sentence (often a noun or pronoun) with a word or expression that identifies or describes the subject.

Be in all its forms—*am, is, are, was, were*—is the most commonly used linking verb.

I **am** an athlete.   The players **are** fast.
Squash **is** an indoor sport.   They **were** hockey fans.

Several other verbs besides the forms of *be* can act as linking verbs.

Other Linking Verbs			
look	remain	seem	become
stay	grow	appear	sound
taste	smell	feel	

Exercise 27   **Completing Sentences with Linking Verbs**

On your paper write a linking verb to complete each of the following sentences. Try to use as many different verbs as you can.

Georgia

1. The air at higher altitudes in Georgia _____ cool in the summer.
2. Georgia _____ one of the southern states.
3. Azaleas and other colorful plants_____ good in the summer.
4. The saws of the lumber mills in the mountains _____ loud and screechy.
5. The Okefenokee National Wildlife Refuge and Stone Mountain Park _____ two popular attractions.
6. The Civil War_____ a topic of great interest, especially in Atlanta.
7. Fishing, hunting, and golfing _____ popular with many Georgians.
8. The population of Georgia _____ more diverse every year.
9. With its many different industries and attractions, Georgia _____ ready for a bright future.
10. Atlanta _____ the site of the 1996 Summer Olympics.

Exercise 28   **Writing Sentences with Linking Verbs**

On your paper write five sentences about yourself, your family, or your day at school. Use a different form of the verb *be* in each sentence.

Identifying Action and Linking Verbs

On your paper make a list of the twenty verbs that appear in the following paragraphs. Identify each verb as either *action* or *linking*.

The Statue of Liberty

[1]In 1884 France presented the United States with a gift as a dramatic gesture of friendship. [2]This spectacular gift was a huge copper statue. [3]Its official name is *Liberty Enlightening the World*. [4]Most people, however, know it simply as the Statue of Liberty. [5]The gift commemorated the hundredth anniversary of the American Revolution. [6]It also celebrated the alliance of France with the colonists during their fight for independence from England. [7]The immense figure of Liberty holds a torch in her right hand. [8]The inscription on the cover of her book reads "July 4, 1776."

[9]Artist Frédéric Auguste Bartholdi first made a nine-foot model of the statue. [10]Gustave Eiffel, a pioneer in the use of metal as an architectural material, created the iron framework for the full-size statue. [11]The completed statue was too large for delivery in one piece. [12]Workers in France dismantled it. [13]The pieces of the statue arrived in the United States in 214 cases.

[14]The French people donated the money for the construction of the statue. [15]Grateful, the people of the United States collected the funds for the massive granite and concrete pedestal. [16]This impressive monument found a permanent home on Liberty Island in New York Harbor. [17]The dedication of the statue by President Grover Cleveland on October 28, 1886, was a great ceremonial occasion.

[18]At 151 feet and 1 inch high, the Statue of Liberty remains one of the largest statues in the world. [19]The monumental lady with the torch quickly became a symbol of American democracy.

Completing Sentences with Action and Linking Verbs

On your paper write a verb to complete each of the sentences below. Identify each verb as an *action* or a *linking* verb.

Those Amazing Hummingbirds

1. Hummingbirds _____ the smallest birds in the world.
2. About nineteen different kinds of hummingbirds _____ in the United States.
3. The ruby-throated hummingbird _____ approximately 3 1/2 inches in length.
4. The hummingbird _____ its wings between fifty and seventy times per second.
5. The rapid wing beating _____ soft and low, like the whirring of a distant motorboat.
6. The bird's wings _____ a blur to the human eye.
7. This rapid wing beating _____ the hummingbird hover in midair.
8. While hovering, the hummingbird _____ its long, slender bill into a flower.
9. The bird _____ the flower's nectar through its long, tubelike tongue.
10. Hummingbirds also _____ insects and may even steal them away from spider webs.

Verb Phrases

The verb in a sentence may consist of more than one word. The words that accompany the main verb are called **auxiliary,** or helping, **verbs.**

Auxiliary Verbs			
FORMS OF *BE*	am, is, are, was, were, being, been		
FORMS OF *HAVE*	has, have, had		
OTHER AUXILIARIES	can, could	may, might	must
	do, does, did	shall, should	will, would

A **verb phrase** consists of a main verb and all its auxiliary, or helping, verbs.

The most common auxiliary verbs are the forms of *be* and *have*. They help the main verb express the various tenses.

We **are working** in the yard.
We **have worked** for the past two weeks.
We **had been working** for an hour before the storm.

The other auxiliary verbs are not used primarily to express time. They are often used to emphasize meaning.

I **should be leaving.**
Could he **have finished?**
Luisa **may** already **be waiting.**

Exercise 31 **Using Auxiliary Verbs**

On your paper write two revisions of each sentence below by changing the italicized verb phrase. Remember that you will probably have to change the main verb as well as the auxiliary verb. Underline the verb phrase in each sentence you write.

SAMPLE   I *am going.*
ANSWER   I <u>have gone</u>.   I <u>might go</u>.

1. Jerry and Sue *will eat* dinner.
2. The rest of the family *has left*.
3. When *did* the Murrays *call?*
4. Janice *has been waiting*.
5. Who *should set* the table?

On your paper write each verb phrase that appears the following sentences. (Some sentences have more than one verb phrase.) Put parentheses around the auxiliary verbs in each phrase. (A word or words that interrupt a verb phrase are not considered part of the verb phrase.)

Fats Waller, a Great Jazz Pianist

1. Fats Waller has been called one of the greatest jazz musicians of the twentieth century.
2. A versatile musician, he could compose, sing, and play several instruments with equal skill.
3. Fortunately, most of his music has been recorded.
4. Waller was already playing the piano at the age of six.
5. He had been taught by his mother, a musician herself.
6. Waller's father, a church deacon, had felt that his son should follow in his footsteps.
7. Nevertheless, young Waller had decided that his life would be dedicated to music.
8. By the age of 16, he was earning $23 a week as a theater organist and had already written his first instrumental composition, "Boston Blues."
9. People must have appreciated Waller's talents.
10. Can you believe that Waller's first song, "Squeeze Me," became a jazz classic?
11. A recording of the song by Louis Armstrong and Earl Hines had already become popular by 1928.
12. By the beginning of the 1930s, Waller had become known not only as a major composer, bandleader, and jazz vocalist but also as the greatest jazz organist of his time.
13. By 1932 he had already composed the song that would become his most famous work, "Ain't Misbehavin'."
14. An earlier Waller song, "Honeysuckle Rose" (1928), has remained a favorite ever since the time it was written.
15. It may not be widely recalled today that Waller had performed for several years on radio before becoming a recording artist.
16. By the mid-1930s, Waller had become famous as a recording star for RCA Victor.
17. At that time, people were buying more records by Waller than by any other African American musician.
18. *Ain't Misbehavin'*, a Broadway show with many of Waller's songs, was declared a hit in 1978, more than three decades after Waller's death.
19. Those people who have seen *Ain't Misbehavin'* will surely never forget the experience.
20. Waller will always have a special place in the history of American jazz.
21. Today we can still enjoy his exuberant style of piano playing.
22. Few musicians have been able to imitate Waller's humorous vocal renditions.
23. Fans should know that Fats's real name was Thomas.
24. Waller's lasting popularity has benefited from new recording technologies.
25. Our musical heritage has been greatly enriched by Fats Waller's talents, despite his death at an early age.

Creating Verb Phrases

On your paper write auxiliary verbs to create a verb phrase for each sentence. Be sure that your completed sentences make sense.

Satellites

1. Satellites _____ defined as artificial objects that orbit celestial bodies.
2. The first satellite, *Sputnik I*, _____ launched in 1957 by the Soviet Union.
3. Satellites _____ study solar radiation, magnetic fields, and atmospheric temperature.
4. Crewed satellites _____ include food, air, and life-support systems for astronauts.
5. One of the earliest crewed satellites _____ named *Skylab*.
6. Astronauts _____ performed experiments in space to find out more about the materials we use on earth.
7. The Hubble Telescope _____ enabled astronomers to learn more about our universe.
8. Many scientists and engineers _____ work long hours to prepare the next satellite for its mission into space.
9. More advanced satellites _____ help meteorologists predict the weather more accurately.
10. Telecommunications companies _____ financing future experiments in space.

Completing Sentences with Verb Phrases

On your paper write a verb phrase to complete each of the following sentences. Be sure that your completed sentences make sense.

James Herriot, Veterinarian and Author

1. Many children and adults _____ a friend in James Herriot.
2. A country veterinarian in Yorkshire, England, Herriot decided after his fiftieth birthday that he _____ books.
3. His first book _____ *If Only They Could Talk*.
4. Herriot had hoped that someone would publish his book and a few people _____ it.
5. It soon became apparent that his book _____ a bestseller.
6. His first two books _____ in the United States in 1972 as one volume entitled *All Creatures Great and Small*.
7. By the time Herriot died in February 1995, his 15 books _____ more than 50 million copies in 20 countries.
8. Critics _____ Herriot's stories as "fresh, clear, pure, and good."
9. Each of his stories features animals that _____ by the country veterinarian himself.
10. *James Herriot's Treasury for Children* _____ a wonderful gift for readers of all ages.

Using Vivid Verbs

Write five sentences about one of your favorite sports. Choose very specific action verbs and verb phrases to convey a vivid sense of the sport.

Exercise 36   **Completing Sentences with Verbs and Verb Phrases**

On your paper complete each sentence in the following paragraph by adding a verb or verb phrase as indicated in italic typeface. Be sure that your completed sentences make sense.

New York's World Trade Center

The massive World Trade Center in New York City [1]*linking verb* a city within a city. About 50,000 people [2]*action verb* in its stores and offices, and another 80,000 or so [3]*action verb* in and out each day. The center [4]*action verb* 110 stories in each of its twin towers, and another 6 levels [5]*action verb* underground. Its dozens of stores, from flower stores to drugstores, [6]*linking verb* attractive and busy. The stores often [7]*action verb* special services to their customers. Clients of the cleaners, for example, [8]*action verb* their clothes in large bags for protection on the subway. The enormous kitchens of the center [9]*action verb* as many as 30,000 people each day. More than 20 restaurants [10]*action verb* inside the buildings. The vast complex even [11]*action verb* its own police station, with a force of 39 officers. The manager's office [12]*linking verb* busy all the time. In fact, it [13]*action verb* over 200 calls for assistance each day. Some people [14]*linking verb* too hot and [15]*action verb* a lower temperature. Others [16]*action verb* themselves out of their offices and [17]*action verb* spare keys. An ambulance [18]*action verb* outside the complex at all times in case of an emergency, and paramedics, with the latest in life-support equipment, [19]*action verb* the life of a seriously ill or injured person. With its impressive population and variety of services, the World Trade Center [20]*linking verb* a small city in the middle of New York City.

Exercise 37   **Identifying Action Verbs, Linking Verbs, and Verb Phrases**

On your paper identify the verb in each of the following sentences as an *action verb* or a *linking verb*. If the verb is a verb phrase, write *verb phrase* as well. Then use the information in the sentence to write a new sentence, using the italicized verb form in parentheses.

SAMPLE   The pangolin and the lizard look similar. (*action verb phrase*)
ANSWER   look; linking verb   The pangolin and the lizard do have similar qualities.

The Pangolin

1. The pangolin has some of the characteristics of a lizard. (*linking verb*)
2. Overlapping scales instead of hair cover the back of this insect-eating mammal. (*linking verb*)
3. These scales feel sharp, similar to a razor in the mouth of a predator. (*action verb phrase*)
4. The pangolin curls itself into a tight ball for protection. (*action verb phrase*)
5. This toothless anteater lives in Asia and Africa. (*linking verb*)

10.4 Adjectives

An **adjective** is a word that modifies a noun or pronoun by limiting its meaning. An adjective tells *what kind, which one, how many,* or *how much.*

round window	**six** oranges	**that** hat	**adult** cat
romantic story	**many** ideas	**these** books	**Scottish** wool
interesting book	**enough** cups	**third** time	**no** reason

Nouns can also be used as adjectives. They tell *what kind* or *which one* about the noun modified.

afternoon class   **music** lesson   **football** practice

Possessive pronouns, such as *our* and *his*, can be considered adjectives because they modify nouns in addition to their usual function as pronouns.

our book   **his** watch   **their** house   **my** hands

Similarly, possessive nouns can be considered adjectives.

Julia's dream   the **knight's** castle   the **Bowers'** car

Adjectives may be used in various positions in relation to the words they modify.

How **obedient** the poodle is!
That **obedient** poodle belongs to her.
The poodle is **obedient**.
The judges considered the poodle **obedient**.
The poodle, always **obedient,** waited by the door.

Many adjectives have different forms to indicate degree of comparison.

POSITIVE	COMPARATIVE	SUPERLATIVE
light	lighter	lightest
heavy	heavier	heaviest
funny	funnier	funniest
sad	sadder	saddest
practical	more practical	most practical
good	better	best
much	more	most
bad	worse	worst

Exercise 38　　Identifying Adjectives

On your paper list the 20 adjectives that appear in the following passage, which describes a scene on a British heath during the last century. Count possessive pronouns as adjectives, but do not count the words *a*, *an*, and *the*.

Literature: A Long Road

Before him stretched the long, laborious road, dry, empty, and white. It was quite open to the heath on each side, and bisected that vast, dark surface. . . . The old man frequently stretched his eyes ahead to gaze over the tract that he had yet to traverse. At length he discerned, a long distance in front of him, a moving spot. . . . Its rate of advance was slow. . . . When he drew nearer he perceived it to be a . . . van, ordinary in shape, but singular in color. . . . The driver walked beside it; and, like his van, he was completely red.

From *The Return of the Native* by Thomas Hardy

Exercise 39　　Completing Sentences with Adjectives

On your paper write an adjective to complete each of the following sentences. Be sure that your completed sentences make sense.

1. The sheepdog trial was held on a _____ field.
2. It was near the edge of a _____ river.
3. The dogs, always _____, waited for the trial to begin.
4. Wearing _____ jackets, the trainers leaned on their long crooks.
5. Soon the judge waved his _____ handkerchief to begin the trial.

Exercise 40　　Discovering How Adjectives Are Formed

Use your dictionary to discover the adjective form that is most closely related to each of the following nouns.

1. literature
2. grammar
3. declaration
4. residence
5. parent
6. science
7. intention
8. might
9. idealism
10. noise

Using Forms of Adjectives

On your paper complete the sentences in each group by writing the correct positive, comparative, and superlative forms of the given adjective.

SAMPLE   **tall**
ANSWERS   The basketball player is **tall**.
           Other players are **taller** than he is.
           The captain of the team is the **tallest** player of all.

bright
 1. The male mandrill is a type of baboon that has a very ____ face.
 2. Scientists think that the colors become even ____ when the baboon gets angry.
 3. During a fight between mandrills, the male with the ____ color usually wins.

good
 4. Most people agree that milk is ____ for you.
 5. Others argue that water is even ____ for you than milk.
 6. Personally, I think fruit juices are the ____.
 7. I like orange juice ____ than grapefruit juice.

tasty
 8. Last night's dinner was ____.
 9. It was ____ than any other meal he has served this week.
 10. Thanksgiving dinner is my candidate for our family's ____ meal.
 11. Is Jack's cooking ____ than Minna's?

large
 12. Compared to Mercury, Earth is a fairly ____ planet.
 13. Saturn is much ____ than Earth.
 14. Jupiter, however, is the ____ planet.
 15. Which is ____, Neptune or Mars?

slow
 16. The tortoise was very ____.
 17. It was much ____ than the hare.
 18. In fact, the tortoise was the ____ animal around.

curious
 19. The detective is ____ about the case.
 20. Her assistant is even ____.
 21. The police captain is the ____ of all.

many
 22. Jack won ____ awards at the sports banquet.
 23. Did he win the ____ awards?
 24. He won ____ awards than he did last year.
 25. The team was surprised that Jack won ____ awards than the quarterback.

Articles

Articles are the adjectives *a, an* and *the*. *A* and *an* are called indefinite articles. They can refer to any one of a kind of person, place, or thing. *A* is used before consonant sounds and *an* is used before vowel sounds. *The* is called a definite article. It refers to a specific person, place, or thing.

INDEFINITE	She found **a** ring.	They spotted **an** iceberg.
	I bought **a** used mask.	He was **an** honorable choice.
DEFINITE	She found **the** ring.	They spotted **the** iceberg.
	I bought **the** used mask.	He was **the** honorable choice.

Exercise 42   **Completing Sentences with Articles**

On your paper write an article to complete each of the following sentences. Then identify each article as *indefinite* or *definite*.

Coral Reefs

 1. Coral reefs are land features formed in _____ ocean.
 2. _____ fringing reef extends from the shore of an island or mainland.
 3. No body of water comes between _____ fringing reef and land.
 4. _____ channel or lagoon comes between a barrier reef and shore.
 5. Charles Darwin first explained _____ formation of coral reefs.
 6. Darwin's theory is _____ one accepted by modern geologists.
 7. Many coral reefs are in _____ Atlantic, Pacific, and Indian oceans.
 8. _____ most famous barrier reef is in Australia.
 9. The Bikini Atoll was the site of _____ underwater atomic explosion in 1946.
10. The coral that forms _____ atoll can be more than 1,000 feet thick.

Exercise 43   **Writing with Different Kinds of Adjectives**

On your paper write an adjective to complete each sentence. The kind of modifier to use in each case is indicated in italics. Be sure that your completed sentences make sense.

The African Elephant

The African elephant is [1]*article* largest of all land animals. [2]*article* mature elephant eats about 300 pounds of plants every day. Some of [3]*possessive pronoun* favorite foods include grass, leaves, roots, bark, and fruit. The [4]*possessive noun* long trunk is actually a nose that serves as a hand. With [5]*possessive pronoun* trunk, the elephant can pick up a small berry or a heavy log. Most African elephants are dark gray with a little pink on the edges of [6]*possessive pronoun* ears. The [7]*possessive noun* big ears brush away flies and other pesty insects. [8]*article* African elephant also has two long, ivory tusks. Elephants use [9]*possessive pronoun* tusks to dig for food, fight, and carry heavy loads. Wild African elephants are found only in areas south of [10]*article* Sahara.

Proper Adjectives

A **proper adjective** is formed from a proper noun and begins with a capital letter.

Rembrandt was a **Dutch** painter.
The **Berlin** Wall came down in 1989.

The following suffixes are often used to create proper adjectives: *-an*, *-ian*, *-n*, *-ese*, and *-ish*. Sometimes there are other changes as well.

PROPER NOUNS	PROPER ADJECTIVES
Alaska	Alaskan
Queen Victoria	Victorian
Vietnam	Vietnamese
Denmark	Danish

Exercise 44   Identifying Proper Adjectives

On your paper list the 10 proper adjectives that appear in the following passage.

The Early Colonization of the Americas

[1]The Spanish colonization of the Americas began in the late 1400s after Christopher Columbus, an Italian explorer, sailed westward from Europe until he reached some Caribbean islands. [2]The great Columbian drama unfolded as hundreds of Native American cultures, including the Aztec and Incan civilizations, collided violently with conquistadors and colonists. [3]A century later, England and France joined in the quest for a North American empire. [4]Some Europeans hoped to acquire great wealth, while others hoped to spread the Christian faith. [5]Still others sought freedom from oppressive European laws and customs.

Exercise 45   Forming Proper Adjectives

On your paper write a proper adjective formed from each of the following proper nouns. Consult a dictionary if you need help.

1. Africa
2. China
3. Mexico
4. Thomas Jefferson
5. William Shakespeare
6. Dakota
7. Spain
8. Confucius
9. Hawaii
10. Senegal

Identifying Adjectives

On your paper write the 20 adjectives, including articles, that appear in the following paragraph.

Mayan Culture

[1] Recent discoveries have revealed new facts about the ancient Maya, who formed one of the oldest societies in Central America. [2] By A.D. 1000 they had already made impressive and original advancements in art and science. [3] Recently, at a site in northern Belize, fortunate archaeologists unearthed the unmistakable remains of an early civilization. [4] This discovery was remarkable and significant, for it pushed back the origins of Mayan culture to 2400 B.C.

Creating Sentences with Adjectives

On your paper write five sentences about someone you know and can picture clearly. In your description include details about the person's appearance, voice, behavior, and personality. Choose adjectives that are especially descriptive to convey a vivid image of the person.

Using Adjectives in Writing

On your paper complete the paragraphs below by replacing each blank with an adjective, including definite and indefinite articles. Be sure that your completed sentences make sense.

Corn

Corn is an important [1]_____ crop in the United States. The country's annual [2]_____ production is more than 6 billion bushels, accounting for almost half the total world production. Illinois is a(n) [3]_____ producer, along with several other [4]_____ states. Most of the corn grown in the United States is used as feed for [5]_____ animals such as hogs, cattle, and chickens. Although corn is a(n) [6]_____ source of energy, it is low in protein.

Each corn plant has a(n) [7]_____ stem, averaging 8 feet in height. The ear of corn is protected by [8]_____ husk. The [9]_____ tassels at the tip of the ear of corn contain pollen.

There are [10]_____ different types of corn, and all of them have a specific use. Sweet corn is often served as a(n) [11]_____ dish at meals. Popcorn is a(n) [12]_____ snack throughout the United States. During the fall, many people use pod corn as a(n) [13]_____ decoration. Even the other parts of the corn plant have [14]_____ uses. For example, corncobs are ground to make abrasives for cleaning [15]_____ engines.

No one knows where or when [16]_____ plants were first farmed, but corn was [17]_____ important staple in the diet of Native Americans by the 1600s. When the [18]_____ colonists arrived in the Massachusetts Bay Colony, Squanto taught them how to grow and harvest corn. Without his [19]_____ help, the [20]_____ colony might not have survived.

10.5 Adverbs

An **adverb** is a word that modifies a verb, an adjective, or another adverb by making its meaning more specific.

The following sentences illustrate the use of adverbs to modify verbs, adjectives, and adverbs.

She **always** waited **patiently.**
verb

The waiting room was **very** noisy and **overly** crowded.
adjective   adjective

Rather oddly, we have **almost** never visited his farm.
adverb   adverb

Adverbs modify by answering the questions *when? where? how?* and *to what degree?*

I will call **tomorrow.**
His phone rings **often.**
The speaker will stand **here.**
Kim **carefully** polished the car.
We were **truly** sorry.

When an adverb modifies a verb, it may be placed in various positions in relation to the verb. When an adverb modifies an adjective or another adverb, it usually comes directly before the modified word.

MODIFYING A VERB

Finally the storm is ending.

The storm **finally** is ending.

The storm is **finally** ending.

The storm is ending **finally.**

MODIFYING AN ADJECTIVE

The snow was **quite** heavy.

Driving was **very** hazardous.

MODIFYING AN ADVERB

It **almost** never snows this heavily.

I **hardly** ever need to wear my boots.

Negative Words as Adverbs

The word *not* and the contraction *n't* are considered adverbs. Other negative words can function as adverbs of time and place.

The plane has **not** landed.　　　They have **hardly** boarded.
The plane is **nowhere** in sight.　　I have **never** flown.

Exercise 49　　**Identifying Words Modified by Adverbs**

On your paper write the word or words that are being modified by the adverb in italics in each sentence.

The Cleaner Wrasse

1. The eel *instinctively* opened its mouth to let the small fish enter.
2. Surprisingly, the eel did *not* intend to eat the small fry.
3. The cleaner wrasse, a tropical fish, is *almost* always welcome to inspect the eel's teeth.
4. Some wrasses, such as blueheads, *thoroughly* clean the teeth of larger fish.
5. They eat the *extremely* tiny creatures and pieces of dead skin that cling to the bigger fish's teeth.
6. *Sometimes* snappers and groupers also go to the "cleaners."
7. One cleaner wrasse is *often* visited by as many as 300 fish in a period of 6 hours.
8. Finding customers is *never* difficult for the bluehead wrasse.
9. Its *especially* bright neon color acts as a kind of undersea advertising.
10. Its dancelike swimming motion attracts customers *also*.

Exercise 50　　**Identifying Adverbs**

On your paper write all the adverb(s) that appear in each sentence below. Then write the word or words each adverb modifies.

A Great Blues Singer

1. Bessie Smith is often considered a great blues singer.
2. She was born into an extremely poor family in Chattanooga, Tennessee.
3. Hardly 14, she was already touring with Ma Rainey and her Rabbit Foot Minstrels.
4. Others have sung songs more matter-of-factly than she.
5. Jazz writers have called her style rhythmically adventurous.
6. In 1923 Smith began to make commercially successful records.
7. Louis Armstrong was one very famous jazz musician with whom she sang.
8. Her greatest fame probably came in the years from 1923 to 1928.
9. Her record *Nobody's Blues but Mine*, which covers the period from 1925 to 1927, remains popular today.
10. Bessie Smith did not survive a tragic car accident in 1937.

Adverbs That Compare

Like adjectives, some adverbs have different forms to indicate degree of comparison. The comparative form of an adverb compares two actions. The superlative form of an adverb compares more than two actions. For adverbs of only one syllable, add *-er* to make the comparative form and *-est* to make the superlative form.

POSITIVE	COMPARATIVE	SUPERLATIVE
runs **fast**	runs **faster**	runs **fastest**
arrived **late**	arrived **later**	arrived **latest**
works **hard**	works **harder**	works **hardest**

When an adverb ends in *-ly* or has more than one syllable, use the word *more* to form the comparative and *most* to form the superlative.

POSITIVE	COMPARATIVE	SUPERLATIVE
walks **quickly**	walks **more quickly**	walks **most quickly**
reads **carefully**	reads **more carefully**	reads **most carefully**
calls **often**	calls **more often**	calls **most often**

Some adverbs do not form the comparative and superlative in the regular manner.

POSITIVE	COMPARATIVE	SUPERLATIVE
feels **well**	feels **better**	feels **best**
behaves **badly**	behaves **worse**	behaves **worst**
cares **little**	cares **less**	cares **least**
throws **far**	throws **farther**	throws **farthest**

Exercise 51 — Forming Comparative and Superlative Adverbs

On your paper write the comparative and superlative forms of each of the following adverbs. Consult a dictionary if you need help.

1. high
2. bravely
3. early
4. surprisingly
5. thoroughly
6. easily
7. low
8. far
9. happily
10. foolishly
11. near
12. softly
13. poorly
14. little
15. close
16. eagerly
17. well
18. fearfully
19. strangely
20. speedily

Using Adverbs That Compare

On your paper write the form of the adverb specified in parentheses.

Balloons

1. The highest recorded plastic balloon flight _____ reached an altitude of more than 150,000 feet. (positive form of *easily*)
2. Seven years later a rubber balloon went 18,000 feet _____. (comparative form of *high*)
3. The longest superpressured balloon flight on record lasted _____ than 300 days. (comparative form of *long*)
4. The _____ the pilot computes the atmospheric pressures, the better is the chance of a successful flight. (comparative form of *carefully*)
5. A balloon can travel so _____ into the atmosphere because its skin can stretch. (positive form of *far*)
6. The balloon that rises _____ is the one that is the lightest. (superlative form of *fast*)
7. In general, a hot-air balloon will rise _____ if the air in it is heated to a higher temperature. (comparative form of *fast)*
8. Some of the earliest balloons were _____ tethered to the earth. (positive form of *carefully*)
9. Scientists are now working even _____ to improve balloon technology. (comparative form of *hard*)
10. Helium is used _____ than hydrogen because it is safer. (comparative form of *often*)

Exercise 53   **Completing Sentences with Adverbs**

On your paper write an adverb to complete each sentence below.

The United States Capitol

1. The hill where the United States Capitol has stood since 1800 is _____ called Capitol Hill.
2. After many delays in construction, some feared that the Capitol would _____ be completed.
3. During the War of 1812, the inside of the Capitol was _____ destroyed by British troops.
4. The dome is _____ impressive, reaching a height of 188 feet.
5. A statue symbolizing freedom stands _____ on top of the Capitol dome.
6. Tourists consider the Capitol a _____ important sight in Washington, D.C.
7. Tourists _____ visit the Library of Congress and the Supreme Court, which are within walking distance of the Capitol.
8. They also see members of Congress, who _____ walk through the corridors on their way to one of the legislative chambers.
9. Statuary Hall _____ contains statues of some famous Americans.
10. Every four years, a new president is _____ sworn in at the Capitol.

Exercise 54   Completing Sentences with Adverbs

On your paper rewrite each sentence, adding the adverb in parentheses. Be sure that you place each adverb in an appropriate position.

Historically Speaking

1. The Greek writer Herodotus is considered to be the first historian. (generally)
2. A practical-minded individual, Herodotus did not worry about the purposes or goals of history. (much)
3. He wondered about the past. (simply)
4. He also asked some intriguing questions about past events. (very)
5. Then he recorded what he had discovered. (carefully)
6. Some people study history for its own sake. (still)
7. They are interested in the past. (truly)
8. Many historians find it challenging to make history relevant to others. (extremely)
9. Students of history learn when they are given the chance to draw their own conclusions about past events. (best)
10. Public officials use the lessons of the past to help find solutions to contemporary problems. (sometimes)

Exercise 55   Positioning Adverbs

On your paper rewrite each sentence adding an appropriate verb-modifying adverb. Then rewrite the sentence again, placing the adverb in a different position.

SAMPLE   Track-and-field star Florence Griffith-Joyner accepted her gold medal.
ANSWER   (a) Track-and-field star Florence Griffith-Joyner proudly accepted her gold medal.
          (b) Proudly, track-and-field star Florence Griffith-Joyner accepted her gold medal.

An Olympic Race

1. Another group of Olympic runners waited for the signal.
2. The starting shot rang out.
3. All eight racers leaped from their starting blocks.
4. The runner from Kenya began to lag.
5. The French contestant was pulling ahead of her.
6. The Kenyan runner exerted her last ounce of strength.
7. The two women were running neck and neck.
8. The Kenyan spectators jumped to their feet as their favorite crossed the finish line.
9. To the strains of her national anthem, the Kenyan runner accepted the gold medal.
10. The French runner shook her opponent's hand.

Following Models

A Tom Swifty is a sentence in which an adverb comments in a humorous way on an action or object mentioned in a quotation. Note the relationship between each adverb and quotation in the following examples:

"Will you hang up these wet clothes?" asked Ben dryly.

"I've never seen such flat land," said the farmer plainly.

(a) For items 1–5, write each Tom Swifty on your paper, completing it with an adverb that comments in a humorous way on the quotation. (b) For items 6–10, write a Tom Swifty of your own, using the adverb provided. Consult a dictionary if you need help.

1. "Please turn on the light," requested Sara _____.
2. "I need the sandpaper," said the carpenter _____.
3. "The temperature is rising," said the weather forecaster _____.
4. "Be careful with that knife!" warned Hiroshi _____.
5. "My arm is aching," complained the pitcher _____.
6. coldly
7. heavily
8. sourly
9. snappily
10. idly

Exercise 57   **Identifying Adjectives and Adverbs**

On your paper write each of the twenty adjectives and twenty adverbs that appear in the following paragraph. (Do not include *a*, *an*, and *the*.)

Hurricanes

[1]Hurricanes are severe storms with extremely strong winds. [2]Storms with this name are always limited to the northern Atlantic Ocean. [3]The same storm in the western Pacific Ocean is not called a hurricane; it is a typhoon. [4]In the Indian Ocean, such storms generally are known as cyclones. [5]A hurricane is defined officially as a storm with winds of seventy-five miles an hour. [6]Such storms usually start in the North Atlantic and move westward. [7]Sometimes they progress northeastward from the Mexican coast. [8]They move at approximately ten miles an hour in the beginning and gradually gain speed. [9]A fully mature hurricane is almost circular. [10]Air pressure in its center, or eye, can be extremely low. [11]In the eye the air barely moves, the atmosphere seems strangely calm, and the sky often looks blue. [12]Clouds that swirl rapidly outside quickly bring violent winds and torrential rains.

10.6 Prepositions

A **preposition** is a word that shows the relationship of a noun or pronoun to some other word in a sentence.

Prepositions begin phrases that end with a noun or pronoun that is called the **object of the preposition.**

> The silverware is **inside** the cabinet. [*Inside* shows the spatial relationship of the silverware and the object of the preposition, *cabinet.*]

> All the guests arrived **before** dinner. [*Before* tells the time relationship between the guests' arrival and the object of the preposition, *dinner.*]

> He brought a gift **for** the host. [*For* relates *gift* to the object of the preposition, *host.*]

Commonly Used Prepositions			
aboard	beneath	in	regarding
about	beside	inside	since
above	besides	into	through
across	between	like	throughout
after	beyond	near	to
against	but*	of	toward
along	by	off	under
amid	concerning	on	underneath
among	despite	onto	until
around	down	opposite	unto
as	during	out	up
at	except	outside	upon
before	excepting	over	with
behind	for	past	within
below	from	pending	without

*meaning "except"

A **compound preposition** is made up of more than one word.

Compound Prepositions		
according to	because of	next to
ahead of	by means of	on account of
along with	in addition to	on top of
apart from	in front of	out of
aside from	in spite of	owing to
as to	instead of	

On your paper list the prepositional phrases that appear in each of the following sentences. Remember that some prepositions are made up of more than one word. (The numeral in parentheses at the end of each item indicates the number of prepositional phrases in that sentence.)

Sonny Rollins, a Great Jazz Saxophonist

1. The great jazz musician Sonny Rollins was born in New York in 1920 to musical parents. (3)
2. Instead of the usual piano, Rollins chose the tenor saxophone for his instrument. (2)
3. Like many jazz musicians, he often improvised on themes within the music. (3)
4. His exceptional album *Moving Out* put him at the top of his profession. (2)
5. During the late fifties and into the sixties, his work became notable for its energy. (3)
6. Rollins took music out of its usual locations and went beyond the usual limits of the saxophone. (3)
7. Sometimes he would play his saxophone outdoors instead of indoors. (1)
8. Another of his experiments involved making the sound from his saxophone bounce off walls. (3)
9. Rollins continued experiments with music throughout his long career. (2)
10. In addition to his experimental work, Rollins played the music for the movie *Alfie*. (2)

On your paper write the preposition that appears in each sentence below. Then rewrite each sentence using a different preposition. You may also need to change the object of the preposition.

1. The basketball game started after seven o'clock.
2. The players eagerly ran onto the court.
3. In spite of the snowstorm, attendance was high.
4. The pep band played loudly during halftime.
5. Aside from a few minor injuries, the game went well.
6. My brother is a cheerleader for the team.
7. He and the other cheerleaders perform during the game.
8. They have attended games throughout the year.
9. They will attend the state tournament with the team members.
10. In addition to cheering, they also like winning.

10.7   Conjunctions

A **conjunction** is a word that joins single words or groups of words.

Coordinating Conjunctions

A **coordinating conjunction** joins words or groups of words that have equal grammatical weight in a sentence.

Coordinating Conjunctions						
and	but	or	so	nor	for	yet

Two **and** two are four.
She is good at algebra **but** not at arithmetic.
We must leave now, **or** we will be late.
The bell rang, **yet** everyone remained seated.
He could not sleep, **nor** would he eat.

When used as a coordinating conjunction, **for** means "for the reason that" or "because."

The children were tired, **for** they had run a long distance.

Exercise 60   **Identifying Coordinating Conjunctions**

On your paper write the coordinating conjunctions that appear in the following sentences.

A Monument to Civil Rights

[1]The civil rights leaders of the 1960s strove to win greater respect, dignity, and political freedom for African Americans. [2]Martin Luther King Jr. was the most famous civil rights leader, but he was not the only person to participate in the struggle. [3]Ordinary citizens, such as Rosa Parks, who refused to sit at the back of a segregated bus, contributed to the fight for justice and equality. [4]Taunts did not deter the civil rights demonstrators, nor did physical abuse.

[5]A new monument in Alabama commemorates the famous heroes of the movement, yet it does not ignore its anonymous heroes. [6]The monument is in the city of Montgomery, for it was there that many famous civil rights demonstrations took place. [7]Made of smooth black granite, the monument is simple, yet it is remarkably powerful. [8]Water flows gently over the flat surface of the stone and collects in a pool. [9]The names of civil rights leaders or the dates of famous events in the struggle are engraved on the stone. [10]The monument was designed by the Chinese American architect Maya Lin, who is famous for her bold and austere monument to the veterans of the Vietnam War.

Correlative Conjunctions

Correlative conjunctions work in pairs to join words and groups of words of equal weight in a sentence.

Correlative Conjunctions		
both . . . and	just as . . . so	not only . . . but (also)
either . . . or	neither . . . nor	whether . . . or

Correlative conjunctions make the relationship between words or groups of words a little clearer than do coordinating conjunctions.

COORDINATING CONJUNCTIONS	CORRELATIVE CONJUNCTIONS
She **and** I were there.	**Both** she **and** I were there.
She **or** I can go.	**Either** she **or** I can go.
	Neither she **nor** I can go.
I met Jean **and** Ed.	I met **not only** Jean **but also** Ed.

Exercise 61	Identifying Correlative Conjunctions

On your paper write both parts of the correlative conjunctions that appear in the following sentences.

Weather Forecasting

1. Just as people are interested in the weather forecast today, so people thousands of years ago tried to predict weather conditions.
2. Methods of predicting the weather have grown not only more complicated but also more accurate.
3. Both modern and ancient cultures have looked to the sky for signs of change in the weather.
4. The predictions of the ancients, whether correct or incorrect, were based on very different methods from those of today.
5. Neither the seemingly essential thermometer nor the equally useful barometer was invented until a few hundred years ago.
6. Both the modern telegraph and the even more recent satellite have made it possible to exchange weather information more rapidly.
7. Satellites are used for early spotting not only of hurricanes but also of tornadoes.
8. Neither high-speed computers nor other advanced technological breakthroughs have revealed all we need to know to predict the weather accurately.
9. The National Oceanic and Atmospheric Administration is responsible for both studying the weather and forecasting it.
10. Weather forecasting is an activity not only of government agencies but also of private companies.

Subordinating Conjunctions

A **subordinating conjunction** joins two clauses, or ideas, in such a way as to make one grammatically dependent upon the other.

The idea, or clause, that a subordinating conjunction introduces is said to be "subordinate," or dependent, because it cannot stand by itself as a complete sentence.

We raked the leaves **because** so many had fallen.
We raked the leaves **before** we had lunch.
When more leaves fall, we will rake again.

The father pushed the baby...

because

she could not push herself.

Common Subordinating Conjunctions			
after	as though	provided (that)	until
although	because	since	when
as	before	so long as	whenever
as far as	considering (that)	so that	where
as if	if	than	whereas
as long as	inasmuch as	though	wherever
as soon as	in order that	unless	while

Exercise 62   Identifying Subordinating Conjunctions

On your paper write the subordinating conjunction that appears in each sentence below. Remember that some subordinating conjunctions are made up of more than one word.

The Art of Mural Painting

1. Although murals are found in many cultures around the world, they have always been a particularly important art form in Mexico.
2. Some of the murals painted by Mayan artists in ancient Mexico still survive, though many are in poor condition.
3. Before the Mexican painter Diego Rivera came on the scene, twentieth-century Mexican murals were relatively unknown.
4. Rivera designed extraordinary murals before he died in 1957.
5. Many of Rivera's murals depict scenes from Mexican history because Rivera believed that Mexicans are defined by their past.
6. After Rivera died, many Mexican American muralists took up his style and themes.
7. Mexican American artists in Los Angeles paint murals wherever they can find space.
8. They paint on public buildings so that their work can be enjoyed by many people.
9. So that the murals can be easily seen, the muralists use bright colors and bold, eye-catching designs.
10. As long as Hispanic culture continues to thrive in the United States, we will surely have many colorful and exciting murals to enjoy.

Completing Sentences with Subordinating Conjunctions

On your paper write a subordinating conjunction to complete each of the following
sentences. Be sure that your completed sentences make sense.

Early Painters

1. We will never know who the earliest painters were _____ they did not record their
   names on their work.
2. The art of painting began as early as the Paleolithic Age, _____ prehistoric hunters
   decorated the walls of their caves.
3. _____ we know the names of some ancient Greek artists, none of their paintings exist
   today.
4. _____ images covered walls, gates, palaces, and temples, it seems likely that professional
   painters lived in Sumeria and ancient Egypt.
5. Decorations on Greek pottery were baked permanently into the surface _____ they
   could be preserved.
6. _____ paintings on wood or walls cannot be baked, many have been lost.
7. Roman painters used a heating process _____ their paintings might be preserved.
8. They discovered that paints weathered better _____ they were mixed with boiling wax,
   resin, and vegetable oils.
9. _____ wealthy Roman citizens admired art, fresco paintings covered the walls of their houses.
10. _____ Roman painters were very skillful, few of their works have endured.

Adding Conjunctions to Make Sentences

On your paper revise the sentences below. Use a coordinating conjunction, correlative
conjunction, or subordinating conjunction to join the two sentences in each item. Try to use
a variety of conjunctions. Make sure your completed sentences make sense.

SAMPLE   It was such a hot day. I rested in the shade.
ANSWER   *Because* it was such a hot day, I rested in the shade.

SAMPLE   Whales are interesting. They are mysterious creatures.
ANSWER   Whales are interesting and mysterious creatures.

Whale Watching

1. In the winter young humpback whales sometimes feed off the coast of Virginia.
   They also feed off the coast of North Carolina.
2. The whale is a warm-blooded animal. It looks like a fish.
3. The whale needs oxygen to breathe. It will drown if submerged too long.
4. Porpoises are considered whales. Dolphins are considered whales.
5. Most whales dive for an average of 3 to 10 minutes. Some of the toothed whales
   can remain submerged for more than 30 minutes.
6. The rib cage of a whale is very flexible. It can withstand great pressure.
7. No one has seen whales mate. Scientists think whales mate once a year.
8. Blue whales are the largest whales. Blue whales are the fastest whales.
9. Blue whales are rare. They can be found in all oceans of the world.
10. Finback whales are a valuable catch. They are the mainstay of the whaling industry.

Conjunctive Adverbs

A **conjunctive adverb** is used to clarify the relationship between clauses of equal weight in a sentence.

Conjunctive adverbs are usually stronger, more precise, and more formal than coordinating conjunctions.

COORDINATING CONJUNCTION	Most people think of deserts as very hot places, **but** desert nights can be quite cool.
CONJUNCTIVE ADVERB	Most people think of deserts as very hot places; **however,** desert nights can be quite cool.

There are many conjunctive adverbs, and they have several uses, as the following examples show:

TO REPLACE *AND*	also, besides, furthermore, moreover
TO REPLACE *BUT*	however, nevertheless, still, though
TO STATE A RESULT	consequently, therefore, so, thus
TO STATE EQUALITY	equally, likewise, similarly

Exercise 65	Identifying Conjunctive Adverbs

On your paper, write the conjunctive adverb in each sentence.

Toltec Civilization

1. The Toltec civilization of ancient Mexico was advanced in arts and architecture; moreover, it produced impressive stonework.
2. Toltec religion centered on Quetzalcoatl; consequently, he appeared in many images.
3. Quetzalcoatl was the name of a deity; furthermore, it was the name of a legendary ruler.
4. Quetzalcoatl was identified with the planet Venus; likewise, he was linked with the wind.
5. Usually he was depicted as a plumed serpent; however, he was often shown as a wind god.
6. The people wished to please Quetzalcoatl; therefore, they built circular temples that presented no sharp obstacles to the wind.
7. There were many different religious ceremonies and rituals; moreover, people played a sacred ball game called *tlatchi* that resembled basketball.
8. The Toltec civilization expanded southward during the tenth century; therefore, the Toltecs dominated the Mayas of the Yucatan.
9. Other nomadic Mexican groups conquered the Toltecs; thus, their civilization declined.
10. The Aztecs soon built their own empire; consequently, art continued to flourish.

Identifying Kinds of Conjunctions

On your paper write the conjunction that appears in each sentence below. Indicate whether the conjunction is a *coordinating*, *correlative*, or *subordinating* conjunction.

The Galápagos Tortoise
1. After they have mated, adult female Galápagos tortoises lay their eggs on the beach.
2. Each tortoise finds a spot of bare soil where she digs a foot-wide pit.
3. She lays 15 to 20 eggs inside the pit and covers them with soil.
4. Neither the male nor the female tortoises watch over the eggs.
5. Baby tortoises are on their own after birth because they are able to find their own food.

Exercise 67   **Creating Sentences with Conjunctions**

Think of a day in which several interesting and varied events happened to you. On your paper write five sentences about that day, using as many conjunctions as possible.

Exercise 68   **Completing Sentences with Conjunctions**

On your paper replace each blank in the following sentences with a conjunction that makes sense. The kind of conjunction to use is stated in parentheses at the end of each sentence.

Modern Tunnel Construction
1. Modern tunnel building is a complicated process; _____, it is a very costly process, involving millions of dollars. (conjunctive adverb)
2. _____ a tunnel under a river costs considerably more than a bridge, it may have certain advantages. (subordinating conjunction)
3. _____ does it allow the unhindered passage of ships, _____ it is less vulnerable. (a pair of correlative conjunctions)
4. A tunnel is a marvelous construction, _____ building one is extremely hazardous. (coordinating conjunction)
5. There are basically three ways to build a tunnel; _____, tunnels may be divided into three types. (conjunctive adverb)
6. A "true" tunnel is dug horizontally through earth _____ rock. (coordinating conjunction)
7. For the cut-and-cover tunnel, a large ditch is dug, a tube is built in the ditch, _____ the tube is covered over. (coordinating conjunction)
8. _____ the first subway in the world, in London, _____ the first on the European continent, in Budapest, were built in this way. (a pair of correlative conjunctions)
9. The trench tunnel involves a kind of cut-and-cover method used _____ the tunnel is dug underwater. (subordinating conjunction)
10. _____ a route is chosen for any tunnel, a careful geologic study is made of the type of earth and rock along the way. (subordinating conjunction)

10.8 Interjections

An **interjection** is a word or phrase that expresses emotion or exclamation. An interjection has no grammatical connection to other words.

Oh, I didn't know that.   **Whew,** it's hot.
Ouch! That hurts!   **Why,** children!

Exercise 69   Identifying Interjections

On your paper write the interjection that appears in each item.

1. Dear me! Whatever shall we do?
2. Oh, don't ask me.
3. Alas! The ship was doomed.
4. This box is heavy. Ugh!
5. Yuck! What a disgusting thought!
6. Phooey! I give up.
7. Wow, it's really snowing out there.
8. Whee! We're sliding all over.
9. Well! This is a surprise.
10. Hey, what's that noise?

Exercise 70   Using Interjections

On your paper replace each blank below with an appropriate interjection from the following list. Remember to add punctuation.

Wow	Oops	Ssh	Ah	Whew
Well	Psst	Yipes	Alas	Ouch

1. _____ That was an amazing catch!
2. _____ I dropped the plate.
3. _____ you are here at last.
4. _____ The stove is hot!
5. _____ the concert is beginning.
6. _____ That was pretty close!
7. _____ it is finally over.
8. _____ come here a second, but do not let anyone see you.
9. _____ That is the wildest thing I have ever heard!
10. _____ It is pouring, and I forgot to shut the windows.

Grammar Review

Parts of Speech

This passage from Marilynne Robinson's novel *Housekeeping* has been annotated to show some of the parts of speech covered in this unit. The narrator is Ruth, the elder of two orphaned sisters who are the main characters of this novel. Read the passage and do the exercises that follow.

Literature Model

from HOUSEKEEPING

by Marilynne Robinson

Common noun

Proper noun

Abstract noun

Adjective

Concrete noun

Linking verb

Relative pronoun

Coordinating conjunction

Personal pronoun

It was a hard winter, too. The snow crested, finally, far above our heads. It drifted up our eaves on one side of the house. Some houses in Fingerbone simply fell from the weight of snow on their roofs, a source of grave and perpetual anxiety to my great-aunts, who were accustomed to a brick building, and to living below ground. Sometimes the sun would be warm enough to send a thick sheet of snow sliding off the roof, and sometimes the fir trees would shrug, and the snow would fall with surprisingly loud and earthy thuds, which would terrify my great-aunts. . . .

For some reason the lake was a source of particular pleasure to Fingerbone that year. It was frozen solid early and long. Several acres of it were swept, for people brought brooms to tend and expand it, till the cleared ice spread far across the lake. Sledders heaped snow on the shore into a precipitous chute that sent them sailing far across the ice. There were barrels on the shore for fires to be built in, and people brought boxes to sit on and planks and burlap bags to stand on around the barrels, and frankfurters to roast, and clothespins to clip frozen mittens to the lips of barrels. A number of dogs began to spend most of their time at the ice. They were young, leggy dogs, affable and proprietary, and exhilarated by the weather. They liked to play at retrieving bits of ice which sped fantastically fast and far across the lake. The dogs made a gallant and youthful →

joke of their own strength and speed, and flaunted an utter indifference to the safety of their limbs. Lucille and I took our skates to school, so that we could go to the lake directly and stay there through the twilight. Usually we would skate along the edge of the swept ice, tracing its shape, and coming finally to its farthest edge, we would sit on the snow and look back at Fingerbone.

    We felt giddily far from shore, though the lake was so solid that winter that it would certainly have supported the weight of the entire population of Fingerbone, past, present, and to come. Nevertheless, only we and the ice sweepers went out so far, and only we stayed.

— Action verb

— Subordinating conjunction

— Preposition

— Possessive pronoun

— Adverb

Exercise 1

Identifying Nouns   The following sentences elaborate on ideas suggested by the passage from *Housekeeping*. On your paper write each of the nouns in these sentences. After each noun write in parentheses *common, proper,* or *collective*, depending upon how the noun is used in the sentence.

SAMPLE   *Housekeeping* is about two sisters and their family.
ANSWER   *Housekeeping* (proper), sisters (common), family (common, collective)

1. The village of Fingerbone, Idaho, endured severe winters.
2. During a particularly bad winter, Fingerbone was nearly buried by a fierce storm.
3. The snowfall was heavy, and temperatures were low.
4. Half of the roof was covered with snow.
5. According to Aunt Lily and Aunt Nona, the house might collapse from the weight.
6. The idea that the house could fall made the aunts nervous.
7. Lily and Nona were even startled by the noise made by huge clumps of falling snow.
8. A crowd of local residents gathered daily at Fingerbone Lake.
9. The lake froze early, well before Thanksgiving Day.
10. A team of sweepers cleared the snow from the icy surface.
11. People packed the snow into a steep chute for sledders to use.
12. The public enjoyed many activities on the ice.
13. One crowd of merrymakers roasted wieners.
14. Another group rode sleds down a snowy hill.
15. Gleefully, a pack of dogs scampered among the throng.
16. Ruth and Lucille were among the throng of townspeople at the festivities.
17. After school the pair of girls went straight to the lake.
18. The sisters skated to the boundary of the swept ice.
19. Later the two skaters rested on a snowbank and looked at the village.
20. Ruth and her sister returned to their home after hours of fun.

Exercise 2

Using Pronouns Effectively   The paragraph below elaborates on ideas suggested by a passage from *Housekeeping* that is not reprinted in this textbook. On your paper write each sentence in the paragraph, substituting pronouns for nouns when a pronoun would make good sense. Do not substitute a pronoun for a noun if the pronoun would make the sentence unclear.

[1]Ruth and Ruth's sister, Lucille, lived in the small town of Fingerbone, Idaho. [2]Ruth's and Lucille's grandfather was originally from the Midwest, but the grandfather had come to Idaho years ago and built the grandfather's home there. [3]Ruth did not remember the grandfather, since the grandfather had died before Ruth was born. [4]Ruth had been raised by Ruth's grandmother until the grandmother died. [5]Then Ruth's great-aunts came to Fingerbone to take care of the two girls. [6]The great-aunts were unfamiliar with rural life and did not really enjoy rural life. [7]The great-aunts felt isolated in Fingerbone because of Fingerbone's small population. [8]The heavy snowfall troubled the great-aunts, and the great-aunts also worried about the great-aunts' nieces. [9]Ruth did not mind the harsh winter, since Ruth had lived in Fingerbone all Ruth's life. [10]Ruth often took Ruth's ice skates with Ruth to school and afterward went to Fingerbone Lake to skate on Fingerbone Lake's frozen waters.

Exercise 3

Completing Sentences with Pronouns   The following sentences elaborate on ideas suggested by a passage from *Housekeeping* that is not reprinted in this textbook. On your paper write the type of pronoun specified in italics for each sentence. Be sure that your completed sentences make sense.

1. *Indefinite* of the winters in Fingerbone, Idaho, were severe.
2. During a particularly harsh winter, the people found simple ways to amuse *reflexive*.
3. *Indefinite* seemed to enjoy sledding down snowy hills and skating on Fingerbone Lake.
4. Ruth and *possessive* sister enjoyed skating on the frozen lake after school.
5. *Personal* were certain that the frozen ice was solid enough to hold them.
6. *Indefinite* seemed to stop the girls from enjoying the great outdoors.
7. Of course, the girls' great-aunts needlessly worried *reflexive* about the weather.
8. The great-aunts also worried about *possessive* nieces.
9. *Interrogative* could blame them?
10. The aunts were not accustomed to rural living, and *demonstrative* was an especially severe winter.

Exercise 4

Identifying Verbs and Verb Phrases The following sentences are adapted from the literary passage. Write on your paper any verbs and verb phrases that appear in the sentences, and label them accordingly.

SAMPLE   Ruth's great-aunts had lived in brick houses all their lives.
ANSWER   had lived—verb phrase

1. The snow had been falling for days.
2. It piled into drifts and covered the eaves of the house.
3. Finally the sun returned to the sky.
4. Sometimes the fir trees would shudder under a heavy load of snow.
5. A dense layer of snow often slid to the ground with an earthy thud.
6. Many weeks of cold weather had frozen the waters of Fingerbone Lake to its very depths.
7. There must have been a dozen children among the skaters.
8. Townspeople had cleared several acres of ice with their brooms.
9. After school Lucille and Ruth skated until twilight, and they would have stayed even later.
10. They would venture farther out than anyone else onto the frozen surface of the lake.

Exercise 5

Identifying Transitive and Intransitive Verbs The following sentences contain verbs that appear in the passage from *Housekeeping*. For each item write *transitive* or *intransitive* on your paper, depending upon the way the italicized verb is used in the sentence.

SAMPLE   Mounds of snow *crested* as high as the windows.
ANSWER   intransitive

SAMPLE   The skaters *brought* extra mittens.
ANSWER   transitive

1. Snow *drifted* against the fence.
2. A child *fell* in the deep snow.
3. The howling blizzard *terrified* the small children.
4. Some neighbors *brought* snowshoes with them.
5. Children *heaped* snow into small hills to build igloos.
6. An expert skier *sped* through the countryside.
7. Ice skaters *flaunted* their skills before crowds.
8. They *skated* around the lake at dizzying speeds.
9. Toddlers *traced* patterns with their feet in the cold, sparkling snow.
10. The frozen lake *supported* hundreds of skaters.

Exercise 6

Identifying Adjectives   The following sentences are about Idaho. On your paper write the adjectives that appear in each sentence. Include pronouns and proper adjectives, but not the words *a*, *an*, and *the*. After each adjective write the word that the adjective modifies.

SAMPLE   Idaho is an unusual setting for a novel about ordinary life.
ANSWER   unusual—setting; ordinary—life

1. Few aspects of life in the state are unremarkable.
2. The lofty Rocky Mountains provide spectacular sights.
3. A large portion of Idaho remains a remote wilderness.
4. Its icy streams provide a suitable habitat for many varieties of trout.
5. The early Native American peoples of the region were expert hunters of the mighty buffalo.
6. After the discovery of gold in the 1860s, many European settlers came to make their homes in Idaho.
7. Hardy miners were prominent among these hard-working settlers in northern sections of Idaho.
8. Because of the hostile landscape, life was difficult for most people.
9. Primitive conditions fostered a generous spirit of cooperation, however.
10. Today farming is a major industry in this large state.

Exercise 7

Expanding Sentences with Adjectives   The following sentences elaborate on the passage from *Housekeeping*. On your paper write adjectives that would make sense in the places indicated by carets. Although there are no specific correct answers, base your choices on the passage.

SAMPLE   Temperatures were ∧, and a ∧ layer of snow blanketed the town.
ANSWER   low, thick

1. In the ∧ village the air was frosty and ∧.
2. The town of Fingerbone looked for a few days like a ∧ and ∧ wonderland.
3. When the ∧ sun returned, ∧ neighbors dug paths from their homes.
4. Ruth's ∧ aunts worried about the ∧ roof.
5. Fingerbone Lake became a ∧ sheet of ice, ∧ for skating.
6. The ∧ townspeople took ∧ pleasure in the lake.
7. ∧ sledders built a ∧ chute of snow.
8. ∧ dogs raced across the ice at ∧ speeds.
9. Ruth and Lucille skated on the ∧ ice and looked back at the ∧ town.
10. Tired but ∧, the girls trudged home in the ∧ twilight.

Exercise 8

Identifying Adverbs   The following sentences are about ice skating. On your paper write each adverb that appears in these sentences and the word that the adverb modifies.

SAMPLE   Skilled ice skaters twirl quite gracefully.
ANSWER   quite—gracefully; gracefully—twirl

1. Experienced skaters move rather rapidly on the ice.
2. Frequently they form special patterns, or figures.
3. In cold climates they often skate outside.
4. Sometimes they glide on frozen lakes and ponds.
5. Safety is very important for all skaters.
6. Wise skaters never skate alone.
7. Professional figure skaters generally perform indoors.
8. Special equipment creates the ice mechanically.
9. Have you ever seen a professional ice show?
10. The skaters dress beautifully and usually perform to music.

Exercise 9

Using Adverbs   Each of the following sentences is based on the information in the passage from *Housekeeping*. On your paper write an appropriate adverb to take the place of the prepositional phrase in italics. The adverb should express the same idea as the prepositional phrase.

SAMPLE   That year winter descended *with much harshness* on Fingerbone.
ANSWER   harshly

1. The snow fell *in heavy masses* for many days.
2. *In a sudden motion* a heavy slab of snow slid from a tree.
3. Ruth's great-aunts looked *with anxiety* at their own snow-laden roof.
4. *To everyone's amazement* the dilapidated roof held up under the weight of the snow.
5. The villagers walked *with eagerness* to the frozen lake.
6. Some sledded *in a reckless way* down a steep chute of snow.
7. The dogs chased pieces of ice that slid *in a quick manner* across the frozen lake.
8. Dogs scampered *in an exuberant fashion* across the ice.
9. For hours Ruth and Lucille skated *with swiftness* on the frozen lake.
10. After twilight the girls returned home *in a weary manner.*

Exercise 10

Identifying Prepositions   The following sentences are based on passages from *House-keeping* not reprinted in this book. On your paper list the prepositions that appear in each sentence. Remember that some prepositions are made up of more than one word. (The numeral in parentheses at the end of each item indicates the number of prepositions the sentence contains.)

1. *Housekeeping* is about two orphaned sisters in Idaho. (2)
2. The novel is narrated by Ruth, one of the sisters. (2)
3. Ruth's grandmother brought order to the household through her insistence on strict attention to chores. (4)
4. After the death of Ruth's grandmother, Ruth's great-aunts came to Idaho and cared for the girls. (4)
5. The great-aunts came from Spokane, Washington, and were unfamiliar with life in a small town like Fingerbone. (4)
6. They moved to Fingerbone in spite of their preference for city life. (3)
7. During crises the aunts took refuge in the repetition of familiar chores. (3)
8. The normal needs of adolescents in the home caused too many changes in routine for the aunts' liking. (4)
9. They fled to the safety of a hotel and left Ruth's aunt, Sylvie, in charge as the girls' guardian. (4)
10. According to Sylvie, life is about change and surprises, not the dull tasks of housekeeping. (3)

Exercise 11

Using Prepositions   Each of the sentences below elaborates on the passage from *House-keeping*. On your paper write a preposition that completes the word or phrase in italics and makes sense in the sentence. More than one preposition may make sense.

SAMPLE   The cold spell lasted _____ *weeks.*
ANSWER   for

1. Because temperatures had remained _____ *the freezing point*, Fingerbone Lake had turned to solid ice.
2. Townspeople _____ *brooms* steadily swept the snow from acres of ice.
3. They dumped snow from sleds into huge mounds _____ *the shore.*
4. Some villagers skated _____ *the frozen surface* almost to the far shore.
5. Sledders raced _____ *a steep hill* of snow.
6. People roasted meat _____ *barrels* on shore.
7. Frozen mittens were clipped _____ *clothespins* to the rims of the barrels.
8. Some of the townsfolk brought boxes to use _____ *chairs.*
9. Dogs scampered playfully _____ *the crowd.*
10. The lake assumed the aspect _____ *an impromptu festival.*

Using Conjunctions   The following sentences tell more about Idaho, the setting for *Housekeeping*. On your paper complete each sentence by writing an appropriate conjunction according to the direction in parentheses. Choose your conjunctions from the list below, which has more conjunctions than you will need.

CONJUNCTIONS

and	or	but	yet
neither . . . nor		not only . . . but also	
although	because	before	if	when	wherever

SAMPLE   Idaho is located in the Rocky Mountains, _____ it is very beautiful.
(Add a coordinating conjunction.)

ANSWER   and

1. _____ you go in Idaho, you are likely to find spectacular scenery.
(Add a subordinating conjunction.)
2. _____ you visit the Snake River Canyon, be sure to see Shoshone Falls.
(Add a subordinating conjunction.)
3. You might fish in one of Idaho's 2,000 lakes in the summer _____ visit the state during the skiing season.
(Add a coordinating conjunction.)
4. _____ Idaho is far from the coast, it has the cold winters typical of the American interior.
(Add a subordinating conjunction.)
5. Winter temperatures often dip below freezing, _____ several feet of snow fall each year.
(Add a coordinating conjunction.)
6. _____ Idaho is the thirteenth largest state in area, it is sparsely populated.
(Add a subordinating conjunction.)
7. _____ Boise, Idaho's capital city, _____ the even smaller city of Twin Falls has a population of over 150,000.
(Add a pair of correlative conjunctions.)
8. Native American communities had inhabited Idaho for centuries _____ the first European explorers arrived in 1805.
(Add a subordinating conjunction.)
9. _____ gold was discovered in Idaho in the 1860s, thousands of prospectors flocked to the state.
(Add a subordinating conjunction.)
10. Today Idaho is famous for its potatoes, _____ few people know that it also has the largest silver mine in the nation.
(Add a coordinating conjunction.)

Exercise 13

Using Interjections   Each of the sentences below relates to the theme of the passage from *Housekeeping*. On your paper replace each blank below with an appropriate interjection from the following list. Remember to add punctuation.

Yikes	Wow	Boy	Well	Ssh
Ah	Whee	Alas	Oops	Uh-oh

1. _____ That was a hard winter.
2. _____ the snow finally crested.
3. _____ Some houses fell from the weight of snow on their roofs!
4. _____ The clumps of falling snow almost hit me!
5. _____ the great-aunts are very nervous.
6. _____ I slipped on some ice!
7. _____ Skating is so much fun!
8. _____ We are really far from shore!
9. _____ Can you hear the snow falling?
10. _____ what a winter wonderland!

Exercise 14

Proofreading

The following passage describes the artist Grandma Moses, whose painting appears on the opposite page. Rewrite the passage, correcting the errors in spelling, capitalization, usage, and grammar. Add any missing punctuation. There are twenty-five errors.

Grandma Moses

[1]Anna Mary Robertson Moses (1860–1961) who was known as Grandma Moses, was born in Greenwich, New York, to a family of Scottish and irish desent. [2]She begun painting at the age of seventy-seven. [3]During the last two decades of her life, Moses painted hundreds of scenes of rural farm life, she became perhaps the most famous folk painter in America.

[4]Encouraged by her father Moses developed her talent for drawing; she, however, had little time to pursue hers interest in art. [5]She married a farmer, Thomas Salmon Moses and bore ten children. [6]She spent much of her life on a dairy farm in the tiny community of Eagle Bridge in upstate new york. [7]She begun to paint seriously only after her arthritis became so crippling that she could no longer work on the farm. [8]A few of her paintings on display at a Eagle Bridge drugstore was discovered by an art collector who happened to pass through town. [9]Somewhat taken aback by her sudden fame, Moses was scandalized when both dealers or tourists began to offer large sums for paintings that she thought were worth only a few dollars'.

[10]Moses paintings are remarkable for their harmony and detail. [11]Although she had no formel training, Moses had a strong intuitive grasp of color, pattern, and design. [12]Recorded the landscapes and customs of her rural countryside with the sensitivity of a poet. [13]Every detail is careful observed: the gray cast of the sky on a snowy morning the steam rising from a locomotive, and the straining muscles of a horse pulling a sleigh.

Anna Mary Robertson ("Grandma") Moses, *Early Skating,* **1951**

[14]Moses's *Early Skating*, like the passage from Marilynne Robinson's novel *Housekeeping*, capture the atmosphere of a small community on a winter day. [15]Although the painting depict New York, whereas the novel is set in Idaho, the mood are the same. [16]There are a playfulness about the two scenes of children cavorting on the ice. [17]There is also a feeling of isolation, as if these two small towns were seperated from the outside world by time and winters snowy blanket.

The following biography of Marilynne Robinson is followed by 10 sentences. On your paper write an appropriate word to complete each sentence. Use the directions in parentheses as a guide. You will need to consult the biography in order to fill in some of the blanks properly.

Marilynne Robinson

Born in 1944, Marilynne Robinson is one of contemporary America's promising new writers. Her first novel, *Housekeeping* (published in 1981), was widely acclaimed for its poetic language, its vivid characterizations, and its keen understanding of human nature. Set in an isolated Rocky Mountain community in Idaho, *Housekeeping* describes two orphaned sisters who are cared for by a number of different guardians, each with her own ideas about what is important in life. This touching story about small-town life earned Robinson the 1982 Ernest Hemingway Foundation Award for Best First Novel. The book was the basis of a critically acclaimed motion picture. Robinson is also the author of a nonfiction book called *Mother Country*. In addition, she has contributed several stories and articles to *Harper's* and other major magazines.

1. The _____ author Marilynne Robinson was born in 1944. (Add a proper adjective.)
2. Robinson _____ her novel *Housekeeping* in 1981. (Add an action verb.)
3. _____ *Housekeeping* was only a first novel, it received much critical attention. (Add a subordinating conjunction.)
4. *Housekeeping* takes place in a remote community in the _____ of Idaho. (Add a proper noun.)
5. The novel was praised for its _____ language and keen understanding of human nature. (Add an adjective.)
6. Critics also _____ applauded its finely drawn and well-developed characters. (Add an adverb.)
7. *Housekeeping* _____ a winner of the Ernest Hemingway Foundation Award for Best First Novel. (Add a linking verb.)
8. The _____ based on the novel was also critically acclaimed. (Add a common noun.)
9. Robinson has not yet published a second novel _____ has written a nonfiction work titled *Mother Country*. (Add a coordinating conjunction.)
10. Some of Robinson's short stories have appeared _____ *Harper's*, the noted literary magazine, as well as other major publications in the United States. (Add a preposition.)

Writing Application

Nouns in Writing   Amy Tan uses nouns in this passage from *The Joy Luck Club* to convey the bustle and confusion a California girl feels traveling in a foreign country for the first time. Examine the passage, focusing especially on the italicized nouns.

> Before the *train* even comes to a *stop*, *people* are bringing down their *belongings* from above their *seats*. For a *moment* there is a dangerous *shower* of heavy *suitcases* laden with *gifts* to *relatives*, half-broken *boxes* wrapped in *miles* of *string* to keep the *contents* from spilling out, plastic *bags* filled with *yarn* and *vegetables* and *packages* of dried *mushrooms*, and camera *cases*. And then we are caught in a *stream* of *people* rushing, shoving, pushing us along, until we find ourselves in one of a dozen *lines* waiting to go through *customs*. I feel as if I were getting on the number 30 Stockton *bus* in *San Francisco*. I am in *China*, I remind myself. And somehow the *crowds* don't bother me. It feels right. I start pushing, too.

Techniques with Nouns   Try to apply some of Amy Tan's writing techniques when you write and revise your own work.

1.   Whenever possible, replace general words with precise concrete nouns. Compare the following:

General Words plastic bags filled with *things*
Tan's Version plastic bags filled with *yarn* and *vegetables* and *packages* of dried *mushrooms*, and camera *cases*

2.   Use proper nouns whenever appropriate to help make your writing more specific.

General Words I am in a foreign *country*. . . . a crowded bus in a *city*. . . .
Tan's Version I am in *China*. . . . the number 30 Stockton bus in *San Francisco*. . . .

3.   Expand single nouns into longer groups of specific words when you wish to provide more details.

Single Noun suitcases
Tan's Version heavy suitcases laden with gifts to relatives

Practice   Practice these techniques by revising the following passage, using a separate sheet of paper. Pay particular attention to the underlined words.

By seven o'clock on that snowy morning, the <u>park</u> was a scene of great activity. A <u>group</u> of <u>dogs</u> was racing across the <u>area</u>, putting <u>birds</u> to flight. Frantic owners followed, shouting the names of their dogs. Squirrels flicked their tails and scampered to safety. Along the pathway, the <u>dog owners</u> stamped their feet in the snow and chatted about <u>things</u>. Others fed birds that chirped and hopped nervously on the path. Before long, <u>children</u> came running through the park, dragging their <u>toys</u> behind them. Their <u>voices</u> blended with all the other <u>sounds</u>. In a moment, the usually serene park had become quite a hectic place.

Parts of the Sentence

11.1 Simple Subjects and Simple Predicates

A **sentence** is a group of words expressing a complete thought.

Every sentence has two basic parts, a *subject* and a *predicate*.

The **subject** is the part of the sentence about which something is being said.

The **predicate** is the part that says something about the subject.

The **simple subject** is the key noun or pronoun (or word or group of words acting as a noun) that tells what a sentence is about.

The simple subject may be a compound noun consisting of more than one word.

The **simple predicate** is the verb or verb phrase that expresses the essential thought about the subject of the sentence.

A simple predicate that is a verb phrase consists of the verb and any helping verbs.

SIMPLE SUBJECT	SIMPLE PREDICATE
Dionne Warwick	will perform.
Owls	were hooting.
José Canseco	ran.
Things	change.

The simple subject is found by asking *who?* or *what?* about the verb.

Exercise 1 **Identifying Simple Subjects and Predicates**

Write each simple subject and each simple predicate. Underline the simple predicates.

The Yo-Yo

1. Donald Duncan was an American inventor.
2. He founded a toy company in the 1920s.
3. A popular Duncan toy was the yo-yo.
4. The yo-yo is a double disc with a string between the discs.
5. The yo-yo moves up and down the string.
6. Duncan used a yo-yo from the Philippines as a model.
7. Prehistoric Philippine hunters used yo-yos as weapons.
8. *Yo-yo* means "to return" in Pilipino.
9. The ancient Philippine people had made their yo-yos of stone.
10. Since the 1950s, Duncan has been making yo-yos out of plastic.

W h o o o o o o o

...was hooting in the night?

11.2 Complete Subjects and Complete Predicates

In most sentences the meaning of the simple subject and the simple predicate is expanded or modified by the addition of other words and phrases.

The **complete subject** consists of the simple subject and all the words that modify it.

The **complete predicate** consists of the simple predicate, or verb, and all the words that modify it or complete its meaning.

COMPLETE SUBJECT	COMPLETE PREDICATE
Talented Dionne Warwick	will perform her biggest hits.
Large owls with bright eyes	were hooting loudly in the dark forest.
The speedy José Canseco	ran all the way home from first base on a double.
Many things	change daily.

Exercise 2 **Identifying Complete Subjects and Predicates**

Write the following sentences on your paper. Underline each complete subject once and each complete predicate twice.

Virginia State Parks

1. The state of Virginia has a fine park system.
2. Virginia state parks offer access to lakes, rivers, and the Chesapeake Bay.
3. Virginia's lakes are fished most heavily in the early fall.
4. Boats can be rented only in the summer months.
5. Canoes are available in many places.
6. Frequent visitors can purchase season tickets for state parks.
7. The variety of trails gives hikers access to many different kinds of terrain.
8. Hilly and flat areas can be reached on the various trails.
9. Some trails lead to the Appalachian Trail.
10. Many families explore the Virginia countryside by horseback.
11. Certain parks have facilities for horse rental.
12. The Virginia state park system provides numerous camping facilities.
13. Campgrounds are located in many different settings.
14. Some parks have on-site exhibits about Virginia's rich history.
15. Parents enjoy these exhibits with their children.

Identifying Complete and Simple Subjects and Predicates

Copy each of the following sentences, and draw a vertical line between the complete subject and the complete predicate. Then underline the simple subject once and the simple predicate twice.

SAMPLE ANSWER   An important <u>event</u> I <u>sparked</u> the civil rights movement in the United States.

Rosa Lee Parks, a Woman of Courage

[1]Rosa Lee Parks made history in Montgomery, Alabama, in 1955. [2]She boarded a bus there late one December day. [3]Parks took a seat at the front of the bus. [4]This action was illegal for an African American person in Alabama at the time. [5]The angry driver ordered Parks to the back of the bus. [6]She ignored his orders courageously. [7]The police arrested Parks for her action. [8]The African American community of Montgomery conducted a year-long boycott of the city buses in protest. [9]A Supreme Court decision in November 1956 made segregation on all public transportation illegal. [10]Many people consider Parks the catalyst of the modern civil rights movement.

Expanding Subjects and Predicates

Expand each of the following sentences by adding words and phrases to both the simple subject and the simple predicate. Write your sentence. Then underline the simple predicate in each sentence.

SAMPLE   Sky darkened.
ANSWER   The blue sky <u>darkened</u> slowly to indigo.

1. The sun set.
2. Night fell.
3. Darkness descended.
4. Frogs croaked.
5. Stars shone.
6. Moon rose.
7. Owls hooted.
8. Possums skulked.
9. People slept.
10. Wind howled.
11. Leaves rustled.
12. Curtains fluttered.
13. The train rattled.
14. Baby cried.
15. Sky lightened.
16. Rooster crowed.
17. The dog barked.
18. Workers left.
19. Cars honked.
20. Day began.

11.3   Compound Subjects and Compound Predicates

A sentence may have more than one simple subject or more than one simple predicate.

Compound Subjects

A **compound subject** is made up of two or more simple subjects that are joined by a conjunction and have the same verb.

The conjunctions most commonly used to join the subjects in a compound subject are *and* and *or*.

> **Tomatoes** and **carrots** are colorful vegetables.
> **Tomatoes** or **carrots** are my favorite vegetable.

Correlative conjunctions may be used to join compound subjects.

> Neither the **tomato** nor the **pepper** grows underground.
> Both the **tomato** and the **pepper** are rich in vitamin C.

When more than two words are included in the compound subject, the conjunction is usually used only between the last two words, and the words are separated by commas.

> **Tomatoes, carrots,** and **peppers** are healthful.

Exercise 5   Identifying Compound Subjects

Write the compound subject in each of the following sentences.

The Planets
1. Jupiter and Saturn are the largest planets.
2. Mercury, Venus, and Earth orbit the sun faster than the other planets.
3. Mars or one of Jupiter's moons could harbor life forms.
4. Both Jupiter and Saturn have many moons.
5. Neither Mercury nor Venus has moons.

Exercise 6   Expanding Subjects

(a) Write five sentences. In each one use a simple subject and a simple predicate.
(b) Expand each sentence by making the subject compound.

SAMPLE ANSWER   **a.** John Hancock signed the Declaration of Independence.
                      b. John Hancock and John Adams signed the Declaration of Independence.

Compound Predicates

A **compound predicate** (or **compound verb**) is made up of two or more verbs or verb phrases that are joined by a conjunction and have the same subject.

> Horses **gallop** and **charge.**

> Nina **inserted** the film, **looked** through the viewfinder, and **snapped** the first photograph.

In compound verbs that contain verb phrases, the helping verb may or may not be repeated before the second verb.

> Sea gulls **will glide** or **swoop** down to the ocean.

A sentence may have both a compound subject and a compound predicate.

>   S   S   P   P
> **Butterflies** and **hummingbirds dart** and **dip** in the air.

Exercise 7 — Identifying Compound Predicates

Write the compound predicate in each of the following sentences.

Dogs and Water

1. Some dogs swim and play in the water as a recreational activity.
2. Other dogs jump into water but then immediately return to shore.
3. Fearful dogs may scratch or whine.
4. Confident dogs can sit quietly in a canoe and enjoy the scenery.
5. I have swum and played in the water with many dogs.
6. Retrievers jump into the water readily and fetch objects for their owners.
7. Some dogs climb up ladders, dive off docks, or rescue people from the water.
8. Water play relaxes dogs and offers them excellent exercise.
9. Exercise increases energy and improves the dog's health.
10. Many dogs may not recognize polluted water and, unfortunately, may drink it.

Exercise 8 — Expanding Predicates

(a) Write five sentences. In each one use a simple subject and a simple predicate.
(b) Expand each sentence by making the predicate compound.

SAMPLE ANSWER
    a. A businessperson bought the Nettlehurst Company.
    b. A businessperson bought and sold the Nettlehurst Company.

Identifying Subjects and Predicates

Copy each of the following sentences on your paper. For each sentence, underline the simple subject(s) once and the simple predicate(s) twice. Note that some subjects and predicates are compound.

Chief Joseph

1. The Nez Percé lived and flourished for centuries in the Northwest.
2. The federal government ordered them away from their lands in 1877 and assigned them to a reservation in Oregon.
3. The government wanted land for many new white settlers and their families.
4. The leader of the Nez Percé at the time was Chief Joseph, a wise and compassionate man.
5. Chief Joseph and the Nez Percé men, women, and children packed their belongings and left their homes.
6. A small group of Nez Percé encountered and killed several white settlers during their journey.
7. Chief Joseph and his advisers foresaw a long and bloody battle with the United States Army as a result of this incident.
8. Chief Joseph therefore sought freedom for the Nez Percé in Canada.
9. He and his outnumbered people fought courageously but finally surrendered to the United States Army just 30 miles from the Canadian border.
10. The Nez Percé accepted land from the United States government on a reservation in Oklahoma and settled there in 1878.

Exercise 10   **Writing Compound Subjects and Predicates**

On your paper expand each of the following sentences by making both the subject and the predicate compound. (You may need to make other changes, too.)

SAMPLE   Birds fly.
ANSWER   Birds and bats fly and eat insects.

School Subjects

1. American history is taught in schools.
2. Children in kindergarten practice simple mathematical concepts.
3. Young children play word games.
4. The school lunch period never lasts long enough.
5. Coaches will teach players useful strategies.
6. Basic algebra is introduced in middle school.
7. Special projects improve students' research skills.
8. Computers will be used more frequently in the future.
9. Geography teaches about other cultures.
10. A longer school year remains a controversial topic.

11.4   Order of Subject and Predicate

In most sentences in English, the subject comes before the predicate. There are exceptions, however, to this usual word order.

Commands

In commands and requests, the subject is usually not stated. The predicate is the entire sentence. The pronoun *you* is understood to be the subject.

[You] **Run**!   [You] **Give** it to me.   [You] Please **be** careful.

Questions

Questions frequently begin with a verb or helping verb or the words *who, whom, what, when, where, why* or *how.*

Was she right?
Have you **read** Gary Soto's stories?
Whom did he invite?

In both of these cases, the subject generally follows the verb or helping verb. To find the subject of a question, rearrange the words to form a statement.

SUBJECT	PREDICATE
She	was right.
You	have read Gary Soto's stories.
He	did invite whom.

Exercise 11   Identifying Subjects and Predicates in Questions and Commands

Write the simple subject and the simple predicate of each of the following sentences. (Remember that the simple predicate may include one or more helping verbs.) If the sentence is a command, write *(You)* as the subject.

Drivers' Licenses

1. Where are drivers' licenses issued?
2. Go to the Department of Motor Vehicles.
3. What kind of preparations should I make?
4. Study the manual carefully.
5. Practice good driving skills every day for about four months before taking the test.

Inverted Order

At times a sentence is written in **inverted order**—that is, with the predicate before the subject. This reversal of the usual order can add emphasis to the subject.

PREDICATE	SUBJECT
Across the field **galloped**	the three **horses.**
In the distance **ran**	a **river.**

Remember, a word in a prepositional phrase is never the subject.

When the word *there* or *here* begins a sentence and is followed by a form of the verb *to be*, the subject follows the verb. The words *there* and *here* are almost never the subject of a sentence.

PREDICATE	SUBJECT
There **is**	a **chill** in the air.
Here **are**	my **thoughts** on the subject.

To find a subject in an inverted sentence, ask "Who?" or "What?"

What galloped across the field? The three horses galloped.
What is in the air? A chill is in the air.

Exercise 12	Reordering Inverted Sentences

On your paper rewrite each of the following sentences so that the complete subject comes before the predicate. Then underline the simple subject once and the simple predicate twice. (Remember that both subjects and predicates may be compound.)

Poisonous Snakes of the United States

1. From under a rock crawled the coral snake.
2. Around the bend swam a water moccasin.
3. In the stream wiggled six small water snakes.
4. There were a dozen hiding along the shore.
5. In the United States live only two types of poisonous snakes.
6. Included in the poisonous category are coral snakes and pit vipers.
7. On the low-lying plains of the American Southeast lives the deadly coral snake.
8. There are circular bands of different colors on the coral snake's body.
9. On some nonpoisonous snakes are similar but incomplete color bands.
10. Among the pit vipers in the United States is the notorious rattlesnake.

Recognizing the Order of Subject and Predicate

Copy each of the following sentences. For each sentence draw a vertical line between the complete subject and the complete predicate, and label each.

SAMPLE ANSWERS

             P
    I Look at that painting.

             P   **S**
On the opposite wall is I another work of art.

   P   **S**
There is I the loveliest statue in the museum.

An African Art Exhibit

1. A visit to an African art exhibit can be a fine educational experience.
2. Many museums offer temporary shows in addition to their permanent collections.
3. Call ahead for information about special displays of African art.
4. Where are the best examples of beadwork, basketry, woodwork, leatherwork, and metalwork?
5. In some museums are beautiful displays of African textiles.
6. Excellent craftsmanship is found in decorative ornaments and ceremonial objects.
7. Here is a Nigerian bronze sculpture of a priest-king.
8. This ancient civilization used sculptures of former kings in memorial rites for the dead.
9. Look at this elaborately carved ceremonial mask.
10. Dancers wore such masks as these at coronations and royal funerals.
11. There are still more African artifacts of great complexity.
12. On the shelf to the left sits a seventeenth-century ivory bracelet from the kingdom of Benin.
13. Notice the intricate carvings of kings on the antique bracelet.
14. From the workshops of Benin came some of Africa's finest bronze figures.
15. Among the most ancient African art objects are terra-cotta figures nearly 1,500 years old.
16. Terra-cotta is a kind of earthenware.
17. Superb bronze and terra-cotta heads were made in Nigeria in the thirteenth century.
18. In the museum's exhibit there are even older examples of African art.
19. Prehistoric cave paintings were discovered in the Tassili Plateau in the Sahara.
20. African people of today still create many such exquisite art objects.

Exercise 14 Writing Sentences

Write five sentences about a topic of your choice. Make at least one sentence a question, one a command, one a statement beginning with *here* or *there*, and one a statement in which a prepositional phrase and the verb precede the subject.

A **complement** is a word or group of words that completes the meaning of a verb.

There are four kinds of complements: *direct objects*, *indirect objects*, *object complements*, and *subject complements*.

Direct Objects

A **direct object** answers the question *what?* or *whom?* after an action verb.

The subject of a sentence usually performs the action indicated by the verb. That action may be directed toward or received by someone or something—the direct object. Nouns, pronouns, or words acting as nouns may serve as direct objects. Only transitive verbs have direct objects.

Carlos served **dinner.** [Carlos served *what?*]

Marie admires **him** deeply. [Marie admires *whom?*]

Carlos served a Mexican **dinner** and a fabulous **dessert.** [Carlos served *what?*]

Exercise 15   **Identifying Direct Objects**

Write the action verb in each sentence. Then write any direct objects and underline them.

American Cowboys

1. North American cowboys copied the style of Mexican cowboys.
2. Historians see the Mexican vaqueros as the first real cowboys.
3. At all times of the year, the vaquero wore a floppy sombrero.
4. This large hat kept snow, rain, or sun off his face.
5. The North American cowboy modeled his own hat on the Mexican sombrero.
6. During branding season the vaqueros roped cows with a sturdy riata.
7. Cowboys in North America lassoed cows with a lariat (from the Spanish word *la riata*).
8. Mexican cowboys protected their shins and thighs with leather chaparejos.
9. In a similar fashion, North American cowboys put leather chaps over their pants.
10. Cowboys also roam the grassy plains, or *pampas*, of Argentina and Uruguay.
11. These plains provide excellent food for cattle or sheep.
12. The cowboys, or *gauchos*, of these areas share many qualities with North American cowboys.
13. For example, *gauchos* wear hats and chaps for protection against the elements.
14. Cowboys in any country do the same sorts of jobs.
15. Cowboys from North and South America would probably tell very similar tales.

Indirect Objects

Kim saved Rosa

An **indirect object** answers the question *to whom? for whom? to what?* or *for what?* after an action verb.

In most cases a sentence may have an indirect object only if it has a direct object. The indirect object will always come between the verb and the direct object.

> Tyrone served his **sisters** dinner. [Tyrone served dinner *to whom?*]

> Greta saved **him** a seat. [Greta saved a seat *for whom?*]

> Kim saved **Rosa** and **José** seats. [Kim saved seats *for whom?*]

> The children gave the worthy **charity** all their savings. [The children gave all their savings *to what?*]

> Marsha gave the **game** her best effort. [Marsha gave her best effort *for what?*]

a seat.

Kim saved Rosa.

Exercise 16   **Identifying Indirect Objects**

For each sentence write the direct object, and list any indirect object(s). (Not all sentences have an indirect object.) Label the objects *DO* and *IO* for *direct object* and *indirect object*.

Careers in Sports

1. Professional sports offer many careers.
2. Television or radio sportscasters broadcast sports events.
3. A good sports announcer gives fans play-by-play descriptions of the game.
4. The announcer tells them anecdotes.
5. Newspaper writers and photographers also cover athletic competitions.
6. Newspapers give their readers sports coverage.
7. Teaching may give a person satisfaction.
8. Managers, coaches, and trainers all bring teams success.
9. Sports also give referees, umpires, and doctors jobs.
10. Athletic events even give hot-dog and peanut vendors work.
11. Some boys and girls contemplate sports careers at a very young age.
12. They give famous basketball stars attention.
13. They show their coaches their dedication to their sports.
14. They tell their friends endless stories about their skill on the court or field.
15. Unfortunately, few young athletes will achieve success as professionals.

Object Complements

An **object complement** answers the question *what?* after a direct object. That is, it *completes* the meaning of the direct object by identifying or describing it.

Object complements occur only in sentences with direct objects and only in those sentences with the following action verbs or with similar verbs that have the general meaning of "make" or "consider":

appoint	elect	render	consider	name
choose	make	call	find	think

An object complement usually follows a direct object. It may be an adjective, a noun, or a pronoun.

> Residents find the park **peaceful.** [adjective]
> Katie appointed me **assistant, treasurer,** and **cook.** [nouns]
> My grandmother considers the property **hers.** [pronoun]

Exercise 17   Identifying Object Complements

Write the object complement(s) that appear in the following sentences. (Not every sentence has an object complement.)

Musical Tastes

1. The Music Club has appointed Felipe president.
2. He finds that honor extraordinary.
3. One member, Maya, thinks Mozart the best composer.
4. Another member, Diane, considers Bach stupendous.
5. Felipe, Maya, and Diane make music a priority.
6. Diane calls Verdi a great composer and a musical genius.
7. Felipe likes chamber music better than opera.
8. Maya thinks opera sublime.
9. Diane names the basso singer Justino Díaz her favorite.
10. Maya finds the voice of Kiri Te Kanawa exquisite.

Exercise 18   Using Object Complements

On your paper complete the following sentences by writing object complements. Then write the letter *A*, *N*, or *P* to identify the object complement as an *adjective, noun,* or *pronoun.*

1. The fearful swimmers found the ocean _____.
2. Generations of fishers consider the ocean _____.
3. Sailors make the ocean _____.
4. Early explorers thought the ocean _____.
5. Surfers call the ocean _____.

Subject Complements

A **subject complement** follows a subject and a linking verb and identifies or describes the subject.

There are two kinds of subject complements: *predicate nominatives* and *predicate adjectives.*

A **predicate nominative** is a noun or pronoun that follows a linking verb and points back to the subject to rename it or to identify it further.

Sopranos are **singers.**

Clearly the star of the opera was **she.**

Many current opera stars are **Italians** or **Spaniards.**

Predicate nominatives are usually found in sentences that contain forms of the linking verb *be.* A few other linking verbs (for example, *become* and *remain*) can be followed by a predicate nominative.

Julia became both a **musician** and an **actress.**
That experience remains a cherished **memory** for me.

A **predicate adjective** follows a linking verb and points back to the subject and further describes it.

Ballerinas are **graceful.**

Ballerinas must be extremely **dedicated.**

Most ballerinas seem **intense** and **hard-working.**

Predicate adjectives may follow any linking verb.

I felt very **carefree.**
Only a few marathoners appear **fresh** even now.
The water tasted **delicious.**
I grew increasingly **tired.**
My sister appeared **weary.**
My friend Tanya looked **exhausted** but **happy.**
The musty room smelled **bad.**
The band sounded **loud.**
The noise became **louder** as we approached the finish line.

Identifying Predicate Nominatives

On your paper write the predicate nominatives that appear in the following sentences. (Not all sentences contain predicate nominatives.)

Dwight D. Eisenhower

1. Dwight Eisenhower was one of seven sons.
2. Eisenhower graduated from West Point with the class of 1915.
3. He had been an average student in high school.
4. During World War II, he rose to the rank of Supreme Allied Commander in Europe.
5. After that, Eisenhower's name became a household word.
6. He was the Republican presidential candidate in 1952.
7. His election was the first presidential victory for the GOP in twenty-four years.
8. Eisenhower was a proponent of "Modern Republicanism."
9. He remained an advocate of reducing the federal government's power.
10. He also was a supporter of higher minimum wages.

Exercise 20 **Identifying Predicate Adjectives**

On your paper write each simple subject and each predicate adjective. Underline the predicate adjectives.

Dinner Is Served

1. The gym was ready for the class banquet.
2. The tables looked beautiful in the soft candlelight.
3. On the walls, portraits of the class members appeared almost alive.
4. Their unwavering gazes seemed lifelike.
5. The music of the combo sounded romantic.
6. All of the students felt ravenous.
7. The onion soup smelled especially good.
8. The food tasted excellent to all of the elegantly dressed diners.
9. The students remained unusually talkative throughout the meal.
10. The chaperones, however, grew sleepy rather early.

Exercise 21 **Using Subject Complements**

On your paper complete the following sentences with nouns, pronouns, or adjectives. Write *PN* or *PA* to indicate if the complement you wrote is a *predicate nominative* or a *predicate adjective*.

1. The most popular sport, in my opinion, is _____.
2. The lifestyles of many prominent players seem _____.
3. Very few athletes become _____.
4. The great majority of athletes are _____.
5. Their lives remain _____.

Identifying Subject Complements

On your paper write all the subject complements that appear in the following sentences. Write *predicate nominative* or *predicate adjective* to identify each. (Five sentences have more than one predicate nominative or predicate adjective.)

Japanese Flower Arrangements

[1]Flower arrangement is an ancient Japanese art. [2]This tradition grew popular in the sixth century. [3]Early flower arrangements were decorations for Buddhist temple altars. [4]Over the centuries the art of flower arrangement became increasingly specific. [5]Important materials in Japanese floral arrangement are leaves, stems, and branches. [6]The lines of the branches should be graceful and sleek. [7]In Western countries blossoms are generally the only important features. [8]The best Japanese floral arrangements look natural and colorful. [9]A Japanese florist must be a designer and an artist. [10]The art of Japanese flower arrangement is both simple and complex.

Exercise 23   Identifying Complements

On your paper write the complements that appear in the following sentences. Next to each complement write the kind of complement it is: *direct object, indirect object, object complement, predicate nominative,* or *predicate adjective.*

A Jazz Musician

 1. Davenport, Iowa, was the home of Leon Bix Beiderbecke.
 2. Mississippi riverboats passing by Davenport gave Bix Beiderbecke his first taste of jazz.
 3. Bix Beiderbecke played the cornet and the piano.
 4. The cornet's sound is mellow and rich.
 5. Bix Beiderbecke carried his cornet with him in a paper bag.
 6. Louis Armstrong once met young Bix on a riverboat.
 7. Beiderbecke's parents were conservative, wealthy Midwesterners.
 8. They did not give Bix any financial assistance for his musical career.
 9. Beiderbecke's reputation is still great in music circles today.
10. In fact, many musicians consider him a true classic of American jazz.

Exercise 24   Writing Sentences with Complements

Write five sentences about a natural phenomenon, such as an eclipse, a thunderstorm, or a sunset. In each sentence use at least one of the four kinds of complements: direct object, indirect object, object complement, or subject complement. Label the complements for each sentence that you write.

Grammar Review

Parts of the Sentence

A member of the Ibo tribe of eastern Nigeria, Chinua Achebe writes about his people in *Things Fall Apart*. Set in the Ibo village of Umuofia around the turn of the century, the novel chronicles the life of a proud young wrestler named Okonkwo. In this passage Okonkwo is just about to go to bed when he hears the town crier, who beats his metal drum and summons the men of the village to a meeting. The passage has been annotated to show some of the parts of sentences covered in this unit.

Literature Model

from THINGS FALL APART
by Chinua Achebe

Direct object

Compound predicate

Subject complement
(predicate nominative)

Subject complement
(predicate adjective)

Complete predicate

Simple subject

Simple predicate

Okonkwo had just blown out the palm-oil lamp and stretched himself on his bamboo bed when he heard the *ogene* of the town crier piercing the still night air. *Gome, gome, gome, gome,* boomed the hollow metal. Then the crier gave his message, and at the end of it beat his instrument again. And this was the message. Every man of Umuofia was asked to gather at the market place tomorrow morning. Okonkwo wondered what was amiss, for he knew certainly that something was amiss. He had discerned a clear overtone of tragedy in the crier's voice, and even now he could still hear it as it grew dimmer and dimmer in the distance.

The night was very quiet. It was always quiet except on moonlit nights. Darkness held a vague terror for these people, even the bravest among them. Children were warned not to whistle at night for fear of evil spirits. Dangerous animals became even more sinister and uncanny in the dark. A snake was never called by its name at night, because it would hear. It was called a string. And so on this particular night as the crier's voice was gradually swallowed up in the distance, silence returned to the world, a vibrant silence made more intense by the universal trill of a million forest insects. ➡

On a moonlit night it would be different. The happy voices of children playing in open fields would then be heard. And perhaps those not so young would be playing in pairs in less open places, and old men and women would remember their youth. As the Ibo say: "When the moon is shining the cripple becomes hungry for a walk."

— Complete subject

— Compound subject

— Direct object

Exercise 1

Identifying Complete Subjects and Complete Predicates   Copy each of these sentences, which are based on the content of *Things Fall Apart*. Draw a line between the complete subject and complete predicate.

1. Okonkwo was going to bed for the night.
2. His palm-oil lamp had been blown out.
3. The comfort of his bamboo bed beckoned him.
4. The hollow metal sound of the town crier's drum aroused everyone from sleep.
5. His message of a morning meeting surprised Okonkwo.
6. A clear note of tragedy in the crier's voice made Okonkwo fearful.
7. Nights without moonlight, such as this one, were always very quiet and sinister.
8. The vibration from the crier's voice could be sensed long after his departure.
9. Children were always silenced on dark, moonless nights.
10. The absence of moonlight changed the outlook of the community completely.

Exercise 2

Writing Sentences with Complete Subjects and Complete Predicates   The following partial sentences draw on ideas in the passage from *Things Fall Apart*. Complete each sentence by writing on your paper either a complete subject or a complete predicate. Do not repeat the exact wording from the novel.

SAMPLE   The town crier _____.
ANSWER   The town crier beat his metal drum.

1. The voice of the crier _____.
2. _____ listened in the darkness.
3. The dark, moonless night _____.
4. Even the bravest villagers _____.
5. _____ roamed the jungle on dark nights.
6. A string _____.
7. _____ trilled in the darkness.
8. Moonlight _____.
9. _____ went outside in the moonlight.
10. Even the older people _____.

Exercise 3

Writing Sentences with Compound Subjects and Predicates   Write on your paper a complete sentence answering each of these questions about *Things Fall Apart*. Begin your sentence with the subject, and follow the directions in parentheses. Then underline and label the simple or compound subject and the simple or compound predicate.

SAMPLE   What two kinds of nights had opposite effects on the people of Umuofia?
(Use a compound subject.)

<table>
<tr><td align="center">COMPOUND SUBJECT</td><td align="center">SIMPLE PREDICATE</td></tr>
</table>

ANSWER   Dark <u>nights</u> and moonlit <u>nights</u>   <u>had</u> opposite effects on the people of Umuofia.

1. What did Okonkwo do to prepare for sleep? (Use a compound predicate.)
2. What sounds broke the silence of the night? (Use a compound subject.)
3. What did Okonkwo do as the crier gave his message? (Use a compound predicate.)
4. What qualities of the night made the crier's message all the more ominous to the villagers? (Use a compound subject.)
5. What things were troublesome on a dark night? (Use a compound subject.)
6. What did the villagers never do in the dark? (Use a compound predicate.)
7. What happened to the sound of the crier's voice? (Use a compound predicate.)
8. What did the villagers do on moonlit nights? (Use a compound predicate.)
9. What groups of villagers would go outside on a moonlit night? (Use a compound subject with three different nouns.)
10. Who would reminisce about the past? (Use a compound subject.)

Exercise 4

Writing Inverted Sentences   The following sentences develop an image or idea suggested by the passage from *Things Fall Apart*. On your paper rewrite each sentence in inverted order, following the instructions in parentheses and making any needed changes.

SAMPLE   A fear of darkness was in the hearts of the villagers.
(Begin the sentence with *There was*.)
ANSWER   There was a fear of darkness in the hearts of the villagers.

1. Okonkwo lay on the bamboo bed. (Begin the sentence with *On the bamboo bed*.)
2. The town crier came down the road. (Begin the sentence with *Down the road*.)
3. Tragic overtones were in the crier's voice. (Begin the sentence with *There were*.)
4. Many a scary creature was out and about. (Begin the sentence with *There was*.)
5. Dangerous animals lurked in the darkness. (Begin the sentence with *In the darkness*.)
6. A snake might hide within any shadow. (Begin the sentence with *Within any shadow*.)
7. The drum faded into the distance. (Begin the sentence with *Into the distance*.)
8. Millions of insects were in the dark jungle. (Begin the sentence with *There were*.)
9. No children were outside on this moonless night. (Begin the sentence with *There were*.)
10. People of all ages appeared on a moonlit night. (Begin the sentence with *On a moonlit night*.)

Exercise 5

Writing Sentences with Predicate Nominatives and Predicate Adjectives The pairs of words that follow are derived from the passage from *Things Fall Apart*. For each pair write a sentence that uses the first word as the subject and the second word as a predicate adjective or a predicate nominative. Do not use Achebe's exact words, and add more than just a verb to the pair of words. After you have written the sentence, indicate whether the second word from the pair is acting as a *predicate adjective* or a *predicate nominative*.

SAMPLE   Umuofia, village
ANSWER   Umuofia was Okonkwo's village in Africa. predicate nominative

1. *Things Fall Apart*, novel
2. Nigeria, country
3. villagers, members
4. Okonkwo, wrestler
5. *ogene*, drum
6. sound, loud
7. message, worrisome
8. morning, time
9. overtone, tragic
10. night, silent
11. people, fearful
12. darkness, time
13. animals, danger
14. string, name
15. trill, persistent
16. silence, extreme
17. villagers, lively
18. children, happy
19. fields, playgrounds
20. elderly, thoughtful

Exercise 6

Identifying Direct Objects and Object Complements The sentences below are based on the content of *Things Fall Apart*. On your paper write the direct object and object complement from each sentence. Write *direct object* and *object complement* to identify each.

1. The town-crier's message made Okonkwo fearful.
2. He considered the crier's tone of voice ominous.
3. The people of his village thought moonless nights menacing.
4. In contrast, the people found moonlit nights comfortable and friendly.
5. The light made their worst fears more bearable.

Exercise 7

Writing Sentences with Direct and Indirect Objects   The following groups of words describe incidents related to the passage from *Things Fall Apart*. Each word is labeled *S* (for *subject*), *DO* (for *direct object*), or *IO* (for *indirect object*). On your paper write a sentence using these words as those parts of the sentence, but do not use the exact wording from the novel. Try to add modifiers or prepositional phrases.

| SAMPLE | lamp (S), Okonkwo (IO), light (DO) |
| ANSWER | A palm-oil lamp gave Okonkwo light at night. |

1. town crier (S), drum (IO), thump (DO)
2. Okonkwo (S), sound (DO)
3. crier (S), instrument (DO)
4. crier (S), villagers (IO), message (DO)
5. Okonkwo (S), tragedy (DO)
6. darkness (S), townspeople (IO), feelings (DO)
7. whistle (S), trouble (DO)
8. distance (S), voice (DO)
9. trill (S), silence (DO)
10. moonlight (S), villagers (IO), courage (DO)

Exercise 8   **Proofreading**

The following passage describes the people and the art of Nigeria. (An example of Nigerian sculpture appears on the opposite page.) Rewrite the passage, correcting the errors in spelling, grammar, and usage. Add any missing punctuation. There are twenty-five errors.

The Art of Nigeria

[1]The country of Nigeria are the most populous nation in West Africa it is more than twice the size of California. [2]Two hundred or more native tribes inhabits modren Nigeria. [3]The largest tribes are the Hausa and the Fulani who live mainly in the north; the Yoruba, in the southwest; the Ibo, in the southeast; and the Ijo, on the southern coast. [4]Each of the tribal groups have their own language but the common language of all the groups are English, reflecting Nigeria's century-long domination by Great Britain. [5]Nigeria finally acheived it's independence from Great Britain in 1960.

[6]Nigerian cultures have produced some of Africas' most impressive art. [7]The Yoruba fashioned magnificent bronze sculptures and the people of western Nigeria produced fine ivory figures. [8]Many of these sculptures and figures was used during the religious ceremonies of the people.

[9]The Ijo who live in the warm and humid region of the Niger River delta, are closely related to their neighbors, the Ibo, who live nearby. [10]The Ijo traditionally venerated many gods, each god was thought to control a particular aspect of everyday life. [11]Some of the Ijo people continues to practice the religion of their ancestors. ➡

[12]On this page are pictured a shrine that is typical of the sacred objects of the Ijo culture. [13]It is made of highly polished wood and showed a figure—possibly a tribal ancestor—sitting on a throne. [14]Generally, such an image was not displayed every day, it was probably created for a special ritual, such as a marriage or a funeral.

[15]In recent years many Nigerians have abandoned their native villages and migrate to large cities. [16]Those who remain in the country still lives close to nature. [17]The Ibo villagers described by Chinua Achebe in *Things Fall Apart* is aware of every sound heard on a moonless night. [18]They attribute some of those sounds to animals and insects; they attributes others to the supernatural. [19]Such sacred objects as this shrine may have symbolized a bridge between the natural and the supernatural world's.

Artist unknown, Ijo shrine, Nigeria

Mixed Review

Exercise 9

The following sentences describe the life of Chinua Achebe. Rewrite each sentence on your paper according to the instructions that appear after each item.

Chinua Achebe

 1. According to many critics, Chinua Achebe's works are insightful.
    (Add *and educational* to create a second predicate adjective.)
 2. A member of the Ibo tribe of Nigeria, Achebe grew up in the village of Ogidi.
    (Add *and graduated from the University College at Ibadan* to expand the complete predicate.)
 3. He spoke the Ibo language first.
    (Add *but learned English as a child* to expand the complete predicate.)
 4. The fifth in a family of six children, Achebe was always a reader.
    (Add *eager* as a modifier of the subject complement.)
 5. Achebe's mother insisted on the best education possible for the family's children.
    (Add *and father* to create a compound subject.)
 6. From his experiences with African life have come Achebe's powerful themes.
    (Rewrite the sentence so that it begins with the complete subject.)
 7. Many of his books give a sense of the effects of colonialism on African culture.
    (Add *readers* to the complete predicate so that it functions as an indirect object.)
 8. Numerous examples of problems caused by colonial rule are in Achebe's works.
    (Rewrite the sentence so that it begins with *There are*.)
 9. Over the years the popular Nigerian author has received many awards.
    (Add *and honorary doctorates* to the direct object.)
10. Chinua Achebe has become an important spokesperson for African people.
    (Add *and has been praised for his eloquent writings* to expand the complete predicate.)
11. Achebe's writings describe African life. (Add *rural* to modify the direct object.)
12. In the southeast section of Nigeria had lived the Ibo for hundreds of years.
    (Rewrite the sentence so that the complete subject comes before the complete predicate.)
13. English helped the unification of Nigeria. (Add *and provided a language for communication with the West* to expand the predicate.)
14. Achebe provides detailed pictures. (Add *his audience* to serve as an indirect object.)
15. Achebe's works present vivid images of life in Nigeria during colonial times.
    (Add words to create a compound predicate.)
16. Many of Achebe's themes were provided by the long presence of the British government in Nigeria. (Rewrite the declarative sentence as a question.)
17. Many stories about religion are in Achebe's work.
    (Rewrite the sentence as an inverted sentence that begins with *There are*.)
18. His readers and followers consider Achebe a rare voice in Nigerian literature.
    (Add *and important* to the object complement.)
19. Achebe is an important figure in twentieth-century African history.
    (Add *literary* to the predicate nominative.)
20. Achebe's works speak to people everywhere. (Add *of all ages* to the predicate.)

Writing Application

Sentence Elements in Writing Jack London uses a variety of sentence elements and patterns in this passage from *The Call of the Wild* to create a lively, engaging prose rhythm. As you read the passage, focus especially on the italicized words.

> Buck's first day on the Dyea beach was like a nightmare. Every hour was filled with shock and surprise. He *had been* suddenly *jerked* from the heart of civilization and *flung* into the heart of things primordial. *No lazy, sun-kissed life was this*, with nothing to do but loaf and be bored. Here was neither peace, nor rest, nor a moment's safety. All was confusion and action, and every moment life and limb were in peril. There was imperative need to be constantly alert; for *these dogs and men were not town dogs and men*. They were savages, all of them, who knew no law but the law of club and fang.

Techniques with Sentence Elements

Try to use various sentence elements and patterns, as London does, when you write and revise your work.

1. Vary sentence length and rhythm by using compound subjects and predicates. Compare the following:

Boring pattern He *had been* suddenly *jerked* from the heart of civilization. He *had been flung* into the heart of things primordial.
London's pattern He *had been* suddenly *jerked* from the heart of civilization and *flung* into the heart of things primordial.

2. Occasionally use repetition for effect in sentences with predicate nominatives.

Boring pattern These dogs and men weren't from towns.
London's pattern These dogs and men were not *town dogs* and *men*.

3. Achieve sentence variety by sometimes using inverted word order.

Visual order This was no lazy, sun-kissed life . . .
London's order No lazy, sun-kissed life was this . . .

Practice Practice these techniques by revising the following passage, adapted from *The Call of the Wild*, combining ideas to expand the basic sentence patterns. Try to write one sentence in inverted order.

Then an old wolf, gaunt and battle-scarred, came forward. Buck writhed his lips into the preliminary of a snarl. He sniffed noses with him. Whereupon the old wolf sat down. He pointed his nose at the moon. He broke out the long wolf howl. The others sat down, too. They howled. Then the call came to Buck in unmistakable accents. He, too, sat down. He howled. . . . And the story of Buck may well end here.

12.1 Prepositional Phrases

A **prepositional phrase** is a group of words that begins with a preposition and ends with a noun or a pronoun called the **object of the preposition**.

> The stairs lead **to the attic**. [*Attic* is the object of the preposition *to*.]
>
> The staircase is too steep **for her**. [*Her* is the object of the preposition *for*.]
>
> They laid carpeting **on the stairs**. [*Stairs* is the object of the preposition *on*.]

For lists of common prepositions, see page 435.

Adjectives and other modifiers may be placed between the preposition and its object. Also, a preposition may have more than one object.

> The staircase leads **to the crowded, dusty attic**. [adjectives added]
>
> The staircase leads **to the attic and the roof**. [two objects]

A prepositional phrase acts in the same way an adjective or an adverb does. Used as an adjective, a prepositional phrase modifies a noun or a pronoun. Used as an adverb, it modifies a verb, an adjective, or an adverb.

> They used the staircase **on the left**. [adjective phrase modifying the noun *staircase*]
>
> Which **of the staircases** leads downstairs? [adjective phrase modifying the pronoun *which*]
>
> **At midnight** you can come downstairs **to the kitchen**. [adverb phrases modifying the verb phrase *can come*]
>
> My grandfather explained that a daily walk is healthful **for him**. [adverb phrase modifying the adjective *healthful*]
>
> She walks very quickly **for a young baby**. [adverb phrase modifying the adverb *quickly*]

Identifying Prepositional Phrases

On your paper write each prepositional phrase that appears in the following sentences. (You will find a total of 25 prepositional phrases.)

Crispus Attucks

[1]Crispus Attucks, a former slave, is a hero of the American Revolution. [2]He was one of five men who died in 1770 during the historic Boston Massacre. [3]At the time, British troops were stationed in Boston. [4]Some sixty men and boys from Boston gathered around a small group of British soldiers. [5]They shouted insults and threw snowballs at the British. [6]Suddenly the soldiers fired into the unruly crowd. [7]Attucks was hit instantly by a bullet and died beside two other men. [8]Later two more men, who were also shot by the British during the attack, died from their wounds. [9]Bostonians throughout the city expressed shock and outrage over the incident. [10]At a trial, however, only two of the soldiers were found guilty, and they were released after a brief period. [11]A monument in Boston honors the memory of Crispus Attucks and the others who perished with him in the Boston Massacre.

Exercise 2 **Identifying Adjective and Adverb Phrases**

On your paper write the word or words each prepositional phrase in Exercise 1 modifies. Then indicate whether each phrase is acting as an adjective or an adverb in the sentence.

Exercise 3 **Expanding Sentences with Prepositional Phrases**

Copy and expand the following sentences by adding at least one adjective phrase and one adverb phrase to each.

> SAMPLE   The new equipment arrived.
> ANSWER   The new equipment for the office arrived by truck.

1. The candle flame flickers.
2. Someone should have asked me.
3. The comedian performed.
4. The gardener pulled the weeds.
5. The children brought flowers.
6. The classroom emptied quickly.
7. I have used a shovel many times.
8. The woman was buying cat food.
9. The farmers drove their tractors.
10. Her cousin will send a letter.

Exercise 4 **Writing with Prepositional Phrases**

Write five sentences that include two or more prepositional phrases. Then underline each prepositional phrase and tell whether it is being used as an *adjective* or an *adverb*.

> SAMPLE ANSWER   Most students <u>in my grade</u> watch television <u>on weekends</u>. (adjective; adverb)

12.2 Appositives and Appositive Phrases

An **appositive** is a noun or pronoun that is placed next to another noun or pronoun to identify or give additional information about it.

> My friend **Paulo** sends me long letters from Brazil. [The appositive *Paulo* identifies the noun *friend*.]

An **appositive phrase** is an appositive plus any words that modify the appositive.

> He is living and working in Brasília, **the capital city.** [The appositive phrase, in bold type, identifies *Brasília*.]

Use commas to set off any appositive or appositive phrase that is not essential to the meaning of a sentence.

> Paulo's brother **Ernesto** also lives there. [The appositive **Ernesto** is essential because Paulo has more than one brother.]
> Dora, **Paulo's only sister,** lives in New York. [The appositive phrase is not necessary to identify Dora.]

Usually an appositive or appositive phrase follows the noun or pronoun it identifies or explains. Occasionally an appositive phrase precedes the noun or pronoun.

> **A skilled mechanic,** Paulo could probably find work anywhere.

Exercise 5   Identifying Appositives and Appositive Phrases

Write the appositives and appositive phrases in the sentences below.

1. Our neighbor Katie Rosenfeld organized the dance.
2. The most tickets were sold by Mia and Vanessa, two tenth graders.
3. After a long search, Greg finally found and booked the band, a fantastic group.
4. A clever class president, Juan Lopez talked his cousin into performing one of the opening comedy acts.
5. Two of Mr. Swanson's art classes, the third and the fifth periods, began work on the decorations a month in advance.

Identifying Appositives and Appositive Phrases

Write the appositive or the appositive phrase that appears in each sentence. Then write the noun or pronoun that is identified or explained by the appositive.

Stars of American Culture

  1. Alvin Ailey, an innovative choreographer, founded a lively modern dance company.
  2. *The Heart Is a Lonely Hunter* is a novel by the acclaimed twentieth-century author Carson McCullers.
  3. The great contralto Marian Anderson was the first African American singer to perform leading roles at the Metropolitan Opera in New York City.
  4. Midori, one of the most brilliant violinists of her generation, launched her career as a very young girl.
  5. The Pulitzer Prize was awarded to Gwendolyn Brooks for *Annie Allen*, a collection of poems.
  6. The Guggenheim Museum in New York was one of the last projects of Frank Lloyd Wright, the greatest modern American architect.
  7. Georgia O'Keeffe, one of the most influential twentieth-century American painters, lived in New Mexico from 1949 to 1986.
  8. Fans admired the jazz vocalist Billie Holiday for the emotionally charged quality of her singing.
  9. Rita Hayworth, the daughter of a Spanish dancer, starred in many American films in the 1940s.
  10. *Nobody Knows My Name* is a collection of autobiographical essays by the author James Baldwin.

Expanding Sentences with Appositive Phrases

On your paper expand the following sentences by adding an appositive phrase to each sentence. Be sure to use commas where necessary.

> SAMPLE   Vitus Bering was the first European to land in Alaska.
> ANSWER   Vitus Bering, a Danish explorer, was the first European to land in Alaska.

  1. The film was nominated for an Academy Award.
  2. The local newspaper printed my letter on its editorial page.
  3. Robert Frost wrote the poem.
  4. Alaska entered the Union in 1959.
  5. Every year New Orleans celebrates Mardi Gras.
  6. The novel is my favorite.
  7. In Washington are many cherry trees.
  8. My favorite singer will be appearing here in concert in July.
  9. Our team won.
  10. The principal of the school has resigned.

12.3 Verbals and Verbal Phrases

A **verbal** is a verb form that functions in a sentence as a noun, an adjective, or an adverb.

A **verbal phrase** is a verbal plus any complements and modifiers.

There are three kinds of verbals: *participles, gerunds,* and *infinitives.* All three types can be expanded into phrases.

Participles and Participial Phrases

A participle is a verb form that can function as an adjective.

A **present participle** is made up of the base form of the verb plus *-ing: falling.* A **past participle** is usually made up of the base form plus *-ed: burned.* Some past participles are irregularly formed.

Participles are often used as adjectives.

No one would eat the **burned** toast.

We were warned to watch out for **falling** rocks.

The **fallen** tree blocked the **winding** road.

A participle may also be used as part of a verb phrase. When a participle is part of a verb phrase, it is not acting as an adjective.

PARTICIPLE AS ADJECTIVE	The **growing** child was curious.
PARTICIPLE IN VERB PHRASE	They saw that he **was growing** stronger.

A **participial phrase** contains a participle plus any complements and modifiers.

Participial phrases can be placed in various positions in a sentence.

We watched the best teams **playing baseball.**

The **badly defeated** team accepted its fate with grace.

The victors, **elated by the victory,** shook hands with the losers.

Throwing their hats into the air, the fans of the victorious team let out a great roar.

A participial phrase at the beginning of a sentence is usually followed by a comma.

Identifying Participles in Sentences

Write the participle that functions as an adjective in each of the following sentences.

1. The blowing trees were etched against the sky.
2. A broken branch scratched against the window.
3. The closed barn doors rattled in the strong wind.
4. Everywhere was evidence of the gathering storm.
5. Shivering, the young boy returned to his chair near the fireplace.

Identifying Participles and Participial Phrases

Write the participial phrase that acts as an adjective in each of the following sentences. Then identify the word each phrase modifies.

Early Native Americans of the Northwest

1. The northwestern coast of North America, extending from southern Alaska to northern California, was the home of many Native American groups.
2. The dense forests inhabited by these groups have a temperate climate and plentiful rainfall.
3. Salmon caught in streams was an important source of food.
4. Knowing the woodlands well, the groups gathered wild fruit.
5. Northwest Native Americans ordinarily lived in houses built of wood.
6. Dressed for battle, they wore armor and helmets as a means of protection.
7. Some of the groups had totem poles decorated with carvings.
8. Displaying great artistic skill, the Northwest Native Americans produced baskets, rattles, masks, and other artifacts.
9. Native Americans of the Northwest had a distinctive culture established over hundreds of years.
10. Determined to find furs and other natural resources, Europeans came into the area in the late 1700s.

Writing Sentences with Participial Phrases

Write five sentences with participial phrases. Then underline each phrase, and write what noun or pronoun the phrase modifies.

SAMPLE ANSWER   <u>Determined to be the next class president</u>, Kevin began his campaign the first day of school.   Kevin

Gerunds and Gerund Phrases

A **gerund** is a verb form that ends in *-ing* and is used in the same way a noun is used.

STRIKE!

> **Eating** is something I enjoy. [gerund as subject]
>
> My grandfather likes **strolling.** [gerund as direct object]
>
> Tony gives **baking** his best effort. [gerund as indirect object]
>
> How much enthusiasm do you feel for **bowling?**
> [gerund as object of preposition]
>
> Rachel's favorite pastime is **painting.**
> [gerund as predicate nominative]
>
> My hobbies, **writing** and **reading,** are quiet activities.
> [gerunds as appositives]

Bowl + ing
is fun!

A **gerund phrase** is a gerund plus any complements and modifiers.

> **Dancing the tango** is not as easy as it looks.
> **Fred Astaire's marvelous dancing** will always be exciting.

The difference between a present participle and a gerund is that a present participle is used as a verb or an adjective and a gerund is used as a noun.

> **Running** around the track, Yuki felt exhilarated. [present participle]
> **Running** gives Yuki a sense of well-being. [gerund]

Exercise 11   **Identifying Gerunds and Gerund Phrases**

List on your paper the gerunds and gerund phrases that appear in the following sentences. The number of gerunds or gerund phrases in each sentence is given in parentheses.

A Spanish Conqueror

1. Conquering was the goal of the ruthless Spanish adventurer Hernán Cortés. (1)
2. His greatest accomplishment was claiming for Spain land in southern Mexico. (1)
3. Capturing territory was a challenging experience, Cortés found. (1)
4. The famous Spaniard enjoyed discovering and exploring new places. (2)
5. Cortés was adept at gaining the trust of some Native Americans. (1)
6. The result was winning the Aztec capital, Tenochtitlán, through the overthrow of Emperor Montezuma. (1)
7. By 1521 Cortés's goals—finding gold, claiming Mexican lands, and conquering native groups—were fulfilled. (3)
8. For several years Cortés was famous for controlling much of present-day Mexico. (1)
9. His trip to Spain in 1528 resulted in his receiving the title of *marquis.* (1)
10. Cortés sailed back to Mexico in 1530 and engaged in ranching and mining. (2)

Infinitives and Infinitive Phrases

An **infinitive** is a verb form that is usually preceded by the word *to* and is used as a noun, an adjective, or an adverb.

When you use the word *to* before the base form of a verb, *to* is not a preposition but part of the infinitive form of the verb.

To stand can be uncomfortable. [infinitive as subject]

Infants first learn **to crawl**. [infinitive as direct object]

Her aim is **to walk**. [infinitive as predicate nominative]

Birds have an instinct **to fly**. [infinitive as adjective]

I am happy **to run**. [infinitive as adverb]

An **infinitive phrase** contains an infinitive plus any complements and modifiers.

We decided **to sail across the lake**.

They wanted **to drive slowly around the park**.

To run in a marathon someday is my secret ambition.

A triathlon requires athletes **to train diligently**.

To complete a triathlon is a success in itself.

Exercise 12	Identifying Infinitives and Infinitive Phrases

Write the infinitive phrase that appears in each of the following sentences.

Mary Cassatt

1. Mary Cassatt was one of the foremost American artists to paint in the Impressionist style.
2. Cassatt grew up in Philadelphia and decided to study at the Pennsylvania Academy of the Fine Arts.
3. In 1868 she went to live in Paris.
4. The great French painter Edgar Degas began to influence her work.
5. Degas helped Cassatt to develop her precise and delicate style.
6. Cassatt often chose to paint portraits of mothers and children.
7. Degas invited Cassatt to exhibit paintings with other Impressionists.
8. Cassatt encouraged her American relatives and friends to purchase the paintings of the French Impressionists.
9. In so doing, Cassatt helped to influence a growing American interest in contemporary art.
10. Today art lovers are able to appreciate Cassatt's work for its own remarkable qualities.

Identifying Verbal Phrases

On your paper write each of the verbal phrases that appears in the following sentences. Write whether each phrase is a *participial phrase*, a *gerund phrase*, or an *infinitive phrase*.

Elephants

1. Elephants have the distinction of being the largest land mammals.
2. Living in the tropical regions of Asia and Africa, they may reach a height of 13 feet.
3. Their tusks, weighing as much as 200 pounds each, can be more than 10 feet long.
4. Their distinctive ears are huge, measuring up to 42 inches in width.
5. Elephants use their fingerlike trunks to pick up objects.
6. Elephants browse all day, feeding on leaves and tall grasses.
7. Elephants can learn to carry logs and to perform in circuses.
8. Training young elephants takes great skill.
9. It can be difficult to handle them, too.
10. Hunted for food and for ivory, elephants now must struggle for their survival.
11. An adult elephant needs to eat about 300 pounds of food a day.
12. The elephant needs to search constantly for food.
13. Weighing about 200 pounds, a newborn elephant stands about 3 feet tall.
14. The adults form a circle around their offspring to protect them from predators.
15. Young elephants amuse themselves by playing with each other.
16. Traveling to many water holes each day, elephants spend a lot of time in and around water.
17. Splashing themselves with muddy water keeps elephants cool.
18. Elephants love to swim in fresh water and are excellent swimmers.
19. Most wild Asian elephants, protected by regional governments, live on preserves.
20. Large predators avoid attacking adult elephants because of their size.

Using Verbal Phrases

On your paper use each of the following verbal phrases in an original sentence. Write whether each phrase is a *participial phrase*, a *gerund phrase*, or an *infinitive phrase*.

1. blaming us for the loud music
2. to test the speakers
3. playing the drums
4. to annoy the neighbors
5. turning down the speakers
6. listening at the door
7. to play more softly
8. upset by all the commotion
9. to make everyone happy
10. putting pads on the floor

Grammar Review

Phrases

The passage below is taken from a novel by the Japanese American writer Yoshiko Uchida. The novel tells of a young Japanese woman who arrives in San Francisco in 1917 to marry a man whom she has never met. In this passage, she contemplates her fate. The passage has been annotated to show many of the kinds of phrases covered in this unit.

Literature Model

from PICTURE BRIDE

by Yoshiko Uchida

Hana Omiya stood at the railing of the small ship that shuddered toward America in a turbulent November sea. She shivered as she pulled the folds of her silk kimono close to her throat and tightened the wool shawl about her shoulders.

She was thin and small, her dark eyes shadowed in her pale face, her black hair piled high in a pompadour that seemed too heavy for so slight a woman. She clung to the moist rail and breathed the damp salt air deep into her lungs. Her body seemed leaden and lifeless, as though it were simply the vehicle transporting her soul to a strange new life, and she longed with childlike intensity to be home again in Oka Village.

She longed to see the bright persimmon dotting the barren trees beside the thatched roof, to see the fields of golden rice stretching to the mountains where only last fall she had gathered plump white mushrooms, and to see once more the maple trees lacing their flaming colors through the green pine. If only she could see a familiar face, eat a meal without retching, walk on solid ground and stretch out at night on a *tatami* mat instead of in a hard narrow bunk. She thought now of seeking the warm shelter of her bunk but could not bear to face the relentless smell of fish that penetrated the lower decks. ➡

Prepositional phrase
(adjective phrase)

Prepositional phrase
(adverb phrase)

Infinitive phrase

Participial phrase
(adjective phrase)

Gerund phrase
(object of preposition)

Why did I ever leave Japan, she wondered bitterly. Why did I ever listen to my uncle? And yet she knew it was she herself who had begun the chain of events that placed her on this heaving ship. It was she who had first planted in her uncle's mind the thought that she would make a good wife for Taro Takeda, the lonely man who had gone to America to make his fortune in Oakland, California.

Appositive phrase

Exercise 1

Expanding Sentences with Prepositional Phrases   The following sentences describe an imaginary journey on a boat. Read through the sentences quickly to get an idea of the scene. Then rewrite each sentence, adding at least one prepositional phrase—either an adjective phrase or an adverb phrase—to the sentence. You can imagine any scene that you wish.

SAMPLE   The voyage was long and tedious.
ANSWER   The voyage to the new land was long and tedious.

1. The ship rocked violently.
2. The boy watched the dark waves.
3. His hair was tossed.
4. He wore a long scarf.
5. The breeze flushed his cheeks.
6. He carried a small suitcase.
7. He was taking a long trip.
8. The previous night he had slept poorly.
9. The boy ate little.
10. Memories flooded his mind.
11. He felt intense longing.
12. He had left his family.
13. All his friends had stayed behind.
14. The ship was crowded.
15. Many people were traveling.
16. Some men sang songs.
17. Small children played games.
18. Young women chatted.
19. Sailors came and went.
20. The captain appeared only once.
21. The boy sat quietly.
22. He had a faraway look.
23. The ship arrived late.
24. A man greeted the boy.
25. The boy's new life had begun.

Exercise 2

Expanding Sentences with Appositives and Appositive Phrases   The following sentences describe Hana Omiya, the main character of *Picture Bride*. Each sentence is followed by a group of words in parentheses. Rewrite each sentence, incorporating the words in parentheses as an appositive or appositive phrase. Use a comma or commas to set off the appositive or appositive phrase from the rest of the sentence.

SAMPLE   The ship sailed toward San Francisco. (a small steamer)
ANSWER   The ship, a small steamer, sailed toward San Francisco.

 1. A solitary figure stood on the open deck. (a small woman with a shawl)
 2. The woman was traveling to America. (Hana Omiya)
 3. She had left her home and was traveling to meet her future husband. (a small village in Japan)
 4. Her father had died, leaving four daughters and a wife behind. (a prosperous landowner)
 5. Of the four sisters, Hana was the only one without a husband. (the youngest)
 6. Hana's mother was determined to find a match for her. (a practical woman)
 7. The idea that Hana should go to America was suggested by another relative. (Uncle Oji)
 8. Oji knew a Japanese man who had gone to California to seek his fortune. (Taro Takeda)
 9. Taro Takeda had opened a small shop in Oakland. (the son of a friend of Oji's)
10. Oji said that Taro would make a good husband. (a hardworking and honest man)
11. Hana's dark eyes were fixed on the horizon. (a barely perceptible line of blue)
12. The bracing scene contrasted with her mood. (a heavy feeling of dread)
13. Familiar faces filled her mind. (now only distant memories)
14. She yearned to see not the ocean but the graceful persimmons and maples. (the trees of home)
15. The discomforts of the trip were becoming unbearable. (seasickness and unpleasant odors)
16. Even more unbearable was her fear. (a constant companion on the voyage)
17. Another land was to be her new home. (a country with strange people and an unfamiliar language)
18. A man totally unknown to her was to be her husband. (her companion for the rest of her life)
19. His picture offered few clues to his character. (a faded photograph)
20. She was overwhelmed by bitterness. (an emotion unfamiliar to her)
21. She longed for familiar customs. (the simple ceremonies of her homeland)
22. She longed as well for the familiar landmarks of her village. (the carefully cultivated gardens and flaming maple trees)
23. Yet she was being hurled toward America. (an unknown wilderness)
24. Would she ever again see her old home? (Oka Village)
25. Tears streamed from her brimming eyes. (drops of sorrow)

Exercise 3

Expanding Sentences with Participial Phrases   The following sentences relate to Hana Omiya and her life. Each sentence is followed by another sentence in parentheses. Combine the sentences, changing the sentence in parentheses into a participial phrase. Be sure to place the participial phrase near the word that it modifies. Note that some of the sentences may be expanded in more than one way.

SAMPLE   Hana stood on the deck of the ship. (She was shivering in her thin clothes.)
ANSWER   Shivering in her thin clothes, Hana stood on the deck of the ship.

1. The woolen shawl offered little warmth. (The shawl was draped over her shoulders.)
2. Her silk kimono made her look like a bird. (Her kimono was fluttering in the wind.)
3. The sea air was damp and cheerless. (The air was rushing past her face.)
4. Hana recalled the warm colors of her village. (She was gazing absently at the sea.)
5. The memory of familiar faces haunted her. (The faces were filled with goodwill.)
6. She recalled the rice fields. (The rice fields were rustling in the breeze.)
7. She longed to see the orange persimmons. (The persimmons were hanging from the bare trees.)
8. Why was she going to America to marry a man? (The man was unknown to her.)
9. Her uncle had described Taro as decent and hardworking. (Her uncle was speaking eagerly.)
10. Hana had decided to leave Japan. (Hana had been longing for a different kind of life.)
11. Her sisters lived in big cities. (Her sisters were married to merchants.)
12. Their lives were monotonous. (Their lives were filled with routine.)
13. Hana did not want to be a bored wife. (A bored wife is trapped in a dull marriage.)
14. At first Hana had looked forward to a new life. (Her life would be filled with excitement.)
15. She dreaded the future now. (She was plagued with uncertainty.)
16. She had reluctantly boarded the ship. (She was leaving her family behind.)
17. Many passengers had stayed in their quarters. (They were exhausted by the trip.)
18. Hana remained on the deck. (She was not accompanied by even a single friend.)
19. She listened to some Russian travelers. (The Russians were singing of home.)
20. The loneliness was as endless as the sea. (The loneliness was stretching before her.)
21. Family members would have made the journey less terrifying. (They would have provided companionship.)
22. Hana would be alone in America, too. (She would be isolated by language.)
23. She listened to the cries of sea gulls. (The gulls followed the ship.)
24. The cries tore at her heart. (The cries reminded her of abandoned infants.)
25. Hana cried. (She lowered her head.)

Exercise 4

Writing Sentences with Gerund Phrases   The exercise that follows focuses on the lives of immigrants who came from Japan to the United States. Each item consists of a question followed by a phrase in parentheses that answers the question. For each item write a sentence that answers the question, using the words in parentheses as a gerund phrase. Note that some of the sentences may be reworded in several ways.

SAMPLE   What is painful? (leaving one's homeland)
ANSWER   Leaving one's homeland is painful.

1. In the late nineteenth century, what was difficult in Japan? (earning a living)
2. What seemed like a good idea? (moving to the United States)
3. What was a first step for many poor immigrants? (signing a work contract)
4. What was impossible for early Japanese immigrants? (becoming an American citizen)
5. What did many Japanese immigrants find practical? (living in California)
6. What was a common job for Japanese families who moved to California? (picking grapes)
7. What did many Japanese immigrants have to accept? (working for low wages)
8. What was a goal for many of them? (owning property)
9. How did many Japanese immigrants survive? (applying skills learned in their native land)
10. What did one Japanese immigrant begin doing? (growing rice on wasteland)
11. What is now an important industry in California? (cultivating rice)
12. How did other Japanese immigrants earn a living? (fishing for abalone, tuna, and sardines)
13. What enterprise did some Japanese families in California develop? (extracting salt from sea water)
14. How did many Japanese businesspeople survive? (banding together in associations)
15. What was one goal of the associations? (lending money to members)
16. As more Japanese families arrived, what became a part of their lives? (maintaining a sense of their cultural heritage)
17. What became prevalent in many parts of the West? (segregating Japanese schools and communities)
18. What helped keep their heritage alive? (wearing traditional dress for special occasions)
19. What was one particularly important tradition? (practicing the ancient tea ceremony)
20. What was another means of preserving cultural ties? (singing traditional songs)
21. What was the only way to cross the ocean before the invention of the airplane? (traveling by boat)
22. What provided the Japanese with a healthy supply of protein? (fishing the ocean waters)
23. What enabled Japanese immigrants to continue to enjoy seaweed, a Japanese staple? (living near an ocean)
24. Over what issue did some Japanese young people in the United States begin to disagree with their elders? (keeping to the traditional ways)
25. What is one value that has enabled many Japanese Americans to succeed? (working hard)

Exercise 5

Writing Sentences with Infinitive Phrases The exercise that follows describes some cultural characteristics and practices of Japanese immigrants to the United States early in the twentieth century. Each of the items consists of a question followed by a phrase in parentheses that answers the question. For each item write a sentence that answers the question, using the words in parentheses as an infinitive phrase.

SAMPLE   What did many Japanese immigrants to the United States hope to do?
(to start a new life in the new land)

ANSWER   Many Japanese immigrants to the United States hoped to start a new life in the new land.

1. What did many Japanese men want to do? (to get married)
2. What was difficult in the United States? (to find a Japanese bride)
3. What did some men return to Japan to do? (to seek a wife)
4. What did other men ask their parents in Japan to do? (to send them a suitable woman for a wife)
5. What did a friend usually agree to do? (to arrange the marriage)
6. What was the young wife forced to do? (to face her frightening and uncertain future with courage)
7. What did the wife need to do? (to travel to America alone)
8. What was wrenching for the picture brides? (to leave their families and their familiar villages behind)
9. What did most wives expect to do in the United States? (to work hard)
10. What did most wives hope to do? (to find economic security)
11. What were Japanese taught as small children? (to control their feelings)
12. What was considered to be proper public conduct for Japanese women? (to be shy and retiring)
13. How was a Japanese wife supposed to act toward her husband? (to act quiet and obedient)
14. What was considered to be a fate worse than death? (to be disgraced)
15. What did Japanese farmers expect their children to do? (to work in the fields)
16. What was the purpose of the large bowl-like hats worn by Japanese fishers? (to protect the head from the sun and ocean spray)
17. What was the reason behind the Japanese custom of removing shoes upon entering the home? (to avoid damaging the floor mats)
18. What did the large windows in Japanese living rooms allow the members of the family to do? (to view the garden outside)
19. What was one thing that Japanese girls liked to do on holidays? (to wear brightly colored kimonos)
20. What was the purpose of cultivating the silkworm in Japan? (to make silk fabric)

Exercise 6

Writing Sentences with Verbal Phrases   Use each phrase below in an original sentence about the excerpt from *Picture Bride*. Forms ending with *-ing* may be used in either participial or gerund phrases.

1. standing at the ship's railing
2. to protect herself from the cold sea winds
3. transported to a new country
4. wishing desperately for her home
5. remembering the beauty of the trees and fields
6. to see the face of someone she knew
7. smelling the strong fish odors
8. anguished about her decision to leave
9. influenced by her uncle's words
10. to meet her husband-to-be

Proofreading

Exercise 7

The following passage describes the artist Andō Hiroshige, whose work appears on the opposite page. Rewrite the passage, correcting the errors in spelling, grammar, and usage. Add any missing punctuation. There are twenty-five errors.

Andō Hiroshige

[1]Andō (or Ichiyu-sai) Hiroshige (1797–1858) the son of a fire-brigade chief, came from a moderately wealthy family and he is expected to follow in his fathers footsteps. [2]However, he soon abandoned his post with the fire brigade and begun to study painting.

[3]Unlike painters in Europe and America, Japanese artists of the period painted predetermined images according to Japans' strict rules of representation. [4]Trying a number of pictorial themes Hiroshige finally settled on landscapes birds, and flowers. [5]Abandoning portraiture and historical subjects he focused on nature themes throughout his life.

[6]Making steady artistic progress Hiroshige experimented with printmaking. [7]Began to make wood-block prints in a style called *ukiyo-e*, which, literally translated, means "floating world." [8]These prints was inexpensively mass-produced for popular consumption. [9]Following an artists specific instructions craftspeople made the prints.

[10]The subject matter of the *ukiyo-e* prints were historical events portraits, and landscapes. [11]Sometimes the prints was even used to teach people, mainly young children about some of the specific elements of Japanese culture. [12]Enabling the populace to have art in their homes printmakers produced countless numbers of such prints. [13]These prints popular and inexpensive works at the time, today are quite valuable. ➡

Andō Hiroshige, *Compound of the Tenjin Shrine at Kameido,* **1856**

[14]The artwork on this page, a typical wood-block print is made in the *ukiyo-e* style. [15]Applied with a separate wood block each color is clear and vivid. [16]Hiroshige combined plants, birds, water, and figures crossing a bridge to form a subtly poetic atmosphere in an everyday seen.

[17]To Hana Omiya, the character in Uchida's *Picture Bride* such an image would undoubtedly recall many fond images of Japan and of all things Japanese. [18]Its delicate desine, decorative colors, hanging leaves, and arched bridge would remind her of the world she had left behind.

Mixed Review

Exercise 8

Read the brief biography of Yoshiko Uchida. Then use the facts in the biography and the guidelines in parentheses to expand the sentences.

Yoshiko Uchida

Yoshiko Uchida was born in Alameda, California, in 1921. Her parents, seeking a better life, had moved to America several years before Uchida was born. Her mother, who was an amateur poet, taught Uchida to love words. As a child, Uchida witnessed the struggles of many Japanese Americans. Many of the Japanese Americans spoke little English but ran their own businesses and earned a reputation as hard workers.

When Uchida was about to begin her final college exams, Japan attacked Pearl Harbor, and the United States entered World War II. Soon afterward the Uchidas, along with thousands of other Japanese American families, were moved to relocation camps. At the camp at the Tanforan Race Track in California, Uchida's family lived in a horse stall; they spent five months there. Uchida spent three years in the grim, dusty camps.

After the war Uchida studied education and taught in a Philadelphia school. She later left her teaching job and traveled to Japan, where she collected folktales and visited her ancestors' tombs. After learning a great deal about Japanese culture, she returned to California and dedicated herself to writing fiction. Uchida has written mostly for children; *Picture Bride* is her first novel for adults. It appeared in 1987.

1. Yoshiko Uchida was born in 1921. (Add an appositive phrase.)
2. Her parents came to America. (Add an infinitive phrase.)
3. Uchida's mother taught her to love words. (Add an appositive phrase.)
4. As a child, Uchida observed many Japanese immigrants. (Add a participial phrase.)
5. Most of them knew few words. (Add an adjective phrase.)
6. Many of the immigrants earned a living. (Add a participial phrase.)
7. The immigrants earned a reputation. (At the end of the sentence, add the preposition *for* and a gerund phrase.)
8. The United States entered World War II. (Add an adverb phrase.)
9. When Pearl Harbor was attacked, Uchida was studying. (Add an adverb phrase.)
10. The Uchidas were sent to the Tanforan Race Track. (Add an appositive phrase.)
11. Thousands were sent to the camps. (Add an adjective phrase.)
12. Uchida's entire family lived in a stall. (Add an adjective phrase.)
13. Uchida lived in the camps. (Add an adverb phrase.)
14. After the war Uchida studied. (Add an infinitive phrase.)
15. She taught school. (Add an adverb phrase.)
16. Later she decided to stop and travel to Japan. (Add a gerund or a gerund phrase.)
17. She went to Japan. (Add an infinitive phrase.)
18. After she returned, she made a decision. (Add an infinitive phrase.)
19. Most is written for children. (Add an adjective phrase.)
20. *Picture Bride* was published in 1987. (Add an appositive phrase.)

Writing Application

Phrases in Writing Note how Mary Stewart uses appositives, participles, and prepositional phrases to enliven this passage from *The Crystal Cave.* As you read, pay particular attention to the italicized words.

> *Behind me* the flow *of bats* had ceased, and the cave was still. *Reassured*, I stayed where I was, *studying myself with interest in the mirror.* My mother had had one once, *an antique from Egypt*, but then, *deeming such things to be vanity*, she had locked it away. Of course I had often seen my face *reflected in water*, but never my body *mirrored*, till now. I saw a dark boy, wary, all eyes *with curiosity, nerves, and excitement. In that light* my eyes looked quite black; my hair was black, too. . . .

Techniques with Phrases Try to apply some of Mary Stewart's techniques as you write and revise your own work.

1. Use prepositional phrases to pinpont location as well as to add specific detail to your sentences. Compare the following:

Imprecise versions The flow of bats had ceased. My eyes looked quite black.
Stewart's versions *Behind me* the flow of bats had ceased. . . . *In that light* my eyes looked quite black. . . .

2. Use appositives to combine short, choppy sentences.

Choppy version My mother had had one once. It was an antique from Egypt.
Stewart's version My mother had had one once, *an antique from Egypt* . . .

3. Use participles and participial phrases to connect ideas and show the relationships between them.

Unclear version I was reassured. I stayed where I was. I studied myself with interest.
Stewart's version *Reassured*, I stayed where I was, *studying myself with interest* . . .

Practice Revise the following passage by adding prepositional phrases to show location and by combining choppy sentences with appositives and participles.

Vinland, or Wineland, is an area of North America. It is believed to have been along the coast. The Vikings probably explored this part before other Europeans did. The Vikings were courageous and skillful. The Vikings began to send ships in about the year 1000. They established no settlements. Leif Eriksson was probably sailing from Norway to Greenland. His ship was blown off course. He came to a land. It had first been sighted a few years earlier by another Viking.

13.1 Main Clauses

A **clause** is a group of words that has a subject and a predicate and is used as a part of a sentence. A **main,** or **independent, clause** has a subject and a predicate and can stand alone as a sentence.

Every sentence must have at least one main clause, but a sentence may have more than one. In each of the following examples, both clauses can stand alone, so both are main, or independent, clauses.

Both the subject and verb of a main clause may be compound.

Exercise 1   Identifying Main Clauses

Copy the following sentences, and underline each main clause. Then write *S* below each subject and *V* below each verb. Be sure that each clause you mark can stand alone as a sentence.

1. The lights dimmed, and the curtain rose.
2. The setting was a magnificent living room, and the audience applauded the sight.
3. Elegantly dressed people entered and spoke, and the host greeted them.
4. One man sat alone by the fire, and several guests and the host talked with him.
5. The butler announced dinner, but the seated man nodded and slumped in his chair.

13.2 | Subordinate Clauses

A **subordinate**, or **dependent**, **clause** has a subject and a predicate, but it cannot stand alone as a sentence.

A subordinate clause must be attached to a main clause in order for it to make sense. Subordinate clauses frequently begin with subordinating conjunctions or relative pronouns. When the subordinate clause comes first, a comma separates it from the main clause.

In the first example, the subordinating conjunction *when* placed before *the audience applauded* creates a word group—*when the audience applauded*—that cannot stand alone as a main clause. Although the clause has a subject and a predicate, it does not express a complete thought.

In the second example, the relative pronoun *who* begins a subordinate clause that comes between the subject and the verb of the main clause. *Who* also serves as the subject of the subordinate clause.

Exercise 2 | Identifying Main and Subordinate Clauses

In each of the following sentences, the first clause appears in italics. On your paper write *main clause* or *subordinate clause* to identify the first clause. (Remember that a subordinate clause cannot stand alone as a sentence.)

Romana Bañuelos, a United States Treasurer

[1]*Romana Acosta Bañuelos was treasurer of the United States from 1971 to 1974*, while Richard Nixon was President. [2]*Though many others have held this position*, Bañuelos was the first Mexican American woman in such a high government post. [3]*Her signature became a familiar sight*, since the treasurer's name is printed on all paper currency. [4]*Because it involves a number of diverse tasks*, the job of treasurer is a challenging one. [5]*When Bañuelos was in office*, she wrote checks for all government agencies. [6]*Whenever currency became worn out*, she oversaw the destruction and replacement of the bills.

[7]*Although Bañuelos grew up in Mexico*, she was born in Arizona. [8]*After she invested in a small tortilla stand in 1949*, the business grew into a 5-million-dollar food company. [9]*Because her tortilla company had become such a success*, Bañuelos undertook another challenge. [10]*In 1964 she founded the Pan-American National Bank of East Los Angeles*, which was the first bank in the United States run by a Mexican American.

13.3 Simple and Compound Sentences

A **simple sentence** has only one main clause and no subordinate clauses.

A simple sentence may have a compound subject or a compound predicate or both. The simple subject and the simple predicate may also be expanded in many other ways. Adjectives, adverbs, prepositional phrases, appositives, and verbal phrases may make some simple sentences seem anything but simple. Nevertheless, as long as the sentence has only one main clause and no subordinate clauses, it remains a simple sentence.

Bobcats stalk. [simple sentence]

Bobcats and lynxes stalk. [simple sentence with compound subject]

Bobcats stalk and pounce. [simple sentence with compound predicate]

Bobcats and lynxes stalk and pounce. [simple sentence with compound subject and compound predicate]

Bobcats silently stalk their prey during the night. [simple sentence expanded with modifiers]

A **compound sentence** has two or more main clauses and no subordinate clauses.

As the following examples show, each main clause of a compound sentence has its own subject and predicate. Notice that the main clauses of a compound sentence are usually joined by a comma and a coordinating conjunction, such as *and, but, or, nor, yet, so,* or *for.*

MAIN CLAUSE 1	MAIN CLAUSE 2

Bobcats stalk, and lynxes pursue.
   S   V   S   V

MAIN CLAUSE 1	MAIN CLAUSE 2	MAIN CLAUSE 3

Bobcats stalk, and lynxes pursue, but house cats slink.
   S   V   S   V   S   V

Two main clauses may also be joined by a semicolon to form a compound sentence.

MAIN CLAUSE 1	MAIN CLAUSE 2

The frightened rabbit ran swiftly; the lynx followed at a close pace.

Identifying Simple and Compound Sentences

Write *simple* or *compound* to identify each sentence.

Climbing Mount Everest

1. Sir Edmund Hillary and Tenzing Norgay, his Sherpa guide, were the first conquerors of Mount Everest.
2. Norgay was already a well-known mountaineer, but Hillary's experience had been limited to climbing in ice and snow in New Zealand.
3. Hillary took photographs of Norgay at the summit, but none of Hillary were taken.
4. Hillary, Norgay, and all the other members of the expedition looked for the easiest and safest route to the top of Mount Everest.
5. Today climbers look for greater challenges and choose the more difficult routes.
6. Hillary once had traveled overland to the South Pole and also had followed the Ganges River to its source.
7. The public and the media had shown considerable interest in Hillary.
8. Fame came with Hillary's successful ascent of Mount Everest, and afterward he raised money for the Sherpa people of Nepal.
9. They had helped Hillary, and in return he generously helped them.
10. Hillary gave lectures and raised funds for schools, hospitals, clinics, bridges, water pipelines, and airstrips in Nepal.

Exercise 4   **Writing Simple Sentences**

Combine each pair of ideas below into a simple sentence. Remember that each sentence must have only one main clause, although it may have a compound subject and/or a compound predicate.

SAMPLE   Arctic explorers are brave. They must receive special training.
ANSWER   Arctic explorers are brave but must receive special training.

1. Robert E. Peary was a brave man. He explored arctic regions.
2. He made his first expedition to Greenland in 1886. Later he made several other trips there.
3. Peary planned a trip to the North Pole. He announced his plans in 1898.
4. He made the trip with his assistant, Matthew Henson. Peary's team also included four Inuit.
5. Peary succeeded in reaching his goal. He arrived at the North Pole on April 6, 1909.

Exercise 5   **Writing Compound Sentences**

Use the information in each item from Exercise 4 to write a compound sentence. Remember that each sentence must have two or more main clauses joined by a comma and a coordinating conjunction or by a semicolon.

SAMPLE   Arctic explorers are brave. They must receive special training.
ANSWER   Arctic explorers are brave, but they must receive special training.

13.4 Complex and Compound-Complex Sentences

A **complex sentence** has one main clause and one or more subordinate clauses.

MAIN CLAUSE	SUBORDINATE CLAUSE

Some areas become deforested because people need wood for fuel.
   S   V   S   V

SUBORDINATE CLAUSE   MAIN CLAUSE

Because people need fuel, they cut down trees
        S   V   S   V

SUBORDINATE CLAUSE

that have grown for many years.
  S   V

A **compound-complex sentence** has more than one main clause and at least one subordinate clause.

MAIN CLAUSE   MAIN CLAUSE

Campers need fuel for cooking, but they should use stoves
    S   V   S   V

SUBORDINATE CLAUSE

that require no wood.
  S   V

Exercise 6   Identifying Subordinate Clauses

Write the subordinate clause in each of the following sentences. If a sentence has no subordinate clause, write *none*.

1. Since the world's supply of wood is limited, environmentalists encourage conservation of timber resources.
2. The United States government controls large areas of national forest and sets the policy for use of the timber.
3. Many states have set aside land for state forests, which may also be used for recreation.
4. People's ideas about forest conservation differ, and opposing groups present arguments that deserve serious consideration.
5. Because opinions on the subject are so different, no simple solution exists.

Identifying Complex and Compound-Complex Sentences

Write the subordinate clause that appears in each of the following sentences. Then write *complex* or *compound-complex* to identify each sentence.

Conservation

1. Energy conservation has become extremely important because millions of energy-consuming devices are in use every day.
2. When builders construct new homes, they should install solar panels and other passive solar devices and as many energy-saving appliances as possible.
3. Although energy-efficient appliances cost more, their use results in long-term savings for the owner, and the environment benefits, too.
4. Because legislators have enacted certain laws, all new cars must be energy efficient.
5. When cars use less gas, the air is cleaner, and people may have less trouble breathing.
6. Though sulfur pollution is a threat to human health, it also damages lakes, wildlife, and buildings.
7. Although water power can generate electricity, hydroelectric dams may cause floods on farmland, in forests, and in wildlife areas.
8. We must always find ways of producing more goods, but at the same time we must reduce the amount of energy that we consume in producing those goods.
9. Conservation and solar power are the keys to a safe future, so we must cautiously use the devices that cool, heat, and transport us.
10. Because our natural resources clearly cannot last forever, we must find better ways of conserving them.

Exercise 8   **Writing Four Kinds of Sentences**

Use your own knowledge and the information below to create four different kinds of sentences about electrical power. Write *simple, compound, complex,* or *compound-complex* to identify each sentence you write.

An electric motor is a source of power.   It can power a speeding train.
It is convenient.   It can run a tiny watch.
It is clean.   Power can come through a wire from an outside source.
It is silent.   Power can come from a battery.
It starts instantly.   An electric car does not pollute.
It stops instantly.   It is expensive to manufacture.
It can be built in almost any size.   It needs frequent recharging.

Exercise 9   **Creating Sentences with Various Structures**

Write a simple sentence. Then rework it, making it into a compound sentence. Now go back to the simple sentence, and rework it to make it part of a complex sentence. Finally, rework your compound sentence into a compound-complex sentence. Label each sentence.

13.5 Adjective Clauses

An **adjective clause** is a subordinate clause that modifies a noun or a pronoun.

An adjective clause normally follows the word it modifies.

The hikers **who reached the peak** were overjoyed.

The trail, **which was rarely used,** had been a difficult one.

I forgot about the blisters **that covered my feet.**

The hiker **whom we appreciated most** carried the food.

The hikers, who were diverted by the natural splendor, arrived later in the day.

Both relative pronouns (*who, whom, whose, that,* and *which*) and the words *where* and *when* may begin adjective clauses.

I will always remember the time **when I hiked to Pike's Peak.**
That is the spot **where we set up camp.**

Sometimes the relative pronoun is dropped at the beginning of an adjective clause.

Our camp was the place **every hiker loved the most.**
[The relative pronoun *that* has been omitted.]

An adjective clause is sometimes essential to a sentence; that is, it is needed to make the meaning of the sentence clear. This kind of adjective clause is called an *essential clause,* or a *restrictive clause.*

One characteristic **that many Native Americans had in common** was a love of dancing. [essential clause]

An adjective clause that is *not* needed to make the meaning of a sentence clear is called a *nonessential clause,* or a *nonrestrictive clause.* It adds information to a sentence, but the sentence would be perfectly logical without it. (Note that a nonessential clause must be set off with commas.)

The Iroquois people of the East, **who were farmers,** thanked the spirits for the gift of food. [nonessential clause]

In the Southwest, **where water is scarce,** the Pueblo people performed rain dances. [nonessential clause]

When choosing between *that* and *which*, use *that* to introduce an essential clause and *which* to begin a nonessential clause.

The Cheyenne hunted buffalo, **which supplied them with meat and skins for clothing and shelter.** [nonessential clause]

The animal **that was most important to the Cheyenne** was the buffalo. [essential clause]

Exercise 10   Identifying Adjective Clauses and the Words They Modify

On your paper write the adjective clause from each sentence. Then write the word the clause modifies. (In one sentence the relative pronoun has been dropped.)

International Dances

1. The Pueblo rain dancers wore outfits with symbols that represented lightning, thunder, clouds, and rainbows.
2. In the eagle dance, the dancers' movements are like those of the eagle, which swoops and dives for its food.
3. Chinese schoolchildren learn dances that require difficult body movements.
4. The Chinese ribbon dance, which has been performed for thousands of years, is often danced with red ribbons.
5. Red, which signifies happiness and good fortune in China, is the favorite ribbon color.
6. A lively dance that is very popular is the square dance.
7. Probably the best-known early American dance is the Virginia reel, which became popular in George Washington's time.
8. Flamenco is a dance form the Gypsies in Spain invented.
9. A flamenco dancer, who is accompanied by a guitarist, typically wears bright and colorful clothing.
10. Folk dances often require steps that are difficult to learn.

Exercise 11   Adding Adjective Clauses to Sentences

On your paper complete each sentence below by adding a noun. Then write an adjective clause to modify the noun.

1. My favorite meal is _____.
2. I will always remember _____.
3. Did you see the _____?
4. I really don't like the _____.
5. I had forgotten all about the _____.
6. Where did you get the _____?
7. Tomorrow I will pick up the _____.
8. This is the _____.
9. Last week I visited _____.
10. We laughed about the _____.

Identifying Essential and Nonessential Clauses

For each sentence in the following pairs, write the adjective clause, and then write *essential* or *nonessential* to identify it.

Sacajuwea Hunter, Olympic Champion

1. a. Sacajuwea Hunter, who lost her legs at an early age, competed in the 1984 Olympics.
  b. One young athlete who competed in the 1984 Olympics lost her legs at an early age.
2. a. She was one of eight disabled women who competed in the 800-meter wheelchair exhibition race.
  b. Sacajuwea Hunter, who competed in the 1984 Olympics, was one of eight disabled women in the 800-meter wheelchair exhibition race.
3. a. Nearly 100,000 people watched the 800-meter wheelchair exhibition race, which was the first such event in Olympic history.
  b. An event that nearly 100,000 people watched was the 800-meter wheelchair exhibition race.
4. a. Bill Greene, who was Sacajuwea Hunter's special-education counselor, urged her to race.
  b. The man who was Sacajuwea Hunter's special-education counselor urged her to race.
5. a. Sacajuwea Hunter, who at 14 was the youngest American in the 1984 Olympics, finished in fourth place overall.
  b. Sacajuwea Hunter was the youngest American athlete who competed in the 1984 Olympics.

Identifying Adjective Clauses

Rewrite the sentences below. Underline each adjective clause. If a clause is nonessential, set it off with commas.

1. In most cultures around the world, people have dances that they use to tell stories.
2. Often the dancers who may wear colorful costumes are accompanied by singing, chanting, or playing of special instruments.
3. Many immigrants who moved to the United States from Europe, Africa, Asia, and South America brought their dances with them.
4. The dances that came from England, Ireland, and Scotland became the basis for American square dancing.
5. Native Americans who are descendants of the earliest inhabitants of this continent still perform colorful ceremonial dances of their own.

13.6 Adverb Clauses

An **adverb clause** is a subordinate clause that modifies a verb, an adjective, or an adverb. It tells *when, where, how, why, to what extent,* or *under what conditions.*

Whenever it rains, the river rises. [The adverb clause modifies the verb *rises.* It tells *when.*]

This canoe can take us **wherever we want to go.** [The adverb clause modifies the verb phrase *can take.* It tells *where.*]

The canoe will be safe **as long as everyone remains seated.** [The adverb clause modifies the adjective *safe.* It tells *under what condition.*]

You are paddling harder **than I am paddling.** [The adverb clause modifies the adverb *harder.* It tells *to what extent.*]

Subordinating conjunctions, such as those listed on page 439, introduce adverb clauses. Being familiar with those conjunctions will help you recognize adverb clauses.

An adverb clause may come either before or after the main clause. Notice how the comma is used when the adverb clause begins the sentence.

The canoe capsized **when the river got rough.**
When the river got rough, the canoe capsized.

Occasionally words may be left out of an adverb clause. The omitted words can easily be supplied because they are understood, or implied. Such adverb clauses are described as *elliptical.*

You are paddling harder **than I am [paddling].**
Paddling made me more tired **than [it made] him [tired].**

Identifying Adverb Clauses

Write the adverb clauses that appear in the following sentences. (Three sentences have more than one adverb clause.)

Yo-Yo Ma, an Outstanding Cellist

 1. Yo-Yo Ma first played the cello on national television in 1962, although he was only seven years old at the time.
 2. Because he had such talent, young Ma already played better than most adults do.
 3. When Ma was only four, his father gave him cello lessons.
 4. His father made a special cello from a viola, since a regular cello was too big for Ma at the time.
 5. When he was big enough, Ma switched to a regular cello.
 6. After his family moved from Paris to New York, Ma studied at the Juilliard School of Music.
 7. Wherever he played, Ma dazzled audiences with his deftness.
 8. Ma continued on the cello while he worked on a degree in the humanities.
 9. A highlight in his career came in 1978, when Ma received the Avery Fisher Prize for his musical talent.
10. Whenever Ma performs, fans can hardly imagine a cellist more talented than he.
11. When Ma played with the Chicago Symphony last year, I saw him in person.
12. The tickets were more expensive than I had expected.
13. Many people attended that evening because Ma's performance earlier that week had received rave reviews.
14. Before Ma appeared on stage, everyone waited impatiently as the orchestra tuned up their instruments.
15. When the great performer finally made his entrance, the audience jumped to their feet and applauded.

Exercise 15   **Using Adverb Clauses in Sentences**

Use each of the following adverb clauses in an original sentence. Vary the positions of the clauses in your sentences.

 1. whenever the first members of the audience arrive
 2. as long as I can hear from the back of the auditorium
 3. unless something happens at the last minute
 4. although she still used her father's old stereo system
 5. because the traffic was so heavy that night
 6. considering that no one was given information beforehand
 7. until everyone finds a place to sit down
 8. before the master of ceremonies could say a single word
 9. since I had decided earlier not to go with them
10. wherever people get together to hear fine music

A **noun clause** is a subordinate clause used as a noun.

You can use a noun clause as a subject, a direct object, an indirect object, an object of a preposition, or a predicate nominative.

NOUN

Campers enjoy the outdoors.
S

NOUN CLAUSE

Whoever camps enjoys the outdoors.
S

NOUN

Footgear affects hikers.
DO

NOUN CLAUSE

Footgear affects whoever walks often.
DO

In the preceding examples, notice that each noun clause is an inseparable part of the sentence's main clause; the main clause is the entire sentence.

Here are some of the words that can be used to introduce noun clauses:

how	when	who, whom
that	where	whoever
what	which	whose
whatever	whichever	why

Here are additional examples of noun clauses.

I do not know **where my hiking boots are**. [direct object]

That is **why I did not join the others**. [predicate nominative]

We will make do with **whatever camping equipment we can borrow**. [object of a preposition]

Sometimes the relative pronoun may be dropped at the beginning of a noun clause.

I believe **we can have a great time outdoors**. [The relative pronoun *that* is omitted.]

Identifying Noun Clauses

Write the noun clauses that appear in each of the following sentences. (Three of the sentences have two noun clauses each. In two sentences the relative pronoun introducing the noun clause has been dropped.)

The Importance of Police Dogs

1. Everyone knows that dogs have a keen sense of smell.
2. What makes their sense of smell valuable is that people can train dogs to sniff out explosives.
3. Specially trained dogs search for whatever explosive device they can find.
4. What the dog finds may save whoever is in danger.
5. Do you believe that police dogs are valuable?
6. Whoever works with a police dog is trained along with the dog.
7. Many police officers say that police dogs make good partners.
8. Whoever says police dogs are vicious animals is misinformed.
9. That these dogs become aggressive upon command is true.
10. Police officers are grateful for whatever help these dogs provide.
11. Most people realize that police dogs will not attack them without cause.
12. They will pay little attention to whoever leaves them alone.
13. The laws of some communities state that police dogs should be muzzled.
14. Another regulation is that they should usually be on leashes.
15. Can you see why their appearance frightens some people?

Exercise 17 **Identifying Subordinate Clauses**

On your paper write the subordinate clause that appears in each sentence. Then write *adverb clause, adjective clause,* or *noun clause* to identify what kind of clause it is.

Sojourner Truth, a Crusader for Justice

[1] Sojourner Truth was a slave who was born in New York in the late eighteenth century. [2] Isabella is what she was called as a child. [3] Whoever has studied her life understands the importance of her work. [4] She fought against slavery wherever she went. [5] When an antislavery law was passed in New York in 1828, Isabella gained her freedom. [6] In 1843, after she took the name Sojourner Truth, she began a series of lecture tours throughout New England and the Midwest. [7] Her speeches expressed her strong belief that all people are equal. [8] She supported herself with proceeds from her biography, which was published in 1850. [9] Sojourner Truth campaigned for a state in the Midwest where freed slaves could have a land of their own. [10] Sojourner Truth was a woman whom everyone admired.

Exercise 18 **Writing Subordinate Clauses in Sentences**

Write four original sentences. In the first, use an adverb clause. In the second, use an adjective clause. In the third, use a noun clause as a subject. In the fourth, use a noun clause as a direct object. Label the clauses.

13.8 Four Kinds of Sentences

A **declarative sentence** makes a statement.

> An owl is hooting.
> I cannot see it.

A declarative sentence normally ends with a period. It is the type of sentence used most frequently in speaking and writing.

An **imperative sentence** gives a command or makes a request.

> Look at that bird.
> Please tell me what it is.

An imperative sentence usually ends with a period. The subject "you" is understood.

An **interrogative sentence** asks a question.

> What kind of bird is that?
> Is the hawk hunting for prey?

An interrogative sentence ends with a question mark.

An **exclamatory sentence** expresses strong emotion.

> Watch out for that hawk's sudden dive!
> What a powerful hunter the hawk is!

An exclamatory sentence ends with an exclamation point.

Exercise 19   Identifying and Punctuating Four Kinds of Sentences

On your paper write *declarative, imperative, interrogative,* or *exclamatory* to identify each sentence below. Then give the correct ending punctuation.

1. Have you ever been to Niagara Falls
2. What an awesome sight they are
3. The falls are on the Niagara River between New York State and Ontario, Canada
4. When you go, I hope that you plan to visit both the American and the Canadian sides
5. Don't miss the boat ride on the *Maid of the Mist*

Exercise 20   Writing Four Kinds of Sentences

Write four sentences about a recent school event. Use one declarative, one imperative, one interrogative, and one exclamatory sentence. Remember to punctuate each sentence correctly.

13.9 Sentence Fragments

A **sentence fragment** is an error that occurs when an incomplete sentence is punctuated as though it were a complete sentence. In general, avoid sentence fragments in your writing.

When you check your work for sentence fragments, look for three things. First, be alert for a group of words that lacks a subject. Then, look for a group of words that lacks a verb, especially a group that contains a verbal form rather than a complete verb. Finally, be careful that you have not punctuated a subordinate clause as a complete sentence.

Often you can correct a sentence fragment by joining it to an idea that comes before or after the fragment. Sometimes, however, you may need to add missing words to form a complete sentence.

FRAGMENT	Toshiko and Kenji are happy together. **Seem to be in love.** [lacks subject]
COMPLETE SENTENCE	Toshiko and Kenji are happy together, and they seem to be in love.
FRAGMENT	The two will marry. **Their new life together.** [lacks verb]
COMPLETE SENTENCE	The two will marry, and their new life together will begin.
FRAGMENT	They are planning an out-of-town wedding. **Many of their gifts arriving in the mail.** [lacks complete verb]
COMPLETE SENTENCE	They are planning an out-of-town wedding. Many of their gifts have been arriving in the mail.
FRAGMENT	On their honeymoon they will be traveling to Italy. **Which they both love.** [has subordinate clause only]
COMPLETE SENTENCE	On their honeymoon they will be traveling to Italy, which they both love.

Greek,
Nike of Samothrace,
200–190 B.C.

Professional writers sometimes use sentence fragments to create a special effect—to add emphasis to what they are saying or to convey realistic dialogue. Remember that professionals use sentence fragments *carefully* and *intentionally*. In most of the writing you do, however, including your writing for school, you should avoid sentence fragments.

Identifying Sentence Fragments

Write on your paper *complete sentence* or *sentence fragment* to identify each of the items below.

The Piñata Game

¹Children in Mexico often celebrate festivals and birthdays with parties. ²By breaking a colorful piñata. ³An earthenware or papier-mâché container covered with crepe-paper streamers. ⁴A piñata is often shaped like an animal or a person. ⁵Filled with nuts, candy, and small toys, it is hung by a rope from the ceiling. ⁶Or—if the party is outdoors—from a tree limb. ⁷The blindfolded children take turns hitting the piñata with a stick. ⁸Not always easy, because an adult raises and lowers the piñata with a rope. ⁹Finally, after many attempts, the break. ¹⁰Children rush to collect the treats scattered about.

Exercise 22 **Correcting Sentence Fragments**

Revise the preceding paragraph by correcting each fragment. Whenever possible, combine the fragments with other sentences in the paragraph.

Exercise 23 **Identifying and Correcting Sentence Fragments**

Add your own words and phrases to rewrite each item that is not a sentence as a complete sentence. Change wording if you need to. For any item that is already a sentence, write *sentence*.

1. Jack and Kera help with the cooking for the family.
2. After they get home from school or on the weekends.
3. Soup, pasta, and grilled cheese sandwiches.
4. Which they like the best.
5. Planning the menu or the grocery shopping.
6. The oven and the stove being broken.
7. To fix cold foods and use the toaster and microwave.
8. Because he was too impatient to wait for the electrician.
9. Juice, pancakes, waffles, and muffins, the favorites for Sunday breakfast.
10. Enjoys fixing special dishes for birthdays and holidays.
11. They both enjoy cooking together.
12. Especially like to make dinner for their parents
13. When their parents let them prepare the whole meal.
14. Whenever they have a chance to help make the refreshments for a party.
15. The twins are especially happy after cleaning up.

13.10 Run-on Sentences

Avoid run-on sentences in your writing. A **run-on sentence** is two or more complete sentences written as though they were one sentence.

There are three basic kinds of run-on sentence.

1. A **comma splice,** probably the most common type of run-on sentence, occurs when two main clauses are separated by a comma rather than a period or a semicolon. To correct this type of run-on, replace the comma with a period (or other end mark of punctuation), and start the new sentence with a capital letter. You can also correct this error by adding a coordinating conjunction after the comma.

RUN-ON	Luis and Fredericka are going to Washington, D.C., with their school, they are very excited.
CORRECT	Luis and Fredericka are going to Washington, D.C., with their school. They are very excited.
CORRECT	Luis and Fredericka are going to Washington, D.C., with their school, **and** they are very excited.

2. Another kind of run-on sentence occurs when two main clauses are written with *no* punctuation between them. To correct this type of run-on, separate the main clauses with an end mark of punctuation or with a semicolon. Still another way to correct the error is to add a comma and a coordinating conjunction between the main clauses.

RUN-ON	They hope to see many famous sights the Lincoln Memorial will surely be among them.
CORRECT	They hope to see many famous sights; the Lincoln Memorial will surely be among them.
CORRECT	They hope to see many famous sights, **and** the Lincoln Memorial will surely be among them.

3. Still another kind of run-on sentence occurs when the comma is omitted before a coordinating conjunction joining two main clauses. To correct this error, simply add the comma before the coordinating conjunction.

RUN-ON	Fredericka and Luis will need to take notes for a written report on their Washington trip but they plan to have fun anyway.
CORRECT	Fredericka and Luis will need to take notes for a written report on their Washington trip, but they plan to have fun anyway.

Distinguishing Between Run-ons and Correct Sentences

On your paper write *correct* or *run-on* to identify each sentence below.

The Amazon River and the Nile River

1. The Amazon River is 3,900 miles (6,280 km) long it is the second longest river in the world.
2. The river flows generally eastward across northern South America and into the Atlantic Ocean through a wide delta in northern Brazil.
3. The Amazon is formed by the junction of two rivers in Peru, the Ucayali and the Marañón.
4. The Amazon has more than 500 tributaries and its river system drains 40 percent of South America.
5. Ships can travel almost the entire length of the river, it has no rapids or waterfalls to obstruct traffic.
6. The Nile is the world's longest river; it flows about 4,160 miles (6,695 km) from its headwaters in Burundi to the Mediterranean Sea.
7. The main part of the river is formed by the joining of two rivers, the Blue Nile and the White Nile.
8. The Blue Nile begins at Lake Tana it flows 1,000 miles to Khartoum.
9. The White Nile is 2,300 miles long, and its source is Lake Victoria.
10. The Blue and the White Nile converge at the city of Khartoum, which is the capital of Sudan.
11. Khartoum was founded as a camp for the Egyptian army in 1821 and developed into a major trading center.
12. Above Khartoum the Nile makes a huge S-curve and then it flows north through Egypt.
13. The Nile valley in Egypt was the location of a great ancient civilization, the tombs of kings and many other historic monuments are preserved there.
14. Dams on the Nile in Egypt have created a water supply for irrigating crops; the dams also produce hydroelectric power for the region.
15. Beyond Cairo the river forms an enormous triangular delta, here the river slows and drops much of its load of sediment before it flows into the sea.

Exercise 25   **Correcting Run-on Sentences by Adding Commas**

Correct each run-on sentence below by adding a comma before the coordinating conjunction.

1. Wilbur Wright was born in Dayton, Ohio, in 1867 and his brother Orville was born in 1871.
2. They ran a weekly newspaper together and then they started a bicycle manufacturing business.
3. The brothers read about aeronautics and they experimented with gliders.
4. Kitty Hawk, North Carolina, had long expanses of rolling sand dunes and the winds there were quite steady and dependable.
5. The Wright brothers tested their gliders on the dunes of Kitty Hawk and in 1903 they made the first powered flight.

Correcting Run-on Sentences with a Period or a Semicolon

Correct each run-on sentence below by adding a period or a semicolon and using correct capitalization.

1. Benjamin Franklin was an important political figure during the period of the American Revolution, he was a man of many other talents as well.
2. He lived in Philadelphia as a young man, there he learned the printing trade.
3. Franklin published an almanac he also experimented with electricity.
4. Franklin started a university, in Philadelphia he also started a lending library.
5. Franklin helped draft the Declaration of Independence he was also one of the signers of the peace treaty that in 1783 formally ended the American Revolution.

Exercise 27 **Correcting Run-on Sentences**

Rewrite the following paragraph, correcting the run-on sentences in any way you wish.

Animal Care in Zoos

[1]The earliest known zoo was established in Egypt around 1500 B.C. a half century later a Chinese emperor built a zoo that covered about 1,500 acres. [2]Today zoo facilities are limited and zookeepers cannot keep every animal on display year-round. [3]In the winter in colder climates, most birds must be brought indoors but zookeepers cannot always keep each bird on view for the public. [4]Many visitors are surprised to see that some animals remain outside all year, penguins, polar bears, bison, and timber wolves are happy outdoors in wintertime. [5]Some animals are always indoors in northern areas, reptiles and small desert animals always have indoor displays. [6]Zookeepers must provide indoor shelters for large animals such as elephants and giraffes how large those shelters must be! [7]Today zoologists understand much more about animal behavior and zoos are being designed that are similar to the animals' natural habitats. [8]Viewers can closely observe animals at animal parks, animals roam free. [9]Zoo kitchens keep a wide variety of foods and food supplements these are used to prepare meals that meet each animal's nutritional needs. [10]Zoos contribute to wildlife conservation, they nurture species that are in danger of becoming extinct.

Exercise 28 **Correcting Sentence Fragments and Run-on Sentences**

Rewrite the following paragraph, correcting all sentence fragments and run-on sentences.

Chinese New Year

[1]The biggest and most popular of all Chinese festivals. [2]The Chinese New Year, an exciting and colorful holiday. [3]Falling anywhere between January 21 and February 19. [4]The New Year is celebrated by Chinese people all over the world, they parade through the streets and set off fireworks. [5]People pay visits to friends they wish them luck and prosperity with a greeting that means "happy greetings, and may you gather wealth." [6]On the final day of the year, preparations are made for a great New Year's Eve supper. [7]All doors are sealed with paper strips and no one may leave or enter until the next morning. [8]Businesses are closed. [9]For days after the new year begins. [10]Children receive presents of money in red envelopes adults give gifts to the poor.

Grammar Review

Clauses and Sentence Structure

As Eudora Welty's novel *Delta Wedding* begins, young Laura McRaven is on her way from her home in Jackson, Mississippi, to Shellmound, the plantation where her cousin Dabney is to be married. It is Laura's first trip alone, and she savors every minute of it. The passage has been annotated to show the types of sentences and clauses covered in this unit.

Literature Model

from DELTA WEDDING

by Eudora Welty

Simple sentence

Complex sentence

Compound-complex sentence

Adverb clause

Adjective clause

Compound sentence

The nickname of the train was the Yellow Dog. Its real name was the Yazoo-Delta. It was a mixed train. The day was the 10th of September, 1923—afternoon. Laura McRaven, who was nine years old, was on her first journey alone. She was going up from Jackson to visit her mother's people, the Fairchilds, at their plantation named Shellmound, at Fairchilds, Mississippi. . . .

In the passenger car every window was propped open with a stick of kindling wood. A breeze blew through, hot and then cool, fragrant of the woods and yellow flowers and of the train. The yellow butterflies flew in at any window, out at any other, and outdoors one of them could keep up with the train, which then seemed to be racing with a butterfly. Overhead a black lamp in which a circle of flowers had been cut out swung round and round on a chain as the car rocked from side to side, sending down dainty drifts of kerosene smell. The Dog was almost sure to reach Fairchilds before the lamp would be lighted by Mr. Terry Black, the conductor, who had promised her father to watch out for her. Laura had the seat facing the stove, but of course no fire was burning in it now. She sat leaning at the window, the light and the sooty air trying to make her close her eyes. Her ticket to Fairchilds was stuck up in her Madge Evans straw hat, in imitation of the drummer [salesman] across the aisle. Once the Dog stopped in the open ➡

fields and Laura saw the engineer, Mr. Doolittle, go out and pick some specially fine goldenrod there—for whom, she could not know. Then the long September cry rang from the thousand unseen locusts, urgent at the open windows of the train. . . .

    From the warm window sill the endless fields glowed like a hearth in firelight, and Laura, looking out, leaning on her elbows with her head between her hands, felt what an arriver in a land feels—that slow hard pounding in the breast.

— Noun clause

Exercise 1

Identifying Main and Subordinate Clauses   The following sentences are based on the passage from *Delta Wedding*. Each sentence contains a clause that appears in italics. On your paper write *main clause* or *subordinate clause* to identify the italicized clauses.

1. *Although she was only nine years old*, Laura was traveling alone.
2. The conductor, *who was watching out for Laura*, would soon light the lamp.
3. *The ticket* that was stuck in Laura's hat *would take her to Fairchilds, Mississippi.*
4. Laura was traveling to Fairchilds *so that she could attend her cousin's wedding.*
5. *She would stay at her cousin's plantation*, which was named Shellmound.
6. *The train was called the Yellow Dog*, although its name was really the Yazoo-Delta.
7. *While the train moved along*, Laura sat quietly in her seat.
8. *The car had a faint smell of kerosene*, which came from the swinging lamp overhead.
9. As the car rocked from side to side, *the lamp swung in a big circle.*
10. Laura could see the unlighted stove just opposite *where she sat.*
11. *Even though it was September*, the weather in the delta was still summery.
12. Because it was a warm day, *all the windows of the train were open.*
13. *Since the windows would not stay open by themselves*, they were propped up with sticks.
14. In the car were yellow butterflies, *which had flown in through the open windows.*
15. While the train was stopped, *Laura could hear the loud sounds made by locusts in the fields.*
16. Laura saw a field of goldenrod *as she looked out the window.*
17. Where the sun shone on them, *the broad fields glowed like a lighted fireplace.*
18. *After the engineer had picked some goldenrod*, the train started up again.
19. Laura could feel the warmth of the windowsill beneath her elbows *as she sat with her head between her hands.*
20. *Because the sun was bright*, Laura's eyes wanted to close.

Exercise 2

Identifying Simple, Compound, Complex, and Compound-Complex Sentences
The following sentences elaborate on ideas in the passage from *Delta Wedding* and tell
something about its author. On your paper write whether each sentence is *simple*, *compound*,
complex, or *compound-complex*.

1. The train's name was the Yazoo-Delta, but people called it the Yellow Dog.
2. It was September 10, 1923, and Laura McRaven was traveling by train to Fairchilds,
   Mississippi, where her cousin was getting married.
3. Nine-year-old Laura watched the countryside pass by.
4. Laura was enjoying the trip, for she was traveling alone for the first time.
5. The car rocked gently as the train hurried along, and the overhead lamp swung round
   and round.
6. The windows, which were held open with sticks of wood, let breezes into the cars.
7. The train had been traveling for a long time, yet the conductor had still not collected
   the tickets from Laura and the salesperson across the aisle.
8. Because the day was warm, no fire burned in the stove.
9. Laura watched while the engineer picked some goldenrod, and she noticed that the
   flowers were especially fine.
10. Though she sat quietly, Laura could feel her heart pounding.
11. While she sat alone on the train, Laura noticed many details inside the railroad car,
    and she observed the passing landscape as well.
12. Because she was traveling alone for the first time, she was unusually aware of her
    surroundings.
13. She compared what she was seeing with her hometown.
14. The author of *Delta Wedding*, Eudora Welty, was born in Jackson, Mississippi, in 1909.
15. When she created the character of Laura McRaven in *Delta Wedding*, Welty created a girl
    whose life was similar to hers.
16. Welty has lived in the Mississippi Delta for most of her life, and the delta landscape is
    familiar to her.
17. Eudora Welty, like Laura, probably traveled by train through the delta as a young girl.
18. Welty says that she has always been aware of words and of the way people speak.
19. As a young girl, she paid attention to the ordinary sights, sounds, and objects of daily life,
    and they formed vivid sensory images that remained with her.
20. When Welty grew up and became a writer, her store of early impressions and memories
    provided a wealth of convincing details for her books and stories.

Exercise 3

Writing Sentences with Adjective Clauses   Use the passage from *Delta Wedding* to rewrite the sentences below. To each sentence add an adjective clause that answers the question in parentheses. Your clause must begin with one of the relative pronouns below. It must contain a verb, and it must be correctly punctuated. There may be more than one correct answer.

RELATIVE PRONOUNS   who   whom   whose   which   that

SAMPLE   The train was heading toward Fairchilds, Mississippi. (What was the name of the train?)

ANSWER   The train, whose name was the Yazoo-Delta, was heading toward Fairchilds, Mississippi.

1. Laura was traveling alone for the first time in her life. (How old was she?)
2. Laura's father had taken her to the train. (How did her father feel about her trip?)
3. Laura was traveling from Jackson, Mississippi. (What was Jackson to Laura?)
4. She was going to visit her mother's family. (Where did Laura's mother's family live?)
5. Laura's journey was taking place on a September afternoon. (What was the weather like?)
6. Laura felt very dressed up for her ride on the train. (What hat was she wearing?)
7. A breeze blew through the open windows. (What did the breeze smell like?)
8. Laura watched the yellow butterflies. (What were the butterflies doing?)
9. One butterfly seemed to be having a race with the train. (Where was the butterfly?)
10. A black lamp swung to the rhythm of the rocking car. (How was the lamp decorated?)
11. The lamp would probably not be lighted during the journey. (What odor did the lamp give off?)
12. The conductor would light the lamp later. (What was the conductor's name?)
13. Mr. Black had not yet collected the tickets. (What promise had he made?)
14. Laura sat in her seat. (Where was her seat?)
15. The stove provided heat for the car in cold weather. (Was the stove being used on this day?)
16. The air made her want to close her eyes. (What was the air like?)
17. Laura imitated the drummer, or traveling salesperson. (Where was his ticket?)
18. Many drummers traveled by train to call on customers. (Where were the customers?)
19. Mr. Doolittle stopped the train. (What was Mr. Doolittle's job?)
20. The engineer picked some goldenrod. (What was the goldenrod like?)
21. Laura wondered to whom Mr. Doolittle would give the goldenrod. (Why did she want to know?)
22. Through the train's open windows Laura heard a cry. (From what did the cry come?)
23. Laura heard locusts. (Where were they?)
24. Laura gazed at the fields. (What did the fields look like?)
25. Laura wanted her journey to end. (How did she feel?)

Exercise 4

Writing Sentences with Adverb Clauses   Use the passage from *Delta Wedding* to rewrite each sentence, adding an adverb clause that answers the question in parentheses. Your clause must begin with one of the subordinating conjunctions listed below, and it must contain a subject and a verb. There may be more than one correct answer for each item.

SUBORDINATING CONJUNCTIONS

after	as if	if	so that	when	wherever
as	because	since	than	whenever	while

SAMPLE   Laura McRaven was traveling to Shellmound.
(Why?)

ANSWER   Laura McRaven was traveling to Shellmound
because her cousin Dabney was getting married.

1. It was an exciting day for Laura. (Why?)
2. Laura sat looking out the window. (When?)
3. Laura felt excited. (Why?)
4. Laura had a ticket to Fairchilds, Mississippi. (Why?)
5. Laura carefully observed everything that went on around her. (Why?)
6. The passenger car swayed back and forth. (When?)
7. Pieces of kindling were being used at the windows of the passenger car. (Why?)
8. There were butterflies inside the car. (Why?)
9. Butterflies flew into the train. (Where?)
10. One butterfly flew alongside the train. (In what manner?)
11. The black lamp over Laura's head swung in circles on its chain. (Why?)
12. The conductor would finally light the lamp. (When?)
13. Laura's father had asked the conductor to look after her. (When?)
14. A fire would be lighted in the stove opposite Laura. (Under what condition?)
15. Laura almost had to close her eyes. (Why?)
16. Laura put her ticket in her hat. (Why?)
17. The passengers would give the conductor their tickets. (When?)
18. The engineer stopped the train. (Why?)
19. The engineer picked goldenrod. (Where?)
20. Laura found the engineer's actions somewhat mysterious. (Why?)
21. Laura heard the locusts. (Why?)
22. The fields glowed in the daylight. (How?)
23. Laura could feel the warmth of the windowsill. (Why?)
24. Laura's heart pounded. (When?)
25. Laura would see her mother's family. (When?)

Exercise 5

Identifying Noun Clauses   The following sentences describe the Mississippi Delta area, to which Laura McRaven was traveling. On your paper write the noun clauses that appear in the sentences. Two of the sentences have two noun clauses each. In one sentence the relative pronoun before the noun clause has been dropped.

1. Does this book explain what the Mississippi Delta is?
2. Whoever has visited Mississippi is probably familiar with the area.
3. That the Mississippi River periodically floods its banks is the reason for the delta's existence.
4. What we now call the Mississippi Delta was formed by whatever deposits of silt the receding Mississippi River floodwaters left behind.
5. You can easily understand why many farmers live in the delta.
6. What attracts many farmers to the delta is that the soil is so fertile.
7. Do you know what makes the delta so famous?
8. One reason for its fame is that the area produces large crops of cotton.
9. You may also have read that large crops of soybeans are grown in the delta.
10. I know that visitors are also attracted by the area's many beautiful plantations.

Exercise 6

Identifying Adjective, Adverb, and Noun Clauses   The following sentences give information about the author of *Delta Wedding*, Eudora Welty. Write the adjective clauses, adverb clauses, and noun clauses that appear in the sentences. Then write *adjective clause*, *adverb clause*, or *noun clause* to identify each clause. One sentence has more than one clause.

1. Author Eudora Welty, who was born in Jackson, Mississippi, is well known for her entertaining and insightful novels and short stories.
2. Because everyone in her family loved to read, there were always many books around Welty's home.
3. After Welty attended Mississippi State College for Women in 1926 and 1927, she was graduated from the University of Wisconsin.
4. Later Welty studied advertising at Columbia University, which is in New York City.
5. Welty's reason for returning to Jackson in 1931 was that her father died.
6. While Welty has traveled in the United States and Europe, most of her work focuses on southern rural life.
7. Welty's stories of human relationships often tell about people who live in small towns.
8. *Delta Wedding*, which was Welty's first full-length novel, was published in 1946.
9. The novel describes a comfortable southern world that would soon change forever.
10. Whoever reads Welty's stories realizes that she believes in the importance of change and love in human life.

Exercise 7

Writing Four Kinds of Sentences On your paper write *declarative*, *imperative*, *interrogative*, or *exclamatory* to identify each of the following sentences. Then rewrite each sentence in the form noted in parentheses.

SAMPLE   The engineer stopped the train. (Rewrite as an imperative sentence.)
ANSWER   declarative
          Engineer, please stop the train.

1. Was the train's official name the Yazoo-Delta? (Rewrite as a declarative sentence.)
2. We call the train the Yellow Dog. (Rewrite as an imperative sentence.)
3. The date was September 10, 1923. (Rewrite as an interrogative sentence.)
4. It was very warm that September day. (Rewrite as an exclamatory sentence.)
5. Were all the train windows open? (Rewrite as a declarative sentence.)
6. Will you open all the train windows? (Rewrite as an imperative sentence.)
7. How delicate the butterflies were! (Rewrite as an interrogative sentence.)
8. Was Laura sitting across the aisle from the drummer? (Rewrite as an imperative sentence.)
9. Laura, put the ticket in your hat. (Rewrite as a declarative sentence.)
10. Laura liked the smell of the kerosene from the lamp. (Rewrite as an interrogative sentence.)
11. Cool breezes came from the woods nearby. (Rewrite as an interrogative sentence.)
12. How beautiful the goldenrod was! (Rewrite as a declarative sentence.)
13. Mr. Doolittle, please give her some goldenrod. (Rewrite as a declarative sentence.)
14. Mr. Doolittle stopped the train in order to pick some goldenrod. (Rewrite as an interrogative sentence.)
15. How loud the cries of the locusts were! (Rewrite as a declarative sentence.)
16. Did Laura look forward to seeing her cousins? (Rewrite as a declarative sentence.)
17. Laura's heart was pounding. (Rewrite as an exclamatory sentence.)
18. Mr. Black promised to look after Laura. (Rewrite as an imperative sentence.)
19. Laura's cousins were going to meet her train. (Rewrite as an interrogative sentence.)
20. Laura had a wonderful time. (Rewrite as an exclamatory sentence.)

Exercise 8

Creating Four Kinds of Sentences For each topic below, write two different kinds of sentences: declarative, imperative, interrogative, or exclamatory. Within the exercise, use each type of sentence at least twice. Use correct punctuation. Label each sentence *declarative*, *imperative*, *interrogative*, or *exclamatory*.

1. things you see in the classroom
2. your trip to school this morning
3. a visit to a new place
4. a person you have talked to today
5. a meal with your friends or family

Exercise 9

Correcting Sentence Fragments   The following paragraph describes Uncle Battle, another character from *Delta Wedding*. Revise the paragraph, correcting any sentence fragments. The fragments may be corrected by combining sentences, by adding words (such as a subject or a verb), or by changing the form of a verb.

SAMPLE	Laura arrived. Her cousins rushing out to meet her.
ANSWER	When Laura arrived, her cousins rushed out to meet her.

[1]At Shellmound, Laura so happy to see Uncle Battle again. [2]A big man, her mother's brother. [3]Always called all the children Skeeta. [4]All of his children exactly like him. [5]Wore tall boots that creaked when he stood up. [6]His hair always combed back over his brow. [7]At mealtime Uncle Battle always carving and serving the turkey. [8]Likely to drive off at any time of the day or night, without a moment's notice. [9]Because he needed to check to see that the plantation work was getting done. [10]Also to protect the plantation's workers from the sheriff.

Exercise 10

Correcting Run-on Sentences   The following sentences elaborate on ideas suggested by the passage from *Delta Wedding*. On your paper revise each sentence, correcting any run-ons. Remember that run-on sentences may be corrected in more than one way. For the sentences that do not contain run-ons, write *correct*.

SAMPLE	It was September 10, 1923, Laura McRaven was on her way to Fairchilds.
ANSWER	It was September 10, 1923. Laura McRaven was on her way to Fairchilds.
ANSWER	It was September 10, 1923, and Laura McRaven was on her way to Fairchilds.

1. Laura was only nine years old, nevertheless, she was traveling alone.
2. Laura's cousins lived at Fairchilds Laura was going to visit them.
3. The day was warm and butterflies flew in and out of the open windows.
4. The breeze kept changing, it would be hot for a while and then it would be cool.
5. Laura wanted to catch every detail of the countryside; however, the sooty air from the train's engine kept making her want to close her eyes.
6. Mr. Black was the conductor, Laura's father had asked him to watch out for Laura.
7. Laura wore a straw hat, she had stuck her ticket in it.
8. The train came to a halt and Mr. Doolittle went into the open fields.
9. Laura couldn't wait to get to Fairchilds she was anxious to see her mother's people.
10. Laura tried to stay calm, but her heart kept pounding.

Exercise 11

Correcting Sentence Structure   The following paragraphs tell about the state of Mississippi. Revise the paragraphs, correcting sentence fragments or run-on sentences. Some sentences are correct, but you may wish to combine them with other sentences. Try to vary your sentence structure, and use correct punctuation.

[1]Mississippi is bordered on the east by Alabama, its southern border is the Gulf of Mexico. [2]On the north by Tennessee, on the west by Arkansas and Louisiana. [3]The Mississippi River actually forms most of the state's western boundary. [4]Jackson, the capital of Mississippi and its largest city. [5]The Yazoo-Mississippi Delta, in western Mississippi, a broad, flat plain with rich, dark soil.

[6]Mississippi has a warm climate and long growing season, its main crops are cotton and soybeans. [7]Much of the southern part of the state covered by pine forest. [8]The Delta National Forest northwest of Jackson. [9]Covers 60,000 acres, has facilities for camping, fishing, and picnicking. [10]The Yazoo River borders the forest and flows into the Mississippi River just above Vicksburg.

Exercise 12

Proofreading

The following passage describes the artist Robert Duncan, whose painting appears on the opposite page. Rewrite the passage, correcting the errors in spelling, grammar, and usage. Add any missing punctuation. There are twenty-five errors.

Robert Duncan

[1]Robert Duncan was borned in Salt Lake City, Utah, in 1952. [2]He spent his summers on his grandfathers' ranch in Wyoming. [3]His grandmother, beleiving in Duncan's talent gave the eleven-year-old boy a set of oil paints and arranged for him to take art lessons [4]Duncan continues to paint in high school. [5]Duncan, however, is largely self-taught he has been painting full-time since 1972. [6]He, his wife, and their six children lives in Midway, Utah. [7]Utahs citizens and rugged landscapes are frequent subjects in his paintings.

[8]Duncan who has visited many museums in Europe and the United States, derived his style from his study of traditional figurative and landscape art. [9]He was particlarly influenced by the work of painters from the turn of the century, such as John Singer Sargent. [10]When Sargent was young he had been influenced by the Impressionists. [11]Who created their paintings with rapid strokes of pure color. [12]Duncan, who uses naturalistic settings and loose brushwork displays his debt to such Realists as Sargent and, indirectly, to the Impressionists. [13]Although his style is at odds with many currents in modren art it has won him modest acclaim. ➡

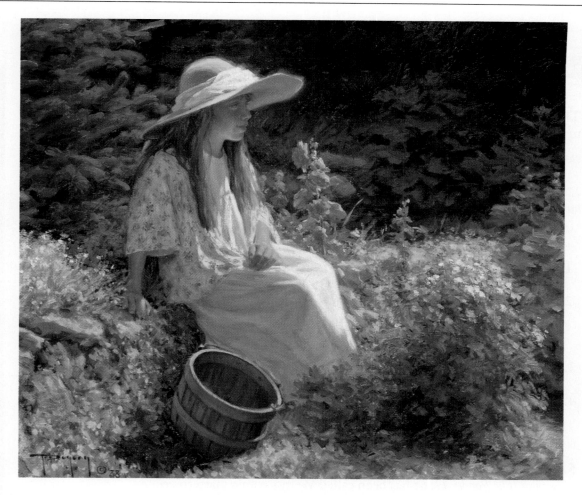

Robert Duncan, *Mandy's Sunhat*, 1988

[14]Duncan portrays many aspects of rural life his goal is to show that all people are fundamentally the same. [15]Often paints outdoors to capture the natural light. [16]He depicts farms gardens, and country people; children are among his favorite subjects [17]Duncan's style, which is romantic and somewhat sentimental is evident in all his paintings.

[18]*Mandy's Sunhat* shows Duncans facility for depicting atmosphere and light. [19]Anyone who has read Eudora Welty's *Delta Wedding* could easily believe that the girl in the painting are Laura McRaven. [20]The youngster in Welty's novel. [21]Can you imagine her stepping off the train and into the open fields

Mixed Review

Exercise 13

The items that follow describe the writing career of Eudora Welty. Revise each item in the manner indicated in parentheses; there may be more than one correct answer.

SAMPLE   Eudora Welty was born in Jackson, Mississippi, in 1909. She is well-known for her entertaining and insightful novels and short stories. (Rewrite as a complex sentence.)

ANSWER   Eudora Welty, who is well-known for her entertaining and insightful novels and short stories, was born in Jackson, Mississippi, in 1909.

Eudora Welty's Published Work

1. Welty's first book of short stories, *A Curtain of Green*, was published in 1941. (Rewrite as an interrogative sentence.)
2. Her novella *The Robber Bridegroom* was published in 1942. It was later made into a successful Broadway play. (Combine the sentences by turning the second sentence into an adjective clause beginning with *which*.)
3. Did Welty publish two collections of short stories between 1949 and 1955? (Write as a declarative sentence.)
4. *The Golden Apples* (1949), her next book after *Delta Wedding*, contained seven related stories about a group of families. The lives of these families were intertwined. (Combine the sentences by turning the second sentence into an adjective clause beginning with *whose*.)
5. Like *The Robber Bridegroom*, Welty's novel *The Ponder Heart* (1954) has been turned into a play. *The Ponder Heart* has been called Welty's comic masterpiece. (Rewrite as a complex sentence.)
6. Welty published almost nothing between 1955 and 1970, but 1970 brought the publication of her novel *Losing Battles*. The novel deals with humorous characters and situations. (Rewrite as a compound-complex sentence.)
7. Welty won the Pulitzer Prize in 1972 for her novel *The Optimist's Daughter*; this event further increased her popularity. (Eliminate the run-on by writing a compound sentence.)
8. One reason for Welty's success is clear. Her fiction is often very humorous. (Combine the sentences by turning the second sentence into a noun clause beginning with *that*.)
9. Besides novels and short stories, Welty has written several works of nonfiction. Including a collection of essays and an autobiography. (Eliminate the fragment by writing a complex sentence.)
10. Many readers pay special attention to Welty's gift for vivid detail and to her wry insights into human nature. (Rewrite as an imperative sentence.)

Writing Application

Clauses and Sentence Structure in Writing   In the following paragraph from "A Day's Pleasure," Hamlin Garland uses a variety of sentence types to capture the reader's interest and to develop a pleasing rhythm and an appropriate mood of relaxation. Notice how the structure of each of Garland's four sentences varies: compound-complex, simple, complex, compound-complex.

> They went into the little sitting room, so dainty and lovely to the farmer's wife, and as she sank into the easy chair she was faint and drowsy with the pleasure of it. She submitted to being brushed. She gave the baby into the hands of the Swedish girl, who washed its face and hands and sang it to sleep, while its mother sipped some tea. Through it all she lay back in her easy chair, not speaking a word, while the ache passed out of her back, and her hot, swollen head ceased to throb.

Techniques with Clauses and Sentence Structure   Try to apply some of Garland's techniques when you write and revise your own work.

1.   Avoid using the same sentence structure repeatedly.

Monotonous structure   She lay back in her chair. She did not speak. The ache passed out of her back.
Garland's version   . . . she lay back in her easy chair, not speaking a word, while the ache passed out of her back. . . .

2.   Use subordination to call attention to some ideas and downplay others.

Equal attention to each idea   She sank into a chair. She was faint and drowsy. She sipped her tea.
Garland's version   . . . as she sank into the easy chair, she was faint and drowsy . . . The Swedish girl . . . sang it to sleep, while its mother sipped some tea.

Practice   Practice these techniques by revising the following series of simple sentences, using a separate sheet of paper. Decide which ideas should be subordinated, and try to use a variety of sentence structures.

The day grew warmer. A strong wind rose, blowing from the south. They were all thirsty. They had only half a barrel of water left. They knew the next watering place was several hours ahead. The sun rose higher. Dust settled on their hair and clothing. It coated the children's bare feet. The woman sat holding the reins. The deep ruts in the trail jolted the wagon. Her back and neck ached. She shaded her eyes against the glare. Nowhere on the wide horizon could she see a tree or a building. In fact, they had seen no other people for two days. Her husband remained confident. Today, though, even he seemed tired.

UNIT

14

Diagraming Sentences

Grammar	Lessons

532

Diagraming is a method of showing the relationship of various words and parts of a sentence to the sentence as a whole.

You begin to diagram a sentence by finding the simple subject. (Keep in mind that a sentence may have a compound subject.) After you have found the subject, find the action or linking verb that goes with it. Write the subject and the verb on a horizontal line. Separate them with a vertical line that bisects the horizontal line. This line indicates the division between the complete subject and the complete predicate.

Athletes train.

subject	action verb

Athletes	train

Adjectives and Adverbs

To diagram a simple sentence with adjectives and adverbs, follow the model diagram below.

A very good athlete must train extremely hard.

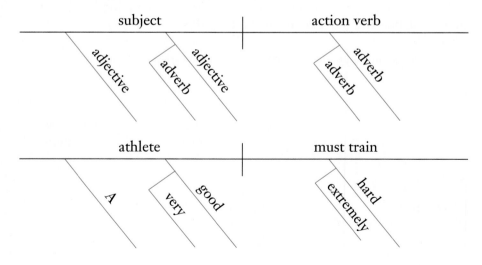

Direct Objects and Indirect Objects

To diagram a simple sentence with an indirect object and a direct object, follow the model diagram below.

Coaches give players guidance.

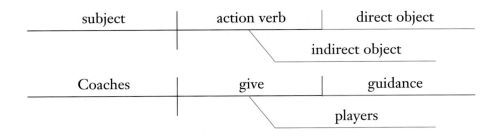

Object Complements

To diagram a simple sentence with a compound subject, a direct object, and an object complement, follow the model diagram below. If the simple subjects in a compound subject are connected by a conjunction, place the conjunction on a dotted vertical line between the subjects. If the simple subjects are connected by a correlative conjunction, such as *both . . . and* or *either . . . or*, place the first part of the conjunction on one side of the line and the second part on the other.

Coaches and players consider practice essential.

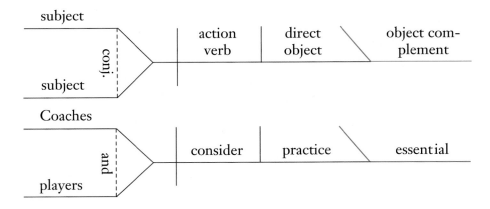

Subject Complements

To diagram a simple sentence with a subject complement (a predicate nominative or a predicate adjective), follow the model diagrams below.

Swimmers are athletes.

Gymnasts are strong and must be coordinated.

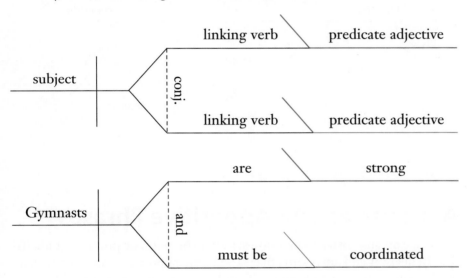

Exercise 1   **Diagraming Simple Sentences**

Using the preceding models as a guide, diagram the following sentences.

1. The muddy field was drying slowly.
2. A coach gave the players instructions.
3. The players and the coach considered the game critical.
4. It was the championship game.
5. The players were ready but felt nervous.
6. They looked calm but felt uneasy.
7. The coach encouraged them.
8. She gave the players a pep talk.
9. The players paid attention and listened silently.
10. They were ready.

Prepositional Phrases

Place the preposition on a diagonal line that descends from the word the prepositional phrase modifies. Place the object of the preposition on a horizontal line that joins the diagonal. The diagonal line on which the preposition is placed should extend somewhat beyond the horizontal on which the object of the preposition is placed, forming a "tail."

Athletes of today set new records at every opportunity during a season.

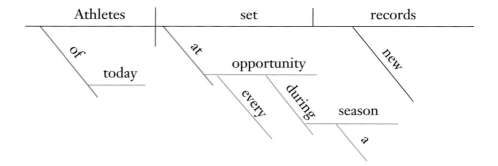

Appositives and Appositive Phrases

Place an appositive in parentheses after the noun or pronoun it identifies. Beneath it add any words that modify the appositive. Any words that modify the noun or pronoun itself, and not the appositive, should be placed directly beneath the noun or pronoun.

The coach, a graduate of the school, preaches team spirit, an important ideal.

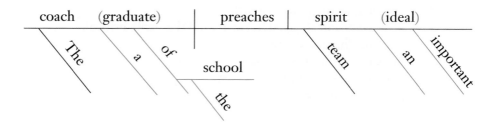

Participles and Participial Phrases

The line on which the participle is placed descends diagonally from the word the participle modifies and then extends to the right horizontally. The participle is written on the curve, as shown below. Add any modifiers and complements to the horizontal line in the same way that you would show the modifiers and complements of an action verb.

Stumbling, the quarterback fell, gracefully completing the pass in midair.

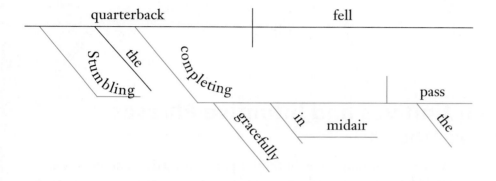

Gerunds and Gerund Phrases

Place a gerund on a "step," adding complements and modifiers in the usual way. Set the gerund or the gerund phrase on a "stilt," and position the stilt according to the role of the gerund. (Remember that a gerund can be a subject, a complement, an object of a preposition, or an appositive.)

Winning is one way of gaining confidence.

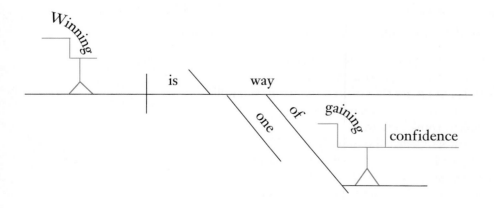

Infinitives and Infinitive Phrases as Adjectives or Adverbs

When an infinitive or an infinitive phrase is used as an adjective or an adverb, it is diagramed like a prepositional phrase.

Teams have a need to travel frequently.

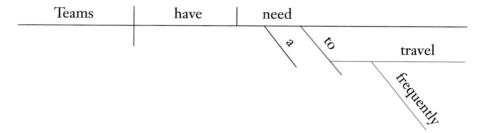

Infinitives and Infinitive Phrases as Nouns

When an infinitive or an infinitive phrase is used as a noun, it is diagramed like a prepositional phrase and then placed on a "stilt" in the subject or complement position.

To triumph is to taste glory.

Exercise 2	Diagraming Simple Sentences with Phrases

Using the preceding models as a guide, diagram the following sentences.

1. People of that time knew nothing about the rest of the world.
2. My cousin Janet got her wish, a part in the play.
3. Thousands of leaves, falling gently, covered the damp sidewalk.
4. Watching television is one way of relaxing.
5. To write well means to think clearly.
6. My grandmother wants to learn about everything.
7. Roaring, the rapidly widening river raced to cover waiting farmland.
8. Eating well is the best revenge.
9. Pedestrians, shadows in the fog, hurried to reach home.
10. Blinking in bewilderment, I stared at the scene before me.

Compound Sentences

Diagram each main clause separately. If the clauses are connected by a semicolon, use a vertical dotted line to connect the verbs of each main clause. If the main clauses are connected by a conjunction, place the conjunction on a solid horizontal line, and connect it to the verbs of each main clause by vertical dotted lines.

Athletes like to win, but they must also learn to lose.

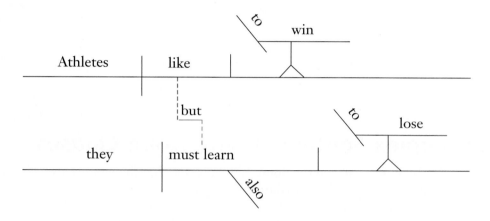

Complex Sentences with Adjective Clauses

Place the main clause in one diagram and the adjective clause beneath it in another diagram. Use a dotted line to connect the relative pronoun or other introductory word in the adjective clause to the modified noun or pronoun in the main clause.

The player whom you like won games that were close.

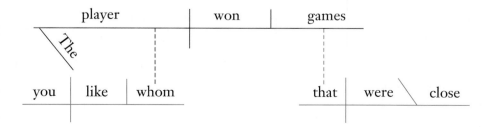

Complex Sentences with Adverb Clauses

Place the main clause in one diagram and the adverb clause beneath it in another diagram. Place the subordinating conjunction on a diagonal dotted line connecting the verb in the adverb clause to the modified verb, adjective, or adverb in the main clause.

Before a game begins, the coach gives encouragement.

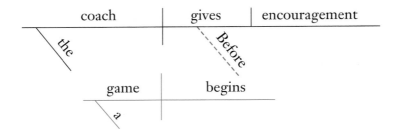

Complex Sentences with Noun Clauses

First decide what role the noun clause plays within the main clause. Is it the subject, direct object, predicate nominative, or object of a preposition? Then diagram the main clause, placing the noun clause on a "stilt" in the appropriate position. Place the introductory word of the clause in the position of the subject, object, or predicate nominative within the noun clause itself. If the introductory word merely begins the noun clause, place it on a line of its own above the verb in the subordinate clause, connecting it to the verb with a dotted vertical line.

NOUN CLAUSE AS SUBJECT

What the coach says is extremely important.

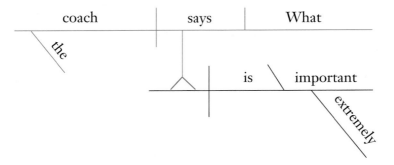

NOUN CLAUSE AS DIRECT OBJECT

The coach knows that the rival may win.

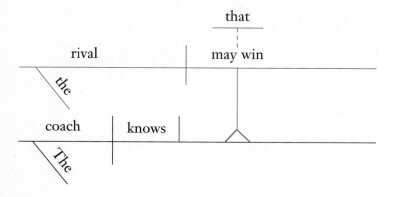

NOUN CLAUSE AS OBJECT OF A PREPOSITION

The coach assigns more practice to whoever needs it.

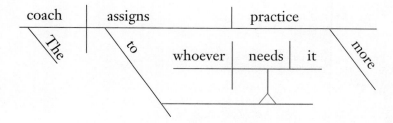

Exercise 3   **Diagraming Sentences with Clauses**

Using the preceding models as a guide, diagram the following sentences.

1. John is the oldest child, and Rebecca is the youngest.
2. The pilot who won last year's competition has sold his airplane.
3. Whenever Manolo remembers, he buys an extra newspaper for Juanito.
4. Whoever wins this game chooses the next one.
5. Everybody knows that Hefflemeyer is the greatest player.
6. After Bettina scored on a jump shot, the score was tied.
7. I liked watching the movie, but the book was better.
8. The team that is better prepared will probably win.
9. Whoever goes first will have the advantage.
10. I want to learn more about what you said.

15.1 Principal Parts of Verbs

All verbs have four **principal parts:** a *base form*, a *present participle*, a *simple past form*, and a *past participle*. All the verb tenses are formed from these principal parts.

Principal Parts of Verbs			
Base Form	**Present Participle**	**Past Form**	**Past Participle**
nail	nailing	nailed	nailed
carry	carrying	carried	carried
ring	ringing	rang	rung
be	being	was, were	been
sit	sitting	sat	sat

The base form (except the base form of *be*) and the past form can be used by themselves as main verbs. To function as the simple predicate in a sentence, the present participle and the past participle must always be used with one or more auxiliary verbs.

Lions **roar.** [base or present form]
Lions **roared.** [past form]
Lions **are roaring.** [present participle with the auxiliary verb *are*]
Lions **have roared.** [past participle with the auxiliary verb *have*]

Exercise 1   **Using Principal Parts of Verbs**

Write the correct form of the principal part of the verb indicated in parentheses.

1. They _____ for an auto dealership. (base form of *work*)
2. They are _____ up sales of minivans and jeeps. (present participle of *ring*)
3. Last month, he _____ 10 people into buying minivans. (past form of *talk*)
4. She is _____ harder than any other salesperson. (present participle of *work*)
5. They have both _____ a bonus and an award. (past participle of *receive*)
6. They are _____ to other salespeople at the award dinner. (present participle of *talk*)
7. They have often _____ techniques with their colleagues. (past participle of *discuss*)
8. Now they _____ a wider audience. (base form of *need*)
9. Their supervisor _____ very proud when they were selected. (past form of *be*)
10. He was actually _____ around in his office. (present participle of *dance*)

15.2 Regular and Irregular Verbs

A **regular verb** forms its past and past participle by adding
-*ed* to the base form.

Regular Verbs		
Base Form	**Past Form**	**Past Participle**
roar	roared	roared
talk	talked	talked
learn	learned	learned

Some regular verbs undergo spelling changes when a suffix beginning
with a vowel is added.

ruffle + **-ed** = ruffl**ed**   spy + **-ed** = spi**ed**   flop + **-ed** = flop**ped**
argue + **-ed** = argu**ed**   tie + **-ed** = ti**ed**   refer + **-ed** = refer**red**

An **irregular verb** forms its past and past participle in some way
other than by adding -*ed* to the base form.

Irregular Verbs		
Base Form	**Past Form**	**Past Participle**
be	was, were	been
beat	beat	beaten
become	became	become
begin	began	begun
bite	bit	bitten *or* bit
blow	blew	blown
break	broke	broken
bring	brought	brought
buy	bought	bought
catch	caught	caught
choose	chose	chosen
come	came	come
do	did	done
draw	drew	drawn
drink	drank	drunk
drive	drove	driven
eat	ate	eaten
fall	fell	fallen
feel	felt	felt
find	found	found
fly	flew	flown
freeze	froze	frozen
get	got	got *or* gotten➝

Irregular Verbs		
Base Form	**Past Form**	**Past Participle**
give	gave	given
go	went	gone
grow	grew	grown
hang	hung *or* hanged	hung *or* hanged
have	had	had
keep	kept	kept
know	knew	known
lay*	laid	laid
lead	led	led
leave	left	left
lend	lent	lent
lie*	lay	lain
lose	lost	lost
make	made	made
put	put	put
ride	rode	ridden
ring	rang	rung
rise*	rose	risen
run	ran	run
say	said	said
see	saw	seen
seek	sought	sought
sell	sold	sold
set*	set	set
shrink	shrank *or* shrunk	shrunk *or* shrunken
sing	sang	sung
sink	sank *or* sunk	sunk
sit*	sat	sat
sleep	slept	slept
speak	spoke	spoken
spring	sprang *or* sprung	sprung
steal	stole	stolen
swim	swam	swum
swing	swung	swung
take	took	taken
teach	taught	taught
tear	tore	torn
tell	told	told
think	thought	thought
throw	threw	thrown
wear	wore	worn
win	won	won
write	wrote	written

*For more detailed instruction on *lay* versus *lie* and *raise* versus *rise*, see Unit 19.

* For more detailed instruction on *sit* versus *set*, see Unit 19.

Writing Principal Parts of Verbs

Copy and complete the chart. Make sure that you have spelled each form correctly.

Base Form	Past Form	Past Participle
1. start		
2. think		
3. climb		
4. stop		
5. hit		
6. occur		
7. grow		
8. skip		
9. fly		
10. deter		
11. murmur		
12. pray		
13. cry		
14. go		
15. swim		
16. flip		
17. insure		
18. steal		
19. wear		
20. submit		
21. write		
22. run		
23. deny		
24. lend		
25. know		

Exercise 3   Using Principal Parts of Irregular Verbs

Write the correct form of the principal part of the verb indicated in parentheses.

1. I _____ breakfast for my family every Sunday. (base form of *make*)
2. Last Sunday I _____ late. (past form of *rise*)
3. I was still _____ in bed when a wonderful aroma hit me. (present participle of *lie*)
4. I almost _____ out of bed with excitement. (past form of *fall*)
5. My brother had _____ to give me a present. (past participle of *choose*)
6. I _____ out of bed and sprinted down the stairs. (past form of *spring*)
7. His choice couldn't have _____ a better one. (past participle of *be*)
8. How could he have _____ what I really wanted? (past participle of *know*)
9. I sat and _____ my teeth into my favorite breakfast. (past form of *sink*)
10. I have never _____ better pancakes. (past participle of *eat*)

Write the principal part of the verb indicated in parentheses.

Arthur Ashe, a Tennis Pioneer

  1. The name Arthur Ashe has ___ to symbolize athletic brilliance and outstanding achievement. (past participle of *come*)
  2. Over the past two decades, the name has also ___ personal integrity and grace. (past participle of *signify*)
  3. Ashe ___ playing tennis in elementary school. (past form of *begin*)
  4. His athletic talent ___ the attention of a local physician, Dr. Robert "Whirlwind" Johnson. (past form of *catch*)
  5. Dr. Johnson ____ talented African American youngsters to play for the U.S. Tennis Association. (past form of *teach*)
  6. Dr. Johnson had ___ tennis lessons to Althea Gibson. (past participle of *give*)
  7. Althea Gibson ___ the first African American to win a championship at Wimbledon, a famous tennis tournament in England. (past form of *be*)
  8. By the age of 18, Arthur Ashe had ___ to national prominence. (past participle of *rise*)
  9. In 1960 and again in 1961, he ___ the Junior Indoor Singles Championship. (past form of *win*)
 10. While he ___ at the University of California in Los Angeles, Ashe was coached by Pancho Gonzales, a tennis champion. (past form of *study*)
 11. In 1963 Ashe was ____ for the Davis Cup Team. (past participle of *choose*)
 12. In 1966 he ____ himself the winner of both the singles and doubles titles in the National Collegiate Athletic Association Championship. (past form of *find*)
 13. In 1968 Ashe's dream of winning at the highest levels of American tennis finally ____ true. (past form of *come*)
 14. He ___ first place at the U.S. National Men's Singles Championship. (past form of *take*)
 15. By the end of 1968, Ashe had ____ all opponents in the men's singles competition of the first U.S. Open tournament. (past participle of *beat*)
 16. Unfortunately, his tournament career ended when he ___ heart surgery. (past form of *undergo*)
 17. As a result of a blood transfusion, Ashe ___ HIV. (past form of *contract*)
 18. Years later, he ____ a news conference and discussed his illness publicly for the first time. (past form of *hold*)
 19. Arthur Ashe ____ in 1993, five months before his fiftieth birthday. (past form of *die*)
 20. Friends who ____ at his memorial service praised Ashe for his professional and humanitarian achievements. (past form of *speak*)

15.3 | Tense of Verbs

The **tenses** of a verb are the forms that help to show time.

There are six tenses in English: *present, past, future, present perfect, past perfect,* and *future perfect.*

Present Tense

The present-tense form of a verb (excluding the third-person singular, which adds an -*s* or -*es*) is the same as the verb's base form. The one exception is the verb *be.*

THE VERB *STAY*	SINGULAR	PLURAL
FIRST PERSON	I **stay.**	We **stay.**
SECOND PERSON	You **stay.**	You **stay.**
THIRD PERSON	She, he, or it **stays.**	They **stay.**
	Jesse **stays.**	The children **stay.**

THE VERB *BE*	SINGULAR	PLURAL
FIRST PERSON	I **am** sad.	We **are** sad.
SECOND PERSON	You **are** sad.	You **are** sad.
THIRD PERSON	She, he, or it **is** sad.	They **are** sad.
	Sheila **is** sad.	The players **are** sad.

The **present tense** expresses a constant, repeated, or habitual action or condition. It can also express a general truth.

> My garden **grows** well in the summer. [not just this summer but every summer: a repeated action]

> Helena **bakes** bread well. [always: a habitual action]

> Gold **is** valuable. [a condition that is generally true]

The **present tense** can also express an action or condition that exists only now.

> Jenny **feels** happy. [not always but just now]
> I **see** a fly on the ceiling. [at this very moment]

The **present tense** is sometimes used in historical writing to express past events and, more often, in poetry, fiction, and reporting (especially in sports) to convey to the reader a sense of "being there."

> Washington and his troops **spend** the winter at Valley Forge.

> The exhausted runner **seems** to stumble, but in a final spurt he **rushes** over the finish line and **wins.**

Past Tense

Use the **past tense** to express an action or condition that was started and completed in the past.

> The orchestra **performed** well.
> The musicians **seemed** pleased.
> The soloist **sang** beautifully.
> The conductor **praised** the musicians.

Nearly all regular and irregular verbs—except *be*—have just one past-tense form, such as *soared* or *began*. The word *be* has two past-tense forms: *was* and *were*.

	SINGULAR	PLURAL
FIRST PERSON	I **was** sad.	We **were** sad.
SECOND PERSON	You **were** sad.	You **were** sad.
THIRD PERSON	She, he, or it **was** sad.	They **were** sad.

Exercise 5   Using the Present Tense

Write a sentence using each of the following verb forms. The content of your sentence should express the kind of present time indicated in parentheses.

SAMPLE   does (a repeated action)
ANSWER   He does his housecleaning on Saturday.

1. sleeps (a habitual action)
2. feel (just now)
3. is (generally true)
4. hopes (at this moment)
5. takes (constant action)
6. opens (at this moment)
7. am (not always, but just now)
8. practices (a repeated action)
9. need (a condition that is generally true)
10. signs (an event in history)

Exercise 6   Using the Past Tense

Write two paragraphs, one using the past tense of verbs 1 through 5 and one using the past tense of verbs 6 through 10.

1. feel
2. catch
3. freeze
4. eat
5. write
6. be
7. give
8. take
9. wear
10. drink

Future Tense

Use the **future tense** to express an action or condition that will occur in the future.

You form the future tense of any verb by using *shall* or *will* with the base form: *I shall study; you will go.*

> Roberta **will send** the telegram.
> I **shall practice** the piano tonight.

The following are other ways to express future time besides using *shall* or *will*:

1. Use *going to* with the present tense of *be* and the base form of a verb.

   > Roberta **is *going to* send** the telegram.

2. Use *about to* with the present tense of *be* and the base form of the verb.

   > Roberta **is *about to* send** the telegram.

3. Use the present tense with an adverb or an adverb phrase that shows future time.

   > Roberta **leaves *tomorrow*.**
   > Roberta **arrives *in the middle of next week*.**

Exercise 7 **Using Expressions of Future Time**

Rewrite each of the following sentences so that the verb is in the future tense. Try to use at least two other ways of expressing future time in addition to *shall* and *will*.

Japan's Classical Theater

[1]Two classmates and I presented a cooperative report on the history of Japanese theater for our literature class. [2]There were three parts to the presentation. [3]First Kate spoke about the form of medieval theater called No. [4]She described the formality and beauty of No plays. [5]Then Miguel covered the history of Japan's Joruri puppet theater. [6]He focused on the extraordinary realism of the colorful and expressive Joruri puppets. [7]I was responsible for information on Kabuki theater. [8]I began with a description of the typical Kabuki stage with its trapdoors and revolving platforms. [9]I explained the stylized and exaggerated movements of Kabuki actors. [10]The report concluded with a demonstration of Kabuki dance.

Exercise 8 **Expressing Future Time in Sentences**

Write five statements or predictions about the future. Your sentences may be as realistic or as unrealistic as you wish. Remember to vary the ways in which you express future time.

SAMPLE ANSWER   Household robots are going to become a reality.

15.4 Perfect Tenses

Present Perfect Tense

Use the **present perfect tense** to express an action or condition that occurred at some *indefinite time* in the past.

You form the present perfect tense by using *has* or *have* with the past participle of a verb: *has stopped, have waited.**

She **has caught** the flu.
They **have brought** a present for us.

The present perfect can refer to completed action in past time only in an indefinite way. Adverbs such as *yesterday* cannot be added to make the time more specific.

Sophia **has completed** her project.
Jack **has wanted** to visit Mexico.

To be specific about completed past time, you would normally use the simple past tense.

Sophia **completed** her project yesterday.
Jack **wanted** to visit Mexico last summer.

The present perfect can also be used to communicate the idea that an action or a condition *began* in the past and *continues* into the present. This use is normally accompanied by adverbs of time or by adverb phrases.

The museum **has displayed** the exhibit for months.
We **have kept** the dogs indoors for a week.

* Do not be confused by the term *present perfect;* this tense expresses past time. *Present* refers to the tense of the auxiliary verb *has* or *have.*

Exercise 9   Using the Present Perfect Tense

(a) Rewrite each of the following sentences, changing the tense of the verb from past to present perfect. (b) Add adverbs or adverb phrases to each new sentence to communicate the idea that an action or condition began in the past and continues into the present.

SAMPLE   We wanted to go to Paris.
ANSWER   **a.** We have wanted to go to Paris.
          b. We have wanted to go to Paris for two years.

1. Lila gave piano lessons.
2. My parents owned two dogs.
3. The trees were in bloom.
4. My friend wrote poetry.
5. The team played with determination.

Past Perfect Tense

Use the **past perfect tense** to indicate that one past action or condition began *and* ended before another past action or condition started.

You form the past perfect tense by using *had* with the past participle of a verb: *had loved, had written.*

> PAST PERFECT   PAST
> She **had been** the captain of the team before I **became** captain.
> [She was captain; she stopped being captain; I became captain.]

> PAST   PAST PERFECT
> Before I **slipped,** many other pedestrians **had slipped** in the
> same place. [They slipped; they finished slipping; I slipped.]

> PAST PERFECT   PAST
> He **had** already **dried** the dishes by the time I **arrived.** [He dried
> the dishes; he finished drying the dishes; I arrived.]

Future Perfect Tense

Use the **future perfect tense** to express one future action or condition that will begin *and* end before another future event starts.

You form the future perfect tense by using *will have* or *shall have* with the past participle of a verb: *will have walked, shall have walked.*

> By summertime I **will have lived** here four months. [The four
> months will be over by the time another future event, the
> coming of summertime, occurs.]

> By the time the astronauts reach the moon, they **will have
> practiced** the maneuver many times.

| Exercise 10 | Writing the Past Perfect and Future Perfect Tenses |

Write the verb in parentheses in the tense indicated in brackets.

1. When the president resigned, he (hold) office for three years. [past perfect]
2. My father projects that forty years from now the majority of people (become) comfortable with voting by computer. [future perfect]
3. Before she realized it, Janice (throw) away the newspaper with the candidates' statements. [past perfect]
4. Peter learned that he (drive) to the wrong polling place. [past perfect]
5. By the time the candidate makes a speech she (rehearse) it for weeks. [future perfect]

Exercise 11   Review: Identifying the Verb Tenses

On your paper write the tense of each italicized verb in the following sentences. Identify the tense as *present*, *past*, *future*, *present perfect*, *past perfect*, or *future perfect*.

Reggae Music

1. Perhaps you *listen* to a style of music known as reggae.
2. This intensely rhythmic music *has been* popular in Jamaica for some time.
3. Jamaican and African folk music and American rhythm and blues *had influenced* the reggae star Bob Marley before he *began* to play music himself.
4. Bands *had performed* reggae in Jamaica for twenty years before it was heard in either the United States or Europe.
5. It *has been* popular in the United States since the 1970s.
6. Before the musical style *took* the name reggae, fans *had called* it by various names—including rudie blues, ska, blue beat, and rock steady.
7. Reggae music *has gained* international fame as a result of two groups, Bob Marley and the Wailers and Toots and the Maytals.
8. By the time it *became* popular outside Jamaica, reggae *had influenced* such rock musicians as Eric Clapton, John Lennon, and the Police.
9. Reggae *will remain* popular because current-day reggae musicians *tour* the United States and Europe.
10. By the time he *completes* his latest tour, Bob Marley's son Ziggy, for example, *will have performed* in dozens of American cities.

Exercise 12   Review: Using Verb Tenses

For each sentence, write the tense of the verb indicated in parentheses.

A Legendary Concert

1. The Woodstock Music and Art Fair _____ to symbolize the hippie culture of the 1960s. (present perfect tense of *come*)
2. By the time Jimi Hendrix played the "Star Spangled Banner," an estimated 500,000 young people _____ in Saugerties, New York, for a weekend of rock and roll. (past perfect tense of *arrive*)
3. At the event Richie Havens _____ for over two hours. (past tense of *sing*)
4. For years a rumor _____ that Joni Mitchell, known for her rendition of the song "Woodstock," was never at Woodstock. (present perfect tense of *persist*)
5. In August 1994, what some had called the "Reunion at Yasgur's Farm" _____ place on the actual site of Woodstock '69. (past tense of *take*)
6. Rock elders such as Joe Cocker and Bob Dylan, who _____ favor with young audiences, performed at the anniversary concert. (past perfect tense of *gain*)
7. I _____ happy that I had the opportunity to attend. (present tense of *be*)
8. By the thirtieth anniversary of Woodstock, many of the "flower children" of the 1960s _____ their fifties. (future perfect tense of *reach*)
9. Do you think they _____ Janis Joplin, Jimi Hendrix, and the other legendary musicians who performed at Woodstock? (future perfect tense of *forget*)
10. I think they still _____. (future tense of *remember*)

15.5 Progressive and Emphatic Forms

Each of the six tenses has a **progressive** form that expresses a continuing action.

You make the progressive forms by using the appropriate tense of the verb *be* with the present participle of the main verb:

PRESENT PROGRESSIVE	They *are* **reading.**
PAST PROGRESSIVE	They *were* **reading.**
FUTURE PROGRESSIVE	They *will be* **reading.**
PRESENT PERFECT PROGRESSIVE	They *have been* **reading.**
PAST PERFECT PROGRESSIVE	They *had been* **reading.**
FUTURE PERFECT PROGRESSIVE	They *will have been* **reading.**

The present and past tenses have additional forms, called **emphatic,** that add special force, or emphasis, to the verb.

You make the emphatic forms by using *do*, *does*, or *did* with the base form of the verb.

PRESENT EMPHATIC	I *do* **read** the newspaper every day.
	Tony *does* **read** it occasionally.
PAST EMPHATIC	Inez *did* **read** the newspaper yesterday.

Exercise 13 **Using the Progressive and Emphatic Forms**

For each of the following sentences, write the progressive or the emphatic form of the verb in parentheses that makes sense in the sentence.

The Modern Bicycle

1. Today more than 75 million Americans (ride) bicycles.
2. Over the years, bicycling (gain) popularity as a form of both exercise and recreation.
3. Even before bicycles began to be widely used for transportation and exercise, numerous organizations already (work) to promote long-distance trips for experienced riders.
4. Today the bicycle (provide) efficient transportation to and from work for many people.
5. Despite the dangers, many people (ride) bicycles in metropolitan areas.
6. Because of accidents involving bicyclists, safety rules (grow) increasingly important.
7. There is no doubt that bicyclists (find) it difficult to ride on busy streets.
8. We can predict that if environmental conditions don't improve, legislators (try) to pass laws to protect bicyclists.
9. Before the recession many cities (plan) to create bikeways, special lanes for bicyclists.
10. To ensure safety for all, new traffic laws (require) bicyclists to ride more carefully.

Identifying Verb Tenses and Their Uses

Explain the difference in meaning between the sentences in each of the pairs below.
Name the tenses and forms used in each sentence.

SAMPLE   **a.** Why was Gloria so secretive?
            b. Why has Gloria been so secretive?

ANSWER   In sentence *a* the action occurred and ended (past). In sentence *b* the action
            occurred in the past and is still continuing (present perfect).

1. **a.** Do you think Anna is writing a birthday poem for the twins' twenty-first birthday?
    b. Do you think Anna has been writing a birthday poem for the twins' twenty-first
    birthday?
2. **a.** Anna had finished the poem by the twins' birthday.
    b. Anna did finish the poem by the twins' birthday.
3. **a.** Michael had been painting a picture for the twins before he left town on a business trip
    to Salt Lake City.
    b. Michael had painted a picture for the twins before he left town on a business trip to
    Salt Lake City.
4. **a.** The twins had been telling everyone not to make a fuss.
    b. The twins told everyone not to make a fuss.
5. **a.** Nonetheless, the twins' friends planned a surprise party.
    b. Nonetheless, the twins' friends were planning a surprise party.
6. **a.** Last year, they forgot to celebrate the twins' birthday.
    b. Last year, they did forget to celebrate the twins' birthday.
7. **a.** I have been shopping for the perfect gift for weeks.
    b. I had been shopping for the perfect gift for weeks.
8. **a.** Marc and Lydia had been arguing before the twins arrived.
    b. Marc and Lydia were arguing before the twins arrived.
9. **a.** The twins looked happy.
    b. The twins were looking happy.
10. **a.** By this time next week, the twins will have begun their thank-you notes.
    b. By this time next week, the twins will begin their thank-you notes.

Exercise 15   **Expressing Past Time in a Paragraph**

Write a paragraph of at least eight sentences about an important event in your past.
Underline five verbs or verb phrases that you have used. Use some progressive and emphatic
forms if possible. (Remember that the perfect tenses, as well as the past tense, can be used
to express past action.)

15.6 Compatibility of Tenses

Do not shift, or change, tenses when two or more events occur at the same time.

INCORRECT	During the concert the pianist **forgot** the notes, and she **stops** in the middle of the piece. [The tense needlessly shifts from the past to the present.]
CORRECT	During the concert the pianist **forgot** the notes, and she **stopped** in the middle of the piece. [Now it is clear that both events happened at nearly the same time in the past.]
INCORRECT	The maestro **leaves** the podium. The audience **gave** him a standing ovation. [The tense needlessly shifts from the present to the past.]
CORRECT	The maestro **leaves** the podium. The audience **gives** him a standing ovation. [It is clear that both events are happening at about the same time.]

Shift tenses to show that one event precedes or follows another.

INCORRECT	By the time we **arrived,** they **ate** dinner. [The two past-tense verbs give the mistaken impression that both events happened at the same time.]
CORRECT	By the time we **arrived,** they **had eaten** dinner. [The shift from the past tense (*arrived*) to the past perfect tense (*had eaten*) clearly indicates that they ate the dinner before we arrived.]

Keep a statement about a general truth in the present tense even if other verbs are in the past tense.

He **remembered** that Boise **is** the capital of Idaho.

Exercise 16   Choosing Compatible Tenses

Find the first verb that appears in each sentence below. Then write the compatible tense of the verb in parentheses.

1. Kim Mason had been saving her earnings to buy a CD player she (sees, had seen) in the window of Music World.
2. It had been almost a year since she (opens, opened) her savings account.
3. By the time she had saved enough money to buy the CD player, it (goes, went) on sale.
4. She purchased the CD player and also (buys, bought) some CDs.
5. Kim learned that saving diligently (is, was) the best way to get what you want.

Making Tenses Compatible

First find the two verbs that appear in each of the following sentences. Then rewrite each sentence, making the second verb compatible with the first verb.

Maxine Hong Kingston: A Writer's Heritage

1. Maxine Hong Kingston was born in Stockton, California, in 1940 and was speaking Cantonese as a child.
2. After she received several scholarships, she attends college at the University of California at Berkeley.
3. Before she switched to English, Kingston studies engineering.
4. Kingston found out in college that she is not a reporter.
5. While she wrote her first book, Kingston supports herself with a full-time job.
6. When *The Woman Warrior: Memoirs of a Girlhood Among Ghosts* was published in 1976, reviewers praise its combination of autobiography, fiction, and history.
7. By the time I finished *The Woman Warrior*, I learned a great deal about Kingston's childhood.
8. Kingston published *China Men* four years after she was writing *The Woman Warrior*.
9. In *China Men* Kingston described her grandfather, who works on the transcontinental railroad in the early 1900s.
10. After I completed *The Woman Warrior*, I had decided to read *China Men* as well.
11. *The Woman Warrior* won the National Book Critics Circle Award for nonfiction in 1976, and four years later, *China Men* had received the National Book Award.
12. Kingston made her debut as a novelist when she has written *Tripmaster Monkey His Fake Book*.
13. This novel tells the story of Wittman Ah Sing, who had been a graduate of Berkeley and a Chinese American hippie.
14. Kingston sets the story in San Francisco in the 1960s and has made Sing a kind of rebel with a cause.
15. The story follows Sing as he will pursue his dream of writing and staging a huge Chinese saga.
16. The novel has been described as surreal and will have been called a bitter and funny tale.
17. In the course of the story, Sing falls in love and also searched for his grandmother in Reno, Nevada.
18. Maxine Hong Kingston is married to Earll Kingston, the actor, and they had had a son, Joseph.
19. Unlike his mother, Joseph Kingston is not a writer; instead, he had been a musician.
20. Maxine Hong Kingston makes her home in Oakland, California, where she continued to write.

15.7 Voice of Verbs

An action verb is in the **active voice** when the subject of the sentence performs the action.

> The student **submitted** her report.

An action verb is in the **passive voice** when its action is performed on the subject.

> The report **was submitted** by the student.

Generally the active voice is stronger, but at times the passive voice is preferred or, in fact, necessary. If you do not want to call attention to the performer or do not know who the performer is, use the passive voice.

> The dinner **was ruined.** [You may not want to identify the culprit.]

> The manuscript **was stolen.** [You may not know who the culprit is.]

You form the passive voice by using a form of the auxiliary verb *be* with the past participle of the verb. The tense of a passive verb is determined by the tense of the auxiliary verb.

> The child **is pleased** by the dog. [present tense, passive voice]

> The child **was pleased** by the dog. [past tense, passive voice]

> The child **will be pleased** by the dog. [future tense, passive voice]

| Exercise 18 | Identifying Active and Passive Voice |

Write the verb in each sentence and tell if it is *passive* or *active*.

Denver International Airport

1. In 1995 the largest airport in North America opened for business.
2. Denver International Airport has been labeled by its supporters as the airport for the twenty-first century.
3. The airport was built on fifty–three square miles of prairie land northeast of the city.
4. Mismanagement and technological mishaps pushed the final cost to almost $5 billion, $3 billion over budget.
5. Three parallel runways are designed to handle ninety–nine aircraft every hour.
6. The control tower, 327 feet tall, will operate even in severe weather.
7. An automated underground transit system and a superhighway of moving sidewalks transport passengers to their gates.
8. Some of the glitches in the $232-million automated baggage system have been corrected.
9. Baggage is no longer shredded by the state-of-the-art system.
10. The baggage system winds for twenty miles beneath the terminal.

Exercise 19   Changing the Voice of Verbs

Rewrite the following sentences, changing active verbs to passive and passive verbs to active. When using passive verbs, drop the performers of the action if they do not need to be identified. Make other wording changes as needed.

SAMPLE   Long-distance health care *was made* possible by new technology.
ANSWER   New technology *has made* long-distance health care possible.

Explorer Robots

1. The explorer robot has been brought to us by new technology.
2. Human beings operate some of these robots.
3. Areas dangerous to people have been explored by these robots.
4. NASA has tested some explorer robots.
5. Marine biologists expect explorer robots to do underwater research.
6. Endurance superior to that of humans is offered by these robots.
7. Therefore, explorer robots can maintain underwater equipment.
8. Pictures of Mars were relayed to Earth by planetary explorer robots.
9. Engineers have designed some explorer robots to help the physically challenged.
10. Scientists predict a great future for explorer robots.
11. A robotic arm has been constructed by engineers at NASA's Jet Propulsion Laboratory.
12. The device can imitate any action of a surgeon's electronic pointer.
13. The arm provides surgeons access to remote regions of the spine and brain.
14. The robotic arm will be tested on humans by medical researchers.
15. Engineers at MIT are developing a surgical robot for fulfilling a surgeon's commands.
16. Two small cameras have been placed inside the robot's head by engineers.
17. The cameras can continually transmit magnified images back to a video console.
18. A surgeon can direct the robot's movements by manipulating surgical tools mounted on the console.
19. For the next century, long-distance operating rooms with fiber-optic cable connectors are envisioned by researchers.
20. However, many obstacles must first be overcome by medical researchers and electronic engineers.

Exercise 20   Writing Sentences with Active and Passive Voice

Write a paragraph of ten sentences describing a process with which you are familiar. Use a combination of active and passive verbs in your paragraph.

Grammar Review

Verb Tenses and Voice

The following literary passage is taken from *Black Boy*, Richard Wright's autobiography. Born in Natchez, Mississippi, in 1908, Wright grew up poor, neglected, and hungry. In this passage he describes a happy memory: the abundant meals that his Aunt Maggie served at her home in Arkansas. The passage has been annotated to show some of the kinds of verbs covered in this unit.

Literature Model

from BLACK BOY: A RECORD OF CHILDHOOD AND YOUTH
by Richard Wright

Passive voice ——

Active voice ——

Past tense of an irregular verb ——

Present tense of an irregular verb ——

Past progressive form ——

. . . At mealtime Aunt Maggie's table was so loaded with food that I could scarcely believe it was real. It took me some time to get used to the idea of there being enough to eat; I felt that if I ate enough there would not be anything left for another time. When I first sat down at Aunt Maggie's table, I could not eat until I had asked:

"Can I eat all I want?"

"Eat as much as you like," Uncle Hoskins said.

I did not believe him. I ate until my stomach hurt, but even then I did not want to get up from the table.

"Your eyes are bigger than your stomach," my mother said.

"Let him eat all he wants to and get used to food," Uncle Hoskins said.

When supper was over I saw that there were many biscuits piled high upon the bread platter, an astonishing and unbelievable sight to me. Though the biscuits were right before my eyes, and though there was more flour in the kitchen, I was apprehensive lest there be no bread for breakfast in the morning. I was afraid that somehow the biscuits might disappear during the night, while I was sleeping. I did not want to wake up in the morning, as I had so often in the past, feeling hungry and knowing that there was no food in the house. So, surreptitiously, I took ➡

some of the biscuits from the platter and slipped them into my pocket, not to eat, but to keep as a bulwark against any possible attack of hunger. Even after I had got used to seeing the table loaded with food at each meal, I still stole bread and put it into my pockets. In washing my clothes my mother found the gummy wads and scolded me to break me of the habit; I stopped hiding the bread in my pockets and hid it about the house, in corners, behind dressers. I did not break the habit of stealing and hoarding bread until my faith that food would be forthcoming at each meal had been somewhat established.

— Past perfect tense

— Past tense of a regular verb

Exercise 1

Identifying Principal Parts of Verbs   The following sentences elaborate on ideas suggested by the passage from *Black Boy*. Each sentence contains an italicized verb in one of four forms: (a) the base form, (b) the past form, (c) the present participle, or (d) the past participle. At the end of the sentence is a second verb in parentheses. First, identify the form of the verb in italics. Then write the verb in parentheses in the same form as the original verb.

SAMPLE   The family *dined* at Aunt Maggie's. (eat)
ANSWER   past form; ate

1. At home in Mississippi, food had often *seemed* scarce. (be)
2. Young Wright *had* the acute, daily ache of hunger. (feel)
3. His stomach frequently was *churning* with discomfort. (growl)
4. Then Wright and his mother *traveled* to his aunt's home in Arkansas. (come)
5. They are *visiting* Wright's Aunt Maggie and Uncle Hoskins today. (see)
6. The kindly pair *welcome* them into their home. (take)
7. Wright *wondered* at the amount of food in the kitchen. (marvel)
8. Later Wright was *devouring* an abundant dinner. (eat)
9. He had *consumed* the food until his stomach ached. (eat)
10. Aunt Maggie *carried* a lavish platter of hot biscuits to the table. (bring)
11. Wright had *grown* fearful that the biscuits would disappear before breakfast. (become)
12. He was even *concealing* extra food in his pocket. (hide)
13. His mother had *found* gummy wads of bread in his pocket. (discover)
14. For many days he *feared* that every full meal might be his last. (think)
15. This fear of hunger *remained* with him for months. (stay)

Exercise 2

Using the Present, Past, and Future Tenses   The following sentences are based on passages from *Black Boy* that are not reprinted in this textbook. On your paper write the tense of each italicized verb according to the directions in parentheses. Use only the present, past, and future tenses; with the exception of *will* to express the future tense, do not use any helping verbs.

SAMPLE   Wright's mother *will bring* her son to Arkansas. (Change to the present tense.)
ANSWER   brings

1. On the train to Elaine, Arkansas, Wright *will become* aware of racism and segregation. (Change to the present tense.)
2. In those days, African Americans and whites *ride* in separate sections of the train. (Change to the past tense.)
3. The naive youngster *wanted* a peek at the whites' part of the train. (Change to the present tense.)
4. His mother *says*, "Quit talking foolishness!" (Change to the past tense.)
5. The travelers *went* to Aunt Maggie and Uncle Hoskins's home to live. (Change to the future tense.)
6. Uncle Hoskins *owned* a prosperous business in town. (Change to the present tense.)
7. Aunt Maggie *will have* plenty of food on the dinner table. (Change to the past tense.)
8. Soon a major calamity *will break* Wright's mood of contentment. (Change to the present tense.)
9. Some white people in town, envious of Uncle Hoskins's success, *murder* him one night. (Change to the past tense.)
10. Aunt Maggie, Wright, and Wright's mother *flee* to safety in another town. (Change to the future tense.)
11. Wright's four years at Jim Hill public school *were* his only opportunity for formal study. (Change to the present tense.)
12. At first the principal *puts* him in the fifth grade. (Change to the past tense.)
13. After studying day and night, Wright *passes* to the sixth grade. (Change to the future tense.)
14. Flushed with success, Wright *thinks* about studying medicine. (Change to the past tense.)
15. In school he *will try* to deter questions about his home and his life. (Change to the present tense.)
16. At noon he *went* to the sandwich shop with some of his classmates. (Change to the future tense.)
17. One of the boys *sensed* Wright's dilemma. (Change to the present tense.)
18. Later he *suggests* that Wright earn some money by selling newspapers published in Chicago. (Change to the future tense.)
19. Slowly Wright *collects* customers in the African American neighborhoods. (Change to the past tense.)
20. Later he *found* out that the newspapers preach the Ku Klux Klan doctrine. (Change to the present tense.)

Exercise 3

Using the Perfect Tenses   Each of the following sentences is based on events in Richard Wright's *Black Boy*. On your paper write the form of the italicized verb that belongs in the place indicated by the caret. Follow the directions in parentheses, using the past participle of the main verb and the appropriate form of the helping verb *have*.

SAMPLE   Before he arrived in Arkansas, Wright ∧ in Mississippi and Tennessee. (past perfect tense of *reside*)

ANSWER   had resided

1. By the time he became a teenager, Wright ∧ in several southern states. (past perfect tense of *live*)
2. Wright ∧ the age of four before he moved from his grandparents' home near Natchez, Mississippi. (past perfect tense of *reach*)
3. When Richard's grandmother ∧ ill for some time, a fire nearly destroyed the Wright home. (past perfect tense of *be*)
4. The fire ∧ through several rooms by the time Wright could flee to safety. (past perfect tense of *tear*)
5. When the adults at last put out the blaze, nearly half the house ∧ down. (past perfect tense of *burn*)
6. Wright ∧ to Arkansas to live with his aunt and uncle. (present perfect tense of *come*)
7. Wright ∧ in Memphis, Tennessee, but he had never lived in Arkansas before. (past perfect form of *live*)
8. For most of her life before she decided to leave Memphis, his mother ∧ against exhaustion and despair. (past perfect tense of *struggle*)
9. Her meager wages ∧ her almost no money for food. (present perfect tense of *leave*)
10. Now that his mother ∧ Wright to his aunt's home, he is finally getting enough to eat. (present perfect tense of *bring*)
11. Because he ∧ constant hunger, at first he eats until his stomach hurts. (present perfect tense of *know*)
12. After he ∧ a meal, he hides bread in his pockets. (present perfect tense of *finish*)
13. His mother often finds gummy wads of bread in the clothes that she ∧. (present perfect tense of *wash*)
14. She realizes what he ∧ and scolds him. (present perfect tense of *do*)
15. In spite of her criticism, she understands why he ∧ the bread. (present perfect tense of *steal*)
16. During his short life he already ∧ great hardship and misery. (present perfect tense of *endure*)
17. In a month or so Wright ∧ the habit. (future perfect tense of *break*)
18. By then he ∧ more confident that food will always be available. (future perfect tense of *become*)
19. Violence tears the family apart when they learn that envious whites ∧ Uncle Hoskins. (present perfect tense of *murder*)
20. By the following morning, mother and son ∧ safety in a nearby town. (future perfect tense of *reach*)

Exercise 4

Using the Progressive and Emphatic Forms   Each of the following sentences is based on events in Richard Wright's *Black Boy*. On your paper write the form of the italicized verb that belongs in the place indicated by the caret. Follow the directions in parentheses, using the present participle of the main verb and the appropriate tense of *be* or the base form of the main verb and the appropriate form of *do*.

SAMPLE   The writer ∧ about the meaning of his life. (present progressive form of *think*)
ANSWER   is thinking

1. A train trip to Arkansas in 1917 ∧ Wright about the realities of the Jim Crow laws that limited the rights of African Americans. (past emphatic form of *teach*)
2. He wonders why whites and African Americans ∧ in separate sections of the train. (present progressive form of *sit*)
3. During the train ride to Arkansas, Wright ∧ about his grandmother's life as a slave before the Civil War. (present progressive form of *ask*)
4. Tonight young Wright ∧ in the home of his Uncle Hoskins. (future progressive form of *sleep*)
5. Although startled at first by all the food served by his aunt, eventually Wright ∧ to Hoskins's home. (past emphatic form of *adjust*)
6. Envious men in town ∧ Uncle Hoskins's life. (past progressive form of *threaten*)
7. One night Aunt Maggie ∧ for Uncle Hoskins's return when a tall boy knocked on the door. (past progressive form of *wait*)
8. The threat ∧ a reality: Uncle Hoskins was murdered. (past emphatic form of *become*)
9. Weeks later a regiment of African American soldiers ∧ with rifles on their shoulders. (future progressive form of *parade*)
10. Soon these troops ∧ in World War I. (future progressive form of *fight*)

Exercise 5

Identifying and Using Voice of Verbs   The following sentences are about Richard Wright and *Black Boy*. First, identify each sentence as being in either the *passive voice* or the *active voice*. Then rewrite each sentence, changing the active voice to the passive or the passive voice to the active.

SAMPLE   *Black Boy* was written by Richard Wright.
ANSWER   passive voice; Richard Wright wrote *Black Boy*.

1. The events in *Black Boy* are recounted by the author with fury and eloquence.
2. The Civil War ended slavery in the United States.
3. Little was done by society about the plight of African Americans.
4. *Black Boy* was written by Richard Wright as a story of protest.
5. Wright's forceful voice has inspired generations of African Americans.

Exercise 6

Making Tenses Compatible The following sentences elaborate on events in the passage from *Black Boy*. On your paper correct the tense of the italicized verb so that the tenses are compatible.

SAMPLE Before Wright came to his aunt's home in Arkansas, he *lived* in Memphis, Tennessee.

ANSWER had lived

1. Aunt Maggie was married to Uncle Hoskins, who *runs* a thriving business near their home in Arkansas.
2. In Memphis Wright *is eating* poorly, but at Aunt Maggie's he ate well.
3. He *sits* shyly at the table when Aunt Maggie brought out the first meal.
4. Aunt Maggie was a fine cook, and she *sets* a variety of savory foods on the table.
5. As Wright *bites* into a biscuit, he recalled his many hungry times.
6. The others had not yet finished their first portion when Wright *takes* a second helping of the food.
7. After his meals Wright *puts* some extra food into a pocket or hid it in the house.
8. Wright's mother *finds* wads of bread when she washed his clothes.
9. Wright controlled his urge to hoard food only after he *becomes* certain of the source of his next meal.
10. In his years in Memphis, Wright *is failing* to gain weight, but in Arkansas, at Aunt Maggie's table, he never went hungry.
11. Wright is hired by a white family who *will want* someone to milk cows, feed chickens, and serve meals.
12. The woman teaches him how to milk and *had shown* him how to gather eggs.
13. When he came into the house, Wright noticed that the dining table *will have been set* for five people.
14. He was appalled that the family habitually *had cursed* each other.
15. When the time came for him to return to school, he *will be* physically tired and emotionally spent.
16. He *clings* to the job, however, because the family never measured how much food he ate.
17. Back home, when he described his meals, his family *feels* envious.
18. In class Wright *will fall* behind with his academic work because he had drifted off to sleep so many times.
19. To keep himself awake and alert, he goes to the water fountain and *ran* cold water over his wrists.
20. Now that he is earning money, he *has bought* sandwiches for lunch.

Exercise 7

Using Verb Tenses in Writing Choose a story you have read recently or seen at the movies or on television. Write ten sentences about the story and the characters. In each sentence, use at least two verbs that are compatible in tense. Write the verbs and label the tenses. Use all six verb tenses in your sentences: present, past, future, present perfect, past perfect, and future perfect.

SAMPLE ANSWER   I recently read a story that I had wanted to read for some time.
read–past tense; had wanted–past perfect tense

Exercise 8

Proofreading

The following passage describes the artist William H. Johnson, whose painting appears on the opposite page. Rewrite the passage, correcting the errors in spelling, grammar, and usage. Add any missing punctuation. There are twenty-five errors.

William H. Johnson

[1]William H. Johnson (1901–1970), one of the most innovative artists of the Harlem Renaissance is born in Florence, South Carolina. [2]One day one of his elementary school teachers founded on Johnson's desk a piece of paper with a remarkable likeness of herself. [3]His teachers and his family, recognizing his talent encourage Johnson to develop his skill as a painter.

[4]When he was seventeen, Johnson moved to Harlem a neighborhood in New York City. [5]Three years later he accepted into the prestigious National Academy of Design, where he won several awards. [6]He gone to Paris in 1926. [7]He was spending twelve years altogether in Europe, nine of them in Scandinavia. [8]There he studied art and met the Danish woman who become his wife. [9]His painting was influenced by the highly expressive works of Vincent van Gogh the famous Dutch Postimpressionist.

[10]Johnson once describes himself as primitive and cultured at the same time. [11]When he come back to the United States, he had refined his hybrid style. [12]Using vivid colors and a delibreatly primitive technique, he painted scenes of contemporary African American life. [13]Poor farm workers city dwellers, soldiers, convicts, musicians, and preachers appear often in his work. [14]The heightened colors and the strong emotional tone of his paintings shows the influence of the European school of painting known as Expressionism.

[15]Soon after World War II ended, Johnson hospitalized for a nervous disorder. [16]Tragically, his last years was spent in mental institutions. [17]His works has continued to be exhibited and praised despite his career's premature end. ➡

William H. Johnson, *Jim*, 1930

[18]*Jim*, a relatively early portrait is painted in a style that Johnson later abandoned. [19]The vivid colors and loose brush strokes is reminiscent of Expressionist techniques. [20]It is not hard to imagine the young Richard Wright as the boy in Johnsons painting. [21]The gaze in Jim's eyes suggest an inner turmoil that seems akin to the physical and spiritual hunger that Wright felt as a boy.

Exercise 9

The following sentences describe the life and literary achievements of the author Richard Wright. Rewrite each sentence, following the directions in parentheses.

SAMPLE   Richard Wright portrayed his childhood and also writes about urban life.
(Change the second verb to make the tenses compatible.)

ANSWER   Richard Wright portrayed his childhood and also wrote about urban life.

Richard Wright

1. Richard Wright was born in a rural region of Mississippi, where his grandparents were enslaved before the Civil War. (Change the second verb to the past perfect tense.)
2. Wright lived in Memphis when his father abandoned the family to a life of poverty. (Change the first verb to the past progressive form.)
3. After he had spent time with relatives in Arkansas and Mississippi, Wright had returned to Memphis. (Change the second verb to the past tense.)
4. In Memphis Wright worked as a postal clerk when he decided to become a writer. (Change the first verb to the past progressive form.)
5. He reads several books that stimulated his interest in becoming a writer. (Change the first verb to make the tenses compatible.)
6. The American author H. L. Mencken wrote one of those books. (Rewrite the sentence in the passive voice.)
7. Financial aid was given to the budding author by the Federal Writers' Project, a government assistance program. (Rewrite the sentence in the active voice.)
8. Before he moved to New York City in 1937, Wright lived for a time in Chicago. (Change the second verb to the past perfect tense.)
9. Wright first wins attention with *Uncle Tom's Children*, a collection of short works of fiction that appeared in 1938. (Correct the error caused by the use of the present tense.)
10. Two years later he published his popular novel *Native Son*. (Rewrite the sentence in the passive voice.)
11. *Native Son* was adapted for the Broadway stage by the noted director Orson Welles. (Rewrite the sentence in the active voice.)
12. Eventually Hollywood turned *Native Son* into a film drama. (Change the verb to the past emphatic form.)
13. When an Argentine film version of *Native Son* appeared in 1951, Wright himself plays the main character, Bigger Thomas. (Correct the error caused by the use of the present tense.)
14. An American studio recently released a film adaptation of *Native Son*. (Change the verb to the present perfect tense.)
15. In fact, the video store in my neighborhood stocks the 1986 version of *Native Son*. (Change the verb to the present emphatic form.)

Writing Application

Verbs in Writing   In this passage from her autobiography *I Know Why the Caged Bird Sings*, Maya Angelou describes the relationship between her grandmother and the aristocratic Mrs. Flowers. As you read, concentrate on Angelou's use of verbs, especially the italicized ones.

> Mrs. Flowers didn't belong to our church, nor *was* she Momma's familiar. Why on earth *did* she *insist* on calling her Sister Flowers? Shame made me want to hide my face. Mrs. Flowers deserved better than to be called Sister. Then, Momma left out the verb. Why not ask "How *are* you, Mrs. Flowers?" With the unbalanced passion of the young, I hated her for showing her ignorance to Mrs. Flowers. It didn't occur to me for many years that they were as alike as sisters, separated only by formal education.

Techniques with Verbs   When you write and revise your own work, try to use verbs as Angelou does.

1. Do not shift tenses when referring to events in the same time frame.

Incorrect version   Mrs. Flowers doesn't belong to our church, nor was she Momma's familiar.
Angelou's correct version   Mrs. Flowers didn't belong to our church, nor was she Momma's familiar.

2. Use the emphatic form and the active voice to make a point.

Unemphatic passive version   Why was Mrs. Flowers called Sister Flowers by her?
Angelou's version   Why on earth did she insist on calling her Sister Flowers?

Practice   Revise the following passage on a separate sheet of paper. Keep verb tenses consistent and use active voice as much as possible.

Maya Angelou has enriched American culture with the many books and poems she had written. Perhaps best known for her multivolume autobiography, she also will have been remembered for the poem she wrote to commemorate the inauguration of President William Jefferson Clinton. She completed the poem several days before Clinton was inaugurated.

Interestingly, an experience was shared by President Clinton and this gifted African American writer: They both spent their childhood in Arkansas and were cared for by grandmothers whom they will remember with great affection.

UNIT

16

Subject-Verb Agreement

Grammar | **Lessons**

A verb must agree with its subject in number and person.

Number can be singular or plural. Singular words indicate one; plural words indicate more than one. A singular subject takes a singular verb. A plural subject takes a plural verb.

With most verbs the only change in form to indicate agreement in person occurs in the present tense. An *-s* (or *-es*) is added to the base form of the verb when its subject is third-person singular.

SINGULAR	PLURAL
She **speaks.**	They **speak.**
He **exercises.**	They **exercise.**
She **pitches.**	They **pitch.**

The linking verb *be* changes in both the present and the past tense.

SINGULAR	PLURAL
He **is** there.	They **are** there.
It **was** sweet.	They **were** sweet.

In verb phrases the auxiliary verbs *be*, *have*, and *do* change in form to show agreement with third-person subjects.

SINGULAR	PLURAL
He **is going.**	They **are going.**
She **is reading.**	They **are reading.**
She **has seen** a movie.	They **have seen** a movie.
Does he **stay** here?	**Do** they **stay** here?

Do not mistake a word in a prepositional phrase for the subject of a sentence.

The simple subject is never within a prepositional phrase. Make sure the verb agrees with the actual subject and not with the object of a preposition.

The *taste* of the cherries **surprises** us. [The subject, *taste*, is singular; *of the cherries* is a prepositional phrase; therefore, the verb, *surprises*, is singular.]

The *spices* in the food **are** interesting. [The subject, *spices*, is plural; *in the food* is a prepositional phrase; therefore, the verb, *are*, is plural.]

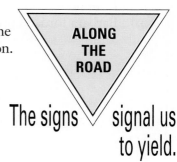

ALONG THE ROAD

The signs signal us to yield.

Making Subjects and Verbs Agree

Write on your paper the form of the verb indicated in parentheses that agrees with the subject of each sentence.

A Class Field Trip

1. Don (is/are) looking forward to the field trip.
2. Carol (wants/want) to take the bus.
3. The teacher (tells/tell) the class about the park.
4. They (is/are) going to the zoo after lunch.
5. The bus driver (waits/wait) for the students to return.

Making Subjects and Verbs Agree When Prepositional Phrases Intervene

Find the simple subject in each of the following sentences. Then write on your paper the form of the verb indicated in parentheses that agrees with the subject of each sentence.

Barbara Jordan: A Prominent Texan

1. Barbara Jordan's years in the U.S. Congress (has/have) given her a unique perspective on American politics.
2. Over thirty years ago, this distinguished graduate of two universities (was/were) first attracted to politics.
3. Jordan, despite many setbacks and difficulties, (has/have) achieved many of her goals.
4. A public speaker with Jordan's exceptional talents (is/are) rare.
5. Politicians from every state (was/were) impressed with Barbara Jordan's address at the 1976 Democratic National Convention.
6. Perhaps Jordan's extraordinary abilities in public speaking (was/were) encouraged by her father, a Baptist minister.
7. African American women, in Jordan's opinion, (needs/need) to make their voices heard in government.
8. Jordan's reputation in political circles (was/were) enhanced by her strong role in the congressional hearings about the impeachment of President Richard Nixon.
9. Jordan, in spite of her popularity among Texas voters, (was/were) planning by 1978 to leave politics for a teaching career.
10. Barbara Jordan's place in history books clearly (seems/seem) secure.

16.2   Agreement with Linking Verbs

Do not be confused by a predicate nominative that is different in number from the subject. Only the subject affects the number of the linking verb.

> The lightest **crate is** two tons. [The singular verb, *is*, agrees with the singular subject, *crate*, not with the predicate nominative, *tons*.]

> Recent **studies** on the behavior of wild animals **are** his topic for the day. [The plural verb, *are*, agrees with the plural subject, *studies*, not with the predicate nominative, *topic*.]

Exercise 3   Making Linking Verbs Agree with Their Subjects

Find the simple subject or subjects in each of the following sentences. Then write on your paper the form of the verb in parentheses that agrees with the subject of each sentence.

Our Endangered Forests and Wildlife

1. The growing threat to America's wild animals (is/are) a national problem.
2. Another problem (is/are) the many acres of forest land we lose each year.
3. Wildlife (remains/remain) a rich and vital part of our national heritage.
4. Animals (is/are) also an important part of our world.
5. Research on plant and animal life (is/are) the means of much scientific discovery.
6. Our forests (is/are) also a wonderful resource for recreation.
7. Not long ago our forest land (was/were) millions of acres more extensive.
8. Growing cities (is/are) part of the problem.
9. By the 1990s one result of deforestation (was/were) high numbers of endangered species.
10. Adequate food (is/are) a necessity for animals.
11. The cost of deforestation (is/are) years of floods and damaging soil erosion.
12. Harmful effects on the wild animals that depend on the forest (is/are) a result of deforestation.
13. The long-term effects of excessive hunting and fishing (is/are) another problem.
14. State governments (is/are) important agencies in protecting our endangered forests.
15. The destructive results (is/are) a disturbance in the balance of nature.
16. Our land (is/are) our home, our heritage, and our gift to the future.
17. Protected lands (seem/seems) the only hope for wildlife.
18. Our forests (remains/remain) an important part of their survival.
19. Efforts by government and private citizens (seems/seem) the solution.
20. We (is/are) all part of the solution.

16.3 Agreement in Inverted Sentences

In an **inverted sentence**—a sentence in which the subject follows the verb—take care in locating the simple subject, and make sure that the verb agrees with the subject.

Inverted sentences often begin with prepositional phrases. Do not mistake the object of the preposition for the subject.

                                           V   **S**

SINGULAR   In the jungle **roars** the *lion.*

                                           V   **S**

PLURAL   In the jungle **roar** the *lions.*

                                                        V   **S**

SINGULAR   In a large cage at the zoo **rests** a noble *lion.*

                                                        V   **S**

PLURAL   In a large cage at the zoo **rest** two noble *lions.*

In inverted sentences beginning with *there* or *here*, look for the subject after the verb. The word *there* or *here* is almost never the subject of a sentence.

                                     V   **S**

SINGULAR   There **is** a *lion* in the jungle.

                                   V   **S**

                     Here **goes** the *ambulance.*

                                   V   **S**

PLURAL   There **are** *lions* in the jungle.

                                   V   **S**

                     Here **go** the two *ambulances.*

In questions an auxiliary verb may come before the subject. Look for the subject between the auxiliary verb and the main verb.

                                   V   **S** **V**

SINGULAR   **Does** that *lion* **live** in the jungle?

                                   V   **S**   **V**

PLURAL   **Do** those *jungles* **contain** lions?

Find the simple subject in each of the following sentences. Then write on your paper the form of the verb in parentheses that agrees with the subject of each sentence.

Dining Out

1. There (is/are) three excellent and unusual restaurants in my neighborhood.
2. In the window of one of the restaurants (hangs/hang) an interesting menu.
3. Over the door of another (swings/swing) an old and elaborate sign.
4. Outside the third (stands/stand) two statues representing servers.
5. (Does/Do) the restaurant owners ever cook and bake?
6. (Is/Are) expert chefs brought in to create mouth-watering specialties to please the demanding clientele?
7. There (is/are) a pleasant decor in all three of these restaurants.
8. Into the restaurants (crowds/crowd) the hungry customers.
9. Here (comes/come) the people who want to eat before they go to the theater.
10. There (gathers/gather) the people waiting to be seated.
11. On one menu (is/are) a picture of an unusual animal.
12. On the sign there (is/are) three pictures of the food served.
13. In the lap of one statue in a corner of the restaurant (rests/rest) a knife.
14. How (does/do) the owner find all the foods for the menus?
15. There (is/are) special menus for children in each restaurant.
16. On each table (is/are) a vase of flowers.
17. On a table in the center of the restaurant (is/are) dishes from other countries.
18. There (is/are) a line of three young men outside the door.
19. (Does/Do) the three men have reservations?
20. Here (comes/come) the third delivery of food for today.

On your paper write the following sentences as inverted sentences. Make sure each verb agrees with its subject.

Team Trophies

1. The prize trophy rests in the office.
2. The members of the team are sitting in the hall.
3. Ten other trophies won by other teams are also in the case.
4. The principal hopes to keep the trophies in the new case. (Write as a question.)
5. The trophy for the basketball tournament is here.

16.4   Agreement with Special Subjects

Collective Nouns

A **collective noun** names a group. Consider a collective noun singular when it refers to a group as a whole. Consider a collective noun plural when it refers to each member of a group individually.

SINGULAR   His ***family* arrives**.
PLURAL   His ***family* are** well.

SINGULAR   The ***committee* decides**.
PLURAL   The ***committee* sign** their names.

Special Nouns

Certain nouns that end in -*s*, such as *mumps, measles,* and *mathematics,* take singular verbs.

SINGULAR   ***Mumps* is** a disease.

Certain other nouns that end in -*s*, such as *scissors, pants, binoculars,* and *eyeglasses,* take plural verbs.

PLURAL   The ***scissors* were** sharp.
               Your ***eyeglasses* need** cleaning.

Many nouns that end in -*ics* may be singular or plural, depending upon their meaning.

SINGULAR   ***Statistics* is** an interesting subject. [one subject of interest]
PLURAL   ***Statistics* show** that women live longer than men. [more than one application of this particular field of study]

Exercise 6   **Using Special Subjects in Sentences**

Write 10 sentences. In each sentence use one of the following nouns as the subject. Make sure each subject agrees with a present-tense verb.

SAMPLE   measles
ANSWER   Measles is a common childhood disease.

1. club
2. politics
3. family
4. fleet
5. audience
6. stairs
7. mathematics
8. news
9. analysis
10. group

Nouns of Amount

When a noun of amount refers to a total that is considered as one unit, it is singular. When it refers to a number of individual units, it is plural.

SINGULAR	Three **dollars is** not too much for that book. [one amount]
PLURAL	Three **dollars are** on the table. [three individual bills]
SINGULAR	Ten **years is** a decade. [one unit of time]
PLURAL	Ten **years have passed.** [ten individual periods of time]

Titles

A title is always singular, even if a noun within the title is plural.

SINGULAR	**Great Expectations is** one of the best-loved novels in English literature.

players is a team.

Five players are
on the court.

Exercise 7   **Making Verbs Agree with Special Subjects**

Find the subject in each sentence. Then write on your paper the form of the verb in parentheses that agrees with the subject.

Roberto Clemente, a Baseball Hero

1. The first baseball team to hire Roberto Clemente (was/were) the Santurce Cangrejeros of Puerto Rico.
2. When Clemente became a professional ball player with the Pittsburgh Pirates in 1954, 50 thousand dollars (was/were) considered a princely salary.
3. Clemente's family (was/were) eager to show its pride in him.
4. Roberto Clemente's impressive offensive and defensive statistics (shows/show) that he was a versatile player.
5. Professional athletics (is/are) a demanding field.
6. Clemente's 18 years in major-league baseball (is/are) considered a long career.
7. Five hours (is/are) a long time for a professional baseball game to last.
8. On December 31, 1972, his team (was/were) all very much shocked to hear that Clemente had died in a plane crash while taking supplies to earthquake victims in Nicaragua.
9. Sometimes a professional athlete's second family (is/are) his or her teammates.
10. Our class agrees that *Homers* (is/are) an appropriate title for a biography of Roberto Clemente.

16.5 Agreement with Compound Subjects

Compound Subjects Joined by *And*

A compound subject that is joined by *and* or *both . . . and* is plural unless its parts belong to one unit or they both refer to the same person or thing.

<table>
<tr><td>PLURAL</td><td>The **lion** and the **tiger are roaring**.
Both **skiing** and **skating are** fun.</td></tr>
<tr><td>SINGULAR</td><td>**Peanut butter** and **jelly is** a favorite combination. [Compound subject is one unit.]</td></tr>
<tr><td></td><td>His **friend** and **companion accompanies** him. [One person is both friend and companion.]</td></tr>
</table>

Compound Subjects Joined by *Or* or *Nor*

With compound subjects joined by *or* or *nor* (or by *either . . . or* or *neither . . . nor*), the verb always agrees with the subject nearer the verb.

<table>
<tr><td>PLURAL</td><td>*Neither* the **lion** *nor* the **tigers are roaring**.</td></tr>
<tr><td>SINGULAR</td><td>*Either* the **lion** *or* the **tiger is roaring**.
Neither the **lions** *nor* the **tiger roars**.</td></tr>
</table>

Exercise 8 — Writing Sentences with Compound Subjects

Write five sentences. In each sentence, use one of the following items as the compound subject. Make the compound subject agree with a present-tense verb.

1. bread and butter
2. neither the players nor the coach
3. both the climate and the geography of the South
4. Aunt Susan or Uncle Harold
5. either a cat or a dog

Many a, *Every*, and *Each* with Compound Subjects

When *many a*, *every*, or *each* precedes a compound subject, the subject is considered singular.

SINGULAR   *Many a* **giraffe** and **elephant lives** in the nature preserve.

Every **chair, bench,** and **table was taken.**

Each **lion** and **tiger is roaring.**

Exercise 9   Making Verbs Agree with Their Subjects

On your paper write the appropriate form of each verb in parentheses.

Leontyne Price, Opera Star

1. The opera expert and the casual listener (agrees/agree) that Leontyne Price is one of the greatest living sopranos.
2. Price's friends and relatives in Mississippi (was/were) influential in her decision to pursue a career in music.
3. When Price undertook four demanding years of formal training in New York, neither her talents nor her ambition (was/were) lacking.
4. Before Price became a star, both Ira Gershwin and Virgil Thomson (was/were) impressed by Price's singing.
5. Price's longtime friend and adviser, vocal coach Florence Page Kimball, (feels/feel) that Price's finest role was that of Bess in Gershwin's *Porgy and Bess.*
6. Neither Price's performance in *The Magic Flute* nor her triumphs in Verdi's operas (has/have) given me as much pleasure as her singing in *Madame Butterfly.*
7. Fortunately, neither serious illnesses nor stage fright (has/have) interrupted Price's long career.
8. To be a successful singer like Price, talent and perseverance (is/are) required.
9. Every note, gesture, and facial expression (is/are) crucial to the success of a performance.
10. Many a performer and audience member (feels/feel) excited when the lights in a theater dim.

16.6   Intervening Expressions

Certain expressions, such as *accompanied by*, *as well as*, *in addition to*, *plus*, and *together with*, introduce phrases that modify the subject but do not change its number. Although their meaning is similar to that of *and*, these expressions do not create compound subjects.

If a singular subject is linked to another noun by an intervening expression, such as *accompanied by*, the subject is still considered singular.

SINGULAR   **Margaret,** *accompanied by* her date, **was** the first girl to dance.

The **pianist,** *as well as* the guitarist, the saxophonist, and the lead singer, **is** late.

Her **course load,** *plus* her extracurricular activities, **was** a lot to handle.

Sleet, *in addition to* snow, **is expected** tomorrow.

Sports, *together with* band, **is** the most popular extracurricular activity.

Exercise 10   Making Verbs Agree with Intervening Expressions

On your paper write the appropriate form of each verb in parentheses.

Becoming a Singer

1. A voice teacher, as well as friends and relatives, (is/are) helpful in encouraging a young singer.
2. Talent, together with perserverance and practice, (makes/make) a successful career possible.
3. The student, accompanied by a pianist, (sings/sing) for the first time tonight.
4. Members of the orchestra, plus the soloist and the teacher, (prepares/prepare) for the evening's performance.
5. The teacher, together with family and friends, (applauds/applaud) the students.
6. The students, in addition to the teacher, (is/are) relieved that the performance went so well.
7. The performers, as well as the audience, (departs/depart) satisfied with the evening.
8. Lessons, in addition to practice, (has/ have) proven valuable.
9. Every student, plus the students' parents, (realizes/realize) the importance of rehearsing.
10. The class, together with the teacher, excitedly (discusses/discuss) the performance.

16.7 Indefinite Pronouns as Subjects

A verb must agree in number with an indefinite pronoun subject.

Indefinite pronouns can be divided into three groups, as shown in the following chart:

Indefinite Pronouns				
ALWAYS SINGULAR	each either neither one	everyone everybody everything no one	nobody nothing anyone anybody	anything someone somebody something	
ALWAYS PLURAL	several	few	both	many	
SINGULAR OR PLURAL	some	all	any	most	none

Plural indefinite pronouns take plural verbs. Singular indefinite pronouns take singular verbs.

SINGULAR   ***Everybody* is** going to the rodeo.
                 No one in the audience **looks** upset.
                 Something in the kitchen **smells** good.
PLURAL   ***Both*** of the children **are** in school this morning.
                 Many of the books **were** donated to the library.

A pronoun from the group labeled singular or plural can be either singular or plural, depending upon the noun to which it refers.

SINGULAR   ***Some*** of the dessert **is** left. [*Some* refers to *dessert*, a
                 singular noun.]
PLURAL   ***Some*** of the commuters **were caught** in the
                 rainstorm. [*Some* refers to *commuters*, a plural noun.]

Exercise 11   Making Verbs Agree with Indefinite Pronoun Subjects

Find the pronoun subject in each sentence and the noun to which it refers.
On your paper write each pronoun, noun, and the form of the verb in parentheses that agrees with the subject.

A Night at the Opera

1. All of the performers of the opera (knows/know) their parts.
2. Few of the soloists (was/were) needed for this particular work.
3. Any of the audience who came late (was/were) handed a program by the usher.
4. Each of the programs left after the performance (was/were) recycled.
5. Most of the audience members (was/were) pleased by the performance.

Exercise 12 — Writing Sentences with Indefinite Pronoun Subjects

Write 10 sentences. In each sentence use one of the following indefinite pronouns as the subject. Make each subject agree with a present-tense verb.

SAMPLE   one
ANSWER   One of my friends owns a racing bike.

1. each
2. many
3. few
4. both
5. neither
6. nobody
7. nothing
8. everything
9. one
10. several

Exercise 13 — Writing Sentences with Indefinite Pronoun Subjects

For each indefinite pronoun listed below, write two sentences, using the pronoun as the subject of both sentences. In the first sentence of each pair, use a singular present-tense verb. In the second sentence, use a plural present-tense verb.

SAMPLE   some
ANSWER   Some of the work is not finished.
         Some of the books are on the shelf.

1. none
2. any
3. most
4. all
5. some

Exercise 14 — Making Verbs Agree with Their Subjects

On your paper write the appropriate form of the verb in parentheses.

Butterflies

1. Almost all of these insects (has/have) some means of protection from enemies.
2. Many of them (excels/excel) at the art of imitation.
3. Some insects, like the tree hopper, (looks/look) like inanimate objects when they rest on a plant stem.
4. Some butterflies, like this one, (has/have) special coloration to startle would-be predators.
5. Some of the members of one group (has/have) subdued colors and fly at night.
6. Both of these (is/are) true butterflies.
7. Protective coloration, as well as spiny larvae, (is/are) characteristic of many butterflies.
8. The monarch butterfly, in addition to the pipe vine swallowtail, (has/have) a bitter taste.
9. Neither of these butterflies (makes/make) a tempting meal for a hungry bird.
10. Many of these birds (avoids/avoid) some butterflies.

Correcting Subject-Verb Agreement

The following paragraph contains 10 errors in subject-verb agreement. Locate the sentences with errors, and rewrite those sentences, using the verb form that agrees with the subject. (Not every sentence contains an error.)

Popular Music

[1]Many people in the cities of Los Angeles, Miami, and New York enjoys several kinds of popular music. [2]While a family in a Jamaican neighborhood in Brooklyn probably listen to reggae music together, a Dominican family in Miami probably like merengue. [3]Many a New Yorker, whether young or old, like jazz and blues. [4]Cuban Americans, as well as people from Puerto Rico, dances to the brassy music known as salsa. [5]The syncopated rhythms of calypso music is popular among people who come from Trinidad. [6]Very popular in the Hispanic communities of Los Angeles is Mexican folk songs called *rancheras.* [7]From the recording studios come one new popular hit after another. [8]Usually thousands of dollars are the sum needed to record a new song. [9]In many American cities neither the Motown tunes of the 1960s nor rock-and-roll have gone out of style. [10]Ask whether your family or friends enjoy a special kind of music.

Exercise 16 **Making Verbs Agree with Their Subjects**

On a separate sheet of paper, rewrite the following paragraphs, replacing each blank with a verb in the present tense.

The boy with black eyes _____ over the rim of the canyon into the valley below. Everything _____ pale, as if the hot midday sun has bleached the colors from the landscape. The boy stands with arms upraised and _____ a stone over the cliff. "One, two, three," _____ the boy as the stone falls, and on "four" he hears it clatter on the rocks. Then he remembers that in one of his pockets _____ the carving of the bird he finished the night before. As polished as river rocks _____ his bird, and as white as sunlight. Quickly, without thinking, the boy from Wide Ruins _____ the bird and _____ it over the cliff. There _____ a brief flash of white, and the bird is gone. Nobody, not even the boy, _____ whether it hits the ground.

The boy listens. No sounds from the valley far below _____ his ears. The silence of his surroundings _____ absolute. Suddenly, faint flutterings _____ a signal to turn his gaze downward. Far below him in the shade of the canyon _____ the valley floor. The boy peers intently, adjusting his gaze from the brightness of sun to the darkness of shadow. In the dimness there _____ a flash of white. _____ his eyes deceive him? Again _____ the white, and then it is gone. Both the valley and the air _____ again still. The boy waits another moment, but there _____ nothing. His family _____ . He turns away from the canyon.

Grammar Review

Subject-Verb Agreement

Simin Daneshvar is from Iran, and her novel *Savushun* describes the fortunes of an Iranian family at the time of the Second World War. The chief characters of the novel are a sensitive young woman named Zari and her husband, Yusof. In this passage, Zari spends a quiet afternoon in her garden with her twin daughters. The passage has been annotated to show some examples of subject-verb agreement covered in this unit.

Agreement between a singular pronoun subject and a singular past form of *be*

An inverted sentence with agreement between an indefinite pronoun subject (referring to the plural noun *flowers*) and the plural past form of *be*

An inverted sentence with agreement between a plural noun subject and the plural past form of *be*

Agreement between a compound noun subject and the plural past form of *be*

Agreement between a singular noun subject and a singular past form of *be*

Literature Model

from SAVUSHUN

by Simin Daneshvar
translated from the Persian
by M. R. Ghanoonparvar

Ten days had passed since Yusof had left for the winter pastures, and the weather in the garden wasn't much better than where he was. Summer always hurried in like this, chasing away spring. It was afternoon and Gholam was sprinkling water on the patio in front of the house. Zari, carrying gardening clippers, was looking for flowers to pick. But there were none worth picking in the garden. Mina and Marjan, chirping like birds, followed their mother from one bush to another. By the stream around the patio there were some cockscombs so wilted and dusty that not even an old hen would have looked at them twice. By another stream, the faces and heads of the snapdragons were all covered with dust. Some more humble plants were straining to close their eyes and sleep as the sun set. The only hope was for the tuberoses, which Gholam claimed would "blossom when there is a full moon." The orange-blossom petals had dried up completely and, under the trees, looked like dried and shriveled brown stars. How one missed winter, when the narcissuses opened at the edge of the streams, and gave their reflections to the passing water as a memento. The water flowed on, losing the ➡

reflections, pouring into the pool without a witness. One could only hear its current. And when spring came, the white and purple violets gracefully greeted the passing water without promise or memento.

Exercise 1

Making Subjects and Verbs Agree When Prepositional Phrases Intervene
Each of the following sentences describes characteristics of the Persian garden. On your paper rewrite each sentence, following the directions in parentheses. In some cases you will need to change the form of the verb to make the sentence correct; in other cases the verb will remain the same.

SAMPLE   For Persians, an image of paradise is created by gardens.
                 (Change *an image* to *images.*)

ANSWER   For Persians, images of paradise are created by gardens.

1. The scene on ancient Persian pottery often depicts garden images. (Change *scene* to *scenes.*)
2. A pool of water usually plays a prominent role in these scenes. (Change *A pool* to *Pools.*)
3. Often, too, the patterns on Persian rugs suggest a garden. (Change *Persian rugs* to *a Persian rug.*)
4. Persian gardens throughout the years have been laid out in four sections. (Change *the years* to *time.*)
5. Pavilions of cypress trees were often built at the center of the garden. (Change *Pavilions* to *A pavilion.*)
6. In Iran some gardens still follow this plan. (Move the prepositional phrase so that it comes directly after the subject.)
7. The pool in such a garden is still an important feature. (Change *such a garden* to *these gardens.*)
8. Sometimes streams from nearby areas supply the water for these pools. (Change *nearby areas* to *a nearby area.*)
9. In some seasons water is provided by sloping tunnels called *qanat* lines. (Move the first prepositional phrase so that it comes directly after the subject.)
10. The length of the *qanat* line varies considerably. (Change *line* to *lines.*)
11. Beneath the surface *qanat* lines connect the valleys to the snow-capped mountains. (Move the first prepositional phrase so that it comes directly after the subject.)
12. Owners of gardens rent the channel for a certain length of time. (Change *gardens* to *a garden.*)
13. From the mountains melting snow thus becomes a source of water. (Move the first prepositional phrase so that it comes directly after the subject.) ➡

14. Varieties of roses dominate Persian gardens. (Change *Varieties* to *A variety.*)

15. A rose with deep aroma has been used in many interesting ways. (Change *A rose* to *Roses.*)

16. Gardeners of certain roses press petals to make fragrant rosewater. (Change *Gardeners* to *A gardener.*)

17. A flavoring from the rose is used in a variety of desserts. (Change *the rose* to *roses.*)

18. The song of a nightingale makes a garden even more delightful. (Change *song* to *songs.*)

19. A common sight in Persian gardens is brightly colored tulips. (Change *A common sight* to *Common sights.*)

20. A plane tree of huge proportions often provides shade for the garden. (Change *A plane tree* to *Plane trees.*)

Exercise 2

Writing Sentences with Intervening Prepositional Phrases   The following sentences describe an imaginary garden. Rewrite each sentence, adding an appropriate prepositional phrase in the place indicated by the caret and choosing the correct form of the verb in parentheses.

SAMPLE   The flower garden ∧ (is/are) beautiful.

ANSWER   The flower garden behind my grandmother's house is beautiful.

1. Flowers ∧ (offers/offer) a spectacle of color throughout the growing season.

2. Some kinds of flowers ∧ (provides/provide) food and nectar for insects and other animals.

3. Fresh flowers ∧ (makes/make) the whole house smell good.

4. Flowers ∧ (adds/add) pleasure to your world.

5. Fragrant roses ∧ (delights/delight) all who behold them.

6. Lilacs ∧ (is/are) a charming sight.

7. The first crocuses ∧ (announces/announce) the coming of spring.

8. A small garden ∧ (needs/need) to be planned carefully.

9. Weeding ∧ (is/are) an important part of caring for a garden.

10. Bulbs ∧ (is/are) planted long before they are expected to bloom.

11. The rich soil ∧ (nourishes/nourish) the flowers.

12. People passing ∧ (enjoys/enjoy) the flowers' beauty and fragrance.

13. A birdbath ∧ (attracts/attract) robins and sparrows.

14. A vegetable garden ∧ (is/are) practical but not necessarily beautiful.

15. Vegetables ∧ (enhances/enhance) one's diet.

16. Fresh vegetables ∧ often (tastes/taste) better than vegetables bought in a store.

17. Surplus crops ∧ (is/are) frozen, dried, or canned.

18. A small herb garden ∧ (provides/provide) fresh seasonings for cooking.

19. Herb gardens ∧ (is/are) easy to take care of.

20. Daily watering ∧ (is/are) a must when rainfall is scarce.

Exercise 3

Making Linking Verbs Agree with Their Subjects   Each of the following sentences describes the scene from the passage from *Savushun*. On your paper rewrite each sentence, following the directions in parentheses. If necessary, change the number of the linking verb.

SAMPLE Gardens in Iran are retreats from the dry countryside. (Change *retreats* to *a retreat.*)
ANSWER Gardens in Iran are a retreat from the dry countryside.

1. Usually Zari's garden is a beautiful sight. (Change *garden* to *flowers.*)
2. Today, however, the main feature of the garden is a cluster of wilted flowers. (Change *a cluster* to *clusters.*)
3. An orange-blossom petal has become a shriveled jumble. (Change *An orange-blossom petal* to *Orange-blossom petals.*)
4. The streams are mirrors for the drooping blossoms. (Change *mirrors* to *a mirror.*)
5. The garden tool is a useless device on such a day. (Change *tool* to *clippers.*)
6. The only animals in the parched garden are birds. (Change *animals* to *surprising sight.*)
7. In winter a flowering plant is a welcome sight. (Change *a flowering plant* to *flowering plants.*)
8. In spring one image of loveliness is the violet. (Change *the violet* to *violets.*)
9. Water is the key to survival for these fragile plants. (Change *key to* to *means of.*)
10. Irrigation systems are the best solution for dry areas. (Change *Irrigation systems* to *An irrigation system.*)

Exercise 4

Making Subjects and Verbs Agree in Inverted Sentences   Each of the following sentences elaborates on an idea suggested by the passage from *Savushun*. First write each sentence on your paper, choosing the correct form of the verb in parentheses. Then rewrite each sentence in inverted order, using the correct verb form.

SAMPLE The hot sun (beats/beat) upon the dry plants.
ANSWER The hot sun beats upon the dry plants.
     Upon the dry plants beats the hot sun.

1. The clippers (is/are) in Zari's hand.
2. The gardener (stands/stand) among some bushes.
3. A gently curving stream (flows/flow) between the towering trees.
4. Some wilted cockscombs (droops/droop) by the side of the stream.
5. Crumbling orange-blossom petals (lies/lie) in the dry dust.
6. The colorful snapdragons (blooms/bloom) near another stream.
7. The limp blossoms (bends/bend) toward the parched earth.
8. The refreshing water (flows/flow) onto the thirsty plants.
9. New growth (comes/come) with frequent waterings.
10. The white tuberose (appears/appear) on cool moonlit nights.

Exercise 5

Making Verbs Agree with Special Subjects   The following sentences are about a panel discussion on the occupation of Iran during the Second World War by Great Britain and the Soviet Union. First write the subject of each sentence, and then write the form of the verb in parentheses that agrees with the subject.

SAMPLE   A panel of experts (prepares/prepare) for discussions of various aspects of the occupation of Iran.

ANSWER   panel prepares

1. Because mumps (is/are) spreading throughout the community, some students will miss the discussion.
2. Binoculars (helps/help) those in the back of the large auditorium to see the speakers.
3. *The Effects of Allied Occupation on Iran* (is/are) a book recommended by one of the speakers.
4. First the audience (learns/learn) about the German influence in Iran at the beginning of World War II.
5. The panel then (discusses/discuss) among themselves the British and Soviet control of Iran in the early 1940s.
6. The group at the podium (disagrees/disagree) about whether that occupation was necessary.
7. Five years (was/were) the length of the Allied occupation of Iran.
8. Our class next (hears/hear) about the economic and social problems in Iran at the time.
9. Thirty thousand (was/were) the approximate number of troops provided by the United States when it joined the occupation in 1942.
10. Statistics (shows/show) that the years of occupation were difficult for Iran.
11. The Committee on International Affairs (sponsors/sponsor) the discussion.
12. The committee (discusses/discuss) the issues thoroughly.
13. Nobody (arrives/arrive) late for the discussion.
14. Six months (has/have) passed since the last panel discussion.
15. A brief synopsis of the events leading to the occupation (is/are) given.
16. The ethics of the occupation (is/are) also discussed.
17. *World War II Military Occupations* (is/are) a book referred to by a speaker.
18. The faculty (is/are) represented by several teachers.
19. The hours spent at the panel discussion (is/are) very productive.
20. Afterwards, our class (is/are) divided on the need for the occupation.

Exercise 6

Making Verbs Agree with Compound Subjects   Each of the following sentences elaborates on an idea suggested by the passage from *Savushun*. On your paper rewrite each sentence, following the directions in parentheses and making any necessary adjustments to the form of the verb.

SAMPLE   Every flower needs water. (Add *and shrub* to the complete subject.)
ANSWER   Every flower and shrub needs water.

1. Mina scampers from bush to bush. (Add *and her sister* to the complete subject.)
2. Zari and the girls look for flowers. (Delete *and the girls* from the complete subject.)
3. Every cockscomb droops. (Add *and orange blossom* to the complete subject.)
4. Many a violet has faded. (Add *and narcissus* to the complete subject.)
5. Each stem withers. (Add *and blossom* to the complete subject.)
6. Zari and Gholam tend the garden. (Delete *and Gholam* from the complete subject.)
7. The stream and the pond supply water for the garden. (Delete *and the pond* from the complete subject.)
8. Many a dried leaf floats on the still water. (Add *and petal* to the complete subject.)
9. The spring and the winter bring fresh foliage. (Delete *and the winter* from the complete subject.)
10. Now Zari and her children want only the safe return of Yusof. (Delete *and her children* from the complete subject.)

Exercise 7

Making Subjects and Verbs Agree When Expressions Intervene   The following sentences describe the situation and characters in *Savushun*. Rewrite each sentence, correcting any errors in subject-verb agreement. If the sentence contains no errors, write *correct*.

1. In the novel *Savushun*, the British army, as well as Soviet troops, occupy Iran.
2. The troops, plus a poor harvest, causes a food shortage.
3. Yusof, as well as Zari, is sympathetic to the hungry nomads and peasants.
4. A tribal leader, accompanied by his brother, bring Yusof news of the peasants' hardships.
5. The peasant population, plus its sheep, is starving.
6. Yusof, accompanied by servants, have gone to his pastures.
7. Yusof, in addition to his foreman, visits the shepherds.
8. Zari, together with Yusof's sister, give food to the poor.
9. Bread, as well as dates, are taken by Zari to hospitals.
10. Famine, together with disease, cause death everywhere.

Exercise 8

Making Verbs Agree with Indefinite Pronoun Subjects   The following sentences describe gardens around the city of Shiraz, the setting of *Savushun*. Rewrite each sentence, replacing the indefinite pronoun in italics with the pronoun in parentheses. If necessary, change the number of the verb.

SAMPLE   *Many* of Iran's historic sites are near Shiraz.
           (One)

ANSWER   One of Iran's historic sites is near Shiraz.

1. *Most* of the sites, such as the tombs of the ancient poets Hafiz and Sadi, feature gardens. (A few)
2. *Both* of these poets are revered in Muslim cultures. (Each)
3. *Either* of their tombs attracts numerous visitors. (Both)
4. *Most* in Iran are familiar with the poems of Hafiz. (Everyone)
5. *Many* enjoy reading his verse in a nearby garden. (Anybody)
6. *Several* of the older gardens have vanished entirely. (Some)
7. *Each* of the area's palaces was decorated with mirrored tile. (Many)
8. *All* are able to imagine the beauty of the palaces. (Someone)
9. *Few* of the ancient gardens have been fully restored. (Several)
10. *Some* of the renovation of the Rose Garden is complete. (Most)

Exercise 9

Proofreading

The following passage describes manuscript illumination; an example by a Persian artist appears on the opposite page. Rewrite the passage, correcting any errors in spelling, usage, and grammar. Add any missing punctuation. There are twenty-five errors.

Persian Illuminated Manuscripts

[1]Illustrated, or illuminated, books was one of the highest art forms in the Islamic world. [2]From the tenth through the sixteenth centuries, manuscript painting was highly cherished for it celebrated the beauty and the power of the writen word. [3]Because in Islam books were considered to be the embodiment of devine revelation, they was treated with reverence. [4]Moreover, written Arabic lend itself to exquisite calligraphy a type of stylized handwriting. ➡

Habib Allah, from *Mantiq at-Tayr (Language of the Birds)*, c. 1600

[5]In Persia and in other Middle Eastern countries, the teachings of the sixth-century prophet Mohammed was often illustrated. [6]Similarly, many literary manuscripts was illustrated in the sixteenth century. [7]The illustration above date from that time. [8]It is taken from a book entitled *Mantiq at-Tayr (Language of the Birds)* which was written by Farid-Al-Din 'Attar. [9]The image of the birds in the garden are quite small intricate, and carfully painted. [10]Parts of the painting is covered with gold leaf, which was used to brighten the scene. [11]The imaje is a rich brocade that represents the idealized realm of the birds. [12]The birds themselves represents creatures of the heavens.

[13]At the upper right of the picture are the figure of a man. [14]This figure can be interpreted in two ways—as a guardian of the birds sanctuary or as a representation of the human threat to that world. [15]The painting, however, mirror the content of the book in reflecting an ideal world rather than an actual world. [16]Therefore, peace and harmony predominates.

[17]Garden-related themes appears in many Persian literary classics. [18]The richly varied colors and textures of nature is found not only in Persia's art but in it's architecture and in the many complex decorative designs that pervade Persian culture. [19]In the illumination at the top of this page, the colors and sounds of the garden calls up visions of natural beauty.

Mixed Review

Exercise 10

The following sentences describe the life and achievements of Simin Daneshvar [sē mēn´ dä´nesh vär´]. For each sentence write the appropriate form of the verb in parentheses.

Simin Daneshvar

1. Simin Daneshvar, as well as her husband, (figures/figure) prominently among contemporary Iranian writers.
2. Daneshvar, along with other Iranian writers, (criticizes/criticize) the lack of freedom in her homeland.
3. Studies at Tehran University (was/were) the foundation for her doctorate in Persian literature.
4. Daneshvar's lectures at Tehran University (has/have) exposed many scholars to her ideas.
5. All of Iran's social classes (is/are) represented in her fiction.
6. Among the greatest influences on her works (was/were) the famous American author O. Henry.
7. *The Quenched Fire* (1948) and *A City as Paradise* (1961) (deals/deal) with women's roles in society.
8. None of the stories in *The Quenched Fire* (has/have) been reprinted because the author was dissatisfied with the work.
9. In Daneshvar's most widely read novel, *Savushun* (1969), the descriptions of suffering (composes/compose) a portrait of the effects of war on common people.
10. Daneshvar's works (is/are) a realistic depiction of social problems in her country.
11. Politics in Iran (does/do) not generally encourage artistic freedom.
12. In Iran a woman who receives a doctorate, especially in Persian studies, (is/are) unusual.
13. There (is/are) many things Daneshvar wants to do to help her country.
14. One of her concerns (is/are) the needs of the people of Iran.
15. All of Iranian society (is/are) the subject of her work.
16. One of Daneshvar's objectives (has/have) been to help women.
17. Daneshvar (is/are) an author and storyteller who takes pride in her work.
18. Both her clear language and her graceful style (gives/give) a compelling picture of life in Iran.
19. I, as well as my best friend, (has/have) a better understanding of life in Iran after reading her books.
20. Persian, the language of Daneshvar's books, (is/are) an ancient language.

Writing Application

Subject-Verb Agreement   In this passage from *House Made of Dawn*, N. Scott Momaday demonstrates several examples of correct subject-verb agreement. Examine the passage, focusing especially on the italicized subjects and verbs.

My grandmother lived in a house near the place where Rainy Mountain Creek runs into the Washita River. Once there *was a lot* of sound in the house, a lot of coming and going, feasting and talk. The *summers* there *were* full of excitement and reunion. The Kiowas are a summer people; they abide the cold and keep to themselves, but when the season turns and the land becomes warm and vital they cannot hold still; an old *love* of going *returns* upon them. The old people have a fine sense of pageantry and a wonderful notion of decorum. The aged *visitors* who came to my grandmother's house when I was a child *were* men of immense character, full of wisdom and disdain.

Techniques with Subject-Verb Agreement   Try to apply some of the techniques used by Momaday when you write and revise your own work.

1.   Be alert to prepositional phrases and other expressions that fall between a subject and its verb. Mentally block them out when you check for agreement.

Incorrect use *visitors* who came to my grandmother's house when I was a child *was*
Momaday's correct use *visitors* who came to my grandmother's house when I was a child *were*

2.   When you check for agreement in inverted sentences, remember that the subject follows the verb. In inverted sentences beginning with *there* or *here*, remember that *there* or *here* is almost never the subject.

Incorrect use there *were* a *lot* of sound in the house
Momaday's correct use there *was* a *lot* of sound in the house

Practice   Practice these techniques by revising the following passage, using a separate sheet of paper. Rewrite the paragraphs, replacing each blank with a verb in the present tense.

At the tip of a high point overlooking the waves far below _____ the town. The handsome houses of the village _____ me of beautifully bound books on a high shelf. The wide windows facing the sea _____ the curve of book spines.

There, stretching into the distance on three sides, _____ the sea. The light glancing off the waves _____ me squint. The screech of gulls _____ the air. A sloop with billowing sails _____ toward the horizon. A fishing boat laden with crabs _____ toward the safety of harbor. The whole scene—cliff, sea, and houses— _____ so picturesque that it _____ like a watercolor.

Using Pronouns Correctly

17.1 Case of Personal Pronouns

Pronouns that are used to refer to persons or things are called **personal** pronouns.

Personal pronouns have three **cases,** or forms, called **nominative, objective,** and **possessive.** The case of a personal pronoun depends upon the pronoun's function in a sentence (whether it is a subject, a complement, or an object of a preposition).

Personal Pronouns			
Case	Singular Pronouns	Plural Pronouns	Function in Sentence
NOMINATIVE	I, you, she, he, it	we, you, they	subject or predicate nominative
OBJECTIVE	me, you, her, him, it	us, you, them	direct object, indirect object, or object of preposition
POSSESSIVE	my, mine, your, yours, her, hers, his, its	our, ours, your, yours, their, theirs	replacement for possessive noun(s)

Exercise 1   Identifying Pronoun Case and Function

On your paper write each personal pronoun in the sentences below. Then write what case each is, and how the pronoun functions in the sentence. One pronoun is used in a contraction.

SAMPLE   I first met him at our neighbor's party.

ANSWER   I—nominative, subject; him—objective, direct object; our—possessive, replacement for possessive noun

1. His parents had just moved into the vacant house next to ours.
2. My mother and father had just been introduced to his mother and father.
3. Maybe they should meet him, too, I thought.
4. We walked up to my mother, and I introduced him to her.
5. She extended her hand and said, "It's certainly a great pleasure to meet any friend of our son's."

The best guitar player was SHE was the best guitar player

Use these rules to avoid errors with the case of personal pronouns.

1. Use the nominative case for a personal pronoun in a compound subject.

   Paul and **I** play the guitar.   **She** and **I** sing duets.

2. Use the objective case for a personal pronoun in a compound object.

   Al's sister visited Al and **her**.   This is between you and **me**.

   Hint: In a sentence with a compound subject or object, try saying the sentence aloud without the conjunction and the other subject or object.

3. Use the nominative case of a personal pronoun after a form of the linking verb *be*.

   The best guitar player is **he**.   The best singer was **she**.

   This rule is changing. In informal speech, people often use the objective case after a form of the linking verb *be*; they say, *It's me, It was her.* Some authorities even recommend using the objective case in informal writing to avoid sounding pretentious. To be strictly correct, however, use the nominative case after the linking verb *be*, at least in formal writing.

4. Be careful not to spell possessive pronouns with apostrophes.

   This sheet music is **hers**.   The instruments are **theirs**.

   It's is a contraction for *it is.* Do not confuse *it's* with the possessive pronoun *its.*

   It's a great day for a walk. Bring me the guitar and **its** case.

5. Use possessive pronouns before gerunds (*-ing* forms used as nouns).

   Your dancing bothers me. He wasn't pleased with **my** singing.

Exercise 2	**Choosing the Correct Case Form**

On your paper write the correct personal pronoun from each pair in parentheses.

Phillis Wheatley, Poet

1. When you and (I/me) think of African American poets, we often forget Phillis Wheatley.
2. Susannah Wheatley, wife of slaveholder John Wheatley, took great interest in Phillis's education, and it was (she /her) who taught Phillis how to read and write English.
3. John Wheatley encouraged Susannah and (she/her) in their studies.
4. (Its/It's) sad that Phillis's health was not good.
5. My knowledge of Phillis Wheatley has increased by (me/my) reading about her.

17.2 Pronouns with and as Appositives

Use the nominative case for a pronoun that is in apposition to a subject or a predicate nominative.

The judges, **she** and **Mrs. Chiu,** will have a difficult task. [*Judges* is the subject of the sentence.]

The winners were the pianists, **Linda** and **he.** [*Pianists* is the predicate nominative.]

Use the objective case for a pronoun that is in apposition to a direct object, an indirect object, or an object of a preposition.

The audience cheered their favorite performers, **Darnell** and **her.** [*Performers* is the direct object.]

The director gave the stage crew, **Lee** and **him,** special thanks. [*Stage crew* is the indirect object.]

The judges explained the rules to both groups, **them** and **us.** [*Groups* is the object of the preposition *to.*]

When a pronoun is followed by an appositive, choose the case of the pronoun that would be correct if the appositive were omitted.

We violinists hope one day to play in a concert hall. [*We* is the correct form because *we* is the subject of the sentence.]

The music teacher handed the scores to **us musicians.** [*Us* is the correct form because *us* is the object of the preposition *to.*]

Hint: When you are choosing the correct pronoun, it is often helpful to say the sentence aloud without the appositive.

| Exercise 3 | Using Pronouns with and as Appositives |

For each sentence in the following paragraph, write on your paper the correct pronoun from the pair in parentheses.

Making a Movie

[1]The writers, Lawrence Kasdan and (she/her), were willing to revise the script. [2]The director worked well with the leads, Harrison Ford and (she/her). [3]The two cinematographers, Gordon Willis and (him/he), were both efficient and creative. [4](We/Us) young actors were lucky to work with such a fine team. [5]There is no question that working on this film had a positive effect on (we/us) beginners.

Using Pronouns with and as Appositives

For each of the following sentences, write on your paper the correct personal pronoun from the pair in parentheses.

The Game of Golf

1. The first lecturers, Anna and (I/me), explained to the class that golf was popularized by the Scottish king James IV and his granddaughter, Mary.
2. The two of them, James IV and (she/her), helped to introduce the game to sports enthusiasts in England and France.
3. We then mentioned that (we/us) Americans often do well in professional tournaments.
4. Nancy Lopez and (he/him), two very successful contemporary golfers, earn top salaries.
5. Hale Irwin and (she/her), two golf masters, were two recent winners of the United States Open.
6. Then the class asked golf experts Anna and (I, me) some questions about the game.
7. Two students, (he/him) and Larry, wanted to know how many Americans actually play the game.
8. (She, Her) and I, the experts, mentioned that the game is enjoyable for all age groups, both older people and (we/us) youngsters, because it emphasizes skill rather than strength.
9. We gave two students, Gayle and (he/him), a putter and a ball.
10. Both of us, Anna and (I, me), felt that our lecture to the class had gone very well.

Exercise 5   **Using Pronouns in Sentences**

On your paper complete the following sentences by replacing each blank with a personal pronoun that makes sense.

Impressionism

1. We art lovers, Claire and _____, have learned to appreciate the contribution made by Auguste Renoir to the art style known as Impressionism.
2. Two leaders in Impressionism were Monet and _____ .
3. The first Impressionist exhibit showcased Degas, Cézanne, and _____ .
4. Viewers were highly critical of the work by Renoir and _____ .
5. Critics were not pleased by _____ using mauve shadows.
6. The painters were derisively called Impressionists because of *Impression, Sunrise*, by Monet, which later became one of _____ more famous paintings.
7. The artists, Renoir and _____, were undaunted by the negative criticism.
8. Although Edouard Manet was never part of the group, he was a good friend of _____.
9. Renoir and _____ sometimes painted together.
10. The Impressionists have left a valuable legacy for _____ art lovers.

17.3 Pronouns After *Than* and *As*

In elliptical adverb clauses using *than* and *as*, choose the case of the pronoun that you would use if the missing words were fully expressed.

> You use a brush more skillfully than **I**. [The nominative pronoun *I* is the subject of the incomplete adverb clause *than I use a brush*.]

> The logic of the problem puzzled Jennifer as much as **me**. [The objective pronoun *me* is the direct object of the incomplete adverb clause *as much as it puzzled me*.]

Some sentences can be completed with either a nominative or an objective pronoun, depending on the meaning intended.

> Art liked Pat more than **I** [liked Pat].
> Art liked Pat more than [he liked] **me**.

In informal speech, people often use the objective rather than the nominative form in sentences such as *He is several years older than me*. In your writing, however, you should be careful to use the correct case.

| Exercise 6 | Using the Correct Pronoun After *Than* and *As* |

Each sentence contains an italicized word or group of words. On your paper rewrite each sentence, substituting the correct pronoun for the words in italics.

Rembrandt van Rijn, Dutch Painter

1. Nobody enjoys Rembrandt's paintings as much as *my family and I*.
2. Few Dutch artists in the seventeenth century could paint as well as *Rembrandt*.
3. Although Rembrandt's father had hoped his son would be a clergyman, few people supported the artist more than *Mr. van Rijn*.
4. It seems Rembrandt's artistic talent astonished his father as much as *his art teachers*.
5. Critics seemed to agree that nobody in Holland could paint better than *Rembrandt*.
6. Rembrandt's rise to fame must have pleased the artist even more than *the leaders of Amsterdam*.
7. As a portrait artist, Rembrandt was sought after much more than *other painters*.
8. Few models seemed as beautiful to Rembrandt as *a girl named Saskia*.
9. On the day of their wedding, it seemed nobody could have been happier than *Rembrandt and Saskia*.
10. Rembrandt's paintings seem to amaze people today even more than the *people of Rembrandt's century*.

Use the nominative pronoun *who* for subjects.

> **Who** won the contest? [*Who* is the subject of the verb *won.*]
> Tell me **who** is in your class. [*Who* is the subject of the noun clause *who is in your class.*]

In questions with an interrupting expression such as *did you say* or *do you think*, it is often helpful to drop the interrupting phrase to determine whether to use *who* or *whom.*

> **Who** do you think will emcee the show? [Think: *Who* will emcee the show? *Who* is the subject of the verb *will emcee.*]

Use the objective pronoun *whom* for the direct or indirect object of a verb or verbal or for the object of a preposition.

direct object

> **Whom** are you introducing first? [*Whom* is the direct object of the verb *are introducing.*]

> **Whom** did you say Maria invited to the party? [*Whom* is the direct object of the verb *invited.*]

> They told him **whom** he could invite to the show. [*Whom* is the direct object of the verb *could invite* in the noun clause *whom he could invite to the show.*]

> Theodore Roosevelt is a president about **whom** I have read quite a bit. [*Whom* is the object of the preposition *about* in the adjective clause *about whom I have read quite a bit.*]

Maria invited **them** to the party.
Maria invited **whom** to the party?

In informal speech, people generally use *who* in place of *whom* in sentences like *Who did you tell?* In writing and in formal speaking situations, however, make the distinctions between *who* and *whom.*

Exercise 7   Choosing *Who* or *Whom*

For each sentence, write on your paper the correct pronoun from the pair in parentheses.

Learning About Holography

1. (Who/Whom) did you say gave you the passes to the Museum of Holography?
2. Setsuko Ishii is the holographic artist about (who/whom) I've been reading.
3. Setsuko Ishii, (who/whom) many consider one of Japan's top holographic artists, has put together an exhibit at the museum.
4. The museum director, (who/whom) our teacher knows, will show us a 20-minute film.
5. The director mentioned several artists (who/whom) he said will exhibit in the future.

Choosing *Who* or *Whom*

For each of the following sentences, write on your paper the correct pronoun from the pair in parentheses.

George Washington Carver, Scientist

1. (Who/Whom) would you say changed forever the way we look at the lowly peanut?
2. George Washington Carver, (who/whom) many consider one of the best scientists of his day, developed hundreds of products from peanuts.
3. Carver, (who/whom) many still admire today, was born on a Missouri plantation in 1861 and left home when he was 10 years old.
4. He was accepted by a college in Kansas, but he was barred from attending by faculty members (who/whom) were prejudiced.
5. Carver was later admitted to Simpson College in Iowa and paid his way by ironing laundry for students (who/whom) were attending the college.
6. Carver, (who/whom) every student of agriculture has studied, made several important discoveries about plants.
7. Booker T. Washington, a scientist (who/whom) Carver greatly respected, invited Carver to work at the Tuskegee Institute in Alabama.
8. Carver, (who/whom) Washington believed to be hard working and imaginative, eventually came up with more than 300 products derived from peanuts, including peanut butter, ink, shampoo, vinegar, and a coffee substitute.
9. For (who/whom) did Carver develop these products?
10. Carver developed them for poor southern farmers, about (who/whom) he was greatly concerned.

Exercise 9   **Using *Who* or *Whom* in Sentences**

On your paper complete the following paragraph by replacing each blank with *who* or *whom*.

Mary Cassatt, an American Painter

¹Mary Cassatt, _____ many students of art admire, was a successful nineteenth-century American painter who spent much of her time in France. ²Her friends, _____ included Edgar Degas, were some of the great French Impressionists. ³Degas, _____ we know primarily for his paintings of ballerinas, greatly influenced Cassatt. ⁴Cassatt also encouraged American collectors to purchase the art of the Impressionists, _____ she considered very important. ⁵_____ are some other American artists influenced by the European Impressionists?

Exercise 10   **Using *Who* or *Whom* in Writing**

Write 10 sentences. In five, use the nominative pronoun *who*. In the other five, use the objective pronoun *whom*.

An **antecedent** is the word or group of words to which a pronoun refers or that a pronoun replaces. All pronouns must agree with their antecedents in number, gender, and person.

Agreement in Number and Gender

A pronoun must agree with its antecedent in number (singular or plural) and gender (masculine, feminine, or neuter).

A pronoun's antecedent may be a noun, another pronoun, or a phrase or clause acting as a noun. In the following examples, the pronouns appear in bold type and their antecedents in bold italic type. Notice how they agree in both number and gender:

> *Helen Keller* did not let an inability to see and hear prevent **her** from graduating *cum laude* from Radcliffe College. [singular feminine pronoun]
>
> *Helen Keller* and *Robert Smithdas* overcame many challenges to earn **their** college degrees. [plural pronoun]
>
> *Octavio Paz* is one of the greatest poets of **his** era. [singular masculine pronoun]
>
> *Walt Whitman* and *Emily Dickinson* are also famous for **their** poetry. [plural pronoun]
>
> The *horseshoe crab,* despite **its** name, is not a true crab but is related to the spider. [singular neuter pronoun]
>
> *Oysters* and *clams* are becoming endangered because of oil spills near **their** breeding grounds. [plural pronoun]

Traditionally a masculine pronoun is used when the gender of the antecedent is not known or may be either masculine or feminine.

> An *author* must capture **his** readers' interest.

This rule touches on an area of controversy and changing language usage, however. Although some people still prefer the traditional use of the masculine pronoun, others prefer to use a more gender-neutral expression. If you do not wish to use a masculine pronoun when the antecedent may be feminine, you can frequently reword the sentence in one of three ways: (1) by using *he or she, his or her,* and so forth, (2) by using a plural pronoun, or (3) by eliminating the pronoun.

> An *author* must capture **his or her** readers' interest.
> *Authors* must capture **their** readers' interest.
> *Authors* must capture readers' interest. [no pronoun]

Agreement in Person

A pronoun must agree in person with its antecedent.

Most problems with agreement in person arise when the second-person pronoun *you* is used incorrectly to refer to an antecedent in the third person. Either change *you* to an appropriate third-person pronoun, or replace it with a suitable noun.

POOR   Suki and James are going to visit the Everglades, where **you** can see storks and alligators.

BETTER   Suki and James are going to visit the Everglades, where **they** can see storks and alligators.

BETTER   Suki and James are going to visit the Everglades, where **tourists** can see storks and alligators.

When the antecedent of a pronoun is another pronoun, be sure that the two pronouns agree in person. Avoid unnecessary shifts from *they* to *you*, *I* to *you*, or *one* to *you*.

POOR   **They** often visit New Orleans, where **you** can enjoy French cooking.

BETTER   **They** often visit New Orleans, where **they** can enjoy French cooking.

POOR   **I** hiked on trails that amazed **you** with their beauty.

BETTER   **I** hiked on trails that amazed **me** with their beauty.

POOR   When **one** travels, **you** can learn a lot.

BETTER   When **one** travels, **one** can learn a lot.

BETTER   When **you** travel, **you** can learn a lot.

Exercise 11   **Making Pronouns and Antecedents Agree**

Complete the following sentences by writing an appropriate possessive pronoun for each blank. Also write the antecedent for each pronoun that you supply.

Sarah Winnemucca, a Piute Spokeswoman

[1]Sarah Winnemucca, the daughter of a Piute chief, was taken by _____ grandfather to California in 1850. [2]Some years later, after she had learned English and Spanish, she moved to Nevada and worked for a stagecoach agent and _____ wife and family. [3]When several bands of Piutes were forced off their ancestral land in the 1860s, Winnemucca served as _____ interpreter. [4]After lecturing in the East about the plight of her people, she moved to the town of Vancouver and taught in one of _____ schools for Native Americans. [5]Winnemucca's book *Life Among the Piutes* was a great success, and it has added to _____ understanding as Americans of an important chapter in Native American history.

Exercise 12   Making Pronouns and Antecedents Agree

In each of the following sentences, find the personal pronoun and its antecedent. If there is an error in agreement, rewrite the sentence in one or more ways to correct the problem. If there is no error, write *correct*.

Ethnic Cuisines

1. A cook who likes unusual food is in luck these days, for they can find plenty of ethnic recipes and special ingredients.
2. A lover of Japanese food can prepare their own shrimp or vegetable tempura.
3. Even an amateur chef can make their own pasta at home, using an electric or hand-cranked machine.
4. A person who is partial to Mexican food can concoct their own hot sauce with tomatoes, onions, and hot green peppers.
5. Shoppers can visit ethnic grocery shops, where they can purchase many hard-to-get ingredients, such as dried Chinese mushrooms, tortilla mix, collard greens, juniper berries, pine nuts, and litchi nuts.
6. People who crave a North African dish can purchase your own couscous and add morsels of meat or fish.
7. A seafood lover might want to try his luck at paella, a delicious Spanish dish that includes shrimp, clams, rice, and vegetables.
8. While sipping bouillabaisse, a fish stew, an American can imagine that they are sitting at a French café.
9. Food lovers can take cooking classes, where you will learn how to prepare lefse and other Norwegian foods.
10. Connoisseurs of ethnic foods know that they can distinguish an Italian meatball from a Swedish one by their different seasonings.

Exercise 13   Making Pronouns and Antecedents Agree in Person

On your paper rewrite each of the following items, eliminating the inappropriate use of *you* by substituting a third-person pronoun or a suitable noun.

José Feliciano: A Success Story

1. Visually impaired people face more obstacles than the sighted, for you must be unusually self-reliant and persevering.
2. José Feliciano is a highly respected visually impaired musician. He grew up in Puerto Rico, where you had to struggle hard to get ahead.
3. When Feliciano was five, he and his family moved to New York, where you hoped to find better opportunities.
4. From his idol, Ray Charles, Feliciano learned that visually impaired people can succeed in the music business. You must learn to expect setbacks and disappointment, however.
5. Feliciano's fans praise his skillful guitar playing. They say that you can expect nothing less than the best from this disciplined musician.

Agreement with Indefinite Pronoun Antecedents

In general, use a singular personal pronoun when the antecedent is a singular indefinite pronoun, and use a plural personal pronoun when the antecedent is a plural indefinite pronoun.

Indefinite Pronouns				
ALWAYS SINGULAR	each either neither one	everyone everybody everything no one	nobody nothing anyone anybody	anything someone somebody something
ALWAYS PLURAL	several	few	both	many
SINGULAR OR	some	all	any	most
PLURAL	none			

> *Each* of the boys must buy **his** own uniform.
> *One* of the women has **her** own diving equipment.
> *Many* of the students bring **their** lunch to school.

Notice that the plural nouns in the prepositional phrases—*of the boys*, *of the women*—do not affect the number of the personal pronouns. *His* and *her* are singular because *each* and *one*, their antecedents, are singular. In speaking, however, people often use the plural pronoun *their*:

> INFORMAL   *Neither* of the boys bought **their** own uniforms.
> FORMAL   *Neither* of the boys bought **his** own uniform.

When no gender is specified, writers traditionally make a masculine pronoun agree with an indefinite antecedent.

> *Everyone* must buy **his** own uniform.

This rule, again, is one that is experiencing a change, because some people today prefer a more gender-neutral wording. If you do not want to use a masculine pronoun when the indefinite pronoun may refer to a female, try rewording your sentence. You might substitute a plural indefinite pronoun or a word like *people* for the singular indefinite pronoun. Or you might eliminate the personal pronoun entirely. (Although some people use two pronouns, many writers consider such wording awkward.)

> *All* must buy **their** own uniforms.
> *People* must buy **their** own uniforms.
> *Everyone* must buy a uniform. [no pronoun]

On your paper indicate which of the following sentences are correct. Then revise each of the incorrect sentences to make it correct. In some cases you will need to change a single word; in others you may wish to revise the entire sentence.

Native American Medicine

1. Many of the Native American nations relied on their shaman, or medicine man, to treat anyone who became ill.
2. All of the herbs in the shaman's collection had special curative powers of its own.
3. Many in the Dakota nation drank powdered skunk-cabbage roots to relieve his asthma.
4. Each of the women in the Cheyenne nation would gather their own stock of wild mint, which was used to treat nausea.
5. Everybody searched for natural remedies for their illnesses; the Cree people chewed the cones of the spruce tree to soothe sore throats.
6. Among the Kiowa anybody with dandruff knew that their scalp should be washed with soaproot.
7. Some of the Utes treated his cuts and bruises with a salve made from the yarrow plant.
8. Many who lived on the frontier owed his life to natural cures.
9. Some of the pioneers ended their bouts with scurvy by eating wild garlic, a plant used by many Native American nations.
10. Today few doctors question the curative powers of Native American medicines, and their respect for the shaman's remedies continues to grow.

Exercise 15   **Using Pronouns in Sentences**

On your paper complete each of the following sentences by writing a personal pronoun that agrees with its indefinite pronoun antecedent.

Early Native American Nations

1. Each of the Native American leaders spoke _____ own language.
2. Few of the Native Americans shared a language with _____ neighbors.
3. Each of the Inuit mothers dressed _____ children in fur parkas, while some children in more southern climates wore little clothing.
4. In some of the Native American nations, everybody carried _____ goods by canoe.
5. Many of the Great Plains groups hunted animals for _____ food.
6. Some of the other Plains nations developed _____ farming skills.
7. Everyone worked hard harvesting _____ crops.
8. Some of the Native Americans in the Southwest foraged for food, and acorns were a mainstay of _____ diet.
9. Many who lived in the Southwest made _____ homes of adobe.
10. In some nations, each of the men had to support _____ own family, while in other nations resources were shared.

Make sure that the antecedent of a pronoun is clearly stated and that a pronoun cannot possibly refer to more than one antecedent.

Vague Pronoun Reference

Do not use the pronouns *this*, *that*, *which*, and *it* without a clearly stated antecedent.

VAGUE	She is an excellent singer, and **this** was evident in the performance last night. [What showed in the performance? Her talent showed, but the word *talent* is not specifically mentioned.]
CLEAR	She is an excellent singer, and **her talent** was evident in the performance last night.
VAGUE	The senator loved public speaking, and **that** greatly helped boost his popularity. [What helped boost his popularity? His speeches did, but the word *speeches* is not specifically mentioned.]
CLEAR	The senator loved public speaking, and **his speeches** greatly helped boost his popularity.
VAGUE	Last week our garage burned, **which** started from a kerosene heater. [What started from a kerosene heater? A fire started, but the word *fire* is not specifically mentioned.]
CLEAR	Last week a fire, **which** started from a kerosene heater, burned our garage.
VAGUE	The Supreme Court is deliberating on the question of the death penalty, and **it** will have a great impact on the nation. [What will have a great impact? The Supreme Court's decision will, but the word *decision* is not specifically mentioned.]
CLEAR	The Supreme Court is deliberating on the question of the death penalty, and **its decision** will have a great impact on the nation.

Ambiguous and Indefinite Pronoun Reference

If a pronoun seems to refer to more than one antecedent, either reword the sentence to make the antecedent clear, or eliminate the pronoun.

When the tickets slipped between the reports, **they** were lost.

UNCLEAR ANTECEDENT   When the tickets slipped between the reports, **they** were lost. [Which word is the antecedent of *they?* Were the tickets or the reports lost?]

CLEAR ANTECEDENT   The tickets were lost when **they** slipped between the reports.

NO PRONOUN   When the tickets slipped between the reports, **the tickets** were lost.

Avoid the indefinite use of the pronouns *you* and *they.*

INDEFINITE   In Japan **you** bow after saying hello.
CLEAR   In Japan **people** bow after saying hello.

INDEFINITE   In some countries **they** take a nap after lunch.
CLEAR   In some countries **people** take a nap after lunch.

Exercise 16   **Making Pronoun References Clear**

For each sentence determine whether the antecedent of the italicized pronoun is clear or unclear. If the antecedent is unclear, rewrite the sentence to make it clear. You may need to reword the sentence or eliminate the pronoun. If the antecedent is clear, write *clear.*

France

1. France is the largest country of western Europe, and *it* is quite beautiful and historic.
2. France has sunny beaches, *which* stretch along the Mediterranean Sea.
3. Their delicious food and wine are important to the French, and *they* are often considered the best in the world.
4. In France *they* really know how to enjoy life.
5. France also plays an important role in world politics, and *this* affects many other countries.
6. Paris is the capital of France, and *it* is also the country's largest city.
7. Paris has been home to many of the world's best artists, and *this* is reflected in the number of masterpieces that have been painted there.
8. When writers and artists arrive in Paris, *they* immediately fall in love with the city.
9. Paris is both cultured and beautiful, *which* impressed American writers Ernest Hemingway and Gertrude Stein.
10. Hemingway met the popular writer F. Scott Fitzgerald in Paris, and *he* helped *him* get his stories published.

| Exercise 17 | Making Pronoun References Clear |

On your paper rewrite each of the following sentences, making sure that all pronoun references are clearly stated.

Politics

1. The governor told the mayor that she would win by a landslide.
2. When the mayor thanked the governor, she was happy.
3. People who wish to vote must get to the polling places before 7:00 P.M., for after that you are turned away.
4. A citizens' group charged that the elections had been fixed, and it angered the officials.
5. The newspaper's editors criticized the politicians, and they argued for full disclosure of the facts.
6. The activists said that some of the politicians in the city had accepted bribes; this was a scandal.
7. Eric's father was mayor of the city, which gave him considerable social status.
8. When several of the newspapers disclosed the mayor's actions, it caused a great decline in his prestige.
9. The city council member told the newspaper reporter that he had manipulated the coverage of the election.
10. The early election returns pleased the senator, which had been widely predicted.

| Exercise 18 | Using Pronouns Correctly |

On your paper rewrite each of the following sentences by eliminating any mistakes in the use of pronouns. Each sentence has one error.

Sports Jargon

1. Sportscasters and us use sports jargon frequently.
2. A word that means one thing in ordinary conversation, sometimes changes it's meaning when applied to sports.
3. Anyone who watches tennis knows that you call an unreturned serve an ace.
4. The same word is used in golf, which refers to a hole in one.
5. In baseball a bean ball is a pitch thrown so near a batter's head that your head is in danger of being hit.
6. The batter must watch each ball carefully and determine it's speed and position.
7. We watched Roger Clemens pitch three shutouts in a row, and him pitching so well seemed almost miraculous to us.
8. The word *eagle* is familiar to my friends and I.
9. No one was more surprised than me to learn that in golf the word *eagle* means "two strokes under par."
10. I always thought I knew sports, but it was her who first made me especially aware of sports jargon.

Grammar Review

Using Pronouns Correctly

In this passage from *The Old Man and the Sea*, an aging Cuban fisher named Santiago sets out for his day's work after 84 days without a catch. A young boy named Manolín has come to see him off. The passage has been annotated to show examples of the kinds of pronouns covered in this unit.

Literature Model

from THE OLD MAN AND THE SEA
by Ernest Hemingway

The boy was back now with the sardines and the two baits wrapped in a newspaper and they went down the trail to the skiff, feeling the pebbled sand under their feet, and lifted the skiff and slid her into the water.

"Good luck old man."

"Good luck," the old man said. He fitted the rope lashings of the oars onto the thole pins and, leaning forward against the thrust of the blades in the water, he began to row out of the harbor in the dark. There were other boats from the other beaches going out to sea and the old man heard the dip and push of their oars even though he could not see them now the moon was below the hills.

Sometimes someone would speak in a boat. But most of the boats were silent except for the dip of the oars. They spread apart after they were out of the mouth of the harbor and each one headed for the part of the ocean where he hoped to find fish. The old man knew he was going far out and he left the smell of the land behind and rowed out into the clean early morning smell of the ocean. He saw the phosphorescence of the Gulf weed in the water as he rowed over the part of the ocean that the fishermen called the great well because there was a sudden deep of seven hundred fathoms where all sorts of fish congregated because of the swirl the current made against the steep walls of the floor of the ocean. Here there were concentrations of ➡

Pronoun in the possessive case

The pronoun *them* in the objective case is used as a direct object. The pronoun agrees in number with its antecedent, *boats*.

Pronoun in the nominative case used as a subject

The pronoun in the nominative case used as a subject agrees in gender and number with its antecedent, *the old man*.

shrimp and bait fish and sometimes schools of squid in the deepest holes and these rose close to the surface at night where all the wandering fish fed on them.

> Pronoun in the objective case used as the object of a preposition

In the dark the old man could feel the morning coming and as he rowed he heard the trembling sound as flying fish left the water and the hissing that their stiff set wings made as they soared away in the darkness. He was very fond of flying fish as they were his principal friends on the ocean. He was sorry for the birds, especially the small delicate dark terns that were always flying and looking and almost never finding, and he thought, the birds have a harder life than we do except for the robber birds and the heavy strong ones. Why did they make birds so delicate and fine as those sea swallows when the ocean can be so cruel? She is kind and very beautiful. But she can be so cruel and it comes so suddenly and such birds that fly, dipping and hunting, with their small sad voices are made too delicately for the sea.

> The pronoun *they* in the nominative case is used as a subject. The pronoun agrees with its antecedent, the irregular plural *fish*.

He always thought of the sea as *la mar* which is what people call her in Spanish when they love her. Sometimes those who love her say bad things of her but they are always said as though she were a woman.

> The pronoun *who* in the nominative case is used as the subject of *love*.

Exercise 1

Choosing Nominative and Objective Pronouns   The following sentences give background information on the passage from *The Old Man and the Sea*. For each sentence determine whether the italicized nominative or objective pronoun is used correctly. If it is not, on your paper write the pronoun as it should appear. If it is used properly, write *correct*.

SAMPLE   Although the old man had been fishing for weeks, finding nothing had not discouraged his young companion or *he*.

ANSWER   him

1. The boy and Santiago had worked together for many years, but now Santiago and *him* would no longer be able to fish together.
2. The boy's parents had made it clear that *they* disapproved of his working with the unlucky old fisher.
3. It was *him* who had brought supper the previous night for the old man and himself to share.
4. Forgetting his parents, the boy had decided, "It is *us* who will eat supper together this evening."
5. Martin, the owner of a nearby restaurant, had kindly provided the supper for Santiago and *he*.

Exercise 2

Choosing the Correct Pronoun Case   The following sentences give background information on the passage from *The Old Man and the Sea*. For each sentence determine whether the italicized pronoun is used correctly. If it is not, write the correct pronoun on your paper. If it is used correctly, write *correct*.

1. Santiago stood by the boat with the other fishers as the fisher and *him* prepared to leave.
2. By *him* fitting the ropes onto the thole pins, the old man secured the boat's oars.
3. Other fishers were near, and Santiago could hear them rowing, although he could not see their boats or *them*.
4. It was *him* who would catch a fish so huge that it would astonish the other fishers.
5. The ocean suddenly became deep, and *it's* current made a deep swirl over the well in the ocean floor.
6. Santiago seemed to realize the ocean was beautiful, but the ocean was also cruel to wildlife and men like *he*.
7. The old man watched the terns and thought, "The gulls and terns have a harder life than *me*."
8. He also pitied the sea swallows, and the sad voices he heard were *their's*.
9. Santiago landed a huge marlin, but *it's* size was a challenge.
10. After sharks bit the marlin's head, Santiago thought that the fish was now *theirs* and his.

Exercise 3

Using Pronouns Correctly with and as Appositives   The following sentences are based on passages from *The Old Man and the Sea* not reprinted in this textbook. For each sentence determine whether the italicized pronoun appears in the proper form. If it does not, write the correct pronoun on your paper. If it is used properly, write *correct*.

1. The restaurant owner sometimes fed the two fishers, the boy and *he*.
2. The two early risers, Santiago and *him*, quietly left the hut and went to the boat.
3. Joe DiMaggio was a great athlete; apparently Santiago's idols were two baseball players, Dick Sisler and *him*.
4. While at sea Santiago caught a dolphin with two fish in its stomach; such catches, *they* and a tuna, were his only food.
5. Santiago loved the terns and often watched two groups of birds, *they* and the swallows.
6. Santiago hooked a marlin that attracted sharks; he had to contend with two powerful species, the marlin and *them*.
7. The other fishers, the boy and *them*, felt sad at the sight of Santiago's poor marlin.
8. The boy might have decided, "Now we will again be partners, Santiago and *me*."
9. He thought, "The villagers, the other fishers and *me*, have never seen such a fish."
10. Tourists showed interest in the fish, but no onlookers, not *them* or the fishers, could fully understand Santiago's experience.

Exercise 4

Using Pronouns After *Than* and *As*   The following sentences are based on passages from *The Old Man and the Sea*. Each sentence contains an italicized word or group of words. On your paper rewrite each sentence, substituting the correct pronoun for the words in italics.

1. Still, the other fishers caught more fish than *Santiago*.
2. They did not even go as far out as *the old man*.
3. The boy might have concluded, "Santiago is braver than *the other fishers*."
4. Not caring as much for the other fishers as he did for Santiago, the boy helped Santiago more than *the others*.
5. The old man rowed as steadily as *the younger fishers*.
6. Later Santiago would seem to vow to the marlin, "You are not as strong as *Santiago*."
7. Although the sea could be cruel to humans, Santiago reflected that it seemed more cruel to birds than to *his fellow human beings*.
8. The sea swallows searched as hard for food as *the terns*.
9. Watching the ocean's ceaseless waves, Santiago wondered whether anything was as cruel as *the ocean*.
10. Did he love anything else as much as *the ocean*?

Exercise 5

Making Pronouns and Antecedents Agree   Each of the following sentences about terns contains an example of pronoun-antecedent agreement. On your paper rewrite each sentence according to the directions in parentheses, changing the pronouns if necessary. In some cases you will also have to change the form of the verb and other words in the sentence.

1. These sea birds make tropical and semitropical islands their habitat. (Change *These sea birds* to *This sea bird*.)
2. The male tern grooms the female's face as part of his courtship. (Change *The male tern* to *Male terns*.)
3. As people watch the terns, their wonder at the birds' behavior increases. (Change *people* to *we*.)
4. Because females build no nest, their eggs appear in odd, even unsuitable, places. (Change *females* to *the female*.)
5. The mother often lays her egg on the edge of a roof or in the fork of a tree. (Change *mother* to *mothers*.)
6. Both of the parent birds take their turn tending the egg. (Change *Both* to *Each*.)
7. Fairy tern eggs hatch 34 days after they are laid. (Change *Fairy tern eggs* to *A fairy tern egg*.)
8. Many of the parents leave their young untended for hours while they search for food. (Change *Many* to *Some*.)
9. A flying fish sometimes finds itself in the throat of a hungry tern. (Change *A flying fish* to *Flying fish*.)
10. Chicks may fall to the ground while their parents are gone. (Change *Chicks* to *A chick*.)

Exercise 6

Choosing *Who* or *Whom*   The following sentences describe the history of Cuba, the setting of *The Old Man and the Sea* and Hemingway's home for many years. For each sentence write on your paper the correct pronoun from the pair in parentheses.

1. When Columbus reached Cuba in 1492, he encountered the Taino, (who/whom) he discovered were farmers.
2. (Who/Whom) did the Spanish Crown appoint to conquer Cuba?
3. The island's mountains offered refuge for the natives, (who/whom) the Spanish treated harshly.
4. The Taino population, to (who/whom) European diseases proved deadly, became greatly reduced.
5. Enslaved Africans, (who/whom) the Spaniards wished to use for mining gold, were imported in 1524.
6. The enslaved people (who/whom) the plantation owners bought toiled long hours in sugar-cane and coffee fields.
7. Hernán Cortés, (who/whom) we know conquered Mexico, used Cuba as a base for his expeditions.
8. (Who/Whom) did you say established Havana as an important port?
9. Ports like Havana offered recreation for sailors, (who/whom) the natives entertained with African drums and Spanish guitars.
10. At sea many dangers threatened these sailors, (who/whom) pirates attacked regularly for their ships' gold.
11. Tobacco growers, (who/whom) the Spanish government regulated, rebelled unsuccessfully as early as 1717.
12. (Who/Whom) did you say told you that the name *criollos* refers to people of Spanish descent?
13. In Haiti enslaved people (who/whom) the American Revolution inspired rebelled and set up a free republic.
14. Enslaved Cubans, (who/whom) the government freed in 1880, revolted several times between 1812 and 1840.
15. Chinese laborers, (who/whom) nervous landowners recruited, added a new ethnic group to the Cuban population.
16. Cubans, (who/whom) Indian, Spanish, African, and Chinese cultures have influenced, share a colorful heritage.
17. In 1895 revolutionary armies, (who/whom) were led by José Martí, demanded Cuba's independence from Spain.
18. American investors, for (who/whom) an independent Cuba would be profitable, rejoiced when America aided the revolutionaries.
19. Cuban independence in 1898 attracted the attention of American businesspeople, (who/whom) invested heavily in Cuba for nearly 60 years.
20. Nonetheless, peasant classes, to (who/whom) fishers like Santiago belonged, continued to live in poverty.

Exercise 7

Making Pronouns and Antecedents Agree   The following sentences are about Hemingway's characters. Each sentence contains an example of pronoun-antecedent agreement. Rewrite the sentences according to the directions in parentheses, changing the pronouns if necessary. In some cases you will also have to change the verb and other words.

SAMPLE   Sports enthusiasts have compared their true experiences to Santiago's fictional one. (Change *Sports enthusiasts* to *A sports enthusiast*.)

ANSWER   A sports enthusiast has compared his true experiences to Santiago's fictional one.

1. Cuban fishers have described their own struggles with a large fish. (Change *Cuban fishers* to *A Cuban fisher*.)
2. In these stories a marlin has fought as long as fifteen hours before it was caught. (Change *a marlin* to *a few marlins*.)
3. Two of Hemingway's skippers have stated their ideas about the true identity of Santiago. (Change *Two* to *Each*.)
4. Are some of the real people who found their way into Hemingway's fiction famous? (Change *some* to *any*.)
5. In fact, readers find themselves drawn to Hemingway's characters because they seem so real. (Change *readers* to *we*.)
6. Have all of Hemingway's wives seen reflections of themselves in his female characters? (Change *all* to *each*.)
7. Any veteran of war might recognize his or her own feelings in Hemingway's soldiers. (Change *Any veteran* to *Veterans*.)
8. All people must fight personal obstacles to maintain their self-respect. (Change *All people* to *Everyone*.)
9. Hemingway characters show their valor amidst violence. (Change *Hemingway characters* to *A Hemingway character*.)
10. The stories, with their familiar conflicts, help us understand real life. (Change *The stories* to *Each story*.)
11. Does any character in the Nick Adams stories take his likes and dislikes from Hemingway's own personality? (Change *any character* to *the characters*.)
12. Did Hemingway's friends in Europe live their lives as desperately as the characters in *The Sun Also Rises*? (Change *friends* to *best friend*.)
13. Did someone like Catherine in *A Farewell to Arms* actually exert her influence on Hemingway's life? (Change *someone* to *women*.)
14. For the narrator in *For Whom the Bell Tolls*, does his experience reflect Hemingway's own experiences in the Spanish Civil War? (Change *narrator* to *characters*.)
15. It is clear that Hemingway created vivid characters because he wrote about people and situations he knew. (Change *Hemingway* to *both Hemingway and Fitzgerald*.)

Exercise 8

Making Pronoun References Clear   The following sentences give background information on the passage from *The Old Man and the Sea*. Each sentence contains an unclear pronoun reference. On your paper rewrite each sentence to make the pronoun reference clear. In some cases you will need to reword the sentence or eliminate the pronoun.

1. Santiago's wife had died years ago, and that must have been a source of almost unbearable pain.
2. Santiago removed his wife's picture from the wall, which made him sad.
3. The boy and the old fisher enjoyed spending time together, and he sometimes ignored his parents' objections.
4. One day while Santiago was talking with the boy, he spoke of his love of fishing.
5. Santiago finally got the huge marlin into his boat, but it had been severely damaged by the sharks.

Exercise 9

The following passage describes the artist Winslow Homer, whose painting appears on the opposite page. Rewrite the passage, correcting the errors in spelling, grammar, and usage. Add any missing punctuation. There are twenty-five errors.

Winslow Homer

[1]Winslow Homer (1836–1910) were one of America's finest watercolorists. [2]Born in Boston, Massachusetts, him, along with his family, moved to the town of Cambridge when he was six. [3]Growing up with his two brothers in the country Homer learned to love the outdoors. [4]This interest in nature preoccupied him for much of their life.

[5]For the first seventen years of his long career, Homer supported himself by doing illustrations for periodicals, including *Ballou's Pictorial* and *Harper's Weekly*. [6]During the four years of the Civil War, it was him who *Harper's Weekly* sent to the front lines in Virginia, where he drawed many illustrations of battle scenes.

[7]Homer's training in illustration enables him to depict dramatic scenes naturally and unsentimentally. [8]His masterful draftsmanship allowed him to create a clear and honest record of landscapes and people as he saw it.

[9]After the war was over, Homer begun to exhibit his paintings, and them were very well received. [10]When he reached his late thirties, he begun making watercolors directly from nature. [11]His' watercolors are forceful, direct, and saturated with pure color. [12]It was later in life that she began to paint large and powerful canvases of the sea. [13]No American painter is more closely associated with scenes of the sea than him.

[14]*Palm Trees, Nassau* is charateristic of Homers' late watercolors. [15]The casual observer may see an apparently simple nature scene, but looking closer, you can see the tension between the calm setting and the coming storm. [16]The trees bend in the rising wind, clouds scud acros the sky, and a red flag (possibly signaling an oncoming hurricane) flutters near the lighthouse. ➡

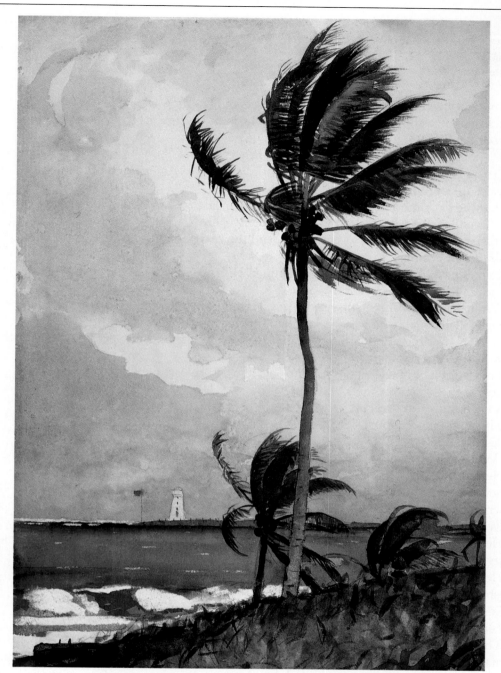

Winslow Homer, *Palm Trees, Nassau,* **1898**

[17]*The Old Man and the Sea* is about an old Cuban fisher whom is confronted with the great power of nature. [18]In the passage from the novel reprinted in this textbook, Hemingway hinting at the seas ominous power. [19]He write, "She is kind and very beautiful. But she can be so cruel . . ." [20]Homers watercolor also evokes this insight.

Mixed Review

Exercise 10

Each of the following sentences describes aspects of Hemingway's life and work. For each sentence choose the proper pronoun from the pair in parentheses and write it on your paper.

Ernest Hemingway

1. Ernest Hemingway, (who/whom) we know was one of America's finest writers, was born in Illinois in 1899.
2. Hemingway's numerous sports activities were balanced by (him/his) playing the cello and writing for his school newspaper.
3. His father was an outdoors enthusiast, and the two of them, (he/him) and Ernest, often took fishing trips to Michigan.
4. It was (he/him) who discouraged Hemingway from enlisting in the army when the United States entered World War I.
5. While driving an ambulance in the war, Hemingway received a wound that might have killed a man who was weaker than (he/him).
6. In Paris after the war, Hemingway met F. Scott Fitzgerald and Gertrude Stein, both of (who/whom) influenced him.
7. These young writers, Fitzgerald and (he/him), were part of what Stein called the Lost Generation.
8. A friendship also grew up between the writer Sherwood Anderson and (he/him).
9. The Lost Generation writers found the politics and morality of (its/their) society destroyed by war.
10. (Who/Whom) would you say is the most admirable character in *The Sun Also Rises*, Hemingway's first novel?
11. Several pieces of Hemingway's writing have found (its/their) way onto the movie screen.
12. Everybody has (his or her/their) favorite Hemingway novel.
13. Hemingway, (who/whom) many know was a journalist, wrote in a spare, unemotional style.
14. He and his third wife bought a home in Cuba in 1940; the couple, Ernest and (she/her), entertained many celebrities.
15. Some of these celebrities remember adventures they had with Hemingway—for example, (their/them) watching bullfights in Spain and hunting in Africa.
16. This lifestyle appealed less to Hemingway's third wife than to (he/him), and the marriage failed.
17. His wartime experience as an ambulance driver and as a news correspondent had (its/their) own profound effects on Hemingway's fiction.
18. Hemingway, (who/whom) Cuba fascinated, stayed in this tropical country even after Castro gained control in 1958.
19. *The Old Man and the Sea*, a best-seller in 1952, led to (his/him) winning the Pulitzer and Nobel prizes.
20. In the years following Hemingway's death in 1961, the novel has retained (its/it's) immense popularity.

Writing Application

Pronouns in Writing In the following excerpt from *Great Expectations* by Charles Dickens, the narrator, Pip, is discussing two other characters, Mr. Jaggers and Mr. Pocket. Examine the passage closely, noting the many italicized masculine pronouns. Focus especially on how Dickens avoids unclear pronoun references.

My guardian took me into *his* room, and while *he* lunched, standing, from a sandwich-box and a pocket flask of sherry (*he* seemed to bully *his* very sandwich as *he* ate it), informed me what arrangements *he* had made for me. I was to go to "Barnard's Inn," to young Mr. Pocket's rooms, where a bed had been sent in for my accommodation; I was to remain with young Mr. Pocket until Monday; on Monday I was to go with *him* to *his* father's house on a visit, that I might try how I liked it.

Techniques with Pronouns Try to apply some of Charles Dickens's writing techniques when you write and revise your own work.

1. Avoid confusion by keeping pronoun references clear. Compare the following:

Unclear reference I was to remain with *him* . . .
Dickens's version I was to remain with *young Mr. Pocket* . . .

2. When you revise sentences containing many pronouns, make sure that each pronoun has a clear antecedent.

Unclear reference I was to go to "Barnard's Inn," to *his* rooms . . .

Dickens's version I was to go to Barnard's Inn, to young *Mr. Pocket's rooms* . . .

Practice Practice these techniques by revising the following passage, using a separate sheet of paper. Eliminate confusion by making the unclear pronoun references clear. Make sure each pronoun has a clear antecedent.

The young child sat cuddled on her grandmother's wide lap, as she rocked the old oak chair back and forth. She loved swaying with her. Wonderful scents wafted past her delicate little nose on the shifting breeze created by the rocking motion. She easily detected the pungent scent of garlic. Had she helped herself to a generous serving of her famous calzones? (Nobody could refuse her spicy creations, and especially not she, who succumbed easily to all cheesy, tomatoey foods.) Less obvious was the almost sterile scent of her heavily starched dress, which she was careful to iron each morning. Her mother had an awful impatience with anything less than perfection, a fact that the young girl on her lap knew only too well.

Using Modifiers Correctly

Most adjectives and adverbs have three degrees: the positive, or base, form; the comparative form; and the superlative form.

The **positive** form of a modifier cannot be used to make a comparison. (This form appears as the entry word in a dictionary.)

The **comparative** form of a modifier shows two things being compared.

The **superlative** form of a modifier shows three or more things being compared.

She ran **swiftly**.

POSITIVE	My cousin is **tall**.
	The cat ran **swiftly**.
COMPARATIVE	My cousin is **taller** than I am.
	My dog ran **more swiftly** than the cat.
SUPERLATIVE	Of the three cousins, Paula is **tallest**.
	I ran **most swiftly** of all.

The following rules will guide you in forming the comparative and superlative degrees of adjectives and adverbs:

In general, for one-syllable modifiers add *-er* to form the comparative and *-est* to form the superlative.

green, green**er**, green**est**
The neighbor's grass always looks **greener** than ours.

loud, loud**er**, loud**est**
That sonic boom is the **loudest** noise I've ever heard.

She ran more **swiftly**.

fast, fast**er**, fast**est**
Her hair grows **faster** than mine.

In some cases adding *-er* and *-est* requires spelling changes.

big, bi**gger,** bi**ggest**
hot, ho**tter,** ho**ttest**
true, tru**er**, tru**est**
dry, dr**ier,** dr**iest**

With some one-syllable modifiers, it may sound more natural to use *more* and *most*.

just, **more** just, **most** just
Of the three, that judge's ruling was the **most just** of all.

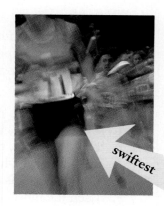

She ran **most swiftly** of all.

For most two-syllable adjectives, add -*er* to form the comparative and -*est* to form the superlative.

> ugly, ugl**ier,** ugl**iest**
> Your mask is **uglier** than mine.
> That is the **ugliest** mask I've ever seen.

If -*er* and -*est* sound awkward with a two-syllable adjective, use *more* and *most*.

> afraid, **more** afraid, **most** afraid
> No one is **more afraid** of spiders than I am.
> Of all of us, I was the **most afraid**.

For adverbs ending in -*ly*, always use *more* and *most* to form the comparative and superlative degrees.

> clearly, **more** clearly, **most** clearly
> Lewis gives directions **more clearly** than most people.
> This candidate explains his views **most clearly** of all.

For modifiers of three or more syllables, always use *more* and *most* to form the comparative and superlative degrees.

> attractive, **more** attractive, **most** attractive
> I think red looks **more attractive** on you than on me.
> That watercolor is the **most attractive** one in the exhibit.

Less and *least*, the opposite of *more* and *most*, can also be used with most modifiers to show comparison.

> Are prepared foods **less economical** than fresh foods?
> I think cabbage is the **least appetizing** of all vegetables.

Exercise 1	Identifying Comparisons

In the following sentences, identify the adjectives and adverbs, and write them on a separate sheet of paper. Then write *positive*, *comparative*, or *superlative* to indicate the degree of comparison.

The Blues

1. A talented blues band can play more softly than a hard-rock band.
2. The slow blues, to my way of thinking, sound the sweetest of all.
3. The sadder the lyrics, the more mellow the melody becomes.
4. The vocalist tells the tale of woe most clearly when the trumpet's tone becomes less strident.
5. Then the most emotional mood is created out of songs that describe the least fortunate circumstances.

18.2 | Irregular Comparisons

A few modifiers form their comparative and superlative degrees irregularly. It is most helpful simply to memorize their forms.

Modifiers with Irregular Forms of Comparison		
Positive	**Comparative**	**Superlative**
good	better	(the) best
well	better	(the) best
bad	worse	(the) worst
badly	worse	(the) worst
ill	worse	(the) worst
far (distance)	farther	(the) farthest
far (degree, time)	further	(the) furthest
little (amount)	less	(the) least
many	more	(the) most
much	more	(the) most

Exercise 2 Making Correct Comparisons

On another sheet of paper, complete the following sentences by writing the correct degree of comparison of the modifier in parentheses.

SAMPLE Which vegetable tastes the _____ of all? (good)
ANSWER best

Space and Space Exploration

1. Are there _____ planets in our solar system than the nine we know about? (many)
2. The distance between Venus and Earth is _____ than that between Mars and Earth. (little)
3. Mercury has the _____ mass of all the planets. (little)
4. The _____ planet from the sun is Pluto. (far)
5. *Voyager I* did a _____ job of photographing Jupiter than its predecessor. (good)
6. One of the _____ space catastrophes ever was the destruction of the *Challenger* spacecraft in 1986. (bad)
7. Of all the descriptions of the motion of the planets, that of the seventeenth-century astronomer Johannes Kepler is the _____. (good)
8. There are _____ celestial bodies in the Milky Way than just our solar system. (many)
9. Some asteroids—small, planetlike objects—have diameters of _____ than 120 miles. (much)
10. A comet, with its bright head and glowing tail, is one of the _____ astronomical sights you will ever see. (good)

Making Correct Comparisons

On another sheet of paper, complete the following sentences by writing the correct degree of comparison of the modifier in parentheses.

SAMPLE   *The Joy Luck Club* is one of the _____ novels I have ever read. (interesting)
ANSWER   most interesting

1. *The Joy Luck Club* is an entertaining book, and it is _____ to read than many other contemporary novels. (easy)
2. The novel is by Amy Tan, perhaps the _____ voice in contemporary Asian American fiction. (lively)
3. *The Joy Luck Club* is a _____ book than some that have recently been on the best-seller list. (long)
4. Maxine Wong is another talented Asian American writer, although Amy Tan is _____ than Wong. (famous)
5. In the book the members of the Joy Luck Club do many things, but their _____ activity is playing mah-jongg. (important)
6. Though she is _____ experienced than the other club members, June Woo is asked to join the mah-jongg game. (little)
7. Though mah-jongg resembles rummy, it is _____. (complicated)
8. It relies _____ on strategy than rummy does. (much)
9. Most people believe, however, that chess is still the _____ of all board games. (challenging)
10. Even so, one can play chess _____ than mah-jongg. (quickly)
11. The club members, who are June's unofficial aunts, are _____ than June and observe traditional Chinese customs. (old)
12. June is _____ to be with friends her own age than she is to be playing games with her aging aunts. (happy)
13. The aunts are the _____ of all when they are reminiscing about their years in China. (content)
14. China seems even _____ away for June than it does for her aunts, for whom China is a distant memory. (far)
15. Eventually, though, June learns that the _____ decision of all would be to abandon her Chinese heritage completely. (bad)
16. From all the aspects of her Chinese heritage, June learns to accept only the _____. (good)
17. The ethnic roots of many Americans are _____ than June's. (remote)
18. Many of us would have to go much _____ back in time to recapture information about our ancestors. (far)
19. Researching, tracing, and studying one's genealogy has become a _____ pursuit than it once was. (popular)
20. There are some people who will travel to the _____ corners of the earth to trace their family histories. (far)

18.3 Double Comparisons

Do not make a double comparison by using both *-er* or *-est* and *more* or *most*.

INCORRECT	A redwood grows more taller than an oak.
CORRECT	A redwood grows taller than an oak.
INCORRECT	Aunt Rosa is my most kindest aunt.
CORRECT	Aunt Rosa is my kindest aunt.
INCORRECT	He will visit us more oftener in the fall.
CORRECT	He will visit us more often in the fall.

Exercise 4 **Correcting Double Comparisons**

Rewrite each of the following sentences, correcting the double comparison.

Thomas Edison, Inventor

1. Many people believe that Thomas Alva Edison was the world's most best inventor.
2. Some people consider him even more greater than Leonardo da Vinci.
3. The phonograph and the electric light are probably Edison's most usefulest creations.
4. Edison was most happiest with his phonograph.
5. He was most proudest of his work on the electric light.
6. Electric light is certainly more safer than candlelight.
7. Edison also took others' inventions, such as the telephone and the typewriter, and made them more better.
8. As a boy, Edison was more curiouser than other children.
9. He worked more harder and longer than his peers.
10. Historians agree that Edison was one of the most fruitfulest inventors of modern times.
11. After electric lights were invented, nights seemed more brighter.
12. People could read or do chores more longer after dark.
13. Before the phonograph was invented, hearing great music was more difficulter.
14. The phonograph and the electric light, though expensive at first, became more cheaper as time went by.
15. Edison was blessed with a more quicker mind than most boys his age.
16. After only three months of formal schooling, he entered the more wider world of work.
17. An accident caused him to become more harder of hearing than he had been before.
18. One of his most earliest inventions was a stock ticker for printing stock-exchange quotations.
19. A more later invention, the movie projector, aided the development of motion pictures.
20. During his lifetime, Edison patented over 1,000 inventions, the most greatest number ever recorded for one person.

Correcting Irregular and Double Comparisons

Rewrite each of the following sentences, correcting the comparisons.

Twins

 1. Mother says that raising twins has been the goodest experience of her life.
 2. When they were born, Laura weighed littler than Lonnie, but she soon caught up.
 3. All of us children had sunny dispositions, but Lonnie's was the most cheerfulest.
 4. Lonnie was always serene, even though his health was worser than it should have been.
 5. When he got sick, Mother used to go through some of the baddest days of her life.
 6. The higher his temperature rose, the more upsetter she became.
 7. The worser he felt, the more time she devoted to him.
 8. "Sometimes," she told us, "I would like to go farrer back in history to an era when people had more time to spend with their children."
 9. Being the oldest, I tried to be the most good, but I made a lot of mistakes.
10. I could have found more frequenter opportunities to lend a hand.
11. As toddlers, the twins tried to see which one could wander more farther from home.
12. Mother or the babysitter would chase them for the gooder part of the morning.
13. We would have appreciated a lesser adventurouser spirit on the twins' part.
14. Mucher peace and quiet was what we wanted.
15. The most happiest day of our lives was the twins' first day of school.

Writing Correct Comparisons

On another sheet of paper, complete the following sentences by writing the correct degree of comparison of the modifier in parentheses. In two sentences you will use *less* or *least*.

Ethnic Cuisine

 1. (Many) Americans than ever before are enjoying the pleasures of ethnic cuisine.
 2. Mexican dishes are usually (spicy) than those prepared north of the border.
 3. Mexican chilies run the gamut in flavor and appearance, but the habañero is the (spicy) one of all.
 4. French food, with its emphasis on sauces and careful methods of preparation, is for some people the (elegant) of all the world's cuisines.
 5. French recipes often call for (rich) ingredients, such as real butter and whole cream, than do American recipes.
 6. Strangely enough, in spite of their eating habits, the French appear to be no (healthy) than Americans.
 7. Mediterranean cultures—Italian, Spanish, Greek, Turkish, Moroccan—rely (heavily) on foods low in cholesterol than do most other cuisines.
 8. For many years Chinese food was the (popular) ethnic cuisine in America, but now Mexican and Tex-Mex foods have more fans.
 9. Chinese delicacies such as dim sum and Peking duck are (common) taste treats than the more ordinary chop suey and chow mein.
10. A quick look at the restaurant listings in the yellow pages will convince you that the (good) words to describe America's food preferences are *ethnic* and *diverse*.

18.4　Incomplete Comparisons

Do not make an incomplete or unclear comparison by omitting *other* or *else* when you compare a person or thing with the group of which it is a part.

UNCLEAR	Mercury is closer to the sun than any planet. [*Any planet* includes Mercury.]
CLEAR	Mercury is closer to the sun than any **other** planet.
UNCLEAR	My aunt has more pets than anyone. [*Anyone* includes the aunt.]
CLEAR	My aunt has more pets than anyone **else.**

Be sure your comparisons are between like things.

UNCLEAR	The grace of a basketball player is more obvious than a baseball player. [The grace of a basketball player is being compared illogically with everything about a baseball player.]
CLEAR	The grace of a basketball player is more obvious than **that of a baseball player.**
CLEAR	The grace of a basketball player is more obvious than a **baseball player's.**
UNCLEAR	The claws of a lion are sharper than a cat. [The claws of a lion are being compared illogically with everything about a cat.]
CLEAR	The claws of a lion are sharper than **those of a cat**.
CLEAR	The claws of a lion are sharper than **a cat's**.

Exercise 7　　Making Complete Comparisons

Rewrite the following sentences to correct the incomplete comparison in each.

Native American Dwellings

[1]Native American homes were just as varied as today. [2]The buffalo-skin dwellings of the Plains groups were more portable than the Wichita. [3]The design of the tepees of the Plains peoples was perhaps more ingenious than any design. [4]Women were responsible for erecting the tepees, and they could do this faster than anyone. [5]Many people think that the tepee was more beautiful than any Native American dwelling. [6]The lodges of the Pawnees were warmer and sturdier than the Plains groups. [7]Because the Pawnees did not move frequently, their homes were less portable than Native American dwellings. [8]The Pueblo groups of New Mexico were probably cooler than anyone, for they lived in well-insulated buildings made of clay. [9]Pueblo dwellings were several stories high, like many city dwellers today. [10]If I could, I would rather live in a tepee than any place.

18.5 *Good* or *Well*; *Bad* or *Badly*

Always use *good* as an adjective. *Well* may be used as an adverb of manner telling how ably or adequately something is done. *Well* also may be used as an adjective meaning "in good health."

Blue is a **good** color for you. [adjective]
You look **good** in blue. [adjective after a linking verb]

You dress **well.** [adverb of manner]
Aren't you feeling **well?** [adjective meaning "in good health"]

Always use *bad* as an adjective. Therefore, *bad* is used after a linking verb. Use *badly* as an adverb. *Badly* almost always follows an action verb.

That was a **bad** idea. [adjective]
The milk tasted **bad.** [adjective following a linking verb]

I feel **bad** about your moving to another state. [adjective following a linking verb]
The faucet is leaking **badly.** [adverb following an action verb]

Exercise 8   **Correcting Errors with *Good, Well, Bad,* and *Badly***

If a sentence contains an error with *good, well, bad,* or *badly,* on your paper write the form that should have been used. If a sentence is correct, write *correct.*

SAMPLE   Marisa did bad on her algebra test.
ANSWER   badly

1. "You'll do good on your tests if you will just remember to study," my mother always tells me.
2. "That's easy for you to say," I always answer. "You were always a good student."
3. I don't feel good enough to study because of this headache.
4. My mother feels badly that I am ill.
5. "Would a little chicken soup taste good to you today?" she inquires kindly.
6. "I'll eat whatever you think will make me well," I respond.
7. "But, really, my head hurts so bad that I don't know that soup will help much," I continue.
8. "I know, but your grandmother always believed that eating good could cure anything," Mom says.
9. "Let's give it a try, then. Maybe it will help me study well for the test, too," I say.
10. "That soup smells so well that I'm starting to feel cured already."

Using *Good*, *Bad*, *Well*, and *Badly*

On your paper complete the following sentences by writing *good*, *well*, *bad*, or *badly*.

Taking a Hike

1. No one can hike _____ without comfortable hiking shoes.
2. Improper equipment can make a hiker or camper feel _____ .
3. _____ planning is absolutely essential for a long and difficult hike.
4. A hike that is planned _____ will not be enjoyable and may be unpleasant.
5. Locating a _____ trail is one important aspect of planning a hike.
6. A hiker who is not feeling _____ can become a serious problem on the trail.
7. Hikers feel _____ if they cannot keep up with their companions.
8. If a hike begins _____, the hikers may become discouraged and decide to turn back.
9. The views along the Appalachian Trail look as _____ as the views that one sees in the Rocky Mountains.
10. Hikers should know their capabilities _____ before they start off on an ambitious hike.
11. I recently took an energetic walk with my friend Arnold, who could not hike _____.
12. Arnold tripped and hurt himself _____ after we had hiked only about a mile and a half.
13. Arnold said that his new hiking boots felt _____, but I thought they looked quite loose on his feet.
14. It also appeared that the soles were too thin to support his weight _____.
15. I felt _____ that he had hurt himself because I had really wanted our hike to go _____.
16. Arnold had been feeling _____ about his girlfriend, but then she suddenly broke up with him.
17. Needless to say, his confidence was _____ shaken.
18. He needed a _____ friend to spend time with him and make him forget his problems.
19. Ever since we were young children, we have gotten along with each other very _____.
20. I will be very disappointed if this misadventure hurts our friendship _____.

Exercise 10

Writing Paragraphs with Modifiers

Write two paragraphs, using each of the phrases below. You can use the phrases for one paragraph in any order.

SAMPLE   danced badly
SAMPLE SENTENCE   Ellie danced badly at her first audition.

Paragraph 1
1. feel well
2. stumbled badly
3. than any other basketball player
4. than those of Patrick Ewing
5. played well

Paragraph 2
6. feel good
7. drove well
8. than any other student
9. failed her driving test badly
10. looked bad

18.6 Double Negatives

In general, do not use a **double negative,** two negative words in the same clause. Use only one negative word to express a negative idea.

INCORRECT	I don't have no stereo equipment.
CORRECT	I do**n't** have **any** stereo equipment.

INCORRECT	We haven't seen no concerts this year.
CORRECT	We have**n't** seen **any** concerts this year.
CORRECT	We have seen **no** concerts this year.

INCORRECT	My parrot never says nothing.
CORRECT	My parrot **never** says **anything.**
CORRECT	My parrot says **nothing.**

The words *hardly* and *scarcely* are also negatives. Do not use them with other negative words such as *not.*

INCORRECT	I haven't hardly finished.	He can't scarcely never be on time.
CORRECT	I have **hardly** finished.	He can **scarcely** ever be on time.

Exercise 11   **Identifying Double Negatives**

On your paper write each double negative in the following sentences. If a sentence is correct, write *correct.*

Working Out

1. I used to think there wasn't no reason for me to exercise.
2. I didn't want no new activity to distract me from my other interests.
3. I hadn't never explored the possibility of joining an aerobics class.
4. Eventually, my friend Ramón convinced me that my negative attitude was neither sensible nor smart.
5. I signed up for an aerobics class at the "Y," but at first I didn't want nobody to watch me make mistakes.
6. The other students never said nothing about my clumsy moves.
7. They didn't seem to have no interest in anything but stepping, jogging, and dancing to the high-energy music.
8. Soon I realized that exercising never gets no harder; it just gets easier.
9. Now I hardly never miss a session.
10. Not even bad weather can keep me from working out.

Correcting Double Negatives

On your paper rewrite the following sentences, eliminating the double negative in each. (Most sentences can be corrected in more than one way.) If a sentence is correct, write *correct*.

Camping

1. When our family goes camping, we like to find a site where there isn't no one around.
2. Don't never pitch your tent on sloping ground, for you will be very uncomfortable.
3. Nobody should never forget to dig a trench around the tent, in case it rains during the night.
4. Can't none of them help us pitch our tent?
5. It's best never to leave no food in your tent, for animals may be attracted to it.
6. One time my sister and I discovered a raccoon in our tent, and after that we didn't leave nothing edible inside.
7. In some wilderness areas, campers aren't allowed to build no fires, and they must cook all their meals on a portable stove.
8. Some campers bring canned food along, but we don't bring none because it is too heavy to carry.
9. My parents always pack dried food because it is light and doesn't never spoil.
10. When it is time to break camp, no one should leave no trash on the ground, and all fires should be put out.
11. Our most memorable camping trip was one I don't never want to repeat.
12. One summer we decided to go to Crater Lake in southern Oregon because we hadn't never been to that site in the Cascade Range.
13. There isn't no more beautiful place in all the world.
14. The lake, originally called Deep Blue Lake, hasn't no inlet or outlet.
15. Nobody can't see it without being amazed by its sapphire-blue color.
16. However, we didn't have no idea about the area's changeable summer weather when we pitched our tent.
17. We hadn't no sooner gone to bed than it began to rain.
18. We didn't get hardly any sleep as the rain poured down, the wind blew, and the temperature dropped.
19. In the morning when we opened our tent flap, we realized we hadn't had no other camping experience like this before.
20. The rain had turned to snow, leaving not a patch of green grass or a brown tree trunk anywhere to be seen.
21. We had never seen nothing like it before in our lives.
22. We wanted something hot to drink, but we couldn't start no fire.
23. There wasn't scarcely any dry firewood around.
24. We decided that we didn't want to spend no more time there, even though the lake looked beautiful surrounded by the snow-covered trees.
25. We just hadn't no idea that it could snow in the Cascades in the middle of summer.

Place modifiers as close as possible to the words they modify in order to make the meaning of the sentence clear.

Misplaced modifiers modify the wrong word, or they seem to modify more than one word in a sentence. To correct a sentence with a misplaced modifier, move the modifier as close as possible to the word it modifies.

MISPLACED **Soaring over the edge of the cliff,** the photographer captured the eagle. [participial phrase incorrectly modifying *photographer*]

CLEAR The photographer captured the eagle **soaring over the edge of the cliff.** [participial phrase correctly modifying *eagle*]

MISPLACED He easily spotted the eagle **with his high-powered binoculars.** [prepositional phrase incorrectly modifying *eagle*]

CLEAR **With his high-powered binoculars,** he easily spotted the eagle. [prepositional phrase correctly modifying *he*]

Place the adverb *only* immediately before the word or group of words it modifies.

If *only* is not positioned correctly in a sentence, the meaning of the sentence may be unclear.

UNCLEAR Dan **only** has art on Monday. [Does Dan have only one class on Monday, or does he have no class on any day but Monday, or is Dan the only person (in a group) who has one class on Monday?]

CLEAR Dan has **only** art on Monday. [He has no other class.]

CLEAR Dan has art **only** on Monday. [He does not have art on any other day.]

CLEAR **Only** Dan has art on Monday. [No other person has art on Monday.]

Soaring over the edge of the cliff, the photographer captured the eagle.

Dangling modifiers seem logically to modify no word at all. To correct a sentence with a dangling modifier, you must supply a word the dangling phrase can sensibly modify.

DANGLING   **Working all night long,** the fire was extinguished. [participial phrase logically modifying no word in the sentence]

CLEAR   **Working all night long,** fire fighters extinguished the fire. [participial phrase modifying *fire fighters*]

DANGLING   **After a valiant effort,** the blaze was still raging uncontrollably. [prepositional phrase logically modifying no word in the sentence]

CLEAR   **After a valiant effort,** the fire fighters still faced a blaze that was raging uncontrollably. [prepositional phrase modifying *fire fighters*]

DANGLING   **Sleeping soundly,** the raucous alarm startled me into consciousness. [participial phrase logically modifying no word in the sentence, since *me* is an object pronoun]

CLEAR   **Sleeping soundly,** I sprang into consciousness at the sound of the raucous alarm. [participial phrase modifying *I*]

Exercise 13   Identifying Misplaced and Dangling Modifiers

On your paper, write the misplaced or dangling modifier from each sentence. If a sentence is correct, write *correct.*

SAMPLE   The police officer saw the tire explode in his binoculars.
ANSWER   in his binoculars

1. Last night Darnell had a flat tire on the way to his job.
2. A motorcycle rider offered to fix the tire with a friendly grin.
3. Coming out from behind some parked cars, neither Darnell nor his helper could see the police officer.
4. Watching the motorcycle rider work, the tire was soon fixed.
5. "I only have trouble on this road," Darnell lamented.

Correcting Misplaced Modifiers

Rewrite each sentence, moving the misplaced modifier closer to the word it modifies.

SAMPLE   I noticed the park walking home from school.
ANSWER   Walking home from school, I noticed the park.

At the Park

1. The sign at the park entrance said, "Children should be with an adult under eight years of age."
2. A little boy was riding around on a bicycle with unmatched shoes.
3. Scampering around the top rung of the jungle gym, Marty noticed a baby squirrel.
4. Helen saw the sand castle her little sister had built on the way home from school.
5. The new paint set was under the swings that he had received for his birthday.

Identifying and Correcting Dangling Modifiers

Rewrite each sentence that needs correction, fixing the dangling modifier. If a sentence has no dangling modifier, write *correct*.

SAMPLE   Waking to the screech of the alarm, the blankets were pulled up over Pete's head.
ANSWER   Waking to the screech of the alarm, Pete pulled the blankets over his head.

Rise and Shine

1. Waking up in the dark, Pete's room seemed mysterious and gloomy.
2. After taking a shower, the sun finally came out.
3. Putting on a short-sleeved shirt, the temperature outside was warm.
4. Shouting from the kitchen downstairs, Pete's dad let him know that juice and cereal were on the table.
5. The school bus pulled up right on time after a hurried breakfast.

Using the Adverb *Only*

Rewrite each of the following sentences, adding the word *only*. Then explain what *only* means in your sentence.

SAMPLE   I sleep late on Saturday.
ANSWER   I sleep late only on Saturday. I don't sleep late on any day except Saturday.

Only on Saturday

1. I wake up early on Saturdays if there's an emergency.
2. The chore I have is mowing the grass.
3. I go to the movies on Saturday afternoons.
4. I eat pizza at my favorite pizzeria, Paul's Place.
5. I can appreciate how much my Saturdays mean to me.

Exercise 17   Correcting Misplaced and Dangling Modifiers

On your paper rewrite the following sentences, correcting any misplaced or dangling modifiers. (Some sentences can be corrected in more than one way.)

Going to the Circus

[1]The Barnum and Bailey circus is a big event, for it comes only to our town once a year. [2]Julio and I arrived early and took our seats inside the tent in high spirits. [3]Dimming the lights, the elephants lumbered into the ring. [4]Swinging their great trunks, the trainers marched the elephants in a circle. [5]On a tightrope high above the ring, we watched the acrobat walk steadily and fearlessly. [6]Three lions were released from a cage growling fiercely. [7]The clown pretended that he had been attacked by the lions, but one girl in the audience only screamed. [8]Galloping around the ring, a woman in a blue sequined dress waved to the crowd on horseback. [9]Julio watched nervously as the trapeze artists leaped through the air clutching his chair. [10]We watched her intently sitting on the bleachers and eating cotton candy.

[11]Facing north, the second ring could be seen quite clearly. [12]The snake charmer only charmed one snake, but it was a big one. [13]A trainer commanded a bear with a chair. [14]Watching the acrobats, the thrills never stopped. [15]Barking furiously, the clowns chased little dogs around the tent. [16]Julio enjoyed photographing the ringmaster with his miniature camera. [17]Knowing what a bad photographer I was, the spectacle itself was enough. [18]The band played a march dressed in star-spangled khaki. [19]Taking their bows, the crowd applauded all the performers. [20]Under the stars our hearts were content as we walked home.

Exercise 18   Review: Correcting Modifiers

The following paragraph contains 10 errors in the use of modifiers. Rewrite the paragraph, correcting the errors.

Ted Williams, Home-Run Ace

[1]Ted Williams is considered one of the most finest baseball players of all time. [2]At the age of 17, a team in San Diego was the team he joined. [3]By 1939 he was playing good enough to start with the Boston Red Sox. [4]From that time until his retirement in 1960, Ted Williams only played baseball with the Red Sox; he never played for no other team. [5]Williams was one of baseball's all-time most greatest hitters. [6]His batting average was higher than most other players. [7]He hit especially good in 1941, when he had a 0.406 batting average. [8]Williams did not play so bad in 1942 either. [9]In both 1941 and 1942 he hit more home runs than any player in the league.

Correcting Modifiers

On your paper rewrite the following sentences, correcting the misplaced, dangling, or other incorrect modifiers in each. (Some sentences can be corrected in more than one way.) If a sentence is correct, write *correct*.

SAMPLE   Winston and Sabah only go out together once a week.
ANSWER   Winston and Sabah go out together only once a week.

Winston and Sabah

1. Walking along the sidewalk, a stone made Winston trip and fall.
2. Winston hadn't hardly time to get to Sabah's house without being late.
3. In a great hurry, the buzzer rang as Sabah ran to the door.
4. Out for a walk, Winston and Sabah walked more farther than they usually did.
5. The yogurt sundaes they stopped to eat tasted well.
6. As they walked to the movies, they saw that a fire had destroyed a neighbor's house and the chimney was only left standing.
7. Sleeping too late the next morning, the school bus left Sabah behind.
8. Sabah felt worser than she had felt in a long time.
9. Walking to school, Sabah bought a stuffed bear from a vendor with fuzzy pink fur.
10. Because she was late, Sabah's teacher reprimanded her.
11. Sabah felt badly that she had overslept.
12. Sabah decided that English grammar was more easier than algebra.
13. She liked English class better than any class.
14. Winston and Sabah only had one class together.
15. Winston wrote an essay about his cat using a ballpoint pen.
16. Sabah wrote a paragraph about her dog concentrating deeply.
17. The teacher announced that both had done good.
18. Hoping to do well on the pop quiz, a silence fell over the classroom.
19. Having fallen asleep, Sabah threw her pencil at Winston.
20. Winston felt well that his friend was looking out for him.
21. Greeting each other enthusiastically, Winston and Sabah met after school.
22. Running in all directions, Sabah waved as their classmates left for home.
23. In the middle of the football field, Winston and Sabah watched the team practice.
24. The bestest player was not at the practice.
25. Starting for home, Winston and Sabah bid each other a fond farewell.

Correcting Modifiers

On your paper rewrite any of the following sentences in which there are errors in the use of modifiers, correcting the errors in your revision. (Some sentences may be corrected in more than one way.) Write *correct* for each sentence that does not contain any errors.

Famous Comic Strips

1. In 1897 the first comic strip appeared in the *New York Journal*, called "The Yellow Kid."
2. The next comic strip to come along was "The Katzenjammer Kids," whose prankster stars, Hans and Fritz, usually behaved bad.
3. Hans and Fritz never gave the Captain and Momma no peace.
4. In "Mutt and Jeff," a strip that started in 1908, Mutt is always more taller than Jeff.
5. "Mutt and Jeff" was one of the most early strips to appear in the newspaper in color.
6. All the comic strips in the early years depended upon slapstick more than any form of comedy.
7. Based on real-life people, the cartoonist of "The Gumps" drew popular characters.
8. The character Andy Gump had a mustache, but he didn't have no chin.
9. First appearing in 1919, Frank King sometimes drew innovative backgrounds for his "Gasoline Alley" strip.
10. People liked this strip very much, especially after the character Uncle Walt adopted little Skeezix.
11. Before "Gasoline Alley" there had been no comic strip in which the characters grew up and aged.
12. Although full of crusading political content, "Little Orphan Annie" also told a good story.
13. The eyes of Little Orphan Annie are larger than most people.
14. For its first 10 years, the "Thimble Theatre" comic didn't have no Popeye in it.
15. "Blondie" was more widely circulated than any comic strip.
16. Dagwood, Blondie's husband, only made huge sandwiches when he raided the refrigerator; he never made an average-sized sandwich.
17. In his pursuit of such bizarre criminals as Flattop and Eighty-eight Keys, a yellow hat and square jaw were the trademarks of the cartoon detective Dick Tracy.
18. In "Peanuts," Pigpen is more dirtier than his friends Charlie Brown, Lucy, and Linus.
19. "We have met the enemy, and he is us," said the comic-strip opossum, Pogo, in a famous comment on the ecological crisis.
20. In spite of its sometimes controversial political remarks, Garry Trudeau won a Pulitzer Prize for his "Doonesbury" strip.
21. The editorial page only runs political cartoons, not comic strips.
22. Solving one problem, another problem always faces the kindly heroine of "Mary Worth."
23. In the strip "Peanuts," Charlie Brown always feels badly after his baseball team loses.
24. Many people believe that "Calvin and Hobbes" is funnier than any comic strip.
25. The strip "Sally Forth" goes more far into women's issues than most of the other strips.

Grammar Review

Using Modifiers Correctly

The passage in this workshop is taken from *An American Childhood,* a memoir by Annie Dillard. In it Dillard recalls her fascination with books that describe the pleasures and perils of rock collecting, one of her hobbies as a child. The passage has been annotated to show the kinds of modifiers covered in this unit.

Literature Model

from AN AMERICAN CHILDHOOD
by Annie Dillard

People who collected rocks called themselves "rockhounds." In the worst of cases, they called their children "pebble pups." Rockhounds seemed to be wild and obsessive amateurs, my kind of people, who had stepped aside from the rush of things to devote themselves to folly. . . .

Some rockhounds had recently taken up scuba diving. These people dove down into "brawling mountain streams" with tanks on their backs to look for crystals underwater, or to pan for gold. The gold panning was especially good under boulders in rapids.

One book included a photograph of a mild-looking hobbyist in his basement workshop: he sawed chunks of Utah wonderstone into wavy, landscapy-looking slabs suitable for wall hangings. Here was a photograph of rockhounds in the field: two men on a steep desert hillside delightedly smash a flat rock to bits with two hammers. Far below stands a woman in a dress and sensible shoes, doing nothing. Here is their campsite: a sagging black pyramidal tent pitched on the desert floor. A Studebaker fender nudges the foreground. The very hazards of field collecting tempted me: "tramping for miles over rough country," facing cold, heat, rain, cactus, rough lava, insects, rattlesnakes, scorpions, and glaring alkali flats. Collectors fell over boulders and damaged crystals. Their ballpoint pens ran out of ink. . . . ➡

Positive form of the adjective *wild*

Positive form of the adverb *recently*

Correct use of *good*

Correctly placed prepositional phrase modifying *men*

Getting back home alive only aggravated their problems. — Correct placement of the adverb *only*
If you bring home five hundred pounds of rocks from an average collecting trip, what do you do with them? Splay them attractively about the garden, one book suggested lamely. Give them away. Hold yard sales. One collector left five tons of rough rock in his yard when he moved. . . .

On the other hand, rock collecting had unique rewards. For example, the thinner you sliced your specimens when you sawed them up, the more specimens you had. In this way you could multiply your collection without leaving home.

Comparative form of the adverb *thin*

Exercise 1

Making Correct Comparisons   The following sentences are about rock collecting. For each sentence, write on your paper the proper comparative or superlative form of the modifier in parentheses.

SAMPLE   Rock collecting is _____ in some areas than in others. (easy)
ANSWER   easier

1. Rock hunting in areas where the ground is already broken, such as quarries and building sites, is _____ than hunting in areas with unbroken ground. (simple)
2. Some rock hunters gather rocks at a local site, whereas others travel _____ than that for specimens. (far)
3. One of the _____ practices to engage in while rock hunting is trespassing on private property. (bad)
4. One of the _____ and most dangerous things a rock hunter can do is to hunt alone on a steep rock wall. (silly)
5. Of the rock hunter's various tools, a rock hammer is the _____ implement for loosening solid rock. (good)
6. To loosen individual crystals, a chisel works _____ than a pocketknife. (good)
7. Museum specimens are often larger and _____ than those kept by amateur rock collectors. (impressive)
8. Minerals can be identified _____ than rocks because the atoms in minerals are arranged in a regular pattern, resulting in the formation of crystals. (quickly)
9. Rocks and minerals cannot always be identified simply by looking at them; _____ testing is often required. (far)
10. Of the various testing methods, the one that is probably used _____ is the streak test. (frequently)

Correcting Double Comparisons   The following sentences are based on passages from *An American Childhood* that are not reprinted in this textbook. Rewrite the sentences, correcting any errors of double comparison. If a sentence contains no errors, write *correct*.

SAMPLE   To outsiders no one seems more crazier than rockhounds.

ANSWER   To outsiders no one seems crazier than rockhounds.

1. The young Annie Dillard liked nothing more better than the natural sciences.
2. She was more curiouser about rocks than she was about stamps or coins.
3. To Dillard rock hunting seemed like the most liveliest of hobbies.
4. The books she read showed rockhounds hunting for specimens in the most wildest places imaginable.
5. Although Dillard obtained her own specimens by less ruggeder methods, she still found the rocks' secrets intriguing.
6. Some plain-looking rocks, when scratched on a rough surface, created streaks of color more brighter than greasepaint.
7. Even the dullest rocks, when cracked open, might reveal lovely crystals inside.
8. Of the rocks in Dillard's collection, the most prettiest was a red one called cinnabar.
9. Many minerals have strange names, but chalcopyrite (a brassy yellow mineral) was the most hardest for Dillard to pronounce.
10. Dillard longed to possess rocks with names even odder than that of chalcopyrite: sillimanite and agaty potch, for example.
11. Dillard was impressed with the fact that the earth is more older than any rock yet discovered.
12. Before she began to read about rocks, she thought they were the most drabbest things imaginable.
13. Only with more further exposure to the subject did she begin to find them fascinating.
14. Once she started her collection, she looked for the most fastest way to expand it.
15. With delight she learned that the more thinner she sliced her specimens, the bigger her collection became.
16. She realized that more sooner or later she would need a larger room for the collection.
17. With time and training, Dillard developed a more stronger descriptive prose than most other authors of her generation.
18. One of her most greatest gifts is her keen eye for detail.
19. All of her most latest books, including her fiction, continue to reflect her strong grounding in nature.
20. It's interesting to note that the seeds of her talent as an adult author were planted much more earlier in a youthful enthusiasm for rock collecting.

Exercise 3

Correcting Incomplete Comparisons The following sentences are about minerals and gemstones. Rewrite the sentences, correcting any errors of incomplete comparison. Some of the sentences can be revised in more than one way. If a sentence contains no errors, write *correct*.

SAMPLE   The value of a diamond is far greater than a ruby.
ANSWER   The value of a diamond is far greater than that of a ruby.

1. On the Mohs scale, which lists minerals by their hardness, the mineral talc is softer than any mineral.
2. Quartz, a mineral that can cut glass, is much harder than talc.
3. Diamonds, among the world's most valuable minerals, are harder than anything in nature.
4. The facets, or flat surfaces, of a diamond are different from an amethyst.
5. Among the stones called beryls, which come in different colors, green is more valuable than any color.
6. Green beryls are called emeralds, and the value of some emeralds is higher than some diamonds.
7. The emeralds from Colombia are finer than those supplied by any South American country.
8. More fine rubies are found in Southeast Asia than anywhere.
9. The appearance of many synthetic rubies is very close to natural rubies.
10. Unlike most other gemstones, pearls are not minerals but an organic material.
11. A gemologist is more interested in the chemical structure of precious stones than any scientist.
12. Unlike other gemstones, such as lapis and malachite, diamonds are not only polished, but also facet-cut.
13. The aquamarine from Brazil is of better quality than Colombia.
14. In Sri Lanka one can find finer sapphires than anywhere.
15. Unlike any rubies, star-rubies contain three sets of needlelike particles that create rays of light.
16. In ancient China, jade was considered more precious than any gemstone.
17. Chinese collectors often valued a tiny piece of jade sculpture over any artifact.
18. The turquoise jewelry created by a Navajo is different from a Zuni.
19. Native American artisans create more exquisite turquoise jewelry than anyone.
20. Today there is a greater selection of unusual gemstones available than at any time in history.

Exercise 4

Choosing the Correct Modifier   The following sentences are based on passages from *An American Childhood* not reprinted in this textbook. For each sentence choose the correct form of the modifier in parentheses, and write it on your paper. Then indicate whether the modifier you have chosen is being used as an *adjective* or an *adverb*.

SAMPLE   To the young Annie Dillard, few hobbies seemed as (good/well) as rock collecting.

ANSWER   good—adjective

1. Dillard obtained the first rocks in her collection from a newspaper boy whom she did not know very (good/well).
2. The newspaper boy had received the rocks as a gift from a (good/well) customer named Mr. Downey.
3. Mr. Downey, an avid rock hunter and collector, could no longer maintain his collection because his health was failing (bad/badly).
4. He had not been feeling (good/well) for several months and decided to give the collection to his newspaper boy, one of the few young people he knew.
5. The newspaper boy felt (bad/badly) because he did not have enough time to devote to the rock collection, and eventually he decided to give it to Dillard.
6. Dillard noticed right away that some of the rocks were attractive; others did not look too (good/well).
7. The fact that he could identify only two stalagmites made the newspaper boy feel (bad/badly) about his right to the collection.
8. Dillard herself was not (good/well) informed about the rocks and minerals when she first accepted the collection.
9. Had someone tested her on the names of Mr. Downey's rocks, Dillard would have done quite (bad/badly).
10. It was (good/well) that Dillard was able to borrow and read several books about rocks and minerals.
11. Dillard became more and more interested in rocks, quickly learning how to identify them (good, well).
12. She discovered that "rockhounds" were people that she got along with very (good, well).
13. She felt (good, well) about the amount of information and assistance some of these rockhounds could provide for her.
14. When she went on rock-finding expeditions, Dillard at first was (bad, badly) frustrated about not knowing what to do when she brought her findings home.
15. The rigors of actually looking for the rocks did not seem (bad, badly) by comparison.

Exercise 5

Correcting Double Negatives   The following sentences are about precious metals. Rewrite the sentences, eliminating any double negatives. Most sentences can be corrected in more than one way.

SAMPLE   Finding precious metals isn't no easy task.
ANSWER   Finding precious metals is no easy task.

1. Gold is a very malleable metal; if you hammer it, it won't never break.
2. Because there isn't no more malleable metal, people began using gold for jewelry thousands of years ago.
3. Nobody never has to worry that gold will tarnish, as many other metals do.
4. You can't make no jewelry out of pure gold, however, for it is too soft.
5. Pure gold is hardly never found; usually it is combined with another metal.
6. For centuries there wasn't nothing more valuable than gold.
7. Silver was also deemed valuable, but there wasn't no interest in platinum.
8. Medieval alchemists tried to create gold, but no one could make none.
9. Few early European explorers of the Americas hadn't never heard about the gold of the Inca and the Aztec.
10. Most prospectors in nineteenth-century America never had no scientific training.

Exercise 6

Correcting Misplaced Modifiers   The following sentences elaborate on ideas suggested by the passage from *An American Childhood*. Rewrite the sentences, correcting each misplaced modifier. If a sentence has no errors, write *correct*.

SAMPLE   Dillard tried to identify unfamiliar rocks consulting books and visiting local museum displays.
ANSWER   Consulting books and visiting local museum displays, Dillard tried to identify unfamiliar rocks.

1. Rockhounds seem eccentric to conventional people, having an unusual obsession.
2. Everyday activities seem unimportant to adventurous rockhounds with their dull routines.
3. Divers find some of the most interesting specimens in mountain streams using scuba-diving equipment.
4. Rockhounds often pan for gold in streams leaving no opportunity unexplored.
5. Some hobbyists might find enough gold to turn a tidy profit in the water.
6. Browsing through a book, Dillard noticed a strange photograph of a rockhound.
7. The picture showed a hobbyist sawing a chunk of wonderstone in his workshop destined for use as a wall hanging.
8. Lugging home huge quantities of rock, the question of practicality gnaws at the hobbyist.
9. The rockhound now begins to search for ideas about unloading his bounty in books.
10. One idea is to sell the specimens to friends occupying too much space.

Exercise 7

Correcting Dangling Modifiers   The following sentences elaborate on ideas suggested by the passage from *An American Childhood*. Rewrite the sentences, correcting each dangling modifier by adding appropriate information. Reword the sentence if necessary. Some sentences can be corrected in more than one way. If a sentence has no errors, write *correct*.

SAMPLE   Finding rock collectors wildly impractical, their hobby was attractive.

ANSWER   Finding rock collectors wildly impractical, Dillard was attracted to their hobby.

1. Calling themselves "rockhounds," rock collectors sometimes called their children "pebble pups."
2. Pausing to reflect, rock hunting began to seem like a wild obsession.
3. Strapping on their heavy tanks, the hunt for rock crystals in mountain streams began.
4. After studying the photographs and reading the anecdotes in books about rock collecting, Dillard decided the hobby was both artistic and adventurous.
5. Sawed into wavy slabs by one hobbyist, its suitability for wall hangings was achieved.
6. After climbing a steep hillside, the flat rock was smashed with two hammers.
7. Pitched in the desert, a tent served as the rockhounds' refuge from the elements.
8. Hunting for unusual rock specimens in wild and isolated places, minor problems like running out of ink arose.
9. After moving to a new home, five tons of rock remained in the rockhound's old yard.
10. Tramping for miles over rough country, their ballpoint pens ran out of ink.

Exercise 8

Proofreading

The following passage describes the artist Georgia O'Keeffe, whose painting appears on the opposite page. Rewrite the passage, correcting the errors in spelling, grammar, and usage. Add any missing punctuation. There are twenty-five errors.

Georgia O'Keeffe

[1]Born in 1887 in Sun Prairie, Wisconsin, art was an early love of Georgia O'Keeffe's. [2]She began studing art while still in her teens. [3]She worked in Chicago as an advertising illustrator in 1909 but she resumed her art studies in 1912. [4]First worked as a teacher for the public school system in Amarillo, Texas. [5]She then taught art at the University of Virginia And more later, she returned to Texas to head the art department at West Texas State Normal College.

[6]Although she had been painting good for some years, O'Keeffe did not produce no important works until 1915. [7]They were large charcoal drawings based on elements in nature showing great promise. [8]These works were seen by the photographer and gallery owner Alfred Stieglitz who admired them very much. [9]O'Keeffe's first exhibition was in 1916 at one of Stieglitzs galleries in New York City. [10]Eight years later O'Keeffe and Stieglitz was married. [11]Every year until her husband's death in 1946, it had an exhibit at one of Stieglitz's galleries. ➡

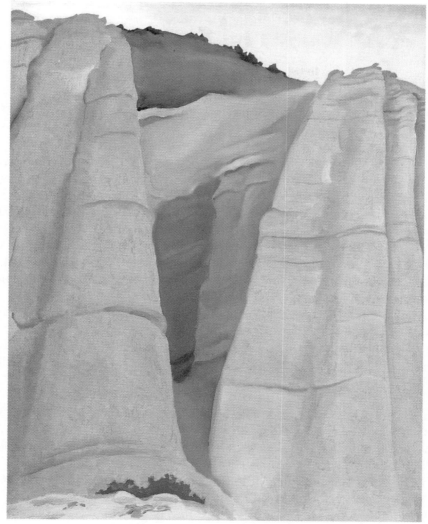

Georgia O'Keeffe, *From the White Place,* **1940**

[12]After visiting New Mexico in 1929, the dessert landscape became O'Keeffe's main subject. [13]She was more happier painting there than anywhere. [14]In the years after her husband's death, she made Abiquiu, New Mexico, her permanant home.

[15]O'Keeffe belonged to the first generation of American abstract artists and drew on her American roots (particularly the vastest landscape of the arid Southwest) more than many of her compatriots. [16]She was not greatly influenced by no European art. [17]O'Keeffe often used large, simplest forms that combined both soft and vivid colors. [18]In many of her works, she exaggeratted the size of an object.

[19]O'Keeffe painted some of the more dramatic landscapes in all America. [20]In her painting *From the White Place,* she used subdued tones and massive shapes more than anything to capture the dry, sun-bleached cliffs of northern New Mexico. [21]A setting such as this would perhaps be attractive to the rockhounds described by Annie Dillard than to most people.

Mixed Review

Exercise 9

Read the following biography of Annie Dillard. Then rewrite the sentences below it, correcting any errors in the use of modifiers. If you need additional information in order to complete any of your sentences, consult the biography.

Annie Dillard

Born and raised in Pittsburgh, Annie Dillard fell in love with nature when, at the age of 10, she discovered *The Field Book of Ponds and Streams* at a local library. Always a fine scholar, Dillard was an honor-society member at Hollins College. For her master's degree, she wrote a paper on Henry David Thoreau, the famous American nature writer to whom she is often compared. Dillard's journal of a year spent alone in rural Virginia became the basis for *Pilgrim at Tinker Creek*, which earned her the 1975 Pulitzer Prize. This vivid and introspective exploration of the natural world remains Dillard's best-known work. She has also published a volume of poetry and several more works of nonfiction, including her fine autobiography, *An American Childhood* (1987).

In 1992 Dillard published her first book of fiction, *The Living*, to great critical acclaim. In this novel she described the harsh life of the pioneers who came to the Pacific Northwest during the nineteenth century. In spite of her successes, Dillard claims to dislike writing because it takes her away from the great outdoors. Of her approach to nature, she has remarked, "I am no scientist. I am a wanderer."

1. Writing vividly about the world of nature and her own experiences, Annie Dillard's books have enjoyed great popularity.
2. Some readers and critics consider her writings about nature as powerful as the classic American author Henry David Thoreau.
3. Born in Pittsburgh, her youth is described vividly in the book *An American Childhood*, an autobiography published in 1987.
4. As a child, Dillard was an avid reader and almost never had no trouble with her schoolwork.
5. She later did good at Hollins College in Virginia and was elected to the school's honor society.
6. After spending a year in rural Virginia, her journal of that period was expanded into her acclaimed best-seller *Pilgrim at Tinker Creek*.
7. *Pilgrim at Tinker Creek* is probably more popular than any book by Dillard.
8. Although it was Dillard's first book, *Pilgrim at Tinker Creek* won her the 1975 Pulitzer Prize as the year's most finest work of nonfiction.
9. Dillard has only published a single volume of poetry.
10. Cooped up in her office, writing often keeps Dillard away from the natural world she loves.

Writing Application

Modifiers in Writing   Good writers are careful about the clear use and placement of modifiers. Notice, for example, the italicized modifiers in the following passage from Flannery O'Connor's *A View of the Woods*.

> No one was particularly glad that Mary Fortune looked like her grandfather except the old man himself. He thought it added greatly to her attractiveness. He thought she was the smartest and prettiest child he had ever seen and he let the rest of them know that if—IF that was—he left anything to anybody, it would be Mary Fortune he left it to. She was now nine, *short*, and *broad* like himself, *with his very light blue eyes, his wide prominent forehead, his steady penetrating scowl, and his rich florid complexion; . . .but she was like him on the inside too. She had, to a singular degree, his intelligence, his strong will, and his push and drive.*

Techniques with Modifiers   Try to apply some of O'Connor's techniques when you write and revise your own work.

1. Use comparative and superlative forms of modifiers when appropriate.

Weak version a smart and pretty child
O'Connor's version the *smartest* and *prettiest* child

2. Place modifiers correctly to make your meaning clear.

Confusing placement *With his very light blue eyes, his wide prominent forehead, his steady penetrating scowl, and his rich floral complexion*, she was now nine, *short* and *broad* like himself. . . .
O'Connor's version She was now nine, *short* and *broad* like himself, *with his very light blue eyes, his wide prominent forehead, his steady penetrating scowl, and his rich florid complexion.*

Practice   Practice using modifiers correctly by revising the following passage on a separate piece of paper.

Margaret watched her friend Linda windsurf sitting on the prow of the small boat. She wondered if she would ever be able to do it as effortlessly. There only was one way to find out. Taking a deep breath, her board was tossed into the water. Then she took another deep breath and plunged in after it. Climbing aboard, her feet were positioned just as Linda had taught her. She began to skim over the water as the wind became stronger. Feeling more freer than a seagull and more playful than a dolphin, suddenly the wind shifted, tossing her off the board. The sea was icy. It had not been icy near the shore. Struggling to the surface, a sobering thought occurred to her. She had a long way to go before she could windsurf in Linda's league.

UNIT

19

Usage Glossary

Grammar | **Lessons**

The glossary that follows presents some particularly troublesome matters of preferred usage. The glossary will give you guidance, for example, in choosing between two words that are often confused. It will also make you aware of certain words and expressions that you should avoid when speaking or writing for school or business.

a, an   Use the article *a* when the word that follows begins with a consonant sound, including a sounded *h*: *a poem, a house.* Use *an* when the word that follows begins with a vowel sound or an unsounded *h*: *an apple, an heirloom.* Use *a* before a word that begins with the "yew" sound: *a European, a unit.*

a lot, alot   This expression is always written as two words and means "a large amount." Some authorities suggest avoiding it altogether in formal English.

> **A lot** of snow fell last night.

a while, awhile   *A while* is made up of an article and a noun. *In* and *for* often come before *a while*, forming a prepositional phrase. *Awhile* is an adverb.

> We'll stop in **a while**.
> We'll stop for **a while**.
> We'll stop **awhile** before hiking to the top of the mountain.

accept, except   *Accept* is a verb that means "to receive" or "to agree to." *Except* is a preposition, a verb, or a conjunction. As a preposition *except* means "but."

> Eric will **accept** the trophy for the team.
> Alanna will not **accept** defeat.
> Everyone will be at the ceremony **except** the captain. [preposition]

affect, effect   *Affect* is a verb that means "to cause a change in; to influence." *Effect* may be a noun or a verb. As a noun it means "result." As a verb it means "to bring about or accomplish."

> The mayor's policies have **affected** every city agency.

> The mayor's policies have had a good **effect** on every agency. [noun meaning "result"]

> The mayor has been able to **effect** his goals in every city agency. [verb meaning "to bring about"]

ain't   *Ain't* is unacceptable in speaking and writing unless you are quoting somebody's exact words. Instead of using *ain't*, use *I am not; she is not; he is not;* and so on.

all ready, already   The two words *all ready* mean "completely ready." *Already* is an adverb that means "before" or "by this time."

> The band was **all ready** to play its last number, but the fans were **already** leaving the stadium.

all right, alright   Always write this expression as two words. Although the expression is often seen in print as one word, most language authorities prefer *all right*.

> She was sick yesterday, but today she feels **all right.**

all the farther, all the faster   These are regional expressions. Use *as far as* and *as fast as* in writing.

> We drove **as far as** we could during daylight hours.
>
> I'm pedaling this bike **as fast as** I can.

all together, altogether   Use *all together* to mean "in a group." Use the adverb *altogether* to mean "completely" or "on the whole."

> For the holidays our family will be **all together** at my grand-mother's house.
>
> My grandmother is **altogether** delighted to have us with her.

amount, number   *Amount* and *number* both refer to quantity. Use *amount* when referring to nouns that cannot be counted. Use *number* when referring to nouns that can be counted.

> Fort Knox contains a vast **amount** of gold.
> Fort Knox contains a large **number** of gold bars.

bad, badly   See Unit 18. 628

being as, being that   These expressions are sometimes used instead of *because* or *since* in informal conversation. In formal speaking and writing, always use *because* or *since*.

> **Because** their car broke down, they could not get here.
> **Since** they did not call, we assumed they were not coming.

beside, besides   *Beside* means "at the side of." *Besides* usually means "in addition to."

> Katrina sat **beside** her mother at the table.
> **Besides** yogurt and fruit, they had homemade muffins.

between, among   In general, use *between* to compare one person or thing with one other person or thing or with an entire group.

> What is the difference **between** Seattle and Portland? [Two cities are compared.]

> What was the difference **between** Pavlova and other ballet dancers? [One dancer is compared with an entire group of dancers.]

In general, use *among* to show a relationship in which more than two persons or things are considered as a group.

> The committee members were arguing **among** themselves.
> You are **among** friends.

Exercise 1   **Making Usage Choices**

For each of the following sentences, choose the correct word or expression from the pair in parentheses.

San Francisco

1. When gold was discovered in California in 1848, miners seeking their fortune traveled there (all the faster/as fast as) they could.
2. Although most prospectors found no gold, some of them discovered that staying on in California as ranchers or farmers was quite (all right/alright).
3. San Francisco has everything residents could want (except/accept) a sunny climate, for the city is often rainy and foggy.
4. In 1906 a terrible earthquake and fire destroyed much of San Francisco, but by 1916 the city had recovered and was (all ready/already) for a major cultural exposition.
5. There are (a lot/alot) of people of Chinese ancestry in San Francisco.
6. About 36,000 of them live in (a/an) area known as Chinatown.
7. The buildings in this district, many of which echo traditional Chinese architectural styles, create a picturesque (affect/effect).
8. Many visitors spend quite (a while/awhile) browsing in the shops on Grant Avenue, Chinatown's main thoroughfare.
9. There (ain't/is not) another Chinese community in the entire Western Hemisphere that is as large as San Francisco's Chinatown.
10. At first the Chinese families who immigrated to San Francisco lived (all together/altogether) in Chinatown, but now many of them have resettled in other parts of the city.

borrow, lend, loan   *Borrow* and *lend* have opposite meanings. *Borrow* is a verb meaning "to take something with the understanding that it must be returned." *Lend* is a verb meaning "to give something with the understanding that it will be returned." *Loan* is a noun. It may be used as a verb, but most authorities prefer *lend*.

> May I **borrow** ten dollars till payday? [verb]
> Will you **lend** me some money? [verb]
> Did the bank give you a **loan?** [noun]

bring, take   Use *bring* to mean "to carry from a distant place to a closer one." Use *take* to mean the opposite: "to carry from a nearby place to a more distant one."

> Will you **bring** me some perfume when you come back from Paris?

> Don't forget to **take** your passport when you go to Europe.

can, may   *Can* indicates the ability to do something. *May* indicates permission to do something or the possibility of doing it.

> You **can** make hot chocolate by dissolving cocoa in warm milk.
> You **may** have a cup of hot chocolate before going to sleep.

can't hardly, can't scarcely   These terms are considered double negatives because *hardly* and *scarcely* by themselves have a negative meaning. Therefore, avoid using *hardly* and *scarcely* with *not* or *-n't*.

> Eduardo **can hardly** tell the twins apart.
> The driver **can scarcely** see through the dense fog.

could of, might of, must of, should of, would of   After the words *could, might, must, should,* or *would,* use the helping verb *have,* not the preposition *of.*

> Some historians say that the United States **could have** prevented the stock market crash of 1929.

> The country **might have** avoided the Great Depression that followed.

> The Great Depression **must have** been a difficult time to raise a family.

different from, different than   The expression *different from* is generally preferred to *different than.*

> The sport of cross-country skiing is **different from** downhill skiing.

For each of the following sentences, choose the correct word or expression from the pair in parentheses.

Kansas City

1. The Missouri River flows (between/among) Kansas City, Missouri, and Kansas City, Kansas.
2. Both cities are situated (beside/besides) the river.
3. If you look at a map, you (can/may) see that the Missouri River forms part of the boundary between Kansas and Missouri.
4. Until the Civil War, Kansas City's economy was based on supplying and outfitting the large (number/amount) of travelers headed west.
5. After the first railroad reached the city in 1869, (alot of/a lot of) things changed.
6. One major (affect/effect) was that the city became a busy cattle-trading center.
7. The city was (already/all ready) a railroad hub, and it soon became a great grain center.
8. A large (amount/number) of Native Americans belonging to the Osage nation once lived in the area that is now Kansas City.
9. Pioneers who settled in the area called the Native Americans living there Osage (being as/because) the pioneers could not pronounce the group's real name, Wazhazhe, which means "We Are the People."
10. (Beside/Besides) the Osage nation, the Kansa, Otoe, and Missouri nations lived in the area where Kansas City now stands.
11. Until the late nineteenth century, visitors to Kansas City (could of/could have) seen people of several Native American nations living around the town.
12. One (can scarcely/can't scarcely) exaggerate the importance of the role played by Native Americans in the history of Kansas City.
13. If you visit Old Shawnee, a restored mission near Kansas City, carry your camera or (borrow/loan) one from a friend.
14. Years ago Native Americans would (bring/take) furs to Fort Osage from far away to exchange for manufactured goods.
15. In the 1870s the federal government resettled many Native Americans from Kansas to Indian Territory in Oklahoma; many historians claim that the plan was carried out (bad/badly).
16. (Being as/Because) most of the Native Americans who were resettled had not chosen to move, many people today feel that the mass movement was unjust.
17. The Cherokee, Chicksaw, Creek, Choctaw, and Seminole peoples each had traditions and customs that were quite (different than/different from) those of the others.
18. The history of all of these Native American nations (would of/would have) been quite different had they not been moved forcibly to Indian Territory.
19. Originally, Indian Territory also included a vast (number/amount) of land in Kansas and Nebraska.
20. When Oklahoma became a state in 1907, the last of the Indian Territory was dissolved, leaving Native Americans in Oklahoma to live (between/among) the general population.

doesn't, don't *Doesn't* is a shortened form of *does not,* which is used with *he, she, it,* and all singular nouns. *Don't* is a shortened form of *do not,* which is used with *I, you, we, they,* and all plural nouns. Authorities usually discourage the use of contractions in formal writing.

> Our state **doesn't** allow people to drive before the age of 17.

> Some foreign countries **don't** require their citizens to attend school.

emigrate, immigrate Use *emigrate* to mean "to leave one country and go to another to live." Use *immigrate* to mean "to come to a country to settle there." Use *from* with *emigrate* and *to* or *into* with *immigrate.*

> Mr. Roh **emigrated** from South Korea.
> He **immigrated** to the United States.

farther, further *Farther* should be used in reference to physical distance. *Further* should be used in reference to degree or time.

> San Antonio is **farther** south than Dallas.
> She did not question him **further.**

fewer, less Use *fewer* when referring to nouns that can be counted. Use *less* when referring to nouns that cannot be counted. *Less* may also be used with figures that are seen as single amounts or single quantities.

> **Fewer** students have enrolled in physics this year than last year.

> This year there is **less** interest in physics among the students.

> We traveled to New York City in **less** than two hours. [*Two* is treated as a single period of time, not as individual hours.]

> It cost **less** than $20.00 to go by train. [The amount of money is treated as a single sum, not as individual dollars.]

good, well See Unit 18.

had of Do not use *of* between *had* and a past participle.

> I wish I **had received** this information earlier.

hanged, hung Use *hanged* when you mean "put to death by hanging." Use *hung* in all other instances.

> The state of New Hampshire **hanged** three convicts between 1900 and 1950.

> The teacher **hung** the bulletin board above her desk.

in, into   Use *in* to mean "inside" or "within" and *into* to indicate movement or direction from the outside to a point within. The preposition *in* suggests a fixed location within a particular area or place. The preposition *into* suggests movement within or between locations.

> Jeanine was sitting outdoors **in** a lawn chair.
> When it got too hot, she went **into** the house.

irregardless, regardless   Use *regardless*. The prefix *ir-* and the suffix *-less* both have negative meanings. When used together, they produce a double negative, which is incorrect.

> **Regardless** of what the critics said, I liked the movie.

Exercise 3   **Making Usage Choices**

For each of the following sentences, choose the correct word or expression from the pair in parentheses.

San Antonio

1. During its early history, San Antonio, Texas, was under the control of no (fewer/less) than six countries.
2. Many people who first settled in San Antonio (emigrated/immigrated) from Spain.
3. The beautiful Spanish mission of San José still looks (good/well) after many years.
4. If you visit San Antonio, (don't/doesn't) miss seeing the old Fort Alamo.
5. To see the Alamo, the site of the famous 1836 battle between Texas and Mexico, you must go (in/into) the center of San Antonio.
6. If the Texas garrison (had/had of) been larger, it might have withstood the Mexican attack.
7. (Irregardless/Regardless) of their defeat at the Alamo, the Texans went on to win the war.
8. Officials (hanged/hung) the flag of the independent Republic of Texas in buildings in San Antonio from 1836 to 1845.
9. During the 1800s pioneers flocked to Texas, pushing the frontier (farther/further) west.
10. The modern city of San Antonio is quite different (from/than) the original Spanish settlement founded hundreds of years ago.
11. (In/Into) the modern city are a number of military bases.
12. The bases (affected/effected) population growth in the region.
13. Because of jobs on the bases, many people (emigrated/immigrated) to the area.
14. The military has (less/fewer) economic importance for the region today.
15. The future of the defense industry in San Antonio is open to (farther/further) study.
16. San Antonio has (less/fewer) residents than Houston or Dallas.
17. At the time of the 1990 census, San Antonio's population was (less/fewer) than 1 million.
18. That population figure is (all ready/already) out of date.
19. It (doesn't/don't) take into account the many people who live in the surrounding metropolitan area.
20. Many people think that there (can/can't) hardly be a better place to live than San Antonio.

this kind, these kinds *Kind* is singular. Therefore, the singular form *this* or *that* modifies *kind*. *This* and *that* should also be used with *sort* and *type (this type, that type, this sort, that sort)*. *Kinds* is plural. Therefore, the plural form *these* or *those* modifies *kinds*. Also use *these* and *those* with the plural nouns *sorts* and *types*.

> **This kind** of bulb should be used in your lamp.
> **These kinds** of lamps are very attractive.
> **This sort** of food is found in many ethnic cuisines.
> **These sorts** of foods are nutritious.
> **That type** of exercise is my favorite.
> **Those types** of exercises are considered good for your heart.

lay, lie *Lay* means "to put" or "to place"; it takes a direct object. *Lie* means "to recline" or "to be positioned"; it never takes an object.

> **Lay** your coat on the bed.
> I am going to **lie** in the sun now.

Problems arise particularly in using the principal parts of these verbs. Notice, for example, that the past tense of *lie* is *lay*. Learn all the principal parts of these verbs.

BASIC FORM	lay	lie
PRESENT PARTICIPLE	laying	lying
PAST FORM	laid	lay
PAST PARTICIPLE	laid	lain

> She **laid** her coat on the bed.
> I **lay** in the sun too long and got sunburned.
> She had **laid** her coat on the bed before the party started.
> I have **lain** in the sun longer without getting as sunburned.

learn, teach *Learn* means "to receive knowledge," and *teach* means "to give knowledge."

> Jon **learned** to play the piano at the age of nine.
> Mrs. Ramos **teaches** us American history.

leave, let *Leave* means "to go away," and *let* means "to allow" or "to permit."

> When you **leave** next week, I will miss you.
> Please **let** me use your dictionary.

like, as *Like* is a preposition and introduces a prepositional phrase. *As* is a subordinating conjunction and introduces a subordinate clause. Many authorities say that it is incorrect to use *like* before a clause.

> Phil plays baseball **like** a professional.

> Teresa is confident, **as** I am, that everything will go well on the expedition.

loose, lose The adjective *loose* means "free," "not firmly attached," or "not fitting tightly." The verb *lose* means "to have no longer," "to misplace," or "to fail to win."

> That ring is so **loose** you are sure to **lose** it.
> Which team do you think will **lose** the game?

passed, past *Passed* is the past form and the past participle of the verb *to pass*. *Past* may be an adjective, a preposition, an adverb, or a noun.

> We **passed** your house on the way to school. [verb]

> Chris had a cold this **past** week. [adjective]

> We drove **past** your house last Sunday. [preposition]

> What time did you drive **past?** [adverb]

> Louise's grandmother always tells wonderful stories about her **past**. [noun]

precede, proceed *Precede* means "to go before" or "to come before." *Proceed* means "to continue" or "to move along."

> Our band **preceded** the homecoming float as the parade **proceeded** through town.

raise, rise The verb *raise* means "to cause to move upward"; it always takes an object. The verb *rise* means "to go up"; it is intransitive and does not take an object.

> **Raise** your hand if you know the answer.
> The rocket will **rise** from the launching pad at 9:01 A.M.

reason is, because *Because* means "for the reason that." Therefore, do not use *because* after *reason is*. Use *that* after *reason is*, or use *because* alone.

> The **reason** I am tired is that I did not sleep last night.
> I am tired **because** I did not sleep last night.

For each of the following sentences, choose the correct word or expression from the pair in parentheses.

New York City

1. New York (lies/lays) near the mouth of the Hudson River in the southeastern corner of New York State.
2. The reason New York is often called a melting pot is (because/that) many ethnic groups have settled there.
3. At the American Museum of Immigration at the base of the Statue of Liberty, exhibits (teach/learn) visitors about the contributions made by people who immigrated to the United States.
4. People from many different cultures (immigrated/emigrated) to Ellis Island over the years.
5. The federal government now (lets/leaves) people visit Ellis Island, where nearly 12 million immigrants entered the country between 1892 and 1954.
6. If you wish to learn more about ethnic America, (like/as) our class did, you can visit the Hispanic Society of America, Japan House, the Museum of the American Indian, and the Jewish Museum.
7. You can admire works by African American artists at the Studio Museum in Harlem and then (precede/proceed) to the Schomburg Center, a library for the study of African American culture.
8. At the Metropolitan Museum of Art, visitors can stroll (past/passed) an Egyptian temple and many exhibits of African and Asian art.
9. In Chinatown, near a large red-brick apartment building that (rises/raises) high above the street, is a bronze statue of Confucius, the venerable Chinese philosopher.
10. Tourists and New Yorkers alike enjoy visiting (these kinds/this kind) of places to learn more about our country's multicultural heritage.
11. New York is still a city in which people of many races and ethnic backgrounds can live together and not (lose/loose) their cultural identity.
12. You can (teach/learn) much about New York City's history by visiting the Museum of the City of New York and the New York Historical Society.
13. The South Street Seaport Museum, which (lays/lies) near the East River, specializes in maritime history.
14. (Preceding/Proceeding) from Manhattan to the Bronx, maritime buffs can also visit the City Island Historical Nautical Museum.
15. The Harbor Festival celebrating the (passed/past) is held on July 4.
16. (As/Like) they did a century ago, traditional sailing ships moor in New York Harbor.
17. They (raise/rise) billowing white sails.
18. When the ships set sail, they (let/leave) many admirers gazing after them.
19. What is the reason (because/that) so many people are intrigued by the sea?
20. (This kind/These kinds) of question is hard to answer.

respectfully, respectively   *Respectfully* means "with respect." *Respectively* means "in the order named."

> The audience listened **respectfully** as the poet spoke.

> Phoenix and Phoenixville are, **respectively,** in Arizona and Pennsylvania.

says, said   *Says* is the third-person singular of the verb *say*. *Said* is the past tense of *say*. Be careful not to use *says* for *said*.

> At dinner last night, Nelson **said** that he wasn't hungry.
> He always **says** that, but he eats everything anyway.

sit, set   *Sit* means "to place oneself in a sitting position." *Sit* rarely takes an object. *Set* means "to place" or "to put" and usually takes an object.

Set is also an intransitive verb when it is used with *sun* to mean "the sun is going down" or "the sun is sinking below the horizon." When *set* is used in this way, it does not take an object.

> Grandpa likes to **sit** on the porch.
> Lian **set** the pots on the stove after the sun **set**.

than, then   *Than* is a conjunction used to introduce the second element in a comparison; it also shows exception.

> Elsa is taller **than** Isabel.
> Our visitor was none other **than** Uncle Al!

Then is an adverb that means "at that time," "soon afterward," "the time mentioned," "at another time," "for that reason," or "in that case."

> My grandmother was a young girl **then**.
> Marguerite finished the book and **then** turned out the light.
> By **then** the party was almost over.
> If it rains, **then** we cannot go.

this here, that there   Avoid using *here* and *there* after *this* and *that*. Use *this* and *that* alone.

> All of us want to read **this** magazine.
> Have you heard **that** story?

where at   Do not use *at* after *where*.

> **Where** is Valley Forge?

who, whom   See Unit 17.

Making Usage Choices

For each of the following sentences, choose the correct word or expression from the pair in parentheses.

Santa Fe

1. Santa Fe, New Mexico, has more sites of historic interest (than/then) most American cities.
2. Tourists in Santa Fe can explore the narrow, winding streets and (than/then) visit museums that display Native American crafts.
3. In summer, audiences (set/sit) in the open-air theater of the Santa Fe Opera.
4. (This/This here) opera house is one of the most famous in the world.
5. Audiences listen (respectfully/respectively) as some of the world's greatest opera singers perform.
6. Native Americans and Spanish colonists were, (respectfully/ respectively), the first two groups to reside in the Santa Fe area.
7. Many of the early Spaniards (who/whom) we know about in this area came to search for fabulous riches.
8. These early Spaniards reported hearing of a man who (said/says) he had seen seven cities of gold in the area.
9. Santa Fe is the place (where/where at) the historic Santa Fe Trail ended.
10. (This/This here) trail was used by pioneers traveling west during the 1800s.

Exercise 6   **Making Usage Choices**

For each of the following sentences, choose the correct word or expression from the pair in parentheses.

Washington, D.C.

1. (Where/Where at) is Washington, D.C., located?
2. The capital of the United States (sets/sits) at what may be considered the dividing line between the North and the South.
3. The city (lies/lays) along the banks of two rivers, the mighty Potomac and its tributary, the Anacostia.
4. When the location was first selected for the capital of the country, some people thought that the choice had been (bad/badly) made.
5. (Between/Among) the two rivers stretched a broad area of what many people considered swamp.
6. They did not believe that a graceful city would (raise/rise) where they saw only bog.
7. (Besides/Beside) the swampy ground, the hot and humid summer climate was a problem.
8. (Like/As) other towns and cities of the time, Washington had streets that were little better than rutted dirt roads.
9. Planes, cars, and trains today (take/bring) 20 million tourists a year to this beautiful city with a multicultural population.
10. In addition, people from many countries and states move to the capital and (teach/learn) to call it home.

For each of the following sentences, choose the correct word or expression from the pair in parentheses.

New Orleans

1. New Orleans, Louisiana, has (a/an) average elevation of one foot above sea level.
2. (A lot/Alot) of levees were constructed along the banks of the Mississippi River to prevent flooding.
3. The Mississippi River flows through Baton Rouge and then (precedes/proceeds) southeast to New Orleans.
4. New Orleans (ain't/is not) only a shipping center.
5. (Being that/Because) New Orleans is picturesque, many people enjoy vacationing there.
6. The temperature in the winter months (doesn't/don't) drop below freezing very often.
7. French and Spanish colonists (preceded/proceeded) Americans in settling New Orleans.
8. Many people from Italy (emigrated/immigrated) to New Orleans.
9. In New Orleans restaurants customers can choose (among/between) French and Creole cuisine.
10. Most visitors enjoy strolling through the streets of the historic French Quarter for quite (a while/awhile), taking in the beautiful architecture.
11. No skyscrapers (raise/rise) above the low skyline of the French Quarter.
12. Visitors need walk no (farther/further) than Basin Street and Bourbon Street to hear jazz.
13. A large (number/amount) of visitors attend concerts at music halls like the famous Preservation Hall.
14. Visitors crowd (in/into) this small hall whenever jazz is being played.
15. In Preservation Hall fans (set/sit) their coats on their laps as they (set/sit) on the crowded wooden benches.
16. Here musicians play jazz (like/as) it was played in the early 1900s.
17. This style of jazz is quite (different from/different than) the style of modern jazz.
18. By February of each year, the citizens of New Orleans are (all ready/already) to hold their famous Mardi Gras festival.
19. During Mardi Gras the city (can scarcely/can't scarcely) accommodate its many visitors.
20. During this celebration it is (all right/alright) to take a vacation from work, dress in elaborate costumes, and take part in carnivals and parades.
21. Although the heat and humidity of New Orleans may (affect/effect) some visitors, the local inhabitants seem to be used to it.
22. Similarly, they (accept/except) without serious complaint the amount of rainfall.
23. It seems the residents are (altogether/all together) used to the climate.
24. (Between/Among) the inhabitants of New Orleans are Creoles, descendants of early French and Spanish immigrants; Cajuns, descendants of refugees from Nova Scotia; and descendants of Santo Domingo slaves.
25. They have all (taught/learned) to live together in harmony.

For each of the following sentences, choose the correct word or expression from the pair in parentheses.

Boston

1. Boston is an (all together/altogether) special place.
2. If it had been more centrally located, Boston (might have/ might of) been the nation's capital.
3. New York City and Philadelphia were, (respectively/ respectfully), the first and second capitals of the United States.
4. In 1773 Bostonians who would not (accept/except) King George III's taxes dumped many pounds of tea into Boston Harbor.
5. They wanted independence from England (bad/badly).
6. They (set/sit) several demands before the English king.
7. The government of the city of Boston has (hanged/hung) plaques at historic sites.
8. Beacon Hill, more (than/then) any other area in Boston, is known for its beauty and historic importance.
9. Boston is a very accessible city. The reason is (because/that) it has an efficient transit system.
10. If you want to get from the suburbs to the city center, just go (in/into) the nearest station of the rapid transit system, and you'll be there in no time.
11. Be sure to (bring/take) a raincoat if you come to Boston in the fall, for it is often stormy.
12. A visitor can tour the Boston Museum of Fine Arts and (then/than) visit the Boston Arts Center.
13. Boston abounds in (this kind/these kinds) of cultural centers.
14. After the Charles River has (passed/past) through the city, it empties into Boston Harbor.
15. People can picnic in the parks (beside/besides) the river.
16. A visitor who likes to walk (can/may) follow the Freedom Trail to many of Boston's historic sites.
17. Along the one-and-a-half-mile-long trail are no (less/ fewer) than 15 historic sites.
18. Guidebooks will (learn/teach) the visitor about places on the trail.
19. The visitor will not (lose/loose) the way because the trail is well marked.
20. Time spent in Boston (can't hardly/can hardly) be forgotten.
21. (Besides/Beside) being a historical treasure trove, Boston is a leader in education.
22. In 1636 Harvard College was founded in what was (than/then) Newtowne.
23. Harvard, the first university founded in the English colonies, had many (less/fewer) students in the 1600s than it does now.
24. (Among/Between) Boston's many institutions of higher learning are Tufts, Boston University, Northeastern University, and the Massachusetts Institute of Technology.
25. If you run, (like/as) I have, along the jogging trail that follows the Charles River, you can glimpse at least three of these universities.

Making Usage Choices

For each of the following sentences, choose the correct word or expression from the pair in parentheses.

Seattle

1. Recently a report (said/says) that Seattle, Washington, is one of America's most attractive cities.
2. (Irregardless/Regardless) of whether or not people choose to live in Seattle, most agree it is a beautiful place.
3. Many tourists (who/whom) the Century 21 Exposition attracted in 1962 later returned to Seattle to live.
4. Seattle is known as the Emerald City, a name (borrowed/loaned) from *The Wizard of Oz.*
5. The city of Seattle (lays/lies) near the Pacific Ocean.
6. (This/This here) location made Seattle a gateway to the Far East.
7. Many Japanese were (between/among) Seattle's early settlers.
8. Other early settlers (emigrated/immigrated) from Scandinavia.
9. A glance at the beautiful Cascade Mountains east of Seattle can easily (raise/rise) one's spirits.
10. This is the mountain range (where Mount Saint Helens is located/where at Mount Saint Helens is located).

Exercise 10   **Making Usage Choices**

For each of the following sentences, choose the correct word or expression from the pair in parentheses.

Atlanta

1. (Leave/Let) us go to Atlanta, Georgia.
2. Atlanta is a larger city (than/then) Birmingham, Alabama.
3. Today's Atlanta is very (different from/different than) the city portrayed in *Gone with the Wind.*
4. Traces of the Old South (can't hardly/can hardly) be found in Atlanta.
5. A devastated city after the Civil War, Atlanta is more than (alright/all right) now.
6. Other cities seeking Atlanta's success have done (like/as) Atlanta has.
7. Because of its location, Atlanta is (all ready/already) well situated as a transportation crossroads.
8. By promoting itself (good/well), Atlanta has attracted national corporations and federal government offices.
9. Some visitors who (could have/could of) seen the *Cyclorama*, a depiction of the Battle of Atlanta and one of the three largest paintings in the world, (passed/past) up the opportunity.
10. Many of those who see the painting agree that its (affect/effect) is striking.

Grammar Review

Usage Glossary

The following quotations, which relate to the themes of friendship and love, have been annotated to show usage items covered in this unit.

Literature Models

QUOTATIONS ABOUT FRIENDSHIP AND LOVE

The relative pronoun *who* in the nominative case because it is the subject of a clause

He who has a thousand friends has not a friend to spare.
And he who has one enemy will meet him everywhere.

From *Sentences* by Ali Ibn-Abi-Talib (seventh century),
translated from the Arabic

Can used to suggest ability

To me, fair friend, you never can be old. . . .

From Sonnet 104 by William Shakespeare

The preposition *into* used to suggest movement from one place to another

I breathed a song into the air,
It fell to earth, I knew not where. . . .
And the song, from beginning to end,
I found again in the heart of a friend.

The preposition *in* used to mean "inside"

From "The Arrow and the Song" by Henry Wadsworth Longfellow

Except used as a conjunction meaning "but"

"Every man's his own friend." "Except sometimes some people are nobody's enemies but their own."

From *Oliver Twist* by Charles Dickens

Like, a preposition, used to introduce a prepositional phrase

For there is no friend like a sister
In calm or stormy weather;
To cheer one on the tedious way,
To fetch one if one goes astray. . . .

From "Goblin Market" by Christina Rossetti

May used to suggest possibility

The process of falling in love at first sight is as final as it is swift . . . , but the growth of true friendship may be a life-long affair.

From *The Country of the Pointed Firs* by Sarah Orne Jewett ➡

Only solitary men know the full joys of friendship. Others have their family; but to a solitary and an exile his friends are everything.

A before a consonant sound; *an* before a vowel sound

From *Shadows on the Rock* by Willa Cather

We have fewer friends than we imagine, but more than we know.

Fewer referring to a noun that can be counted

From *The Book of Friends* by Hugo von Hofmannsthal, translated from the German by Mary Hottinger and Tania and James Stern

Among those whom I like or admire, I can find no common denominator, but among those whom I love, I can: all of them make me laugh.

The relative pronoun *whom* in the objective case because it is a direct object

From *The Dyer's Hand* by W. H. Auden

"Love, Umi, means something very different from 'falling in love,' " Daddyji said. "It's not an act but a lifelong process. . . ."

Different from rather than *different than*

From *The Ledge Between the Streams* by Ved Mehta

Exercise 1

Making Usage Choices   The following sentences describe friendships between famous artists. For each item choose the correct word or expression in parentheses, and write it on your paper.

1. Though they were very (different from/different than) each other in temperament, the Dutch painter Vincent van Gogh and the French painter Paul Gauguin were close friends.
2. The French artist Edgar Degas noted the similarities (between/among) his drawing style and that of his friend, the American artist Mary Cassatt.
3. (Beside/Besides) Degas, Cassatt was also friendly with several other Impressionist painters.
4. (Being as/Since) Berthe Morisot's close friend, fellow French painter Edouard Manet, so admired one of her paintings, she gave it to him as a gift.
5. The friendship may have influenced Morisot's work more (than/then) it influenced that of Manet.

Exercise 2

Making Usage Choices   The following sentences describe more friendships between famous artists. For each item choose the correct word or expression in parentheses, and write it on your paper.

1. Spanish artist Pablo Picasso and French artist Georges Braque had a great (affect/effect) on each other's work.
2. They are known as the founders of Cubism, which was an (all together/altogether) new style of art for its time.
3. In the 1920s the Russian artist Wassily Kandinsky and the Swiss artist Paul Klee were colleagues at the Bauhaus, a school of architecture and design in Berlin, (where they taught painting/where they taught painting at).
4. An artistic friendship between two Americans, the painter Georgia O'Keeffe and the photographer Alfred Stieglitz, (preceded/proceeded) their marriage.
5. Stieglitz (hanged/hung) O'Keeffe's paintings in his gallery.

Exercise 3

Making Usage Choices   The following sentences describe friendships between famous writers. For each item choose the correct word or expression in parentheses, and write it on your paper.

1. In Rome in the first century B.C., the poet Virgil was supported, (like/as) his friend and fellow poet Horace also was, by the patron Maecenas.
2. (This/This here) article says that the writers Edith Wharton and Henry James were friends.
3. The authors Gustave Flaubert and Ivan Turgenev exchanged letters faithfully for two decades; (this kind/these kinds) of long-term correspondence is now rare.
4. Flaubert and Turgenev had (all ready/already) published some of their most famous novels when they met in 1863.
5. *Madame Bovary* and *Fathers and Sons*, by Flaubert and Turgenev, (respectfully/ respectively), remain classics.
6. Herman Melville befriended his fellow American writer Nathaniel Hawthorne, (who/whom) he greatly admired.
7. During these authors' lifetimes, Hawthorne's works were more widely read (than/then) Melville's.
8. The novelists Joseph Conrad and Ford Maddox Ford thought it was (all right/ alright) to collaborate on two novels.
9. In the course of their friendship, the American poets Elizabeth Bishop and Marianne Moore (must of/must have) enjoyed each other's lively wit and humor.
10. The poet Joseph Brodsky received much support from his fellow Russian poet Anna Akhmatova before he was forced to (immigrate/emigrate) to the United States.

Exercise 4

Making Usage Choices   The following sentences describe famous fictional friendships and romances. For each item choose the correct word or expression in parentheses, and write it on your paper.

1. In Arthur Conan Doyle's works, Sherlock Holmes investigates a great (amount/number) of criminal cases.
2. Horatio tells his dear friend Hamlet, one of Shakespeare's tragic heroes, that he has seen the ghost of Hamlet's father (raise/rise) from the dead.
3. Romeo and Juliet, Shakespeare's famous young lovers, (can't/can't hardly) bear to be apart from each other.
4. By the end of Jane Austen's novel *Pride and Prejudice*, Elizabeth Bennet thinks she (passed/past) judgment on Mr. Darcy much too quickly.
5. In Emily Brontë's *Wuthering Heights*, Cathy's brother, who feels (bad/badly) about her impending marriage, tries to prevent the match and causes a tragedy.
6. In Tolstoy's novel *War and Peace*, Prince Andrei and Pierre are devoted friends, (irregardless/regardless) of their opposing personalities.
7. Huckleberry Finn and Tom Sawyer have (a lot/alot) of adventures together in Mark Twain's novels.
8. At the outset of Herman Melville's *Moby Dick*, Ishmael is terrified to find that he is (laying/lying) beside the bizarre-looking Queequeg, but they later become close friends.
9. Unhappy at school, the orphan Jane Eyre, Charlotte Brontë's main character, finds comfort for (a while/awhile) in a friendship with the sweet but sickly Helen Burns.
10. Although Cervantes's character Don Quixote (looses/loses) touch with reality, his squire and friend, Sancho Panza, maintains common sense.

Exercise 5

Making Usage Choices   The following sentences describe relationships from mythology and folklore. For each item choose the correct word or expression in parentheses, and write it on your paper.

1. In Homer's *Iliad*, Achilles (borrows/lends/loans) his armor to his dear friend Patroclus, who lacks armor of his own, but Patroclus is nevertheless killed in battle.
2. Because Orpheus cannot (accept/except) the death of Eurydice, he enters the underworld to try to retrieve her.
3. In a tale told by Ovid, the parents of Pyramus and Thisbe tell the young lovers they (cannot/may not) marry.
4. The reason Pyramus stabs himself is (that/because) he believes a lioness has killed Thisbe.
5. Orestes, with his friend Pylades, goes (in/into) the palace of Clytemnestra to avenge Orestes' father's death.

Exercise 6

Making Usage Choices The following sentences describe collaborations in science. For each item choose the correct word or expression in parentheses, and write it on your paper.

1. In 1903 the inventors Orville and Wilbur Wright altered aviation history with the first sustained flight; its distance was (fewer/less) than 150 feet.
2. The French chemist Marie Curie, working (beside/besides) her husband, Pierre Curie, discovered the element radium.
3. The Curies' work caused scientists to (raise/rise) their hopes about treating certain medical problems.
4. The Swiss psychologist Carl Jung and the Austrian founder of psychoanalysis, Sigmund Freud, worked (good/well) together for a brief time.
5. Jung (might of/might have) supported Freud's ideas initially, but he later disputed many of Freud's doctrines.
6. The discovery of the DNA double helix by James D. Watson and Francis H. C. Crick (farther/further) advanced our understanding of biology.
7. Their discovery, in turn, spurred a great (amount/number) of research into the role of DNA in the human body.
8. The anthropologists Louis and Mary Leakey and the team of Don Johanson and Tom Gray, working in Tanzania and Ethiopia (respectfully/respectively), made astounding archaeological discoveries.
9. The first lunar landing succeeded through cooperation (between/among) Neil Armstrong, Buzz Aldrin, and Michael Collins of the *Apollo 11* spaceflight.
10. (All together/Altogether) there were sixteen Apollo space missions.

Exercise 7

Proofreading

The following passage describes the artist John Singer Sargent, whose painting is reproduced on the opposite page. Rewrite the passage, correcting any errors in spelling, grammar, and usage. Add any missing punctuation. There are twenty-five errors.

John Singer Sargent

[1]John Singer Sargent, a famous portrait and landscape painter of the passed century was born in Italy in 1856. [2]His father, a physician and his mother, a amateur painter, were wealthy New Englanders. [3]They spend alot more time in Europe then in America, however. [4]Sargent begun his studies in Florence at the age of fourteen. [5]And moved to Paris four years later. [6]He discovered in Paris that he preferred to paint directly on the canvass without making preliminary sketches.

[7]When he was still younger then twenty-one, Sargent made his first trip to the United States. [8]He became instantly popular his portraits were in great demand in Boston and ➡

John Singer Sargent, *Carnation, Lily, Lily, Rose,* **1886**

New York for awhile. [9]He quickly made a name for himself in London and immigrated there permenently in 1884.

[10]While living in London, Sargent cultivated influential friends; between these were the painter Edwin Abbey and the writer Henry James. [11]Sargents taste for aristocratic life are reflected in his portraits of upper-class people. [12]Although it may look as if Sargent painted all the faster he could, he actually labored over each piece until he achieved the affect he wanted. [13]He never excepted anything but the best from himself.

[14]As the art world turned increasingly toward modernism and abstraction, Sargent's realistic style gradually fell out of fashion. [15]His great talent as a painter however, was never challenged. [16]The Sargent work above show Sargent's extraordinary technique. [17]This here painting echoes the love and friendship expressed in the quotations that appear in this review.

Mixed Review

Exercise 8

The following sentences provide information about the authors of the quotations in this review. For each sentence write the correct word or expression from parentheses.

1. Ali Ibn-Abi-Talib, (who/whom) was married to Mohammed's daughter, became a leader of Islam.
2. The division of Islam between Shiites and Sunni (can/may) be traced back to events that occurred during the lifetime of Ali Ibn-Abi-Talib.
3. If you could (bring/take) only one writer's works to a desert island, the plays of William Shakespeare might suffice.
4. (Accept/Except) for *King Lear*, I prefer Shakespeare's comedies to his tragedies.
5. In narrative poems such as *Hiawatha* and *The Courtship of Miles Standish*, Henry Wadsworth Longfellow explored the events and folklore of the American (passed/past).
6. Longfellow combined the epic form of poetry with (a/an) simple and sentimental style that was his own.
7. It (can/may) be fair to say that Charles Dickens ranks among the most popular English writers of all time.
8. Most of Dickens's novels, (as/like) *Nicholas Nickleby*, first appeared in installments in periodicals.
9. Christina Rossetti, (like/as) her brother, Dante Gabriel Rossetti, was an English poet known for vivid imagery.
10. (Beside/Besides) writing lyrical religious poetry, Christina Rossetti specialized in writing verses for children.
11. The stories and novels of Sarah Orne Jewett give readers a sense of lingering (a while/awhile) in the countryside of the author's native Maine.
12. Christina Rossetti and Sarah Orne Jewett died in 1894 and 1909, (respectively/respectfully).
13. Her childhood in Nebraska had a great (affect/effect) on Willa Cather.
14. One reason Willa Cather was able to create strong characters who embody the pioneer spirit is (because/that) she knew many such people when she was growing up.
15. Hugo von Hofmannsthal, an Austrian writer, wrote (fewer/less) lyric poems as he grew older.
16. Von Hofmannsthal, a poet, dramatist, and essayist, wrote the text for some operas composed by Richard Strauss during the (passed/past) century.
17. The poet W. H. Auden (emigrated/immigrated) from England in 1939 and became an American citizen.
18. I listened (respectfully/respectively) when our teacher told us that Auden won the Pulitzer Prize in 1948 for *Age of Anxiety*.
19. Although the Indian-born author Ved Mehta had become completely blind by the age of three, he (preceded/proceeded) to excel in college and in his profession.
20. Ved Mehta owns a summer home on the island of Isleboro, which (sets/sits) in Penobscot Bay off the coast of Maine.

Writing Application

Usage of *Lie* in Writing

In this passage from *Of Wolves and Men*, Barry Holstun Lopez uses several forms of the intransitive verb *lie*. Read the passage, concentrating on the italicized verb forms.

It is now late in the afternoon. The wolf has stopped traveling, has *lain* down to sleep on cool earth beneath a rock outcropping. Mosquitoes rest on his ears. His ears flicker. He begins to waken. He rolls on his back and *lies* motionless with his front legs pointed toward the sky but folded like wilted flowers, his back legs splayed, and his nose and tail curved toward each other on one side of his body.

Techniques with Usage of *Lie*

Try to use correct principal parts of the verb *lie* when you write and revise your own work.

1. Learn the difference between *lie* and *lay*. Remember that *lie* means "to recline" or "to be positioned." *Lie* never takes an object. *Lay*, on the other hand, takes a direct object. *Lay* means "to put" or "to place."

Incorrect use He rolls on his back and *lays* motionless . . .
Correct use He rolls on his back and *lies* motionless . . .

2. Learn the principal parts of the verb *lie: lie, lying, lay, lain.*

Incorrect use The wolf has stopped traveling, has *laid* down . . .
Correct use The wolf has stopped traveling, has *lain* down . . .

Practice Practice these techniques by revising the following passage, on a separate sheet of paper. Replace each set of parentheses with the correct form of *lie* or *lay*.

When I got home from school, I was exhausted. I (   ) down my backpack, which felt like a ton of bricks, and wanted nothing more than to (   ) down and lose some of my weariness. First, though, I had to (   ) out the ingredients my father would use to make his famous chicken stew. I trudged to the kitchen, where I found the cat (   ) in its own private patch of sunlight. It has probably (   ) there all day, I thought with resentment. I'd be (   ) there myself if I didn't have to go to school and to work and then home to do chores. "How long have you (   ) there, Hercules?" I demanded. A wheezy purr was its only response, so I picked up the hairy critter and (   ) it outside the kitchen door. Then I quickly (   ) out the food on the counter next to the stovetop before finally (   ) my own weary body to rest on my bed.

UNIT
20

Grammar

Capitalization

Lessons

20.1 Capitalization of Sentences

Capitalize the first word of every sentence, including the first word of a direct quotation that is a complete sentence.

One of the first computers was large enough to fill a two-car garage.

Henry Ford said, "**T**hinking is the hardest work there is, which is the probable reason why so few engage in it."

Unless it begins a sentence, do not capitalize the first word of a quotation that cannot stand as a complete sentence.

Although astronauts must learn how to use computers, experts say most astronauts are "**c**omputer users, not computer wizards."

Do not capitalize an indirect quotation. An **indirect quotation** gives the meaning of an original statement without repeating it word for word. It is often introduced by the word *that*.

This letter from a computer camp states that **s**wimming, hiking, and archery will be offered this summer.

Capitals form the top of Greek columns.

Exercise 1   **Capitalizing Quotations**

Rewrite any incorrect sentences that follow, correcting any errors in capitalization. If a sentence is correct, write *correct*.

Franklin's Wisdom

1. Writer and publisher Benjamin Franklin observed, "nothing should be expressed in two words that can be as well expressed in one."
2. He advised writers to choose words that were "Smooth, clear, and short, for the contrary qualities are displeasing."
3. Franklin believed that writers should rarely, if ever, use synonyms or words that have almost the same meaning as other words.
4. He said, "words should be the most expressive that the language affords."
5. He recommended that words be so placed "As to be agreeable to the ear in reading."

Capitalize the first word of a sentence in parentheses that stands by itself. Do not capitalize a sentence within parentheses that is contained within another sentence.

Games can be tools for learning about computers. (**M**any programmers think that programming itself is the best game of all.)

They were looking for software (**t**hey hoped to buy no more than three or four programs) that they could use in writing reports.

Exercise 2 — Capitalizing Within Parentheses

Rewrite each item that is incorrect, correcting the capitalization. If an item is correct, write *correct*.

1. He went in through the back door. (he hoped no one would notice him.)
2. He expected to be nervous facing a huge crowd (ironically, no one was even in the room).
3. When he heard the noise (Someone was sneaking up behind him), he turned quickly.
4. Eventually the audience filled with young adults (no children were allowed).
5. His speech was very well received. (his wife always knew that it would be.)

Exercise 3 — Capitalizing Sentences

Rewrite correctly any of the following sentences that have errors in capitalization. Write *correct* if a sentence has no errors.

Words to Ponder

1. the great Indian leader Mohandas Gandhi said, "civilization is the encouragement of differences."
2. The Chinese American novelist Maxine Hong Kingston remarked, "you can be a writer at any time. you don't have to worry about talent."
3. Eleanor Roosevelt wrote, "No one can make you feel inferior without your consent."
4. the civil rights leader Dr. Martin Luther King Jr. wrote that nonviolence is a powerful weapon. (he described nonviolence as a "sword that heals.")
5. The Russian-born sculptor Louise Nevelson said, "I never liked the middle ground—the most boring place in the world."
6. the Spanish philosopher and statesman José Ortega y Gasset wrote, "living is a constant process of deciding what we are going to do."
7. The Native American poet Simon J. Ortiz answered the question "why do you write?" by saying, "Your children will not survive unless you tell them something about them."
8. Albert Einstein wrote that Imagination is more important than knowledge.
9. The American abolitionist Frederick Douglass wrote, "if there is no struggle, there is no progress."
10. Margaret Mead (She was an anthropologist) wrote, "today's children are the first generation to grow up in a world that has the power to destroy itself."

20.2 Capitalization of Proper Nouns

Capitalize a proper noun.

Proper nouns name particular persons, places, things, or ideas. In proper nouns composed of several words, capitalize only the important words. Do not capitalize articles, coordinating conjunctions, and prepositions of fewer than five letters.

1. Names of individuals

Seiji **O**zawa	**S**equoya
Sally **R**ide	**S**teffi **G**raf
Mark **T**wain	**J**esse **J**ackson
Charles de **G**aulle	**C**atherine the **G**reat

2. Titles of individuals

Capitalize titles used before a proper name and titles used in direct address.

Dr. Henry Ramirez	**C**hief Sitting Bull
Princess Caroline	**P**rime **M**inister John Major
General Robert E. Lee	**S**ecretary of **S**tate Jefferson
Mother **T**eresa	**M**s. **J**ones
Pope John Paul II	**S**enator Dole
Congresswoman Schroeder	Aye, aye, **C**aptain. [direct address]

In general, do not capitalize titles that follow a proper name or are used alone. Most writers, however, capitalize *president* when referring to the current president of the United States.

Lawton Chiles, the **g**overnor of Florida, met with the **P**resident last evening at the White House.

In general, capitalize a title that describes a family relationship when it is used with or in place of a proper name.

Have you met **A**unt Flora?	*but*	Have you met my **a**unt?
Please ask **G**randfather.		Please ask your **g**randfather.
What did you say, **M**other?		What did my **m**other say?
After a moment **M**other spoke.		After a moment my **m**other spoke.

3. **Names of ethnic groups, national groups, and languages**

Native **A**mericans	**I**talian
Laotians	**S**wahili
Mexicans	**J**apanese
Scots	**L**atin

4. **Names of organizations, institutions, political parties and their members, and firms**

Food and **D**rug **A**dministration
Girl **S**couts of **A**merica
Utah **S**tate **U**niversity
the **C**ongress
the **D**emocratic party
a **R**epublican
Bank of **A**merica
General **E**lectric

The word *party* is not capitalized. Do not capitalize common nouns such as *court* or *university* unless they are part of a proper noun.

She was appointed judge of the **F**irst **D**istrict **C**ourt.
Mr. Tavares was a witness in **t**raffic **c**ourt.
He became interested in science at the **u**niversity.

Exercise 4   **Capitalizing Names and Titles**

Rewrite the following items if they are incorrect, adding capital letters as necessary. If an item is correct, write *correct*.

1. george allen, the governor of Virginia
2. senator barbara boxer
3. aunt luisa and her mother
4. the progressive party
5. mount vernon college
6. our secretary of the interior
7. attorney general janet reno
8. securities and exchange commission
9. Sign here, general.
10. small claims court
11. chrysler corporation
12. chief justice john marshall
13. scotch-irish
14. hernando de soto
15. bishop john walker
16. What did you mean, grandfather?
17. 4-h club
18. Please respond, mr. secretary.
19. arabic
20. vietnamese americans
21. commodore matthew c. perry
22. mothers against drunk driving
23. We saw your uncle last night.
24. speaker of the house gingrich
25. the university

5. Names of monuments, buildings, bridges, and other structures

the **E**iffel **T**ower
Vietnam **V**eterans **M**emorial
World **T**rade **C**enter
Golden **G**ate **B**ridge
the **P**arthenon
Sears **T**ower
Lincoln **T**unnel
Hoover **D**am
Shea **S**tadium
the **W**hite **H**ouse

The World Trade Center

is a center of commerce.

6. Trade names

Chevrolet   **C**heerios
Kleenex   **F**riskies cat food
Xerox   **L**ifesavers

7. Names of documents, awards, and laws

the **C**onstitution   **P**ulitzer **P**rize
Fifth **A**mendment   a **G**rammy
Emancipation **P**roclamation   **B**ill of **R**ights
Treaty of **P**aris   **E**nvironmental **P**rotection **A**ct

Do not capitalize short prepositions that appear as part of the name.

8. Geographical terms

Capitalize the names of continents, countries, states, counties, and cities, as well as the names of specific bodies of water, topographical features, regions, and streets.

Asia   **L**ake **H**uron
Africa   **B**iscayne **B**ay
Mexico   **G**rand **C**anyon
Virginia   **B**lue **R**idge **M**ountains
Oregon   **C**ape **C**od
Dade **C**ounty   the **S**ahara
Dallas   **M**iddle **E**ast
Atlantic **O**cean   **S**outhern **H**emisphere
Mississippi **R**iver   **M**ain **S**treet
Great **P**lains   **P**rince **E**dward **I**sland

9. **Names of planets and other heavenly bodies**

Pluto	the constellation **S**corpio
Mars	**N**orth **S**tar
the **B**ig **D**ipper	the **M**ilky **W**ay

Do not capitalize the words *sun* and *moon*. *Earth* is capitalized only when it is used in conjunction with the names of the other planets. It is never capitalized when used with the definite article *the*.

Venus and **M**ars are **E**arth's closest planetary neighbors.
The astronauts took many photographs of the **e**arth.

10. **Compass points**

Capitalize the words *north*, *east*, *south*, and *west* when they refer to a specific area of the country or the world or when they are part of a proper name. Do not capitalize them when they merely indicate direction.

the **N**orth	*but*	**n**orth of 42nd Street
the **W**est **C**oast		the **w**est **c**oast of Africa
South **P**acific		**s**outh of Bangor
East Lansing		**e**ast of the school

11. **Names of ships, planes, trains, and spacecraft**

U.S.S. *Constitution*	*Spirit of St. Louis*
Challenger	*Yankee Clipper*

12. **Names of most historical events, eras, and calendar items**

Reconstruction	**W**ashington's **B**irthday
Middle **A**ges	**L**abor **D**ay
Ming **D**ynasty	**W**orld **W**ar **II**
the **C**rusades	**B**attle of **H**astings

Do not capitalize a historical period when it refers to a general span of time.

the **t**wenties
the **t**enth **c**entury

Capitalize the days of the week and the months of the year, but do not capitalize the names of the seasons (*spring, summer, autumn, fall, winter*).

We met on a **M**onday in **M**arch; it was the first day of **s**pring.

13. Religious terms

Capitalize names of deities, religions and their denominations and adherents, words referring to a supreme deity, and religious books and events.

God	**M**uslims
Allah	**Q**uran
Christianity	**N**ew **T**estament
Russian **O**rthodox	the **A**lmighty
Protestants	**H**anukkah
Jews	the **S**econd **C**oming
Buddhism	**F**our **N**oble **T**ruths

14. Names of school courses

Capitalize only those school courses that are the name of a language or the title of a specific course. Do not capitalize the name of a subject.

Advanced **A**lgebra *but*	**a**lgebra
Spanish	**g**eography
Music 101	**m**usic
World **C**ultures II	**w**orld **h**istory

15. Titles of works

the ***O**dyssey*	[epic poem]
"**T**he **G**ift of the **M**agi"	[story]
the *Los Angeles Times*	[newspaper]
"**H**ome on the **R**ange"	[song]
Information Please Almanac	[reference book]

Do not capitalize articles, coordinating conjunctions, or prepositions of fewer than five letters unless they appear as the first word of the title itself.

Capitalize articles (*a*, *an*, and *the*) at the beginning of a title only when they are part of the title itself. It is common practice not to capitalize (or italicize) articles preceding the title of a newspaper or a periodical. Do not capitalize (or italicize) the word *magazine* unless it is part of the title of a periodical.

"**T**he Fifty-first Dragon"	**t**he *Christian Science Monitor*
"**A** Marriage Proposal"	**a** *Newsweek* **m**agazine

Capitalizing Proper Nouns

Write the following items, adding capital letters where necessary.

SAMPLE jefferson memorial
ANSWER Jefferson Memorial

   1. antioch college
   2. jacqueline bouvier kennedy
   3. library of congress
   4. the *wall street journal* and *time* magazine
   5. portuguese, spanish, and latin
   6. the capitol
   7. aunt lydia and uncle ted
   8. the speaker of the house, newt gingrich
   9. the magna carta
  10. national urban league
  11. amy tan's *the kitchen god's wife*
  12. the oscars
  13. sunday, march 5
  14. the eastern hemisphere
  15. hispanics
  16. pikes peak
  17. aunt vanessa
  18. venus, pluto, mars, and earth
  19. my favorite classes are calculus II and my history class
  20. *the world book encyclopedia*
  21. "the legend of sleepy hollow"
  22. ivory soap
  23. fourth of july
  24. the uss *maine*
  25. fifth avenue in new york city

Exercise 6 **Identifying Reasons for Capitalization**

On your paper explain why you capitalized or did not capitalize each of the items in Exercise 5.

SAMPLE Jefferson Memorial
ANSWER name of a monument

For each sentence below, find the words with capitalization errors and write them correctly.

Early Settlers in America

1. Early in the Seventeenth Century, king james I of England gave a trading company the right to send settlers to live in north america.
2. The settlers, among them captain John Smith, set sail in the Company's ships, the *godspeed*, the *discovery*, and the *susan constant*.
3. After crossing the atlantic ocean, the Settlers founded jamestown, Virginia, the first permanent British settlement in north america.
4. In 1619 a ship owned by holland brought the first africans to the colonies in america.
5. The pilgrims, a group of English puritans, landed a good distance North of Virginia, in present-day massachusetts, in december of 1620.
6. Squanto, a native american, helped the pilgrims survive their first harsh Winter in the Settlement named plymouth.
7. Wall street in New York city is named after a wall built in 1653 by colonists from holland who feared an attack by the British.
8. In 1681 william penn, the english quaker leader, together with a group of quakers, founded the City of Philadelphia on the Delaware river.
9. In philadelphia members of all religious groups were allowed to worship god and interpret the bible in their own way.
10. In 1704 the first issue of a successful colonial newspaper, the *boston newsletter*, was printed.
11. Samuel de Champlain, who built the first french settlement in north America at quebec, established friendly ties with the powerful algonquian nation.
12. Among the hundreds of french explorers who explored the area around the great lakes was father marquette, a Priest.
13. La salle claimed the entire valley of the mississippi River for France and named the area louisiana in honor of king Louis XIV.
14. The southern section of the carolinas, South Carolina, attracted scots, germans, and emigrants from the west Indies.
15. In the winter of 1634, some 200 settlers, many of them catholics, sailed into the chesapeake bay and established the colony of maryland.
16. In 1649 lord baltimore secured the passage of the toleration act, guaranteeing freedom of worship for all Christians.
17. In 1636 the first colonial college, harvard, was founded in massachusetts.
18. Two of the early Presidents of the college were the reverend increase mather and his son cotton.
19. Among the required subjects were greek, latin, and theology.
20. In the north, schoolchildren were taught not only to read but also to write about god from the *new england primer*.

20.3   Capitalization of Proper Adjectives

Capitalize proper adjectives (adjectives formed from proper nouns).

Most proper adjectives fit into the following categories:

1. **Adjectives formed from names of people**

Napoleonic era	**J**acksonian ideals
Victorian customs	**M**arxist revolutionary
Georgian architecture	**D**ickensian character

2. **Adjectives formed from place names and names of national, ethnic, and religious groups**

Chinese acupuncture	**H**ispanic studies
Saharan winds	**I**sraeli dances
Midwestern accent	**N**orwegian accent
European languages	**B**uddhist temple

   Many proper nouns do not undergo a change in form when they are used as adjectives.

United **N**ations calendar	**T**hanksgiving dinner
New **O**rleans cooking	**P**assover meal
Beethoven sonata	**M**onday night
Kodak camera	**R**epublican victory

Exercise 8   Using Proper Adjectives

Form a proper adjective from each of the proper nouns listed below.

SAMPLE   Queen Elizabeth I
ANSWER   Elizabethan

1. Thomas Jefferson
2. Guatemala
3. Pablo Picasso
4. South America
5. Alaska
6. Japan
7. Islam
8. Greece
9. Easter
10. Navajo
11. William Shakespeare
12. Australia
13. Michigan
14. Paris
15. Hanukkah
16. Middle East
17. Malaysia
18. Joseph Stalin
19. African American
20. Pacific Ocean

For each sentence below, find the words with capitalization errors and write them correctly.

The Triumph of Kathleen Battle

1. Kathleen Battle, a talented contemporary american Opera singer, is celebrated for the purity of her voice.
2. Born in the City of Cleveland, Ohio, she studied at the College Conservatory of music at the university of Cincinnati.
3. In addition to being one of the favorite Sopranos at the Metropolitan Opera House in New York city, she has won ovations in many european Opera Houses.
4. Battle is best known for her roles in mozart operas, including *the magic flute.*
5. She has worked closely in many Concerts and on many Musical Recordings with James Levine, a well-known Conductor.
6. In 1988 Battle sang in New York's central park with the italian star luciano Pavarotti.
7. Later that year she traveled to the far east and sang in Tokyo with the spanish opera star Placido Domingo.
8. One of her greatest triumphs was her role in *antony and cleopatra,* an opera based on a shakespearean play.
9. The Opera recounts the story of Mark Antony, a Roman Consul, who is bewitched by the charms of queen Cleopatra of Egypt.
10. Although they often appeared in broadway musicals, few african American singers won major roles in opera.
11. In recent years, however, Kathleen Battle, Leontyne price, and Jessye norman have reversed that trend.
12. Battle is scheduled to perform at the tallest opera house, a 42-story building on wacker drive in Chicago, illinois.
13. She may sing excerpts from italian operas written during the Nineteenth Century.
14. It is unlikely that she will sing one of the long Arias from a wagnerian opera.
15. My Aunt Julia is taking her Mother to the concert as a mother's day present.
16. It is believed that the first opera was *dafne,* written by jacopo Peri and introduced in florence, italy, in 1597.
17. This Winter, Battle's outstanding recording of spirituals was nominated for a grammy.
18. Battle may one day follow in the steps of the Contralto marian anderson and sing at the Lincoln memorial.
19. Do you think the daughters of the american revolution will invite her to perform at constitution hall in Washington, d.c.?
20. I would like Battle to be invited to sing when the democratic party meets to nominate its next Candidate for President.

The chart below reviews which words should be capitalized.

Summary of Capitalization Rules	
Capitalize	**Do Not Capitalize**
She gave us thirty pages of reading for homework. (**S**he said we needed to do it.)	For homework (**s**he said we needed to catch up) she gave us thirty pages of reading.
He said, "**L**et me drive."	He said that **h**e would drive.
Then **F**ather smiled at me.	My **f**ather wants to retire.
Captain **A**hab	The **c**aptain paced the deck.
Texas **S**tate **U**niversity	a **u**niversity in Texas
Lawrence **H**all of **S**cience	the **s**cience **m**useum in town
Prell shampoo; **I**vory soap	Bring **s**oap and **s**hampoo.
Bill of **R**ights	an animal **b**ill of **r**ights
Pacific **O**cean; **G**hirardelli **S**quare; **S**anta **C**lara **A**venue	the **s**quare where the two **a**venues meet near the **o**cean
Neptune; **M**ercury; **E**arth	**s**un; **p**lanets; the **e**arth
the **K**orean **W**ar	the **w**ar in the former Yugoslavia
the **B**ible; **H**alloween	**s**acred **b**ook; **h**olidays
Russian; **E**nglish **L**iterature I	**f**oreign **l**anguage; **l**iterature
Third **D**istrict **C**ourt	**s**mall **c**laims court
the **F**ar **E**ast	the **f**ar **e**astern tip of **K**orea
the **I**ce **A**ge	the **t**wentieth **c**entury
"**T**he **F**all of the **H**ouse of **U**sher"	the **s**tory
the *Dayton Daily News*	the **b**ook, **n**ewspaper, or **m**agazine
Tuesday; **J**uly	**s**pring; **f**all

Exercise 10   Using Correct Capitalization in a Dialogue

Write several sentences of dialogue between you and a friend about a country you would like to visit and the sights you would like to see. Use a variety of proper nouns and proper adjectives. Capitalize all sentences, quotations, proper nouns, and proper adjectives correctly.

Write the letter of the one item that is correctly capitalized in each of the following pairs.

 1. **a.** James Baldwin wrote, "one cannot deny the humanity of another without diminishing one's own."
    b. James Baldwin wrote, "One cannot deny the humanity of another without diminishing one's own."
 2. **a.** university of California
    b. University of California
 3. **a.** General George Patton
    b. general George Patton
 4. **a.** The English stage actress Rachel Kempson is the mother of Vanessa and Lynn Redgrave.
    b. The English stage actress Rachel Kempson is the Mother of Vanessa and Lynn Redgrave.
 5. **a.** Georgia O'Keeffe's painting *New York night* is done mostly in dark colors.
    b. Georgia O'Keeffe's painting *New York Night* is done mostly in dark colors.
 6. **a.** *A Raisin In The Sun*
    b. *A Raisin in the Sun*
 7. **a.** European History I and physics
    b. European History I and Physics
 8. **a.** a Buddhist temple on Homan Avenue
    b. a buddhist temple on Homan avenue
 9. **a.** I wished that summer would not fade so quickly.
    b. I wished that Summer would not fade so quickly.
10. **a.** West of the Colorado River
    b. west of the Colorado River

Georgia O'Keeffe's
New York Night

New York at night

Grammar Review

Capitalization

Immortalized in Garrison Keillor's radio show *A Prairie Home Companion* is the fictional town of Lake Wobegon. Keillor's book *Lake Wobegon Days* grew out of the radio show. This passage from the book has been annotated to show some of the rules of capitalization covered in this unit.

Literature Model

from LAKE WOBEGON DAYS

by Garrison Keillor

Place names

Compass point,
not capitalized

Proper adjective

First word of a
sentence

Name of a firm

Title not capitalized
because not followed
directly by an individual's name

Trade name

First word of a full sentence in quotation
marks

The town of Lake Wobegon, Minnesota, lies on the
shore against Adams Hill, looking east across the blue-
green water to the dark woods. From the south, the highway aims for the lake, bends hard left by the magnificent
concrete Grecian grain silos, and eases over a leg of the hill
past the SLOW CHILDREN sign, bringing the traveler in on
Main Street toward the town's one traffic light, which is
almost always green. A few surviving elms shade the street.
Along the ragged dirt path between the asphalt and the
grass, a child slowly walks to Ralph's Grocery, kicking an
asphalt chunk ahead of him. It is a chunk that after four
blocks he is now mesmerized by, to which he is completely
dedicated. At Bunsen Motors, the sidewalk begins. . . . The
boy kicks the chunk at the curb, once, twice, then lofts it
over the curb and sidewalk across the concrete to the island
of Pure Oil pumps. He jumps three times on the Bunsen
bell hose, making three dings back in the dark garage. The
mayor of Lake Wobegon, Clint Bunsen, peers out from the
grease pit, under a black Ford pickup.

Incorporated under the laws of Minnesota but omitted
from the map due to the incompetence of surveyors, first
named "New Albion" by New Englanders who thought
it would become the Boston of the west, taking its ultimate
name from an Indian phrase that means either "Here we
are!" or "We sat all day in the rain waiting for [you]," Lake

Wobegon is the seat of tiny Mist County, the "phantom county in the heart of the heartland" (Dibbley, *My Minnesota*), founded by Unitarian missionaries and Yankee promoters, then found by Norwegian Lutherans who straggled in from the west, having headed first to Lake Agassiz in what is now North Dakota, a lake that turned out to be prehistoric, and by German Catholics, who, bound for Clay County, had stopped a little short, having misread their map, but refused to admit it.

A town with few scenic wonders such as towering pines or high mountains but with some fine people of whom some are over six feet tall, its highest point is the gold ball on the flagpole atop the Norge Co-op grain elevator south of town on the Great Northern spur, from which Mr. Tollefson can see all of Mist County when he climbs up to raise the flag on national holidays, including Norwegian Independence Day, when the blue cross of Norway is flown. (No flag of Germany has appeared in public since 1917.) Next highest is the water tower, then the boulder on the hill, followed by the cross on the spire of Our Lady, then the spire of Lake Wobegon Lutheran (Christian Synod), the Central Building (three stories), the high school flagpole, . . . etc.

- Book title
- Name of a religious group
- General time period, not capitalized
- Name of a holiday
- First word of a sentence in parentheses that stands by itself
- Name of a building

Exercise 1

Capitalizing Sentences   For each sentence below, find the words with capitalization errors and write them correctly. If a sentence has no errors, write *correct*.

1. the imaginary town of Lake Wobegon has been called "The little town that time forgot and decades cannot improve."
2. Keillor claims the town is not on any map because of surveying errors. (it is supposedly in central Minnesota.)
3. Keillor states that One early explorer thought Lake Wobegon was the headwaters of the Mississippi River.
4. A statue of an unknown Norwegian (the town was settled largely by Scandinavians) is a major landmark.
5. There is also a stone carved with Viking runes. (runes are old alphabetical symbols.)
6. A settler from Boston said that no civilized society could find comfort in the town.
7. later she said, "Providence has led us here."
8. The young woman (She had come west as a missionary) married a French trapper.
9. In his broadcasts, Keillor said, "that's the news from Lake Wobegon, where all the women are strong, all the men are good-looking, and all the children above average."
10. he also described the residents of Lake Wobegon as "Skeptical of progress."

Exercise 2

Capitalizing Proper Adjectives and Proper Nouns For each of the following sentences, find the words that contain errors in capitalization and write them correctly. If a sentence has no errors, write *correct*.

1. Though lake wobegon characters seem ordinary, many famous americans, both real and imaginary, have minnesota roots.
2. Sinclair Lewis, a nobel prize winner, set his novel *babbitt* in a town that resembled his birthplace, sauk Centre.
3. Charles Lindbergh, a minnesota native of swedish descent, made the first solo flight across the atlantic ocean.
4. The Mayo Clinic founders, Drs. Charles and William Mayo, established their famous hospital in Minnesota.
5. The Minnesota-born actress and singer Judy Garland won worldwide popularity as Dorothy in *The Wizard of Oz*.
6. Ole Rölvaag, a Minnesotan of scandinavian ancestry, wrote novels about pioneers in the dakotas.
7. Eugene McCarthy, who was a united states senator from Minnesota, sought the democratic party's nomination for President in 1968.
8. John S. Pillsbury, a founder of pillsbury, a food-products company, served as a republican Governor of Minnesota for three terms.
9. The minnesota-born author F. Scott Fitzgerald depicted the decaying morality of society in the years following world war I.
10. The paul bunyan and hiawatha legends, both based on fictional heroes, are set in the minnesota frontier.

Proofreading

Exercise 3

The following passage describes the artist Grant Wood, whose painting appears on the opposite page. Rewrite the passage, correcting the errors in spelling, capitalization, grammar, and usage. Add any missing punctuation. There are twenty-five errors.

Grant Wood

[1]Grant Wood (1892–1941) was born on a farm outside the small town of anamosa, Iowa. [2]He studied at the Handicraft Guild in Minneapolis and at the Art institute of Chicago. [3]Before he began military service in 1918, he worked as a schoolteacher, an interior decorator and a metalworker. [4]After World war I ended, he returned to Iowa to teach Art.

[5]Wood made several trips to Europe over the next decade, and he studied at a parisian art school. [6]His European travels reflected his discontent with american art, and his early works recall those of the french painters of the late nineteenth century. [7]Wood later had a change of hart and began to concentrate on American subjects. [8]Eventually, he, along with thomas Hart Benton, was ranked as one of America's great regional painters. ➡

Grant Wood, *Stone City, Iowa,* **1930**

[9]Wood is best known for his portrayals of the land and the people of the midwest. [10]His pictures are finely detailed his landscapes are reduced to round shapes, and his people are witty caricatures. [11]His technique was influenced by the lush and detailed paintings of the flemish masters. [12]He was also influenced strangely enough, by the stylized pattern on his Mother's dishes. [13]His best-known work, *American gothic,* is typical of his mature style. [14]The painting, which was completed in the 1930s, show a man holding a pitchfork and standing with his wife in front of a farmhouse.

[15]Wood, who painted very slowly produced relatively few major works during his lifetime. [16]In *Stone City, Iowa,* the painting on this page, neither his skill as an Artist nor his reverence for the rural countryside are missing. [17]Woods gently ironic realism is like that of Garrison Keillor. [18]Each poke fun at the obsesive orderliness—both physical and moral— of the people who live in the small towns of the Midwest. [19]Do so with respect and tenderness.

Mixed Review

| Exercise 4 |

For each of the following sentences, find the words that contain errors in capitalization and write the words correctly. If a sentence has no errors, write *correct*.

Garrison Keillor

1. Garrison Keillor was born in 1942 in Anoka county, Minnesota, to parents of scottish descent.
2. After finishing High School, he entered the University of Minnesota. (he earned a degree in english in 1966.)
3. Keillor had written earlier for the *Anoka herald*, and he became Editor of the literary magazine at the University.
4. Hoping to work as a journalist, Keillor went East to New York after college, but he soon returned to minnesota.
5. in 1974 he sold a story about the Grand ole Opry to the *New Yorker* for $6,000 (More money than he had ever seen).
6. In the Spring of 1974, Keillor and his Wife and son traveled by train through the Northern rockies.
7. In idaho the Keillor family boarded an old bus heading for Washington. (the train they had been traveling on had derailed.)
8. From portland they took the southbound train, the *coast starlight*, to San Francisco.
9. On the trip Keillor started a story titled "the lake wobegon memoir," but it was stolen from his briefcase in the Train Station.
10. Years later in the Eighties, Keillor would write *Lake Wobegon Days*, a book that he insists Is not as fine as his lost story.
11. The book has been described as an unforgettable portrait of why we "are what we are" and why being smart "doesn't count for much."
12. In july 1974 Keillor began hosting *a Prairie Home Companion*, a radio show on Public Radio in Minnesota.
13. Keillor has said that one of his Great-Uncles, Uncle Lew (his Grandmother's brother), inspired some of the show's homespun characters.
14. The imaginary sponsors for the humorous show were Raw bits Cereal and a pet shop called Bertha's kitty boutique.
15. In the show Keillor talked about the unitarian missionaries who started the town and the arrival of the first settlers, norwegian lutherans and german catholics.
16. He described albion college and its crazed founder, the reverend watt.
17. Students at the college studied latin, poetry, penmanship, and moral psychology I.
18. On Groundhog Day the Sons of Knute sponsored an ice melt contest.
19. The radio show was a recipient of the peabody award.
20. At times Garrison Keillor has lived in Wisconsin and in new york city.

Writing Application

Capitalization in Writing In "Skeletons in the Attic," Clara Spotted Elk describes how Native Americans regained the skeletal remains of their ancestors. As you read the passage below, pay special attention to the use of capitalization.

> Millions of **A**merican **I**ndians lived in this country when **C**olumbus first landed on our shores. After the western expansion, only 250,000 Indians survived. **W**hat happened to the remains of these people who were decimated by the advance of the white man? Many are gathering dust in **A**merican museums.
>
> **I**n 1985, I and some **N**orthern **C**heyenne chiefs visited the attic of the **S**mithsonian's **N**atural **H**istory **M**useum in **W**ashington, **D.C.**, to review the inventory of their **C**heyenne collection. After a chance inquiry, a curator pulled out a drawer in one of the scores of cabinets that line the attic. There were the jumbled bones of an **I**ndian. "**A K**iowa," he said.

Techniques with Capitalization Like Clara Spotted Elk, you should apply the rules of capitalization when you write and revise your own work.

1. Capitalize proper nouns that name monuments, bridges, buildings, and other structures. Do not capitalize common nouns unless they are part of a proper noun.

   Proper noun the attic of the **S**mithsonian's **N**atural **H**istory **M**useum
   Common noun the attic of the **m**useum

2. Capitalize adjectives formed from proper nouns but not those formed from common nouns.

   Proper adjective **C**heyenne collection
   Common adjective **c**hance inquiry

Practice Practice the rules of capitalization by revising the following paragraph on a separate sheet of paper. (You will need to capitalize twenty-five additional words.)

The explorer christopher columbus landed on what is now the island of san salvador in the late fifteenth century. Although he thought he had landed in india (because he thought so, he mistakenly called the people he found indians), he really landed in the bahamas, a chain of islands, cays, and reefs lying southeast of florida. At the time, the continent of north america was home for a wide array of independent cultural groups. since that time, archaeologists have discovered artifacts left by these pre-Columbian (that is, "before columbus") societies. Some of these artifacts are displayed in natural history museums such as the museum of natural history in new york city. Federal agencies such as the national park service in the department of the interior also house native american collections.

Punctuation, Abbreviations, and Numbers

Lessons

There are three punctuation marks used at the ends of sentences: the period, the exclamation point, and the question mark.

21.1 The Period

Use a period at the end of a declarative sentence and at the end of an imperative sentence—a polite command or request.

DECLARATIVE SENTENCE	Track practice is held twice a week.
IMPERATIVE SENTENCE	Please sign up for two track events.

Exercise 1   Identifying Use of the Period

Identify each of the following sentences that should end with a period by writing *declarative* or *imperative* on your paper. If a sentence is neither a declarative sentence nor a polite command, write *no period*.

The Swim Team

1. Our swim team will hold its first meeting next Tuesday
2. The first big swim meet will take place in one month
3. Please sign up in the gym
4. My specialty is the backstroke
5. Do you want to become a winner
6. We won three gold medals at the last swim meet
7. Be sure to wear your goggles
8. To remain on the team you must maintain good grades
9. We have a lot of fun during practice
10. After practice we often get together at the restaurant across the street
11. Have you heard us sitting there talking about swimming
12. If you learn something about the sport, our conversations will be livelier
13. The ancient Greeks trained their soldiers to swim so they could cross rivers
14. In medieval times swimming was unpopular because people feared the water might be unhealthful
15. In the nineteenth century the British discovered that Native Americans used a swimming method similar to the modern crawl
16. Development of the flutter kick inspired the Australian crawl, the most common stroke today
17. Tell me how swimming became part of the modern Olympic games
18. There are four basic categories of Olympic swimming events: freestyle, backstroke, breaststroke, and butterfly
19. Have you heard that some Olympic swimmers have become movie stars
20. John Weissmuller, who won five Olympic gold medals in the 1920s, played Tarzan in the movies in the 1940s

21.2 | The Exclamation Point

Use an exclamation point to show strong feeling and indicate a forceful command.

Oh, no!	Look out!
What lovely weather!	Wake up!
Hurrah!	Get going!

21.3 | The Question Mark

Use a question mark to indicate a direct question.

Who would like a part-time job?
Which call should I answer first?

Do not place a question mark after an indirect question (one that has been reworded so that it is part of a declarative sentence).

He asked whether I needed a work permit.
I wondered why such a document was needed.

Exercise 2   **Using End Punctuation**

On your paper rewrite the following sentences, adding periods, exclamation points, and question marks where necessary. You will add 20 marks in all.

First Aid

1. Don't you think that everyone should learn about first aid I think it's crucial
2. First aid is the immediate medical care given to an ill or injured person First aid can save lives
3. Oh, if only people realized the importance of first aid So many people could be helped
4. An instruction manual by John S. Kelly, published by the U.S. Bureau of Mines, has useful information about first aid Will you get it from the library
5. The primary goals of first aid are to treat serious injuries, prevent infection, and make the injured or ill person as comfortable as possible Other problems are less important
6. If you come upon an injured person, try to send for medical help right away Don't panic
7. Are you the person best qualified to take charge If two of you know first aid, the one with more experience and training should take charge, and the other one can assist
8. If people are crowding the injured person, make them stand at a distance Be firm
9. Once you have sent for help and the patient is lying still, ask yourself which injuries require immediate attention Which are less critical
10. Because of possible broken bones or internal injuries, move an injured person only if it is absolutely necessary How vital this is

Colons to Introduce

1. Lists

Use a colon to introduce a list, especially after a statement that uses such words as *these, the following,* or *as follows.*

> The science test on Friday will cover **these** areas: the circulatory system, the digestive system, and the nervous system.

> He requested the following: a hammer, a screwdriver, four nails, and a level.

Do not use a colon to introduce a list if the list immediately follows a verb or a preposition.

> The best nonanimal sources of protein **are** soybeans, wheat germ, brewer's yeast, nuts, seeds, and whole grains. [The list follows the verb *are.*]

> My sister likes to top her hamburger **with** lettuce, tomato, mustard, ketchup, and relish. [The list follows the preposition *with.*]

2. Illustrations or restatements

Use a colon to introduce material that illustrates, explains, or restates the preceding material.

> I often wish that my parents had had more than one child: they worry too much about me.

A complete sentence following a colon is generally not capitalized.

3. Quotations

Use a colon to introduce a long or formal quotation. A formal quotation is often preceded by such words as *this, these, the following,* or *as follows.*

> Mrs. Hopkins asked us to write an essay on **the following** African saying: "It is the rainy season that gives wealth."

Poetry quotations of more than one line and prose quotations of more than four or five lines are generally written below the introductory statement and indented on the page.

> In his long poem *The Other Pioneers,* Roberto Félix Salazar describes some of this nation's early settlers:
>
> > Now I must write
> > Of those of mine who rode these plains
> > Long years before the Saxon and the Irish came.

Other Uses of Colons

Use a colon between the hour and the minute of the precise time, between the chapter and the verse in biblical references, and after the salutation of a business letter.

| 12:30 A.M. | Genesis 7:20–24 | Sir: |
| 4:00 P.M. | Ruth 1:16–18 | Dear Ms. Snow: |

Exercise 3   **Using the Colon**

For the items below, write each word or number that should be followed by a colon. Then write the colon itself. For any sentence that does not need a colon, write *correct*.

SAMPLE   Any of these will work as substitutes ketchup, chili sauce, or salsa.
ANSWER   substitutes:

The Game of Chess

1. Many people enjoy playing these board games chess, checkers, and pachisi.
2. Chess may have spread from place to place in the following order India, Persia, and Spain.
3. There are several board games that resemble chess checkers, the Japanese game *go*, and Chinese checkers.
4. In chess each player has the following playing pieces one king, one queen, two bishops, two knights, two rooks, and eight pawns.
5. The qualities essential to a good chess player are a good memory, a quick mind, and foresight.
6. In some ways chess is like war it pits two "armies" against each other.
7. The *Encyclopaedia Britannica* notes that chess players use strategies of attack and defense aimed at the surrender of the opponent's king. The encyclopedia continues as follows "Nevertheless, the game is only a rather limited simulation of war or, in Freudian terms, a sublimation of that aggressive impulse."
8. The Old Testament has the following to say about war

   They shall beat their swords into plowshares
   and their spears into pruning-hooks;
   nation shall not lift up sword against nation,
   neither shall they learn war anymore.
   —Isaiah 2 4

9. A regional chess tournament typically takes place on a three-day weekend, with two rounds each day at the following times round 1 occurs from 1100 A.M. to 100 P.M. and round 2 from 500 P.M. to 730 P.M.
10. In addition to the type of chess that most people play, other types include blindfold chess, lightning chess, postal chess, and computer chess.

21.5 | The Semicolon

Semicolons to Separate Main Clauses

Use a semicolon to separate main clauses that are not joined by a coordinating conjunction (*and, but, or, nor, yet,* and *for*).

> Paul Robeson was an excellent singer and actor; he was also a talented football player.
>
> Paul Robeson was an excellent singer and actor, **and** he was also a talented football player.

Use a semicolon to separate main clauses joined by a conjunctive adverb (such as *however, therefore, nevertheless, moreover, furthermore,* and *subsequently*) or by an expression such as *for example* or *that is.*

In general, a conjunctive adverb or an expression such as *for example* is followed by a comma.

> Robeson appeared in many plays and musicals; for example, he starred in *Othello* and *Porgy and Bess.*
>
> Robeson appeared in *Show Boat* in 1926; subsequently, he acted in the films *Jericho* and *Song of Freedom.*

Exercise 4 **Using Semicolons and Commas in Clauses**

On your paper rewrite the following sentences, adding semicolons and commas where necessary.

Ancient Bridges

1. An early type of bridge was a tree trunk thrown across a stream another type was a primitive suspension span of twisted bamboo.
2. In 500 B.C. the Persian king Xerxes created a "bridge" of boats over the Bosporus Strait his purpose was to rapidly deploy ground troops into ancient Greece.
3. The finest ancient bridges were built by the Romans nearly 2,000 years ago for example the semicircular arch bridge over the Tagus River in Spain is still standing.
4. In the Middle Ages Europeans began to build bridges with pointed arches however these features had been invented by Persian and Muslim engineers many years earlier.
5. In 1973 the Bosporus Bridge created the first road link between Europe and Asia since King Xerxes's bridge of boats more recently, a second bridge was built across that same waterway.

Semicolons and Commas

Use a semicolon to separate the items in a series when the items contain commas.

> Some of the powerful African kingdoms that flourished before the sixteenth century were Kush, which dominated the eastern Sudan; Karanga, which was located around Zimbabwe in southern Africa; Ghana, Mali, and Songhai, which successively controlled the Niger River in West Africa; and Benin, which had its center in what is now Nigeria.

Use a semicolon to separate two main clauses joined by a coordinating conjunction when the clauses already contain several commas.

> The rule of Mansa Musa, the Moslem emperor of the African kingdom of Mali from 1312 to 1337, is remembered for military success, trade expansion, and Moslem scholarship; but this period is probably most noteworthy as a golden age of peace and prosperity.

Exercise 5   Using Semicolons with Items Containing Commas

For the following sentences, write each word that should be followed by a semicolon and add the semicolon.

Ancient Kush

1. The heroes of the ancient kingdom of Kush were King Kashta, Prince Piankhi, and Piankhi's brother, Shabako, and they and their Kushite successors ruled Egypt for almost 100 years.
2. The Kushites, like the ancient Egyptians they conquered, worshipped Ra, the god of sky and sun, Isis, the great mother goddess, Osiris, the god of the underworld, and Horus, the son of Isis and Osiris.
3. In early times Kush was famous for its ebony, ivory, gold, silver, incense, wood, and precious gems, but later its most precious resource became iron.
4. The gifts of the Nile River included rich soil for farming, water for irrigation, and a route for trading, and Kush was one of many societies that benefited from these gifts.
5. On its way to the Mediterranean Sea the Nile River passes Khartoum, Sudan, Merowe, Sudan, Aswan, Egypt, Luxor, Egypt, and Cairo, Egypt.

For the sentences below, write each word that should be followed by a semicolon. Then write the semicolon itself.

Louise Nevelson, Sculptor

1. The sculptor Louise Nevelson lived in a number of places in Europe and the United States, including Kiev, Ukraine, Rockland, Maine, Munich, Germany, and New York City.
2. At the age of 5, Nevelson moved to Rockland with her family she lived there for 15 years.
3. Nevelson's family name was Berliawsky at the age of 20 she married Charles Nevelson and moved to New York.
4. Nevelson studied art under Hans Hofmann, the abstract painter who used primary colors in explosive contrasts she also studied with the muralist Diego Rivera.
5. Many artists are not willing to struggle however, Louise Nevelson worked for years without money or fame.
6. Nevelson's first one-woman sculpture show was in 1940 after that she became world renowned.
7. Nevelson made sculptures with found objects her artworks were large and intricate.
8. Nevelson used many materials in her sculptures nevertheless, her wooden assemblages in black and white are the best known.
9. A pioneer in environmental art, Nevelson created walls of framed sculptures her large-scale works sometimes take up an entire room.
10. Nevelson's art was influenced by multimedia sculpture as well as Cubism and Surrealism in addition, the art of Africa and pre-Columbian America affected her work.
11. Her life spanned most of the twentieth century she was born in 1900 and died in 1988.
12. She collected old parts of furniture subsequently, she used such objects in her famous black-box sculptures.
13. The black boxes are arranged like shelves along a wall however, their effect is almost musical, with changes in tone and rhythm.
14. Nevelson's decorated walls reached the height of their development in the 1950s nevertheless, she continued to explore new artistic avenues.
15. In some of her later works, she employed aluminum, steel, and Plexiglas she became interested in working with these materials as time passed.
16. From an early emphasis on somber blacks and whites, she turned to brighter materials for example, she gave a white and gold finish to the sculpture known as Transparent Sculpture VI.
17. At first the untrained eye may find Nevelson's art difficult to understand however, close attention increases the viewer's appreciation for her imagination.
18. Nevelson's works can be seen in the Whitney Museum in New York City she also created an all-white chapel in Saint Peter's Lutheran Church in New York City.
19. There are several books that describe Nevelson's life and art one is a biography by John Gordon.
20. Other noted twentieth-century sculptors include Henry Moore, Alberto Giacometti, Alexander Calder, and Claes Oldenburg their styles are all fairly distinct from each other.

21.6 The Comma

As you study the rules for comma usage, keep in mind that to *separate* elements means to place a comma between two equal elements. To *set off* an element means to put commas before and after it.

Commas and Compound Sentences

Use commas between the main clauses in a compound sentence.

Place a comma before a coordinating conjunction (*and, but, or, nor, yet,* or *for*) that joins two main clauses.

I am not going to the concert, for I am too busy.

Many of the prospectors searched for years, but others struck gold immediately.

You may omit the comma between very short main clauses that are connected by a coordinating conjunction unless the comma is needed to avoid confusion.

Mara washed the dishes and Jim dried them. [clear]

We visited Miami and the Everglades are next. [confusing]

We visited Miami, and the Everglades are next. [clear]

Exercise 7   **Using Commas in Compound Sentences**

For each sentence below, write the word that should be followed by a comma. Then write the comma itself.

The Everglades

1. We wanted to visit the Everglades National Park and we tried to learn as much as possible about the area before taking our trip.
2. These large marshlands are located in southern Florida but they once extended all the way to the Gulf of Mexico.
3. The northern part of the Everglades has been drained to provide more dry land and this area is now used for farming.
4. A hundred years of dredging, draining, and land clearing have taken their toll yet the Everglades have managed to survive.
5. We must work diligently to protect the Everglades or we will lose a unique ecological system.

Commas in a Series

Use commas to separate three or more words, phrases, or clauses in a series.

> A chair, a table, and a sofa were the room's only furnishings.
>
> The cat ran out of the house, across the lawn, and down the street.
>
> I rounded third, headed for home, and slid in safely.
>
> Read carefully, take good notes, and outline the chapter.

No commas are necessary when all of the items are connected by conjunctions.

> It was a sunny and hot and humid day in July.

Nouns that are used in pairs (*thunder and lightning, table and chairs, bread and butter*) are usually considered single units and should not be separated by commas. If such pairs appear with other nouns or groups of nouns in a series, they must be set off from the other items in the series.

> My favorite breakfast is bacon and eggs, toast, and milk.

Exercise 8   **Using Commas in Series**

For each sentence below, write the words that should be followed by commas. Then write the commas.

Our Scottish Terrier

1. We decided to get a Scottish Terrier to be our family's companion watchdog and friend.
2. Terriers were originally used to dig for small furry game engage their quarry underground and drive it out of the hole.
3. Today terriers are prized for their curiosity high spirits and friendliness.
4. Monty likes to take long walks ride in the car and eat all kinds of food.
5. We enrolled Monty in an obedience school where he learned to sit to stay and to heel.
6. The instructor told us that the secret to successful dog training is praise patience and persistence.
7. Sometimes Monty runs across the street sits in the neighbors' yard and watches their cat.
8. When he refuses to come, we try to entice him with a treat toy or ride in the car.
9. Monty's favorite toys are a squeaky soccer ball a rubber hamburger and a rope bone.
10. Everyone in our family agrees that Monty is a good friend valued family member and loving pet.

Commas and Coordinate Adjectives

Place a comma between coordinate adjectives that precede a noun.

Coordinate adjectives modify a noun equally. To determine whether adjectives are coordinate, try to reverse their order or put the word *and* between them. If the sentence still sounds natural, the adjectives are coordinate.

> Pepper is a good, obedient, gentle dog.

Do not use a comma between adjectives preceding a noun if they sound unnatural with their order reversed or with *and* between them. In general, adjectives that describe size, shape, age, and material do not need commas between them.

> Jelani grew up in a small white frame house.

Commas may be needed between some of the adjectives in a series but not between others.

> I like to read in our bright, cozy family room.

In the preceding sentence *and* would sound natural between *bright* and *cozy*, but it would not sound natural between *cozy* and *family*.

Exercise 9   **Using Commas in Sentences**

On your paper rewrite the following sentences, adding commas between coordinate adjectives, items in a series, and main clauses. If a sentence needs no comma, write *correct*.

Arthur Schomburg, Collector

1. Arthur Schomburg led a long active productive life.
2. He grew up in Puerto Rico studied in the Virgin Islands and came to the United States in 1891.
3. Schomburg was an author and historian but he is best known as a collector of literature about African American culture.
4. Schomburg was also an important figure in the literary artistic and musical movement known as the Harlem Renaissance.
5. His collection included over 10,000 books and manuscripts and pamphlets.
6. The Carnegie Corporation bought the collection donated it to the New York Public Library and named it in Schomburg's honor.
7. The Schomburg Collection has a wide reputation because it has more books on African American history and literature than any other library in North America.
8. The collection is housed in a tall modern brick building in the Harlem neighborhood.
9. Users of the collection study African American history literature art or music.
10. You may find that your own local library has a collection of books about African American culture or that a nearby historical society has some information about local African American families.

Commas and Nonessential Elements

1. Participles, infinitives, and their phrases

Use commas to set off participles, infinitives, and their phrases if they are not essential to the meaning of the sentence.

> She watched, puzzled, as the man in the yellow hat drove away.

> A customer, complaining loudly, stepped up to the counter.

> I have no idea, to be honest, what you would like for a graduation present.

Do not set off participles, infinitives, and their phrases if they are essential to the meaning of the sentence.

> The man standing by the door is my father. [The participial phrase tells *which* man.]

> My mother's car is the one parked in the driveway. [The participial phrase identifies the car.]

> She went to medical school to become a doctor. [The infinitive phrase tells *why*.]

> To become a doctor had been her goal for years. [The infinitive phrase is used as the subject of the sentence.]

> I wanted to go home. [The infinitive phrase is used as the direct object.]

2. Adjective clauses

Use commas to set off a nonessential adjective clause.

A nonessential (nonrestrictive) clause can be considered an extra clause because it gives additional information about a noun. Because an extra clause adds to the basic meaning of a sentence, it is set off by commas.

> Atlanta, which is the capital of Georgia, is the transportation center of the Southeast. [*Which is the capital of Georgia* is a nonessential clause.]

Do not set off an essential adjective clause. Because an essential (restrictive) clause gives necessary information about a noun, it is needed to convey the exact meaning of the sentence.

> People who are afraid of heights do not like to look down from balconies or terraces. [*Who are afraid of heights* is an essential clause.]

3. Appositives

Use commas to set off an appositive if it is not essential to the meaning of a sentence.

A nonessential (nonrestrictive) appositive can be considered an extra appositive; it calls for commas.

> Nelson Mandela, the president of South Africa, was freed from a South African prison in 1990.

> My mother lives in Escondido, a town near San Diego in southern California.

A nonessential (nonrestrictive) appositive is sometimes placed before the noun or pronoun to which it refers.

> An insurance executive, Charles Ives wrote music in his spare time. [The appositive, *An insurance executive*, precedes the subject of the sentence, *Charles Ives.*]

An essential (restrictive) appositive gives necessary information about a noun and is not set off.

> The word *fiesta* came into English from Spanish. [The appositive, *fiesta*, is needed to identify *word.*]

| Exercise 10 | Using Commas with Nonessential Elements |

On your paper rewrite the following sentences that need commas, adding commas as necessary. If a sentence needs no commas, write *correct*.

The Great Red Ape

1. Junior the oldest male orangutan in the National Zoo in Washington, D.C., is a favorite of visitors.
2. The orangutan whose formal name is Atjeh is a Great Red Ape.
3. He is a member of a species created by zookeepers who cross-bred two subspecies of orangutans.
4. Many scientists have lately been surprised to learn that Sumatran and Bornean orangutans are more genetically different from each other than lions are from tigers.
5. Being so different from each other they probably would not interbreed in nature.
6. The organization overseeing zoo programs in the United States has called a halt to the interbreeding of Sumatran and Bornean orangutans.
7. The hybrids that are now in zoos will not reproduce.
8. Critics of the policy disagreeing vocally claim that the hybrids are being treated as second-class apes.
9. These critics' argument that the existence of the Great Red Ape does not endanger the zoos' mission to emphasize conservation represents a controversial viewpoint.
10. A long-lived animal the orangutan can survive as long as sixty years.

Commas with Interjections, Parenthetical Expressions, Conjunctive Adverbs, and Antithetical Phrases

Use commas to set off interjections (such as *oh* and *well*), parenthetical expressions (such as *on the contrary, on the other hand, in fact, by the way, to be exact,* and *after all*), and conjunctive adverbs (such as *however, moreover,* and *consequently*).

Well, we'd better be going home.
Oh, I don't know.
We have to leave, unfortunately.
Last night, on the other hand, we could have stayed longer.
We said we'd be home early; consequently, we must leave now.
You might want to come with us, however.

Use commas to set off an antithetical phrase.

An **antithetical phrase** uses a word such as *not* or *unlike* to qualify what precedes it.

You, not I, deserve this honor.
Bicycles, unlike cars, cause no pollution.

| Exercise 11 | Using Commas |

On your paper rewrite the following sentences, adding commas where they are needed. If a sentence needs no commas, write *correct*.

Sequoya and the Cherokee Language

1. Most Native American languages unlike European ones were not written down before the eighteenth century; consequently it was difficult for people to learn them.
2. The Cherokees thought that writing was the privilege of certain people.
3. Like many other Native American groups in fact the Cherokees used smoke and drum signals to communicate with people some distance away.
4. Sequoya for example saw the need for a way of writing down his language.
5. Having considered the idea for some time he realized how valuable a written language would be.
6. He had been hurt in a hunting accident; therefore he had the leisure to think about a writing system.
7. Specifically he began to draw marks on twigs and stones.
8. People at first laughed at Sequoya's dream; however they soon began to change their minds about him.
9. Sequoya produced the first Cherokee alphabet making it possible for his tribe to write messages and record its history.
10. Sequoya who became successful despite the doubts of others was sent to Washington, D.C., in 1828 to represent the Cherokees.

Commas with Other Phrases and Clauses

1. Introductory prepositional phrases

Although a comma after a short introductory prepositional phrase is not incorrect, it is necessary only if the sentence would be misread without the comma.

> To those outside, the house appeared deserted. [comma needed to prevent misreading]

> At the last moment we decided not to go. [comma not needed]

Do use a comma after a long prepositional phrase or after the final phrase in a succession of phrases.

> On the extremely steep and rocky cliff, the mountain climbers carefully found their footholds.

> On the afternoon of the day of the game, we made a banner.

Do not use a comma if the phrase is immediately followed by a verb.

> On the stone above the front door of the building was the date.

2. Introductory participles and participial phrases

Use commas to set off introductory participles and participial phrases.

> Purring, the kitten curled up in my lap.
> Sitting in a tree, my little sister called down to us.

3. Adverb clauses

Use commas to set off all introductory adverb clauses.

> Although I like country music, I did not want to hear his entire collection.

> Until she arrived, I thought that no one was coming.

Also use commas to set off internal adverb clauses that interrupt the flow of a sentence.

> Evan, after he thought about it awhile, agreed with our idea.

In general, do not set off an adverb clause at the end of a sentence unless the clause is parenthetical or the sentence would be misread without the comma.

Exercise 12   Using Commas with Phrases and Clauses

On your paper rewrite the sentences that need commas, adding commas as necessary. If a sentence needs no additional commas, write *correct*.

I. M. Pei

1. To most people the name I. M. Pei means good taste and quality of design.
2. Among contemporary architects throughout the world Pei's name is unquestionably one of the best known and most respected.
3. Because his firm has frequently combined a beautiful and practical design with an affordable budget Pei is considered a gifted architect.
4. Among Pei's most successful designs are the East Building of the National Gallery of Art in Washington, D.C., and the pyramidal entrance to the Louvre in Paris.
5. Architects unlike artists must seek to harmonize a building's appearance with its purpose.
6. After a series of problems with the John Hancock Tower in Boston Pei's firm lost some business.
7. Pei and his staff gradually regained their hands-on reputation after the problems with the John Hancock Tower were resolved.
8. For a resort hotel in mainland China Pei created a design that pleased everyone.
9. Having been born in China Pei was happy to design a structure for his native land.
10. Although Pei has become highly successful as an architect he continues to welcome new challenges.

Exercise 13   Using Commas with Phrases and Clauses

Rewrite the sentences that need commas adding commas as necessary. If a sentence needs no commas, write *correct*.

Corn in the Americas

1. When it was recently determined that corn was first cultivated in the Americas only 4,700 years ago many scientists were puzzled.
2. Before this discovery they had thought that people in central Mexico started farming corn about 7,000 years ago.
3. Perplexed the scientists are trying to figure out if an earlier example of cultivated corn could have existed.
4. About 9,000 years ago in the Middle East around the Jordan River valley both plants and animals were domesticated.
5. If they do not locate an earlier sample scientists may have to rethink the chronology of civilization in the Western Hemisphere.
6. One famous botanist after he studied the matter cautioned his fellow scientists not to be too hasty.
7. In other parts of Mexico still older corn may be found.
8. Growing wild a plant that is similar to domesticated corn still exists in many regions of Mexico.
9. Scientists believe that ancient people once they discovered the wild corn plant began to cultivate it.
10. After it was discovered by the rest of the world corn became the third largest crop grown.

Additional Uses of Commas

1. Titles of people

Use commas to set off titles when they follow a person's name.

> Alan Wong, M.D. Maureen O'Connor, mayor of San Diego
>
> Jorge Gonzalez, Ph.D., will speak on Thursday.

2. Addresses, geographical terms, and dates

Use commas to separate the various parts of an address, a geographical term, or a date.

> Anaheim, California, is the home of Disneyland.
>
> Her address is 9 Lee Road, Nome, AK 99762.
>
> Friday, March 15, 1995, was the day I got my driver's license.

Use the following forms for letter writing.

> 90 Sherwick Road
> New Bedford, MA 02745
> July 7, 1997

Do not use commas if only the month and the day or only the month and the year are given.

> October 31   September 1996

3. References

Use commas to set off the parts of a reference that direct the reader to the exact source.

> Odysseus becomes reunited with his son Telemachus in the *Odyssey*, Book 16, lines 177–219.

4. Direct Address

Use commas to set off words or names used in direct address.

> Nathaniel, do you know where Kathleen is?
> I can order the book for you, sir, if you like.

5. Tag Questions

Use commas to set off a tag question.

A tag question (such as *shouldn't I?* or *have you?*) emphasizes an implied answer to the statement preceding it.

> You've already seen this film, haven't you?

6. Letter Writing

Place a comma after the salutation of an informal letter and after the closing of all letters.

Dear Dolores,   Very truly yours,

Misuse of Commas

In general, do not use a comma before a conjunction that connects a compound predicate or compound subject.

INCORRECT	She started the car, and drove down the hill. [compound predicate]
CORRECT	She started the car and drove down the hill.
INCORRECT	The adults playing softball, and the children playing soccer argued in the field. [compound subject]
CORRECT	The adults playing softball and the children playing soccer argued in the field.

Do not use only a comma to join two main clauses that are not part of a series. Use a coordinating conjunction with the comma, or use a semicolon.

INCORRECT	John Wayne worked in Hollywood for almost 50 years, he made more than 200 films.
CORRECT	John Wayne worked in Hollywood for almost 50 years, and he made more than 200 films.

Do not use a comma between a subject and its verb or between a verb and its complement.

INCORRECT	What you do with your money, is your business.
CORRECT	What you do with your money is your business.
INCORRECT	For the overnight camping trip you will need, a sleeping bag, a towel, soap, and a toothbrush.
CORRECT	For the overnight camping trip you will need a sleeping bag, a towel, soap, and a toothbrush.

Exercise 14   Using Commas with Various Elements

On your paper rewrite the following letter, adding twenty commas.

1516 Evergreen Road
Bonita CA 92002
October 5 1997

Dear Belinda

Your mother has told me that you would like some advice about a good diet. She wrote that you want to lose about twenty pounds. I hope that she has misunderstood your goal Belinda because you would be quite thin if you lost that much weight wouldn't you?

I have enclosed a copy of an article about diet and weight loss that was published in the May 6 1996 issue of *News in America* page 22. Ruth Smith M.D. the author is a specialist in nutrition. In November 1990 I heard Dr. Smith speak at a conference in Washington D.C. and I have a great deal of respect for her knowledge. You will read this article carefully won't you?

I am looking forward to visiting your family at Thanksgiving. I haven't seen any of you since I was in San Diego on May 14 1989 for a convention. When I visit this year I hope we'll be able to spend some time together Belinda.

Love
Aunt Miriam

Exercise 15   Using End Marks, Colons, Semicolons, and Commas

On your paper rewrite the following sentences, adding all necessary punctuation.

The Movies

1. In the 1939 movie *The Wizard of Oz* a cyclone sweeps Dorothy out of rural Kansas and deposits her in the wild wonderful land of the Munchkins
2. You've surely seen and enjoyed *The Lion King* haven't you
3. As my grandmother remembers Shirley Temple a famous adorable and talented child star of the 1930s appeared in dozens of films
4. Movies such as these from the 1930s and 1940s have stood the test of time *Gone with the Wind It's a Wonderful Life* and *Treasure of the Sierra Madre*
5. To be honest most of Hollywood's films about cowboys and pioneers and Native Americans don't reflect the cold cruel facts of history
6. Quite a few movies by the way have been inspired by comic strip characters *Batman* and *Superman* are two outstanding examples
7. Robert Redford best known for his acting directed *A River Runs Through It* as well as *Quiz Show* and other outstanding movies
8. According to my great-grandfather who will soon be eighty-five the comedy *The Gold Rush* starring Charlie Chaplin opened in May 1925
9. Because of their outstanding acting in *The Miracle Worker* both Anne Bancroft who played Annie Sullivan and Patty Duke who played Helen Keller won Academy Awards
10. If you ask me movie stars who perform their own stunts are taking unnecessary foolish childish chances their efforts should reflect their true talent which is acting

On a typewriter indicate the dash with two hyphens (--). Do not place a comma, semicolon, colon, or period before or after a dash.

If you use a computer, you may make a dash with a certain combination of keystrokes. Refer to the manual of your word-processing program for instructions.

1. Dashes to Signal Change

Use a dash to indicate an abrupt break or change in thought within a sentence.

> A small stand sells sugar loaves—the gift to bring when invited to dinner—sugar for the mint tea and for the sweet pastry, so flaky and light, that they bake.
>
> Anaïs Nin

2. Dashes to Emphasize

Use a dash to set off and emphasize supplemental information or parenthetical comments.

> It was a shiny new car—the first he had ever owned.
>
> A shiny new car—the first he had ever owned—was his most prized possession.

Do not overuse dashes in your writing.

Exercise 16   Using Dashes

For each sentence below, write the phrase that should be set off with dashes. With the phrase write the dash or dashes.

SAMPLE He waxed and polished the old car a waste of time before he tried to sell it.
ANSWER —a waste of time—

1. Uncle Raymond by the way, he's my mother's brother-in-law was the proud owner of a new foreign car.
2. He had purchased the sedan at the start of a driving tour of Europe his first visit to the place he called the Old Country.
3. When he brought the car back to the United States, he realized it had a few drawbacks especially the cost of maintenance.
4. Ironically, this car from northern Europe a region of frigid, snowbound winters performed poorly on icy roads in the upper Midwest.
5. The car proved its worth, however, after Uncle Raymond was involved in a major accident a highway pileup on Route 1 that totaled some of the other vehicles but left his car undamaged.

Parentheses with Supplemental Material

Use parentheses to set off supplemental material.

Commas and dashes as well as parentheses can be used to set off supplemental material; the difference between the three marks of punctuation is one of degree. Use commas to set off supplemental material that is closely related to the rest of the sentence. Use parentheses to set off supplemental material that is not important enough to be considered part of the main statement. Use dashes to set off and emphasize material that interrupts the main statement.

> Many contemporary women's fashions (business suits and low heels) show the influence of Gabrielle "Coco" Chanel.

A complete sentence within parentheses is not capitalized and needs no period if it is contained within another sentence. If a sentence in parentheses is not contained within another sentence (if it stands by itself), both a capital letter and a period are needed.

> The unisex trend (it still seems to be popular) was started by Chanel, who wore a man's trench coat.

> Chanel introduced the world's most famous perfume, Chanel No. 5. (This scent is still in great demand.)

Exercise 17 **Using Parentheses**

Rewrite the following sentences, adding parentheses where needed.

New Mexico

1. Albuquerque this fast-growing city is headquarters for a large computer chip manufacturer has a hot-air balloon fiesta every October.
2. The "sky city" of Acoma in this clifftop site Native Americans have lived for hundreds of years is a place to view handsome geometric pottery.
3. The altitude of Santa Fe and Taos 5,000 to 7,000 feet helps to explain the cold winters that these two cities frequently get.
4. Bandelier National Monument contains fascinating cliff dwellings carved out of the volcanic rock by the Anasazi people. the Anasazis mysteriously disappeared from the pueblo long before the Spanish arrived.
5. Los Alamos named after the Spanish word for poplar trees is where the atomic bomb was developed in the 1940s.

Parentheses with Other Marks of Punctuation

1. With a comma, semicolon, or colon

Place a comma, semicolon, or colon *after* the closing parenthesis.

> Despite the simple clothes that Chanel designed and wore (the little black dress became her uniform**),** she became wealthy.

> In the early 1950s women wore long skirts with cinched waists and high heels (the Dior look**);** Chanel helped change that.

2. With a question mark or an exclamation point

Place a question mark or an exclamation point *inside* the parentheses if it is part of the parenthetical expression.

> Chanel believed that simplicity and practicality were more important than obviously expensive, complicated-looking clothes (who would not agree today**?).**

> Chanel exerted little influence on fashion during World War II (1939–1945), but she reopened her fashion house in 1954 (when she was seventy**!).**

Place a question mark or an exclamation point *outside* the parentheses if it is part of the entire sentence.

> Did you know that Chanel introduced many of today's fashion classics (sweaters, costume jewelry, sling-back shoes**)?**

> How amazed I was to find out that it was Chanel who made a suntan fashionable (in the 1930s**)!**

Exercise 18 — Using Parentheses

Rewrite the following sentences correctly, adding parentheses where they are needed.

1. Roger he lived next door to us for years had a great love for baseball.
2. Amarillo from the Spanish word for "yellow" is a town in the Texas Panhandle.
3. It was a December night the first winterlike night of the month, and snow was falling.
4. That song is it by Handel or Mozart? always reminds me of Paula, for she used to play it constantly when we were in college together.
5. He was aggressive, overbearing, mean, and who would have thought it possible! completely devoted to his dachshund.
6. Anorexia can have serious even tragic consequences if not treated properly.
7. Some people I am not one of them think that Elvis Presley was devastatingly handsome.
8. Do you believe in love at first sight forgive the cliché?
9. It was an extraordinary feat: she threw the javelin 245 feet about 75 meters!
10. Otis was an Air Force pilot during the Persian Gulf War the war against Iraq.

Quotation Marks for Direct Quotations

Use quotation marks to enclose a direct quotation.

Place quotation marks around the quotation only, not around purely introductory or explanatory remarks. Generally separate such remarks from the actual quotation with a comma. (For the use of colons to introduce quotations, see page 695.)

> A famous poster asks, "What if they gave a war and nobody came?"

> A Pawnee poem reminds us of "the sacredness of things."

Do not use a comma after a quotation that ends with an exclamation point or a question mark.

> "What is the question?" Gertrude Stein asked.

When a quotation is interrupted by explanatory words such as *he said* or *she wrote*, use two sets of quotation marks.

Separate each part of the quotation from the interrupting phrase with marks of punctuation before and after the phrase. If the second part of the quotation is a complete sentence, begin it with a capital letter.

> "A thing of beauty," wrote John Keats, "is a joy forever."

> "It wasn't just that Babe Ruth hit more home runs than anybody else," said Red Smith. "He hit them better, higher, and farther."

Do not use quotation marks in an indirect quotation (a quotation that does not repeat a person's exact words).

> ORIGINAL QUOTATION   "Dance is life at its most glorious moment," said Pearl Lang.
> INDIRECT QUOTATION   Pearl Lang said that dance is life's most glorious moment.

Use single quotation marks around a quotation within a quotation.

> President John F. Kennedy said, "I am one person who can truthfully say, 'I got my job through the *New York Times.*'"

In writing dialogue, begin a new paragraph and use a new set of quotation marks every time the speaker changes.

> He looked at me proudly. "Was it so hard to do, Daughter?"
> "Not so hard as I thought." I pinned the brooch on my dress.
> "I'll wear it always," I said. "I'll keep it forever."
> Kathryn Forbes

Writing Dialogue Correctly

Copy the following sentences, setting them up correctly as a dialogue.

[1]"I need help," Robert said. [2]"What happened?" I asked. [3]"I just locked the car keys in the trunk," he responded. [4]"How did you ever happen to do such a thing?" I demanded. [5]"I set them down there while I was looking for my house keys, which are missing, too."

Exercise 20   Using Quotation Marks with Direct Quotes

Rewrite the following sentences, adding quotation marks where they are needed. For sentences that need no changes, write *correct*.

1. My method for remembering the numbers of days in all twelve months was given by my first-grade teacher, who said, Thirty days hath September, April, June, and November. All the rest have thirty-one, excepting February and that has twenty-eight.
2. These are the times that try men's souls, warned eighteenth-century American pamphleteer and patriot Tom Paine.
3. Poet Bliss Carman writes, There is something in the autumn that is native to my blood/Touch of manner, hint of mood.
4. According to poet Bliss Carman, there is something about the autumn that is native to her blood—a touch of manner and a hint of mood.
5. Describing the false sense of good days ahead that Indian summer frequently inspires, poet Emily Dickinson writes, These are the days when skies put on the old, old sophistries.
6. If you were coming in the fall, writes Dickinson in another poem, I'd brush the summer by/With half a smile.
7. Poet T.S. Eliot tells us that for him April is the cruelest month.
8. April is the cruelest month, writes Eliot, breeding lilacs out of the dead land, mixing memory and desire.
9. Shall I compare thee to a summer's day? wrote Shakespeare. Thou art more lovely and more temperate.
10. At her sixtieth birthday party, the guest of honor said, This occasion inspires me to repeat the words of that old song, Though it's a long, long time from May to December, the days grow short when you reach September.

Quotation Marks with Titles and Unusual Expressions

Use quotation marks to enclose titles of short works, such as short stories, short poems, essays, newspaper and magazine articles, book chapters, songs, and single episodes of a television series.

"The Legend of Sleepy Hollow" [short story]
"The Raven" [poem]
"On the Duty of Civil Disobedience" [essay]
"Steven Spielberg's Newest Film" [newspaper article]
"The 1980s in America" [chapter]
"If I Had a Hammer" [song]
"Division of the Spoils" [episode in a television series]

(For the use of italics with titles of longer works, see page 719.)

Use quotation marks to enclose unfamiliar slang and other unusual or original expressions.

My cousin uses the expression "the cat's meow" to describe something she likes.

The 1920s were known as the "roaring twenties."

Be careful not to overuse quotation marks with expressions like these. Generally, use quotation marks only the first time you use the expression in a piece of writing.

Exercise 21   **Using Quotation Marks with Titles and Expressions**

Rewrite the following sentences, adding quotation marks where they are needed.

1. Before they began to write their essay, Sara and Miguel read the short story The Gift of the Magi.
2. Sara decided the title Giving to the Other Person would be good.
3. Miguel suggested adding his poem Time for Others at the end.
4. The teacher asked Miguel to explain the term the giving tree in the first paragraph.
5. Stephanie remarked, Your essay is going to be so good that I really think you ought to submit it to the school paper.

Quotation Marks with Other Marks of Punctuation

1. With a comma or a period

Always place a comma or a period *inside* closing quotation marks.

> "The frog does not drink up the pond in which it lives," states a Native American proverb.

> Henry David Thoreau humorously advises, "Beware of all enterprises that require new clothes."

2. With a semicolon or a colon

Always place a semicolon or a colon *outside* closing quotation marks.

> Her father said, "We cannot go"; her mother said, "Perhaps we can go next year"; her elder brother just shrugged his shoulders.

> This is what I think of Lady Ōtomo's poem "My Heart, Thinking": it is romantic and powerful.

3. With a question mark or an exclamation point

Place the question mark or the exclamation point *inside* the closing quotation marks when it is part of the quotation.

> A famous sonnet by Shakespeare begins with these words: "Shall I compare thee to a summer's day?"

> She said, "I never want to hear from you again!"

Place the question mark or the exclamation point *outside* the closing quotation marks when it is part of the entire sentence.

> I've finally memorized all of "Paul Revere's Ride"!
> Why do you keep saying, "I'm sorry"?

If both the sentence and the quotation at the end of the sentence need a question mark (or an exclamation point), use only one punctuation mark, and place it *inside* the quotation marks.

> When did he ask, "Would you like to go to the movies?"

Rewrite the following sentences, adding quotation marks where they are needed. For the sentences that need no changes, write *correct*.

Gabriela Mistral and Pablo Neruda

1. When Chilean poet Gabriela Mistral received the Nobel Prize for literature in 1945, the Swedish Academy said that Mistral had almost become a legend.
2. The poem Close to Me, which appears in Gabriela Mistral's first book, *Despair*, is a lullaby that is sung by a mother to a young child.
3. The refrain sleep close to me! appears at the end of each verse of the poem.
4. In his introduction to a collection of Mistral's poems, the African American poet Langston Hughes implies that her language is simple and direct.
5. Even when she sings the commonplace in life, writes critic A. Ortiz-Vargas, there is always a restraint, a dignity in her tone.
6. Ortiz-Vargas goes on to say, Sometimes her song soars high as on eagle wings, but more often it is rooted in the fertile region of her own heart.
7. Ortiz-Vargas writes, There is never any gaiety in her poetry—nor lightness—for her emotions are always ardently passionate; many other critics agree with his view.
8. The phrase a cry from the heart could be used to describe many of Mistral's verses.
9. Do you know Mistral's powerful poem about motherhood, Song of Virgo?
10. In his introduction to *Selected Poems of Gabriela Mistral*, Langston Hughes writes: Mildred Adams wrote, Gabriela's clarity and precision, her passion and that characteristic which can only be called her nobility of soul are accepted as ideals.
11. Another Chilean poet, Pablo Neruda, has been described by Luis Monguió in this way: a son of the New World, surging, creating, and coming to be, in quest of his destiny.
12. Neruda, like Mistral a Nobel Prize winner, says of his work, It is a poetry impure as the clothing we wear, or our bodies, soup stained, soiled with our shameful behavior.
13. In his poem You Flame-Foot! Neruda writes, Those feet of yours—pint-sized, no bigger than bees, how they eat up the shoe leather!
14. In his introduction to Neruda's *Selected Poems*, Monguió writes this about the critic Montesinos, Montesinos has said of the old Spanish baroque, It is the art of denying oneself nothing.
15. Poetry, to quote Neruda, is useful and usable; true and virtuous.
16. Have you read Neruda's famous poem Walking Around?
17. In it the poet compares Monday morning to an oil slick.
18. In Ode with a Lament, Neruda mourns, Only with waves at my back can I love you.
19. Juan Jimenez has said of Neruda, He is a great poet; a great, bad poet.
20. Neruda, in Monguió's view, seeks his salvation not in fantasy but in realism.

21.10   Italics (Underlining)

Italic type is a special slanted type that is used in printing. (*This is printed in italics.*) Indicate italics on a typewriter or with handwriting by underlining. (<u>This is underlined</u>.) When using a computer, find out the special keystrokes needed for italics by referring to the manual for the software you are using.

1. Italics with Titles

Italicize (underline) titles of books, lengthy poems, plays, films and television series, paintings and sculptures, and long musical compositions. Also italicize the names of newspapers and magazines, ships, airplanes, and spacecraft.

Great Expectations [book]	*Gone with the Wind* [film]
Romeo and Juliet [play]	*Starry Night* [painting]
Nova [television series]	*Grand Canyon Suite* [musical work]
The Thinker [sculpture]	the *Oakland Tribune* [newspaper]
Sports Illustrated [magazine]	*Spirit of St. Louis* [airplane]
USS *Enterprise** [ship]	*Columbia* [spacecraft]
Snow-Bound [long poem]	

*Do not italicize abbreviations such as USS that precede the name of a ship.

Italicize (underline) and capitalize articles (*a*, *an*, *the*) written at the beginning of a title only when they are part of the title itself. It is common practice not to italicize (underline) the article preceding the title of a newspaper or a magazine. Do not italicize the word *magazine* unless it is part of the title of a periodical.

A Light in the Attic	but	a *National Geographic* magazine
The Red Badge of Courage		the *Chicago Tribune*

2. Italics with Foreign Words

Italicize (underline) foreign words and expressions that are not used frequently in English.

The motto of the U.S. Marine Corps is **semper fidelis** ("always faithful").

Do not italicize a foreign word or expression that is commonly used in English.

I eat **croissants** for breakfast.

3. Italics with Words and Other Items Used to Represent Themselves

Italicize (underline) words, letters, and numerals used to represent themselves.

> Do not start a sentence with *and* or *but*.

> She was too superstitious to say the number aloud, so she handed the elevator operator a piece of paper on which she had written **13**.

> Replace all of the number signs (**#**'s) with the word **number**.

Exercise 23   **Using Italics**

Write the words in each sentence below that should be italicized. Underline the words.

Women in the Olympics

1. In the book Golden Girls by Carli Laklan, you will find information about the many women who have won Olympic medals.
2. The ancient Greeks based the first Olympics on the concept of arete, which means "excellence in every area of life—physical, moral, and intellectual."
3. The author of Golden Girls notes that the earliest games featured just one event, the stade, a 200-yard footrace; the English word stadium comes from the Greek word stade.
4. The word Olympics comes from Olympia, the name of the Greek city where the first Olympic games were held in 776 B.C.
5. Sonja Henie, who won three gold medals in figure skating at three successive Olympic games, gained recognition as a movie star with her first film, One in a Million.
6. Peggy Fleming won a gold medal in figure skating at the 1968 Grenoble Olympics; she skated to Tchaikovsky's Pathétique.
7. With the financial backing of the publishers of the Chicago Tribune, Gertrude Ederle, who had won the gold medal for swimming in 1924, became the first woman to swim the English Channel in 1926; the French tug the Alsace followed her with a jazz band on board "to keep up her spirits."
8. Wilma Rudolph, who overcame serious illnesses in childhood, was the first American woman to win three gold medals in track and field; she later became a commentator for the radio series Olympic Odyssey.
9. After the 1984 Olympics gold-medal winners Florence Griffith-Joyner and Jackie Joyner-Kersee were featured in Time, Life, Newsweek, the New York Times, and Sports Illustrated.
10. Many of the Olympic gold medalists have been on television series ranging from Saturday Night Live to 20/20.

21.11 The Apostrophe

Apostrophes with Possessives

1. Pronouns

Use an apostrophe and -*s* for the possessive of a singular indefinite pronoun.

Do not use an apostrophe with other possessive pronouns.

everybody**'s** problem	*but*	**its** owner
each other**'s** parents		**whose** talents
one**'s** beliefs		The bikes are **theirs**.

2. Singular nouns

Use an apostrophe and -*s* to form the possessive of a singular noun, even one that ends in -*s*.

the woman**'s** team	San Francisco**'s** earthquake
the class**'s** election	Robert Burns**'s** poetry
the princess**'s** career	Cape Hatteras**'s** beauty
the box**'s** lettering	Groucho Marx**'s** biography

There are some exceptions to this rule, however. To form the possessive of ancient proper nouns that end in -*es* or -*is*, the name *Jesus*, and expressions with words such as *appearance* and *conscience*, just add an apostrophe.

Euripides**'** plays	Jesus**'** teachings
Acropolis**'** structure	for appearance**'** sake
Hercules**'** feats	conscience**'** teachings

3. Plural nouns ending in -*s*

Use an apostrophe alone to form the possessive of a plural noun that ends in -*s*.

the countries**'** treaty	the Joneses**'** picnic
the trees**'** leaves	the Greens**'** barbecue

4. Plural nouns not ending in -*s*

Use an apostrophe and -*s* to form the possessive of a plural noun that does not end in -*s*.

women**'s** clubs	Women**'s** Bar Association
oxen**'s** harness	mice**'s** squeaks

5. Compound nouns

Put only the last word of a compound noun in the possessive form.

> my sister-in-law**'s** office
> the court-martial**'s** effect
> attorney general**'s** job
> the chief of staff**'s** order

6. Joint possession versus individual possession

If two or more persons (or partners in a company) possess something jointly, use the possessive form for the last person named.

> Claude and Louise**'s** children
> Johnson and Johnson**'s** baby-care products
> Abbott and Costello**'s** antics

If two or more persons (or companies) possess an item (or items) individually, put each one's name in the possessive form.

> Tina Turner**'s** and the Rolling Stones**'** songs
> Chrysler**'s** and the American Motor Company**'s** cars

7. Expressions of time and money

Use a possessive form to express amounts of money or time that modify a noun.

The modifier can also be expressed as a hyphenated adjective. In that case, no possessive form is used.

one dollar**'s** increase	*but*	a one-dollar increase
five minutes**'** drive		a five-minute drive
ten days**'** wait		a ten-day wait

Exercise 24	**Using Apostrophes with Possessives**

Copy the phrases below, adding apostrophes and whatever else is needed to make the italicized parts possessive. If a phrase is correct, write *correct*.

  1. the *Smiths* car
  2. a book of *hers*
  3. one *lawyer* opinion
  4. the *children* playground
  5. *Johnson and Goldberg* main office
  6. *Orestes* father
  7. *somebody* mistake
  8. two *weeks* worth of laundry
  9. the *editor in chief* orders
 10. *Larry and Joel* bicycles

Apostrophes with Special Plurals

Use an apostrophe and *-s* to form the plural of letters, numerals, symbols, and words used to represent themselves.

Italicize (underline) the letter, numeral, symbol, or word but not the apostrophe and the *-s*.

> Your *q*'s look like *g*'s, and your *5*'s look like *S*'s.
> She told me to replace the *henceforth*'s with *therefore*'s.

Apostrophes in Contractions

Use an apostrophe in place of letters omitted in contractions.

A **contraction** is a single word made up of two words that have been combined by omitting letters. Common contractions combine a subject and a verb or a verb and an adverb.

you'd	*formed from*	you had, you would
you're		you are
who's		who is, who has
it's		it is, it has
won't		will not

Use an apostrophe in place of the omitted numerals of a year.

the class of '94	the '92 campaign

Exercise 25   **Using Apostrophes**

Write the words from the following sentences that require an apostrophe or an apostrophe *-s*. Mark them as needed.

Women and Literature

[1]Imagine that you were making a list of writers names for a new encyclopedia about female authors. [2]Under the *a*s youd include Louisa May Alcott, whos best known for *Little Women*, and Isabel Allende, author of *The House of the Spirits*. [3]Maya Angelou, who wrote *I Know Why the Caged Bird Sings*, would surely be on everyones list. [4]The *b*s would include the names of Toni Cade Bambara and Gwendolyn Brooks. [5]Both Bambaras novels and Brooks poems focus on the lives of African Americans and on womens issues. [6]Nikki Giovanni is a poet whod be listed under the *g*s; her books include *Black Feeling* and *My House*. [7]At least five twentieth-century authors names would be listed under the *m*s: Carson McCullers, Edna St. Vincent Millay, Margaret Mitchell, Marianne Moore, and Toni Morrison. [8]Millays and Moores names would be found on anyones list of talented poets; McCullers and Morrisons names are familiar to lovers of prose. [9]Most people don't know that Margaret Mitchells *Gone with the Wind* took ten years labor to write; it was finally published in 36. [10]In the entry about the novelist Katherine Anne Porter, youd want to mention Porters great-great-grandfathers name: Daniel Boone.

21.12 The Hyphen

Hyphens with Prefixes

A hyphen is not ordinarily used to join a prefix to a word. There are a few exceptions, however. If you are in doubt about using a hyphen, consult a dictionary. You should also keep in mind the following guidelines:

Use a hyphen after any prefix joined to a proper noun or a proper adjective. Use a hyphen after the prefixes *all-*, *ex-* (meaning "former"), and *self-* joined to any noun or adjective.

mid-Atlantic	pre-Renaissance
all-city	trans-Pacific
ex-coach	all-American
self-confidence	post-Elizabethan

Use a hyphen after the prefix *anti-* when it joins a word beginning with *i-*. Also use a hyphen after the prefix *vice-*, except in *vice president.*

anti-intellectual
vice-mayor
vice president

Use a hyphen to avoid confusion between words beginning with *re-* that look alike but are different in meaning and pronunciation.

re-cover the couch	*but*	recover the ball
re-store those cans		restore your confidence
re-lease the car		release the brake

The offensive end recovered the ball.

Exercise 26   **Using Hyphens with Prefixes**

On your paper write each word in the following sentences that needs a hyphen. Add the hyphen.

Colonial America

1. In the preRevolutionary War era, there was a slow growth of antiBritish sentiment.
2. The average individual living in the midAtlantic colonies, for example, was beginning to feel more selfconfident about taking control of the government.
3. America was a land of opportunity where an exindentured servant could become a property owner, although the transformation sometimes required an allout effort.
4. After the Boston Tea Party, the colonists would have been doubly resentful had the British resent tea shipments into Boston Harbor.
5. The main place in the colonies where antiindependence feelings remained surprisingly strong was New York.

Hyphens with Compounds and Numbers

1. Compound adjectives

Use a hyphen in a compound adjective that precedes a noun.

In general, a compound adjective that follows a noun is not hyphenated.

dark-green eyes	*but*	Her eyes are dark green.
a fifteen-year-old aunt		His aunt is fifteen years old.
a well-liked reporter		That reporter is well liked.

An expression made up of an adverb ending in *-ly* and an adjective is not hyphenated.

a nicely behaved dog	a fairly close race
a slightly rusted exterior	a hastily written report

2. Compound numbers

Hyphenate any spelled-out cardinal or ordinal compound number up to ninety-nine or ninety-ninth.

sixty-four	sixty-fourth
eighty-two	eighty-second

3. Fractions used as adjectives

Hyphenate a fraction used as an adjective (but not one used as a noun).

one-eighth teaspoon	*but*	one eighth of a teaspoon
one-quarter cup		one quarter of a cup
one-half pound		one half of a pound

4. Connected numerals

Hyphenate two numerals to indicate a span.

pages 30-56	1986-1990

Hyphens to Divide Words at the End of a Line

Words are generally divided between syllables or pronounceable parts. Because it is frequently difficult to determine where a word should be divided, check your dictionary.

In general, if a word contains two consonants occurring between two vowels or if it contains a double consonant, divide the word between the two consonants.

foun-tain	struc-ture
lin-ger	sup-per
profes-sor	tomor-row

If a suffix has been added to a complete word that ends in two consonants, divide the word after the two consonants.

pull-ing	point-less
meaning-ful	strong-est

Exercise 27   Using Hyphens

Hyphens must be added to five of the following sentences. On your paper rewrite those sentences, adding the hyphens where they are needed. Then make a list of all the italicized words, showing where each would be divided if it had to be broken at the end of a line.

Sally Ride, Astronaut

1. Sally Ride was thirty one in 1983 when she became the first American woman to *orbit* the earth.
2. She was also the *youngest* American astronaut to go into orbit.
3. At Swarthmore College, where she did her undergraduate work, Sally Ride won a national tennis tournament for *college* students.
4. Astronaut Ride received her *doctorate* from Stanford University.
5. Dr. Ride said that one third of the *scientists* at NASA are women.
6. A thirty four year old Russian woman, Svetlana Savitskaya, *orbited* the earth about eight months before Dr. Ride.
7. Astronauts are *resourceful*, self confident, healthy, highly educated, and experienced in their special fields of study.
8. By the year 2010 space flight may become *common*; within your lifetime thousands may be taking trips into space every year.
9. Well known ex astronauts such as John Glenn and Neil Armstrong were viewed as all American heroes for years after their space *missions*.
10. Astronaut trainees must learn to live in an almost *weightless*, low gravity environment.

21.13 Abbreviations

Abbreviations are shortened forms of words. Abbreviations save space and time and prevent unnecessary wordiness. For instance, *M.D.* is more concise and easier to write than *Medical Doctor.* Most abbreviations take periods. If you are unsure of how to write an abbreviation, consult a dictionary.

Use only one period if an abbreviation occurs at the end of a sentence that would ordinarily take a period of its own.

If an abbreviation occurs at the end of a sentence that ends with a question mark or an exclamation point, use the period *and* the second mark of punctuation.

> Gerry left at 8:00 **A.M.**   Did she leave at 8:00 **A.M.?**

Capitalizing Abbreviations

1. Abbreviations of proper nouns:

Capitalize abbreviations of proper nouns.

> 109-46 Queens **Blvd.**   **Rev.** Billy Graham
> **N.** Michigan **Ave.**   **U.S.** Congress

2. Abbreviations formed from initial letters:

Abbreviations of organizations and government agencies are often formed from the initial letters of the complete name. Such abbreviations, whether pronounced letter by letter or as words, omit periods and are written with capital letters.

> YWCA   NAACP   IRS
> NASA   UNICEF   CBS

3. Abbreviations related to dates and times

Capitalize the following abbreviations related to dates and times:

A.D. (*anno Domini*), "in the year of the Lord" (since the birth of Christ); place before the date: **A.D.** 5

B.C. (before Christ); place after the date: 1000 **B.C.**

B.C.E. (before the common era; equivalent to *B.C.*); place after the date: 164 **B.C.E.**

C.E. (common era; equivalent to *A.D.*); place after the date: 66 **C.E.**

A.M. (*ante meridiem*), "before noon"; place after exact times: 7:45 **A.M.**

P.M. (*post meridiem*), "after noon"; place after exact times: 2:30 **P.M.**

ZIP-Code Abbreviations

In ordinary prose spell out state names. On envelopes, however, abbreviate state names as shown in the following list.

Alabama	**AL**	Kansas	**KS**
Alaska	**AK**	Kentucky	**KY**
Arizona	**AZ**	Louisiana	**LA**
Arkansas	**AR**	Maine	**ME**
California	**CA**	Maryland	**MD**
Colorado	**CO**	Massachusetts	**MA**
Connecticut	**CT**	Michigan	**MI**
Delaware	**DE**	Minnesota	**MN**
Florida	**FL**	Mississippi	**MS**
Georgia	**GA**	Missouri	**MO**
Hawaii	**HI**	Montana	**MT**
Idaho	**ID**	Nebraska	**NB**
Illinois	**IL**	Nevada	**NV**
Indiana	**IN**	New Hampshire	**NH**
Iowa	**IA**	New Jersey	**NJ**
New Mexico	**NM**	South Dakota	**SD**
New York	**NY**	Tennessee	**TN**
North Carolina	**NC**	Texas	**TX**
North Dakota	**ND**	Utah	**UT**
Ohio	**OH**	Vermont	**VT**
Oklahoma	**OK**	Virginia	**VA**
Oregon	**OR**	Washington	**WA**
Pennsylvania	**PA**	West Virginia	**WV**
Rhode Island	**RI**	Wisconsin	**WI**
South Carolina	**SC**	Wyoming	**WY**

The ZIP-code form for the District of Columbia is **DC.** In ordinary prose, however, use periods to write **Washington, D.C.**

| **Exercise 28** | **Using Abbreviations with Capital Letters** |

On your paper write the abbreviations for the italicized words or phrases in the following sentences. If the terms should not be abbreviated, write *correct.*

1. My aunt lives near Washington, *District of Columbia.*
2. The *Internal Revenue Service* is responsible for collecting federal taxes.
3. The House of Representatives will be in session today from 10:00 *ante meridiem* to 4:00 *post meridiem.*
4. President William Clinton took office in *anno Domini* 1993.
5. The senior senators from *Illinois, California,* and *South Carolina* are having lunch together this week.

Using Abbreviations

Use abbreviations for some personal titles.

Titles such as *Mrs., Mr., Ms., Sr.,* and *Jr.* and those indicating professions and academic degrees (*Dr., Ph.D., M.A., B.S.*) are almost always abbreviated. Titles of government and military officials and members of the clergy are frequently abbreviated when used before a full name.

Ken Griffey **Sr.** and
Ken Griffey **Jr.**

Mrs. Roosevelt	**Sen.** Nancy Kassebaum
Harry Connick **Jr.**	**Gen.** Colin Powell
Rosalyn Ying, **Ph.D.**	Myron Greene, **D.D.S.**

Abbreviate units of measure used with numerals in technical or scientific writing. Do not abbreviate them in ordinary prose.

The abbreviations that follow stand for both plural and singular units:

ENGLISH SYSTEM

ft.	foot	**mi.**	mile	**tbsp.**	tablespoon
gal.	gallon	**oz.**	ounce	**tsp.**	teaspoon
in.	inch	**pt.**	pint	**yd.**	yard
lb.	pound	**qt.**	quart		

METRIC SYSTEM

cg	centigram	**l**	liter
cl	centiliter	**m**	meter
cm	centimeter	**mg**	milligram
g	gram	**ml**	milliliter
kg	kilogram	**mm**	millimeter
km	kilometer		

Exercise 29   Using Abbreviations of Titles and Measurement Units

On your paper write the abbreviations for the italicized words or phrases in the following sentences. If the terms should not be abbreviated, write *correct.*

1. *Senator* Robert Dole was majority leader for the 104th Congress in 1995.
2. *Doctor* C. Everett Koop was surgeon general during the administration of President George Bush.
3. Harvey J. McCarthy *Junior* will testify before a Senate subcommittee during the first week of February.
4. I believe that the Washington Monument stands 555 *feet* 5 1/8 *inches* high.
5. Bethesda, Maryland, a suburb of Washington, is located 8 *miles* (14.8 *kilometers*) from the Capitol.

21.14   Numbers and Numerals

In nontechnical writing some numbers are spelled out, and some are expressed in figures. Numbers expressed in figures are called *numerals*.

Regular Uses of Numbers and Numerals

In general, spell out cardinal and ordinal numbers that can be written in one or two words.

New Hampshire is one of the original **thirteen** states.
There are **twenty-seven** students in the class.
Alaska was the **forty-ninth** state to join the Union.

Spell out any number that occurs at the beginning of a sentence.

Sixteen hundred fifteen delegates attended.
Eleven thousand people live in that town.

In general, use numerals to express numbers that would be written in more than two words.

Mount Mitchell, the highest mountain in the eastern United States, is **6,684** feet tall.

In 1790 the total population of the United States (according to the first census) was **3,929,214.**

In 1984 Joe W. Kittinger covered **3,535** miles in eighty-three hours and fifty-three minutes, setting a new record for balloon flight.

Very large numbers are often written as a numeral followed by the word *million* or *billion*.

The surface area of the earth is close to **197 million** square miles.

If related numbers appear in the same sentence and some can be written out while others should appear as numerals, use all numerals.

Edgar ranked **5th** in the class; his brother ranked **119th.**
They ordered **38** doll houses and **112** toy robots.

Special Uses of Numbers and Numerals

1. Money, decimals, and percentages

Use numerals to express amounts of money, decimals, and percentages.

$897 million   **1.2** kilograms   **5** percent

Amounts of money that can be expressed in one or two words, however, should be spelled out.

forty-five cents   **two thousand** dollars

2. Dates and time

Use numerals to express the year and day in a date and to express the precise time with the abbreviations A.M. and P.M.

The U.S.S.R. launched *Sputnik I* on October **4, 1957.**

She went to the meeting at **4:15 P.M.**

Spell out expressions of time that do not use A.M. or P.M.

She set her alarm clock for **five** o'clock.

To express a century when the word *century* is used, spell out the number. Likewise, to express a decade when the century is clear from the context, spell out the number.

The **twentieth** century saw great technological advances.

The Great Depression of the **thirties** was an economic crisis.

When a century and a decade are expressed as a single unit, use numerals followed by an -*s*.

1930s   **1400s**

3. Addresses

Use numerals for numbered streets and avenues over ten and for all house, apartment, and room numbers. Spell out numbered streets and avenues of ten or under.

1654 West **66th** Street   **4** North Main Street
Apartment **8C**   **20 Second** Avenue

4. References

Use numerals for page, line, act, and scene numbers and the like.

Look on pages **20** and **59** for information about Pablo Casals.
Read lines **1–80** in Book **I** of the *Iliad.*
We rehearsed *Act **2**, Scenes **3** and **4**,* of the play.

Using Numbers and Numerals

On your paper rewrite each sentence below, correcting the errors with numbers or numerals. If a sentence has no errors, write *correct*.

1. Please come to our meeting on October 4 at eight thirty P.M.
2. It will be held at 153 3rd Street.
3. Our speaker will discuss everyday life in the 16th century.
4. Then two group members will read *Act One, Scenes 1 and 2*, from *Hamlet*.
5. The admission charge for tonight only will be $3.50.

Using Numbers and Numerals

For each sentence below, write correctly any number or numeral that should be changed to a different form.

Althea Gibson, Tennis Star

1. In 1957, the year she turned 30, Althea Gibson became the 1st African American tennis player to win the championship in the annual tennis tournament at Wimbledon in England.
2. Gibson traveled three thousand five hundred miles from her home in New York City to Wimbledon, but the distance that she traveled from being a 13-year-old high school dropout to a renowned tennis champion was even greater.
3. Gibson was born on a farm in South Carolina on August twenty-fifth, 1927; she was the oldest of 5 children.
4. For many years she lived with her family at 135 West 143rd Street in Harlem, and she spent her free time playing basketball at the One Hundred Thirty-fourth Street Boys Club with a team called the Mysterious 5.
5. When she was a lanky girl of fifteen (she would eventually be five feet eleven inches tall), she started taking tennis lessons from a 1-armed coach named Fred Johnson.
6. In 1947, when Gibson was 19, she played in 9 tennis tournaments and won the singles title in every single one.
7. Through the late 40s and into the early 50s, Gibson concentrated on both her tennis and her education.
8. She went back to high school, finishing 10th in her class, and then went to college, graduating in 1953 at the age of twenty-five.
9. 49 minutes was all the time it took Gibson to win the championship at Wimbledon in 1957.
10. After Wimbledon she won a one-hundred-thousand-dollar contract to play exhibition tennis matches and, in 1960, the women's professional singles title; she later became a professional golfer.

On your paper rewrite the following sentences, correcting the errors in punctuation, abbreviations, and numbers. There may be several errors in each sentence.

1. In the travel section of Campbells Bookshop, I looked at books about Kenya Switzerland and Mexico.
2. The travel sections most informative book about Mexico I should know because I visited there last year had lavish colorful realistic photographs of people landscapes and architecture
3. Before I took it off the shelf my eyes were drawn to a book titled America bc written by Harvard professor Barry Fell phd.
4. Skimming through it I realized it had been misplaced for its subject was actually archaeology not one of my interests instead of travel.
5. My sights in case you are interested are focused on the people and places of the world as it looks in the 20th century not some mud covered artifacts from over 2,000 years ago.
6. While I looked at travel books Jane and Rafael wandered into other sections.
7. Jane went to the literature section for she wanted a copy of Wuthering Heights.
8. On her way Jane spied a book of quotations with an attractive bright red cover.
9. Picking it up she thumbed through the thick white pages.
10. Then her eye fell on a familiar saying Ask me no questions and Ill tell you no lies.
11. Oh she said to herself. I didn't know that Oliver Goldsmith first wrote that line in his play She Stoops to Conquer.
12. Rafael in the meantime hurried to the compact disc videotape and audiocassette section.
13. A music student he was hoping to find a videotape of Mozarts Magic Flute.
14. May I help you? inquired Mrs Kato a sales clerk.
15. Rafael who wanted to browse first thanked her and then headed for the neatly arranged video packages.
16. Mozarts opera was not on the shelf but Rafael found twenty one copies of a new release, James Galway Plays Mostly Mozart.
17. With all out enthusiasm he grabbed a copy paid for the tape and came looking for me.
18. Having found the travel books I wanted I had moved to the humor section to find a birthday present for my brother.
19. I thought I might give him a book of cartoons perhaps Gary Larsens The Far Side, but Rafael nixed that idea.
20. Rafael suggested James Thurbers Fables for Our Time.
21. I especially like The Unicorn in the Garden he said referring to his favorite fable. Then he added Your brother will like it.
22. Jane arrived next, having bought Wuthering Heights and the book of quotations.
23. I have no self restraint she explained. I wish I could buy out the whole store.
24. Laughing I admitted that I had found approximately thirty five books I would have liked to buy.
25. With our arms laden with the purchases we had made we left the bookstore and headed for the post office where I mailed the Thurber book to my brother.

Grammar Review

Punctuation, Abbreviations, and Numbers

In *Arctic Dreams* Barry Lopez describes the landscapes of the North and the people and animals who live there. In the following passages, which have been annotated to show some of the rules of punctuation covered in this unit, he describes the Arctic's most magnificent creature: the polar bear.

Literature Model

from **ARCTIC DREAMS**
by *Barry Lopez*

Colon to introduce a sentence that explains the preceding material

Commas to separate elements in a series

Comma to separate two main clauses joined by a coordinating conjunction

Parentheses to set off supplemental material

Hyphen in a compound adjective preceding a noun

Semicolon to separate two main clauses

The polar bear is a creature of arctic edges: he hunts the ice margins, the surface of the water, and the continental shore. The ice bear, he is called. His world forms beneath him in the days of shortening light, and then falls away in the spring.

Polar bears vary in size, and their weights can change dramatically during the year. (Very large polar bears may stand 12 feet on their hind legs and weigh 2000 pounds. The number of 12- and 13-foot bears weighing 2200 or 2400 pounds that have been reported, however, says more about unadjusted scales, stretched hides, and wishful exaggeration than about polar bears.) Bears eat prodigiously in the spring, lightly in late summer, and lightly or not at all (in the case of denning females) during the winter. An adult male might weigh between 550 and 1700 pounds and measure 75 to 100 inches from tip of nose to tip of tail.

The Polar Eskimos of northwest Greenland call the polar bear *pisugtooq,* the great wanderer. On the basis of mark-and-recapture studies and radio-tracking information, scientists have determined that individual bears wander largely within a local area; but some, indeed, are long-distance travelers. A polar bear tagged in Svalbard, for example, showed up a year later near Nanortalik, ➡

Greenland, 2000 miles to the southwest. Another bear, a female, traveled a straight-line distance of 205 miles in two days. Polar bears have also been found far afield in unlikely places, at the crest of Mount Newton in Svalbard, for example, 6600 feet above sea level, or 30 miles inland on the Greenland ice cap. An American crew on the ice island Alpha saw a female and her cub at 84°N in December 1957.

❦

Thor Larsen, a biologist who has observed polar bears in Svalbard for more than fifteen years, when I asked him about their hunting behavior, said, "Cats. They are like big cats." Fast? "It is absolutely unbelievable how fast they are—oh, do they come fast." Shrewd? "Yes. They are making judgments at every point about what to do. And they are patient."

— Period at the end of a declarative sentence

— Commas to set off a nonrestrictive appositive

— Quotation marks for dialogue

— Dash to mark an abrupt break

— Question mark to indicate a direct question

Exercise 1

Using End Punctuation   Rewrite each sentence, correcting any errors in end punctuation. If a sentence contains no errors, write *correct*.

1. How is the arctic region commonly defined.
2. Geographers describe it as the region around the North Pole lying north of the Arctic Circle.
3. The Arctic can also be defined as the area north of the tree line, which is the area where trees cannot grow.
4. How the Arctic has always fascinated people?
5. People wonder who first reached the North Pole?
6. Robert E. Peary attained this goal on April 6, 1909.
7. Can you imagine a blizzard that, in Peary's words, "surpasses in fury the sandstorms of the Sahara."
8. Imagine an immense, ice-covered ocean?
9. Water temperatures in the Arctic remain near the freezing point of salt water—about 29 degrees Fahrenheit or minus 1.7 degrees Celsius?
10. "On this great frozen Sahara of the North," wrote Peary, "the wind never ceases to blow."
11. Did you realize that many other adventurers besides Peary have explored the Arctic.
12. As recently as 1995 a group began an expedition!
13. Their goal was to traverse the Arctic by going "over the top of the world".
14. They set out from the European side of the Arctic during the winter months.
15. How surprising many people found that departure date?

Exercise 2

Using Colons and Semicolons   Rewrite each sentence, correcting any errors in the use of colons and semicolons. If a sentence contains no errors, write *correct*.

SAMPLE   Arctic winters are cold and long: summers are cool and short.
ANSWER   Arctic winters are cold and long; summers are cool and short.

1. The Arctic includes parts of the following regions; Greenland, Canada, Alaska, Russia, Finland, Sweden, and Norway.
2. Some geographers include Iceland in the Arctic: others, however, exclude it from the region.
3. These are the minerals that have been discovered in the Arctic; gold, tin, nickel, copper, and coal.
4. The climate is harsh: nevertheless, the Arctic is home to a variety of animals and plants.
5. Two features of the area are permafrost and lack of rainfall.

Exercise 3

Using the Comma   Rewrite each sentence, adding the material in parentheses in the place indicated by the caret. If the material in parentheses is *not* essential to the meaning of the sentence, add commas. If it is essential, do not add commas.

SAMPLE   The Arctic ∧ is home to many animals. (a region of extreme cold)
ANSWER   The Arctic, a region of extreme cold, is home to many animals.

1. Caribou ∧ migrate in huge herds. (similar to reindeer)
2. ∧ the caribou might not seem threatened. (No)
3. ∧ this animal has, however, been overhunted. (As a prime resource for the peoples of the Arctic)
4. Caribou are prized for their meat ∧. (which is extremely nutritious)
5. Another arctic animal ∧ is the musk ox. (that lives on the tundra)
6. ∧ musk oxen can easily withstand the bitter chill of the Arctic. (Wrapped in their dense wool)
7. Snowshoe hares ∧ seek the protection of the taiga, the forests of the Arctic North. (unlike musk oxen)
8. The taiga is also the habitat of the hare's archenemy ∧. (the lynx)
9. In 1986 ∧ Fred Buemmer estimated that fifteen thousand polar bears remained in the Arctic. (the writer)
10. A remarkable sight along the shoreline is polar bears hunting their favorite prey ∧. (the harp seal)

Exercise 4

Using the Comma   Rewrite each sentence, adding or deleting commas where necessary.

1. In general arctic animals have only two major defenses against the harsh pervasive cold.
2. Voracious eating helps animals to stay warm and insulation minimizes heat loss.
3. A seventy-pound sea otter for example frequently will eat fifteen pounds of food in an average day.
4. An otter's typical diet includes sea urchins mollusks and fish.
5. Life is feast or famine for wolves; consequently a single meal may be 25 percent of a wolf's body weight.
6. Fur, and fat, and feathers are all insulation devices that shield arctic animals from the intense cold.
7. The musk ox's long, glossy skirt of coarse, guard hair is undeniably its most striking feature.
8. Musk oxen will in fact seek shelter during severely cold weather, but their thick fur provides such excellent insulation that they routinely endure extremes of minus forty degrees Fahrenheit in the open air for prolonged periods.
9. Nature insulates many animals, but leaves humans unprotected.
10. For warmth the Inuit dress in animal skins; indeed they have long copied the animals' survival strategies.

Exercise 5

Using the Dash and Parentheses   Rewrite each sentence, adding dashes or parentheses where necessary. Use the marks of punctuation indicated in parentheses at the end of each sentence.

SAMPLE   Eric the Red he was a Norse chieftain explored Greenland in the tenth century. (parentheses)

ANSWER   Eric the Red (he was a Norse chieftain) explored Greenland in the tenth century.

1. The Dutch navigator Willem Barents a sea is named for him led a mission of exploration in 1597. (dashes)
2. Barents's arctic expedition the first in recorded history set out to survive a winter in the Far North. (dashes)
3. The Dutch were looking for a Northeast Passage a northern route from Europe to the Pacific. (dash)
4. Vitus Bering the strait between Asia and North America bears his name was a Dane in service to Russia during the eighteenth century. (parentheses)
5. The strait usually frozen from October to June is a mere fifty-five miles wide. (parentheses)

Exercise 6

Using Quotation Marks and Italics Rewrite each sentence, adding quotation marks or italics (underlining) where necessary. For the sentences that contain no errors, write *correct*.

1. In his book Arctic Dreams, Barry Lopez describes his first encounter with a narwhal.
2. According to the chapter of the book entitled Lancaster Sound, narwhals are very mysterious.
3. "We know more about the rings of Saturn, Lopez writes, than we know about the narwhal.
4. The scientific name of this whale consists of two Greek words: Monodon monoceros.
5. The first part of this name literally means "one tooth, and the second part means one horn."

Exercise 7

Using the Apostrophe Rewrite each sentence, adding or deleting apostrophes where necessary. If a sentence has no errors, write *correct*.

1. Another of Barry Lopezs major books is entitled *Of Wolves and Men*.
2. In this widely acclaimed work, Lopez studies wolve's behavior.
3. Minnesota's and Canada's wolves have drastically declined in number, Lopez reports.
4. Wolves are so shy that some people havent spotted one even after a three-month stay in the woods where wolves live.
5. Its surprising how many myths feature wolves as major characters.

Exercise 8

Proofreading

The following passage describes the artist Rockwell Kent, whose painting appears on the opposite page. Rewrite the passage, correcting the errors in spelling, usage, and grammar. Add any missing punctuation. There are twenty-five errors.

Rockwell Kent

[1]Rockwell Kent (1882–1971) was born in Tarrytown Heights a small town on the Hudson River north of New York City. [2]He was strongly influenced by these 3 teachers William Chase, Robert Henri and Abbott Thayer. [3]These men, all prominent artists portrayed American life with a clear and unsentimental eye.

[4]When he was in his early twenties. [5]Kent developed a strong interest in the landscape people, and culture of the Arctic and the Antarctic. [6]Like many other young men of his time Kent had become interested in Alaska and the Yukon after reading the novels of Jack London. [7]Kent, like London, lived an adventurous life, spending much of his time in the harsh cold climates that he loves. [8]He trap lobsters in Maine, sailed through treacherous ➡

Rockwell Kent, *The Trapper,* 1921

waters off the tip of South America and lived in the hinterlands of Alaska, Newfoundland, and Greenland.

[9]Kent were also a gifted writer. [10]He wrote and illustrated several books, including *Wilderness* (1920), which describes his travels through Alaska and *Voyaging Southward from the Strait of Magellan* (1924), which tells of his seafaring adventures in South America. [11]Kent received wide praise for the powerful evocative wood engravings that appeared in the books he illustrated during the 1920's and 1930s. [12]Developed a boldly graphic style that used strong but simple patterns and decorative designs. [13]His interest in simplicity and stylized forms is apparent in *The Trapper* which depicts a solitary man trudging through a bleak landscape.

[14]Kent would have been the ideal illustrater for Barry Lopez' *Arctic Dreams*. [15]The book was published in 1986, 15 years after Kents death). [16]Both men felt a deep affinity for the harsh landscape of the Arctic and the struggles endured by your inhabitants. [17]Lopez writes in *Arctic Dreams*, "I came to believe that people's desires and aspirations were as much a part of the land as the wind, solitary animals, and the bright fields of stone and tundra.

Mixed Review

Exercise 9

The following sentences are about Barry Lopez. Rewrite each sentence, correcting all errors in punctuation. For a sentence that contains no errors, write *correct*.

Barry Lopez

1. Barry Lopez one of Americas' foremost writers on nature was born in 1945.
2. He grew up in the postwar world of the 1950's an optimistic era in American history.
3. A precocious child Lopez began to demonstrate a gift for keen observation careful thought and precise writing even during grade school.
4. Lopez attended a prestigious privately-funded midwestern university.
5. Soon after his graduation from the University of Notre Dame (in 1966), Lopez became a full time writer.
6. However most writers (even those with great talent, find they must hold another job in order to pay for these daily necessities food shelter and clothing.
7. Isnt it ironic that Lopez said, "I never thought I would be able to make a living as a writer?"
8. "Arctic Dreams" a celebration of animals and people in the frozen Arctic was published in 1986, it earned the Francis Fuller Victor Award in nonfiction from the Oregon Institute of Literary Arts, in 1987.
9. A literary award is not simply a great honor, it also helps persuade a publisher to accept future manuscripts from a struggling young author.
10. Among the animals Lopez describes are these; polar bears, narwhals, musk ox, and caribou.
11. Most Americans you should realize, have never seen these animals in their natural habitat and they enjoy observing them vicariously through "armchair travels
12. Arctic Dreams—the work won a National Book Award explores human being's relationship with the landscape.
13. Like the nature writer, Peter Matthiessen, with whom he has been compared), Lopez of course has traveled widely in search of material for his books.
14. Other writers—William Least Heat Moon springs to mind, describe in great detail the ordinary landscapes, that are closer to home.
15. Nature which most of us take for granted is frequently the springboard that an author uses to exercise the imagination.
16. Splendidly detailed Lopezs books convey impressive amounts of carefully researched information.
17. Some readers might wonder how Lopez had the patience not to mention the time to catalog such an impressive array of facts and figures?
18. In an interview, Lopez once stated, "Writers work with metaphors.
19. For those who may have forgotten a metaphor, according to the dictionary is: a figure of speech in which a word or phrase literally denoting one kind of object or idea is used in place of another to suggest a likeness or analogy between them."
20. It is legitimate to ask whether the natural world has ever had a more thorough and eloquent chronicler than Barry Lopez?

Writing Application

Commas and Parentheses in Writing

In the following passage from *Of Wolves and Men*, Barry Lopez gives the reader a palpable sense of the wolf's reality by his attention to detail. His careful use of commas and parentheses clarifies his message and contributes to the effect. Examine the passage, focusing on the commas and the italicized words.

> The wolf weighs ninety-four pounds and stands thirty inches at the shoulder. His feet are enormous, leaving prints in the mud along a creek (*where he pauses to hunt crayfish but not with much interest*) more than five inches long by just over four wide. He has two fractured ribs, broken by a moose a year before. They are healed now, but a sharp eye would notice the irregularity. The skin on his right hip is scarred, from a fight with another wolf in a neighboring pack when he was a yearling.

Techniques with Commas and Parentheses

Try to apply some of Barry Lopez's techniques when you write and revise your own work.

1. Use commas to set off material not essential to the meaning of a sentence.

Careless Style He has two fractured ribs broken by a moose a year before.
Lopez's Style He has two fractured ribs, broken by a moose a year before.

2. Use parentheses to set off material that is purely incidental to the meaning.

Confusing Style His feet are enormous, leaving prints . . . along a creek, *where he pauses to hunt crawfish but not with much interest*, more than five inches long . . .
Lopez's Style His feet are enormous, leaving prints . . . along a creek (*where he pauses to hunt crayfish but not with much interest*) more than five inches long . . .

Practice On your paper practice these techniques by revising the following passage, adding commas, capitalization, parentheses, and other forms of punctuation where appropriate.

The West Highland white terrier commonly known as the Westie is an imaginative hunter of badgers otters, rabbits and rats. It is a "small game" dog weighing twenty pounds or less. Its fur should be double-coated, with the outer coat consisting of straight hard hair about two inches long. The ideal Westie should measure about eleven inches around the withers withers is a term borrowed from horse breeding that refers to the ridge between the shoulder bones. The ears should be small and terminate in a sharp point. Be sure to keep them free of fringes. The tail ideally measuring about six inches in length is the Westie's pride and joy and should be carried gaily.

Inside Resources

The lessons in this unit give you the skills necessary to prepare and deliver a speech, take a test, use a dictionary, and find books in the library. Each lesson is complete, concise, and easy to use.

Unit 23 **Library Resources**

23.1 **Arrangement of a Library**

Although the word *library* comes from *liber*, the Latin word for "book," modern libraries offer many resources in addition to books. Knowing how a typical library is organized can help you open up a wealth of information.

Stacks The stacks, or shelves, hold fiction and nonfiction books. Fiction books are works of the imagination, such as ... Nonfiction books, which are fact based rather than imaginative, include books about such subjects as science, history, and philosophy.

Circulation Desk A librarian or assistant librarian helps you check out books that you intend to remove from the library. When you have questions, someone at the circulation desk usually can help answer them.

Catalogs Both the card catalog and computer catalog contain information about books in the library and give their location.

Young Adult and Children's Section Fiction and nonfiction books for younger readers are often grouped in a separate part of the library.

Audio-Visual Materials Records, audiocassettes, compact discs, videos, and slides are usually grouped in a separate area of the library. Ask a librarian which audio-visual materials you can check out.

Reference The reference area holds encyclopedias, dictionaries, almanacs, atlases, and other reference materials. Some libraries have a reference librarian to help answer questions and locate specific information. Most reference materials cannot be checked out.

Newspapers and Periodicals Newspapers, and periodicals, which include magazines and journals, are published on a regular schedule. Current issues of newspapers and periodicals are kept in a general reading area. The *Readers' Guide to Periodical Literature*, an index that can help you locate specific articles, is kept in either the periodical or reference area.

Exercise 1

In which section of the library might you find these items?

1. *Newsweek* (a magazine)
2. *Hammond Contemporary World Atlas*
3. *The Phantom of the Opera* (an audiocassette of the musical)
4. *All Quiet on the Western Front* (a novel)
5. *Encyclopedia of Baseball*

728 *Library Resources*

Arrangement of a Library 729

Graphics help you comprehend complex information at a glance.

Wordworks

Puns and Tom Swifties

Ever Seen a Horse Fly?

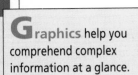

Remember when you were a kid and loved to tell silly riddles like "What's black and white and red (read) all over?" (a newspaper). This riddle is an example of a pun, or a play on words.

Shakespeare loved puns. So did Lewis Carroll, author of *Alice in Wonderland*. Here's how Mock Turtle describes his education to Alice:

"I only took the regular course."
"What was that?" enquired Alice.
"Reeling and Writhing, of course, to begin with," the Mock Turtle replied; "and then the different branches of Arithmetic—Ambition, Distraction, Uglification, and Derision."

The puns in this passage are double-sound puns—words that sound similar to other words. Homophone puns are based on different words that sound the same, such as *red* and *read*. Homograph puns are based on words that are spelled and pronounced the same but have different meanings. Benjamin Franklin used this type of pun when, after signing the Declaration of Independence, he told the gathering of revolutionaries, "We must all hang together or, most assuredly, we shall all hang separately!"

Some of the funniest puns are "Tom Swifties." In the Tom Swift stories, created by Edward Stratemeyer, Tom and his cronies never just plain said anything—they said it *happily* or *humidly* or *speedily* or in some other adverbial way. The humor in Tom Swifties occurs when the adverb describing how something is said forms a pun on what the speaker is saying, for example: "I love pancakes," said Tom flippantly.

"Try This Game," Said Tom Playfully

Match each quotation with a punning adverb below.

1. "These cherries aren't quite ripe," said Tom _____.
2. "This fire needs repair," said Tom _____.
3. "My dog just had puppies," said Tom _____.
4. "Come in out of the rain," said Tom _____.
5. "We studied the body's circulatory system," said Tom _____.

A. literally B. tartly C. dryly D. vainly E. flatly

Wordworks 721

Wordworks pages like this one provide a humorous look at how we use and misuse our language. These features appear in the first unit in Resources, which puts you in command of basic facts about the English language.

Resources and Skills

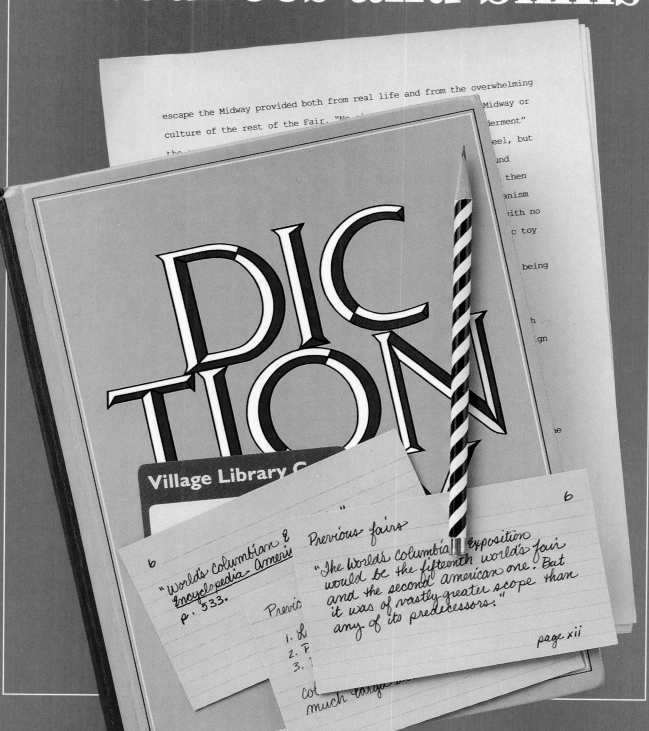

escape the Midway provided both from real life and from the overwhelming

culture of the rest of the Fair. "No ... Midway or

... eel, but

... and

... then

... anism

... ith no

... c toy

... being

... h

... gn

... e

DIC TION

Village Library C

6

"World's columbian & Encyclopedia Amer... p. 533.

Previous fairs

"The World's columbia Exposition would be the fifteenth world's fair and the second american one. But it was of vastly greater scope than any of its predecessors."

Previo...

1. L...
2. P...
3. ...

Col... much large...

page xii

Part 3 Resources and Skills

UNIT 22

Sources of English Words

Twenty years ago the following news item probably wouldn't have made much sense to most Americans. Can you imagine why?

> Muslim fundamentalists in Iran took to the streets today to support a conservative ayatollah's call for a renewed commitment to the Islamic revolution.
>
> Meanwhile, in Israel, Palestinian leaders urged support for the intifada being waged in the West Bank and Gaza.

The words *ayatollah*[1] (referring to a Muslim religious leader) and *intifada* "struggle" were unknown to most English-speaking people two decades ago. These words come from Arabic, a language with which few Americans are familiar. Yet by 1990 these words were routinely used in both broadcast and print news. How did these words find their way into English?

[1] Words from Arabic and from African and Native American languages are given in their English spellings throughout the unit.

A Living Language

Like all living languages, English is continually changing. The adoption of foreign words into English vocabulary, called borrowing, is not a new phenomenon. In fact, it's been going on from the time the language first began to take shape around A.D. 450. English has been borrowing words from conquerors and conquered, missionaries, trading partners, immigrants and a variety of other sources.

So when events in the Middle East commanded the world's attention during the latter part of the twentieth century, English simply borrowed the words it needed to describe what was happening in that region of the world. The more often such words were used, the less "foreign" they sounded, and they came to be used routinely in speech and writing.

As fresh ideas evolve and innovative technologies are developed, new English words are created to describe them. These words may be words borrowed from other languages, existing words taking on new meanings, acronyms, blends, compounds, or newly coined words, as the following examples and the chart show.

Kwanza   (borrowing from Swahili: seven-day African American cultural festival)

rap   (old word, meaning "to knock quickly," taking on a new meaning: a form of music)

AIDS   (acronym for *a*cquired *i*mmune *d*eficiency *s*yndrome)

exercycle   (blend of existing words *exercise + bicycle*)

skateboard   (compound of existing words)

cellulite   (new word for fatty deposits on the hips and thighs, coined in 1971)

In the next four lessons, you'll be introduced to some of the history and mechanisms that continue to shape the language we use. No matter where the words we speak originated, they illustrate a vital feature of English—adaptability. English is alive.

Some Recent Additions to the English Vocabulary

Borrowed Words
- perestroika (Russian: restructuring)
- contra (Spanish: literally "against"—rebel guerrilla fighter)
- satay (Thai: skewered grilled meat)

Old Words, New Meanings
- scan (to transfer words and images into electronic files)
- mouse (hand-operated device for controlling movement on a computer screen)

Acronyms
- MIRV (*m*ultiple *i*ndependently targeted *r*eentry *v*ehicle—a missile with two or more warheads)

Blends
- modem (modulator/demodulator—device for transferring computer files from one computer location to another via telephone lines)

Compounds
- virtual reality (lifelike computer simulation of the real world)
- laser disc (grooveless disc on which digital data is stored and replayed by a laser beam scanning the surface)

Exercise 1

Skim the contents of several popular magazines, such as news, personality, and special-interest magazines. Look for words that you think are in the process of being assimilated into English. These might be words from foreign languages (often italicized) or words that have been created, or adapted from existing words, to name new ideas, technologies, events, consumer goods, and so on. Make a list of the words *you* find, and define each word.

Eponyms

Making History

Have you ever wondered why men, boys, and sometimes whole groups of people are called *guys*? Well, here's the story. **Guy Fawkes was an English traitor who plotted to murder the king. Fawkes was hanged for his treason in 1606, but each year on November 5 (Guy Fawkes Day), the British burn a straw figure of Guy Fawkes in effigy. Originally, any ragged or odd-looking men—men who resembled Fawkes's straw effigy—were called *guys*. Today the word refers to men, boys, or people in general.**

François Boucher, *Madame de Pompadour* (detail), 1756

Guy Fawkes is an eponym. An eponym is a person whose name is the source for the name of someone or something. William Penn, for example, is the eponym for Pennsylvania. Madame de Pompadour (pictured at the right) gave her name to a hairstyle.

Some people have become eponyms because of their inventions or achievements. The Ferris wheel is named for George W. G. Ferris, who invented this popular ride. Louis Pasteur gave his name to pasteurization—the process of sterilizing milk and other bacteria-rich liquids.

Other people have become eponyms because their names were associated with a certain thing. Jules Léotard, for example, was a nineteenth-century French circus performer whose costume included a form-fitting body stocking—what we today call a leotard. Similarly, Samuel Maverick was a Texas cattle rancher who, unlike his fellow ranchers, refused to brand his cattle. These unbranded cattle became known as *mavericks*, and the word *maverick* has now come to mean anyone who refuses to go along with the group.

Eponymous Explorations

Look at the list of definitions on the left, and match them with their eponyms on the right.

1. A wind instrument
2. A type of car engine
3. A temperature scale
4. A railroad sleeping car
5. A unit of electricity

A. Rudolf Diesel
B. Adolphe Sax
C. George Pullman
D. James Watt
E. Gabriel Fahrenheit

22.2   Conquest and Conversion

The year is A.D. 449, and throughout the British Isles the apprehensive mood of the Celtic people is reflected in the low, gray clouds of the winter sky. The Roman legions that have enforced the rule of law in this distant outpost of the Empire have withdrawn back to Rome in what will prove to be a futile effort to repel invading barbarians from the north. The once-invincible Empire is collapsing.

Meanwhile, poised for attack just across the English Channel are three fierce Germanic tribes—the Angles, the Saxons, and the Jutes. The Celts enlisted the aid of these tribes to fight off the Picts and Scots, who attacked the Celts from the west and the north (the areas we now know as Ireland and Scotland). The Germanic warriors have routed the Picts and Scots but now will turn on their Celtic hosts, driving the Celts into the mountains of what are today Wales and Scotland. A new culture will take root on the island of Britain, and its principal language will be Anglo-Saxon, or Old English.

Emissaries from the Pope

Almost as soon as Old English was established, it began to change. Many of the language changes were due to foreign influences. Both Celtic and Anglo-Saxon already had been influenced by Latin because of the dominance of the Roman Empire. That influence increased during the sixth century when Pope Gregory, the spiritual leader of the Roman Catholic church, sent missionaries to Britain to convert the Anglo-Saxons to Christianity.

Latin into English		
Latin	**Old English**	**Modern English**
schola	scōl	school
magister	magister	master
altare	altar	altar
candela	candel	candle
vinum	wīn	wine
cuppa	cuppe	cup
templum	tempel	temple

The monks opened schools where they taught Latin to the Anglo-Saxon people. In addition, religious services were routinely conducted in Latin. Most written texts were also in Latin. As you might expect, many Latin words, especially those pertaining to school and religion, became part of the Anglo-Saxon vocabulary.

Invaders from the North

Starting around 800 the conquering Anglo-Saxons were given a taste of their own military medicine. Vikings from the Scandinavian countries to the north began raiding Engla Land (Land of the Angles) much as the Angles, Saxons, and Jutes had invaded Britain 400 years earlier. This sporadic warfare continued for over 200 years. By the eleventh century, many Norse had settled in Engla Land, and again English underwent change with the addition of Scandinavian words.

Significantly, the Scandinavians contributed three Danish words: the personal pronouns *they, their,* and *them.* This is an unusual case of one language borrowing pronouns from another language. Generally, pronouns are firmly entrenched in a language, and the native forms are not readily displaced.

Scandinavian into English		
Old Norse	**Middle English**	**Modern English**
kalla	callen	call
sæti	sete	seat
skinn	skin	skin
skȳ	sky	sky
bāthir	bothe	both
deyja	dien	die
fēlagi	felawe	fellow

Exercise 2

Each of the following words from modern English was originally borrowed from either Latin or a Scandinavian language. Use a dictionary to discover the origin of each word. Give its Latin or Scandinavian form as well as its Old or Middle English form.

1. discipline
2. low
3. skull
4. priest
5. Sabbath
6. take

Spoonerisms

Time Wounds All Heels

Have you ever made some unintentionally humorous or embarrassing slip of the tongue, such as telling someone to "ship up or shape out" when you meant to say "shape up or ship out"? Well, if that's the case, you're in good company.

At the turn of this century, an English clergyman and educator named William Spooner (pictured at right) acquired a reputation for habitually making such humorous blunders. It seems the Reverend Spooner's brain anticipated what his tongue was about to say, and he would often transpose the sounds from one word to another.

For example, when steering a prominent member of his congregation away from a reserved pew, he supposedly offered this assistance: "Let me sew you to another sheet." Another time, to the amusement of his congregation, when Spooner was delivering a sermon about half-formed wishes, he announced, "We all know what it is to have a half-warmed fish within us." The Reverend Spooner became so notorious for these linguistic bungles that people began calling them spoonerisms.

Everyone makes such slips now and then. The technical term for this normal process is metathesis. Other practitioners of the art besides Spooner include the meteorologist who forecast "rain and slow, followed by sneet" and the radio announcer who, while describing the audience at a world championship bout at Madison Square Garden, informed his listeners, "I see the beautiful Mrs. DePuyster Van Courtland looking gorgeous in her stunning white gownless evening strap."

Scrambled Sayings

Unscramble the following spoonerisms.

1. Is the bean dizzy?
2. a blushing crow
3. You have tasted a whole worm.
4. Someone is occupewing my pie.
5. a well-boiled icicle

22.3 | A Conqueror from France

The English weren't the only people to be harassed by Scandinavian warriors. Coastal areas of France were also attacked and settled. The French called the invaders *Normans*, the Old French word for "Northmen." The region of France settled by the Normans became known as Normandy.

In 1066 the seventh Duke of Normandy, William the Conqueror (pictured at right), was embroiled in a dispute for succession to the English throne. The dispute ended when William defeated King Harold II at the Battle of Hastings. William became king, and the Norman Conquest, as William's victory came to be called, altered the English language.

Parlez-vous français?

Because the conquering Normans were from France, French became the language of the aristocracy in England. The working classes still spoke English, but after several decades of French rule, English was borrowing liberally from the French language. Words relating to religion, the arts and sciences, military affairs, social life, clothing, manners, and food were taken from French.

The vocabulary of food provides an interesting example of how social class influenced the development of English. Farmers and herders were part of the working class, so the names of the animals they tended are

The Norman Invasion, 1066

SCOTLAND

IRELAND

ENGLAND

WALES

Hastings

NORMANDY

BRITTANY   MAINE

FRANCE

X Battle of Hastings
↶ Route of William I
   of Normandy

from Old and Middle English: *cou (cow)*, *cealf (calf)*, *sceap (sheep)*, *deor (deer)*, and *swin (swine)*. When these animals were prepared as elaborate dishes for the nobility, their names shifted from English to Old and Middle French: *buef (beef)*, *veel (veal)*, *moton (mutton)*, *veneison (venison)*, and *porc (pork)*.

English Borrowings from French	
Social Life	peasant (paisant), court (court)
Food	roast (rostir), sausage (saussiche)
Government	authority (auctorité), constable (conestable)
Housing	palace (palais), tower (tor)
Religion	chaplain (chapelain), saint (saint)
Arts and Sciences	music (musique), medicine (medicine)
Military	charge (chargier), powder (poudre)

Plague and War

During the fourteenth century, a terrible plague, known as the Black Death, swept across Europe and Asia. Some historians think that nearly one-fourth of the European and Asian population died from the plague during this period.

In England the plague left businesses in the towns without sufficient workers. Eventually, these jobs were filled by peasants, who spoke only English, because no proper aristocrat was about to become a tradesperson. In addition, the Hundred Years' War, which began in 1337, between England and France caused French culture to decline in favor. Soon French became a language studied only in school. English, with significant French influence, was again the principal language of England.

Exercise 3

Look up these words in a dictionary. Write the Old or Middle French word from which each of the following English words was derived.

1. bacon
2. porch
3. castle
4. boil
5. prayer
6. judge
7. gentle
8. courage
9. lieutenant

Puns and Tom Swifties

Ever Seen a Horse Fly?

R emember when you were a kid and loved to tell silly riddles like "What's black and white and red (read) all over?" (a newspaper). This riddle is an example of a pun, or a play on words.

Shakespeare loved puns. So did Lewis Carroll, author of *Alice in Wonderland.* Here's how the Mock Turtle describes his education to Alice:

"I only took the regular course."
"What was that?" enquired Alice.
"Reeling and Writhing, of course, to begin with," the Mock Turtle replied; "and then the different branches of Arithmetic—Ambition, Distraction, Uglification, and Derision."

The puns in this passage are double-sound puns—words that sound very similar to other words. Homophone puns are based on different words that sound the same, such as *red* and *read.* Homograph puns are based on words that are spelled and pronounced the same but have different meanings. Benjamin Franklin used this type of pun when, after signing the Declaration of Independence, he told the gathering of revolutionaries, "We must all hang together or, most assuredly, we shall all hang separately!"

Some of the funniest puns are "Tom Swifties." In the Tom Swift stories, created by Edward Stratemeyer, Tom and his cronies never just plain said anything—they said it *happily* or *hurriedly* or *speedily* or in some other adverbial way. The humor in Tom Swifties occurs when the adverb describing how something is said forms a pun on what the speaker is saying, for example: "I love pancakes," said Tom flippantly.

"Try This Game," Said Tom Playfully

Match each quotation with a punning adverb below.

1. "These cherries aren't quite ripe," said Tom _____.
2. "This tire needs repair," said Tom _____.
3. "My dog just had puppies," said Tom _____.
4. "Come in out of the rain," said Tom _____.
5. "We studied the body's circulatory system," said Tom _____.

A. literally B. tartly C. dryly D. vainly E. flatly

22.4　Commerce, Culture, and Settlement

Throughout its early history, English acquired most of its new words from invaders and conquerors. By the Middle Ages, however, trade had led to peaceful contacts with distant cultures whose languages further enriched the English word bank.

algebra   cipher   sugar

When traders came back from the Middle East, their cargoes of exotic imports included sugar. In Middle English sugar was called *sucre*, from the Arabic *sukkar*. Arabic was also the source of the name for the mathematical discipline of algebra, *al-jabr*; and for the numeral cipher, from the Arabic *sifr*. Later, commercial contacts with Spain added *vanilla (vainilla)*, *brocade (brocado)*, and *embargo (embargar)* to the English vocabulary.

Cultural Exchange

The exchange of goods between nations led inevitably to an exchange of culture. For example, William Shakespeare's *The Merchant of Venice*

Some English Borrowed Words		
Language	**Word**	**Date into English**
French	shanty (chantier)	1822
	depot (dépôt)	1795
Dutch	cookie (koekje)	1786
	snoop (snoepen)	1832
German	quartz (quarz)	1631
	nix (nichts)	1789
Yiddish	bagel (beygel)	1932
	klutz (klotz)	1960
Italian	ravioli (ravioli)	1611
	piano (pianoforte)	1803
Algonquian	hominy (rockahominy)	1629
	caucus (caucauasu)	1763
Spanish	alligator (el legarto)	1568
	cannibal (canibal)	1553

(1597) was based on a story written by the Italian author Giovanni Fiorentino. In contrast, Shakespeare's *Othello* (1604), adapted from an Italian story by Cinthio, was itself adapted in 1887 by Italian composer Giuseppe Verdi for his opera *Otello*. Such cultural exchanges, particularly in the field of music, led to cultural word borrowings by English. From Italian, English borrowed *stanza (stanza)*, *studio (studio)*, and *violin (violino)*.

Settling North America

As English-speaking people settled North America, contact with Native Americans soon added new words to the settlers' vocabularies. From both the Natick and Narraganset languages came *squash (askootasquash)* and from the Natick came *moccasin (mokussin)*. The chart below shows additional borrowings from Native American languages.

Borrowings from Native American Languages

tomato: from the Nahuatl word *tomatol*

cocoa: from the Nahuatl word *cacahuatl*

chipmunk: from the Algonquian, exact word unknown

Native American languages were just one influence on the English settlers' speech. The Spanish who settled in what is now the southwestern United States added *corral (corral)* and *rodeo (rodear)*. The Dutch contributed *bakery (bakkerij)* and *sleigh (slee)*. Africans brought to America in the slave trade added *gumbo* (from the Bantu *gombo*) and *banjo* (from the Kimbundu *mbanza*).

Exercise 4

Look up the following words in a dictionary. From what language was each word borrowed?

1. coleslaw
2. afghan
3. delicatessen
4. lariat
5. moose
6. tycoon

Euphemisms

Burt's Gone West

W ell," said the young man with a sigh, "Burt bought the farm this morning. Who would have thought the old guy would cash in his chips so soon? His wife's been checking out a few resting places in the memorial park. We'll all be pushing up daisies soon enough."

No, this young man isn't talking about real-estate transactions, a poker game, or gardening. He's talking about death, an unpleasant subject that most people would just as soon avoid mentioning. When people talk about it, they often employ euphemisms to soften this unpleasant fact of life.

A euphemism is an agreeable or neutral word or phrase used in place of another word or phrase that is considered harsh, insensitive, or offensive. People have created euphemisms to cover a wide variety of subjects, especially anything having to do with the human body. The concern to avoid mention of the human body was taken to absurd lengths during the Victorian era.

The Victorian era, named for Queen Victoria of England, was characterized by extreme modesty and propriety. For example, not only was it considered indecent to display one's legs, it was even thought improper to say the word *leg.* Instead, Victorians said *limb.*

Belly was another Victorian no-no. Much preferred were *tummy* and *breadbasket.* And at the dinner table, no proper Victorian, eyeing the roast chicken, would dream of shocking the other diners by requesting a breast or a thigh. *White meat* and *dark meat* became the accepted euphemisms.

Euphemistically Speaking

Try to match the words on the left with their euphemisms on the right.

1. fire	A. intelligence gathering
2. dirty	B. terminate
3. retreat	C. underprivileged
4. spying	D. strategic withdrawal
5. poor	E. unhygienic

CAT scan of human brain

Do you know what a CAT scan is? A hard drive? How about a quasar, a simulcast, or an enkephalin? All of these words are fairly recent additions to the English vocabulary, made necessary by the advance of science and technology and the need to name and describe new things, ideas, and concepts.

As the world changes, so does English. New words are invented to name and describe space exploration, computers, medical science, social movements—any new aspect of any people's culture.

Compounds and Blends

These new words arise through a variety of methods. Some are compounds, such as *meltdown*, which describes the uncontrollable burning of the fuel rods in a malfunctioning nuclear reactor. Another new compound is *cross-training*, a physical workout that combines several different types of exercise, such as running, swimming, weight lifting, and rowing.

Blending, another way new words are formed, occurs when parts of two or more words are blended into one. *Simulcast*, the process of broadcasting a program simultaneously on radio and television, is a blend of *simultaneous* and *broadcast*. *Jazzercise*, a popular form of aerobic dance, is a blend of *jazz* and *exercise*.

Acronyms

Acronyms are yet another way new words enter English. *CD*, for example, stands for *compact disc*, thin, round, silver-colored disks that contain laser-etched, digitally coded music and information. In 1963,

New Words in English			
	Word	**Date**	**Source**
Compounds and Blends	hands-on	1969	hands + on
	launch pad	1958	launch + pad
	Medicare	1955	medical + care
Acronyms	VCR	ca. 1971	*video*cassette *r*ecorder
	RV	ca. 1980s	*r*ecreational *v*ehicle
	laser	1957	*l*ight *a*mplification by *s*timulated *e*mission of *r*adiation
Existing Words, New Meanings	aerobic	1967	From "requiring air or free oxygen"; exercise that increases oxygen intake
	network	1940	From "interconnecting wires"; group of interconnected individuals who exchange

when the U.S. Postal Service wanted to speed up delivery, the service urged that all mail include a *ZIP* code, for *z*one *i*mprovement *p*lan.

Existing Words with New Meanings

Around the time of World War II, military scientists working with radar discovered short radio waves that travel in straight lines. They called this particular type of radio wave a microwave. Today, however, say *microwave* and most people assume you mean a small oven that cooks food quickly using microwave radiation. The word has taken on a new meaning.

Launder is another such example. It has always meant "to wash in water." Today it also means "to 'cleanse' money obtained from illegal or disreputable sources." Similarly, *rap* once meant "to knock." Today, *rap* is a style of music based on rhymed verses spoken to a particular beat.

Exercise 5

Make a list of new words you and your friends use in casual conversation. Most, if not all, of these words will be slang, but chances are they have their roots in other words. Which are completely new creations? Compounds or blends? Are any acronyms? Are any existing words with new meanings?

Slang

Awesome, Daddy-O!

The scene: Lou's Short Orders Deluxe on a rainy Sunday in 1952. A woman walks in and seats herself at the counter. After a quick glance at the menu, she tells the waitress she'd like two scrambled eggs on toast and some coffee. The waitress turns to the kitchen and yells, "Adam and Eve on a raft—wreck 'em—and a cup of jamoch!"

A young man who's already ordered toast and orange juice decides he'd like a couple of eggs as well. The waitress sighs and shouts to the cook, "Make that toast cackle!" A mother orders a hamburger for her daughter—"Hitch old Dobbin to a bun!" the waitress calls out.

Such colorful and inventive language was once part of the atmosphere in every American diner. The words and phrases are slang, popular, informal, faddish, and nonstandard speech. The use of slang is probably as old as language itself, but early examples of slang are difficult to document because most slang has a very brief life span. What is popular today is often long forgotten by tomorrow.

Consider a case in point. When you're leaving a party today, you might say "Catch you later" or "I'm outta here." In the 1960s you would have said "Let's split"; in the 1940s, "Let's amscray" (pig Latin for "scram"), and in the Roaring Twenties, the popular expression was "Twenty-three skiddoo!" A few years from now, the expression will change again. That's the nature of slang.

Generations of Slang

How have slang expressions changed over the years? You can find out by conducting a slang survey. First make a list of popular slang expressions you and your friends use. Assign each word to a category—such as "used when leaving," "means up-to-the-minute," and so on. Ask your parents for comparable expressions from their youth. Then do the same with your grandparents or any individuals who are, say, 70 or 80 years old. Share the results of the survey with your classmates.

Slang

1920
the cat's meow
anything desirable

1940
mess around
to kill time, hang out

1950
dig
to understand

1960
groovy
wonderful

1970
far out
great, wonderful

1980
excellent
first-rate

Library Resources

23.1   Arrangement of a Library

Modern libraries offer many resources in addition to books. Here is a typical organization.

Stacks The stacks, or shelves, hold fiction and nonfiction books. Fiction books are works of the imagination, such as novels and short-story collections. Nonfiction books, which are based on fact rather than imagination, are written about subjects such as science, history, and philosophy.

Circulation Desk A librarian or assistant librarian helps you check out books that you intend to remove from the library. When you have questions, someone at the circulation desk usually can help answer them.

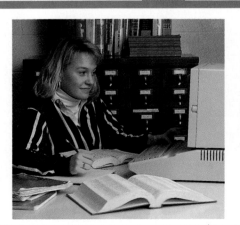

Catalogs Both the card catalog and computer catalog contain information about books in the library and give their location.

Young Adult and Children's Section Fiction and nonfiction books for younger readers are often grouped in a separate part of the library.

Audio-Visual Materials Records, audiocassettes, compact discs, videos, and slides are usually grouped in a separate area of the library. Ask a librarian which audio-visual materials you can check out.

Reference The reference area holds encyclopedias, dictionaries, almanacs, atlases, and other reference materials. Some libraries have a reference librarian to help answer questions and locate specific information. Most reference materials cannot be checked out.

Newspapers and Periodicals Newspapers, and periodicals, which include magazines and journals, are published on a regular schedule. Current issues of newspapers and periodicals are kept in a general reading area. *The Readers' Guide to Periodical Literature,* an index that can help you locate specific articles, is kept in either the periodical or reference area.

Exercise 1

In which section of the library might you find these items?

1. *Newsweek* (a magazine)
2. *Hammond Contemporary World Atlas*
3. *The Phantom of the Opera* (an audiocassette of the musical)
4. *All Quiet on the Western Front* (a novel)
5. *Encyclopedia of Baseball*

When you are searching for information about a particular subject, first decide which resource will provide the information you need. If you are conducting research for a paper, you might want to begin with more general types of resources, such as encyclopedias and dictionaries, and then refer to more specific books, articles, and tapes later.

Identify	**Look up**	**Find**	**Check out**
your resource as specifically as possible—by subject, title, or author.	your resource in the card catalog or in the *Readers' Guide to Periodical Literature*.	your resource in the stacks or in the young adult, audiovisual, reference, or periodical section.	your resource at the circulation desk, unless the material is restricted to in-library use only.

Using Catalogs

Trying to find a particular book in a library filled with books may seem overwhelming. If you know even a little about the book you want, however, you can use the card catalog to find what you need.

Card Catalog   The deep, narrow drawers of the card catalog contain cards similar to the ones below for each book in the library. Catalog cards are arranged in alphabetical order.

875
    Byrd, Richard Evelyn, 1888–
      Alone [by] Richard E. Byrd; decorations by Richard E. Harrison. New York, G. P. Putnam's sons, 1938.
    ixp., 2 l., 3-296 p.

    1. Byrd Antarctic
2. Antarctic regions

G875.B9A2
Library of Congress

875   Alone.
    Byrd, Richard Evelyn, 1888–
      Alone [by] Richard E. Byrd; decorations by Richard E. Harrison. New York, G. P. Putnam's sons,
    ixp., 2 l., 3-296 p.

    1. Byrd Antarctic
2. Antarctic regions

G875.B9A2
Library of Congress

875   Antarctic regions.
    Byrd, Richard Evelyn, 1888–
      Alone [by] Richard E. Byrd; decorations by Richard E. Harrison. New York, G. P. Putnam's sons, 1938.
    ixp., 2 l., 3-296 p. illus. 21 cm.

    1. Byrd Antarctic expedition. 2d, 1933-1935.
2. Antarctic regions. 3. Solitude. I. Title.

G875.B9A2   919.9   38—27911
Library of Congress   [59u²2]

A call number is printed in the upper left-hand corner of each card in the catalog. This number is also printed on the spine of the book. Because library books are arranged on the shelves by call numbers, knowing the exact call number allows you to locate a book easily.

Most fiction books have two cards: an author card and a title card. Nonfiction books usually have three cards in the catalog: an author card, a title card, and a subject card. Some books will also have cross-reference cards, such as the examples below. Some libraries arrange subject cards separately in a subject index. In that case author and title cards are together in an author/title index.

See card

Antarctic expeditions.

see

Antarctic regions.

See cards direct you to other ways a subject is listed in that particular library.

See also card

Antarctic regions. See also

South Pole

See also cards lead you to other possible subject headings or related subjects.

Computer Catalog   Some libraries have a computer catalog that contains the same information as a card catalog. Computer catalogs have separate ways to search for authors, titles, and subjects. For example, if you were looking for *The Good Earth* by Pearl S. Buck, you might enter *good earth* under the title search. You would then see a list of all the books that the library owns with titles that begin with the words *good earth*. Each item would be numbered; for more detailed information you would enter the item number of the book you want. The example at right shows the first listing among the four possible listings for *good earth*. Follow the on-screen prompts to operate the computer catalog, or ask a librarian to help you with the computer, if you need assistance.

```
Buck, Pearl S. (Pearl Sydenstricker), 1892-1973.
    The good earth / Pearl S. Buck. -- New York :
    The John Day Company, c1931.
    375 p. ; 22 cm.
    Spec copy: signed by the author.

LOCATION:  Olin Library
CALL NUMBER:  PS3503 U198 G65 1931
    Not charged out.  If not on shelf, ask at
    Circulation Desk.
LOCATION:  Special Collections (non-circulating)
CALL NUMBER:  PS3503 U198 G65 1931
```

Call numbers and circulation information are included in computer catalog listings. Some computer catalogs are connected to printers so that you can print out listings.

Understanding Classification Systems

Once you have found the information you need in the catalog, you are ready to look for a specific book in a particular section of the library, often in the stacks. All libraries use a system to categorize their collections and physically organize their materials. Most libraries use either the Dewey Decimal System or the Library of Congress Classification.

Dewey Decimal System   In 1876 librarian Melvil Dewey created a system that groups books into 10 broad categories based on general areas of thought and study. In a library using the Dewey Decimal System, books are shelved according to the following categories.

Dewey Decimal System			
Category Numbers	Major Category	Examples of Subcategories	Sample Book Titles
000–099	General works	Encyclopedias, bibliographies	*The Lifetime Reading Plan* *The Cambridge Encyclopedia of China*
100–199	Philosophy	Ethics, psychology	*The Senses of Animals and Men* *Sleep and Dreams*
200–299	Religion	Theology, mythology	*Greek Gods and Heroes* *What Is Islam?*
300–399	Social sciences	Sociology, education	*Society and Change* *World Perspectives in Education*
400–499	Language	Dictionaries, foreign languages	*A Hog on Ice and Other Curious Expressions* *The Story of English*
500–599	Sciences	Chemistry, astronomy, math	*From Zero to Infinity* *How to Make and Use a Telescope*
600–699	Technology	Medicine, engineering	*How Things Work* *The Artificial Heart*
700–799	Arts	Painting, music, theater, sports	*Women Artists* *African Roots of Jazz*
800–899	Literature	Poetry, plays, essays	*Life with Father* *A Street in Bronzeville*
900–999	History and geography	Ancient history, biography, travel	*Isaac Newton: Reluctant Genius* *A History of Mexico*

These general categories contain subcategories—the more specific the topic, the more specific the classification number. Additional categories are indicated by adding a decimal and more numbers. For example, look at the Dewey Decimal number below for *The Ultimate Skateboard Book*.

700   The arts   A book about the arts would be listed in the 700s.

790   Recreation and performing arts   A book about recreation would be further categorized as 790.

796   Outdoor games   A book about outdoor games would be classified as 796.

796.2   Games requiring equipment   Additional categories are indicated by adding a decimal and more numbers.

796.2

Books are shelved by Dewey Decimal number and then by author. For instance, two books about African American society would both be filed in the 301.45 section, but a book by W.E.B. Du Bois would appear before a book by Henry Louis Gates.

Many libraries that use the Dewey Decimal System do not assign classification numbers to fiction books. Instead, the first line of the call number is either an *F* or *Fic* to indicate a fictional work, and the second line contains the first three letters of the author's last name. Fiction works are organized alphabetically on the shelves by authors' last names. If a library has more than one book by the same author, those books are also alphabetized by title.

Library of Congress Classification   Some libraries use the Library of Congress Classification, or LC. This system divides books into 21 general categories; each category is assigned a letter, as shown in the chart on the next page. Many libraries with a large number of books that cover a vast number of subjects use the LC.

Like the Dewey Decimal System the LC has subcategories, identified by additional letters and numbers. Study the following LC call number for the book *Planets* by Carl Sagan.

QB   The general category is Q for science, and the minor category is B for astronomy.

601   The number 601 stands for a category within astronomy.

.S34   Divisions within a category are indicated by letters and numbers to the right of a decimal point.

Library of Congress Classification System			
Category Letter	Major Category	Category Letter	Major Category
A	General works	N	Fine arts
B	Philosophy, psychology, religion	P	Language and literature
		Q	Science
C–F	History	R	Medicine
G	Geography, anthropology, recreation	S	Agriculture
		T	Technology
H	Social sciences	U	Military science
J	Political science	V	Naval science
K	Law	Z	Bibliography and library science
L	Education		
M	Music		

Special Sections Special categories of books, such as reference, biography, and oversize, are often grouped in separate sections. Letters above the call number indicate that a book is in a special section. For example, a *B* denotes a biography. The call number on the catalog card matches the number on the spine of the book.

R or *Ref* identifies a reference book. You would find a book having this Dewey Decimal number in the reference area.

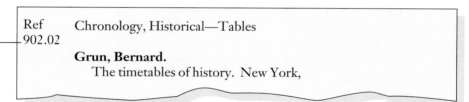

> Ref 902.02   Chronology, Historical—Tables
>
> **Grun, Bernard.**
>   The timetables of history. New York,

Checking the Shelves

Once you have the call number of a resource, you are ready to continue your investigation in the stacks or in a special section.

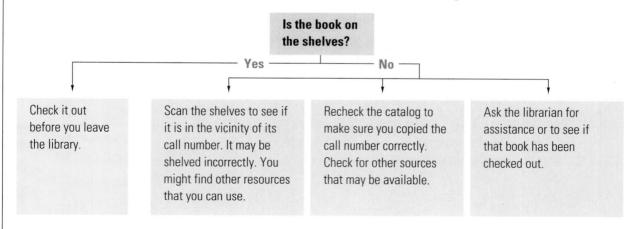

Is the book on the shelves?

Yes —————— No

Check it out before you leave the library.

Scan the shelves to see if it is in the vicinity of its call number. It may be shelved incorrectly. You might find other resources that you can use.

Recheck the catalog to make sure you copied the call number correctly. Check for other sources that may be available.

Ask the librarian for assistance or to see if that book has been checked out.

Use the card catalog or computer catalog to find a book for each of the following topics. List the author, title, call number, and publication date of the books you find.

1. How to speed-read
2. Astronomy
3. Stand-up comedy
4. Indonesia
5. General background information for stage crews
6. Inventors
7. Trends in twentieth-century Japanese literature
8. Family life in Mexico
9. A book by Margaret Mead
10. A collection of letters
11. A book by Paule Marshall
12. Robots
13. A history of soldiers
14. Korean folktales
15. The economy of Nigeria
16. A book on the American Civil War by Shelby Foote
17. A trip through China
18. Mathematics and numbers
19. Sensory perception
20. Great speeches

23.3   Using a Periodicals Index

Looking at newspapers and periodicals can be especially helpful if you are studying current events. Newspapers and periodicals, such as magazines and journals, provide the best source of up-to-date information.

Locating Periodicals and Newspapers

Recent issues of magazines, journals, and sometimes newspapers are often kept on open shelves in a reading area. Back issues of newspapers are usually stored on microforms, which are small photographs of printed pages. Reproduced on either microfilm (filmstrips) or microfiche (film cards), microforms can be viewed on a special machine that enlarges the photographs so they can be read. Some of these viewing machines also allow you to make photocopies. Back issues of magazines are either bound in hardback volumes, grouped by month or year, or stored on microforms.

Using the *Readers' Guide*

Special reference books called indexes help you find the most recent periodicals information. One widely used index of periodicals is the *Readers' Guide to Periodical Literature*. Articles from more than 175 magazines are indexed by author and subject. Paperback editions of this index are published every two weeks, larger paperback editions covering a three-month period are published quarterly, and hardbound volumes of a year's entries are issued annually. The following annotated excerpts from the *Readers' Guide* show you how to read the information in the index.

Subject heading

Article title and title enhancement

Magazine citation

***See also* cross-reference**

Author of article

> **BASEBALL RECORDS**
> Henderson steals way into baseball history by topping
> Lou Brock. il pors *Jet* 80:46–7 My 20 '91
> Wizard of Whiff, Sultan of Swipe [N. Ryan's no-hitter
> and R. Henderson's 939th stolen base]. W. Shapiro.
> il por *Time* 137:55 My 13 '91
> **BASEBALL THROWING**
> *See also*
> Pitching (Baseball)
> **BASEMENTS**
>
> Waterproofing
> *See* Waterproofing
> **BASES (MILITARY)** *See* Military bases
> **BASHFULNESS IN CHILDREN**
> The bold and the bashful. G. Cowley il *Newsweek* 117
> Special Issue: 24–5+ Summ '91

The magazine citation tells you exactly where the article can be found. It lists the name, volume number, page numbers, and date of the periodical in which the article appears.

***See* cross-reference**

Subheading

Author entry

> **BASS TOURNAMENTS** *See* Fishing—Competitions
> **BATAVIA (N. Y.)**
> Social conditions
> Back to Batavia. B. Kauffman. *The American Scholar*
> 60:223–33 Spr '91
> **BATCH FILES (COMPUTER SCIENCE)**
> Serve up better-looking, more useful batch files.
> C. DeVoney. *PC Computing* 4:182 Ap '91
> **BATES, KAREN GRIGSBY**
> Are you my mother? il *Essence* 21:49–50+ Ap '91
> **BATHROOMS**
> The bathroom. il *Good Housekeeping* 212:180 Ap '91
> Lively bath in the treetops. il *Southern Living* 26:126
> Ap '91

Using the excerpts from the *Readers' Guide* on the opposite page, answer the following questions.

1. Who is the author of the article about computer batch files?
2. Where in the *Readers' Guide* would articles about bass tournaments be listed?
3. Which magazine contains an article by Karen Grigsby Bates?
4. Under what subject heading would you look for articles about waterproofing a basement?
5. Who are the subjects of the article entitled "Wizard of Whiff, Sultan of Swipe," listed under the heading "Baseball Records"?
6. In which magazine would you find an article about Batavia, New York?
7. On which page in *Good Housekeeping* does an article about bathrooms appear?
8. What is the title of G. Cowley's article about bashfulness in children?
9. Which magazine features an article about the breaking of Lou Brock's baseball record?
10. How many articles about bathrooms are listed in this edition of the *Readers' Guide?*

23.4   Using Reference Works

Knowing what library materials are available and how to use them can help you find information quickly and easily for class assignments and research papers. If you want to track down specific details, such as names, dates, or other facts, or if you just want to satisfy your curiosity about something, most research begins in the reference area.

General Reference Works

You probably know about and use many general reference works, such as encyclopedias, almanacs, and atlases. When conducting research, ask a librarian about specialized reference works, such as specialized encyclopedias and various literary reference works, that might provide more detailed information.

An encyclopedia yearbook, a separate volume in a set of encyclopedias, contains the most recently available information for the year prior to the yearbook's publication. Yearbooks contain current information, such as annual chronologies, obituaries, and in-depth articles on political, cultural, and social events, not included in the regular volumes of the encyclopedia.

Using General Reference Works to Answer Questions		
Question	**Where to Look for an Answer**	**Examples of Sources to Check**
Were any Civil War battles fought in Indiana?	**Encyclopedias** include general information on a variety of topics.	• *Grolier Encyclopedia* • *World Book Encyclopedia* • *Encyclopaedia Britannica*
Who were the recipients of Pulitzer Prizes in letters for fiction and for general nonfiction in 1989?	**Almanacs and yearbooks** provide statistics, lists, and detailed information on recent issues.	• *Information Please Almanac* • *Guinness Book of World Records*
What is the coldest month of the year in Lima, Peru?	**Atlases** are collections of maps. They often include special maps on climate, land use, history, and other features.	• *Hammond Contemporary World Atlas* • *Times Atlas of World History* • *Cambridge Atlas of Astronomy*
Where was Ernest Hemingway born?	**Biographical reference works** include short life histories of noteworthy individuals, both living and deceased.	• *Webster's New Biographical Dictionary* • *Current Biography* • *Dictionary of American Biography*

Specialized Reference Works

Literary reference works provide information both about writers and about their work. Literary criticism or biographical information on authors is collected in several different sources, such as the *Literary Criticism Series* and *Contemporary Authors*. Books of quotations, such as Bartlett's *Familiar Quotations*, index well-known sayings. If you know the first line of a poem or even just part of a title, poetry indexes, such as *Granger's Index to Poetry*, can help you find a specific poem.

A library's collection of news clippings, pamphlets, and brochures on current events and topics is called the vertical file. This material is arranged alphabetically by subject and is usually stored by the library in a set of file cabinets.

Parts of a Book

Using all parts of a book, not just the main text, can help you determine whether a book has the information you need. Some information, including the introduction, table of contents, copyright page, and title page, is found in the front of a book, before the main text. The pages after the main text contain other useful sources, such as the appendix, glossary, bibliography, and index.

Using a Book Effectively	
Questions	**Where to Look for an Answer**
Does this book have more than one author?	The **title page** contains the complete book title, edition number, and names of authors or editors.
Will this book contain information about developments in this field during 1990?	The **copyright page** tells when a book was first published and when it was updated.
Will this book contain information on my topic?	The **table of contents** identifies the main topics covered in the book.
Was the author intending to thoroughly inform, persuade, or briefly analyze?	The **introduction, preface,** or **foreword** indicates the author's purpose in writing the book.
Will I be able to trace any of the quotations cited by this author to their original sources?	The **bibliography** lists information sources for material covered in the book.
Would this be a good source of visuals I could adapt and re-create to use in an oral presentation?	The **appendix** contains additional information, such as maps, charts, tables, illustrations, or graphs.
If this book is highly technical, will I be able to easily understand the terms used?	The **glossary** alphabetically lists special or unfamiliar terms used in the book.
Have the individuals I am researching been written about in this book? If so, how much is written about them?	The **index** lists alphabetically all people, places, events, and significant topics covered in the book.

Exercise 4

Use this textbook or the reference works in your school library to answer the following questions.

1. How many composition units are in this book?
2. How many pages are in the index of this book?
3. Who won the Academy Award for best actress in 1988?
4. Were Herod and Herod Antipas the same person? Explain your answer.
5. Where is Mount Kilimanjaro?
6. What are Guatemala's chief crops?
7. Who wrote the poem "The Waste Land"?
8. Who was the first person recorded as running one mile in less than four minutes?
9. Which planet was the most recently discovered?
10. When did Henry "Hank" Aaron retire as a baseball player?

Using Dictionaries

24.1 General Dictionaries

Through its alphabetical listing of words with their definitions, called entries, dictionaries can tell you about almost everything. Most dictionaries fall into one of the categories below.

Unabridged Dictionaries
250,000 or more entries

Characteristics
- Extensive word histories
- Detailed definitions
- May be in several volumes
- Found mostly in libraries

Examples
- *Random House Dictionary of the English Language*
- *Webster's Third New International Dictionary*

College Dictionaries
About 150,000 entries

Characteristics
- Detailed enough to answer most questions on spelling or definitions
- Widely used in schools, homes, and businesses

Examples
- *Random House Webster's College Dictionary*
- *American Heritage Dictionary of the English Language*
- *Webster's New World Dictionary*

School Dictionaries
90,000 or fewer entries

Characteristics
- Base definitions on students' backgrounds
- Emphasizes common words

Examples
- *Macmillan Dictionary*
- *Webster's School Dictionary*

The Organization of Entries

With many entries to search through, how do you find the one you want? Guide words, the first and last words listed on the page, can help you locate entries much more quickly than if you simply browse. The sample dictionary page opposite shows the organization of word entries and how to use guide words and the pronunciation key.

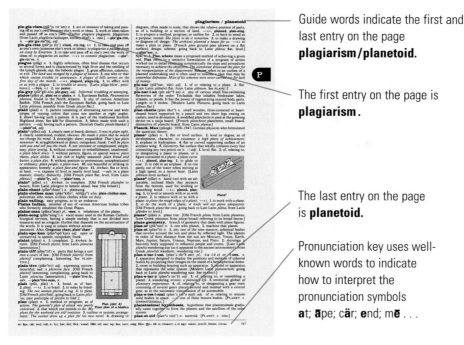

Guide words indicate the first and last entry on the page
plagiarism/planetoid.

The first entry on the page is
plagiarism.

The last entry on the page is
planetoid.

Pronunciation key uses well-known words to indicate how to interpret the pronunciation symbols
at; **ā**pe; **c**ä**r; **e**nd; m**ē** . . .

If you do not know how to spell a word, you can usually find it in a dictionary if you try to sound it out. You may also want to look at the tips for improving your spelling presented in Unit 26. The following tips suggest other ways of finding unfamiliar words.

Tips on Finding Unfamiliar Words

1. Consider whether the word contains silent consonants. They might appear at or near the beginning of a word, such as *k* in *knife* and *h* in *rhyme*. Silent consonants may also appear in the middle of a word, such as *b* in *debt* and *gh* in *night*.

2. Consider alternative spellings of consonants. For example, the *sh* sound can be spelled several ways, as in these words: *ocean, tissue, election, chandelier, special, conscious,* and *sugar.*

3. Consider alternative spellings of vowels. Some vowel sounds are formed by combinations of vowels, such as the *ā* sound in *paid, suede, eight, obey,* and *break.*

4. Check a larger dictionary. Even if you have the right spelling in mind, a school dictionary may not contain the word you need. If you can't find the word in a college or unabridged dictionary, try the above tips again.

The Main Entries

The main part of a dictionary consists of word entries and their definitions. Other information is given as well. The entry for *forbid* on the next page shows some of the main information in an entry.

The entry word is listed first.

The pronunciation is indicated by symbols.

Inflected forms, such as past tense and past participle for a verb, are sometimes listed.

The part or parts of speech that the word takes are indicated.

The etymology explains the history of a word.

for·bid (fər bid′, fôr-) **-bade** (-bad′, -bād′) or **-bad** (-bad′), **bid·den** or *(archaic)* **-bid**, **-bid·ding**, *v.t.* **1.a.** to command (someone) not to do something; refuse to allow: *I forbid you to go out.* **b.** to prohibit (something); ban: *to forbid the wearing of makeup.* **2.** to command to keep away from; bar or exclude from: *I forbid you the car.* **3.** to stand in the way of or make impossible; hinder; prevent: *The snowstorm forbids air travel.* [Old English *forbēodan* to prohibit, restrain.]
Syn. 1. Forbid, prohibit mean to order that something not be done. **Forbid** suggests a direct command from an authority who expects to be obeyed: *The airline forbids smoking on takeoff and landing.* **Prohibit** implies a legal order, as by statute, or a less arbitrary command: *The law prohibits smoking on the subways.*

Syllabication   The entry word indicates how to divide, or hyphenate, a word of more than one syllable. Notice how *for·bid* is divided by the dot. A word entry may also indicate when a word is a solid compound, such as *folklore*, a hyphenated compound, such as *follow-up* when used as a noun or an adjective, or two words, such as *folktale*.

Synonyms   When an entry includes synonyms, words with similiar meanings, it often also includes examples to help you distinguish between the meanings. Compare the synonyms *forbid* and *prohibit* in the example above.

Homographs   Words that are spelled the same but have different meanings and histories are called homographs. They are listed separately and identified by small, raised numerals after the word. If pronunciation varies between different homographs, these pronunciations are noted in the entry. Two separate entries are listed below for *meal*.

Some homographs, like meal[1] and meal[2], have the same pronunciations.

Notice the different etymologies for these homographs.

meal[1] (mēl), *n.* **1.** the food served and eaten at one time or occasion. **2.** one such regular time or occasion for eating. [bef. 900; ME *mel*, OE *mǣl* measure, fixed time, occasion, meal, c. OFris *mel* (meal)time, OHG *māl*, ON *māl*. Go *mēl* time, hour] **—meal′less,** *adj.*
meal[2] (mēl), *n.* **1.** a coarse, unsifted powder ground from the edible seeds of any grain: *barley meal.* **2.** any ground or powdery substance, as of nuts or seeds. [bef. 900; ME *mele*, OE *melu*, c. OFris *mele*, OS, OHG *melo*, ON *mjǫl*; akin to Go *malan*, L *molere* to grind; cf. MILL[1]] **—meal′less,** *adj.*

de·pre·ci·ate (di prē′ shē āt′), *v.*, **-at·ed, -at·ing. —***v.t.* **1.** to reduce the purchasing value of (money). **2.** to lessen the value or price of. **3.** to claim depreciation on (a property) for tax purposes. **4.** to represent as of little value or merit; belittle. **—***v.i.* **5.** to decline in value. [1640–50; < LL *dēprētiātus* undervalued, ptp. of *dēpretiāre* (in ML sp. *dēpreciāre*) = L *dē-* DE- + *-pretiāre*, der. of *pretium* PRICE + *-ātus* -ATE¹] **—de·pre′ci·at′ing·ly,** *adv.* **—de·pre′ci·a′tor,** *n.* **—Usage.** See DEPRECATE.

Cross-references direct you to other main entries for information that may help you understand a word's meaning and when to use it.

dep·re·cate (dep′ ri kāt′), *v.t.*, **-cat·ed, -cat·ing.** . . . **—Usage.** The most current sense of DEPRECATE is "to express disapproval of." In a sense development still occasionally criticized. DEPRECATE has come to be synonymous with the similar but etymologically unrelated word DEPRECIATE in the sense "belittle": *The author deprecated the importance of his work.* In *self-* compounds, DEPRECATE has almost totally replaced DEPRECIATE in modern usage: *She charmed the audience with a self-deprecating account of her career.*

Usage information explains the differences between the uses of certain words.

Cross-references The entry for *depreciate* lists a cross-reference to *deprecate*. The usage information for *deprecate* shows you that *depreciate* and *deprecate* sometimes have the same meaning; however, *deprecate* has almost totally replaced *depreciate* in certain situations.

Usage Information Some definitions may be preceded by usage labels. These labels indicate when to use a particular definition of a word. For example, the label "baseball" appears before a definition of the term *hit-and-run*. The label tells you that the definition that follows is used only when describing a baseball play. The following chart describes different kinds of usage information.

Usage Information in Dictionary Entries		
Type of Information	**Description**	**Example**
Capitalization	Indicates when a word or a particular meaning of a word needs to be capitalized	**southeast** . . . **3. the Southeast.** southeastern part of the United States.
Out-of-date usage	Labels words as obsolete—no longer used—or archaic—once used commonly but now used only in special contexts	**quick** . . . **1.** *Archaic.* living; alive.
Special field usage	Indicates with subject labels a definition that is restricted to a particular study or area of reference	**fly²** . . . **8.** *Baseball.* to hit a fly ball.
Regional usage	Indicates how a word is used in a certain geographical area	**tonic** . . . **5.** *Chiefly Eastern New Eng.* soda pop.
Usage note	Provides general guides for using (or not using) words in particular situations	**scorcher** . . . **2.** *Informal.* an extremely hot day.

Other Information in Dictionaries

In addition to a greater number of word entries, some larger dictionaries include separate biography and geography sections. A biography section alphabetically lists names of important people and provides brief details about them. Names of cities, countries, and other geographical areas and information about them are alphabetically listed in the geography section. These sections usually appear at the back of the dictionary, after the main entries.

Exercise 1

Use a school or college dictionary to answer the following questions.

1. Who was Ho Chi Minh?
2. How is the word *passerine* hyphenated?
3. What is the plural of *hero*?
4. What are the guide words for the page on which *hakim* is listed?
5. What does *try* mean in the game of rugby?
6. What are the origins of the two homographs of *fair*?
7. What synonyms are given for *fashion*?
8. Is *Draconian* always capitalized? Explain your answer.
9. Does the word *queue* rhyme with *me* or with *you*?
10. What is the origin of *cantaloupe*?

24.2 Thesauruses

One special type of dictionary is a collection of synonyms, also known as a thesaurus. Such a book can help a writer choose just the right word in a given context. Even though a thesaurus is a type of dictionary, it is used in the opposite way from most dictionaries. You usually refer to a dictionary to find the meaning of a certain word. You refer to a thesaurus when you know the meaning you want to convey but need a specific word to express that meaning.

Thesaurus Formats

The best-known thesaurus is *Roget's*, first developed by British doctor Peter Mark Roget, in 1852. Roget organized large lists of words into broad categories, such as *color* and *honor*. He then developed an index to the categories. This original thesaurus format is still used. To use this type of thesaurus, you first check the index. Then refer to one of the lists of possible synonyms given in the index.

Dictionary-style Entries

A dictionary-style thesaurus, which organizes words alphabetically rather than in categories, is also widely used. In the dictionary format each word entry is followed by several synonyms and cross-references to related major categories. A major category includes nouns, verbs, adjectives, and adverbs all related to one main idea. Most major category entries also include cross-references to antonyms. The following entry for the major category *generality* shows the main parts of a thesaurus entry.

GENERALITY

Nouns—**1**, generality, generalization; universality, broadness, collectivity; average; catholicity, catholicism; miscellany, miscellaneousness; prevalence; DISPERSION.

2, everyone, everybody [and his brother]; all hands, all the world and his wife; anybody. *Colloq.*, whole kit and caboodle. *Slang*, the works.

Verbs— be general, prevail, be going about; generalize, render general.

Adjectives—general, generic, collective; broad, comprehensive, sweeping; encyclopedic, widespread, dispersed; universal, catholic, common, all-inclusive, worldwide; ecumenical; transcendental; prevalent, prevailing, rife, epidemic, besetting; all over, covered with; every, all; unspecified, impersonal; customary (see HABIT).

Adverbs—generally, in general, generally speaking; always, for better or worse; for the most part, in the long run; whatever, whatsoever; to a man, one and all, all told.

Antonym, see SPECIALITY.

Major categories appear in boldfaced, capital letters.

In this thesaurus synonyms are listed by part of speech.

Cross-references to other major categories appear in capital letters.

Antonyms can be located by referring to the cross-reference at the end of an entry.

Exercise 2

Using a thesaurus, find one synonym for each word below. Then find one antonym for each word listed below. Finally, write an original sentence to illustrate the meaning of either the synonym or the antonym for each word listed. You may wish to check the exact meaning of each word in a dictionary before you use it in a sentence.

1. ability (noun)
2. defeat (verb)
3. modesty (noun)
4. move (verb)
5. strong (adjective)
6. fear (noun)
7. courtesy (noun)
8. difficult (adjective)
9. growth (noun)
10. talk (verb)

Vocabulary

25.1   Building Vocabulary

With Marcie's helpful tips whispered in her ear, Peppermint Patty might yet develop a stronger vocabulary. Like any student, the better she understands words and their meanings, the better equipped she will be to communicate with others.

Developing Your Vocabulary

You probably hear or read at least one new word a day. What do you do when you come across a word you don't know? Rather than skipping over or tuning out an unfamiliar word, you can develop strategies for learning and remembering the new words you encounter. The following steps suggest ways to strengthen your vocabulary.

Steps in Learning and Remembering a New Word

1. **Notice** new words while reading or listening. You might want to keep a new-word journal in which you record unfamiliar words and their meanings.

2. **Understand** the meaning of a new word by studying the context—the surrounding words that are familiar—or checking a dictionary, or doing both.

3. **Verify** your understanding of a word with someone else. A teacher or a friend may be able to tell you if you correctly understand the meaning of a word.

4. **Use** the new word in your speaking and writing. For one week, try to use the new word at least once a day. You might want to double-check the meaning to be sure you're using the word appropriately.

You might also want to study vocabulary with someone—a friend or a small group of classmates. Then you can share your journals, agree to use new words with each other, and help each other figure out the meanings of some items. Your teachers will support you in your efforts. The chart below suggests a few ways to increase your vocabulary, both on your own and with other people.

Tips for Discovering New Words
1. Read extensively in a variety of areas. The more time you spend reading quality material, the more new words you are certain to encounter.
2. Use a thesaurus. Especially when you write, challenge yourself to use new vocabulary. Try to replace "worn out" verbs, such as forms of the verb *to be,* with vivid verbs.
3. Play word games. There are many word games on the market that can be challenging and fun, but you might enjoy inventing a game of your own.

Learning from Context

An unfamiliar word nearly always appears among other words that are familiar to you. These surrounding words provide the context of the new word. Thinking about the meaning of the rest of the phrase, sentence, paragraph, or passage and analyzing how the unknown word fits into that meaning helps you figure out the meaning of the new word.

Analyzing Specific Clues   Writers often supply clues that help you figure out the meanings of unfamiliar words. Notice how the sentence structure provides clues to the meaning of *mélange*.

> Our last talent show had a *mélange* of acts: classical vocalists, jugglers, gymnasts, tap dancers, and performance artists.

The colon tells you that examples of the acts follow. Because the examples are diverse, you might guess that *mélange* means "a mixture." In the following sentence, clue words can help you determine the meaning of *impediment*.

> The Postal Service allows no *impediment,* such as bad weather, to prevent the delivery of mail.

The clue phrase is *such as.* Bad weather is an example of an impediment. You can figure out that the Postal Service does not let any obstacle, like bad weather, get in its way. *Impediment* means "obstacle."

The chart on the next page describes different types of context clues and the specific clue words that help you interpret them. In the "Example" column, the clue words are in bold type. The unfamiliar words and the words that indicate a definition are in italics.

Interpreting Clue Words		
Type of Context Clue	**Clue Words**	**Example**
Definition: The meaning of the unfamiliar word is stated in the sentence.	that is in other words or also known as which means	The lecturer was *verbose;* **in other words,** he was *long-winded.*
Example: The meaning of the unfamiliar word is explained through one familiar case.	like for example such as for instance including	The paramedic quickly checked Amy's *vital signs,* **including** her *pulse rate and body temperature.*
Comparison: The unfamiliar word is similar to a familiar word or phrase.	also likewise similarly resembling identical	Joan's friend testified to her *veracity;* **likewise,** her teacher said Joan's *honesty* was evident to all who knew her.
Contrast: The unfamiliar word is the opposite of a familiar word or phrase.	but on the other hand on the contrary unlike however	Rachel is always *punctual,* **unlike** Brendan, who is usually *late.*
Cause and effect: The unfamiliar word describes a cause in a sentence in which the effects are understood.	because since therefore as a result consequently	Maria felt the stranger was being *intrusive* **because** he *asked too many personal questions.*

Analyzing the General Context   What if the context of an unfamiliar word has no specific clue words? You can still interpret unfamiliar words when the context clues are more general. After figuring out the part of speech of the unfamiliar word, you can try to figure out the idea of the word from supporting and contrasting details, as shown in the following examples.

> Because your friend Jesse was reading a book about the field of *ornithology*, she went to the library to view some of John James Audubon's famous drawings of birds.

How can you figure out the meaning of *ornithology?* You know from the passage that ornithology is a field of study. You also know that Jesse wanted to look at drawings of birds while she was reading about that subject. Therefore, you might deduce that *ornithology* is the study of birds.

The satellite was 670 miles from Earth at its *apogee* but only 260 miles away at its *perigee*.

What are the meanings of *apogee* and *perigee*? You know these two words are nouns since they are both objects of a preposition in a prepositional phrase. The particular measurements cited must be significant. You might guess that the *apogee* is the farthest point away from Earth in the satellite's orbit, while the *perigee* is the closest point.

You can see that being a good word detective helps you figure out unfamiliar words. Paying attention to all the surrounding details and to the general tone of a passage can help you learn many new words. If you carefully examine the context, you can often wait until a more convenient time to consult a dictionary or a more knowledgeable source. Checking to see if you guessed correctly, however, is a good habit to form.

Exercise 1

Each of the following passages contains an italicized word that may be unfamiliar to you. Determine the meaning by examining the context, looking for the different types of context clues described in the chart on page 780. Write the italicized word and its meaning. Then indicate the strategy used in each case by writing either *definition, example, comparison, contrast,* or *cause and effect.* Check your work in a dictionary afterward to see how close you came to figuring out the word meanings.

1. Like the other volunteers, Gayle did not expect payment for her *gratis* performance at the community center.
2. Copper is highly *malleable*, that is, easily shaped.
3. The first day of winter was *balmy*, and the days that followed were similarly mild.
4. Because this room is so small, you don't need a *stentorian* voice to be heard.
5. The village was *enshrouded*, or covered, in a thick fog.
6. Although Eduardo is an *immaculate* housekeeper, his twin sister, Mercedes, is an untidy person.
7. Michael's *acrophobia* was intense; likewise, his father also had an overwhelming fear of heights.
8. *Contiguous* countries, such as the United States and Canada, usually have border patrols.
9. Before the accident my car bumper was perfectly *symmetrical;* however, it is now uneven.
10. Teresa joined a *philately* club because she enjoyed looking at stamps from different countries.

Another way to understand words is by analyzing their parts. The main part of a word is its root. When this is a complete word, it is called a base word. A root can be thought of as the "spine" of the word: it gives the word its backbone of meaning. It is often combined with a prefix (a part attached to the beginning), a suffix (a part attached to the end), or another root. Prefixes and suffixes often change the direction of a word's meaning. Look at the following example.

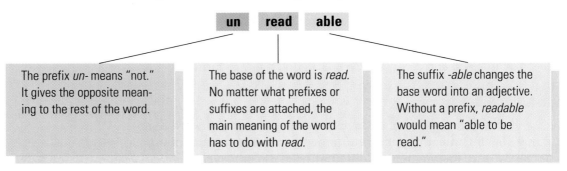

The prefix *un-* means "not." It gives the opposite meaning to the rest of the word.

The base of the word is *read.* No matter what prefixes or suffixes are attached, the main meaning of the word has to do with *read*.

The suffix *-able* changes the base word into an adjective. Without a prefix, *readable* would mean "able to be read."

Analyzing its parts, you can see that the word *unreadable* means "not able to be read."

Word Roots

While prefixes and suffixes can change a word's meaning, remember that the root gives the word its central meaning. The following words have the same root.

therm: ?

You may know that a meter is a unit of measure and that a thermometer measures heat. You may also know that *static* can mean "motionless" and that a thermostat is a device that keeps the amount of heat steady. Finally, you may know that *geo* means "earth" and that *geothermal* means "related to heat produced by the earth." Since all three words in the chart above concern heat and contain the root *therm*, you can infer that *therm* has something to do with heat. If you didn't know the meaning of one of the words above, you could begin to figure it out by using what you know about *therm*. The table opposite shows some words that share roots.

Analyzing Word Roots		
Words	**Meanings**	**Roots**
animate unanimous	having life being of one mind	*anima* means "mind" or "life"
anarchy archives	without government government records	*arch* means "rule" or "govern"
beneficial benevolent	good, helpful inclined to do good	*ben* means "good"
recede proceed	go back, yield again go forward	*ced* means "go"
contradict dedicate	to say the opposite of to say when giving	*dic* and *dict* mean "say" or "speak"
facsimile factory	a thing made similar to another a place where things are made	*fac* and *fact* mean "make"
general generate	affecting whole class to start or create	*gen* means "class" or "origin"
hydrant dehydrate	a large pipe used to draw water to remove water	*hydr* means "water"
manuscript manual	document written by hand done by hand	*man* means "hand"
portable porter	capable of being carried one who carries	*port* means "carry"
science omniscient	knowledge about the natural world knowing everything	*sci* means "know"
stringent unrestricted	binding, severe not bound, free	*string* and *strict* mean "bind"
traction extract	friction when pulling across a surface to pull out	*trac* means "draw" or "pull"
vivacious revive	full of life, lively bring back to life	*viv* means "live" or "alive"

Prefixes

Prefixes are syllables attached before a root to alter or enhance its meaning. Though the English language does not contain as many prefixes as suffixes, prefixes are still important tools for understanding and learning new words.

A prefix can sometimes completely change the meaning of a word. For example, the prefix *un-* gives the opposite meaning to any word to which it is attached. The following chart shows other valuable prefixes and their meanings. Notice that some prefixes have more than one meaning and that sometimes several different prefixes can convey the same meaning.

Analyzing Prefixes		
Words	**Meanings**	**Prefixes**
circumstance circumference circumvent	surrounding conditions distance around a circle avoid by going around	*circum-* means "around" or "about"
demote deduction	move down in rank conclusion drawn from reasoning	*de-* means "from" or "down"
disapprove disassociate	to not approve to not associate	*dis-* means "not"
hypersensitive hyperbole	overly sensitive much exaggeration	*hyper-* means "excessive"
illegal immortal insignificant irresponsible	not legal not mortal not significant not responsible	*il-, im-, in-,* and *ir-* mean "not"
misspell misogamy	spell badly hatred of marriage	*mis-* means "do badly" or "hate"
precede premonition	go before advance warning	*pre-* means "before"
submarine subhuman	beneath the ocean less than human	*sub-* means "beneath" or "less than"

Suffixes

Suffixes have their own meanings and can be added to the ends of base words to create new words with new meanings. Besides having specific meanings, however, suffixes also have grammatical functions. For example, the suffix *-ness* means "state of," "act of," or "quality of." In addition to creating a new meaning, this suffix also turns the base word *deaf,* which is an adjective, into an abstract noun. Therefore, *deafness* is a noun meaning "the state, act, or quality of being deaf." As you study the chart on the next page, notice that the spelling of the root may change when a suffix is added.

Analyzing Suffixes			
Words	**Meanings**	**Suffixes**	**Part of Speech Formed**
movable peaceable visible	able to be moved capable of peace able to be seen	*-able* and *-ible* mean "capable of" or "able to be"	Adjective
occupant dependent	one who occupies one who depends	*-ant* and *-ent* mean "one who does an action"	Concrete noun
quicken moisten deepen	cause to be quick make moist make deep	*-en* means "to become"	Verb
parenthood childhood	state of being a parent state of being a child	*-hood* means "condition" or "state"	Abstract noun
dentist scientist	one who fixes teeth one who special-izes in science	*-ist* means "one who"	Concrete noun
evenly closely slowly	in an even manner in a close manner in a slow way	*-ly* means "in the manner or way mentioned"	Adverb
joyous courageous	full of joy full of courage	*-ous* means "full of"	Adjective
suspension civilization	state of being suspended state of being civil	*-sion* and *-tion* mean "the state of being something"	Abstract noun

Exercise 2

Copy the words below onto a separate sheet of paper. Then draw one line under the prefix in each of the words. Circle the root or the base word. Draw two lines under the suffix. Then write the meaning of the original word.

1. unfriendly
2. procession
3. dissatisfy
4. incredible
5. transmission
6. circumnavigation
7. incorruptible
8. omnivorous
9. repentance
10. intermediation

UNIT
26 Spelling

26.1 | Improving Your Spelling

One of your goals as a writer is to clearly communicate your ideas to your audience. If your writing is filled with misspelled words, your ideas may be lost.

You can improve your spelling—and help make your writing understood—in several ways. First, you can learn some basic spelling rules. Second, you can learn to spell.

Basic Spelling Rules

The following rules, examples, and exceptions will help you master the spellings of many words.

Spelling *ie* and *ei* Many writers find the rules for certain combinations of letters, like *ie* and *ei*, difficult to remember. One helpful learning strategy is to develop a rhyme to remember a rule, like the following rhyme for the *ie* and *ei* rule.

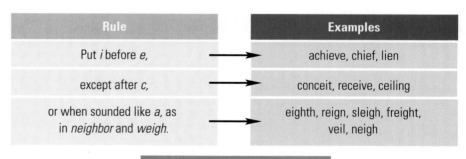

Rule		Examples
Put *i* before *e*,	→	achieve, chief, lien
except after *c*,	→	conceit, receive, ceiling
or when sounded like *a*, as in *neighbor* and *weigh*.	→	eighth, reign, sleigh, freight, veil, neigh

Exceptions
seize, leisure, weird, height, either, forfeit, protein

Spelling *-cede, -ceed,* and *-sede* Because various letters in the English spelling system are sometimes pronounced the same way, it is often easy to make slight spelling errors. The similarity of pronunciation between *c* and *s* accounts for the confusion in spelling words ending in *-cede, -ceed,* and *-sede*. Because there are only four exceptions, however, you should be able to memorize them.

Rule	Examples
Spell the *sēd* sound as *cede.*	concede, recede, intercede

Exceptions
One word uses *-sede* to spell the *sēd* sound: *supersede.*
Three words use *-ceed* to spell the *sēd* sound: *proceed, exceed, succeed.*

Spelling Unstressed Vowels   Notice the vowel sound in the second syllable of the word *or-i-gin.* This is the unstressed vowel sound, and it can be spelled several ways. Dictionary respellings use the schwa symbol (ə) to indicate it. To help spell words with unstressed vowels correctly, try thinking of a related word in which the syllable containing the vowel sound is stressed. The chart below shows examples of this process.

Spelling Unstressed Vowels		
Unknown Spelling	**Related Word**	**Word Spelled Correctly**
leg_l	le**gal**ity	legal
fant_sy	fan**tas**tic	fantasy
host_le	hos**til**ity	hostile
opp_site	op**pose**	opposite

Adding Prefixes   When adding a prefix to a word, keep the original spelling of the word. If the prefix forms a double letter, keep both letters.

dis- + appear = disappear   ir- + regular = irregular
mis- + direct = misdirect   co- + operate = cooperate

Suffixes and the Silent e   Many English words end in a silent letter *e.* Sometimes the *e* is dropped when a suffix is added. The following chart shows when to keep and when to drop the *e.*

Adding Suffixes to Words with Silent *e*	
Rule	**Examples**
When adding a suffix that begins with a consonant to a word that ends in silent *e,* keep the *e.*	place + -ment = placement rare + -ly = rarely
Common exceptions	awe + -ful = awful judge + -ment = judgment ➡

Adding Suffixes to Words with Silent *e* (continued)	
Rule	**Examples**
When adding a suffix that begins with a vowel or *y* to a word that ends in silent *e*, usually drop the *e*. **Common exceptions**	excite + -able = excitable shine + -y = shiny *mile + -age = mileage*
When adding a suffix that begins with *a* or *o* to a word that ends in *ce* or *ge*, keep the *e* so the word will retain the soft *c* or *g* sound.	change + -able = changeable trace + -able = traceable
When adding a suffix that begins with a vowel to a word that ends in *ee* or *oe*, keep the *e*.	agree + -able = agreeable see + -ing = seeing canoe + -ing = canoeing

Suffixes and the Final *y*   When adding a suffix to a word that ends in a consonant + *y*, change the *y* to *i*. Do not change the *y* to *i* when the suffix begins with *i*.

> try + -ed = tried   copy + -ing = copying

When adding a suffix to a word that ends in a vowel + *y*, keep the *y*.

> joy + -ous = joyous   convey + -ed = conveyed
> boy + -ish = boyish   play + -ing = playing

Doubling the Final Consonant   When adding a suffix to a word, you sometimes need to double the final consonant before adding the suffix. You double the consonant when adding a suffix that begins with a vowel to a word that ends in a single consonant preceded by a single vowel, if the original word

- is a one-syllable word
  dip + -ing = dipping   stop + -age = stoppage

- has an accent on the last syllable and the accent remains there after the suffix is added
  occur + -ence = occurrence   repel + -ing = repelling

- is a prefixed word based on a one-syllable word
  reset + -ing = resetting

Based on the preceding rule, you would not double the final consonant when

- the accent is not on the last syllable
  develop + -ing = developing

- the accent shifts when the suffix is added
  refer + -ence = reference

- the final consonant is preceded by two vowels
  train + -ing = training

- the final consonant is preceded by another consonant
  remind + -er = reminder

- the word ends in a consonant and the suffix begins with a consonant
  reck + -less = reckless

Adding -ly   When adding -ly to a word that ends in a single l, keep the l. When the word ends in a double l, drop one l. When the word ends in a consonant + le, drop the le.

real + -ly = really   dull + -ly = dully   terrible + -ly = terribly

Adding -ness   When adding -ness to a word that ends in n, keep the n.

sullen + -ness = sullenness   keen + -ness = keenness

Forming Compound Words   When joining a word that ends in a consonant to a word that begins with a consonant, keep both consonants.

after + noon = afternoon   key + board = keyboard

Forming Plurals   English nouns form plurals in many ways. Most nouns simply add s. The following chart shows other ways of forming plural nouns and some common exceptions to the patterns.

General Rules for Plurals		
If the Noun Ends In	**Then Generally**	**Example**
ch, s, sh, x, or z	add -es	wish ➤ wishes crutch ➤ crutches
a consonant + y	change y to i and add -es	cannery ➤ canneries baby ➤ babies
a vowel + y	add -s	day ➤ days key ➤ keys
a vowel + o	add -s	studio ➤ studios stereo ➤ stereos
a consonant + o **Common exceptions**	generally add -es but sometimes add -s	potato ➤ potatoes cargo ➤ cargoes silo ➤ silos halo ➤ halos
f or ff **Common exceptions**	add -s change f to v and add -es	reef ➤ reefs leaf ➤ leaves
lf	change f to v and add -es	half ➤ halves wolf ➤ wolves
fe	change f to v and add -s	life ➤ lives knife ➤ knives

A few plurals are exceptions to the rules listed on the previous page or present some other special problem, but they are easy to remember. The following chart lists these plurals and some examples.

Special Rules for Plurals	
Special Case	Examples
To form the plural of proper names, add either -s or -es.	D'Amico ➤ D'Amicos Sanchez ➤ Sanchezes
To form the plural of one-word compound nouns, follow the general rules for plurals.	penknife ➤ penknives blackberry ➤ blackberries
To form the plural of hyphenated compound nouns or compound nouns of more than one word, generally make the most important word plural.	father-in-law ➤ fathers-in-law attorney general ➤ attorneys general
Some nouns have irregular forms. These nouns do not follow any rules.	man ➤ men ox ➤ oxen
Some nouns have the same singular and plural form.	series ➤ series deer ➤ deer

Learning to Spell New Words

As you read, note unfamiliar words that you meet as well as words that you recognize but that look hard to spell. As you write, pay attention to any words that you have difficulty spelling. Then try the simple process shown below to learn to spell those words.

Say It
Look at the printed word, and say it out loud. Then say it again, pronouncing each syllable.

Visualize It
Without looking at the printed word, imagine seeing the word printed or written. Try to picture the word spelled correctly.

Write It
Look at the printed word, and write it. Then write it again without looking at the printed word.

Check It
Check what you have written against the printed word. Did you spell the word correctly? If not, try the process again.

Remember that the dictionary is a source for finding the correct spelling of words. You might ask, How can I look up a word if I don't know how to spell it? Typically you will be able to spell enough of a word to find it in the dictionary. If you don't find a word in the first place you look, think of other probable spellings. Once you have located the correct spelling of a word, use the process described above to learn the word.

In each group of words, find the one word that is misspelled. Write the word correctly. Cite the rule that applies to the spelling of the word. If the word is an exception to a rule, note that as well.

1. biege, conceit, thief
2. exceed, supercede, accede
3. definite, editor, abdumen
4. enjoiment, daily, carriage
5. truly, arguement, brownness

26.2   Spelling Difficult Words

Clearly, some words are more difficult to spell than others. As you have learned, not all words follow basic spelling rules. But you can learn to spell even the most difficult words.

One very useful strategy for learning difficult words is to develop a personal word list. What words are especially difficult for you? What words do you frequently misspell? Include those words in your personal word list. Study the words, using the four-step process you learned in Lesson 26.1, page 790.

Another helpful strategy for learning to spell difficult words involves developing memory devices. For example, if you have trouble remembering how many *e*'s are in the word *cemetery*, you might think of how we get there with *e*'s (ease). Puns, like this one, can help you remember how to spell difficult words.

Frequently Misspelled Words

Following is a list of words that many people often misspell. Which words on the list do you have difficulty spelling?

Words Often Misspelled

absence	arctic	cafeteria	commercial
accidentally	attendant	canceled	complexion
accommodate	ballet	canoe	concede
adviser	beautiful	catastrophe	conscientious
alcohol	benefited	cemetery	convenient
allot	buffet	changeable	definite
all right	bureau	choir	deodorant
answer	business	colonel	descend ➡

Words Often Misspelled (continued)

discipline	hippopotamus	occasion	rhythm
disease	humorous	original	schedule
efficiency	hygiene	pageant	separate
eligible	immediate	pamphlet	sincerely
embarrass	incidentally	parallel	succeed
environment	jewelry	pastime	sufficient
essential	laboratory	permanent	supersede
exceed	leisure	pharmacy	technique
familiarize	library	physical	technology
fascinating	license	physician	theory
February	maintenance	pneumonia	traffic
foreign	mischievous	precede	truly
forty	misspell	preferable	unanimous
funeral	molasses	proceed	usually
genius	muscle	receipt	vacuum
government	necessary	recognize	variety
guarantee	neighborhood	recommend	versatile
height	niece	restaurant	Wednesday

Easily Confused Words

Some words are easily confused because they contain similar sounds. Other confusing words are homophones, words that have the same pronunciation but different meanings and spellings. Study the following list of easily confused words. Are there any words on the list that you confuse?

Words Often Confused

affect	to influence; to act upon I'm sure that sad movie will affect her mood.
effect	a result What effect did the punishment have on him?
altogether	entirely Mom is altogether pleased with my report.
all together	everyone in one place We waited all together at the bus stop.
capital	a city that is the seat of government On our trip we stopped in Jefferson City, the capital of Missouri.
capital	wealth The company invested its capital.
capitol	a building in which a legislature meets In the capitol we observed the Senate in session. ➡

formally	politely; officially; according to custom or rule
	Because our visitor was so important, we addressed him formally.
formerly	previously
	The principal was formerly a teacher.
holy	sacred
	Religious travelers make pilgrimages to holy places.
holey	having holes
	You should probably stop wearing that holey jacket.
wholly	completely; fully
	I am wholly satisfied with your story.
its	possessive pronoun
	The United States celebrated its bicentennial in 1976.
it's	contraction of *it is*
	It's not about winning; it's about fair play.
lose	to misplace; to drop
	Did you lose your assignment on the way to school?
loose	free; not confined; not tight
	My clothes are loose since I lost 10 pounds.
passed	moved through; elapsed; completed satisfactorily
	I passed you in the hall several times today.
past	the time before the present; gone by; ended; over
	You can't change the past.
stationary	fixed; unmoving
	For a moment the plane appeared stationary in the sky.
stationery	writing paper and envelopes
	Rhonda wrote me a letter on hot pink stationery.
than	in comparison with
	You studied harder today than I have ever seen you study.
then	at that time; next
	He did his chores, and then he played a computer game.

Exercise 2

For each sentence below, determine which word in parentheses correctly completes the sentence.

1. The ambulance (passed, past) us.
2. Our teacher was (formerly, formally) a stockbroker.
3. (Its, It's) beginning to snow.
4. (Then, Than) what do you do?
5. I always seem to (loose, lose) my keys.

27 Study Skills

27.1 Taking Notes in Class

Taking notes of classroom lectures and teachers' directions gives you a written record of important information for later use. In addition, taking notes can help you do the following:

- organize ideas
- recognize relationships among different topics
- evaluate information
- identify points you find confusing

Many students take notes in the form of an outline. For information on outline form, see Lesson 7.2 in Composition, pages 322–325. The chart below lists other suggestions on how to take class notes.

Tips on Taking Notes

1. Write down only key words and phrases. Focusing on main points allows you to continue to listen while you write.

2. Underline or star main ideas. Highlighting the most important points makes reviewing easier.

3. Revise your notes after class. Clarifying your organization and adding details makes your notes more complete.

4. Keep your notes in a folder or notebook. Having a separate folder for each class helps you keep your notes organized.

Organize your notes by class, date, and topic for easy reference.

To save time, use symbols and numerals instead of words.

Life in an ecosystem   Sept. 28 Biology
Ecosystem: plants, animals, and physical environment
of their community
     Types of biomes
          1. rain forest — Amazon   4. tundra — Arctic
          2. desert — Sahara, Gobi   5. deciduous forest
          3. grassland — U.S. Plains   6. taiga — N. Asia

Watch a television program or listen to a radio broadcast, and take notes on what you observe and hear. You might choose a talk show, a news program, a documentary, or even a drama or play. The point is to practice your note-taking skills by recording as best you can what happens during the program.

In a small group, have one student read aloud from an encyclopedia article for five minutes. Other students in the group should take notes as the student reads. After the reading, the students taking notes should compare notes. What can you learn from your classmates about how to take good notes?

27.2   Studying Outside of Class

Your teacher usually determines what learning activities happen in class. Outside of class, though, you're responsible for allocating your study time and learning material. The first step in studying efficiently is to learn to manage your study time.

Using Study Time Wisely

By preparing yourself to study and organizing your work, you can make the most effective use of your time. Following are some suggestions to help you use your study time well.

Divide large assignments into smaller tasks. Reading 4 pages of a textbook each night is easier than trying to read 20 pages every fifth night.

Select a place to study. By using the same place for studying each day, you will begin to associate that place with studying.

Make a monthly assignment calendar. By writing down due dates, test dates, and notes about tasks to complete, you can see at a glance what work you need to do and when.

Gather necessary materials. If possible, leave study supplies such as pencils and a dictionary at your study place.

When you sit down to study, follow these tips to help you make the best use of your study time.

Tips on Studying Effectively
1. Focus on one assignment at a time. Try to stay on your task until you accomplish your goal.
2. Take short breaks after reaching a goal. Stretching, walking, or having a light snack can help keep you alert.
3. Write down questions about what you are studying. This gives you a written record of what to ask your teacher or classmates.
4. Review material before stopping. Even a short review will greatly increase the amount of material that you remember.

Reading Efficiently

Reading is probably the most important way of learning information. Whether you're looking for the year Simón Bolívar was born, trying to analyze his personality, or reviewing his accomplishments, you're reading. In each case, however, you're reading in a different way. The following chart shows you three different styles of reading and when you might use them.

Hints on Using Three Reading Styles		
Style	**Description**	**Purpose**
Skimming	Glancing over the text to identify main ideas by reading chapter and lesson titles, words in bold or italic type, and topic sentences	• Previewing material before a study session • Reviewing before a test • Deciding whether a book covers a subject you're interested in
Scanning	Glancing over the text in search of specific information by looking for key words	• Reviewing key terms • Looking for a detail to support an opinion • Searching a book to see if it covers a particular topic
In-depth Reading	Reading over the text carefully to absorb new ideas and facts	• Learning the material for the first time • Evaluating the information presented • Preparing to explain the information to someone else

When you sit down to study, follow these tips to help you make the best use of your time.

The Quran According to a Muslim tradition, the angel Gabriel revealed divine messages to Muhammad over a 22-year period. Faithful Muslims wrote down or memorized these messages, but they were not compiled into one written collection until after Muhammad died. Then his successor, Abu Bakr, ordered Muslims to retrieve these messages from wherever they could be found, from the ribs of palm-leaves and tablets of white stone and from the breasts of men. It took 20 years before the messages were compiled into the holy book of Islam, the Quran, whose name means recital. For all Muslims, the Quran is the final authority in matters of faith and practice.

Written in Arabic, the Quran is believed to contain God's message as revealed to Muhammad. This message is expressed in stories, legends, and poems. Some of the stories—such as Noah's ark and Jonah in the belly of the whale—are variations of those found in the Bible.

░░░	**Skimming**
——	**Scanning**
——	**In-depth reading**

Using the SQ3R Method

One way to increase your efficiency when studying material for the first time is to follow a five-step process known as the SQ3R method. The steps are described below.

Survey	Question	Read	Record	Review
Preview the material by skimming. Read heads, highlighted terms, and the first sentence of each paragraph. Look at all pictures and graphs.	Ask questions about the material. Your questions might begin with *who, what, when, where, why,* and *how.*	Read the selection carefully. Identify the main idea of each section. Take notes, and add questions to your list.	Write answers to your questions without looking at the text. Make brief notes about additional main ideas or facts.	Check your answers in the text. Continue to study the text until you can answer all questions correctly.

You can apply the SQ3R method to studying any subject. If you use the method regularly, it will become a habit. You may find that this habit brings several benefits, including the following:

- You remember more of what you read.
- You develop specific questions about information that is unclear.
- You are better prepared for class discussions and lectures.

Evaluating What You Read

The more you think about what you read, the better you will remember it. Hence, if you get in the habit of evaluating material as you read it, you will find that you learn it better.

Identifying Facts and Opinions Most of what you read includes both facts and opinions. A fact is a statement that can be verified or proved true. How do you prove something is true? One way is through direct experience—something you saw or experienced yourself. If someone says it is raining outside, you can step outside and see for yourself.

Proof also might come from an authoritative source, such as a reference book or an expert on the subject. Did the Inca emperor Pachacuti come to power in 1438? You could check the date in an encyclopedia.

An opinion is a personal judgment. Since opinions are expressions of someone's beliefs or feelings, they cannot be proved true or false. While people generally can agree on facts, they often disagree about opinions. Opinions are most convincing when supported by evidence.

The following chart shows examples of facts and opinions. Learning how to distinguish between them will help you evaluate what you read.

Distinguishing Between Facts and Opinions	
Statement	**Fact or Opinion**
1. Computers now do much of the assembly line work that formerly was performed by factory workers.	Fact: Examining factories over the last 20 years would verify this statement.
2. Computerized manufacturing is bad because it causes people to lose their jobs.	Opinion: Computerized manufacturing may actually cause some unemployment, but whether it is good or bad is a value judgment.
3. Many kinds of vegetation and wildlife live in areas known as wetlands.	Fact: You could check this statement by reading studies done by biologists or visiting a wetland yourself.
4. The federal government should protect wetlands from pollution.	Opinion: Facts could be used to support or oppose this statement, but the statement is an opinion. People often disagree on the proper role of the federal government.

Interpreting Figurative Language Writers use figurative language to make their texts more interesting and to express their ideas more clearly. Figurative language is a word or phrase used in an imaginative way rather than in a literal sense. You will see figurative language most often in novels, short stories, poems, and advertising. The text below includes several examples of figurative language.

> The dancers, clad in silks of green and blue, took their positions as the curtain rose. The music floated softly upward from somewhere below the stage and gathered like mist about their feet. As the melody swelled, their frozen forms melted into a celebration of movement. They swept across the floor, colorful rivers seeking their own paths along the barren landscape of the stage.

The dancers were not so cold they were actually "frozen." Rather, they were as motionless as if they were frozen.

Describing how the dancers would "melt" into "rivers" suggests the dancers' graceful, fluid movements.

Exercise 3

Read a newspaper article, an editorial, or a column and identify 10 statements in the piece as either facts or opinions. Then decide whether the writer presents any facts to support the statements that are opinions. Share your comments with your class, and discuss whether or not the piece contains mostly facts or mostly opinions.

Exercise 4

Select a short passage from a novel or short story that uses figurative language. Rewrite the passage, changing the figurative language to literal language. Which style is more effective—the figurative or literal? Why?

Exercise 5

Find a three- or four-paragraph passage in a history or science textbook. Rewrite the passage, expressing the same information but using figurative language.

Read the following sentence quickly: In 1990 the proportion of American women in the labor force was 63 percent among women aged 16–24, 74 percent among women aged 25–54, 45 percent among women aged 55–64, and 8 percent among women aged 65 and over. Did you grasp all of that? Probably not. The mass of numbers in the sentence makes the information difficult to comprehend at a glance. To present numbers and other facts that are difficult to communicate clearly in sentences, writers often use charts, tables, graphs, and maps. The rest of this lesson will give you tips on how to interpret each of these types of visuals.

Tables

Tables separate information into categories so you can compare information easily. The following table shows the percentage of women in the workforce in seven countries in 1990. Notice how much more easily you can pick out information from the chart than from the first sentence in the above paragraph.

Across the top of the chart and down the left-hand side are the categories of information in the chart.

Compare information across columns. Among which age group were the most women in the labor force in Japan?

Compare information between rows. In which country was the percentage of women workers aged 55–64 highest in 1990?

Percentage of Women in the Workforce, 1990				
	16–24 Years Old	25–54 Years Old	55–64 Years Old	65+ Years Old
United States	63	74	45	8
Canada	66	76	36	4
France	34	73	31	2
Italy	41	49	10	2
Japan	45	64	47	16
Sweden	68	91	66	5
United Kingdom	73	73	37	3

To find out what percentage of Japanese women aged 25–54 were in the workforce in 1990, you would first read down the left-hand column in the table to find Japan. Then you would read across the top of the table until you reached the age group "25–54." Moving down the column of numbers to the row even with Japan, you would see that 64 percent of Japanese women between the ages of 25 and 54 were in the workforce in 1990.

Bar Graphs

In bar graphs each quantity is shown as a bar. The length of the bar reflects the amount. Because the bars are separate and distinct, writers often use bar graphs to compare quantities. In this bar graph, the consumption of vegetable protein in five world regions (horizontal axis) is compared using the measurement of grams per person per day (vertical axis). The bars provide a quick way to see who consumes the most and the least vegetable protein.

Daily Consumption of Vegetable Protein

The height of the bar represents the amount of vegetable protein consumed.

Each bar represents a different region.

In the bar graph shown here, the bars run vertically. In many bar graphs the bars run horizontally. In these, the vertical axis indicates the categories being compared, and the horizontal axis indicates the quantities being compared.

Flow Charts

Flow charts show the steps in a process. Arrows connect the steps to show how one flows into the next. For example, a flow chart might show the steps a bill goes through in becoming a law or the stages in the life of a frog. The flow chart below shows the selection process for a Supreme Court justice.

The president nominates a candidate. → The Senate considers the nominee's qualifications. → The Senate votes on the nomination.

If the Senate approves the nominee, he or she becomes a Supreme Court justice.

If the Senate rejects the nominee, the president nominates another candidate.

Identify where the process begins. Arrows show the steps in the process.

At some stages more than one result may occur.

Cluster Diagrams

Another way to show the relationship among ideas is through a cluster diagram. To create a cluster diagram, first write your main topic in the center of a piece of paper. Then, as you think of ideas related to it, write those. Connect each new idea with the ones related to it.

Cluster diagrams are a great method of connecting ideas you learn in class. The diagram below shows a cluster diagram about South American rain forests. Notice how the diagram shows the relationships among ideas.

The central idea is listed in the center of the diagram.

Each new idea creates the possibility of another cluster.

If you expanded the diagram, what ideas might you add?

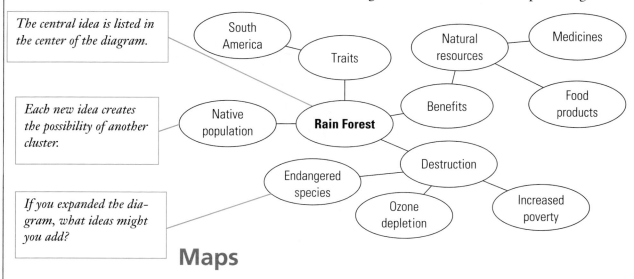

South America

Traits

Natural resources

Medicines

Native population

Rain Forest

Benefits

Food products

Endangered species

Destruction

Ozone depletion

Increased poverty

Maps

Maps are a representation of a portion of the earth. Political maps show features that are created by or reflect the culture of people, such as countries, cities, or roads. Physical maps show the natural features of the earth, such as mountains, rivers, and plains. This map shows both political and physical features.

A blue line on a landmass indicates a river.

Why would you use a map such as this one?

Using the color key, you can determine that the Greeks occupied most of southern Italy.

ITALY 500 B.C.

12°E   16°E

ALPS

ETRURIA

ADRIATIC SEA

APENNINES

Tiber River

Rome

42°N

LATIUM

TYRRHENIAN SEA

Strait of Messina

38°N

SICILY

N

Greeks
Etruscans
Latins

0   50   100 miles
0   50   100 kilometers

AFRICA

Political and physical maps usually show large land areas: the world, a country, a state, a city. Maps can also show smaller areas: the houses in a neighborhood, the buildings on a college campus, or the location of rooms in a building. Architects use a type of map, a floor plan, to help them visualize their ideas. Below is an example of a floor plan that you might see in a history book. It shows the layout of a palace built in Morocco about 1,000 years ago.

Breaks in the lines used to show walls indicate doors or windows.

Different colors and patterns distinguish separate areas and their uses.

Main entrance ▶

- ■ Walls of main building
- ☐ Walls of service buildings
- ☐ Covered areas
- ▨ State hall
- ■ Watercourse
- ☐ Open areas
- ■ Garden

Exercise 6

Create a table showing the increase in the number of female scientists between 1970 and 1986.

In 1970 around 23 percent of social scientists were women. About 17 percent of mathematical scientists and about 14 percent of natural scientists were women. Among physicians 10 percent were women. Only 2 percent of engineers were women. By 1986 women constituted 46 percent of social scientists, 36 percent of mathematical scientists, 23 percent of natural scientists, 18 percent of physicians, and 6 percent of engineers.

Exercise 7

In a group of four to six students, develop a cluster diagram. One student should choose a broad subject and write it down. Members of the group should take turns adding ideas to the diagram. Once you've filled the page, analyze the connections and discuss their meanings.

Taking Tests

28.1   Classroom Tests

Learning the material is the most important step in preparing for a test. In addition, though, you can get ready for a test by learning how to answer the types of questions that you will see on the test.

This lesson will show you some strategies for answering different types of objective test items. An objective test item is one that asks for very specific information about material that you have studied.

Multiple-Choice Items

A multiple-choice item includes an incomplete sentence or a question and several responses. You are to pick the response that best completes the sentence or answers the question. Consider the following tips.

Tips on Answering Multiple-Choice Items

1. Read the item carefully. You need to know what information you are looking for.

2. Read all the responses. Even if the first one seems right, a later response may be better.

3. Eliminate any responses that are clearly incorrect. Eliminating incorrect responses helps you focus your attention on the responses that might be correct.

4. Be cautious about responses that contain absolute words—*always, never, all,* or *none.* Since most statements have exceptions, absolute statements are often incorrect.

Here is an example of a multiple-choice question. In this case you are given a statement with a missing word. You are to choose the response that, when placed in the blank, will make the statement correct.

Though the stories were written by Arab writers, a does not complete the sentence correctly.

The sentence structure indicates that the answer is a female, so b and d are incorrect. The correct answer is c.

```
In The Thousand and One Nights, _____
prevents her execution by telling tales of
high adventure to her husband.

a. an Arab writer        c. Scheherazade
b. Sinbad                d. an unnamed man
```

Here is another multiple-choice item. This one is phrased as a question. You are to select the best answer to the question.

> Which of the following statements
> concerning the book *Native Son* is accurate?
>
> a. It was written by Richard Wright.
> b. It takes place in the North.
> c. It is a work of fiction.
> d. all of the above

Though a sounds correct, read all of the responses before answering.

Select this response only if you are sure that at least two of the responses are correct. In this case, d *is correct.*

True-False Items

A true-false item asks you to decide whether a statement is true or not. Many true-false items include some information that is true and some that is false. If any part of a statement is false, the entire statement is considered false. For the answer to be true, the entire statement must be true. Look at the statement on word usage below. Why is it false?

> The word *affect* is usually a verb meaning
> "to influence," and the word *effect* is
> always a noun meaning "the result."

The first part of this sentence is true, but the second is not because effect *can also be a verb meaning "to cause." The correct answer is* false.

Short-Answer Items

Short-answer items ask for specific information. Therefore, they are usually best answered with precisely phrased complete sentences. Also, since these items may ask you to supply several pieces of information, your answers to these items may be worth more than answers to other questions. For example, look at the following question, which might appear on an earth science test.

> Why is soil erosion viewed as both helpful
> and harmful to people?

The question above asks you for more than a list of the effects of soil erosion. In your answer you should clearly distinguish between effects of soil erosion that are viewed as helpful and those that are viewed as harmful. Soil erosion is seen as helpful because it breaks up rocks and earth, moving rich soil to valleys and the mouths of rivers. Erosion is seen as harmful because it often strips farmland of valuable topsoil and threatens crop production.

Fill-in Items

Fill-in items usually consist of a sentence with one or more blanks for you to fill in. The number of blank spaces provided often indicates the number of words needed in the response. Your answer should make the statement true and also grammatically correct. Consequently, rereading the statement with your answer included will help you check whether your choice is correct. Try to answer the fill-in question below.

Notice that the order of the planets is important. The only correct answer is Mercury, Venus, *and* Earth.

```
In our solar system, the first three
planets in order from the sun are _____,
_____, and _____.
```

On some tests you might be given a list of words from which to choose your answers. If so, complete the ones you're sure of first. If answers from the list can be used only once, cross them off as you use them. As you reduce the number of possible answers, you increase your chances of finding the correct answers to the harder items. For example, assume that you can answer the first two items below, but not the third.

```
1. Astronomers believe that the sun is a
   star in the _____ galaxy.
2. The _____ revolves around the earth
   about once a month.
3. The second closest star to the earth is
   _____.

Milky Way              moon
Andromeda              Alpha Centauri
quasar
```

After answering *Milky Way* for the first item and *moon* for the second, only three possible responses remain. Since the structure of the sentence suggests that the correct answer is the name of a star, and star names are capitalized, you can eliminate *quasar*. Choosing between only two answers improves your chances of choosing correctly. What is the correct answer? *Alpha Centauri*.

Matching Items

Fill-in items with the responses given are similar to matching items. However, instead of writing in the word, you write down the letter or number of the correct response. In matching items you have two sets or lists of items and must match those in the first column or group to those in the second. Reading the directions carefully helps you know what type of match you should make. Some common matches are

- terms and their definitions
- events and the dates they occurred
- causes and their effects
- chemical elements and their symbols

Whatever the subject, compare the lists. Do they include the same number of items? Will every item be used exactly once? If so, you can cross out each one as it is used. Just as you used the process of elimination to help you with fill-ins, you can use it again here. In the following example, match each country with its capital. Each city is used only once.

```
1. _____  Japan           a. New Delhi
2. _____  Uruguay         b. London
3. _____  India           c. Montevideo
4. _____  Great Britain   d. Cairo
5. _____  Egypt           e. Tokyo
```

As with other test items, answer the ones you're sure of first. Note, however, that if each response is used only once, you'll have to make two changes if you change an answer.

Time Management

Tests usually last one class period or less. Since the time is limited, you need to use it efficiently. The chart below gives a few suggestions for using your time wisely.

Tips for Allocating Time During a Test

1. Spend the first few minutes preparing. Reading the directions carefully will help you answer items appropriately.

2. Answer the items you are sure of. Skipping difficult items will allow you to respond to all of the items you know.

3. Return to the difficult items. Using the strategies learned in this lesson, give the best answers you can.

4. Spend the last few minutes reviewing your answers. Taking time to check your answers will help prevent simple mistakes.

Read the passage below, and use the test-taking strategies in this lesson to help you complete the items that follow.

Over the centuries Japan's Kabuki theater has grown and flourished. Continuing a tradition that historians have traced back to the 1600s, Kabuki plays are still performed in Japan to large audiences. Kabuki theater seems to have originated as a new form of drama to satisfy the lavish and melodramatic tastes of a new social class in Tokugawa, Japan.

When the lower and middle classes of society began to increase in the urban centers, they sought new forms of entertainment. The name *kabuki* means "to lean in the direction of fashion," reflecting Kabuki theater's popular origins.

Kabuki dramatizes subjects ranging from historical events to daily life. With elaborate costumes, exaggerated movements, and amazing special effects (including snowstorms and fires), Kabuki theater is a spectacular event. Sometimes the stories make fun of political figures. During the 1600s, government officials banned some performances they felt were too controversial. If anything, this censorship seems to have made Kabuki all the more popular.

1. Which of the following is true of Kabuki theater?
   a. It is an old art form.
   b. It can be controversial.
   c. It is still performed today.
   d. all of the above

2. True or False: Kabuki has a name appropriate to its origins.

3. Like many popular films today, Kabuki theater makes spectacular use of elaborate staging and _____ _____, such as snowstorms and fires.

4. How did the government's ban on certain political plays affect public opinion of Kabuki?

5. For each effect in the following list, choose the cause from which that effect most directly resulted.

   a. bans on Kabuki by the government
   b. increase in the popularity of Kabuki
   c. desire for a new form of drama
   ___ rise of a new social class
   ___ ridicule of political figures
   ___ censorship of performances

28.2 Standardized Tests

To compare large numbers of students, schools often give standardized tests, tests that have been given to similar groups of students around the country. By studying these test results, experts develop standards of performance. Most standardized tests fall into one of three categories:

- Ability tests evaluate general learning skills, such as how well you can read, write, or use logic.
- Achievement tests evaluate knowledge in specific content areas, such as how much you know about biology or world history.
- Aptitude tests evaluate individual talents and interests, such as whether you prefer working in groups or alone.

Standardized tests contain several types of items. Becoming familiar with the kinds of questions most often used on standardized tests will improve your chances of scoring well.

Reading Comprehension Items

How well you understand what you read is measured by reading comprehension items. These items usually include a long passage about a literature, social studies, or science topic, and several questions about the passage. You should be able to answer all of the questions, based on the information in the passage. These questions often require you to

- identify main ideas
- recognize details supporting main ideas
- figure out information that is not stated in the passage

The last type of item, also known as an inference item, requires you to come to a conclusion that is based on the information in the passage but is not explicitly expressed. As you read the following passage and the items that follow it, notice the suggestions for how to respond to the items.

Siddharta Gautama, the founder of Buddhism, began his life as a Kshatriya prince. Born the son of a prince in northern India around 566 B.C., Gautama was raised in luxury. As a young man he continued to live a sheltered life, shielded from sickness and poverty. Tradition states that one day Gautama's charioteer drove him around his estates, and for the first time Gautama saw sickness, old age, and death. Shocked at these scenes of misery, Gautama decided to find out why people suffered and how suffering could be ended. At the age of 29, he left his wife and newborn son and wandered throughout India in what is known as the Great Renunciation.

1. Which sentence best summarizes the most important information in this passage?
   a. Gautama was raised in luxury in India.
   b. Gautama was born around 566 B.C.
   c. Gautama left home at the age of 29.
   d. Gautama wanted to know why people suffered.

2. Based on this passage, Gautama seemed to be
   a. proud of his achievements
   b. concerned about others
   c. angry about his family's situation
   d. eager to meet other people

Vocabulary Items

Standardized tests often evaluate your vocabulary knowledge through varieties of multiple-choice items. Sometimes you may be asked to complete a sentence by filling in the meaning of a word, as in the item below.

A preliminary step is taken _____.
a. before any other step in a process
b. during the most important stage of a process
c. after all other steps in a process are completed
d. only when necessary to complete a process
e. only if the first step of a process fails

One tip for completing vocabulary items is to analyze the parts of an unknown word. See Unit 25, pages 778–781, for more information on how to build your vocabulary. Notice that the word *preliminary* begins with the letters *pre-*. If you recall other words that begin with these letters, such as *precede, preface,* and *prepare,* you may realize that *pre-* often means "first" or "early." Using this knowledge, you might correctly determine that the answer is *a*.

A different type of vocabulary item, an analogy, tests your ability to analyze the relationships between words, not just your understanding of the meanings of words. Consider the words *healthy* and *robust*. What is the relationship between them? They are synonyms, words that have the same meaning. Now examine the pairs of words at the top of the next page. Which pair has the same relationship as *healthy* and *robust*?

```
Healthy is to robust as

a. sociable is to disagreeable
b. haughty is to arrogant
c. mumble is to mouth
d. student is to teacher
e. gaggle is to goose
```

> *"Sociable" is the opposite of "disagreeable." "Haughty" and "arrogant" are synonyms. Mumble is something you do with your mouth. A student learns from a teacher. A "gaggle" is a collection of geese.*

None of the choices listed has anything to do with being healthy. However, the relationship between each pair of words is different. Only in *b* are the words synonyms. Hence, *b* is the correct answer.

Some analogy items are shown in a different format. Each pair of words is separated by a colon, with a double colon used after the first pair. However, this format still requires you to choose the pair of words with the same relationship as the first. What is the relationship below?

```
carpenter : hammer::

a. swimmer : athlete
b. hospital : doctor
c. waiter : tray
d. inept : awkward
e. inane : ridiculous
```

One strategy for answering analogy items is to create a simple sentence in your mind that states the relationship between the first pair of words—for example, A carpenter uses a hammer. Then try each pair of words in that sentence. For *a* you would come up with the statement, A swimmer uses an athlete. Since this sentence makes no sense, you could conclude that the relationship between *swimmer* and *athlete* is not the same as the relationship between *carpenter* and *hammer*. After trying each pair of words in the sentence, you would find that *c* makes the most sense.

Grammar, Usage, and Mechanics Items

Standardized tests often include sections evaluating your ability to recognize and use standard English. Items may ask you to find grammatical errors in sentences, point out misused words, or choose the best way to correct an awkward or incorrect sentence.

English usage items often show a sentence with several underlined and lettered sections. As you read the sentence, decide if one of the underlined parts contains an error, and mark the corresponding letter on your answer sheet. If the sentence contains no error, mark that choice; it usually follows the sentence. Examine the following item.

> The competition between Michelle and I
> $\quad\quad\quad$ a $\quad\quad\quad\quad\quad\quad\quad\quad\quad\quad$ b
> became more intense as the school year
> $\quad\quad\quad$ c $\quad\quad\quad\quad\quad$ d
> progressed. no error
> $\quad\quad\quad\quad\quad\quad$ e

Some usage questions test your knowledge of homonyms, words that sound alike but have different spellings and meanings. Given a list of phrases that contain homonyms, you might be asked to find the one item with a word used incorrectly or the one item with no errors. In the following example find the response in which all words are used correctly.

> a. a heard of cattle
> b. a jury of your peers
> c. a steal beam
> d. to much sun

Correction items ask you to correct a mistake as well as to recognize it. Usually only one part of the given sentence is underlined. Each response is a possible correction. You have to choose the response that best corrects the error in the sentence. Often one of the choices will look identical to the underlined section. Choose it if you feel the sentence contains no error. Here is an example of a sentence correction item.

> Ms. Hasan is the best of the two candidates running for mayor.
>
> a. is the best of the two
> b. is the more better of
> c. is the very best of
> d. is the better of

Test-taking Strategies

Certain test-taking strategies will help you as you take a test. The chart on the next page lists some strategies you might use.

Tips on Taking Standardized Tests

1. Skip difficult items at first. Since standardized tests are usually timed, focus on answering items you know. You can return to skipped items later.

2. Mark only your answers on the answer sheet. Since the test is machine-graded, stray marks might be read as wrong answers.

3. Frequently compare the item numbers on your test and answer sheet. This helps you avoid putting your answers in the wrong spaces.

4. If you have time, check your answers. If the test does not penalize you for wrong answers, guess the answers for all items you did not have time to complete.

Exercise 2

Use the test-taking strategies described in this lesson to help you complete the following items.

1. Choose the phrase that best completes this sentence:
   A transatlantic message is one that _____.
   a. travels under a body of water
   b. goes across the ocean
   c. is sent by passengers on a ship
   d. is always about navigation

2. Find the pair of words with the same relationship as the given pair.
   player : team : :
   a. conductor : baton   d. soldier : army
   b. engineer : bridge   e. cat : Siamese
   c. United States : country

3. Where is the error in the following sentence?

   Our teacher <u>was pleased</u> that <u>all of us</u> <u>have passed</u> the exam,
               a   b   c
   and <u>we were happy</u> that the test was over. <u>no error</u>
         d   e

4. Which item includes a word that is used incorrectly?
   a. a strong ally   c. the capital building
   b. gives good advice   d. the bare facts

5. Correct the underlined section in the following sentence.
   I wanted to remind her that the party starts at seven o'clock, but she <u>had already went</u> out the door.
   a. had already went   c. had went
   b. had went already   d. had already gone

Listening and Speaking

29.1 | Listening with a Purpose

In the telephone game, one person in a group whispers a story to his or her neighbor. That person repeats the story to the next person, who tells the next person, and so on. The final person then tells the story aloud. After several retellings, the story has usually changed in unpredictable ways. With better listening skills, people would repeat the story more accurately and enjoy the telephone game less.

Listening in Class

Next to reading, listening is probably the most important skill you have for learning new information. Study the chart below to gain tips on how to listen effectively in class.

Tips for Effective Listening

1. Think about what you hear. Sorting out the main ideas in your mind helps you identify the points to remember.

2. Write down the important information. This gives you a written record of what you learned.

3. Notice verbal clues. Clues such as "another reason" or "in summary" help you organize the information you are hearing.

4. Listen for helpful information your teacher offers. Your teacher might indicate what material is most important or will appear on a test.

5. Organize your thoughts and notes after class. You will have a chance to fill in missing information while the material is still fresh in your mind.

Interpreting Vocal Clues How your teacher says something may also give you clues about what information is important. To emphasize a point, a teacher might speak more quickly and loudly. Another teacher might speak more slowly and quietly to add emphasis to each word.

Interpreting Nonverbal Signs Teachers also may communicate nonverbally. For example, a teacher might emphasize a key point with an emphatic gesture or a change in facial expression.

Listening to Television and Radio

Outside of class, you may listen to news programs, documentaries, and talk shows that provide information about current events. As you listen, you should also develop your skill at evaluating what you hear. Is this information true? What perspective does it represent? Who would disagree with this? The chart below presents some statements you might hear on a typical news report along with questions to ask about each.

Evaluating News Statements	
Sample Statement	**Questions to Ask**
1. An unidentified source close to the president said there will not be a summit on peace this fall.	Why wouldn't the source give his or her name? Is the source unable to back up the information?
2. Statistics gathered by a Washington-based research group show that high-fat foods may not harm most people's health.	Who was the research group? Who paid the group to conduct the research? Have other research groups challenged these findings?
3. A popular supermarket tabloid has published a story linking the governor to a ring of drug smugglers.	Is a supermarket tabloid believable? Do the news reporters seem to take the story seriously?
4. A radical political organization today vowed to continue its illegal protests.	Who considers this organization radical? What makes its protests illegal?
5. The candidate today charged that her opponent failed to be on hand for 30 roll-call votes.	Is 30 votes many to miss or a low number? Were these votes important? Were any of the votes close?

Exercise 1

Choose a partner, and prepare an interview. Each person should role-play someone famous. The partners should take turns interviewing each other for 15 minutes. Then each student should introduce his or her partner's character to the class. The person interviewed will evaluate how well the partner listened by noting how accurate the introduction was.

Exercise 2

Follow a nightly newscast for one week. Keep a journal of the topics covered and the questions that you thought of as you listened. In a class discussion, explain how the stories developed during the week and whether or not any of your questions were eventually answered. Write a two-page report summarizing the experience.

29.2　Speaking Effectively

Speaking effectively involves more than responding to a question with correct information or reacting to another's statement. It involves using the type of communication most appropriate to the situation—and different situations call for different types of communication. You probably already adjust your speaking style to match your situation. However, to be sure you're doing this appropriately, review the chart below. The chart can also help you better understand the differences between informal, semiformal, and formal communication.

Types of Speaking Situations		
Type	**Traits**	**Examples**
Informal	• Involves little planning or preparation • Often covers many topics • Much interaction among speakers	conversations introductions
Semiformal	• Involves some preparation by the speaker • Covers a subject chosen for a specific purpose • Moderate interaction between speaker and audience	class discussions announcements
Formal	• Involves extensive preparation by the speaker • Covers a specific topic and purpose • Interaction between speaker and audience limited and controlled	class report graduation speech dramatic reading

Preparing Spoken Comments

Just as you practice a dance routine before a recital or important plays before a game, you need to practice spoken comments before you give them. In general, the more formal the speaking situation is, the more you should prepare for it. To help you speak effectively, follow the steps outlined in the flow chart on the facing page. You may notice that preparing a speech is similar to preparing a piece of writing.

Prewriting	Drafting	Revising	Practicing	Presenting
• Find an appropriate topic. • Consider what your audience knows and how much time you have to speak. Do any necessary research.	• Organize your ideas by writing a preliminary outline. • Identify your main ideas and supporting information. • Put your outline on note cards.	• Review the organization of information. • Improve word choices. • Add transitions.	• Read the speech aloud. • Critique your delivery. • Time your speech.	• Be organized. • Deliver your speech in a clear, strong voice.

Presenting Yourself and Your Ideas

Many speakers, from students to experienced politicians, get nervous before delivering a speech. Here are a few tips to help you remain calm.

Tips for Relaxing

1. Writing the word *relax* several places in your note cards will remind you to take it easy.

2. Taking a deep breath before you begin will help you calm down.

3. Speaking to one person in your audience at a time will help you speak in a normal tone of voice.

In addition to staying relaxed, you want to deliver a speech that will capture the attention of your listeners. Here are a few suggestions for how to speak effectively.

Tips for Effective Speaking

1. Pause after each important point. This gives people time to take in what you've said.

2. Use gestures to help explain your material. By pointing to a place on a map or using your hands to show the size of a fish you caught, you help your audience visualize what you are discussing.

3. Look people in the eye. Making eye contact with individuals in your audience helps you keep your audience's attention.

4. Vary the tone and pitch of your voice. Letting your voice rise and fall naturally and get louder and softer will make your speech sound more conversational.

When you deliver a speech, you are doing the talking. However, your audience is also communicating with you. With practice you can read the signals the audience is sending you and then adapt your speech. Following are suggestions about how to interpret audience signals.

Communicating with Your Audience	
Audience Signals	**Speaker Response**
1. People are staring out the window or fidgeting in their chairs.	People are probably getting bored. Try to use a more emotional or exciting tone of voice.
2. People are frowning or appear to be asking each other questions.	People might be confused. Try to review key points, using new examples.
3. People are leaning forward in their chairs and appear to be struggling to hear you.	People may be unable to hear. Besides speaking more loudly, scan the room for other sources of noise, such as fans, that can be reduced.
4. People are attentive, smiling, and nodding their heads in an affirmative manner.	People are listening closely. Keep doing just what you've been doing.

Exercise 3

With a group of four or five classmates, analyze the following topics (or develop more topics on your own) as possible subjects for a three-minute speech. Decide how the topics can be narrowed, what your class would like to hear, and how much research the topics would require.

- women in sports
- fairy tales and nursery rhymes in history
- minority roles in World War II
- high school course requirements

Exercise 4

Choose one of the topics you discussed in Exercise 3, and prepare a speech on it. In small groups each student should prepare and deliver part of his or her speech. Other members of the group should make suggestions on how to improve the presentation. Use these suggestions to help you practice and deliver your speech to the entire class.

29.3   Working in Groups

As a member of a group, you need certain skills that you don't use when working alone. For example, group work requires more communication skills, more organizational skills, and more interpersonal skills than does working alone. However, group work has several advantages. The members of a group can

- benefit from the special skills and knowledge of each member
- work together to accomplish tasks that one person could not do alone
- get feedback on their ideas and proposals

Because of these advantages, you may often find yourself part of a group. You might be part of a group that is doing a science research experiment, reviewing for a social studies test, or trying to raise money for a school project.

Roles in Groups

In a group every member has a role to play. Each member is partially responsible for the successful functioning of the group. However, two people in a group usually have special roles to play, the chairperson and the recorder. The various roles of group members are described below.

Chairperson
Announces discussion topic
Keeps discussion focused
Moves group toward a decision

Recorder
Writes down all ideas
Reads ideas to be reviewed
Records final decisions

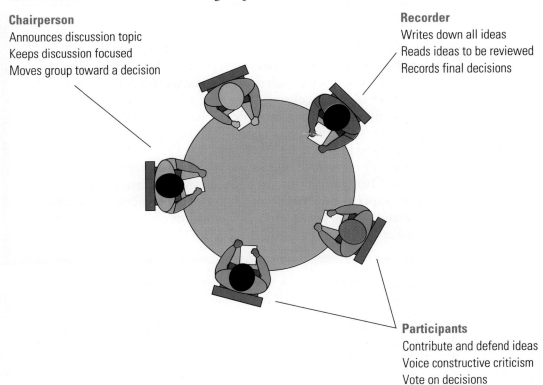

Participants
Contribute and defend ideas
Voice constructive criticism
Vote on decisions

Group Procedures

Certain procedures will help any group to stay on its task and function more smoothly. For example, if everyone follows common courtesy, such as not interrupting one another, the group will function better. Below are additional suggestions to help a group work well.

Tips for Working in a Group

1. Listen to other group members. You may want to jot down suggestions, examples, and other comments made by people in the group.

2. Help members stay on track. When the discussion is wandering, say something like, "I think we should remember that our goal is . . ."

3. Criticize ideas, not individuals. Focus on supporting or opposing ideas rather than people.

4. Accept criticism of your ideas from others. Assume that everyone in the group is trying to help. They are not trying to belittle you.

5. Encourage quiet members to participate. Pull people in with phrases such as "You've been quiet. What do you think of this idea?"

Exercise 5

Working in a group of five or six students, decide the following issue: What is the most crucial problem facing high school students today? Select a chairperson and a recorder for your group. In addition, select an observer, a person to keep track of how well the group is functioning. The observer should notice if everyone is participating, if people are being courteous, if the group is staying focused, and so on.

After 30 minutes of discussion, ask the observer to evaluate the group. Then write a summary of your own evaluation of the group experience. Discuss such items as your feelings of comfort or anxiety in the group and whether or not you think you'd enjoy a career that requires much group work.

Exercise 6

Attend a meeting of the school board, city council, or some type of committee. Write a one-page summary evaluating how well the group worked together.

Index

B

Bad, badly, 628
Bar graphs, 801
Base words, 543, 544
   See also Word roots
Be. See Linking verbs; Helping verbs; Passive voice
Being as, being that, 650
Beside, besides, 651
Between, among, 651
Bias
   and opposing arguments, 292
   overcoming attitudes, 307
   See also Sexist language
Bible
   capitalization, 684
   references to, 696
Bibliography, 771
   final, 333, 334–335
   working, 319, 333
Bibliography cards, kinds of, 319
Biography, 34–37
   write a response to a, 37
   See also Autobiography
Biography section, in dictionary, 776
Blends, 746, 757, 758
Book, parts of a, 770–771
Borrowed words, 746, 748, 749, 752, 754
Borrow, lend, loan, 652
Brainstorming, 23, 27, 101, 107, 139, 141, 147, 179, 191, 194, 201, 225, 259, 265, 307
Bridges, capitalizing names of, 677
Bring, take, 652
Buildings, capitalizing, 677
Business letters, 696

C

Calendar items, capitalizing names of, 678
Call numbers, 763
Can, may, 652
Can't hardly, can't scarcely, 652
Capitalization
   of abbreviations, 728–729
   of articles in titles of works, 679
   of compass points, 678
   of direct quotations, 673

   of geographical names, 677
   of historical events and periods, 678
   names of family members, 675
   names of persons, 675
   names of school courses, 679
   names of ships, 678
   of nationalities, 676
   of proper adjectives, 427, 682
   of proper nouns, 405, 608, 675–685, 691
   of sentences, 673–674, 687
   summary of capitalization rules, 684
   titles of literary works, 679
   titles of persons, 675
   of trade names, 677
   in writing, 691
Card catalog, 760, 762–763
Case forms of personal pronouns. *See* Personal Pronouns
Cause-and-effect diagram, 233
Cause-and-effect writing, 232–235, 274
   as context clue, 780
   eliminating errors in, 291
   literature model in, 232
   organization, 86, 88, 226, 234
   revising, 234
   thesis statement in, 233
   transitions for, 91, 234
Characters, 108
   in descriptive writing, 144–147, 148–151
   in expository writing, 253
   in narratives, 172, 175
Charts, 801
Chronological order, 86, 174, 272
Circulation desk, 760
Civics, writing topics in, 52, 70, 105, 293
Classification in expository writing, 236–239, 274
   definition of, 236–237
   drafting, 237, 238
   literature model in, 236
   prewriting, 237
   revising, 238
Classroom tests. *See* Tests
Clauses
   adjective, 396, 507–508, 539, 703

   adverb, 510, 540, 599, 705, 706
   definition of, 501
   diagraming, 539–541
   elliptical, 510, 599
   essential/nonessential, 396, 507, 703
   main, 501
   noun, 512, 541
   punctuation of, 396, 507, 510, 703, 706
   subordinate, 502, 600–601
Climax, in short story. *See* Narrative Writing, conflict in
Closing of letter. See Letter writing
Clustering, 16, 19, 52, 141
Coherence, in paragraphs, 90–92, 93, 96
Collaborative learning. *See* Cooperative Learning
Collecting, in prewriting, 65
Collective nouns, 406
   and subject-verb agreement, 381, 576–577
Colons
   in biblical references, 696
   in expressions of time, 696
   to introduce, 695, 779
   parentheses with, 713
   quotation marks with, 695
   before quotations, 695
   after salutation of business letter, 696
Combining Sentences. *See* Sentence combining
Commas
   with addresses, 708
   with adjective clauses, 396, 507, 703
   with adverb clauses, 510, 706
   with antithetical phrases, 705
   to avoid confusion, 700
   in compound sentences, 378–379, 503, 700
   with conjunctive adverbs, 705
   and coordinate adjectives, 702
   with coordinating conjunctions, 378–379, 503, 517, 709
   with geographical terms, 708
   with interjections, 397, 705
   in letter writing, 709

Copyright page, 771
Correlative conjunctions, 438, 440
  diagraming, 534
Could of, might of, must of, should of, would of, 652
Creative writing, 26–29, 144–147, 172–175, 188–190, 192–194
Critical analysis
  of biography, 34–37
  of character descriptions, 148–151
  characters in, 108
  comparing and contrasting myths in, 260–263
  explaining theme in, 106–109
  of movie, 276–280, 302–305
  plot in, 108
  in reader-response journal, 30–33
  sentence combining in, 370–374
  setting in, 108
Critical listening, 814–815
Critical thinking
  analyzing cause and effect, 232–233
  analyzing characters, 148–151
  analyzing and drawing conclusions about context clues, 779–781
  analyzing and drawing conclusions about words, 782–785
  classifying ideas, 236–237
  constructing a logical argument, 282–284, 299–300
  critical listening, 814–815
  evaluating a logical argument, 290–292
  evaluating evidence, 286–288
  organizing ideas, 78–79
  in writing a topic sentence/thesis statement, 78–79, 324–325
Cross-curricular writing topics.
  in art, 17, 89, 93, 109, 135, 179, 187, 195, 223, 235
  in civics, 52, 314
  in geography, 164
  in literature, 212, 305

  in music, 143, 297
  in science, 85, 231
  in social studies, 13, 97, 122, 274
Cross-references, in dictionaries, 775

D

Dangling modifiers, 392, 632
Dashes
  for emphasis, 711
  to signal change, 711
Dates
  abbreviations for, 727
  commas in, 708
  numerals for, 730–731
Declarative sentences, 514, 693
Definite article, 426
Definitions
  as context clues, 780
  in dictionary, 773–775
  in expository writing, 222, 225
Demonstrative pronouns, 411
  as adjectives, 423
Dependent clauses. *See* subordinate clauses
Descriptive writing, 124–164
  analysis of character descriptions, 148–151
  connotation of words in, 136–137, 164
  creating an overall impression in, 131–133, 164
  describing an imaginary person in, 144–147, 164
  describing an imaginary place in, 135, 139, 141–143, 164
  descriptive language in, 136–139, 164
  drafting, 127, 134, 137, 153–154
  editing, 128, 146, 155
  explaining theme in, 106–109
  literature models, 130–131, 134, 136, 140, 145, 156–162
  mood in, 131
  portfolio in, 164
  presenting, 149, 155, 164
  prewriting, 126, 133, 141, 153
  revising, 128, 131–132, 138, 142, 150, 154

  sentence combining in, 354–357
  spatial organization in, 133
  topic sentence in, 132–133
  transitions in, 134
Details
  in a character description, 149
  checking for, in revising, 132, 142, 150
  creating mood with, 142
  in creating suspense, 194
  in expository writing, 218, 224–227
  in a feature article, 252, 253
  in a news story, 244
  ordering, 80, 86–89, 227. *See also* Order of importance; Organization
  in a personal essay, 20
  in a screen play, 129
  spatial organization, 87
  supporting, 80, 132, 224–227
Dewey decimal system, 764–765
Diagraming sentences, 533–541
Diagrams. *See* Graphic tools
  in planning classification, 237
Dialogue
  developing, 181–182
  editing, 181
  in narratives, 180–183, 210
  prewriting, 182
  punctuation of. *See* Quotation marks
  uses of, 180
  writing, 182, 183
Dictionary
  biography section in, 776
  cross-references in, 775
  geography section in, 776
  guide words in, 772–773
  homographs in, 774
  main entries, 773–774
  organization of entries in, 772–773
  syllabication in, 774
  synonyms in, 774
  usage information in, 775
  using, 772–776, 790
Different from, different than, 652

L

Languages, capitalizing names of, 676
Latin, words from, 748
Laws, capitalizing names of, 677
Lay, lie, 656
Leads
    for feature article, 251, 253
    writing effective, 251
Learn, teach, 656
Leave, let, 656
Lend, loan, borrow, 652
Less, fewer, 654
Let, leave, 656
Letters
    apostrophe to form plural of, 723
    as letters, 721
Letter writing
    business, 696
    colons in, 696
    commas in, 709
    hints for, 9
    persuasive, 285
Library
    arrangement of, 760–761
    call number, 763
    card catalog, 760, 762–763
    checking the shelves in, 766
    classification systems in, 764–765
    computer catalog, 760, 763
    Dewey decimal system, 764–765
    general reference works in, 769–770
    locating books and other resources in, 762–763
    locating periodicals and newspapers in, 767–769
    Readers' Guide to Periodical Literature in, 768–769
    specialized reference works in, 768–770
    using, 74
    using parts of book, 770–771
Library of Congress classification, 765–766
Lie, lay, 656
Life map, 23
Like, as, 657
Limerick, 28, 29
Limiting words, 291, 294–295

Line graphs, 245
Linking verbs, 417
    nominative case after, 596
    subject-verb agreement with, 573
Listening. *See also* Speaking
    in class, 814
    with a purpose, 814
    to television and radio, 815
Listing, 66, 79, 131, 141, 229
Lists, colon to introduce, 695
Literary analysis, 32, 106–109
    author reflections on, 4–8, 124–125
    biography, responding to, 34–37
    comparison of literature to other endeavors, 63
    and connotations of words, 136–138
    and dialogue, value of, 182
    elements of literature, 261
    essay questions, analysis of, 254–258
    expository writing, discussion of, 219
    expository writing, varieties of, 222
    movies, analysis of, 302–304
    plagiarism, avoiding, 321
    and poetry, 26–29
    point of view, identifying, 196–198
    reader-response journal, 30–33
    and self-discovery, 10–13, 22–24
    themes, identifying, 106–107
    See also Writing about Literature
Literature. For a complete list of works herein, see p. xxii
Literature, responding to, 51, 121, 163, 211, 273, 313
    See also Writing about Literature
Literature, writing topics in, 129, 171, 199, 219, 281, 305
    in reader-response journal, 30–33
    about biography, 34–37
    See also Critical analysis
Loan, borrow, lend, 652
Logic
    analyzing opponent's, 292

eliminating faulty, 290–291
Logical argument, constructing, 282–284
Logical organization, 323, 338
Loose, lose, 657, 793
Lose, loose, 657, 793

M

Magazine articles
    capitalization of titles, 679
    punctuation, 716
Magazines
    and presenting, 103–104
Main clauses, 501
Main idea. *See also* Thesis statement; Topic sentence
    to develop, 95
    implied, 83
    in paragraph, 79
    supporting evidence, 83–84
    and unity, 82–84
Main verb, 419
Many a, compound subjects joined by, 382–383, 579
Maps, to explain and describe, 245, 802–803
Matching tests, 806
May, can, 652
Measure, abbreviations of units of, 729
Mechanics, on standardized tests, 811–812
    See also Capitalization; Punctuation
Metaphor, in poetry, 27
Metric system, 729
Might of, must of, should of, would of, could of, 652
Misplaced modifiers, 392, 632–633
Modifiers
    dangling, 392, 393, 632
    irregular comparison of, 623–624
    misplaced, 392–393, 632–633
    See also Adjectives; Adverbs
Money, numerals for, 731
Money expression, forming possessive of, 731
Monuments, capitalizing names of, 677
Mood, and setting, 130–131

Movie reviews
    drafting, 280
    evaluating a movie in, 304
    examining elements in, 303
    prewriting, 278–279, 304
    providing background
        information, 302
    revising, 280
    writing, 305
Multiple-choice items, on tests,
    804–805
Music, writing in, 143, 297
*Must of, should of, would of, could
    of, might of,* 652
Myths
    comparing and contrasting two,
        260–263
    definition of, 260, 261

N

Narrative writing, 164–211
    analyzing point of view in,
        196–199
    anecdotes in, 184–187, 212
    basics of, understanding,
        172–174
    building on ideas in, 174
    conflict, development, 176–178
    dialogue, 180–182
    sports narrative, 188–191
    suspense, creating, 173–174
    characters in, 172, 212
    conflict in, 172, 174, 176–179,
        200–203, 212
    creating suspense in,
        192–195
    dialogue in, 180–183, 212
    drafting, 169, 172–175, 177,
        185, 194, 201–202, 209–210
    editing, 170, 181, 194, 197, 203
    generating ideas for, 173
    literature model, 172, 178, 184,
        190, 193, 197, 198, 204–210
    plot in, 172, 175, 212
    portfolio in, 212
    presenting in, 170–171, 185,
        203, 212
    prewriting in, 167, 173–175,
        177, 208–209
    revising, 169, 210–211
    sentence combining in,
        358–361

setting in, 172, 212
on sports, 166–171, 188–191,
    212
suspense writing in, 192–194
telling stories in, 172
Narrator
    first-person, 196, 197, 199
    third-person limited,
        196–199
    third-person omniscient, 196,
        198, 199
National groups, capitalizing
    names of, 676
Nature writing, Case Study in,
    214–219
Negatives, double, 631
Negative words, as adverb, 430
Network tree, 68
Newspapers
    capitalization of titles, 679
    as forums for presenting,
        102–104
    locating, in library, 761,
        767–769
Nominative case, for personal
    pronoun, 595
Nominatives, predicate, 469
Nonessential appositives,
    commas with, 397, 704
Nonessential clauses, 507–509
    commas with, 396, 507, 703
Nonessential elements, commas
    with, 703
Nonessential phrases, commas
    with, 396, 483, 485, 703
Nonrestrictive clauses, 507
Nonverbal communication,
    814, 817–818
Nor, compound subjects joined
    by, 382, 578
Note taking, 319–321, 794–795
    research paper, 318–321
    See also Study skills
Nouns
    abstract, 404
    amount, nouns of, 577
    collective, 381, 406, 559
    common, 405, 445
    compound, 722
    concrete, 404
    definition of, 401
    in direct address, 708
    as direct object, 466

gerund as, 487
infinitives and infinitive
    phrases as, 538
as object complement, 468
possessive, 403
as predicate nominative, 469
proper, 405, 675–681, 690, 728
singular and plural, 402
special, and subject-verb
    agreement, 576
using precise, 137, 139, 404
verbals as, 485–489
Noun clauses, 512
    diagraming, 540–541
    as object of preposition, 541
Nouns of amount, and subject-
    verb agreement, 380–381,
    576–592
Number, amount, 650
Number, pronoun-antecedent
    agreement in, 602–606
Numbers
    apostrophe to form plural of,
        723
    hyphens in, 725
    spelling out, 730
Numerals, 730–733

O

Object complements, 468
    diagraming, 534
Object of the preposition, 435
    noun clause as, 541
Objective case for personal
    pronouns, 595–598
    See also Objects
Objective tests, 804–808
Objects
    direct, 466, 534, 541
    indirect, 455, 467, 520, 534
Observing
    and letter writing, 6
    and literature, 32
    with poetry, 26–29
    public speaking, audience
        reaction, 818
    See also Critical Thinking;
        Point of view
Omniscient point of view. *See*
    Point of view
On Assignment, 9, 59, 129, 171,
    219, 281

Open-market forums, 104
Opinions, distinguishing between facts and, 798
Or, compound subjects joined by, 382, 578
Oral histories, 76
Oral presentations, 104
Order of importance
  in cause-and-effect, 232–242
  in descriptive writing, 130–134
  in persuasive writing, 286–288
  in research writing, 316–328
  in writing process, 86–92
  See also Organization
Organization
  cause-and-effect, 86, 88, 226, 227, 234
  chronological, 86, 174
  effect-to-cause pattern, 227
  importance, 86, 88
  logical, 245, 338
  spatial, 86, 87, 133, 135
Organizations
  abbreviations of, 727
  capitalizing names of, 653
Outline, 322–323
  correct form for, tips on, 322
  for autobiographical sketch, 23
  for class notes, 794
  for essay test, 256
  for research paper, 322–323, 326–327
  in writing process, 79
Overgeneralizations, avoiding, 294–295

P

Paragraphs
  adding examples or incidents to, 84
  adding facts and statistics to, 84
  definition of, 78
  pronouns in, 92
  repetitions in, 92
  revising, 94–97
  structure of, 78–80
  supporting details in, 83–84
  synonyms in, 92
  topic sentence in, 82–83
  transitions in, 91
  writing coherent, 90–93
  in writing process, 79–80

Parentheses
  capitalization of first word of sentence in, 674
  with other marks of punctuation, 713
  to set off supplemental material, 712
Parenthetical documentation, 332
Parenthetical expressions, commas with, 397, 705
Participial phrases, 485, 489
  commas to set off, 485, 706
  diagraming, 537
Participles, 485
  as adjectives, 485
  commas to set off, 706
  diagraming, 537
  past, 485
  present, 485
Parts of speech
  adjectives, 423
  adverbs, 429
  conjunctions, 437
  interjections, 443
  nouns, 401
  prepositions, 435
  verbs, 414
Passed, past, 657, 761
Passive voice, of verb, 558
Past participles, 485
  confusion between past form and, 390
  improper use of, 391
Past, passed, 657, 761
Past perfect tense, 552
Past tense, 414, 549
Peer editing, 100, 227, 247, 283
Peer response. *See* Peer editing
Periodicals, locating, in library, 761, 767–769
Periodicals indexes, using, 767–768
Periods
  with abbreviations, 727
  to end declarative sentence, 514, 693
  to end imperative sentence, 514, 693
  quotation marks with, 717
Person, pronoun-antecedent agreement in, 602–606
Personal pronouns, 408

nominative case for, 595–596, 599
  objective case for, 595–596, 599
  possessive case for, 595–596
Personal response to literature, 51, 121, 163, 211, 273, 313
  See also Literary analysis
Personal writing
  adding details to, 20
  autobiography, 21–25, 52
  about biography, 34–37
  definition of, 19
  distinguishing fact from opinion, 290–292
  drafting, 7, 40
  editing, 8, 41
  literature models, 10, 14, 18, 24, 26, 27, 28, 39, 42–50
  personal essay in, 18–21
  poetry, 26–29
  portfolio for, 52
  presenting, 52
  prewriting, 6, 39
  process of, 10–41
  reader-response journal in, 30–33, 35
  recognizing bias. *See* Bias
  revising, 8, 40
  selecting topic for, 19–20
  self-portraits in, 10–13
  sources for, 11
  thesis statement for, 20
  word choice in, 20
Personification, in poetry, 27
Persuasive writing
  checking reasoning in, 290–293, 314
  connotations in, 296
  constructing logical argument in, 282–285
  drafting, 280, 283, 307–308
  editing, 280, 288, 304, 309
  editorials in, 298–301, 314
  effective use of evidence in, 286–289
  letter-writing, 285
  limiting words in, 294–295
  literature models in, 288, 292, 298, 308, 310–312
  movie reviews in, 276–280, 302–305, 314
  portfolio in, 314
  presenting, 309, 314, 391

Sensory details
  in narrative writing, 190
  in poetry, 27
  in suspense writing, 194
  in writing process, 83
Sentence combining, 350–374
  in description, 354–357
  in exposition, 362–365
  literature-based activities,
    370–374
  in narration, 358–361
  in persuasion, 366–369
Sentence fragments, 515
  correcting, 515
  use of, by professional writers,
    515
Sentences, 457
  capitalization of, 673–674
  complete predicate in, 457
  complete subject in, 457
  complex, 505
  compound, 503
  compound-complex, 505
  compound predicate in, 460
  compound subject in, 460, 462
  declarative, 514, 693
  definition of, 457
  diagraming, 533–541
  exclamatory, 514, 693
  fragments, 515
  imperative, 514, 693
  inverted, and subject-verb
    agreement, 574–575
  interrogative, 514, 693
  parts of, 457
  run-on, 378–379, 517, 709
  simple, 503
  simple predicate in, 457
  simple subject in, 457
  subject of, 457
  topic. *See* topic sentence
  varying, 514
  word order in, 463–464
Sentence Writing exercises,
    404, 407, 409, 417, 422, 428,
    442, 460, 465, 471, 475, 482,
    486, 504, 506, 513, 514, 550,
    555, 559, 578, 582, 601, 626,
    629, 684
Sequence of events, Plot and
    writing process, 62, 230
  See also Organization

Series
  commas in, 398, 701
  semicolons in, 697–698
Set, sit, 659
Setting, 108
  in expository writing, 253
  in narratives, 195
Sexist language, avoiding, 605
Ships, capitalizing names of, 678
Short-answer tests, 805
Short stories, 182, 186, 194, 197,
    198, 201, 204–210
  See also Story writing
*Should of, would of, could of,
    might of, must of*, 652
Simile, in poetry, 27
Simple predicates, 457, 503
Simple sentences, 503
Simple subjects, 457, 474, 503
Sit, set, 659
Skimming, 796
Slang, 727
Social studies, writing topics in,
    13, 97
Sound effects, in poetry, 27
Spacecraft, capitalizing names
    of, 678
Spatial order, 86, 87, 133, 135
  in descriptive writing, 133
Speaking
  oral presentations, 104
  preparing spoken comments,
    816
  presenting yourself and your
    ideas, 817–818
  in writing conference, 40, 112,
    153, 202, 266, 308
  See also Listening
Special nouns, and subject-verb
    agreement, 576
Spelling
  adding *ly*, 789
  adding *ness*, 789
  cede, ceed, sede, 786
  doubling final consonant, 788
  easily confused words, 792
  editing for, 163
  forming compound words, 789
  forming plurals, 789
  learning to spell new words,
    790
  list of frequently misspelled
    words, 791–792

prefixes, adding, 787
suffixes and silent *e*, 787
suffixes and final *y*, 787
unstressed vowels, 787
  See also Nouns, Plurals; Verbs
Spider map, 19, 52
Spoonerisms, 750
Sports narrative, 188–191
  Case Study in, 166–171
  editing, 170
  finding idea for, 167
  literature model, 190
  prewriting, 167–168, 189–191
  publishing, 170
  researching, 168
  writing, 169, 188–191
SQ3R study method, 797–798
Standardized tests, 809–813
  analogies on, 810–811
  grammar, usage, and mechanics
    items on, 811–812
  reading comprehension items
    on, 809–810
  test-taking strategies, 812–813
  types of, 809
  vocabulary items on, 810–811
States, abbreviations for, 728
Stationary, stationery, 793
Statistics, adding to paragraph, 84
Story ideas, generate, 69
Story writing, 172–175. *See also*
    Narrative writing
Student models, 12, 15, 20, 22,
    28, 30, 32, 34, 36, 65, 88, 138,
    146, 148–149, 182, 186, 188,
    194, 198, 221, 234, 238, 258,
    260, 300, 304, 342–347
Study skills
  analyzing graphics and illustra-
    tions, 800–803
  classification of library systems,
    764–766
  classification of subject,
    236–239
  comparison frame, use of, 262
  evaluation of reading, 798–799
  evidence study of, 287
  graphics in, 245, 800–801
  information, finding of, 318
  interview, conducting, 75
  logic, 290–292
  logical argument, 282–284

Study skills *(continued)*
    outline for research, 322–323, 326–327
    reading efficiently, 796–797
    SQ3R study method in, 797–798
    taking class notes, 319, 794–795
    time management in, 795–796
    See also Tests
Style, develop your own, 350–353, *and following exercises*
Subject
    complete, 458
    compound, 460, 503
    noun clause as, 512, 540
    position of, in sentence, 460
    simple, 457
    word order of, 463–464
Subject-by-subject comparisons, 242
Subject complements, 469, 535
    predicate adjective, 469
    predicate nominative, 469
Subject-verb agreement, 571–593
    and collective nouns, 381, 576
    and compound subjects, 382–383, 578–579
    diagraming, 533
    and indefinite pronouns, 385, 581
    with intervening expressions, 380, 383, 580
    in inverted sentences, 380–381, 574
    with linking verbs, 573
    and nouns of amount, 381, 577
    and predicate nominatives, 380
    with special nouns, 576
    with *there*, 574
    with titles of works, 577
Subordinate clauses, 502, 600
    adjective, 507–508
    adverb, 510
    noun, 512
    and varying sentence structure, 531
    who, whom in, 600

Subordinating conjunctions, 439, 502, 510
Suffixes, 784–785
    spelling words with 786, 787, 788
Summary statement, in research paper, 341
Superlative form of modifiers, 423, 431, 621–623
Supporting your opinion. *See* logical argument
Supplemental materials, parentheses to set off, 712
Supporting details
    adding to expository writing, 224–227
    criteria for selecting, 225–226
    organizing, 226
Suspense writing, 192–195
    drafting, 194
    foreshadowing in, 192
    literature model in, 193
    withholding information in, 193
Syllables, 774
    hyphens to indicate, 726
Symbols, apostrophe to form plural of, 723
Synonyms
    in dictionaries, 774
    in paragraph writing, 92
    See also Thesaurus

T

Table of contents, 771
Tables, 245, 800
Tag questions, commas to set off, 708
Take, bring, 652
Teach, learn, 656
Technology, impact of, on language, 757–758
Tense of verbs. *See* Verbs
Tests. *See also* Study skills
    essay, 254–258
    fill-in items, 806
    multiple-choice items on, 804–805
    objective, 804–807
    preparing for, 804, 805
    for short-answer items, 805
    standardized tests, 809–810

    strategies for taking, 812–813
    time management in, 257, 807
    for true-false items, 805
Than, pronouns after, 599
Than, then, 659, 793
That there, this here, 659
Theme, in literature
    explaining, 106–109
    identifying, 107
    writing about, 108
Then/than, 659, 793
There, and subject-verb agreement, 574
Thesaurus, 138, 295, 776
    dictionary-style entries in, 777
    formats in, 776
These kinds, this kind, 659
Thesis statement, 222
    for cause-and-effect writing, 233
    for essay test, 255
    for personal essay, 20
    for research paper, 324–325
    See also Topic sentence
They, indefinite use of, 389
Thinking skills. *See* Critical Thinking Skills
Third-person limited narrator, 196–199
Third-person pronoun. *See* Pronouns
Third-person omniscient narrator, 196, 198
This here, that there, 659
This kind, these kinds, 656
Time
    abbreviations for, 727
    colon in expressions of, 696
    forming possessive of, in expressions, 722
    numerals for, 730–731
    using transitions to show, 91
Time lines, to organize facts and statistics, 84
Time management
    for study skills, 795–796
    for tests, 257, 807
Title page, 771

Titles of persons
  abbreviations of, 729
  capitalizing, 675
  commas with, 708
Titles of works
  articles in, 719
  capitalizing, 679
  italics with, 719
  quotation marks with short,
    716
  and subject-verb agreement,
    577
Tom Swifties, 753
Topic, finding a, 19, 250
Topic sentence, 78, 80, 131
  in descriptive paragraph, 132
  stating main idea in, 82–83
  See also Thesis statement
Trade names, capitalizing, 677
Trains, capitalizing names of,
    678
Transitions
  in descriptive writing, 134, 135
  in paragraph writing, 91
  in persuasive writing, 284
  in process writing, 229, 230
Transitive verbs, 415
True-false tests, 805

U

Underlining. *See* Italics
Understood subject, 463
Unity, checking for, 94, 96
Unusual expressions, quotation
  marks with, 716
Usage
  special problems in, 518, 520
  on standardized tests,
    811–812
  subject-verb agreement,
    571–584
  verb tenses and voice,
    548–559
Usage information, in
  dictionaries, 775

V

Vague pronoun references,
  avoiding, 607–608
Venn diagrams, 241, 243

Verbals
  definition of, 485
  gerunds, 487
  infinitives, 488
  participles, 485
Verb phrases, 419, 485
  definition of, 485
  gerunds, 487
  infinitives, 488
  participles, 485
Verbs
  action, 190, 415
  active voice of, 558
  agreement with subject,
    571–592
  auxiliary, 419
  commands, 463
  compatibility of tenses, 556
  definition of, 414
  emphatic forms of, 554
  future tense of, 550
  helping, 419
  incorrect tense in, 390–391
  intransitive, 415
  irregular, 544–545
  linking, 417, 573
  passive voice of, 558
  past tense of, 549
  present perfect tense of, 551
  present tense of, 548
  principal parts of, 543
  progressive forms of, 554
  regular, 544
  shifts in, 556
  tenses of, 414, 548–569
  transitive, 415
  Troubleshooter for, 389–391
  unnecessary shift in tense, 389
  voice of, 558–559
Viewpoint. *See* Point of view
Visual learning. *Writer's Choice*
  contains numerous
  instructional visuals. 16,
  79, 88, 90, 96, 189, 222, 228,
  230, 244, 245, 291, 317, 529
Vocabulary
  developing, 778–779
  eponym, 747
  learning from context,
    779–781
  prefixes, 783
  recognizing parts of a word,
    782–785

roots of words, 782
  on standardized tests,
    810–811
  suffixes, 784
  See also Words
Vocal clues, interpreting, in
  listening, 814

W

Webbing. *See* Clustering
Well, good, 628, 632
Where at, 659
Who, in questions and
  subordinate clauses,
  600
Who, whom, 600
Wholly/holey/holy, 793
Whom, in questions and
  subordinate clauses, 600
Whom, who, 600
Word maps, 235
Word processing. *See* Computer
  option
Word roots, 782–783
Words
  acronyms, 757
  apostrophe to form plural of,
    723
  blending, 757
  compounds, 757
  connotations of, 136–137
  prefixes, 783–784
  roots of, 782–783
  suffixes, 784–785
  See also Vocabulary
*Would of, could of, might of, must
  of, should of*, 652
Writer's Portfolio, 52, 122, 164,
  212, 274, 314, 348
Writing about art, 17, 29, 69,
  73, 81, 83, 87, 89, 93, 109,
  129, 134, 135, 139, 143, 147,
  187, 191, 195, 223, 235, 239,
  243, 253, 285, 296, 297, 453,
  477, 497, 529, 591, 617, 669
Writing about literature
  analyzing character
    descriptions, 148–151
  analyzing point of view in a
    narrative, 196–199
  analyzing setting, 195

Acknowledgments *(continued from page v)*

Text

4 Sandra Cisneros, courtesy of Susan Bergholz Literary Services. 5 From *Blacks* by Gwendolyn Brooks. Copyright © November 1991 by Third World Press, Chicago. 10 Copyright © 1976 by N. Scott Momaday. All rights reserved. Printed in the United States of America. 14 From *Anne Frank: The Diary of a Young Girl* by Anne Frank. Copyright © 1967 by Doubleday & Company, Inc. 18 From *It Was on Fire When I Lay Down on It* by Robert Fulghum. Copyright © 1988, 1989 by Robert Fulghum. Reprinted by permission of Villard Books, a division of Random House, Inc. 24 From *Kareem* by Kareem Abdul-Jabbar, with Mignon McCarthy. Copyright © 1990 by Kareem Abdul-Jabbar. Reprinted by permission of Random House, Inc. 26 From *Selected Poems* by Langston Hughes. Copyright 1926 by Alfred A. Knopf, Inc., and renewed 1954 by Langston Hughes. Reprinted by permission of the publisher. 27 From *Verses from 1929 On* by Ogden Nash. Copyright 1932 by Ogden Nash. First appeared in the *New Yorker*. By permission of Little, Brown and Company. 28 From *Lots of Limericks: Light, Lusty, and Lasting.* Copyright © 1961 by Louis Untermeyer. Published by Doubleday & Company, Inc. (l); From *Cricket Songs*, Japanese haiku translated by Harry Behn. © 1964 by Harry Behn. Reprinted by permission of Marian Reiner (r). 32 "Reflection" from *A Light in the Attic* by Shel Silverstein. Copyright © 1981 by Shel Silverstein. Reprinted by permission of HarperCollins Publishers. 33 From *Blacks*, published by The David Company, © by Gwendolyn Brooks in 1987. From *Selected Poems of Langston Hughes* by Langston Hughes. Copyright © 1926 by Alfred A. Knopf, Inc. and renewed 1954 by Langston Hughes (b). 37 From *The Autobiography of Malcolm X* by Alex Haley. Copyright © 1965 by Grove Press. 42 From *I Know Why the Caged Bird Sings* by Maya Angelou. Copyright © 1969 by Maya Angelou. Reprinted by permission of Random House, Inc. 55 Reprinted by permission. 56 Reprinted with permission of G.K Hall, an imprint of Macmillan Publishing Company, from *Spanish Surnames in the Southwestern United States* by Richard Donovon Woods and Grace Alvarez-Altman. Copyright © 1978 by Richard Donovon Woods and Grace Alvarez-Altman. 58 Reprinted by permission of *Vista*. 62 From *In Search of Our Mothers' Gardens* by Alice Walker. Copyright © 1983, 1982, 1981, 1980, 1979, 1977, 1976, 1975, 1974, 1973, 1972, 1971, 1970, 1967 by Alice Walker. All rights reserved. Published by Harcourt Brace Jovanovich. 71 From *Desert Exile: The Uprooting of a Japanese American Family*, by Yoshiko Uchida. Copyright © 1982 by Yoshiko Uchida. Published by University of Washington Press. 76 From *Hannah's Daughters: Six Generations of an American Family 1876–1976* by Dorothy Gallagher. Copyright © 1976 by Dorothy Gallagher. Published by Thomas Y. Crowell. 80 Excerpt from "A View of the Woods" from *The Complete Stories* by Flannery O'Connor. Copyright © 1957, 1965 by the Estate of Flannery O'Connor. Reprinted by permission of Farrar, Straus & Giroux, Inc. 82 Copyright © by Sandra Cisneros 1989. From "My Name" published in *The House on Mango Street*. Published in the United States by Vintage Books, a division of Random House, Inc., New York, and distributed in Canada by Random House of Canada Limited, Toronto. Originally published, in somewhat different form, by Arte Publico Press in 1984 and revised in 1989. Reprinted by permission of Susan Bergholz Literary Services, New York. 87 From *I Tell You Now: Autobiographical Essays by Native American Writers*, edited by Brian Swann and Arnold Krupat. Copyright © 1987 by the University of Nebraska Press. 92 Excerpt from *House Made of Dawn* by N. Scott Momaday. Copyright © 1966, 1967, 1968 by N. Scott Momaday. Reprinted by permission of HarperCollins Publishers. 114 Reprinted by permission of The Putnam Publishing Group from *The Kitchen God's Wife* by Amy Tan. Copyright © 1991 by Amy Tan. 127, 128 Gary Ross and Anne Spielberg, courtesy of Creative Artist Agency. 130–131 From *The Return of The King* by J. R. R. Tolkien.

Copyright © renewed 1983 by Christopher R. Tolkien, Michael H. R. Tolkien, John F. R. Tolkien and Priscilla M. A. R. Tolkien. Reprinted by permission of Houghton Mifflin Company. All rights reserved. 134 From *The Crystal Cave* by Mary Stewart. Copyright © 1970 by Mary Stewart. 136 Excerpt from *A Wrinkle in Time* by Madeleine L'Engle. Copyright © 1962 and renewal copyright © 1990 by Madeleine L'Engle Franklin. Reprinted by permission of Farrar, Straus & Giroux, Inc. 140 Reprinted by permission of Don Congdon Associates, Inc. Copyright © 1949, renewed 1977 by Ray Bradbury. 145 Reprinted with the permission of Atheneum, an imprint of the Macmillan Publishing Company. From *Tehanu: The Last Book of Earthsea*, by Ursula K. LeGuin. Copyright © 1990 by the Inter-Vivos Trust for the LeGuin Children. 153 From *The Once and Future King* by T.H. White. Copyright © 1958 by Putnam Publishing Group. 156 From *The Crystal Cave* by Mary Stewart. Copyright © 1970 by Mary Stewart. Reprinted with permission by William Morrow & Company, Inc. 169 Reprinted courtesy of *Sports Illustrated* from the July 2, 1990, issue. Copyright © 1990, The Time Inc. Magazine Company. "Salute to an Amazing Ironman" by Lisa Twyman Bessone. All Rights Reserved. 172 Excerpt from "The Circling Hand" from *Annie John* by Jamaica Kincaid. Copyright © 1983, 1984, 1985 by Jamaica Kincaid. Reprinted by permission of Farrar, Straus & Giroux, Inc. 178 Reprinted from *Growing Up* by Russell Baker © 1983. Used with permission of Contemporary Books, Inc., Chicago. 182 From *Merlyn's Pen: The National Magazine of Student Writing*, October/November 1990, Vol. VI, No. 1. Reprinted by permission of *Merlyn's Pen*. 184 From *The Life of Langston Hughes Volume II: 1941–1967, I Dream A World* by Arnold Rampersad. Copyright © 1988 by Arnold Rampersad. Oxford University Press, Inc. 186 From *Merlyn's Pen: The National Magazine of Student Writing*, April/May 1989, Vol. 4, No. 4. Reprinted by permission of *Merlyn's Pen*. 190 From *Season Ticket: A Baseball Companion* by Roger Angell. Copyright © 1989 by Ballantine. 193 From *Contemporary Latin American Short Stories* edited by Pat McNees Mancini. Copyright © 1974 by CBS Publications, The Consumer Publishing Division of CBS Inc. Published by Ballantine Books. 195 From *Elements of Literature Fourth Course*. Copyright © 1989 by Holt, Rinehart and Winston, Inc. 201, 204 Copyright © by Julia Alvarez 1991 from *How the García Girls Lost Their Accents*, Algonquin Books of Chapel Hill. First published in *The Writer's Craft*, 2nd ed., ScottForesman Co., 1988. Also published in *Unholy Alliances: New Fiction by Women*, Cleis Press, 1988. Reprinted by permission of Susan Bergholz Literary Services, New York. 217, 218 Theresa Larkin, courtesy of *Audubon* magazine. 220 From *The Secret House* by David Bodanis. Copyright © 1986 by David Bodanis. Reprinted by permission of Simon & Schuster. 224 From *Light Elements: Essays in Science from Gravity to Levity* by Judith Stone. Copyright © 1991 by Judith Stone. Published by Ballantine Books. 228 From *Rubber Legs and White Tail-Hairs* by Patrick F. McManus. Copyright © 1987 by Patrick F. McManus. Reprinted by permission of Henry Holt and Company, Inc. 232 Copyright © 1985 Carl Sagan and Ann Druyan. All rights reserved. Reprinted by permission of the author. 236 From "For the Love of Loons" by Sue Hubbell. Copyright © *Smithsonian*. Published March 1989. Reprinted with permission of Darhansoff & Verrill Literary Agency. 240 From *The Doomsday Book of Animals: A Natural History of Vanished Species* by David Day. Copyright © 1981 by London Editions/David Day. Published by the Viking Press. 244 Text: Jeffrey Brune/© 1991 *Discover* Magazine. 249, 252 From "Searching for Medicinal Wealth in Amazonia" by Donald Dale Jackson. Copyright © *Smithsonian*. Published February 1989. 254 From *The Straight Dope* by Cecil Adams. Copyright © 1984. Published by Chicago Review Press. 266, 268 Reprinted with permission of Charles Scribner's Sons, an imprint of Macmillan Publishing Company, from *Of Wolves and Men* by Barry Lopez. Copyright © 1978 Barry Holstun Lopez. 277 Melanie McFarland, courtesy of *New Expressions* magazine. 288 Copyright © 1988 by The New York Times Company. Reprinted by permission. 292 Copyright © 1988 by The New York Times Company. Reprinted by permission. **298** Copyright © 1988 by The New York Times Company. Reprinted by permission. **304** © Copyrighted July 5, 1991, Chicago Tribune company, all rights reserved, used with permission. **444** Excerpt from *Housekeeping* by Marilynne Robinson. Copyright © 1980 by Marilynne Robinson. Reprinted by permission of Farrar, Straus & Giroux, Inc. **472** Excerpt from *Things Fall Apart* by Chinua Achebe. Copyright © 1959 by Chinua Achebe. Reprinted by permission of William Heinemann Limited. **490** Excerpt from *Picture Bride* by Yoshiko Uchida. Reprinted by permission of Northland Publishing. **520** Excerpt from *Delta Wedding* by Eudora Welty. Reprinted by permission of Harcourt Brace Jovanovich, Inc. Copyright © 1945, 1946, 1973 by Eudora Welty. **560** Excerpt from *Black Boy* by Richard Wright. Copyright © 1937, 1942, 1944, 1945 by Richard Wright; copyright © renewed by Ellen Wright. Reprinted by permission of HarperCollins Publishers, Inc. **584** Excerpt from *Savushan* by Simin Daneshvar. Reprinted by permission of Mage Publishers. **610** Excerpt from *The Old Man and the Sea* by Ernest Hemingway. Reprinted with permission of Charles Scribner's Sons, an imprint of Macmillan Publishing Company. Copyright 1952 by Ernest Hemingway; renewal copyright 1980 by Mary Hemingway. **638** Excerpts from *An American Childhood* by Annie Dillard. Copyright © 1987 by Annie Dillard. Reprinted by permission of HarperCollins Publishers Inc. **686** Excerpts from *Lake Wobegon Days* by Garrison Keillor. Copyright © 1985 by Garrison Keillor. Used by permission of Viking Penguin, a division of Penguin Books USA, Inc. **734** Excerpts from *Arctic Dreams* by Barry Lopez. Reprinted with permission of Charles Scribner's Sons, an imprint of Macmillan Publishing Company. Copyright © 1986 by Barry Lopez.

Photos

AR=Art Resource, New York; EF=Eric Futran; RJB=Ralph J. Brunke; SB=Stock Boston, Inc.; SK=Stephen Kennedy; TIB=The Image Bank, Chicago.

Front cover David Madison Photography; (b) Aaron Haupt. **1** Joan Miró, *Chiffres et constellations en amoureux de sa femme*, 1941, gouache on paper, 45.8 x 38.2 cm, Gift of Mrs. Gilbert W. Chapman © 1992 The Art Institute of Chicago. Photo by RJB. © 1992 The Art Institute of Chicago. Photo by RJB. **4** © John Dyer 1991. **5** RJB. **6** RJB (t); © David Muench (b). **7** RJB (t); © John Dyer (b). **8** John Dyer 1991 (t); RJB (b). **9** EF (t, b). **10** © The Estate of John Lennon, 1989. **14** © AFF/ AFS Amsterdam, the Netherlands. **16** RJB. **17** Private Collection. **21** © Boston Athenæum. **22** U.S. SPACE CAMP® Photo. **26** © D. Taylor/H. Armstrong Roberts. **29** Courtesy Fundación Rufino Tamayo/AR. **31** *Lord of the Flies* courtesy of Castlerock Entertainment/Columbia Pictures (t); EF (b). **34** UPI/ Bettmann Newsphotos. **36** © Ron Tom, Globe Photos. **43** © 1991 Bequest of Maxim Karolik. Courtesy, Museum of Fine Arts, Boston. **45** Courtesy Bernice Steinbaum Gallery, New York. **47** Courtesy of the Evans-Tibbs Collection, Washington, D.C. **50** Courtesy of the collection of the B. R. Brazeal Family, Atlanta, Georgia. **54** Jeff Williams. **55** EF (b). **56** Courtesy Carmen Chavez (tl); Courtesy Lorenzo Chavez (tc, tr); EF (b). **57** © Manuel Chavez/*The Houston Post*. **58** EF. **59** EF. **60** © Nippon Television Network, Japan. **64** © Matthew Naythons/SB. **69** © The Museum of Fine Arts, Houston. Museum purchase with funds provided by the Museum Collectors. **72** EF. **73** © 1985 The Estate of Keith Haring. **74** Private Collection. **76** © Dorothy Gallagher/The Estate of Hannah Lambertson Nesbitt. **80** The Metropolitan Museum of Art, Gift of Frederic H. Hatch, 1926. **81** Collection of the Chase Manhattan Bank, N.A. **83** The Bridgeman Art Library Ltd./AR. **87** SCALA/AR. **89** Iran, late 12th-, early 13th-century. Ceramic 3 3/8 x 8 1/2". The Brooklyn Museum 86.227.61. Gift of the Ernest Erickson Foundation. **93** Carl Van Vechten Gallery of Fine Arts, Fisk University, Nashville, Tennessee. **94** *The Far Side* © 1990 Universal Press Syndicate. Reprinted with permission. **102** © The Peninsula

Outlook. **104** © Bob Daemmrich/The Image Works. **108** ©1981 Paramount Pictures Corporation. All Rights Reserved. **109** Beatrice Whitney Van Ness (American, 1888–1981). *Summer Sunlight*, circa 1936. Oil on canvas. National Museum of Women in the Arts. Gift of Wallace and Wilhelmina Holladay. **115** © Tomie Arai 1988. **120** Courtesy Bluett and Sons, London/Bridgeman Art Library, London. **121** EF (l, r). **124** John Dougan. **125** EF. **127** Photofest. **129** Albright-Knox Art Gallery, Buffalo, New York. **130** © Frank Siteman/SB. **133** © Budd Symes (l, c); © Superstock (r). **134** © Nancy Thill. **135** Courtesy of Koplin Gallery, Santa Monica, California. **139** Marc Chagall. *Paris Through the Window*. 1913. Oil on canvas, 53 1/2 x 55 3/4". Solomon R. Guggenheim Museum, New York. Gift, Solomon R. Guggenheim, 1937. Photo: David Heald. Copyright Solomon R. Guggenheim Foundation, New York. **142** © 1989 Masahiro Sano/The Stock Market. **144** Courtesy Holly Solomon Gallery, New York. **147** Courtesy Walter Gruen, Mexico City. **148** © David Wenzel. **163** EF (l); RJB (r). **166** EF. **168** EF (l,r). **169** © Rick Browne/SB (t); EF (b). **170** © Tracy Frankel 1989 (t); RJB (c); © Mario Ruiz (b). **171** RJB. **173** © Bob Daemmrich/SB. **176** Photofest. **179** Courtesy of the artist and J. Cacciola Gallery. **180** *Calvin and Hobbes* © 1985 Universal Press Syndicate. Reprinted with permission. **187** Courtesy Frumkin/Adams Gallery, New York. Private Collection. **188** © Nicholas Foster/TIB. **191** Courtesy Washburn Gallery, New York. **192** Grant Wood, *Death on Ridge Road*, 1935 oil on Masonite, 32 x 39" Collection Williams College Museum of Art, Williamstown, Massachusetts. Gift of Cole Porter, 47.1.3. **193** EF. **195** © Patricia Gonzalez. **196** © 1991 Sherry Rayn Barnett/Michael Ochs Archives. **207** Courtesy the Chapingo Chapel of the National School of Agriculture and the Instituto Nacional de Bellas Artes, Mexico. **209** © 1990 Thames and Hudson, Ltd., London. Photo by David Lavendar. **211** EF. **214** David Smart. **215** © Art Wolfe. **216** David Smart. **217** © Charles C. Place. **218** David Smart (t, b). **219** © Catherine Karnow 1991. **220** RJB. **223** © Don Beatty 1984. **224** © Obremski/TIB. **232** © NASA. **233** © Scott Anger/Gamma Liaison. **235** Courtesy of the Evans-Tibbs Collection, Washington, D.C. **239** © Reprinted with permission from Clear Light Publishers from *Old Father Story Teller* by Pablita Velarde. ISBN 940666-10-3. **243** 1991 Spaulding Collection. Courtesy, Museum of Fine Arts, Boston. **244** © Andrew Christie/© 1991 *Discover* Magazine. **248** © Mike Mazzaschi/SB (l); Mark J. Plotkin/Conservation International (r). **253** © Jake Rajs/TIB. **254** © Slug Signorino. **269** Nancy Schutt © 1988. **271** Courtesy of the Thomas Burke Memorial Washington State Museum, Catalog Number 2.5E 1543. Photo by Eduardo Calderon. **273** RJB (l); EF (r). **276** Scott Raffe (t, c, b). **277** EF. **278** Photofest (l, c, r); EF (t); Photofest (l, r). **279** © 1985 Universal City/Photofest © EF (b). **280** Scott Raffe. **280–281** RJB. **281** © Morray Alcosser/TIB. **282** © Camera Five. **285** © 1991 Field Museum of Natural History, Chicago, Neg # A 108764 c, Cat. # 8258. **286** © Julie Houck/SB. **290** © L. Roberts/H. Armstrong Roberts. **294** *For Better or Worse* © 1990 Lynn Johnston. Reprinted with permission of Universal Press Syndicate. **296** SCALA/AR. **297** Picasso, Pablo. *Two Acrobats with a Dog*. Paris, spring 1905. Gouache on cardboard, 41 1/2 x 29 1/2". Collection, The Museum of Modern Art, New York. Gift of Mr. and Mrs. William A. M. Burden. **302** Photofest. **311** Collection New York State Museum. Photo by Peter T. Furst. **313** EF (l); RJB (r). **316** Chicago Historical Society. ICHi-1893. **317** © P. and G. Bowater/TIB. **322** SK. **326** Courtesy of the U.S. Department of the Interior, National Park Service, Edison National Historic Site, West Orange, New Jersey. **330** © Photoworld 1991/FPG International (l); Courtesy of General Motors Corp. (r). **336** The Bettman Archive. **413** © Bob Daemmrich/SB. **423** © The Telegraph Colour Library/FPG International. **439** © Steve Woit/SB. **453** Anna Mary Robertson Moses (Grandma Moses) 1860–1961 *Early Skating*. (1951) tempera or oil on masonite 17 7/8 x 24" The Brooklyn Museum 83.122.1. Bequest of R. Thorton Wilson. **467** © Shawn Weimer 1991/Lifestyles (t); © Kent Fleming 1991/Lifestyles (b). **477** The Metropolitan Museum of Art, The Michael C. Rockefeller Memorial Collection, Gift of the Matthew T.

Mellon Foundation, 1960. **497** The Metropolitan Museum of Art, Rogers Fund, 1936. (JP 2517). **515** Giraudon/AR. **529** © Robert Duncan; **548** ©The Estate of Harold Edgerton. Courtesy of Palm Press, Inc. **558** © Don Smetzer//TSW. **567** National Museum of American Art, Washington, D.C./AR. **577** © Jerry Wachter/F.O.S. **591** The Metropolitan Museum of Art, Fletcher Fund, 1963. (63.210.11). **617** The Metropolitan Museum of Art, Amelia B. Lazarus Fund, 1910. **621** © Benn Mitchell/TIB (t); © David Brownell/TIB (c); © Janeart Ltd./TIB (b). **645** Courtesy of The Phillips Collection, Washington, D.C. **669** Tate Gallery, London/AR. **677** ©Steve Elmore/TSW-Click/Chicago Ltd. **685** © NAA-Thomas C. Woods Memorial Collection, Sheldon Memorial Art Gallery, University of Nebraska—Lincoln (t); © Joseph Pobereskin/TSW (b). **689** Joslyn Art Museum, Omaha, Nebraska. **714** © Gino Beghe Encore Art Prints, New York. **724** © Elyse Lewin/TIB.

729 © Chuck Solomon/F.O.S. **739** Rockwell Kent. *The Trapper*. 1921. Oil on canvas. 34 x 44". Collection of Whitney Museum of American Art. Purchase 31.258. **747** The Bridgeman Art Library Ltd./AR. **748** The Bettman Archive. **749** The Bettman Archive. **750** © The Hulton-Deutsch Collection, London. **751** The Bettman Archive. **753** Courtesy of The Lilly Library, Indiana University, Bloomington, Indiana. **755** © 1987 Jon Feingersh/SB (l); © Robert Frerck/Odyssey Productions (c); © Andre Gallant/TIB (r). **756** By permission of Johnny Hart and Creators Syndicate, Inc. **757** © Jay Freis/TIB. **758** © 1990 Bill Horsman/SB. **760** SK (t, b). **761** SK. **772** RJB. **778** © PEANUTS reprinted by permission of UFS, Inc. **795** SK. **802** © 1986 Courtesy of Collier, Macmillan Publishers, London. Photo by RJB. **Back cover** Aaron Haupt.

Picture Research by Ligature, Inc.